THE

ESSENTIAL

BAKER

THE

ESSENTIAL

BAKER

THE COMPREHENSIVE GUIDE TO BAKING

WITH CHOCOLATE, FRUIT, NUTS, SPICES,

AND OTHER INGREDIENTS

CAROLE BLOOM, CCP

BICENTENNIAL
1807
WILEY
2007
BICENTENNIAL

JOHN WILEY & SONS, INC.

Published by John Wiley & Sons, Inc., Hoboken, New Jersey
Published simultaneously in Canada

For general information about our other products and services, please contact our Customer Care Department within the United States at (800) 762-2974, outside the United States at (317) 572-3993 or fax (317) 572-4002.

Wiley also publishes its books in a variety of electronic formats. Some content that appears in print may not be available in electronic books. For more information about Wiley products, visit our web site at www.wiley.com.

Library of Congress Cataloging-in-Publication Data:

Bloom, Carole.
    The essential baker : the comprehensive guide to baking with
chocolate, fruit, nuts, spices, and other ingredients / Carole Bloom.
        p. cm.
    Includes index.
    ISBN: 978-0-7645-7645-4 (cloth)
1. Baking.   I. Title.
    TX763.B575 2006
    641.8'15—dc22   2006005473

Printed in the United States of America
10 9 8 7 6 5 4 3 2 1

CONTENTS

THIS BOOK is dedicated to
the memories of my
grandmother Anna and my
father, for inspiring me.
And to my mother, an
amazing role model and an
avid baker. This book is
also dedicated to aspiring
bakers everywhere, and as
always, to my extraordinary
husband, Jerry.

ACKNOWLEDGMENTS

WRITING A BOOK is a huge project, especially one as comprehensive as this, which I fondly refer to as "my creative octopus." It would be absolutely impossible to complete a project like this without the support and encouragement of a great team.

First and foremost, I want to thank my husband, Jerry Olivas. There are not words adequate to express my gratitude for his assistance, not only with my work, but with every aspect of my life. He gladly pitches in on any task, whether it's coming up with a brilliant idea and helping me follow through on it, planning fabulous vacations, fixing my computer, making me laugh, making a pot of tea, cleaning the cat box, watering the garden, or washing dishes. It might sound like he has nothing to do but help me but, in fact, he has his own demanding professional life, which he manages to juggle better than anyone I know while keeping his sense of humor at the same time. And, believe it or not, he still manages to find time to catch those Southern California waves. Jerry's name should be on the cover of this book along with mine. He has helped in every way possible, including tasting every recipe, many more than once. Without his assistance, it would have taken much longer to write this book.

My thanks go to my literary agent, Susan Ginsburg, of Writer's House. I had seen Susan for ten years at the annual conference of the International Association of Culinary Professionals and always liked her. When it came time for me to find a new agent, I immediately turned to her, knowing that we would have a good relationship. This project came alive shortly after Susan and I agreed to work together, and for that I am very appreciative.

I am delighted to have had the opportunity to work with my editor, Pam Chirls. Her guidance and suggestions throughout this project have taught me much. She is a sensitive and caring editor, who always strives to produce the very best possible. Many thanks to Christina Solazzo, Pam's incredibly capable assistant, for always responding so quickly to my requests.

Thanks to copyeditor Ann Martin Rolke for her great attention to detail, which helped to make this book the best it can be. Thank you to production manager Leslie Anglin for so skillfully guiding my book through production and to everyone at Wiley who has helped this book to come to life. Also, many thanks to Gypsy Lovett, Associate Director of Publicity at Wiley, and Carrie Bachman, independent publicist, for being so excited about working on my book and doing such a great job.

I worked with photographer Glenn Cormier fifteen years ago when we shot the photographs for my first book, *Truffles, Candies, & Confections*. I'm thrilled with his beautiful photographs for this book. He is extremely creative and a master at composing and getting just the right shot. My thanks also go to Glenn's assistant, Ben Carufel, who made our photography sessions go very smoothly and thoroughly enjoyed tasting everything I prepared to be photographed.

Thank you to colleague Shirley Corriher, known as the *food sleuth*, who was always available when I called with questions and always had an answer.

Kitty Morse, fellow prolific cookbook author, has been a good friend of mine for many years. Kitty and I support each other's endeavors and are always there to cheer each other on. We've shared many stories "from the trenches" and many great meals together with our husbands.

Nicole Aloni, former caterer and fellow cookbook author, is one of my dearest friends. Nicole and I have spent many hours together "talking shop" while sharing a glass of wine and enjoying each other's company. She has been an inspiration throughout this endeavor. And thanks to Diane Phillips, colleague and friend, a real inspiration, who is always ready to share ideas and contacts.

Monique Renart, owner with her husband, Jacques, of Bubby's Gelato in Encinitas, CA, makes the most sublime gelato and sorbet. Monique is a good friend, a fabulous cook, and an avid baker. Her feedback on many of the recipes in this book was most helpful.

Good friend Lesa Heebner is always very supportive and insightful. I always look forward to Lesa's e-mails and her words of encouragement, especially while I've been working on this project.

My mother, who enjoys baking, is always supportive and proud of my work. My cats, Tiger and Casanova (who really is a lover boy), kept me company while I worked in my office, sleeping on my desk and my lap, and generally providing hours of great entertainment with their antics. They enrich my and Jerry's lives immeasurably.

Many colleagues provided me with ingredients and equipment to use in developing and testing the recipes in this book. My heartfelt thanks go to Robert Steinberg of Scharffen Berger Chocolate Maker, Gary Guittard of E. Guittard Chocolate, Bernard Duclos of Valrhona Chocolate, Rand Turner of El Rey Chocolate, Chef Ida Rodriguez of Melissa's/World Variety Produce, Julie Lynn York of Land O'Lakes Butter, Craig Nielsen of Nielsen-Massey Vanilla, Abbie Leeson of Royal Pacific Foods/The Ginger People, and Mary Rodgers of Cuisinart. Thanks also to Aliza Ciceronne, Culinary Program Coordinator at Sur La Table in Carlsbad; Penny Lake, owner, and Eleanor Burnett, manager, of Bo Danica, a gorgeous tabletop shop in La Jolla; and to Jodi Dickson, owner of The Poached Pear, another beautiful tabletop shop in Carlsbad, for lending me many plates and linens to use for photography.

I want to thank all of the tasters who cheerfully ate my experiments and gave me feedback: good friends Nicole Aloni, Kitty and Owen Morse, Monique and Jacques Renart, Lesa Heebner, Bonnie and John Manion; my neighbors Sam and Semra Gurol and their friends, who called one evening moaning about how delicious the chocolate desserts were; my ice skating pals at Iceoplex in Escondido, especially Susie and Darlene, who always looked forward to what I brought; the San Diego chapter of the Baker's Dozen; the board of the San Diego chapter of Les Dames d'Escoffier, who were very receptive; and most of all my husband, Jerry, who ate everything I baked. After all, someone had to do it.

INTRODUCTION

BAKING IS ONE of my true loves. It's so gratifying to bring together great ingredients in a way that results in so much pleasure. There is such a myriad of wonderful flavors and aromas, it's simple, and it's fun.

One of the things I really love about baking is the satisfaction of being able to get your hands into it and be creative. There is a great sense of accomplishment and all the good feelings that come with that. And it's nice to hear the sighs of joy from family and friends.

I'm often asked how I learned to bake. I can't exactly remember, but it must have had to do with my grandmother and my father. I can still smell and taste the coffee cakes that they used to bake. I would watch them and help when they would let me. And I was always an official taster. They set me on the baking course and I really haven't turned back since then.

This book has been in my head for a long time. It's a culmination of everything that I like to bake, from my work in the pastry kitchens of many restaurants and hotels and my culinary travels throughout the United States and the world. I have learned a lot from others in my culinary journeys. It's hard to pick any one situation or person, but I will say that some of the chefs that I worked under in the United States and Europe were very influential in showing me how to apply good techniques. I've had my flops and still do, occasionally, but most importantly, I've learned from them.

The purpose of this book is to share all of my baking knowledge and skills with you so that you can become an accomplished baker. You will learn how easy it is to bake great cakes, pies, muffins, cookies, scones, and much more. For novice bakers, this is a good first baking book because it does not assume any previous baking experience. For experienced bakers, this book will help you refine your knowledge and skills. There are over 250 recipes, with many variations.

What makes this baking book unique? All of the recipes are organized by primary ingredient. These include Fruit and Vegetables; Nuts and Seeds; Chocolate; Dairy Products; Spices and Herbs; and Coffee, Tea, Liqueurs, and Spirits. Organizing the recipes in this fashion means that you can easily go right to a section that has the particular ingredient that you would like to use. For example, if you want to bake something with peaches, go to the Fruit and Vegetables section and more specifically, to the Stone Fruit chapter. If you would like to bake with hazelnuts, go to the Nuts and Seeds section, and then to the chapter on Nuts. There are several recipes in this book that focus on less commonly used primary ingredients or components. Some of these are pomegranates, persimmons, mangoes, passion fruit, quinces, cocoa nibs, and mascarpone.

The recipes in this book are laid out in an extremely easy-to-use format. They may be different from what you are used to, but I can assure you, you will like the way they are presented because it quickly gives you the information you need in the order in which you use it. All recipes start with an introductory headnote that often contains suggestions for serving. Next, to the right of the headnote I give a list of Essential Gear with the equipment and supplies you need in the order in which they are used. Directly below the headnote is a table layout that lists the ingredients on the left with

I have learned a lot from others in my culinary journeys.

I invite you to share my love of baking.

the steps that apply to them on the right. This allows you to first organize everything you need to make the recipes, including the ingredients, then you simply work down through the recipe by following the steps that are directly across from their ingredients. This not only makes it very simple to make the recipe, but prevents confusion and the possibility of mistakes. This format makes it seem as if I am right there in the kitchen with you. Also, below the list of Essential Gear I give suggestions for Keeping (storing), Streamlining, Making a Change (variations), Troubleshooting, Adding Style (decorating), and Recovering from a Mishap.

The book begins with a complete section on basic ingredients, such as flour, sugar, and fats. Then I turn to an important section on equipment and supplies, where you find information on everything you need. Techniques are covered after this, and they're all there, along with a thorough section on Baking Language. The recipes follow. The book ends with a list of weight and measurement equivalents, comparative volume of baking pan sizes, a metric conversion chart, and a very thorough list of sources for baking ingredients and equipment.

It wouldn't be fair if I didn't mention that the Chocolate section has some "to die for" recipes. This is one of my baking specialties, so I went all out here. There is a good deal of introductory information about dark, milk, and white chocolate, cocoa, and specialty chocolates, such as cocoa nibs and gianduia. In addition, there are four chocolate tasting charts: for dark chocolate, milk chocolate, white chocolate, and cocoa. There are more than fifty-five recipes in this section.

There are several ways to use this book. For the novice baker I recommend you read through all of Section One before you begin baking, paying particular attention to the Techniques chapter. For more experienced bakers, I suggest you scan through Section One and pick out information that builds on your existing knowledge and skills. For very experienced bakers I invite you to go straight to the recipes. When you are ready to bake a recipe, there is no need to follow any particular order. Just pick one that you like and go for it. Some are more involved than others, requiring more ingredients, equipment, and time. By scanning through the recipe you want to make, you will be able to determine this. Because the recipes are arranged by a particular ingredient, such as berries, pumpkin, macadamia nuts, dark chocolate, sour cream, or cinnamon, I recommend that you choose your favorite. You should feel free, of course, to reference the Section One material on ingredients, equipment and supplies, and techniques at any time.

This may be the only baking book you will ever need. I know that is a bold statement, but I really believe this. All the foundation knowledge and skills to be a great baker are found in this book, and these are enhanced with numerous more advanced techniques and tips. And there is a very wide range of recipes in this book that will satisfy everyone. I invite you to share my love of baking.

I.

BAKING

ESSENTIALS

EFORE STARTING ANY JOURNEY, it's important to pack your bag with everything you will need. Even if you've been on the journey before, you should check to see if you need any new things. For the baker, this means having the necessary ingredients, equipment, and supplies on hand and having a good grasp of the techniques that you will be using. ✳ Baking ingredients can encompass a wide variety. There are the basics, such as flour and sugar. That's easy enough. But within these, there are different types, such as cake flour and brown sugar. Having a good understanding of all the various baking ingredients will help you to get the most out of them. ✳ Using the correct baking equipment makes the job easy and assures success. There is nothing more frustrating than getting halfway through a recipe and finding out that you're missing something. Bowls, pans, measuring utensils, spatulas, and a variety of other tools need to be on hand, as well as supplies, like cardboard cake rounds and parchment paper. ✳ I've always thought of techniques as the easy part of baking. Of course, you must know the various techniques and when to apply them. But learning them is a snap. I think of them as little tricks that streamline the process and help guarantee that whatever I bake turns out great. ✳ By using this section you will make your baking journey the very best it can be.

BEST BAKING

PRACTICES

EVERYONE WANTS to be a great baker, and it's actually easy to be one. The following are a few general ground rules that will help you to become the best baker you can be. They are all focused on helping you be efficient and effective at baking. You can think of these as practical advice tips. But the first question is, "What will I bake?"

RECIPES BY INGREDIENTS

When I am deciding what to bake, my thought process first goes to the ingredients I like and what my guests will like. For example, I like berries, so I say to myself, "What can I bake with berries, like raspberries or blackberries?" My husband is a big fan of nuts, so when I'm baking something for him I think about nuts, like almonds and hazelnuts. I have a group of friends who often come for dinner who love spices. For them I want to bake something with anise or ginger or perhaps vanilla. All of the results can come in different forms, such as cakes, pies, or cookies. This is why I decided to organize this book by major ingredients. I truly believe that this is the way most people relate to baking. Navigating through this book is very easy because all you need to do is search out your favorite ingredient and you will find several recipes that use that ingredient as the primary component. It's as simple as that.

BEFORE BAKING

Before beginning any baking, you want to be totally prepared. First, review the recipe you have selected to make sure you have all the necessary ingredients, including any you may want to use for variations. Next, do an inventory of your equipment and utensils and make certain they are in good working order. This includes checking the accuracy of your oven temperature. Following this, see if there are any supplies you need, such as aluminum foil. Read through the recipe to be sure you understand what needs to be done, in which order, and the possible need to prepare component parts. If there is any particular technique that is unfamiliar or you need to review, you should study that area in the Techniques chapter. One final thing that I like to do is premeasure and set out all of my ingredients and everything else I need to make the recipe, including the bowls I'll use and cooling racks. If you are going to make more than one recipe at a time, extra planning is needed. But don't tackle too much at one time. Two different recipes at one session is pretty much my limit.

ORGANIZING YOUR BAKING ENVIRONMENT

I am very big on organizing my baking area. There is nothing more frustrating to me than getting halfway through a recipe and not being able to find something I need or realizing that there is no room to set something down. Having your ingredients, equipment, utensils, and supplies easily accessible will make your baking efficient and easy and make you want to bake more often. Keeping your flour and sugar in canisters and your spices nicely separated in individual jars is definitely the way to go. For large baking equipment, such as your mixer and food processor, keep them on the countertop so they are easy to reach. Lugging these in and out of a cabinet is a pain. Have your utensils separated into drawers, such as one specifically for spatulas, or keep them in canisters so they are close at hand. Storing all those measuring cups and spoons in the same place is also a good idea. And be sure to set up a separate drawer or a shelf for baking supplies. A lot of room is not needed for baking, but having enough open space on countertops and tables can save you from last-minute shuffling and stacking. And, it's worth mentioning, taking a few minutes now and then to clean up while you're baking will help lighten the load at the end.

PRACTICE MAKES PERFECT

It's easy to say "practice makes perfect"—and it's so true—but practice takes time and energy. My first recommendation is that you don't rush the baking process. Make sure to set aside enough time and, if possible, limit the number of distractions. I know that sometimes this is not easy. Read through the recipe slowly and double check as you go. Don't take shortcuts unless you are absolutely sure they work. Making a note or two as you work through the recipe is advisable. You may discover a more efficient way of doing something. After you have made a recipe a few times it will become like second nature, but always do a quick review of the base recipe just to make sure you don't forget anything. Even to this day, I always keep the recipe for whatever I make close at hand. If you have a mishap, don't be discouraged. Learn from your mistake and try again. Of course the biggest benefit of practicing baking is all the great baked goods you can share with your family and friends. And there is plenty of practicing to do.

ESSENTIAL

INGREDIENTS

THESE ARE the basic ingredients that are indispensable to baking. They are building blocks, and without them it would be practically impossible to bake. From these basic ingredients, with the addition of a few others, it's possible to create countless cakes, cookies, pies, tarts, quick breads, muffins, scones, and other baked goods. Choose the best quality ingredients you can get because it will make a discernible difference in your baked goods.

FLOUR

Flour comes from the finely ground meal of wheat and other grains. Unless stated otherwise, wheat flour is used for the recipes in this book. To make flour, the germ and bran of wheat is broken open and removed, leaving the endosperm or the heart of the grain, which is milled.

Flour has several roles in baking. It provides structure because it contains protein, which, when combined with the liquid in a recipe, produces gluten. This forms springy, elastic bonds and allows the mixture to hold air, which is what enables baked goods to rise. The amount of protein varies by the type of flour, and this determines the strength and rising ability of the flour. An easy way to tell the protein content of flour is to read the nutritional label on the package. It will state the grams of protein per ¼ cup.

Flour that is high in protein is the best to use for bread, while flour that is lower in protein, such as all-purpose flour, is better for other baking, where you want a more tender product.

Flour also provides texture to baked goods. It contains starch, and when combined with liquid the starch expands and forms a web that holds other ingredients together. In this way it also acts as a thickener.

Flour adds color to baked goods because its natural sugars caramelize during baking and turn golden. This is what gives cookies, cakes, pies, and other baked goods their appetizing golden brown visual appeal. The caramelizing of the sugar also adds to the delicious aromas during baking.

When dusted on the work surface, flour prevents dough from sticking when it is rolled out. It also prevents baked goods from sticking to their pans by coating the pans. A fine coating of flour also helps keep ingredients such as dried fruit and nuts from sinking to the bottom of a batter.

Bread flour is made from hard wheat and has the highest protein content, about 16 percent, which allows it to hold the largest amount of gas produced by yeast, and to rise to its highest capacity.

All-purpose flour is a blend of hard and soft wheat flours and has a medium protein content, usually about 12 percent. It is the most widely used flour for baked goods. All-purpose flour is available both unbleached and bleached. The color of unbleached flour is ivory or pale yellow and that of bleached flour is pure white. Unbleached flour is aged naturally, which takes about four months, during which time it turns lighter in color, almost white, from oxidation. Bleached flour is made with the use of chemicals. All white flour is enriched with vitamins because milling removes them. Unbleached and bleached flour can be used interchangeably in any recipe in this book that calls for all-purpose flour. Buy a recognizable brand to be sure you're buying a quality product that will consistently be the same. All-purpose flour comes in 2-, 5-, and 10-pound bags and is found in the baking aisle of most supermarkets.

Pastry flour is made from soft wheat. It has less protein than all-purpose flour and slightly more protein than cake flour, about 9 percent. Pastry flour is used for some pastries and delicate cakes. Pastry flour is usually found in natural or health food stores in bins where you can choose the amount you want to buy.

Cake flour is also made from soft wheat and is the most finely milled flour. It is the lowest in protein, about 8 percent, which produces delicate crumb and texture in cakes and other baked goods. Cake flour comes in 2-pound boxes that are usually found in the baking section of supermarkets.

Self-rising flour is all-purpose flour with the addition of baking powder and salt. It is not used for any of the recipes in this book because I prefer to be in control of the amount of baking powder and salt in my recipes. Also, baking powder loses its potency after about six months, and unless you know how long the flour has been stored, it's a good bet that the baking powder has passed its prime.

Whole-wheat flour is milled with the germ and bran. This produces a heavy, dense flour that retains more nutrition than white flour. Whole-wheat flour is available as both all-purpose and pastry flour. Because the fat is left in the wheat germ, whole-wheat flour has a tendency to become rancid quickly. Always buy it in small quantities that will be used quickly. However, baking with all whole-wheat flour produces heavy baked goods. Adding a little whole-wheat flour to baked goods give them a toasted flavor that is intriguing.

It's very important to use the type of flour that a recipe calls for, or the outcome will be very different than the recipe promises. Never use bread flour for baking anything other than bread. And don't use all-purpose flour for making bread. Here is a formula that you can use if you need to use all-purpose flour in place of cake flour and vice versa.

Flour Substitution
- To replace 1 cup of all-purpose flour, use 1 cup plus 2 tablespoons cake flour.
- To replace 1 cup of cake flour, use 1 cup minus 2 tablespoons all-purpose flour and add 2 tablespoons cornstarch, or sift together ½ cup all-purpose flour and ½ cup cornstarch.

In choosing flour, be aware that there are regional differences in the protein content of flour that will have a definite effect on the outcome of your baked goods. For example, flour made in the southern United States is soft, with an average protein content of about 8 percent, the same as cake flour. This is great to use for cakes but would not work at all if used for baking bread. Most all-purpose flour in Canada is made with hard wheat and will produce tough cakes and pies if not blended with some cake flour. If these are the only types of flour available, you will have to add a little hard wheat flour, such as bread flour, to southern flour to create an equivalent all-purpose flour, and add a little soft wheat flour, such as cake flour, to Canadian flour to do the same. Read the label to find out the protein content per cup of the flour you are using. Then sift with the same amount of either hard or soft wheat flour to approximate all-purpose flour.

Store white flour in an airtight container—to prevent it from coming in contact with moisture—in a dark, dry place at room temperature for up to 6 months. It can also be stored in the refrigerator for up to 6 months or in the freezer for up to 2 years. Store whole-wheat flour in the refrigerator for up to 3 months or in the freezer for up to 6 months.

SUGAR AND OTHER SWEETENERS
The primary role of sugar and other sweeteners is to provide sweetness, but they have countless other uses in baking. Sugar is a very versatile ingredient. Sugar and other sweeteners provide moisture to baked goods. They add flavor and tenderness, and help determine the texture. Sugars contribute color by caramelizing when heated, and they aerate mixtures, stabilize whipped egg whites, and are also used for decoration.

Sugar is hygroscopic, which means it draws moisture and holds onto it. This prolongs the life of baked goods by keeping them fresh for a longer period. Sugar also absorbs water during the process of mixing ingredients together. By doing this it keeps gluten from developing because it keeps the proteins in the flour from absorbing too much of the water. This contributes to the tender crumb and texture of many baked goods.

One of the main roles of sugar is to contribute flavor to baked goods. The use of sugar is what sets apart sweet baked goods and desserts from savory baked goods.

Sugar provides color because it caramelizes when it's heated over its melting point. This helps the surface of baked goods to brown, which adds flavor and texture, and increases their ability to hold onto moisture.

When sugar and butter or another fat are creamed together, the sugar crystals become evenly spread among the fat. Air gets trapped around the crystals and then expands during baking, which helps lighten the final product.

Sugar interacts with the proteins in whipped eggs to stabilize the structure. This means that sugar allows eggs to whip to their maximum volume. It also means that the mixture is elastic and can hold air and the gases that develop from leavening agents in a foam type of cake. In the same way, sugar stabilizes whipped egg whites, which aids in making meringues and leavening other baked goods.

Sugar delays the temperature at which eggs set during baking, allowing the maximum amount of steam to develop within a mixture, which means that cakes rise to their greatest height.

Sugar is also used to decorate baked goods. Confectioners' sugar is often dusted on the top of a finished product. Coarse-grained pearl or sanding sugars make an attractive topping for cookies and other baked items.

Sugar is refined from either sugar cane or sugar beets. The package will state that it contains cane sugar. If it doesn't, then the sugar is made from beets. Sugar beets are easier to grow and process than cane, so sugar made from beets is more widely available than cane sugar. Sugar from both cane and beets is 99.95 percent pure sucrose and they generally react the same way in baking. However, the remaining .05 percent of the composition of sugar is made up of different trace minerals, which sometimes cause problems. For most home bakers, though, this won't be noticeable.

Granulated sugar, also called table sugar and fine sugar, is the most common form of sugar and the most widely used sweetener. It is all-purpose and is what we know as "regular" sugar. Granulated sugar is white, free-flowing, and highly re-fined from either sugar cane or sugar beets. It comes in 1-, 2-, and 4-pound boxes and 5- and 10-pound bags, and is readily available in supermarkets. Granulated sugar also comes in the form of sugar cubes. If you only have sugar cubes on hand and need sugar for baking, it's easy to break them up by pulsing them in the work bowl of a food processor with a steel blade for a minute or two.

Superfine sugar, also known as bar sugar and caster or castor sugar, is more finely granulated than regular sugar. The crystals of superfine sugar are the most uniform of all of the sugars. It dissolves very easily and leaves no trace of grittiness behind. This makes it ideal to use for meringues and fine-textured cakes and to dissolve in liquids. Superfine sugar and granulated sugar can be substituted for each other in recipes, but superfine sugar is easier to cream with butter. You can simulate superfine sugar by pulsing granulated sugar in the work bowl of a food processor with a steel blade for thirty seconds to one minute. Superfine sugar (also called ultrafine) comes in 1-pound and 4-pound boxes labeled "Baker's Sugar," and can be found in the baking section of many supermarkets.

Unbleached cane sugar is made from sugar cane that is processed less than granulated white sugar, but the crystal size is the same. It is a light blond color and can be used in place of granulated sugar in any application. It comes in 1-pound bags and is available in natural and health food stores and in specialty food shops.

Organic sugar, also labeled "evaporated cane juice," is made from organically grown sugar cane. It is minimally processed, so it retains a light blond color. The grains are slightly larger than granulated or superfine sugar, but easily dissolve in batters. Organic sugar is available in 1-, 1$\frac{1}{2}$-, and 4-pound bags in natural and health food stores.

Confectioners' sugar, also called powdered sugar and icing sugar, is granulated sugar that has been ground to a fine powder and sifted. Confectioners' sugar contains about 3 percent corn-starch to prevent caking due to moisture absorption. It dissolves very easily and is used in icings and frostings, to flavor whipped cream, and for some delicate cakes, cookies, and tart doughs. It's also widely used to dust and decorate baked goods. Confectioners' sugar has a tendency to get lumpy when it sits, so it's a good idea to sift it before use. Confectioners' sugar comes in 1-pound boxes and 2-pound plastic bags. It is widely available in the baking section of supermarkets. Organic confectioners' sugar is available at natural and health food stores in 1-pound bags.

Coarse sugar, also called decorators' or pearl sugar, is white sugar that is processed into large grains about the size of lentils.

Coarse sugar is primarily used for garnishing baked goods. One of its valued characteristics is that it doesn't break down at high temperatures as easily as other sugars do, so it's not prone to color changes. This sugar is found in specialty shops and through sources listed in this book (see page 625).

Crystal or sanding sugar is white sugar that has been processed into large grains that are four to six times the size of granulated sugar. It is used mainly for decoration on top of baked goods. This type of sugar catches and reflects light to give the baked goods a sparkling appearance. Rainbow sugar is crystal or sanding sugar that is colored with food coloring. Crystal or sanding sugar is found in specialty shops and through sources listed in this book (see page 625).

Sugar keeps indefinitely if stored in an airtight container at room temperature in a cool, dry place. Once I open a bag of sugar, I prefer to transfer it from its original bag to a clear, wide-mouth airtight canister; it's easy to put measuring cups into the canister and I know the sugar is protected from exposure to moisture.

Brown sugar is made from white sugar to which molasses is added back after initial removal. This is what gives brown sugar its soft, moist texture and distinctive rich flavor. The grains are softer than white sugar, so it doesn't create as much volume as white sugar when creamed with fat. Because brown sugar traps air between its crystals, it needs to be packed into the measuring cup for a reliable measurement. Free-flowing brown sugars are less moist than regular brown sugar and have a texture that is more like granulated sugar. Because these sugars hold less moisture, they don't tend to get hard like regular brown sugar. Store brown sugar in an airtight container in a cool, dry place. If it becomes hard, there are a few methods to soften it. Place a slice of apple on a small piece of waxed paper and put this in the container with the brown sugar. Within a day, the sugar will absorb the moisture from the apple. In many cookware shops you can buy a small bear-shaped piece of terra cotta that can be moistened and placed in the sugar container to keep the sugar soft. Another method is to place the brown sugar in a bowl, add a small amount of water, cover with aluminum foil, and soften in a low oven (250°F) for about five minutes.

Light brown sugar has a small amount of molasses added to it. It can replace white sugar in some recipes but does contribute a more full-bodied flavor and more color. I often like to add a little brown sugar to baking recipes to increase the flavor. My recipes state whether to use light brown or dark brown sugar.

Dark brown sugar has more molasses than light brown sugar. This gives it a very distinct, deep flavor. Light and dark brown sugars can be substituted for each other as long as you are aware that there will be a noticeable difference in flavor. If a recipe calls for light brown sugar but all you have is dark brown, you can make a cup of light brown sugar by mixing ½ cup of dark brown sugar with ½ cup of granulated sugar. Both light and dark brown sugars come in 1-pound boxes and 2-pound plastic bags, and are widely available in the baking section of supermarkets.

Demerara sugar is a type of raw sugar that has been processed to remove any impurities. It is named for the area of Guyana from which it comes. This is a light brown sugar with large crystals that are slightly sticky and dissolve slowly. Demerara sugar can be used in place of brown sugar. Because of its relatively large crystals it works well as a topping and decoration. Demerara sugar comes in 1-pound bags and is found in natural and health food stores and in specialty food shops.

Muscovado or Barbados sugar is a specialty type of raw sugar that is finer grained than Demerara sugar. It is available in both light and dark brown and has a strong molasses flavor with coarse crystals that have a slightly sticky texture. Muscovado sugar can be used in place of light or dark brown sugars. It comes in 1-pound bags and is found in natural and health food stores and in specialty shops.

Turbinado sugar is another type of raw sugar that retains some of its molasses. It is a light blond color with coarse crystals and tastes much like light brown sugar. Turbinado sugar can be used in place of brown sugar in many baking recipes. It is available in 1½-pound bags, marked "sugar in the raw," in supermarkets and specialty food shops.

Never use sugar substitutes for baking. Most of them don't react at all well when heated, are several times sweeter than sugar, and don't provide the same texture as sugar.

LIQUID SWEETENERS

Corn syrup is a thick liquid sweetener made by mixing cornstarch with acids or enzymes. It comes in both light and dark styles. Light corn syrup is clarified to remove any impurities. Dark corn syrup, which has a more pronounced flavor, gets its color and flavor from the addition of refiners' syrup or caramel. Both light and dark corn syrups are used in baking. Corn syrup is hygroscopic, meaning that it attracts moisture, and is sometimes used as an interfering agent to keep sugar from crystallizing while cooking. Corn syrup increases the life of baked goods by adding moisture and adds texture due to its thick consistency. Corn syrup is readily available in glass bottles in supermarkets.

Honey is a sweet thick liquid made by honeybees from the nectar of various flowers. The flavor varies depending on the area where it is produced and the type of flowers the bees have fed upon. Honey is named for the type of flower that is the primary source for the nectar, such as buckwheat, thyme, clover, and lavender. There are regional specialty honeys around the world. Honey is composed of approximately 18 percent water and is hygroscopic. It also acts an interfering agent to prevent sugar crystallization. Honey adds flavor, sweetness, texture, and moisture to baked goods. It is available in both glass and plastic jars and bottles. It keeps for years, but crystallizes with age. To liquefy crystallized honey, heat the opened jar or bottle in a microwave oven on low power or in a pan of warm water on medium heat. Honey is available in supermarkets and specialty food shops.

Molasses comes from sugar cane and is extracted during the refining process. Light and dark molasses are the result of the first and second refining. Dark molasses is preferable for use in baking. If sulfur is used in the refining process, the molasses is labeled "sulfured," or "robust-flavor." Because the sulfur leaves a residue that is noticeable in the flavor, unsulfured molasses is preferable for baking. Molasses is deep in color with a rich, strong, distinctive flavor. It contains between 20 and 24 percent water and provides moisture to baked goods, which helps extend their shelf life. It also adds sweetness and color to many baked goods. Molasses is available in supermarkets and some natural and health food stores.

Maple syrup is made by boiling the sap of the sugar maple tree until most of the water evaporates. It is sweet with a rich, aromatic flavor. Maple syrup is graded according to the color. The delicately flavored pale golden syrups are classified as Grade AA or Fancy. Grade A, and Grade B syrups are slightly deeper in color with stronger flavors. Grade C is very dark with robust flavor and is not readily available to consumers. Maple syrup adds sweetness, moisture, and texture to baked goods. Use pure maple syrup, not the cheap imitation, which is made by adding maple flavor to corn syrup. Maple syrup is available in supermarkets and specialty food shops.

Store all liquid sweeteners at room temperature in a cool, dry place until opened. Once opened, store them tightly covered in the refrigerator. Bring them to room temperature before using. Store honey at room temperature because it will crystallize in the refrigerator.

FATS

Fats are among the most important ingredients in baking. They contribute flavor, color, moisture, texture, and richness. They tenderize and help leaven batters and doughs.

Fat holds moisture and limits the development of gluten in batters and doughs by coating the gluten strands. Fat traps air between layers of dough that turns to steam in the heat of the oven. This is what allows puff pastry to rise to such dramatic heights and is what creates flaky pie crust. When solid fat is creamed with sugar, air becomes trapped in the mixture that swells when baked and results in a tender product. Fats not only provide flavor to baked goods, but contribute a distinct texture to them. Coating the inside of baking pans with fat keeps baked goods from sticking and makes it easy to remove them from the pans without breaking.

The type of fat chosen and the method used to combine it with the other ingredients in a recipe determine the degree of tenderness and richness in the result. In cookies, the type of fat used determines how much they will spread.

Solid Fats

Butter is by far the first choice for baking because it provides the very best flavor. I always use unsalted butter because it has a clean, pure flavor that is unmatched. Salt acts as a preservative. By using unsalted butter you are assured that it is fresh. Also, by using unsalted butter you can control the amount of salt in the recipe, since different brands of butter contain different amounts of salt. Unsalted butter is more expensive than salted butter because it is more perishable. Unsalted butter is sometimes inaccurately called sweet butter, but sweet butter actually refers to butter made from sweet cream and can be either salted or unsalted. Unsalted butter should be stored wrapped tightly in plastic in the refrigerator for up to two weeks. Butter easily picks up other flavors, which is one of its valued characteristics for baking, but this means it should be kept away from strongly flavored food in the refrigerator. Butter can also be frozen, very well wrapped, for up to four months. If it is frozen, defrost it in the refrigerator, at room temperature, or in a microwave oven on low power for 5- to 15-second bursts. If you're not sure about whether to use butter that's been stored, check the coded date on the package. This date is four months after production, and the butter should be used by then.

Butter in the United States has a minimum of 80 percent fat. There are some European-style brands of butter that range between 82 and 86 percent fat. The other ingredients in butter are water and milk solids, and different brands of butter contain varying amounts of moisture. This has a direct effect on the outcome of your baked goods. Too much moisture in butter produces baked goods that are tough, and it affects the way butter melts. If you notice wetness on the surface of butter, this is an indication that it has too much moisture and is not the best choice for baking. The wetness on the surface can also be an indication that condensation is forming when it is taken out of the refrigerator. I usually use the same brands of butter for baking that I have used previously because I know they work well. Always choose butter that is firm when cold. If it is soft when cold, it contains too much moisture. For all of the recipes in this book, I used Land O' Lakes unsalted butter with excellent results.

Butter is churned from cow's milk. The color of butter changes throughout the year depending on the cows' diet. In the winter, butter is pale yellow, so some manufacturers add annatto, a natural coloring, to ensure consistency in the color, making it the same deep yellow as butter made in the summer months.

Butter is sold in 1-pound packages that are divided into sticks and in 1-pound solid blocks. It is much more accurate to measure butter by weight than by tablespoons, but the wrappers on sticks of butter are marked by tablespoons. Two tablespoons of butter weigh 1 ounce.

When a recipe calls for butter to be "at room temperature," it needs to be soft enough to mix with other ingredients yet not so soft that it begins to turn to liquid. To bring cold butter to room temperature, let it stand on the countertop until it is soft enough to hold the indentation of your finger. The time this takes will vary depending on the weather, the time of year, and where you live. It can be anywhere from a half hour to overnight. Although it's not my favorite method because it's too easy to overdo it, butter can be softened in a microwave oven on low power for 5- to 15-second bursts. Cut the butter into small pieces and place on a piece of waxed paper or in a microwave-safe bowl. Turn the butter after each burst to help it soften evenly. The texture should be the same as if you let it soften at room temperature. Each microwave oven is different, so be familiar with yours. When I moved into a new house I routinely melted several pounds of butter in the microwave oven by mistake until I realized that my new microwave was more powerful than my old one.

When a recipe calls for melted butter, melt it in a small saucepan over low heat or in a microwave oven on low power for 30-second bursts. Check it after each burst to see if it is melted.

Butter has a low melting point, and is very easy to burn with too much heat.

Whipped butter is not suitable for baking because it has air whipped into it that changes its structure. This means that it won't act the same way as solid butter when used in baking.

Margarine is a substitute for butter that was created by a French chemist in the late nineteenth century. Originally it was made from animal fats, but today it is made from hydrogenated vegetable oils and skim-milk solids that are processed to a spreadable consistency. Hydrogenation means that hydrogen gas is pumped into the vegetable oils to transform them from liquid into a solid. Salt, preservatives, and emulsifiers are also added. Margarine is softer and oilier than butter and has a higher melting point. I do not recommend using margarine in place of butter because it doesn't have the same mouthfeel or flavor as butter, and it won't react the same way in recipes.

Vegetable shortening is made from vegetable oils that are hydrogenated. Shortening is intended to stay the same consistency at varying temperatures. It's virtually tasteless and solid white in color. It has the same type of texture as lard, which makes it useful in pie doughs, although personally I sacrifice the flakiness for the flavor of butter. Vegetable shortening has the tendency to pick up other flavors easily, so it should be stored tightly covered in the refrigerator away from strongly flavored foods, for up to one year.

Lard is made from rendered and clarified pork fat and has the highest amount of fat of all the solid fats. It also has a low moisture content. These two qualities are the reason it works so well to make flaky pie crusts and biscuits. Lard is soft and pliable even when it's cold from the refrigerator. The best type of lard is leaf lard, from the area around the kidneys. Buy lard from a reputable source so you know there is regular turnover. Lard that sits on the shelf too long gets rancid and will taste that way. Store lard tightly wrapped in the refrigerator or at room temperature, according to the directions on the label.

Oils

Oils come from vegetables, nuts, seeds, and fruits and are often used in baking, particularly vegetable oils that don't have strong flavors, such as safflower oil and canola oil. Occasionally olive oil is used for baking. When a recipe calls for olive oil, I always use cold-pressed extra-virgin olive oil because the oil is delicate and flavorful. Oil, like other fats, makes moist and tender cakes and muffins because it coats the proteins in flour and prevents them from forming gluten.

Oils maintain their liquid state at room temperature. If stored in the refrigerator some of them become cloudy, but once they are brought to room temperature they become clear again. All oils should be stored in a dark, dry, cool place. Heat and oxidation lead to rapid breakdown. Oils can turn rancid over time. It's a good idea to smell and taste your oils periodically to make sure that they are not rancid, which would impart an unpleasant flavor to your baked goods.

EGGS

Eggs have a very big role in baking. They provide texture, structure, color, moisture, flavor, richness, tenderness, and leavening. They act as an emulsifier, holding fat and other ingredients together to create silky, smooth textures. Eggs are excellent thickeners because their proteins set with heat. When egg whites are whipped to firm peaks, they act as a leavener by holding air inside of a mixture as it sets in the oven. Eggs and egg whites are often used to glaze the tops of some baked goods, giving them excellent color and crisp texture.

Eggs consist of the white, which is composed of water with some protein, and the yolk, which contains protein, fat, cholesterol, vitamins, and minerals. All eggs are graded for both quality and size. Quality is determined by their physical condition and age. Candling is a technique used by those who grade eggs. It allows them to look inside the egg with strong light and distinguish the size of the air compartment between the shell and the egg. When an egg ages, the air pocket increases as the egg loses moisture due to oxidation. See http://www.aeb.org/LearnMore/EggFacts.htm.

Egg size is classified by weight. Jumbo eggs weigh 30 ounces per dozen; extra-large 27 ounces; large 24 ounces; medium 21 ounces; small 18 ounces; and peewee 15 ounces. All the recipes in this book use Grade AA extra-large eggs. Grade AA is the highest grade of eggs available. I prefer to use them because I am sure of their consistent quality. I find it easy to buy extra-large eggs at several markets. If a different size egg is used, adjustments have to be made to the recipe in order to have an accurate outcome. When a recipe calls for up to 4 eggs, you can use either extra-large or large to obtain approximately the same results. When a recipe calls for more than 4 extra-large eggs, you can add 1 more large egg for every one over 4 (use 6 large eggs when the recipe calls for 5 extra-large).

Buy eggs that are as fresh as possible. Check the date on the carton and look for cracked eggs, which is a definite sign that they can be carrying salmonella bacteria. Personally, I've never had the problem of eggs with salmonella, but it is something to be aware of in raw eggs. Children, the elderly, pregnant women, and those with compromised immune systems should not eat raw eggs. It's unusual to find recipes using raw eggs these days and there are none in this book, so it shouldn't be a concern.

I had an eye-opening experience when I was in New Zealand a few years ago. My husband and I stayed at a lovely bed-and-breakfast inn. On our first morning we came down to breakfast and ate the most amazingly fresh eggs. I remember distinctly saying, "Ah, that's how fresh eggs taste." Unfortunately, the eggs we buy in the supermarket come nowhere close to tasting like eggs freshly culled from hens' nests. I'm very lucky to have a friend who has four chickens—"the girls" as we fondly call them. Whenever I see my friend Bonnie she brings me eggs. I guard them and carry them home like the little treasures that they are.

Contrary to popular belief, there is no nutritional difference between white and brown eggs. The color comes from the type of hens. Either color of egg is fine to use for baking. Just be sure they are the correct size and that they are fresh.

If you need more egg whites than egg yolks for a recipe and don't have them in the freezer, you can use liquid fresh egg whites. These are available in the dairy case of some supermarkets and natural or health food stores. Eggology is the brand I use. This product is 100 percent pure liquid egg whites that have been pasteurized and checked for salmonella bacteria. They don't contain preservatives or coloring, so you can be comfortable that they are safe. These will last for up to four months in the refrigerator and can also be frozen. The only disadvantage is that because they are pasteurized, these egg whites won't whip to the same volume as those from a freshly cracked egg. Dried egg whites can also be used to replace fresh egg whites. All you have to do is mix them with water to create the equivalent of fresh egg whites. Follow the instructions on the can for the correct amounts. Just Whites is the name of this product, which can be found in the baking section of supermarkets or specialty catalogues. The shelf life of dried egg whites is unlimited, which makes this product very appealing to keep on hand.

Egg substitutes are not suitable for baking. Because they are approximately 80 percent egg whites with no egg yolks, they don't work the same as whole eggs in baked goods. Some brands of egg substitutes contain various other ingredients, such as tofu, oils, and nonfat milk, which won't react in the same way as a real egg when used for baking.

Store eggs in the coolest part of the refrigerator in their original carton with their pointed ends down, which keeps the air cell stable and therefore keeps the eggs fresher. If eggs are stored on the door of the refrigerator, they are subject to temperature changes and won't last as long. Although they can be kept longer than the date on the carton, eggs are freshest if used by that date. If you're not sure that an egg is fresh, put it in a bowl of cold water. If the egg floats, the air pocket between the egg and the shell has increased and the egg is too old.

Egg whites can be stored in the refrigerator in a tightly covered container for up to four days. If you need to keep them longer, freeze them. An easy way to tell how many egg whites you have is to freeze them in ice cube trays. Each cube is one egg white. Another way to determine the amount is in a liquid measuring cup. Three extra-large egg whites measure $1/2$ cup.

Egg yolks can be frozen with $1/2$ teaspoon of sugar blended into each yolk to keep them from becoming lumpy. I don't advise freezing them, though, because the resulting texture is grainier than fresh eggs. They can be used for a very few recipes, but in general, defrosted egg yolks are not a good choice for baking. Use them for scrambled eggs, waffles, pancakes, or French toast instead. The amount of sugar is so small that it's not noticeable once cooked. Whole eggs don't freeze well at all.

LEAVENERS

These are the ingredients that help baked goods rise. When mixed with other ingredients, leaveners produce carbon dioxide gas, which becomes trapped within the structure and stabilizes it. In this way, they lighten baked goods by lifting the structure of them. No small feat! Although eggs and butter can act as leaveners by trapping air that rises during baking, and yeast is a natural leavener, chemical leaveners are our concern here. The two primary chemical leaveners are baking powder and baking soda. Cookies, cakes, quick breads, muffins, scones, and biscuits all rely on chemical leaveners to help them rise.

Baking powder is composed of two parts of a baking acid, such as cream of tartar, and one part baking soda. The tartaric acid in the mixture activates the baking soda. A little cornstarch is also added to baking powder to absorb moisture and stabilize the mixture. There are three main types of baking powder: single-acting (also called fast-acting), which reacts when mixed with liquid; slow-acting, which reacts when heated; and double-

acting, the most common type, which reacts first when moistened and again when heated. Most baking powder sold in the United States is double-acting.

Baking powder is perishable and loses its potency after approximately six months. Check the expiration date on the bottom of the can and replace it within a short time of that date. If you're not sure of the effectiveness of your baking powder, here's an easy test: Combine 1 teaspoon baking powder with $1/2$ cup hot water. If the baking powder bubbles vigorously, it's still effective. If not, throw it out and buy a new can.

Homemade Baking Powder

• In a pinch, it is possible to make your own quick-acting baking powder by combining 1 teaspoon baking soda with 2 teaspoons cream of tartar and 1½ teaspoons cornstarch. This mixture should be used immediately after mixing, as it loses its effectiveness rapidly.

Because baking powder is a balance of both acid and alkaline, it is most often combined with other ingredients that are not acidic. Baking powder begins to react as soon as it is moistened, so it is always combined first with the dry ingredients in a recipe. When the liquid is added and mixed, the recipe should be baked immediately, before the baking powder loses its effectiveness. It's important to sift baking powder well with the other dry ingredients so it is evenly distributed and because it tends to clump together when it sits for a while. Otherwise there may be lumps of it throughout the baked goods, which is not appealing, and it won't be able to do its job well.

Baking powder has $1/4$ the rising power of baking soda, so if you decide to substitute baking powder for baking soda, you need to make the equivalent adjustment in the amount. However, I don't recommend substituting one for the other, unless it's absolutely necessary. Baking recipes are well-tuned formulas and are not as forgiving about substitutions as recipes for general cooking. Also, if too much baking powder is used, it will have the opposite effect and cause the baked goods to fall in the oven rather than rise. This is because too many air bubbles develop and the structure simply can't support them. The usual amount of baking powder to use for 1 cup of flour is 1 teaspoon. Adding too much baking powder causes another problem as well. It adds an easily detectable metallic taste, which is unpleasant. Avoiding aluminum-based baking powders solves part of this problem. Rumford is a good brand of non-aluminum based baking powder. Baking powder comes in 10-ounce cans and is readily available in the baking section of supermarkets. Non-aluminum baking powder is found in natural and health food stores and specialty food shops.

Baking soda, also called bicarbonate of soda, is an alkaline ingredient that works best when combined with an acid ingredient such as natural cocoa powder, chocolate, molasses, brown sugar, honey, sour cream, yogurt, buttermilk, or citrus juice. This combination of alkaline and acid ingredients efficiently produces carbon dioxide gas bubbles, which aid in leavening baked goods. Baking soda reacts when moistened. For this reason it should always be mixed with the other dry ingredients in a recipe first and baked immediately after they are combined with the liquid ingredients.

Baking soda is four times as powerful as baking powder. If you substitute baking soda for baking powder, it's important to make the required adjustment in the amount. Also, if substituting baking soda for baking powder, it is necessary to adjust other ingredients in the recipe to make sure there is the correct balance of acid and alkaline. If there is not enough acid present in the recipe, the baking soda won't work properly. In general, it's not a good idea to substitute one for the other.

Using too much baking soda produces an unpleasant soapy taste. To prevent this, use no more than one teaspoon of baking soda for each cup of an acidic ingredient in a recipe and use baking powder if more leavening if necessary. The usual amount of baking soda to use for 1 cup of flour is $1/4$ teaspoon.

Baking soda easily absorbs odors, and it is often used to do so in refrigerators. Keep the box of baking soda used for baking tightly covered to prevent this. Baking soda keeps for up to 1 year. If you're not sure of its potency, dissolve $1/2$ teaspoon in $1/2$ teaspoon vinegar and see if it bubbles energetically. If not, it needs to be replaced. Baking soda comes in 1-pound boxes that are readily available in the baking section of supermarkets. Store baking powder and baking soda tightly covered in a dry, cool place.

SALT

Salt is a natural, edible, white crystalline mineral that comes either from salt mines or is evaporated from sea water pools. It is technically known as sodium chloride. Salt is used to enhance and enliven flavors in baking. It should not impart its own flavor, but should serve to add depth and to heighten the flavor of the overall product. Salt also adds color to the crust of many baked goods. Salt does not stabilize egg whites when they are whipping. In fact, it does exactly the opposite. It diminishes the stability of the egg

white foam and causes it to become dry. Salt does, however, add flavor, so always add it right at the end when whipping egg whites.

Table salt is the most common form of salt. It is a fine-grained, refined salt with additives to prevent it from clumping, so it flows freely. Table salt is often iodized, indicating that iodine is added to it. Iodine is a trace element that is essential to the human body.

Kosher salt has no additives. It is much larger grained than table salt and thus is half as salty per teaspoon. It is a favorite of many bakers because of its texture.

Sea salt, derived from evaporated sea water, is also a favorite choice of many bakers. Like kosher salt, sea salt is less salty per teaspoon than table salt. Many people feel that sea salt is sweet. This is probably due to the minerals it contains.

Most recipes that call for salt use table salt, but it is fine to substitute kosher salt or sea salt. I actually prefer to use both kosher salt and sea salt in place of table salt in all my baking recipes. All the recipes in this book were developed using kosher salt and sea salt. Sea salt is available in both coarse and fine grains. When I use sea salt for baking, I always use the fine-grain type. Different brands of sea salt have differing amounts of minerals in them depending on where they are made. New Zealand, Britain, and Italy all export excellent sea salt.

Rock salt is an unrefined, inedible gray salt that comes in large chunky crystals. It is used to help freeze ice cream and is not used for baking.

Many people try to avoid salt in their food because they think it is not healthy. Leaving salt out of a recipe may not seem like much, but it definitely has an impact on the finished product. Many baked goods seem flat without salt. Since only a small amount is called for in baking recipes, I highly recommend that you use it.

Table salt is widely available in supermarkets. Kosher salt and sea salt are generally found in natural and health food stores, gourmet shops, and specialty food shops. Store salt in a cool, dark, dry place, indefinitely.

PARTICULAR ESSENTIALS

Cream of tartar is a by-product of the wine-making industry. It is tartaric acid, a fine white crystalline acid salt that is deposited as a residue on the sides of wine casks during fermentation. This is refined to make the product we buy on supermarket shelves. The main role of cream of tartar is to stabilize egg whites as they whip by combining with the proteins to firm them, so the egg whites can rise to their full volume. It is also used to prevent sugar from crystallizing as it cooks. Cream of tartar is one of the components of baking powder and in this way is used as a leavener. Cream of tartar is found in the baking section of stores and is available in 1½-ounce jars.

Cornstarch is a fine white powder milled from the inner grain of corn. Its primary role is as a thickener for custards and sauces. Because cornstarch has no protein as flour does, it has the ability to thicken more quickly than flour. This same characteristic causes cornstarch to be clear when heated rather than opaque, which is what happens when proteins coagulate with heat. Cornstarch has double the thickening power of flour, so only half the amount is needed in place of flour. Because cornstarch does not contain proteins, it is also used occasionally to replace a small amount of all-purpose flour in a cake or other baking recipe to create the same type of delicate texture as that of cake flour (see page 4). Cornstarch must be cooked completely so it doesn't leave any taste or unpleasant dry texture behind. Cornstarch comes in 1-pound boxes and is found in the baking section of supermarkets.

Tapioca is a starch that comes from the root of the cassava or tropical manioc plant. Like cornstarch, it is used primarily as a thickener, but is also used to make a pudding or custard dessert. Tapioca comes in the form of beads or pearls, although it can be found in some health and natural food stores in the form of flakes, and is also available in the form of flour. There are both regular and instant varieties of tapioca. The regular type has to be soaked for at least two hours to activate it before it is cooked. Instant tapioca requires no soaking before it is used.

Tapioca is clear when thickened and maintains a slight chewy texture. Because it is clear, tapioca is a great choice for thickening glazes for the top of fruit tarts. It's also an excellent thickener for two-crust pies because it needs to be entirely surrounded by liquid in order to set up correctly. Regular tapioca, also known as pearl tapioca, is the best choice for making tapioca pudding or custard because it keeps its soft, chewy texture when cooked.

Pearl tapioca is best cooked in the top of a double boiler with liquid so it becomes clear before it is mixed with other ingredients. If tapioca is overheated it becomes stringy, which is unappetizing. Because tapioca doesn't break down when frozen and defrosted, it is an excellent thickener for fruit fillings and sauces that need to be frozen.

Tapioca flour is ground from the beads or pearls and can be used in place of cornstarch. Tapioca is widely available in supermarkets and can be found in many Asian and Latin American markets.

Gelatin is a thickening agent that comes from collagen, which is a protein found in the connective tissue and bones of animals. Culinary gelatin comes from pigskin. The primary use of gelatin is to set mousses, puddings, fillings, and other desserts. Gelatin is colorless and tasteless. It comes in two forms: powder and clear paper-thin sheets or leaves. The powder is available in premeasured ¼-ounce (2¼ teaspoons) envelopes and in bulk. The sweetened, flavored, colored gelatin dessert that is sold in small packages is totally different from pure gelatin and won't work for making desserts.

Gelatin is activated when wet and must be soaked before use to plump the granules and soften them so they can be melted to a smooth consistency. To soften powdered gelatin, sprinkle it over a small amount of cold water and let it sit for 5 minutes, then heat it in the top of a double boiler over moderate heat. To soften sheets of gelatin, soak them completely in cold water for a minimum of 10 minutes, until they are soft and very pliable. Squeeze out the water and melt the gelatin sheets in a small saucepan over low heat until it liquefies. However, if gelatin is heated too much it loses its setting ability. Likewise, it doesn't freeze well. Use gelatin as soon as it is melted or it will start to set up and become too difficult to mix into anything.

The best way to add gelatin to any mixture is to whisk it in quickly so it is evenly distributed. In general, 1 envelope (2¼ teaspoons) of gelatin will gel 2 cups of liquid. It takes 4 leaves or sheets of gelatin to set the same amount as 1 envelope of powder gelatin.

Leaf or sheet gelatin is more commonly used in Europe and by professional chefs, while powdered gelatin is the primary form used by home cooks in the United States. Powdered gelatin is readily available in the baking section of supermarkets and can be found in bulk in health and natural food stores. Leaf gelatin is available in gourmet shops and many shops that specialize in cookware and baking ingredients. My personal preference is leaf gelatin because I became so used to working with it in Europe. Gelatin needs time to set up, so don't plan on turning a jelled dessert out of its mold immediately. The minimum amount of time to allow for gelatin to set up is four hours, and it continues to set up over two days. Pineapple, mango, papaya, kiwi fruit, fresh figs, passion fruit, and guava all contain an enzyme that attacks gelatin in its uncooked state. When these fruits are cooked there is no problem about setting them with gelatin.

Store cream of tartar, cornstarch, tapioca, and gelatin tightly covered in a cool, dark, dry place indefinitely.

ESSENTIAL

EQUIPMENT AND

SUPPLIES

FOR THE BEST results in baking, you always want to use the right equipment and tools. Don't feel that you have to own every piece on the following list. Start with the basics and add to them as you need and want to. Always buy the very best quality you can afford because good-quality equipment will last a lifetime and you won't have to waste time and money replacing it. Keep your eyes open for sales at cookware shops and department stores. And don't forget to let your family and friends know about your new hobby so they can add to your stock with gifts. Storing your equipment and tools so they are easy to reach and use will make your time in the kitchen fun. For example, if your mixer is tucked away in a cabinet where it's hard to reach, you may think twice about lifting it out, but if it sits on the countertop ready to be used, you'll be much more inspired to bake. The same is true of your baking utensils and other smaller equipment. Organize them in drawers, on small racks, or in open canisters or crocks that sit on the counter.

BASIC TOOLS
Bowls

Having a variety of sizes of bowls on hand will make baking easy. It's a good idea to have bowls of both glass and stainless steel because they are used for different tasks. Glass bowls and some hard plastic bowls easily go into the microwave oven, while stainless steel doesn't. Mixing bowls should have a flat bottom so they can stand up easily. A good way to get started is to buy a set of bowls of graduated sizes that nest together. Whenever ingredi-

ents are mixed together in a bowl, make sure there is enough room for them to be stirred or mixed without falling out of the bowl. And when cream, eggs, or egg whites are whipped, the bowl needs to be large enough to hold the mixture as it increases in volume. I like to measure out most of my ingredients and place them in bowls, so they are at my fingertips when I'm baking. In my cabinet I keep a stack of several bowls for this purpose that hold 1 to 2 cups of ingredients.

Cooling Racks

It's important to elevate freshly baked goods on a cooling rack so air can circulate around them completely. Otherwise steam can build up and the bottom can become soggy. There are several shapes and sizes of cooling racks: round, rectangular, and square. Some cooling racks hold one cake pan; others can hold two. I recommend that you buy sturdy cooling racks that won't collapse, with $1/2$-inch-high feet. These will serve you well for years. It's a good idea to keep several cooling racks on hand so they are always available when you need them.

Knives

Good-quality knives will last for many years and will make many kitchen chores such as slicing, cutting, and chopping easy. The best way to choose a knife is by how it feels in your hand and the tasks that it will be used for. You want the weight of the knife to do the work instead of having to put your body weight behind it. It's important to keep your knives very sharp. I use a stone to sharpen my knives, but there are good-quality knife sharpeners available. If you don't feel comfortable sharpening your own knives, check with a local cookware shop or market to see if they have a knife sharpening service. A dull blade is more dangerous than a sharp one and is the easiest way to get cut. High-carbon stainless steel is a good material because it won't rust, it allows the knife to be sharpened easily, and it holds an edge. The handles of knives are made of a variety of materials, such as hardwood or plastic. An 8-inch chef's knife is a good all-purpose size to have. I also recommend having a 10-inch chef's knife for chopping chocolate and cutting large items. And having a good paring knife is invaluable for many small cutting and peeling tasks. For slicing cakes horizontally, it's best to use a serrated knife with a long blade. The one I use has a 14-inch blade and easily cuts clean layers. Store knives in a knife block or rack to avoid damage. Never wash knives in the dishwasher. Wash and dry them by hand immediately after using.

Rubber Spatulas

These are invaluable in the kitchen for mixing ingredients together, scraping down the sides of mixing bowls, and stirring mixtures as they cook. Rubber spatulas come in different sizes; some have short handles about 6 inches long and other have long handles, $8^1/2$ to 9 inches long. I like to use both for different tasks. For stirring chocolate and working with a small amount of ingredients, I use the short handle type. For mixing and stirring cake batters, custards, and fillings and many other tasks, I prefer the spatulas with long handles. There are regular rubber spatulas, which are usually white, and those made of silicone or other materials that are heat-resistant and come in a rainbow of colors, including black. The heat-resistant spatulas are excellent for stirring hot mixtures as they cook, but can be used for any other tasks that call for a rubber spatula. Make sure that you can tell the difference between the regular rubber spatulas and the heat-resistant variety. The heat-resistant spatulas have peel-off labels on their handles that give the amount of heat they can take. Some withstand heat up to 450°F, others to 600°F, while others go as high as 900°F. It's important to know which is which when you use them.

Rubber and silicone spatulas don't hold onto flavors because they are not porous, like wooden spoons. The heads of many of the spatulas can be removed from the wooden handle so they can be washed in the dishwasher.

I like to keep a large crock full of rubber and silicone spatulas on my kitchen counter next to my stovetop and near my mixer. They are easy to reach whenever I need one. These spatulas can also be stored in a drawer with other utensils.

Rolling Pins

A rolling pin is a long, thick, smooth cylinder that is essential for rolling out pie, tart, and many types of cookie dough. Some rolling pins have handles at each end, while others are solid hardwood cylinders with no handles. Standard-size rolling pins are $2^1/2$ to 3 inches thick and 12 to 18 inches long. Rolling pins are made of a variety of materials: glass, ceramic, copper, stainless steel, plastic, marble, Teflon, and wood. And there is a new generation of rolling pins that are covered with silicone that helps to keep them from sticking to doughs. The most efficient rolling pin is a heavy-duty one because its weight allows the rolling pin to do most of the work. American rolling pins have a metal dowel that runs through the center of a wood cylinder with handles on each end. Hardwood, such as beechwood or boxwood, is the preferred material for rolling pins because of its weight and strength. Which type of rolling pin you use is a matter of personal preference. My favorite rolling pin is a French-style solid hardwood cylinder with no handles that is about 2 inches thick and 20 inches long. It allows me to feel the thickness of the dough and gives me more control than a rolling pin with handles. Also, there's no need to worry about running the handles over the dough. There is also a tapered hardwood French rolling pin that is thicker in the center with tapered ends. This design makes it easy to rotate the pin and to roll out circles of dough. Rolling pins should be wiped off or hand-washed and dried after use, never soaked in water or put in the dishwasher. Store rolling pins where they are easy to reach.

Pastry Brushes

Pastry brushes are used for a variety of tasks in the baker's kitchen, such as applying glazes to the top of pies and tarts, applying egg washes or liquid to the top of scones, cream puffs, and profiteroles, washing down the sides of the pan when cooking sugar mixtures, buttering the inside of pans and molds, brushing chocolate onto surfaces, and brushing excess flour off of dough after it is rolled out. It's best to use pastry brushes made from natural bristles so they won't tear or scratch the dough or melt if they come in contact with heat. Pastry brushes look like paintbrushes. They have wooden handles and come in a variety of widths from $1/2$ inch up to 4 inches. There are also pastry brushes made from several quills of goose feathers sewn together. These are used for delicately applying glazes to the top of fruit. And there is a new generation of pastry brushes made of silicone that are very flexible. It's best to have at least a couple of pastry brushes. I keep pastry brushes used for butter and chocolate separate from those used for glazes and washing down the sides of pans, or especially from those used for savory foods, so they don't contaminate each other. Never wash pastry brushes with wooden handles in the dishwasher. Use hot, soapy water to clean them immediately after they are used, and dry them with the bristles facing up.

Pot Holders

These are essential for removing anything from the oven or for handling hot pots on the stovetop. There are many types of potholders, from simple squares to long mitts. Pot holders come in a variety of materials, ranging from cloth to silicone. Use whichever feels most comfortable. Keep potholders near the oven and stovetop so they are always easy to find.

Ruler

A ruler comes in very handy to measure the size of squares and rectangles when cutting brownies and bar cookies, to measure the size of slices of cakes, pies, tarts, and shortbread, and to measure dough as it is being rolled out. A plastic ruler can be washed in the dishwasher.

Scissors

Scissors are used for many chores in the baker's kitchen. Cutting parchment paper, trimming the points off of pastry bags, chopping large pieces of dried fruit, and opening packages are only some of their uses. I keep a sharp pair of scissors (three-inch blades) with a plastic-coated handle in a drawer that is easy to reach.

Sifters and Strainers

These tools are used to aerate and mix together dry ingredients, such as flour, confectioners' sugar, cocoa powder, ground spices,

baking powder, and baking soda. Strainers are also used for rinsing fruit and for straining purées and glazes. I keep a variety of sizes of strainers on hand. Strainers with plastic rims and mesh can easily be washed in the dishwasher. For sifting large quantities of dry ingredients I like to use a drum sieve, which is a large shallow sifter, because it's easy to push the ingredients through by hand.

Timers

I used to think I didn't need a timer because I would easily remember how long things had been in the oven. After I burned several cakes and batches of cookies, though, I decided that a good timer was in order. There are several types of timers available. Buy one that is reliable, easy to read, and easy to use. Always set a timer for the minimum amount of time called for in a recipe. It's easy to add more baking time if needed, rather than over-baking. If I leave the kitchen when something is baking, I take my timer with me, so I won't miss hearing it when it rings.

Vegetable Peeler

This tool is used to remove the outer skin from fruits and vegetables. Peelers have either a stationary blade that is held in place by a Y-shaped handle or a swivel blade. Either works very well. Whichever you use is a matter of personal preference. Choose a peeler with a carbon-steel blade that keeps its edge and is razor sharp or a stainless-steel blade that is equally sharp. There is also an ultra-sharp ceramic blade that holds its edge much longer than steel.

Whisk

Whisks are used to whip air into ingredients, to mix ingredients together, and to stir hot mixtures as they cook. A whisk is a tear drop-shaped, hand-held utensil made of many thin looped stainless-steel wires attached to a handle, usually made of wood or metal, and there are silicone-coated whisks, used for hot mixtures. The wires come in a variety of thicknesses and lengths, making some whisks more flexible than others. There are mini whisks as small as 3 inches long and standard whisks ranging from 10 to 14 inches long. Flat whisks are used for folding cake batters and other mixtures. Whisks with coiled springs are used for beating eggs.

Wooden Spoons

Wood does not conduct heat and doesn't scratch the surfaces that it comes in contact with, making it an excellent choice for stirring hot custards and other mixtures as they cook. Wooden spoons with straight or flat edges cover more surface on the bottom of the pan than those that are round, although the round ones are better for small pans. Do not soak wooden spoons in water or wash them in the dishwasher as that causes them to splinter and deteriorate.

Zester

This six-inch-long hand-held tool is designed to remove the aromatic outer rind or zest from citrus fruit, without removing the inner white pith, which is bitter. A zester has five small sharp holes in the end of a short metal strip attached to a handle made of plastic or wood. To use a zester, place the holes against a citrus fruit and pull from top to bottom with even pressure, which removes the zest in tiny threads.

MEASURING UTENSILS
Measuring Cups

There are two types of measuring cups: dry and liquid. It's important to use the correct type of measuring cup for the ingredient, or the measure will be inaccurate.

Dry measuring cups are used to measure dry ingredients, such as flour, sugar, and cocoa powder. They come in nested sets in graduated sizes of $1/4$ cup, $1/3$ cup, $1/2$ cup, and 1 cup. There are also 2-cup sizes available. There are two ways to use these measures; the scoop and sweep method and the spoon and sweep method. For the scoop and sweep method, the measuring cup is scooped into the ingredient and a flat utensil, like the back of a knife, is used to level off the ingredient at the top of the cup. For the spoon and sweep method, the ingredient is spooned into the cup until it reaches the top, then it is swept off evenly with a flat utensil. Because these measures are used so frequently, it's a good idea to keep at least two sets on hand.

Liquid measuring cups are used for liquid ingredients such as milk, cream, water, molasses, honey, oils, and corn syrup. They are made in a variety of materials including glass, plastic, and metal. There is room at the top of the cup above the line of measure that allows the liquid to slosh around without spilling out.

Also, liquid measuring cups have a pour spout at the top and are marked along the side with various levels of measure, such as $1/4$ cup, $1/3$ cup, $1/2$ cup, $2/3$ cup, $3/4$ cup, and 1 cup or more. In order to get a true measure of the ingredient, liquid measures should be read at eye level, not looking down at them, although Oxo has designed liquid measuring cups that are made to be read from above. Keep at least two liquid measuring cups on hand. I like to use clear glass or plastic measuring cups so it's easy to see the ingredient and the line of measure.

Measuring Spoons

Measuring spoons come in sets of graduated sizes: $1/4$ teaspoon, $1/2$ teaspoon, 1 teaspoon, and 1 tablespoon. A $1/8$-teaspoon measuring spoon is also available separately. Measuring spoons come in both metal and plastic. They are used to measure small amounts of both liquid and dry ingredients and should be filled even with their top edge. I like to detach the measuring spoons from their ring and store them separately in small jars on the countertop or arrange them in a drawer by size. This makes it much easier to quickly find the size I need and is also more efficient.

Scales

Scales are very helpful for measuring butter and chocolate, especially if you buy it in bulk. There are three types of scales: spring, balance, and electronic. A spring scale is easy to use. It has a bowl or pan that sits on a platform and reads in either ounces and pounds or grams and kilos, or both. It works by using a spring device attached to a dial that registers the weight. It can be set to zero each time a new ingredient is added to the bowl. Spring scales tend to lose their elasticity over time, which makes them less accurate. A balance scale works by balancing weights against the ingredient until an accurate weight is reached. Electronic scales display a digital readout of the weight of the ingredient. A bowl or pan is placed on top of the scale to hold the ingredient being weighed and the scale can be set to zero (tare). Electronic scales are the most accurate and can record weights up to ten pounds. They can also be set to zero each time a new ingredient is added. Some models can weigh in both ounces and grams. I use a Salter electronic scale. It has a cover that fits over the weighing platform to protect it when not in use, and the scale can be turned off to save the battery. It has a slim footprint and sits on my kitchen counter near my mixer, so it's always within reach.

MIXING TOOLS
Hand-Held Mixer

A good-quality hand-held mixer with variable speeds will be able to mix every recipe in this book, although it may take slightly longer than using an electric stand mixer. Portability is a plus because you can take it anywhere. Hand-held mixers have two detachable beaters that fit into a housing that holds the motor.

Electric Stand Mixer

A heavy-duty electric stand mixer with adjustable speeds, a flat beater (also called a paddle), and a wire whip attachment is one of the most important tools in the baking kitchen. It will mix ingredients without moving around on the countertop and it allows you to have your hands free to add ingredients as they mix. There are several brands and styles of mixers. Some stand mixers have stationary heads with a handle that brings the bowl up to the beater and others have a head that tilts back. Still others have a bowl that rotates while the beater mixes. KitchenAid makes incredibly reliable mixers. For twenty-two years, I used a 5-quart KitchenAid mixer that never skipped a beat and now I have a 6-quart Professional KitchenAid mixer. KitchenAid also makes a 4½-quart mixer that comes in a wide variety of colors. Buy the best quality mixer you can afford because it will last for many years. It's a good idea to have an extra mixing bowl, flat beater, and wire whip attachment if you're going to do much baking because it allows you to accomplish several tasks without having to stop and clean equipment. My mixer sits on my countertop, where it's always ready to be used.

Food Processor

A heavy-duty food processor consists of a squat motor base with a central drive shaft that holds a sturdy, covered, heavy plastic work bowl. Although there are several blades, the S-shaped steel blade is the most versatile. A food processor is a valuable tool for chopping and grinding nuts and for mixing many types of tart and pie pastry and cookie doughs. Extra bowls and blades can be bought. If you use your food processor a lot, it's worth having an extra set so you don't have to waste time washing and drying the bowl and blade between uses. A small amount of nuts or other ingredients may be unevenly chopped in a large food processor. For these tasks, I find a mini processor to be the ideal tool. I have both a large-capacity and a mini Cuisinart food processor on my kitchen counter, where they are easy to reach.

SPECIALTY TOOLS
Biscuit Cutter

A biscuit cutter is a round metal ring, about 2½ inches wide and 1 inch high, open at the top and bottom, that is used to shape biscuits and scones. Some biscuit cutters have a handle at the top making them easy to hold. A good biscuit cutter should be sharp at the bottom rim so it can easily cut through the dough without a lot of work. To make clean cuts, first dip the biscuit cutter into flour and shake off the excess. Cut straight down through the dough, without twisting the cutter, because this would seal the edges of the dough and keep the biscuits or scones from rising as they bake.

Cake-Decorating Turntable

A turntable looks like a lazy Susan with a tall base and is used to assemble and decorate cakes. It makes it easy to reach all sides of a cake without having to move around it yourself. The taller base raises the cake above counter height to bring it closer to eye level, which helps to make the work more precise. Turntables are made from cast iron and plastic. A squat base, about 4 inches high, holds a thin, flat plate. An adjusting metal screw in the base controls the firmness of the plate. This helps in controlling the speed at which the plate can be turned. Most turntables have plates that are 12 inches in diameter, which is the size most often used. But other size plates can be purchased. Fourteen-inch and 16-inch diameters and a 12 × 16-inch rectangle are also available. Cakes are assembled on the turntable, one layer at a time. For decorating, a cake is placed on the turntable and it is slowly rotated, making it easy to accurately apply icing and decorations. Never place a metal turntable in water, because this will cause it to rust. Wipe off the turntable with a damp sponge immediately after use and dry it.

Cherry Pitter

This tool is used to remove the pits from cherries, and looks like a large pair of metal tweezers with an L-shaped (or V-shaped) strip of metal above a plunger at the wide end. The plunger sits above a small cup that holds a cherry. When the device is squeezed together, the metal strip pushes the plunger into the cherry and removes the pit. This tool is available at specialty cookware shops.

Coffee Grinder

For grinding spices such as whole allspice berries and whole cloves, I use a small Krups Touch-Top coffee grinder. This type of grinder allows me to control the fineness of the grind. I keep a clean coffee grinder in the cabinet with my spices and use it only for that purpose. I wipe out the bowl of the grinder with a damp cloth and dry thoroughly after each use. You can also use a bit of vinegar to remove any lingering spice flavor.

Citrus Reamer

This tool is used to extract the juice from citrus fruit. It is a ribbed, pointed cone attached to a handle. The pointed end is pushed into the center of half a lemon, lime, or orange and twisted, which releases the juice from the fruit. Citrus reamers are made of either wood or plastic and are available at cookware shops and supermarkets.

Cookie Cutters

There are a myriad of cookie cutters to choose from. Some cookie cutters come in nesting sets of various sizes and many others are available individually. And, there are many seasonal shapes and theme-related cookie cutters. All cookie cutters are made from either metal or sturdy plastic, about 1 inch high, open at both the top and bottom, with some cutters having handles at the top. Buy cookie cutters that are sharp with well-soldered or sealed seams, so they won't lose their shape when you use them. Dip cookie cutters into flour and shake off any excess to make cutting easy.

Crème Brûlée Dishes

Shallow porcelain or glazed ceramic dishes about 1 inch high and 4 or more inches wide with fluted edges and a smooth interior are used for baking crème brûlée. The wide surface is necessary for caramelizing the top of the custard.

Custard/Pot de Crème Cups

These are individual serving-size cups that are deep and flat-bottomed with flared sides that are wider at the top than at the bottom. Custard cups are about 2 inches deep and 3 inches wide at the top, with no handles. They are ribbed on the outside and smooth inside. They are made of glazed ceramic or porcelain. Pot de crème cups are similar, but they have small loop handles on each side, are slightly rounder and fatter, and have a lid that fits snugly on top.

Dredger

A dredger is a type of sifter that looks like a large salt shaker about $3\frac{1}{2}$ inches high and $2\frac{1}{2}$ inches in diameter. It has a handle on the side and either a perforated top or an arched mesh screen. Dredgers are made of either aluminum or sturdy plastic. A dredger is used for lightly dusting or sifting a small amount of cocoa powder, confectioners' sugar, or flour on surfaces of baked goods or on countertops that are used for rolling out dough. I keep one dredger in my pantry full of cocoa powder and another full of confectioners' sugar. Dredgers can be washed in the dishwasher. Be sure they are completely dry before filling.

Dough Scraper

This tool is also called a pastry scraper and a dough cutter. It is used to cut straight down through dough, to clean a work surface after rolling out dough, for gathering up chopped ingredients to transfer them to a mixing bowl, and for scraping out a bowl. Dough scrapers are made of either firm yet flexible plastic or nylon and stainless steel with a stainless steel or wood handle on top. The plastic or nylon scrapers are about $4\frac{1}{2}$ inches wide and $3\frac{1}{2}$ inches high and should fit comfortably in the hand. They look like a half-moon, flat on one edge and rounded on the other. Metal scrapers are a bit larger, measuring about 6 by 3 inches, with all their edges flat.

Flexible-Blade Spatula

This tool has a narrow, long, metal blade with a rounded end and straight sides attached to a wooden handle. The metal blade is moderately flexible, yet maintains firmness. Flexible-blade spatulas come in a large variety of sizes, ranging from a 3-inch blade to a 16-inch blade. The size of the blade to use depends on the task and the personal preference of the user. I find the most useful are a 3-inch blade for small tasks, and 8-inch and 10-inch blades. Flexible-blade spatulas have a myriad of uses in the baking kitchen, such as applying fillings and icings to layer cakes, cookies, and brownies; glazing cakes; spreading batters; releasing some baked goods from baking pans; and moving cakes and pastries from one place to another.

Graters

Microplane makes several stainless-steel graters with non-clogging teeth set into firm plastic handles that perform specific tasks in the kitchen. They have specialty graters designed for chocolate, hard cheeses, citrus zest, apples, fresh ginger, and hard spices, such as nutmeg and cinnamon. These graters are razor sharp and make quick work of grating whichever ingredient they are used for. I keep several Microplane graters in a tall ceramic container on my kitchen counter. These graters can be washed in the dishwasher.

Ice Cream Scoop

An ice cream scoop with a 1½-inch-wide bowl is the perfect tool for scooping out drop cookie dough into uniform sizes. There are several types of ice cream scoops, but the easiest to use for cookie dough has a round bowl at one end of a tall shaft that has a lever on the handle. When the lever is squeezed, it moves an arc-shaped strip of metal in the bowl from side to side, which releases the mixture.

Offset Spatula

This is a hand-held tool with a flexible stainless-steel blade. The blade has a bend or angle near the handle that is stepped down about 1 inch from the handle, forming a Z-like shape. The tip of the blade is round and blunt. Offset spatulas come in several sizes, with the length of the blade ranging from 3 to 12 inches. The special shape is very handy for evenly spreading batter in a shallow pan because the handle doesn't hit the side of the pan. An offset spatula is also used to fill and ice cakes, for decorative work, and for moving cake layers and cookies from one place to another. I keep a small offset spatula with a 3-inch

blade and a large one with a 12-inch blade in a drawer with other baking tools.

Pastry Bags and Tips

These are used to shape batter and dough into cookies, cream puffs, and profiteroles; to fill sandwich cookies and pastries; to pipe filling into pre-baked tart shells; and to decorate cakes and other baked goods. Pastry bags are shaped into cones, wider at the top and narrow at the tip. The tip sometimes has to be cut off slightly to hold special tips. Pastry bags are fitted with tips made from metal or sturdy plastic. Pastry bags are made from a variety of materials: disposable plastic, nylon, polyester, canvas, and plastic-lined cloth. Nylon and polyester bags are my choices because they are lightweight and can be washed and reused many, many times. Pastry bags can also be shaped out of parchment paper, especially useful when you need only a small bag. Twelve and 14-inch are the most useful sizes for pastry bags because they hold enough without being overfilled and don't have to be refilled frequently.

Pastry tips are available in a myriad of sizes and openings that form various shapes. I prefer to use large pastry tubes that are 2 inches tall because they are easy to keep out of the garbage disposal when they are hand washed and easily fit in the dishwasher. A couple of basic sizes will handle most tasks: a plain, round ½-inch-wide opening and an open star tip.

Pastry Crimper

This tool is used to close and seal the edges of pie and pastry dough to keep the filling from coming out during baking. There are a couple of types of crimpers. One is a round, hollow wheel with indentations, which sits on the end of a round wooden handle. As it rolls along the pastry dough, it makes fluted edges. The other type of crimper is a thin wheel with wavy edges on top of a round wooden handle. It also cuts fluted edges as it is rolled along the rim of the pastry dough.

Pastry Pincher

This tool looks like a large pair of tweezers. It is about 4 inches tall and each leg is approximately 1 inch wide with serrated grooves or teeth at the bottom. It is used to pinch or crimp the sides of pie shells to give them a finished look with a decorative design.

Pie Weights

These are used to weight pie and tart doughs when they are baked without a filling. They keep the sides of the dough from collapsing and the bottom from puffing up. Pie weights are round ceramic or metal pellets. There is also a 10-foot-long stainless-steel beaded chain that is used as a pie weight. The weights are placed on top of aluminum foil or parchment paper that is used to line the shell; otherwise they would bake into the crust, except for the pie chain, which can sit directly on the dough. They should fill the shell almost full because they also help conduct heat to the sides and top of the shell. When the pie or tart shell is set, the foil and weights are lifted off. I use a mixture of uncooked rice and beans as pie weights. I keep them in a jar in my baking pantry and use them only for this purpose.

Soufflé Dish

A soufflé dish is deep and round with straight sides, made of white porcelain or glazed ceramic. It is typically smooth on the inside and fluted on the outside. Soufflé dishes are available in a variety of sizes, from individual—measuring 4 inches in diameter and 2³/₄ inches deep—up to 2 quarts, about 9 inches in diameter and 4 inches deep. Soufflés are baked and served in the same dish. Custards can also be baked in soufflé dishes. Individual soufflé dishes are sometimes called ramekins.

Strawberry Huller

This tool looks like a wide, V-shaped pair of metal tweezers with gripping surfaces on each rounded end. It is used to remove the leaves and cores from strawberries. Grasp the strawberry leaves with the huller and squeeze the sides together to hold them. Then twist and pull the huller to remove the leaves and their core from the berry.

Thermometers

Because accuracy is so important in baking and making desserts, having reliable thermometers is a necessity.

• *Oven thermometer*
An oven thermometer is essential for maintaining a consistent temperature because the oven can naturally fluctuate as much as fifty degrees during use. Also, most ovens have hot spots, and it's a good idea to be familiar with your oven's details. An oven thermometer is suspended from one of the oven racks by a small hook at its top or it can sit on the oven rack. Oven thermometers usually have a dial with a pointer that displays the temperature, making them easy to read. Always check the temperature in your oven after it's preheated and before you bake anything. This gives you a chance to adjust the temperature up or down, as needed, and prevents under- or over-baking.

• *Candy (sugar) thermometer*
A candy or sugar thermometer is designed to read temperatures in the range of 100° to 400°F. It also indicates the stages of cooked sugar, such as soft-ball, hard-ball, hard-crack, etc., and reads in two-degree gradations. This is essential, because one or two degrees in either direction can make a difference in the cooked sugar mixture. Choose a thermometer with clear markings and numbers, so it's easy to read. There are a few types of thermometers to choose from. An instant-read thermometer has either a dial or digital readout that sits at the top of a metal stem. Make sure the dimple of the stem is embedded in the mixture but not touching the bottom of the pan to get an accurate reading. There are also digital thermometers with a probe to register the temperature of the mixture. These have a clip that attaches a probe to the side of the pan and a readout unit that sits on the counter nearby. And there is a thermometer with a remote transmitter and receiver that can span up to 100 feet. Some of these thermometers also have alarms that flash and beep to let you know when the mixture has reached the desired temperature. There is a new liquid material that has replaced mercury in thermometers because of the safety issue. I like to use a Taylor candy thermometer that has a 3-inch-wide metal body and holds the glass thermometer, with this liquid, by metal prongs. It also has a foot at the bottom that sits on the bottom of the pan and keeps the glass thermometer suspended in the mixture so it takes an accurate temperature reading, rather than reading the temperature of the bottom of the pan.

• *Infrared thermometer*
There is a new generation of infrared thermometers made by Raytek. This type of thermometer is worked by aiming the unit at the mixture and pressing a trigger, then the thermometer instantly registers the temperature and shows it on an LCD display. One model also has a thin metal probe to place in the mixture to take its temperature.

BAKING PANS
Baking Sheet

This pan, also called a jelly-roll pan, is a firm, flat sheet of metal with 1-inch-high straight sides and a rolled rim. Baking sheets come in a couple of different sizes. I prefer to use 12 × 17-inch baking sheets. Buy baking sheets that fit in your oven and allow at least 2 inches of space around them on all sides, so air can circulate evenly. Generally, baking sheets are made of aluminum or heavy-gauge steel, which conduct heat evenly and quickly. I prefer to use heavy-weight baking sheets so they won't buckle in the heat of the oven. I also prefer light-colored baking sheets, because the dark ones conduct heat faster, which bakes more quickly and can develop a crust on the outside of baked goods. There are also air-cushioned baking sheets that hold a layer of air between two layers of metal, and baking sheets that are non-stick. Baking sheets are used for several tasks, such as holding the batter for jelly-roll or roulade cakes; baking galettes; baking cookies, scones, and biscuits; and holding tart and tartlet pans, springform pans, and muffin pans as they bake.

Cookie Sheets

Cookie sheets are flat and firm, with two or three open sides and a 1-inch rolled rim on one or two sides. Having flat sides allows air to circulate evenly around and over the cookies as they bake. As with baking sheets, cookie sheets are made of aluminum and should be heavy so they don't warp in the oven. There are also dark steel, non-stick, and air-cushioned cookie sheets, which all bake slightly differently. The dark and non-stick cookie sheets bake faster than plain aluminum and the air-cushioned cookie sheets bake softer, less crisp cookies. Cookie sheets come in several sizes. Buy the largest size that fits in your oven and leaves enough room for air to circulate. Having at least two cookie sheets allows you to bake a batch of cookies on both oven racks at the same time without having to wait in between. You can also use baking sheets or jelly-roll pans for baking cookies.

Cake Pans

• Layer cake
These pans are round with straight sides and come in a range of sizes from 3-inch diameter up to 24-inch diameter. Look for pans with smooth, well-sealed seams. The layer cakes in this book call for 9-inch round cake pans. I prefer to use cake pans that are at least 1½ to 2 inches deep because there is enough room for the cake batter to rise without spilling over the top. There are also layer cake pans that are 3 to 4 inches deep, but if a pan is too big for the amount of batter it holds, the cake will be dry. Layer cake pans made from aluminum or heavy-gauge steel conduct heat efficiently and evenly. Dark or black steel pans conduct heat more quickly and cause a crust to develop on the outside of the cake layers, which is not always desirable. Layer cake pans made with a non-stick coating release cakes easier with a little greasing, but often the cake batter has a hard time holding onto the sides of the pan and may not rise as well. There is also a new generation of pans or molds made from silicone. These are extremely flexible and can stand up to high heat in the oven. Since they are so flexible, they need to be placed on a baking sheet for extra support to go in and out of the oven. These easily peel off a cake when it is cool.

• Bundt
This is a special, deep cake pan with a center tube and deeply grooved, rounded, sculpted sides, in a pattern that repeats around the pan. This pattern transfers onto the cake as it bakes. There are several patterns of Bundt pans and they are available in a variety of materials, such as heavy-duty aluminum, heavy-gauge steel, and non-stick. They come in 9- and 10-inch diameters and also in mini-size, resembling a muffin pan. The nice thing about Bundt pans and fluted tube pans (see below) are that the grooves and flutes provide a good guide for cutting into individual slices.

• Tube
A straight-sided tube pan is also called an angel food cake pan, because it is the pan of choice for baking angel food cakes. This pan is also used to bake chiffon cakes and some pound cakes. The pan is 10 inches in diameter and 4½ inches deep and is made of heavy aluminum. The straight sides allow the airy cakes to climb up them as they rise. There is a center tube that helps conduct heat and bake the center of the cake. Some tube pans have metal "feet" or extensions above the rim of the pan. Their purpose is to hold the pan steady when it is turned upside down and left to cool. Angel food and chiffon cakes are cooled this way because the cake would collapse onto itself if it were to sit on its bottom. If the pan has no feet, it is hung by the center tube over a large funnel or bottle while the cake cools. Some tube pans

have removable bottoms that can be pushed up and away from the sides to release the cake when it is cool.

• Fluted tube

Also called a swirled tube, this pan is a version of the above tube pan, with swirled, grooved designs that imprint on the cake as it bakes. It is generally used to bake butter cakes, tea cakes, and coffee cakes.

• Loaf

This is a rectangular pan designed specifically for baking loaf cakes and quick breads. The standard-size loaf pan used for the recipes in this book is 9 × 5 × 3 inches. Loaf pans are made from a variety of materials including glass, ceramic, aluminum, tinned steel, and black or blue steel. I use Pyrex™ glass loaf pans.

• Square

Eight-inch and 9-inch square baking pans are used to bake brownies and some bar cookies. These are 2 inches deep with straight sides and squared corners. I use both Pyrex™ square glass pans and heavy-duty aluminum square pans. The glass pans can be washed in the dishwasher.

• Rectangular

Rectangular baking pans are used for baking bar cookies and for forming shortbread, and are available in both glass and heavy-duty aluminum. The size I use most often is 13 × 9 × 2 inches. I also use rectangular pans that measure 11 × 7 × 2 inches.

• Springform

These pans are used for baking cheesecakes, soufflé cakes, mousse cakes, and any other delicate cakes that can't be turned upside down to remove them from the pan. Springform pans have expandable sides secured by a clamp. When the clamp is opened, the sides of the pan expand and release the bottom. This makes it very easy to remove a cake from the pan. Springform pans are 3 inches deep with straight sides and range in diameter from 4 to 12 inches. The pans used for the recipes in this book are 9 and 9½ inches in diameter. Springform pans are available in aluminum, stainless steel, and non-stick heavy gauge aluminum. Springform pans often sit on a baking sheet or in another pan that holds water when they bake. For this reason it's important that the bottom fit very snugly into the sides. When I

bake cheesecakes that sit in a water bath, I always wrap the bottom of the springform pan with a double layer of heavy-duty foil to prevent water from seeping into the cake.

Madeleine Pan

Also called a madeleine plaque or sheet, this unique flat, rectangular, tinned-steel or aluminum pan is used for baking the special tea cakes known as madeleines. Each plaque holds twelve 3 × 1¾ × ½-inch, shell-shaped, ribbed indentations that hold the batter and give the tea cakes their characteristic shape. There are also miniature madeleine pans that have from 24 to 40 indentations and large pans that hold as few as 8 cakes. Madeleine and mini-madeleine pans are also made in silicone.

Muffin Pan

This is a rectangular heavy aluminum or tinned-steel baking pan. Standard-size muffin pans have twelve 3 × 1¼- or 1½-inch-deep cup-shaped cavities that hold the batter for muffins, cupcakes, and small cakes. Muffin pans are lined with pleated paper baking cups to hold the batter or the cavities are greased and floured so it's easy to remove the muffins or cakes. Some muffin pans are made with a non-stick surface, and there are silicone muffin pans that easily release the muffins after they are baked.

Pie Pan

Also called a pie plate and pie dish, this pan is used exclusively for baking pies. It is round with sloped sides about 1½ inches deep. Pie pans are made of tinned steel, aluminum, glass, and ceramic and some have a non-stick interior. They range in diameter from 8 to 12 inches, with 9 inches being the most popular. Deep-dish pie pans are slightly deeper (about 2 inches) than standard pie pans. Pies baked in ceramic pie pans need to bake slightly longer to bake evenly. I prefer to use Pyrex™ glass pie pans because it's very easy to see how the pie looks as it bakes, and they brown the crust evenly because they conduct heat so well.

Tart and Tartlet Pans

Tart pans are made of tinned steel or black steel with fluted, straight sides and a removable bottom. When the tart is completely cool, the tart pan is placed over a bowl that is smaller than the bottom of the pan and the sides of the tart pan are gently pulled away. The classic shape for tart pans is round but there are many other shapes, including square, wide rectangle, and narrow rectangle. In this book I use 9-inch and 11-inch round tart pans, 4½-inch round individual tartlet pans, a 9-inch square, and a 12 × 8-inch rectangular tart pan, all with removable bottoms. All of these pans are 1 inch deep. Individual tartlet pans do not have removable bottoms and are available in a myriad of sizes and shapes, some with un-fluted sides. There are also silicone tartlet pans that come in a sheet, resembling a muffin pan. I use 2½-inch-diameter fluted-edge tartlet pans that are 1 inch deep with slightly sloped sides. Tart and tartlet pans need to be placed on a baking sheet before they go into the oven. Because most of the doughs that are baked in tart and tartlet shells are rich with butter, the pans do not need to be greased. Also, the dough shrinks as it bakes and doesn't stick to the pans. Many recipes call for tart and tartlet shells to be baked blind without a filling. For tart pans, they are lined with aluminum foil and tart weights (see page 20). For tartlet pans, place another pan of the same shape and size on top of the dough to act as a weight while the shell bakes and becomes set. Hand wash and thoroughly dry tart and tartlet pans before storing so they don't rust. I store my tart pans nested together by graduating sizes on a slide-out shelf in the cabinet right below my mixer and food processor. My tartlet pans inhabit a drawer (because I have so many of them) under my cook top.

POTS AND PANS
Double Boiler

A double boiler is necessary when melting chocolate and cooking delicate custard mixtures, such as lemon curd, because it insulates and provides a consistent source of heat for melting and cooking ingredients evenly and for holding them at a constant temperature without burning. A double boiler consists of two pans that fit snugly together. The bottom pan, which is larger, holds a small amount of water that transfers delicate heat to the ingredients in the top pan. It's important that the pans fit tightly so no water or steam from the bottom pan can escape and mix with the ingredients in the top pan, and so that the top pan doesn't float around in the water. A double boiler can be made from a saucepan and a bowl that fit tightly together. Always keep

the water level in the bottom pan low (about 1 inch) so it doesn't touch the top of the bowl. Using a glass pan for the bottom allows you to see the level of the water and how hot it becomes. Be sure to use a double boiler that has enough room to hold the ingredients and leaves room for stirring.

Copper Sugar Pan

Copper is the best material for evenly and consistently conducting heat. For this reason, it is the ultimate material for cooking sugar mixtures. Unlined copper pans with straight sides and a pour spout are designed especially for cooking sugar mixtures. The copper pan used for cooking sugar must be unlined because the tin usually used for lining does not have the same resistance to high heat as copper and would melt. The pans make it easy to see the color changes as sugar cooks. I have both 1-quart and 2-quart solid copper sugar pans that I use exclusively for cooking sugar mixtures. Copper sugar pans must be kept very clean so there is no foreign material to contaminate the sugar mixture. It's not necessary to add cream of tartar to sugar mixtures cooked in a solid copper pan. If sugar sticks to the pan, fill it with water and bring it to a boil. To clean copper, use a solution of salt and vinegar or lemon juice. Rub this mixture all over the pan briskly, rinse completely, and dry with a soft towel.

Saucepans

One-half quart, 1-quart, 2-quart, and 3½-quart saucepans are used the most in the baking kitchen. They are used for heating liquids, cooking sugar mixtures, cooking custards and other fillings, and heating glazes. Good-quality, heavy-duty saucepans are the best choice because they last a very long time and don't burn their contents. They should have a non-reactive surface so they don't taint any ingredients with a metal taste. I have used Le Creuset enameled cast-iron saucepans for over twenty-five years. The light-colored interior makes it easy to see what is happening as mixtures cook. I also use Calphalon and Analon saucepans.

SUPPLIES
Aluminum Foil

One of the major uses of aluminum foil is to cover baked goods for storage at both room temperature and in the refrigerator or freezer. It helps to seal out air and maintain freshness longer. Foil is also used to line baking sheets, especially for meringues, and for lining pans for brownies and some bar cookies to make it easy to lift them out of the pan when cool. It is also the perfect choice for lining containers to store some cookies and other baked goods.

Cardboard Cake Rounds, Rectangles, and Squares

Corrugated cardboard rounds, rectangles, and squares are placed underneath cakes and tarts to give them stability while they are being assembled, served, and transported. These precut pieces come in a huge variety of sizes and shapes. They are available at cookware and craft shops and through many online sources and catalogs.

Non-Stick Pan Liners

Silicone (Silpat) pan liners are non-stick and are reusable. They come in different sizes and can't be cut to fit, so be sure to buy the sizes you need for your pans.

Parchment Paper

Greaseproof and non-stick, food-safe parchment paper has a wide variety of uses in the baking kitchen. It is most often used to line baking sheets and the bottom of baking pans, so baked goods don't stick. In many cases, such as when baking cookies, using parchment paper eliminates the need to butter and flour pans, which is a great time saver and reduces clean-up work. Parchment paper is also used for rolling out some pastry, pie, and cookie doughs, and to make pastry cones for decorative work. It is available in rolls and sheets, in pre-cut circles, or in triangles used to make pastry cones.

Plastic Wrap

Plastic wrap has many uses in the baking kitchen. It covers pre-measured ingredients so they don't dry out or lose flavor from exposure to air. It covers dough that is mixed and needs to chill in the refrigerator to keep it from picking up other flavors. It covers cake layers after they are cool and before they are assembled with filling, so they don't become crusty. And it covers many finished baked goods to keep them fresh. Use a good quality plastic wrap that clings tightly.

Rice Paper

Rice paper is an edible, almost transparent paper made from rice flour. It is flavorless and comes in rectangular, round, or square sheets. It is used to line the pan for Panforte. Rice paper should be kept completely dry or it will dissolve. It is available where cake decorating supplies are sold and in some Asian markets.

Storage Containers

Plastic containers of various sizes are very useful for storing ingredients as well as cookies, brownies, scones, and other baked goods when they are completely cool. Containers with tight-fitting lids create a seal that keeps the items inside protected from air and moisture. I like to label and date containers with what they contain so I know how long the contents have been kept.

Waxed Paper

Waxed paper is aptly named because it is coated with wax on both sides. For this reason, it's not good for lining baking pans because it has a low melting point. But it has many other uses. I use waxed paper to sift dry ingredients onto so it's easy to move them around and to add them to a mixing bowl while the beater is moving. Waxed paper is used to shape cookie doughs into rolls or cylinders and to wrap them for chilling before they are cut. I like to roll out pie and pastry dough between sheets of lightly floured waxed paper. This makes it easy to move the dough as it's being rolled so it's always at the right angle, and it keeps the counter cleaner than rolling directly on it. Waxed paper is also used to line containers that hold cookies and other baked goods to separate them so they don't crowd or crush each other.

ESSENTIAL

TECHNIQUES

USING THE CORRECT technique for each recipe makes baking easy and fun and can make the difference between opening the oven and taking out a perfectly baked cake or one that falls. It takes the same amount of time to follow the proper technique as it does to guess. This chapter gives you all the essential techniques you need to make perfect cakes, pies, tarts, cookies, scones, muffins, and many other desserts. Refer back to this chapter as often as you need to and with any question you may have as you bake.

PREPARATION TECHNIQUES
In order to be successful at baking and to enjoy the experience, one of the most important steps is to be prepared with your supplies and ingredients so they will be ready to use and at your fingertips when you need them. Some of this can be done several hours to days in advance of baking. Everyone leads busy lives these days, so any shortcuts and advance steps minimize time spent in the kitchen.

Supplies

• *Cutting parchment paper to fit cake and other baking pans*
Place the cake or other baking pan on top of a piece of parchment paper that's larger than the pan. Use a pencil to trace the outer edge of the pan. Remove the pan and use sharp scissors to cut out the shape slightly inside of the traced line. The parchment will fit exactly to the bottom of the cake or other baking pan. To cut out two shapes at the same time, fold a large piece of parchment paper in half or use two pieces.

• *Making a parchment paper pastry cone*
Buy ready-made parchment paper triangles or cut your own from parchment paper. Parchment paper pastry cones are made from triangles that have two equal-length sides and a base that is larger than the sides. Hold the triangle in front of you with the wide end toward you and the top point facing down. Curve the right corner in and bring it down to the bottom point, so they line up evenly. Use one hand to hold the two points together. With your other hand, take the left point of the triangle and wrap it around the outside, bringing it down to meet the other two points. This forms a cone. Fold the back (seamed) edge of the cone down to the center a couple of times and secure the back seam with a piece of clear tape. You should have an open cone. Make up several parchment paper pastry cones to have on hand.

• *Preparing a new pastry bag*
New pastry bags need to have about ¹/₂ inch cut off at the tip to make room for the decorating tube or tip to fit. Measure before cutting and remove only enough to fit the smallest tube or tip you will use with the pastry bag. To do this, place the pastry tube in the bag with the widest end up and press the tube so it fits all the way against the tip of the bag. A little of the pastry tube should be sticking out. Make a pencil mark where you want to make the cut. Take the tube out of the bag and cut with sharp scissors along the mark, then replace the tube in the bag.

• *Lining square or rectangular pans with foil*
I like to do this when I bake brownies and bar cookies because this makes it easy to lift them out of the pan when cool. Also, once they're cut, it's easy to get the first one out without having it break and crumble. This also works well for baking loaf and pound cakes. To line a pan with foil, cut a piece that's several inches larger than the pan. Hold the foil over the pan and use the edges of the pan as a guide. Mark the foil by pinching it where you will fold it, then place the foil on the countertop and

fold all four edges toward the center. Place the folded foil in the pan and unfold. Use your fingertips to press the foil into the bottom and against the edges so it fits tightly, taking care not to make any holes in the foil. Tightly fold any excess foil around the outer edges of the pan. When the brownies, bar cookies, or loaf cake are cool, unfold the excess foil and use it to lift them from the pan.

• *Preparing cake pans*

Practically every cake recipe, except angel food and chiffon cakes, calls for the pan to be greased and floured, which prevents the cake from sticking to the pan. Often, the pan is also lined with a piece of parchment paper. Apply softened butter to the inside of the cake pan either with a paper towel or clean fingers. Apply melted butter with a pastry brush set aside for that purpose or use a paper towel. With either method, pay close attention and be sure to coat all the grooves and seams on the inside of the pan. Decorative pans, such as Bundt pans, have many curves and grooves. The cake can stick to any place on the pan that is not coated. To dust the pan with flour, place a generous amount (1 to 2 tablespoons) of flour in the pan. Hold the pan over the sink and shake and tilt it so the flour sticks to the pan. Turn the pan upside down and shake it to remove any excess flour. If using a parchment paper liner, butter it first, then place it in the bottom of the pan, butter-side up.

Non-stick baking spray also helps to keep cakes from sticking to their pans. Baker's Joy is a spray of flour and oil that is designed for coating baking pans. I also like to use Ever-Bake and Baker's Release Spray, non-stick sprays made from canola oil. Use non-stick spray instead of butter and flour.

INGREDIENTS
Butter

• *Bringing butter to room temperature (softening butter)*

Unless a recipe specifies otherwise, butter should be at room temperature before using. This means that it should be pliable enough to hold the indentation of a finger, but not so soft that it turns into liquid. There are two ways to bring butter to room temperature. One is to let it stand at room temperature until it reaches the correct consistency. How long this takes depends on the time of year and where you live. If it's summer and very hot, butter will soften quickly. In the winter it will take longer to reach a soft texture. Butter can also be softened in a microwave oven.

Use low power for 5- to 15-second bursts and check the butter carefully after each burst. If you're softening a stick or larger piece of butter, turn it after each burst, so that different surfaces are exposed. This helps the butter to soften evenly. Also, be familiar with your microwave oven because they are all different and it's very easy to melt butter in a powerful microwave.

• *Melting butter*

There are two ways to melt butter: on the stovetop or in a microwave oven. For either technique, cut the butter into small pieces, so it will melt quickly and evenly.

To melt butter on the stovetop, place the pieces in a small to medium heavy-duty saucepan over low heat. It takes a few minutes to melt butter this way. To melt butter in a microwave oven, place the pieces in a microwave-safe bowl, leaving extra room. Heat it on medium power for 1 minute. Check the butter to see if it's melting and heat again on medium power for 1 minute. Check it again and, if it's not completely melted, heat it on medium power for another 30 seconds. It may be necessary to repeat this if the butter isn't completely melted. If the butter is very hot, let it cool briefly before using.

Chocolate

• *Chopping chocolate*

Chop chocolate with a large chef's knife on a cutting board or use a chocolate chipper, a tool that looks like a large, wide fork. Work with a chunk of chocolate that isn't too big and unwieldy. To encourage even melting, chocolate needs to be chopped very finely, about the size of matchsticks. To make chocolate chunks, chop or cut chocolate into pieces that are about 1/2 inch.

• *Grinding chocolate*

Place small chunks of chocolate in the bowl of a food processor fitted with a steel blade. Add other dry ingredients called for in the recipe, such as flour, sugar, or cocoa powder. Pulse the mixture until the chocolate is very finely ground, about two minutes. Don't grind the chocolate without other dry ingredients because the heat of the motor may melt it.

• *Melting chocolate*

Place finely chopped chocolate in the top of a double boiler over low heat. You can make a double boiler with a saucepan and a bowl. Make sure the top pan or bowl fits snugly to the bottom pan so no water or steam can escape and mix with the chocolate. If this happens, the chocolate will "seize" and become like mud. Keep the water level in the lower pan very low, about an inch, and don't let it touch the bottom of the top pan or bowl. Have the top pan or bowl and all utensils completely dry. A drop or two of water will cause the chocolate to seize. Keep the heat under the bottom pan very low because the heat will accumulate and build as the chocolate melts. Stir the chocolate often with a rubber spatula to help it melt evenly. When three-fourths of the chocolate is melted, turn off the heat under the bottom pan and continue to stir the chocolate until it is completely melted. There will be enough residual heat in the bottom pan to melt the remaining chocolate. When all the chocolate is melted, remove the top pan of the double boiler and wipe the bottom and sides very dry (see page 373 for more information).

Chocolate can also be melted in a microwave oven. Place finely chopped chocolate in a microwave-safe bowl and melt on low power for 30-second bursts. Stir with a rubber spatula after each burst to help ensure that it is melting. Repeat as often as necessary until the chocolate is completely melted.

• *Shaving chocolate and making chocolate curls*
It's easiest to shave chocolate and make curls if the chocolate is not too cold. If it is too cold, the chocolate will splinter and break and make it difficult to obtain nice shavings. On the opposite side, many people have warm hands and simply holding a piece of chocolate makes it start to melt. If this is the case, hold the chocolate with a paper towel while shaving. Use a chunk of chocolate or a large bar so there is enough surface to work from. Place a large piece of waxed paper under the chocolate to catch the shavings or curls.

Hold the chunk or bar of chocolate and rub it firmly against a fine grater. Microplane makes a grater specifically for shaving chocolate. Instead of a grater, you can use a small, sharp knife. Push the knife away from you, down the length of the chocolate piece. Or use a vegetable peeler to run along the side of the chocolate chunk or bar. Turn the chocolate piece occasionally and change the side you are working on.

Try not to handle the shavings or curls too much, so they don't melt or break. Use the waxed paper to transfer them to a container for storage or directly to the top of the cake or other dessert for decoration. Store chocolate shavings and curls in an airtight plastic container in a cool, dry place, such as a pantry, not in the refrigerator, where they may form condensation.

• *Tempering chocolate*
Tempering gives chocolate a glossy sheen and a smooth appearance. It also sets cocoa butter, which is part of chocolate, at a stable point so the chocolate holds its good looks and breaks with a crisp snap.

To temper chocolate I use either of the following methods. Note that it's best to temper no less than 6 ounces and no more than 2 pounds of chocolate at a time.

QUICK TEMPERING METHOD
Chop the chocolate into very small pieces and set aside one-third of them. Melt the remaining two-thirds in the top of a double boiler over hot water, stirring often, or in a microwave oven on low power for 30-second bursts, stirring after each burst. This ensures even melting. The chocolate should not be heated over 120°F or it will burn (110°F for white chocolate), so if the water in the bottom pan boils, it will send too much heat into the top pan of chocolate. If this happens, immediately remove the top pan from the water and stir the chocolate vigorously to cool it down. Replace the water in the bottom pan of the double boiler and place over very low heat. When the chocolate is melted, remove the top pan of the double boiler from the heat and wipe it completely dry. Stir in the remaining chopped chocolate in three batches. Make sure each batch is completely melted before adding the next. When all the chocolate has been added, test it (see below) to be sure it is tempered.

CHUNK TEMPERING METHOD
Chop three-fourths of the chocolate into very small pieces and leave one-fourth in a large chunk. Melt the chopped chocolate in the top of a double boiler over hot water, stirring often, or in a microwave oven on low power for 30-second bursts, stirring after each burst. This ensures even melting. Remove the top pan of the double boiler from the heat and wipe it completely dry. Stir the chocolate briefly to cool it, then add the remaining chunk and stir to reduce the temperature.

For either method, if the chocolate is too warm after finishing the process, either add more finely chopped chocolate or continue to stir the chunk around until the chocolate cools. If the chocolate is too cool, warm it over hot water until it reaches the right temperature.

To test the temper, use a spatula or spoon to place a drop of chocolate directly underneath your lower lip. See how it feels. It should feel comfortable—neither too hot nor too cold—to be at the correct temperature. Or spread about 1 teaspoon of the tempered chocolate on a piece of aluminum foil. Either place the foil in the refrigerator for about 2 minutes, let it stand in front of an electric fan, or use a hair dryer on low setting with no heat. With any of these methods the chocolate should set quickly, have a glossy sheen, and show no streaks if it is correctly tempered. If you want to use a chocolate or instant-read thermometer to test the final temperature of the chocolate, use this chart as a guideline:

Finished Temperature Ranges for
Tempered Chocolate
Dark Chocolate: 88° to 91°F
Milk Chocolate: 85° to 88°F
White Chocolate: 84° to 87°F

To hold the temper of chocolate while using it to dip, place the bowl or pan over a pan of water that is two degrees warmer than the chocolate. You can use an instant-read thermometer to test the water temperature. If you do this, wipe it completely dry after each use and take care not to dip the thermometer into the chocolate. Change the water often while dipping to keep it at the right temperature but take care not to mix any water with the chocolate, which will cause it to seize up and become unusable. Another way to hold the temper is to place the bowl of chocolate on a heating pad set at its lowest temperature. In either case, be sure to stir the chocolate often while dipping, so it doesn't build up around the sides of the bowl and become too cool.

Eggs

• *Separating*

Several recipes require eggs to be separated into their two individual parts—whites and yolks. This is done so that the whites and yolks can be whipped separately, a technique that adds air, which aids in leavening when baked. It's easiest to separate eggs when they are cold, but egg whites whip to their fullest volume when warm. I recommend separating eggs while cold, then tightly cover the bowls with plastic wrap and let the whites and yolks warm up to room temperature before using them.

It's important to be careful not to mix together the egg whites and yolks while separating them. Any stray amount of yolk (fat) in the whites will keep them from whipping to their fullest volume. The best way to prevent this is to separate the eggs individually over a small bowl before adding the yolks and whites to separate larger bowls.

There are three methods for separating eggs: the shell-to-shell method, the egg separator method, and the hand method.

For the shell-to-shell method, break the shell against a sharp surface (the side or rim of a bowl, a countertop, or sink) as close to the center of the egg as possible. Gently pull the two sides of the shell apart and keep the egg yolk in one side while holding the shell up. Hold the two sides of the shell close together, tilt them so the openings face each other, and allow the egg white to drip from the shell into a bowl underneath. While holding the shells close together, carefully pass the egg yolk back and forth from one side of the shell to the other and let the egg white drop out of the shell into the bowl. Place the egg yolk in another bowl.

Use a tool called an egg separator for the egg separator method. This tool has a flat bottom with a small bowl in the center that holds the egg yolk while the egg white drips through slots that surround the center bowl. Place the egg separator over a bowl. Crack the egg and place it into the center of the separator. The egg white will drip out in the bowl underneath. Place the egg yolk in another bowl.

For the hand method, break the shell against a sharp surface as close as possible to the center of the egg. Pull the two sides of the shell apart and place the egg in the center of your cupped hand. Separate your fingers and let the egg white drip out into a bowl underneath. The egg yolk will stay in your palm. Place the egg yolk in another bowl.

• *Freezing egg whites*

Egg whites freeze very well and keep for several months in the freezer. Put them in an airtight plastic freezer container and tightly seal the top. Place a large piece of masking tape on the front of the container and, with an indelible marker, write the date and the number of egg whites. Another way to freeze egg whites is to put them into the cavities of an ice cube tray. Each cavity holds one egg white. When they are frozen, transfer the egg whites to a freezer bag and seal it tightly.

• *Using frozen egg whites*

Defrost the egg whites overnight in the refrigerator, at room temperature, or in a microwave oven on low power for 30-second bursts. Check them after each burst, so they don't become overheated. Defrosted egg whites work as well as fresh ones. Make sure they are warmed up to room temperature before whipping them.

• *Bringing eggs to room temperature*

Most baking recipes work best with eggs at room temperature. The easiest way to bring them to room temperature is to take them out of the refrigerator and let them stand on the kitchen counter until they have warmed. This takes about a half hour. If you don't have time for this method, place them in a bowl of hot, but not boiling, water for a couple of minutes. Eggs can also be warmed in the microwave oven on low power for 10-second bursts. Check them after each burst by feeling them in your hand to see how warm they are. This method can be tricky because it's easy to cook the eggs, so proceed with caution.

• *Warming eggs and sugar over hot water*

This technique involves placing the mixing bowl containing eggs and sugar over hot, but not boiling, water and whisking together constantly for a few minutes. Whisking keeps the ingredients from becoming too warm. The purpose of this technique is to blend the two ingredients together well and to help them whip to their maximum volume.

Fruit

• *Blanching fruit*

To remove the skin from peaches, use a technique called blanching. To do this, bring water to a boil in a large saucepan or stockpot over high heat. Using a sharp knife, score a small X in the bottom of each peach. Add the peaches and let them boil for 1 or 2 minutes. Use a slotted spoon or skimmer to remove the peaches from the boiling water. Then starting at the X, use a small sharp knife to gently peel the skin off of the peaches. It should slip off easily. If the peaches are too hot, peel them under cold running water.

Nuts

• *Toasting*

Toasting brings out the flavor of nuts. Spread them in a single layer in a cake pan, pie pan, or jelly-roll pan and toast in a 350°F oven. Toast all nuts, except hazelnuts, for 5 minutes, then shake the pan or stir the nuts, and toast for another 3 to 5 minutes, un-

til they turn light golden brown. Toast hazelnuts for 15 to 18 minutes. Nuts burn quickly, so be sure to check them frequently as they toast. An easy way to tell when they're ready to come out of the oven is if their skins are split. Another indication is aroma. If you can smell them, then they're most likely done.

When the nuts are toasted, remove the pan from the oven and transfer them to a cool pan so they don't continue to cook on the hot pan, then place the cool pan on a cooling rack and let the nuts cool completely

• *Skinning*

The skin of hazelnuts has a slightly bitter flavor, so it's best to remove as much of the skins as possible. To skin hazelnuts, transfer them from the hot pan to a kitchen towel and fold the towel up around them. Leave them in the towel for 10 minutes, then rub them together to remove most of the skins. Some of the skins will stick, which is fine.

Blanching is the best way to skin almonds. Do this by dropping them into a large pan of boiling water for 1 minute. Use a slotted spoon or a skimmer to remove them from the boiling water and immediately put them in a bowl of cold water, which stops them from cooking. Leave them in the cold water for a minute or two. Drain the almonds, pat them dry, and gently squeeze them between your fingers. They will easily pop out of their skins.

• *Chopping*

Chop nuts on a cutting board using a chef's knife with an 8- to 10-inch blade. Be sure the blade of the knife is sharp. Start with no more than 1 cup of nuts or they will be flying in all directions. Place the nuts in the center of the cutting board. Position the blade of the knife on top of the nuts and, hold the knife by the handle. Place your other hand over the top of the blade to help steady it. Rock the knife back and forth and in an arc over the nuts while applying downward pressure. Lift the knife occasionally to gather in more nuts. Gather the chopped nuts into the center of the cutting board and repeat the chopping motion until they are the size you want.

Nuts can also be chopped in the work bowl of a food processor fitted with a steel blade, but the chop is not as even as it is if done by hand. Also, it's too easy to over-process the nuts and wind up with nut paste. To chop nuts in a food processor, add 1 tablespoon of sugar for each cup of nuts to keep them from turning to paste. For nuts that have more oil, such as hazelnuts, Brazil nuts, and macadamia nuts, add 2 tablespoons sugar for each cup. Pulse the nuts and sugar together until they are chopped to the size you need. If you are chopping a small amount of nuts in a food processor, it's best to use a mini processor to obtain an even chop.

• *Grinding*

The best way to grind nuts is in the work bowl of a food processor fitted with a steel blade. All nuts have a high content of natural oil that is released when they are ground. As above for chopping, add 1 tablespoon of sugar for each cup of nuts to keep them from turning to paste and add 2 tablespoons of sugar for nuts with more oil. Pulse the nuts and sugar together until they are as finely ground as you want. This takes anywhere from 30 seconds to 2 minutes.

If I'm grinding nuts for a specific recipe, I take the sugar from the amount called for in the recipe. However, I like to have some ground nuts on hand for those times that I'm inspired to bake and don't have a lot of time. They keep very well in the freezer. The extra tablespoon or two of sugar used for grinding the nuts doesn't make a noticeable difference in the recipe.

When grinding almonds, it's easier to get a more consistent texture if you start with sliced or slivered rather than whole almonds.

• *Toasting coconut*

There are three ways to toast coconut: in the oven, on the stovetop, and in a microwave oven.

To toast coconut in the oven, spread it in a single layer in a cake pan or on a rimmed baking sheet and toast in a 325°F oven for 15 to 20 minutes, stirring frequently, until golden brown.

To toast coconut on the stovetop, heat a medium or large, heavy-duty sauté or frying pan over medium heat. When the pan is hot, add the coconut and cook, stirring often, until it turns light golden brown. This takes 2 to 3 minutes. Remove the pan from the heat and immediately transfer the coconut to a cool pan or plate so it doesn't continue cooking in the hot pan.

To toast coconut in a microwave oven, spread it in a single layer in a microwave-safe plate or pan. Heat it on high power for 1 minute. Stir or shake the coconut and heat again on high power for 1 minute. Again stir or shake the coconut. It may need to be heated again for 30 seconds to 1 minute.

Dry Ingredients

• *Sifting*

It's not necessary to sift all-purpose flour before measuring it for baking, but I do recommend sifting cake flour because it tends to get lumpy when it sits for a while. It's also a good idea to sift dry ingredients such as confectioners' sugar, cornstarch, cocoa powder, baking powder, and baking soda before combining them with other ingredients because these all tend to be lumpy. My favorite sifter is a large plastic strainer with a fine-mesh screen. Place the strainer over a large piece of waxed paper, parchment paper, or a bowl and push the ingredients through with a spoon or your hand, or shake the strainer gently from side to side.

MEASURING AND WEIGHING TECHNIQUES

In general, with savory cooking it's easy to add extra ingredients without causing any problems. Baking, however, is much more precise and requires that the quantity of ingredients specified in a recipe is exact. It's a must to use correct measuring techniques to ensure the success of your baked goods.

Measuring Dry Ingredients

For accuracy, be sure to use dry measuring cups for measuring dry ingredients, such as flour, sugar, confectioners' sugar, cocoa powder, and cornmeal. Dry measuring cups are designed so they can be leveled off at the top. It's not possible to do this in liquid measuring cups because there is extra room at the top to allow the liquid some room for movement. There are two main methods for measuring dry ingredients: scoop and sweep, and spoon and sweep.

For the scoop and sweep method, scoop the measuring cup into the dry ingredient, heaping it over the top. Take care not to tap the cup or hit it on the counter top because this causes the ingredient to pack down and gives an incorrect measure. Use the flat side of a knife or spatula to sweep across the top of the measuring cup and remove any excess. The remaining ingredient should be flush to the top of the measuring cup. Use this method to measure small quantities of dry ingredients with measuring spoons such as baking soda, baking powder, cream of tartar, and spices.

For the spoon and sweep method, loosely spoon the ingredient into the measuring cup and sweep off the excess at the top with a flat implement.

Brown sugar holds a lot of air between its crystals that needs to be squeezed out for an accurate measure. To measure brown sugar, scoop the sugar into the measuring cup, then press it down firmly with your hand or a spatula. Add more brown sugar to the cup as needed and press it down, until it's flush with the top of the measure.

Measuring Semi-Solid Ingredients

Peanut butter and sour cream can be difficult to measure because some of it stays in the measuring cup. These are measured in the same way as dry ingredients, with dry measures. To measure these ingredients, I like to use a measuring cup that is designed so that the bottom pushes up and pushes the ingredient out, after the ingredient has been measured and leveled off at the top. Another way to measure these ingredients and not lose any is to line the measuring cup with plastic wrap, letting some hang over the edges. To remove the ingredient, lift up the plastic wrap and scrape off any leftovers of the ingredient with a spatula.

Measuring Liquid Ingredients

Liquid ingredients should be measured in a liquid measuring cup with a pour spout. These measuring cups have extra room at the top for the liquid to move around. For an accurate reading, place the measuring cup on a flat surface and read it at the level of the lines on the side. There is a new style of liquid measuring cups made by Oxo that are slanted rather than straight. These are designed to be read from above, so you don't have to squat down to see the lines on the side of the cup.

Honey and molasses are sticky, which makes it hard to measure them accurately. To prevent them from sticking to the measuring cup, lightly oil the cup or spray it with non-stick cooking spray before measuring them.

Measuring and Sifting Dry Ingredients; Sifting and Measuring Dry Ingredients

It's important to read recipes carefully so you understand how they call for the ingredients to be handled. If a recipe calls for dry ingredients to be measured and sifted, measure first and then sift. If it calls for the dry ingredients to be sifted and measured, sift first and then measure. It may not sound like much of a differ-ence, but there is a distinct difference in the quantity obtained with each of these methods.

Measuring Butter

Weighing butter is the most accurate way to measure it. A stick of butter weighs 4 ounces and measures 8 tablespoons. Two tablespoons of butter weigh 1 ounce. The wrappers on sticks of butter are marked into tablespoons. Use these as a guide as long as the wrappers are on straight. If you don't have a kitchen scale, measure butter in dry measuring cups. The butter must be soft to measure this way. Place the butter in the measuring cup and press it down to eliminate any air bubbles. Level off the butter at the top of the dry measuring cup with the flat side of a spatula or knife. Use a rubber spatula to scrape the butter out of the measuring cup. One stick of butter measures $1/2$ cup.

Measuring Chocolate

Block or bulk chocolate must be weighed on an accurate kitchen scale. I chop a large piece of chocolate into small pieces and place these in a bowl or other container to weigh, taking into account the weight of the bowl or container. If you're using chocolate bars that are marked into pieces, break off the amount you need. It's a good idea to re-check the amount on a kitchen scale, if you have one. Measure chocolate chips and cacao nibs in dry measures, the same as other dry ingredients (see above).

MIXING TECHNIQUES

Mixing is the technique that combines ingredients into a homog-enous blend. There are several methods for mixing.

Stirring

Stirring is the technique for lightly mixing ingredients. Use low speed if mixing with an electric mixer. Stirring can also be ac-complished by hand using a rubber spatula or a spoon. To do this, start at the center of the bowl and use a circular motion that moves to the outside edge of the bowl. The idea is to blend the ingredients together so they are no longer separate and are evenly distributed. The key here is not to stir too vigorously; if the flour protein is triggered, the mixture will become tough or too many air bubbles will be created, which will make the mixture rise too high in the oven and then fall because the overall structure won't be strong enough to support it.

Folding

This is a mixing technique that's used to combine a light mixture with a heavy mixture while retaining the air that's been whipped into them. This is a method of gently stirring and is always done by hand, never by machine. To fold, place the lighter mixture (whipped egg whites or whipped cream) on top of the heavier mixture (batter). Use a long-handled rubber spatula and bring the blade of it down through the center of the bowl and sweep it around the inner edge of the bowl, bringing it toward you. Give the bowl a quarter turn in the opposite direction and bring the blade of the rubber spatula along the bottom and up through the center, which raises some of the bottom mixture up. Repeat this process quickly, but gently, many times until the mixture is completely blended. Some recipes call for a small amount of the light mixture to be mixed into the heavier mixture first, which helps to lighten the heavier mixture and make it easier to blend, before the rest of the light mixture is folded in.

Beating

Beating involves a quicker and more dynamic circular action that incorporates air into the mixture and creates a smooth blend. An electric stand mixer with a flat paddle attachment or a hand-held mixer is the best tool for beating. Work at medium speed for best results.

• Creaming
This technique is widely used in baking and refers to the method of beating fat, such as butter and other ingredients (usually sugar) together until they are smooth and homogenous. The ingredients should be so well combined that it's impossible to distinguish them separately. For best results the butter should be at room temperature, but not too soft. Use an electric stand mixer with the flat paddle attachment or a hand-held mixer on medium speed. Start with the butter and beat it until it is very smooth and fluffy, one to two minutes. Add the sugar and beat together until well combined, another minute or two. Stop occasionally and scrape down the sides and bottom of the bowl with a rubber spatula to be sure they are mixing evenly.

Whipping

Whipping is the most vigorous and rapid form of mixing in a circular motion that incorporates the most air into a mixture. Medium-high to high speed using an electric stand mixer with the wire whip attachment, a hand-held mixer, or an immersion blender is the best way to accomplish whipping.

• Whipping until foamy
This involves whipping the ingredient (usually eggs or cream) on medium speed until it begins to gain volume and has small bubbles on the surface. If adding other ingredients, such as cream of tartar to egg whites or vanilla extract to cream, the best time to add them is at the foamy stage.

• Holding a ribbon
This is the stage that refers to the consistency of a batter or mixture—usually eggs and sugar—beaten or whipped until it is very thick and pale colored. Whip the mixture with an electric stand mixer using the wire whip attachment or a hand-held mixer on medium to medium-high speed for about 5 minutes. To tell if the mixture is thick enough, dip a rubber spatula into it and lift if up. Let the mixture drip from the spatula into the bowl. The mixture should very slowly fall back on itself in a ribbon-like manner and hold its shape for a few seconds before dissolving back into the bowl.

• Whipping egg whites
Egg whites whip best when they are at room temperature. (See above section, Preparation Techniques: Eggs, for more information.) Whip them in the bowl of an electric stand mixer with the wire whip attachment or in a large mixing bowl with a hand-held mixer. Make sure the bowl has enough room for the egg whites to triple in volume. Start with medium speed and increase it to medium-high as the egg whites gain volume. Check often while the whites are whipping to see that they don't become grainy and start to separate, which are symptoms of overwhipping.

Egg whites won't whip if they are in contact with any fat. This means that a stray drop or two of egg yolk or other fat will cause problems and is the reason why it's important to keep the yolks and whites completely away from each other when separating eggs. To prevent this problem, make sure that any utensils used for whipping egg whites are clean and grease-free. To do this, use lemon juice or vinegar to wipe the bowl and beaters before using. Be sure to wipe them completely dry to remove any lingering traces of the lemon juice or vinegar.

To aid egg whites in reaching their maximum volume, add a little cream of tartar, usually 1/4 teaspoon for 3 to 5 extra-large egg whites, when they start to form bubbles. This stabilizes them and allows them to hold onto the air that's whipped in.

• *Whipping cream*

It's easier to whip cream that is very cold rather than warm because cold cream holds onto the air whipped into it. Use an electric stand mixer with the wire whip attachment or a hand-held mixer, and chill the bowl and beater either in the refrigerator or freezer for about a half hour before whipping cream. Or place the mixing bowl in a larger bowl of ice water while whipping the cream. Start by whipping the cream on medium speed or it will splash out of the bowl. As the cream gains volume, turn the speed up to medium-high. Watch the cream carefully because it can very quickly go from the right point to overwhipped, which will turn into butter. If you mistakenly whip the cream a bit too firm, add another tablespoon or two of cream and whisk it in on medium speed to make the cream a smoother consistency.

• *Soft peaks*

This is the stage where the ingredient (egg whites or whipping cream) is whipped until it forms peaks that can barely hold their shape. If you scoop a small amount of the ingredient from the mixing bowl onto a spatula and hold it upright, you will see that the peak curves to one side and does not stand straight up.

• *Firm peaks*

This is the stage where the ingredient (egg whites or whipping cream) is whipped until it forms peaks that stand upright with a solid shape. There is a distinction, though, between firm peaks that hold their shape well and stiff peaks that are too rigid to mix with other ingredients. Egg whites whipped to firm peaks will look glossy and smooth. If you scoop a small amount of the ingredient from the mixing bowl onto a spatula and hold it upright, you will see that the peak holds its shape but has some elasticity to it. If egg whites are overwhipped, they will look lumpy and dry

and will separate. There really is no remedy for overwhipped egg whites.

Adding Eggs to Mixtures

Follow the directions in each recipe for when to add the eggs. Sometimes they are lightly whisked together before they are added to a mixture. Other times, the recipe calls for the eggs to be added one at a time and to mix well after each addition. When eggs are added to a mixture of butter (or other fat) and sugar, they tend to sit on top. When this happens, stop mixing and scrape down the sides and bottom of the bowl with a rubber spatula. This helps the mixture blend together. Another thing that happens when eggs are added to a butter and sugar mixture is that the mixture looks curdled. Don't worry about this because when the dry ingredients are added, the curdled look disappears.

Adding Dry Ingredients While the Mixer Is Running

Since I recommend sifting over a large piece of waxed paper or parchment paper, it's very easy to use the same paper to add the dry ingredients to the mixing bowl. Fold or gather the paper in half, hold it over the edge of the mixing bowl, and sprinkle the dry ingredients in. Most recipes call for the dry ingredients to be added in a few stages. This lets the batter absorb them and facilitates even mixing.

Adding Dry and Wet Ingredients Alternately

Occasionally a recipe calls for dry and wet ingredients to be added alternately. If all of the dry ingredients were added before the wet ingredients, the mixture would be too firm and difficult to stir. Adding the dry and wet ingredients alternately keeps the mixture in an even balance and creates a smooth blend.

GENERAL BAKING TECHNIQUES
Where to Bake in the Oven

Most baked goods do best when placed on the center rack in the oven. Many recipes call for the oven racks to be adjusted to the upper and lower thirds of the oven. When this is the case, the recipe will tell you to switch the pans partway through baking, which allows the pans to bake evenly. If the source of heat is in the bottom of the oven, then whatever is closest to the bottom will bake and brown quicker. When two cakes are baked on the same oven rack, be sure there is enough space between them—at least a couple of inches—so the air can circulate around them for even baking.

Know Your Oven

Every oven bakes differently. Some ovens run hotter than others and many ovens have hot spots, areas that are hotter than the rest of the oven. A good way to check the temperature of your oven is with an oven thermometer. I like to use one that hangs on the oven rack. I move it around to different areas in the oven periodically to check for hot spots. If the oven is too hot it will over-bake whatever is in it. Several years ago, I taught a class at a local cooking school and everything I made burned. I was so embarrassed! I had set the ovens at the temperature called for in my recipes, but it did no good. After class I asked the cooking school owner to have the ovens checked. A couple of days later she called to tell me that the ovens were running 100 degrees too hot. No wonder everything burned!

Use a Timer

Set a timer for the least amount of time specified in the recipe you are following. Check to see if the item is done. If not, extend the baking time a few more minutes, and check again. A timer allows you to concentrate on other things while you are baking. I used to think I would remember to check what I had in my oven and turned my attention to other activities. After I burned several cakes and batches of cookies, I decided that using a timer was in order.

Cooling Baked Goods

Cool all baked goods on a cooling rack. This allows air to circulate completely around and underneath. Some cookie recipes recommend transferring the cookies from the baking pan directly to the rack. To do this, use a flat, wide spatula to wedge under the cookies. Some cake recipes recommend cooling the cake in the pan for 15 to 20 minutes, removing the cake from the pan, and cooling completely on a rack. Be sure to read each recipe for specific instructions.

Storing and Freezing Baked Goods

Most baked goods can be held at room temperature for a day or two after baking, as long as they are well wrapped. Each recipe states the optimal way to store. Many baked goods can be frozen with good results. To freeze, wrap very well in several layers of plastic wrap and aluminum foil to avoid freezer burn. If the item fits, place it in a freezer bag. Defrost frozen items slowly in the refrigerator for at least 12 hours. I generally recommend defrosting overnight. Then bring the baked goods to room temperature to develop the best flavor.

CAKE TECHNIQUES
Testing Cakes for Doneness

There are three ways to test cakes for doneness. Use a cake tester or a toothpick and push it into the cake, either in the center or about 2 inches in from the outer edge. The recipe will tell you what to look for. In most cases, the tester or toothpick should be dry or have a few crumbs clinging to it. Another way to tell if a cake is done is to lightly touch it on top. If it springs back and doesn't hold the indentation of your fingertips, it's done. The third way to test for doneness is to observe the appearance of the cake. The cake should look risen and set in the center, and the edges should be starting to pull away from the sides of the pan.

Turning Cakes out of Their Pans

Run a thin-bladed knife or metal spatula carefully around the inside edge of the cake pan. Be very careful not to cut into the cake, but simply to loosen it from the sides of the pan. Place a cooling rack over the top of the cake pan, hold the pan by the outer rim, and invert the pan onto the rack. Lift the pan off and peel off the layer of parchment paper from the bottom of the cake. Leave the cake to cool completely on the rack.

Cutting a Cake into Horizontal Layers

To cut a cake into layers, use a long, thin, serrated knife. Place the cake on a flat surface or on a cake turntable. With one hand, hold the blade of the knife parallel to the work surface with the edge of the knife against the side of the cake about halfway from the top. Place your other hand on top of the cake to help stabilize it. Make a shallow cut, about one inch deep, into the side of the cake all the way around, using the hand on top of the cake to turn it as you cut. Holding the knife flat and steady against the side of the cake, continue to turn the cake against the knife, while applying pressure to the knife so it will cut deeper through the cake. Continue to turn the cake and hold the knife so it cuts into the cake. Take care not to twist or turn the knife, which will cause it to make an uneven cut. When you feel the resistance of the cake against the knife begin to decrease, very carefully bring the knife through to the furthest edge of the cake. At this point I usually move my free hand to the side of the cake. The trick here is that you don't want to cut the palm of your hand by bringing the knife out of the center of the cake too quickly while holding your hand against the side of the cake. Use a cardboard cake circle or a cookie sheet to fit under the top layer of the cake and slide it off. Place the bottom layer on a cardboard cake circle or a serving plate for assembly. To cut a cake into 3 equal layers, follow the same technique but make the first cut ⅓ of the way down from the top of the cake.

Assembling and Frosting Layer Cakes

With the bottom layer of the cake on a serving plate, place 3- to 4-inch-wide strips of waxed paper so they fit under the cake and stick out to cover the plate. Overlap the strips so they will keep the serving plate clean while you frost the cake. Or place the layer of cake on a decorating turntable or on a large piece of waxed paper on a countertop. Mound about ½ to ¾ cup of frosting in the center of the cake layer. Use a metal, flexible-blade spatula, held with the blade parallel to the top of the cake, and push the mound from the center to the edges of the cake, turning the cake layer slowly as you spread the frosting. Take care to keep the blade of the spatula on top of the frosting, so crumbs aren't picked up and mixed with the frosting. Push the frosting just to the outer edges of the cake. Place another cake layer on top of the frosting, lining up the edges evenly, and spread with frosting in the same way. Repeat the same process with the remaining cake layers, including the top of the cake.

To frost the sides, hold the flexible-blade spatula perpendicular to the cake. Place a small mound of frosting on the top end of the spatula and press this into the sides of the cake. With a slight back-and-forth motion in the wrist, spread the frosting on an area of the side. Turn the cake about one-quarter and repeat. When the sides are covered, hold the spatula flat against the side and turn the cake against it. This builds up a lip at the top edge of the cake and removes excess frosting.

To smooth the top of the cake, run the flexible-blade spatula under hot water and dry it. Hold the spatula at the top edge of the cake almost flat to the top. With a gentle motion, pull the spatula in from the outer edge to the center of the cake, smoothing the top lip of frosting. Repeat this process until the lip around the top edge is even and the top of the cake is smooth.

Decorating the Sides of a Cake with Chopped Nuts, Shaved Chocolate, or Shredded Coconut

Place the frosted cake on a large piece of waxed or parchment paper on a smooth, flat surface. Use your cupped hand to press the finely chopped nuts, shaved chocolate, or shredded coconut into the sides of the cake up to, but not over, the top edge. Some of the nuts, chocolate, or coconut won't stick. If there are any bare spots, try again to press the nuts, chocolate, or coconut into the sides. Turn the cake periodically to give yourself a comfortable working area.

Transferring a Finished Cake to a Serving Plate

Use a flexible-blade spatula to slide under the cake cardboard and lift one side of the bottom of the cake so you can place your hand underneath it. Balance the cake on your spread hand and have the serving plate close to the cake. To prevent the cake from sliding or cracking, use a sturdy spatula and don't lift the side of the cake at a steep angle. Again, use the flexible-blade spatula to help guide the cake onto the serving plate. Place one side of the cake (at a shallow angle) on the serving plate, remove your hand, and use the spatula to gently lower the cake. This keeps you from making any finger marks in the side of the cake.

Filling and Shaping a Rolled Cake

After the cake is baked and while it is still hot, use a small, sharp knife to loosen the edges from the sides of the pan. Place a sheet of parchment paper over the top of the cake and cover with a kitchen towel. Then invert the jelly-roll pan and lift it off the cake. Gently peel the parchment paper off of the back of the cake and discard.

Starting at one long end, roll the cake up with the towel and parchment paper and leave it to cool, seam-side down, to room temperature. When ready to fill the cake, carefully unroll it and use a long-bladed offset spatula to evenly spread the filling over the cake, leaving a one-inch border at the long end that is farthest away from you. Remove the towel and use the parchment paper as a guide to help support the cake while you roll it up.

To make a tight cake roll, pull about one-third of the parchment paper over the top of the cake. Then place a ruler flat against the parchment that covers the top of the cake and push it against the roll while pulling the bottom part of the parchment paper towards you. This resistance motion of simultaneously pushing against the cake while pulling the parchment under the cake toward you compresses the roulade.

Freezing Cake Layers, Cupcakes, Quick Breads, and Muffins

These all freeze very well for at least three months. When they are completely cool, wrap them very securely in several layers of plastic wrap and aluminum foil. If they fit, put them in a freezer-safe bag. Place a large piece of masking tape on the outside wrapping and use an indelible marker to label and date each item. Defrost overnight in the refrigerator and bring to room temperature before serving.

Freezing Assembled Layer Cakes

Cakes assembled with buttercream and ganache freeze very well, but whipped cream and fresh fruit fillings do not. If you can find a cake box that is the right size (cake decorating and supply stores sell these, as do some bakeries), place the cake in the box and wrap the box snugly with several layers of plastic wrap and aluminum foil. To freeze the cake without a box, place it on a flat surface in the freezer on a baking sheet lined with waxed or parchment paper and let it freeze uncovered. Then wrap the cake loosely in several layers of plastic wrap and aluminum foil. Place a large piece of masking tape on the outside wrapping and use an indelible marker to label and date each cake. Defrost the cake overnight in the refrigerator, unwrap, and bring to room temperature before serving.

Pressing a Crumb Crust into Springform Pans

Once the crumbs are finely ground or crushed to make a crust, transfer them to the springform pan. Use a spoon, the bottom of a glass, a ramekin, or a small bowl to press the crumbs into the bottom of the pan evenly. Press the crumbs as far into the corners of the pan as possible so that there's not a thick build up there. Use your fingers or a spoon to press the crumbs into the edges.

Unmolding Springform Pans

Very carefully run a thin, sharp knife around the edges of the pan to make sure the cake is not sticking. Take care not to run the knife into the side of the cake. Open the clamp on the side of the pan, which expands the rim, and gently pull the outer rim up and away from the cake.

Using a Water Bath to Bake Cheesecake and Custards

A water bath insulates the baking custard and adds humidity to the oven from the water that evaporates. This keeps cheesecakes and custards from overheating and therefore cracking on top, because they don't lose as much moisture as they do when baked without a water bath. For cheesecakes, wrap the bottom of the pan tightly with heavy-duty foil to prevent water from seeping into the cake. Place the cake and/or custard cups in a larger pan (larger cake pan or roasting pan) on the oven rack. Pour boiling water into the bottom pan until it reaches halfway up the sides of the cake pan or custard cups. The bottom pan should be sufficiently large to hold enough water so it won't all evaporate. For example, for a 9-inch round cake pan, use a 12-inch round cake pan for the water bath.

Freezing Cheesecakes

Cheesecakes freeze best without their topping or garnish. When the cheesecake is completely cool, do not remove it from the pan. Cover the top of the cake pan with a piece of waxed paper. Wrap the entire cake snugly in several layers of plastic wrap and aluminum foil. Place a large piece of masking tape on the outside wrapping and use an indelible marker to label and date each cake. Defrost the cheesecake overnight in the refrigerator. Unwrap the cake, and garnish, if you choose, before serving.

Cutting Round Cakes, Pies, and Tarts into Serving Pieces

First, decide how many pieces you want to cut. Cakes, pies, and tarts that are 9 or 10 inches in diameter can easily be cut into 8 to 12 pieces. Cutting an even number is the easiest way to go. Use a sharp knife. Mark the outer rim of the cake where you want to make the cuts. Place the tip of the knife in the center of the cake, pie, or tart. Plunge it straight down and cut firmly toward the outer edge. Cut the dessert in half and then into quarters. Cut each quarter into equal-sized servings.

Cutting Rolled Cakes into Serving Pieces

First, determine how many pieces you want to cut. Mark the top length in half and quarters to ensure even slices. Then cut across the width of the cake using a serrated knife.

Cutting Cheesecake into Serving Pieces

Use a sharp knife with a thin blade. Fill a pitcher or clean vase with hot water. Dip the blade of the knife in the water and dry it off with a towel. This ensures a smooth cut. Repeat this process before each slice. Follow the above instructions for cutting a round cake.

DOUGH TECHNIQUES
Cookie Dough

Chill most cookie doughs before baking to prevent them from spreading too much in the oven. This is helpful for many types of drop cookies, most rolled cookies, and all refrigerator cookies. Also, the dough for rolled cookies needs to chill before it's rolled out or it will need too much flour when it is rolled, which will make it tough. Most cookie doughs freeze beautifully. Be sure to wrap them snugly in layers of plastic wrap and place them in a freezer-safe bag to avoid freezer burn. Place a large piece of masking tape on the outside wrapping and use an indelible marker to label and date them. Defrost the dough overnight in the refrigerator before using. If the dough is too firm, let it stand at room temperature until it is pliable enough to work with.

Bake cookies of the same size together on a baking sheet, so they bake evenly. And leave enough room between the cookies for them to spread. One to two inches works well.

• *Drop cookies*
Use a spoon or a small ice cream scoop to portion out drop cookies.

• *Rolled cookies*
If the dough is too cold, let it stand at room temperature for a short while to become pliable. Or you can soften it in a microwave oven on the lowest power for 5-second bursts. Test it after each burst by pressing your fingers into the dough to make sure it's not too soft.

Roll the dough on a smooth, flat surface lightly dusted with flour or between sheets of lightly floured waxed or parchment paper. Roll from the center toward the outer edges and give the dough a quarter turn after a few strokes. This helps roll out the dough evenly and ensures that it's not sticking. Brush off the dough with a wide pastry brush to remove any excess flour, which will make the dough tough.

Work with one-half or one-third of the dough at a time while keeping the rest covered and chilled.

Use cookie cutters to cut out cookies. Dip the cutters into flour and shake off the excess to keep them from sticking to the dough. Press the cutters straight down firmly into the dough and then lift them off without twisting. Cut the cookies as close together as possible to get the maximum number from the dough. After cutting the cookies, gather the scraps, press them together, and chill, if necessary, for 10 to 15 minutes. Re-roll the scraps and cut into cookies. Don't re-roll dough more than two times or it will become tough from too much flour and handling. Transfer the cut cookies to lined baking sheets with a flat metal spatula. This helps them keep their shape.

• *Refrigerator cookies*
SHAPING REFRIGERATOR COOKIE DOUGH INTO ROLLS
Once the dough is mixed, it needs to be shaped into rolls that can be cut after chilling. Place a large piece of waxed paper on a flat surface. Put the cookie dough on one half of the waxed paper, taking care not to handle it very much. Pull the waxed paper over the dough and position your fingertips on top of it, in the center. Use a gentle back-and-forth motion to start shaping the dough into a roll. Continue the same motion, moving your fingertips toward the ends until the roll is the preferred size and thickness. Use a ruler to check the size of the roll called for in each recipe. Wrap the roll tightly in the waxed paper, twisting it at both ends to seal the cylinder. Chill the dough thoroughly before slicing. To freeze rolls of refrigerator cookie dough, tightly wrap them in several layers of plastic wrap and place them in freezer bags.

SLICING REFRIGERATOR COOKIE DOUGH

To slice the rolls into individual cookies, use a sharp knife on a cutting board. Cut straight down from the top of the roll to the bottom into uniform pieces. To keep the round shape of the roll, give it a quarter turn after every 6 to 8 slices. If the dough starts to soften while you are working with it, wrap it in waxed paper, chill for another 10 to 15 minutes, then continue slicing.

• Bar cookies and brownies

To prevent bar cookies from over- or under-baking, use the size of pan called for in each recipe. Test bar cookies and brownies for doneness with a cake tester or toothpick inserted into the center or at least two inches in from the outer edge. Each recipe will state what to look for, but in general, the tester should have only a few crumbs clinging to it.

Cool the cookies or brownies completely before cutting. To cut bar cookies and brownies into uniform sizes, use a ruler and a sharp knife. For clean cuts, dip the knife into hot water and dry it between cuts. Getting the first bar cookie or brownie out of the pan can be problematic. It always seems to break. To prevent this, be sure to cut all the way through and use a small offset metal spatula. Another way to make it easy to get the first one out is to line the pan with aluminum foil that extends over the sides (see page 23). Use the foil to lift the cookies from the pan when they're cool and peel the foil away from the sides.

• Sandwich cookies

Make sure the cookies are completely cool before filling them. Use cookies that are the same size for each sandwich pair. Forming sandwich cookies is quick and easy. Place a small amount of the filling (about one teaspoon) in the center of the flat side of one cookie and top it with the flat side of another cookie. Press the cookies together gently to spread the filling to the outer edges. If there is too much filling it will spill over the edges. Some sandwich cookies have the center cut out of the top cookie, which lets the filling show through. Use a spoon or a pastry bag (see page 19) to fill sandwich cookies.

• Filled cookies

Prepare both the filling and the dough before working with the cookies and have them both at the same temperature.

• Hand-formed cookies

To make the dough for these cookies easy to work with, chill it for at least fifteen minutes before shaping. To keep the dough from sticking to your hands, dampen them with cold water before shaping the cookies. Hand-formed cookies are often shaped into balls. To do this, pinch off a piece of dough a little smaller than the size of a walnut and roll it between your palms. Roll the balls into uniform sizes so they will bake evenly.

Crescents are another popular shape for hand-formed cookies. To shape crescents, roll about one tablespoon of dough into a log by placing your fingertips on top of the dough and rolling it in a back-and-forth motion. Or shape the dough into a ball and then roll it into a log between your palms. Bend both ends of the log toward yourself into a crescent.

Biscotti fall into the category of hand-formed cookies. These cookies are baked twice, which gives them their characteristic crunchy texture. For the first baking, the dough is shaped into loaves. Most recipes divide the dough into 2 or 3 loaves. Dust your hands lightly with flour so the dough won't stick. Each recipe gives the dimensions for the loaves. Bake the biscotti for the time specified in each recipe, then let the loaves stand at room temperature for 15 to 20 minutes, to set. Transfer the loaves to a cutting board and slice each on the diagonal into $1/2$- to $3/4$-inch-wide pieces with a sharp serrated knife. Return the slices to the baking sheets with their sides exposed and bake another 10 to 15 minutes, until firm and set. Cool completely on racks. Biscotti keep very well in an airtight container at room temperature.

• Molded cookies

Some molded cookies are baked in the mold and turned out while warm to keep their shape. Madeleines are baked this way. They are made with a thin batter that is spooned or piped into the molds.

Other molded cookies are shaped in the mold and turned out to bake. Flour the mold generously to keep the dough from sticking to it. Press the dough firmly into the mold and use a small dowel or rolling pin to roll over the dough to make it even and spread into all the crevices of the mold. To remove the dough from the mold, use your fingertips to loosen one corner of the dough. Hold the mold at a 45-degree angle to the countertop and gently tap. The dough should release easily. Brush off any excess flour with a pastry brush or your fingers.

Springerle is another type of molded cookie with a design imprinted on the dough. For this type of cookie, roll out the dough as for rolled cookies (see page 37). Use a single mold to press the design into the dough or use a special rolling pin carved with designs to roll over the dough and make the imprints. Use a sharp knife to separate the individual cookies before baking.

Filo Dough

Filo dough dries out quickly and becomes brittle when exposed to air. When working with filo dough, keep it covered with a large piece of plastic wrap and a damp kitchen towel. Most filo dough is sold in frozen packages that need to be defrosted before use. Defrost the package overnight in the refrigerator.

Pastry Dough for Pies and Tarts

• *Rolling out dough*
Roll out dough on a smooth, flat, even, lightly floured surface or between sheets of lightly floured waxed or parchment paper. This makes it easy to clean up, and it's easy to check to make sure the dough isn't sticking. The type of rolling pin to use is personal preference. I like to use a solid French baton (not tapered) without handles because it makes me feel that I am in close touch with the dough and I can get my weight behind it (not that I'm a big person). Start rolling from the center of the dough and push away from yourself. Turn the dough a quarter turn to the right and repeat. Turning the dough helps to roll it out evenly and to make sure it's not sticking. If using waxed or parchment paper, check the paper often to make sure it's not too wrinkled. If it is, peel the paper off of the dough and sprinkle the dough lightly with more flour, if needed. Turn the entire package over and peel off the other piece of waxed or parchment paper. Keep rolling and turning the dough until it reaches the size you need. Roll the dough a couple of inches larger than the pan. To see if the dough is at the right size, hold the pan over the dough.

• *Fitting pie and tart dough into the pan*
Once the dough is rolled to the size you need, run an offset spatula under the dough to make sure it's not sticking. If using waxed or parchment paper, check the bottom piece of paper for the same reason. Then flip the dough package over and peel off the waxed or parchment paper. Place the rolling pin at one end of the dough and loosely roll the dough up around the rolling pin without the bottom piece of paper. Place the tart or pie pan directly underneath the rolling pin and gently unroll the dough into the pan. Carefully lift up the sides of the dough and fit it against the bottom and sides of the pan, without stretching or tearing, which will cause the dough to shrink as it bakes. If the dough is in a tart pan, press it against the sides of the pan so it will hold the indentations of the fluted edge. To remove the excess dough at the top of a pie pan, trim it off with a sharp knife or kitchen scissors. If the dough is in a tart pan, simply run the rolling pie over the top edges to cut the dough off evenly.

Instead of rolling the dough around the rolling pin, you can use the waxed or parchment paper to transfer the dough to the pan. Center the paper over the pan, turn it upside down, and gently lower the dough into the pan. Peel off the paper.

Another method for fitting pie dough into the pan is to loosely fold it in half, then in half again. Place the point of the dough in the center of the pie pan and unfold the dough carefully so it doesn't stretch or tear. Fit the dough against the sides of the pan and trim off any excess dough at the top.

One more method for placing pie dough in the pan is to carefully fit your hands underneath it and lift it into the pie pan. Be very careful not to stretch or tear the dough.

• *Pressing a crumb crust into tart pans*
Use a spoon, the bottom of a glass, a ramekin, or a small bowl to press the crumbs into the bottom of the pan evenly. Press the crumbs as far into the corners of the pan as possible. Use your fingers or a spoon to press the crumbs into the sides. To prevent the utensils and your hand from becoming sticky when pressing the crumb crust into the pan, cover them with a piece of plastic wrap or a plastic bag.

• *Forming tartlets*
Tartlet pans come in many shapes and sizes. The easiest way to line them with dough is to invert the tartlet pan over the dough and cut out around it, leaving a rim of ¾ to 1 inch. Fit the dough evenly into the tartlet pan and up the sides, pressing to fit it into the fluted edges. Use your fingers to press against the top edge of the pan or run a rolling pin over the top to remove excess dough.

• *Freezing pie and tart dough*

Pie and tart dough can be frozen up to three months. Form the dough into a disk and wrap it securely in several layers of plastic wrap. Place the dough disk in a freezer bag. Place a large piece of masking tape on the outside of the bag and use an indelible marker to label and date the package. Defrost the dough overnight in the refrigerator and let stand at room temperature until pliable enough to roll.

Pie and tart dough can also be frozen after it is fit into the pan. Wrap the pan snugly in several layers of plastic wrap and aluminum foil and place it in a freezer bag. Label and date the package. Defrost overnight in the refrigerator.

• *Decorative pie edges*

There are several ways to decorate the edges of pies to make them look unique and special. Dip your fingertips into flour and shake off any excess before working with the dough. If the dough becomes too soft, refrigerate it for 15 to 20 minutes so it firms up. If your hands are very warm, run them under cold water or plunge them into a bowl of ice water, then dry them before working with the dough.

CRIMPING

Press the tines of a fork into the dough all around the top edge in an even pattern. Or use a pastry crimper, a specially designed tool (see page 19) that seals the edges of top and bottom pie crusts together and makes a decorative design.

FLUTED EDGE

Place the index finger of one hand on the inside rim and the thumb and index finger of the other hand about an inch apart on the outside rim. Press the dough between your fingers to form a V. Repeat this all around the rim of the pie pan, turning the pan as needed.

CRIMPED FLUTED EDGE

After fluting the edge, use the tines of a fork to crimp every other flute.

ROPE

Using both index fingers or your thumb and index finger of one hand, press the dough together between them and twist it slightly to one side to make a wavy rope effect. Repeat this all around the rim of the pie pan.

PASTRY CUT-OUTS

Roll out any scraps of pie dough to the same thickness as the dough in the pie pan. Use decorative cookie cutters dipped in flour to cut out shapes. Brush one side of the dough cut-outs lightly with beaten egg and press them onto the edges of a single-crust pie or on top of a double-crust pie.

• *Double-crust pies*

Many pies have both a bottom and top crust. There are a few different ways to arrange the top crust to give it a distinctive flair. When making the dough for a double-crust pie, divide it into two equal pieces. Wrap one piece of the dough tightly in plastic wrap and chill while rolling out the bottom dough.

PLAIN TOP CRUST

Roll out the dough between sheets of lightly floured waxed or parchment paper to the desired thickness. Turn the dough package often while rolling and check to make sure the paper is not sticking or too wrinkled. Roll the dough to a size a few inches larger than the pie pan so it will fit over the filling without stretching. Brush the edges of the bottom crust in the pan with water or an egg lightly beaten with a teaspoon of water or milk to help the two crusts stick together.

Roll the dough around the rolling pin and unroll it over the pie filling. Or loosely fold the dough into quarters, position it over the filling, and unfold. Or use the waxed or parchment paper to lift the dough over the pie pan. Turn it upside down and gently lower the dough over the filling. Peel off the waxed or parchment paper. Use a sharp knife to make several slits starting from the center and going toward the outer edge or make free-form cuts in the top pie dough. Or use a decorative cutter to make designs in the crust. All of these serve to release steam as the pie bakes. Fold the edges of the top crust over the bottom crust edges to prevent the filling from leaking and crimp or flute the edges as described above.

LATTICE CRUST

Roll the dough as above for a plain top crust and trim the edges with a sharp knife or pastry wheel. Peel off the top piece of waxed or parchment paper. Use a ruler and a plain or fluted-edge pastry wheel to cut $1/2$-inch-wide strips of dough. If the dough is soft, place a baking sheet under the waxed or parchment paper and transfer the lattice to the baking sheet. Chill in the freezer for 5 to 10 minutes.

Simple lattice: Use a long, metal, flexible-blade spatula to lift and transfer the dough strips to the top of the pie. This helps to keep their shape and prevents them from tearing or breaking. You can, however, use your hands to transfer the dough strips. Place half of the strips evenly spaced across the top of the pie. Turn the pan 90 degrees and place the remaining strips evenly spaced on top of the pie.

Woven lattice: Take the center strip and place it in the center of the pie. Place an outer strip parallel to the center strip and at the outer edge of the pie. Repeat on the other side. There should be 3 strips across the pie. Turn the pie 90 degrees and place 3 more strips across the pie, evenly spaced. Turn the pie 90 degrees and place 2 dough strips in between the first 3 strips. Turn the pie once more and place the remaining 2 dough strips between the remaining 3 strips. The lattice should have a woven look. You can also make the lattice on a piece of floured waxed or parchment paper and then transfer it to the top of the pie. Invert the paper over the top of the pie and gently lower the lattice onto the pie.

Another way to achieve the woven lattice is to place half of the pastry strips evenly spaced across the pie, leaving at least an inch of space between them. Carefully fold back every other strip to the center and place a pastry strip across the pie perpendicular to the first strips. Unfold the pastry strips and fold back the strips that weren't folded the first time. Place another pastry strip across the pie, leaving at least an inch of space between the strips. Repeat this process until the top is covered with the lattice.

Twisted lattice: Cut the dough strips about an inch longer than for a plain lattice crust. Twist the strips in several places before placing them on top of the pie to form a lattice.

Whichever type of lattice you make, finish the edges. Use a sharp knife or kitchen scissors to trim the bottom pastry crust and the lattice strips evenly to a ¾-inch overhang. Brush the edges of the bottom pie dough with water or an egg lightly beaten with a teaspoon of water or milk to help the crust and lattice stick together. Fold the edges of the lattice over the bottom crust edges and press them to seal together. Leave the edges plain or crimp or flute them together (see page 000).

PIE CRUST MADE FROM DECORATIVE CUT-OUTS

See Pastry Cut-outs (page 40) for how to make cut-outs. Instead of a solid top crust for a pie, make cut-outs from the dough for the top crust. Overlap them slightly on top of the pie to form an attractive crust. Brush the edges of the bottom pie dough with water or an egg lightly beaten with a teaspoon of water or milk to help the bottom crust and the cut-outs stick together.

• *Forming galettes*

Galettes are rustic-style tarts that are shaped free-form, without a pan. Roll out the pastry dough into a large circle following the instructions above for rolling out dough (see page 39). Line a baking sheet or large pizza pan with parchment paper or a non-stick liner. Transfer the dough to the baking sheet by loosely rolling the dough up around the rolling pin. Position the rolling pin over the baking sheet and unroll the dough. Or use the waxed or parchment paper to transfer the dough to the baking sheet. Center the paper over the baking sheet, turn it upside down, and gently lower the dough onto the sheet. Peel off the paper. Place the filling in the center of the pastry dough, leaving a 2- to 3-inch border. Fold the dough border over the edge of the filling, making evenly spaced pleats around the rim.

• *Baking blind: Pie and tart shells*

In order to bake pie and tart shells with no filling, they need to be weighted to keep the shells from collapsing on themselves. Preheat the oven to the temperature called for in the recipe. Place the pie or tart shell on a baking sheet. Line the shell with a large piece of parchment paper or aluminum foil (shiny side down) that extends over the sides. Fill the paper or foil with pie or tart weights, or rice or beans or a combination (these can be reused many, many times) of both. Bake the shell for 12 minutes. Lift off the parchment or foil and weights. Pierce the bottom of the shell lightly in several places with a fork or sharp knife to release the air. For a partially baked shell, which will be baked again with its filling, continue to bake for another 5 to 8 minutes, until the shell is set but not colored. For a completely prebaked shell, continue to bake for another 10 to 15 minutes, until the shell is set and golden colored. Remove the shell from the oven and cool completely on a rack.

• *Baking blind: Tartlet shells*

Line each tartlet shell with foil and weights. Or place a second tartlet mold that's the same shape and size over the dough and press down lightly. Bake for 8 minutes, then lift off the foil and weights or the top tartlet mold and continue to bake another 8 to 10 minutes, until the shells are set and golden colored. Remove the shells from the oven and cool completely on a rack.

• Preventing the edges of pies and tarts from over-browning

There are times when the outer edges of the pie or tart brown too quickly while there is still a fair amount of baking time left. There are a couple of ways to keep the edges from becoming too dark. Make a ring of aluminum foil that covers the outer edges of the pie or tart. To do this, take a large piece of foil and use an inverted pie or tart pan or a bowl to trace onto the center of the foil. Cut out the center circle with scissors and place the foil over the top of the pie or tart. For tarts, invert the outer rim of a tart pan (without the bottom) that is larger than the tart over it. You can also buy pre-formed pie edge protectors that are reusable.

• Unmolding tarts and tartlets

To prevent the outer rim of the tart pan from sliding down your arm (which would be painful if it's still hot), use this method to unmold tarts. Take a bowl or can that is smaller than the tart pan and turn it upside down, so the bottom faces up. Center the tart pan on top of the inverted bowl or can. Gently pull on the side rim of the tart pan to loosen it and let it slide down. Lift the tart up and place it on a cooling rack or the kitchen counter. To remove the bottom of the tart pan, use a large, wide spatula to ease between the bottom of the tart and the bottom of the pan. Gently slide the tart onto a cardboard cake circle or a serving plate.

Remove tartlets baked in two-piece pans the same way as tarts. To remove tartlets from solid tartlet pans, let them cool completely on a rack. As the tartlets cool, the sides of the dough will shrink slightly. Lightly tap the tartlet pan on a countertop or table at a slight angle and the tartlet should slip out of the pan.

• Glazing fresh fruit tarts and tartlets

I prefer to use a goose-feather brush for glazing. It doesn't push the fruit around as a natural-bristle pastry brush sometimes does. Dip the tip of the feather into the glaze and lightly brush the top and sides of the fruit. Take care not to build up a thick layer of glaze, which is not attractive. The purpose of the glaze is to seal the fruit from the air and make it glisten.

Puff Pastry

• Rolling out puff pastry

Whether you are working with homemade or store-bought puff pastry, it's important that the dough be cold when rolling it out

or the butter will begin to seep out, which will keep it from rising as it bakes. If the dough becomes too soft when you are working with it, slide it onto a baking sheet, cover with plastic wrap, and let it chill in the refrigerator for at least 30 minutes. Always roll out puff pastry on a cool surface, such as a marble or a countertop that is lightly floured to prevent the dough from sticking. As you roll the dough be careful not apply too much pressure toward the edges or to actually roll over them, which will cause them to compress and retard their ability to rise. As you roll the dough, turn it toward yourself often. This makes it easy to roll it evenly. Maintain the rectangular shape of the dough and keep the sides straight as you roll it out. This allows the dough to rise evenly when it bakes. Let the dough rest, tightly covered with plastic wrap in the refrigerator, after it is shaped and before baking for at least 1 hour and as long as 2 days. This allows the gluten in the dough to relax and results in less shrinkage, but there is always some shrinkage with puff pastry. When cutting the dough, use a sharp knife or cutter and cut straight down through the layers without twisting. This keeps the edges from sticking together so they will rise uniformly.

• Freezing puff pastry

Puff pastry can be frozen for as long as 1 year with no loss in flavor or texture, as long as it is very well wrapped to prevent freezer burn. Defrost puff pastry in the refrigerator overnight before rolling it out. Defrosted puff pastry can be frozen again 1 or 2 times without damage to its structure or flavor. If you need only a portion of puff pastry, cut the frozen dough with a sharp serrated knife.

• Baking puff pastry

Puff pastry always bakes in a very hot oven. It bakes best from its frozen state because the initial blast of hot air from the oven shocks the cold dough into rising and helps it to bake evenly. Be sure to follow the baking directions in each recipe. Sometimes it's necessary to control the amount that the dough rises or it will become unwieldy. To do this, pierce the dough with a fork or the tip of a sharp knife before placing it in the oven to bake. This allows steam to escape and keeps the dough from rising too high.

DECORATION AND GARNISHING TECHNIQUES

These techniques will give the final touch to your baked goods and make them look delicious enough to eat.

Dusting with Confectioners' Sugar and Cocoa Powder

Place the confectioners' sugar or cocoa powder in a fine-mesh strainer and lightly dust the top of cakes, cookies, brownies, or cupcakes. To create a design, place a paper doily on top of a cake, cupcakes, or brownies, dust with confectioners' sugar, cocoa powder, or a combination of both, and lift off the doily. Or use a stencil to make a design on top of the cake. Stencils can be bought,or you can make your own by cutting a design into a piece of cardboard or heavy paper. When lifting off the doily or stencil, lift it straight up so none of the confectioners' sugar or cocoa powder falls onto the cake and spoils the design. Another way to create a design is to lay strips of paper at even intervals across the top. Lay them straight, at a diagonal, or in a diamond shape. Dust heavily with confectioners' sugar, cocoa powder, or a combination, and carefully lift off the paper strips. To create a contrasting design, first dust the surface with confectioners' sugar or cocoa powder. Place a stencil or paper strips on top and dust with the opposite color.

Drizzling with Chocolate

Dip the tines of a fork into melted chocolate. While holding your hand slightly above the baked goods, swing it back and forth, letting the chocolate drop off. Another way to drizzle is to use a parchment paper pastry bag filled with chocolate (see Piping and Writitng with Chocolate, below).

Dipping in Chocolate

To dip partway in chocolate, hold the item (a cookie, for example) firmly between your thumb and forefinger. Dip into a bowl of tempered chocolate (see page 27) halfway or on the diagonal. Remove from the bowl and let the excess chocolate drip off to prevent a puddle from forming underneath. Place the dipped item on a baking sheet lined with waxed or parchment paper.

To dip completely in chocolate, use a chocolate-dipping tool or a heavy plastic fork with the two middle tines removed. Place the item in the bowl of tempered chocolate and use the tool or fork to swirl it around and coat it completely. With the dipping tool or fork, lift the item from the chocolate, hold it over the bowl to let the excess drip off, and place it on a lined baking sheet.

Drizzling with a Glaze or Icing

Place the glaze or icing in a liquid measuring cup. Pour it over the top in a slow, steady stream.

Using a Parchment Paper Pastry Cone

To fill the bag and keep both hands free, stand the parchment paper pastry cone in a tall glass or jar. Use a rubber spatula or spoon to fill the cone with batter or jam, or pour a liquid into the bag. Don't fill the cone more than halfway, to prevent the filling from oozing out. Fold both sides of the top into the center and fold the top down to seal. Use a sharp pair of scissors to snip off a small opening at the pointed end. Hold the pastry cone directly over and about an inch above the surface of the item to be decorated. Apply light pressure with one hand to push the filling out of the cone and use the other hand to stabilize the bag. Release the pressure on the cone to stop the flow.

Piping and Writing with Chocolate

Use tempered chocolate for piping and writing so it won't become dull and streaky (see page 27). The easiest way to pipe and write with chocolate is with a parchment paper pastry cone (see above) because it's disposable. Use a sharp pair of scissors to snip off a very small opening at the pointed end. Hold the pastry cone about an inch above the surface and straight or at an angle that's comfortable for you. Apply light pressure to the pastry cone with one hand while using the other hand to stabilize it. To stop the chocolate from coming out the pointed end, release pressure on the pastry cone. You can write in any style you like with chocolate, such as cursive or block letters. It's always a good idea to practice first on a piece of waxed or parchment paper before writing on a cake or pastry. To pipe an edge design, it's helpful to use a turntable.

Using a Pastry Bag with Pastry Tips and Tubes

There are two types of pastry tips: small decorative ones and large tubes. If using the small, decorative tips, it's easiest to use a coupler to fit them into a pastry bag. The coupler is a two-piece plastic device. One piece fits inside the pastry bag and sticks partway out. This piece has threads across it. The second piece is an open ring that holds the pastry tip. The ring twists onto the threads of the first piece. It's very easy to change decorative tips this way because all you have to do is unscrew one and put on another. Large pastry tubes fit into the pastry bag and part sticks out through the opening. I prefer to use large pastry tubes because I like the size of the designs they make, and I don't have to bother about using a coupler, but both types work well.

Filling a Pastry Bag

To fill the pastry bag and keep your hands free, stand it in a tall glass or jar. Fold the top edge of the pastry bag toward the outside and down a few inches to form a cuff. Use a rubber spatula or spoon to fill the bag no more than halfway or it will be difficult to work with. Fold the cuff up, hold the pastry bag by the top end, and press the filling toward the tip. Twist the pastry bag tightly at the point where the filling stops. To release any air in the bag, squeeze a little of the contents back into the bowl. To refill the pastry bag, fold the cuff back and repeat.

Using a Pastry Bag

Hold the pastry bag about an inch above the surface of the item to be decorated. To form mounds, hold the bag straight above the surface. For other shapes, hold the bag at a slight angle with the top end toward you. Apply light pressure with one hand to push the filling out of the bag and use the other hand to stabilize the bag. To stop the contents from coming out of the bag, stop applying pressure.

Making Piped Decorations

A few simple decorations dress up many baked goods. Whipped cream, whipped ganache, and buttercream are the right consistency to use for piped decorations. There are three piped decorations that I use most of the time: star, rosette, and shell. These are formed using an open-star pastry tube, number 5 or 6. All pastry tubes and tips have a number etched into them. All of these decorations can also be used to create borders by piping them very close together.

- *Star*

To make a star, hold the pastry bag upright about an inch above the surface of the item to be decorated. Squeeze out a small amount of filling. Stop squeezing and lift the bag directly away from the star. How long you squeeze determines the size of the star.

- *Rosette*

To make a rosette, hold the pastry bag upright about an inch above the surface of the item to be decorated. Squeeze out the filling and move the pastry tube counterclockwise in an arc to make a tight circle, ending at the same point where you started. Release the pressure and lift the tube away by pulling it to the side (reverse these instructions if you are left-handed).

- *Shell*

To make a shell, hold the pastry bag upright about an inch above the surface of the item to be decorated. Squeeze out the filling, allowing it to fan out a little, then pull the tube toward yourself while squeezing with a little less pressure. Lower the tube to the surface, forming a tail. Release the pressure and pull the tube toward yourself to form a point. To form a shell border, overlap the next shell on the tail of the previous one.

To make a reverse shell border, start the shell shape as above, then curve your hand slightly to the right and draw the tail toward the left. Reverse the next shell so it goes from left to right. Repeat to form a border.

PRESENTATION

Now that you've made some great baked goods, you'll want to serve them in a way that makes them look good. Use serving plates and platters that are the right size for your baked goods. For example, serve a 9-inch round cake or tart on a 12-inch round platter so there is a border around it. For an elegant layer cake, use an elegant serving plate, perhaps crystal, silver, or glass. For cupcakes, try using an oval or rectangular platter. Cookies look great served in baskets lined with attractive napkins. The idea is that you want to use the type of serving platter that fits the size of the item and is appropriate to the occasion. This is your opportunity to be creative and have fun showing off what you've baked. Keep your eyes open for interesting serving pieces at tabletop and cookware shops, garage sales, antique shows and shops, and the many other places you go.

ESSENTIAL BAKING

LANGUAGE

THE FOLLOWING TERMS are often used to describe techniques for baking and the various stages of baked goods. Knowing what these words mean will make your baking experience much more enjoyable. Please refer back to this list anytime you encounter a word in this book that is not clear.

BAKE BLIND

This is the technique for baking a pastry shell without a filling. The unfilled pastry shell is pierced evenly with a fork to keep it from puffing up during baking. The shell is lined with aluminum foil or parchment paper and weighted to keep it from collapsing during baking. Halfway through baking, the foil or paper and weights are removed and the set pastry shell continues to bake until it is browned (see page 41).

BATTER

Batter is an uncooked mixture that is the basis for many baked goods, including cakes, quick breads, muffins, and crêpes. It generally consists of flour, eggs, and a liquid ingredient, like milk or cream. Butter, sugar, and flavoring ingredients are often added to the mixture. A batter can be either thick or thin.

BEAT

The technique of beating involves rapidly and vigorously mixing ingredients in a circular motion to change their consistency. Beating makes batters smooth and it adds volume to egg whites and cream by incorporating air into them. Beating can be done either by machine with an electric mixer or by hand (see page 32).

BLANCH

This is a technique for loosening and removing the outer skins of nuts and fruit. The nuts or fruit are plunged into a pan of boiling water and left for approximately one minute. Then they are removed with a strainer, skimmer, or tongs and plunged into cold water to stop the cooking process. The skins then easily slip off the nuts or peel off the fruit (see page 29).

BLEND

"To blend" means combining ingredients together so they are smooth and uniform in appearance and texture. Blending can be accomplished by hand or by machine, such as with a food processor, electric mixer, or blender (see page 31).

CHILL

The technique of chilling involves reducing the temperature of food by stirring it over ice water or placing it in the refrigerator. Chilling firms the texture of many types of dough and batters before they are baked.

CREAM

There is no cream involved; rather, this is a technique for mixing or beating together softened fat and other ingredients, like sugar, until they are smooth, creamy, light, and well blended. You should beat the softened fat first to make it fluffy and light before adding the sugar, then continue to beat the mixture until it is so well combined that it's not possible to discern the individual ingredients. Creaming traps air that expands when heated in the oven, which helps to raise baked goods. Creaming is most easily accomplished with an electric stand mixer and a flat beater attachment (see page 32).

CRIMP

This technique is used for sealing the edges of pastry or pie shells by pinching or pressing them together. Crimping forms an attractive, decorative, fluted edge. It is accomplished with a fork, the back of a knife blade, a crimper, or fingers. This raised rim helps to hold in the filling. A crimper is a hand-held tool that looks like a large pair of tweezers. It is used to imprint decorative designs into and to seal the edges of pie and pastry shells (see pages 19 and 40).

CURDLE

This is what occurs when a mixture coagulates or separates into liquid and solid elements. Curdling takes place in milk and milk products, custards, and sauces, and when eggs are added to beaten butter. Too much heat causes the liquid in eggs, milk, and cream to cook and thicken or gel into clumps, which results in a curdled mixture. Constant stirring and cooking over low heat help to prevent this from occurring. Another method of prevention is to slowly stir a small amount of hot liquid into eggs before mixing them with the remainder of the liquid. This brings the eggs up to the temperature of the liquid without curdling. This method is also called tempering. Lemon juice and other acids can cause some mixtures to curdle. If curdling happens when eggs are added to butter, scrape down the sides and bottom of the mixing bowl with a rubber spatula and slowly beat the mixture until smooth.

CUT IN

The technique of cutting in is for combining solid fat, such as butter, with dry ingredients, such as flour, until the mixture is in small pieces. This technique is used with many pie and pastry doughs. The pieces of fat should be about the size of small peas. This helps the dough to become flaky because, as the pieces of fat melt during baking, steam fills the areas left and aids in rising. If the fat pieces are too tiny they will melt into the dough. Cutting in is accomplished using a pastry blender, a fork, two knives, fingers, a food processor, or a stand mixer with the flat beater attachment. Use chilled fat and utensils and work quickly when cutting in, so the fat will not melt and lose its shape.

DASH

A term of measurement for very small amounts of seasonings. This measures between $1/16$ and $1/8$ teaspoon.

DOUGH

Dough is an uncooked mixture of flour, fat, sugar, liquid (water, milk, cream, or eggs) and other ingredients that is the basis for many baked items. Dough is thicker than batter and should be firm enough to knead or roll.

DRIZZLE

This is a technique for lightly pouring a liquid over a surface in a thin, slow, steady stream. Some coffee cakes, quick breads, cookies, and other baked goods are drizzled with a thin sugar glaze or icing or with piping chocolate as a decoration after baking, or they may be drizzled with melted butter before baking.

DUST

To dust is to lightly sprinkle or coat pastry dough, pastries, cakes, confections, or baking pans and work surfaces with a powdery substance such as flour, confectioners' sugar, cocoa powder, or finely ground nuts.

FIRM PEAKS

This is the stage where the ingredient (egg whites or whipping cream) has been whipped until it forms peaks that stand upright with a solid shape and are slightly pointed.

FLUTE

This is the technique for forming a decorative V-shaped or scalloped design on the raised outer edge of a pastry shell or pie crust before it is baked (see page 40).

FOLD

Fold is a very common term in baking. It is the technique used to combine a light (egg whites or whipped cream) and a heavy (batter or custard) mixture and, in the process, retain the air that has been whipped into the lighter mixture (see page 32).

GARNISH

To garnish is to embellish baked goods with edible decorations such as confectioners' sugar, cocoa powder, nuts, fruit, or whipped cream. A garnish normally complements an ingredient in the baked item.

GLAZE

A glaze is a thin, shiny coating for baked items that is either brushed or poured on. There are many types of glazes, including jam glazes, chocolate glazes, confectioners' sugar glaze, caramel glaze, and egg wash.

GREASE

This is what you do to prepare a baking pan with fat, such as butter, by rubbing it over the inside of the pan. The purpose of greasing the pan is to prevent the baked item from sticking to the pan. Baking pans are also dusted lightly with flour after they have been greased. Baking pans can also be prepared by spraying them with a non-stick coating.

GRIND

Grinding is a procedure that reduces food, such as nuts and seeds, to very tiny pieces or to a powder consistency with a food processor or other utensil.

KNEAD

This is the technique for working dough or other substances, such as marzipan, until smooth and supple. To knead, gather the dough into a ball on a smooth work surface. Push it away from you with the heel of your hand while pressing it down, then gather it back into a ball, folding it over itself. Give the dough a quarter-turn and repeal the process until the desired smooth, elastic texture is reached.

MELT

Melting turns an ingredient from a solid into a liquid by using heat.

MIX

"To mix" means to combine two or more ingredients by blending or stirring so that the resulting mixture is well integrated and the ingredients are evenly distributed (see page 31).

PINCH

A pinch is a measurement for dry ingredients that can be held between the tips of the thumb and forefinger of one hand. This amount measures the equivalent of $1/16$ teaspoon.

PIPE

The technique of piping involves forcing a mixture, such as buttercream, choux pastry, icing, or chocolate, from a pastry bag to form shapes or decorative designs. Piping must be done steadily and evenly while the pastry bag is held either straight up or at an angle above the piping surface. The shape of the tip used determines the design and shape of the piped material. Piping is often done using a parchment paper pastry cone to hold icing or melted chocolate (see pages 19 and 43).

PREHEAT

"Preheat" means to bring an oven up to a specific temperature before baking. The initial blast of hot air from a preheated oven is important to develop the structure of baked goods and to create a crisp outer crust.

PUREE

Foods are pureed when they have been processed to a soft, smooth, thick texture in a food processor or a blender, or by passing through a sieve.

REST

When you allow pastry dough to relax, it is called "resting." This lets the gluten in the flour relax, causing the dough to be less elastic when it is rolled out.

RIBBON

This is the consistency of a batter or mixture, such as eggs and sugar, that has been beaten until it is very thick and pale colored. When the whisk or beater is lifted above the bowl, the batter drops slowly onto the mixture in the bowl in a ribbon-like pattern. This ribbon holds it shape for a few seconds before it sinks into the mixture (see page 32).

ROLL OUT

This means to shape pastry, tart, or pie dough into a larger piece to fit a specific pan. This is accomplished with a rolling pin on a smooth, flat surface (see page 39).

SCALE

This is the term for a method of measuring ingredients by their weight (see page 16). It is also the term used by professional bakers to mean increasing or decreasing the yield of a recipe.

SCANT

"Scant" indicates that you want slightly less than what is called for, as in "a scant cup."

SCORE

Scoring involves making shallow cuts partway through dough to mark it for portions that will be cut all the way through before or after baking or to make decorative designs.

SCRAPE DOWN

You scrape down to remove batter or dough from the sides of a mixing bowl by using a rubber or plastic spatula or pastry scraper. The spatula or pastry scraper is run around the side of the bowl under the batter or dough, gathering it up, and the dough or batter is added to the bulk of the mixture in the bowl. This ensures that all of the ingredients are evenly mixed.

SEIZE

When something becomes so thick that it is impossible to stir, it has seized. "Seizing" is the term used to describe chocolate when it is mixed with a small amount of liquid or when it comes in contact with steam. When this happens, the chocolate becomes a lumpy mass that is unusable.

SET

"To set" is to bake or stand until firm or solid.

SIFT

This technique involves aerating dry ingredients such as flour, cornstarch, and confectioners' sugar, to lighten the ingredient and break up any lumps. The ingredient is placed in a sifter, strainer, or drum sieve and pushed through the mesh screen. This process separates the ingredient and adds air to it. Sifting results in a finer texture in baked goods.

SIMMER

This is the technique for cooking a liquid mixture at a low temperature, approximately 185°F, with bubbles barely breaking around the outer edges.

SOFTEN

When the consistency of a food changes from firm to soft, either by heat or by letting it stand at room temperature, it has softened. When butter stands at room temperature, it softens.

SOFT PEAKS

This is the stage where the ingredient (egg whites or whipping cream) is whipped until it forms peaks that can barely hold their shape. If a small amount is scooped from the mixing bowl onto a rubber spatula and held upright, the peak curves to one side or the other and does not stand straight up.

SPRINKLE

This is when you lightly scatter small particles of dry ingredients or a liquid over the surface of a mixture or baked goods.

STIR

This is the technique for mixing ingredients together in a slow circular motion until they are thoroughly combined. Stirring is accomplished using a spoon, rubber spatula, or a whisk (see page 15).

STRAIN

The technique of straining is used for filtering, pressing, sifting, and pureeing liquid or dry ingredients, which removes lumps and results in a smooth texture. Straining indicates that the solids are eliminated.

TEMPER

You temper to bring an ingredient to its proper temperature or texture by mixing it with another ingredient or by stirring it to either cool or warm to a particular temperature. Eggs are tempered by mixing a small amount of hot liquid into them while mixing before they are added to a hot liquid. This slowly brings the eggs up to the temperature of the hot liquid so they are not cooked too quickly when added back into the liquid.

TEMPERING

Tempering is the technique used for stabilizing the cocoa butter in melted chocolate that is used for dipping and molding so it doesn't have unsightly white steaks and dots. Tempering gives chocolate a shiny, unblemished appearance, a smooth texture that breaks with a crisp snap, and makes chocolate easy to remove from molds because it shrinks as it cools. There are several methods for tempering and all involve heating chocolate so that it melts completely, cooling it by stirring to below the melting point of cocoa butter, and heating again to an exact temperature (see page 27).

TOSS

"To toss" means to gently mix ingredients by lifting or stirring several times to combine them.

UNMOLD

You unmold by removing baked goods from the pan or container that gives them their shape. Baked goods are inverted onto a cooling rack or serving plate and their pans are lifted off. Before they are unmolded, baked goods generally sit in their baking pans on a cooling rack for 10 to 15 minutes. This allows steam to build up, which helps release them from the pans.

WHIP

This technique involves stirring rapidly in a circular motion to incorporate air into a substance, such as cream or egg whites, which expands its volume. Whipping is accomplished either by hand with a whisk or rotary beater or by machine with an electric mixer (see page 32).

ZEST

"To zest" means to remove the colored outer rind of citrus fruit that contains the fruit's sweet flavor and perfume in its essential oils. A Microplane grater or a tool called a zester, which separates the zest from the bitter white pith, is used to zest (see page 16). Citrus zest is used to flavor baked goods, creams, and custards, as well as for decoration, and it can be candied.

II.

FRUIT AND VEGETABLES

THERE ARE SO MANY GREAT CHOICES when baking with fruits and vegetables, it's hard to decide what to make. Stone fruits, berries, and tropical fruit are some of my favorites, but there are many more fruits to choose from. For something a little different, try quince and figs. For vegetables, rhubarb tops my list. ✳ Seasons and availability determine to a great degree what you make. But, over and above that, personal preference and the quality of fruits or vegetables that you can find will help you in making your choice. A lot can go into selecting and handling fruits and vegetables, so care needs to be taken. ✳ In this section you will find many recipes that focus on a particular fruit or vegetable. Don't be overwhelmed because there are so many great things to bake. Just choose the fruit or vegetable that you and/or your guests like the most. Or maybe, choose two things to bake for your family or friends. The "wow" factor comes easy with these when you see and taste them.

STONE FRUIT

WHEN I FIRST think about stone fruit, I imagine sitting in the backyard on a warm summer day eating a juicy, fresh, sweet peach or working my way through a handful of sweet cherries, one by one. My next thought is about all the scrumptious baked desserts that can be made with stone fruits. The possibilities are nearly limitless, so it was hard to narrow down what to include in this chapter. The recipes you find here are my family's favorites. I don't think you will be disappointed.

Spring and summer are the seasons when stone fruits are at their finest. Cherries appear first in May, followed by apricots, peaches, plums, and nectarines. Because commerce can move agricultural goods all over the world fairly rapidly, it is possible to get fresh stone fruit from anywhere in the world no matter what the season. Stone fruits are available in the produce section of supermarkets and produce stores, but I like to buy mine at the local farmer's market because I know the fruit is very fresh and often there are more varieties available.

TIPS AND TECHNIQUES

When selecting stone fruits, choose those that look good, with even color and only minor blemishes. Watch out for mold and decay, which is often on the underside of the fruit. Also, check for any tears or cracks in the skin.

When choosing stone fruits, it's important to feel them. Generally they shouldn't be too hard or too soft. Softness means the meat of the fruit is less juicy and possibly even dried out and mealy. Stone fruits should have a pronounced sweet aroma. Watch out for odd and sometimes chemical aromas, which mean there may still be a residue of sprays that were used on the fruit. One of my mottos when I'm selecting stone fruit is, "If it doesn't smell good, it won't taste good." If you can taste-test the stone fruit before you buy it, you will be able to see inside, smell the flesh, get some good mouthfeel, and most important, see if it tastes like it should.

Sometimes you must buy fruit before it is fully ripe because that is the only way you can get it. This is where I have a cautionary note to make. A big problem with underripe fruit is that it may have been picked too early and/or kept in cold storage too long. This means that it may not ripen fully. If you have this problem, my advice is not to buy from that purveyor again, if possible.

However, to ripen stone fruits, simply leave them out in the open at room temperature, away from direct sunlight, until they are fragrant and give slightly when touched. Once a day, turn the fruit around so all sides get exposed to the light and air evenly.

Make sure to handle stone fruits with great care. They are easy to bruise, dent, tear, and poke holes into. All stone fruits must be thoroughly washed in cold water with very mild soap or a specified produce wash (so there won't be any soapy taste) before using to remove any pesticide residue. Don't wash them until you are ready to use them, or they may become moldy.

Apricots, nectarines, plums, and cherries don't need to be peeled for use. For apricots, nectarines, and plums, simply wash and dry them, then cut them in half around the center, gently twist the two sides against each other until they separate, and remove the stone. For cherries, remove their stems and use a cherry pitter or a small sharp knife to remove the center stone. Often it's necessary to remove the skin from peaches using a technique called blanching. To do this, bring water to a boil in a large saucepan or stockpot over high heat. Using a sharp knife, score a small X in the bottom of each peach. Add the peaches to the hot water and let them boil for 1 or 2 minutes. Use a slotted spoon or skimmer to remove the peaches from the boiling water. Then, starting at the X, use a small sharp knife to gently peel the skin off of the peaches. It should slip off easily. If the peaches are too hot, peel them under cold running water.

Apricot Frangipane Tart

FRANGIPANE is a classic French almond cream that is used as the filling for tarts and other pastries. This tart is a medley of complementary flavors. Almond pastry dough holds the frangipane filling, then apricot halves are fanned out over the top of the frangipane, which bakes up around them, leaving them nestled in a golden blanket. The top of the warm tart is brushed with apricot glaze, making it glisten. **Makes one 9 1/2-inch round tart, 8 to 12 servings**

ALMOND PASTRY DOUGH

1 cup all-purpose flour
1/2 cup sliced or slivered
   almonds
2 teaspoons granulated sugar
1/4 teaspoon salt

In the work bowl of a food processor fitted with the steel blade, combine the flour, almonds, sugar, and salt. Pulse until the almonds are very finely ground, about 1 minute.

4 ounces (8 tablespoons,
   1 stick) unsalted butter,
   chilled

Cut the butter into small pieces and add to the almond mixture. Pulse until the butter is cut into very tiny pieces, about 30 seconds. The texture should be sandy with very tiny lumps throughout.

2 teaspoons fresh lemon
   juice
2 to 3 tablespoons ice water
Finely grated zest of 1 large
   lemon

In a small bowl, combine the lemon juice, 2 tablespoons of water, and the lemon zest. With the food processor running, pour this mixture through the feed tube. Process until the dough wraps itself around the blade, 30 seconds to 1 minute. If the dough seems dry, add the remaining tablespoon of water and process until the dough comes together.

Turn the pastry dough onto a large piece of plastic wrap. Shape into a flat disk and wrap tightly in a double layer of plastic wrap. Chill in the refrigerator until firm before using, about 2 hours. Chilling the dough relaxes the gluten in the flour so it won't be too elastic and will roll out easily. It also firms up the butter in the dough so it will need less flour when rolled out. If the dough is too firm, it will splinter and break when rolled out. Let it stand at room temperature for 10 to 15 minutes before rolling to become more pliable.

On a smooth, flat surface, roll out the pastry dough between sheets of lightly floured waxed or parchment paper to a large circle about 11 inches in diameter. Carefully peel the paper off the top of the dough. Brush excess flour off the dough, then loosely roll the pastry dough around the rolling pin without the other piece of paper. Place

Essential Gear

- Food processor
- Rolling pin
- 9 1/2-inch round fluted-edge tart pan with removable bottom
- Electric stand mixer and flat beater attachment or large mixing bowl and hand-held mixer
- 1/2-quart saucepan
- Cooling rack
- Medium-size fine-mesh strainer
- Goose-feather pastry brush

Keeping

The tart can last for up to 3 days in the refrigerator. Place a piece of waxed paper over the top of the tart, then tightly cover it with aluminum foil.

Streamlining

The pastry dough can be made in advance and kept in the refrigerator tightly wrapped in a double layer of plastic wrap for up to 4 days. To freeze for up to 3 months, wrap the dough snugly in several layers of plastic wrap and place it in a freezer bag. Use a large piece of masking tape and an indelible marker to label and date the contents. If frozen, defrost overnight in the refrigerator before using. The dough can also be fit into the tart pan and kept tightly covered in the refrig-

the tart pan directly underneath the rolling pin and carefully unroll the pastry dough onto it.

Gently lift up the sides and ease the pastry dough into the bottom and sides of the tart pan, pushing it lightly into the fluted edges. Trim off the excess pastry dough by running the rolling pin over the top of the pan. Or use your fingers to press against the top of the pan to trim the excess pastry dough.

Place the tart pan on a jelly-roll pan and chill while preparing the filling.

Center a rack in the oven and preheat it to 375°F.

FRANGIPANE FILLING

1 cup sliced almonds
½ cup granulated sugar

In the work bowl of a food processor fitted with the steel blade, combine the almonds and sugar. Pulse until the almonds are very finely ground, about 1 minute.

1 extra-large egg, at room temperature
½ teaspoon pure vanilla extract
½ teaspoon almond extract

Add the egg, vanilla, and almond extract and pulse several times to blend together well.

2½ ounces (5 tablespoons) unsalted butter, softened

Cut the butter into small pieces and add to the almond mixture. Pulse several times to blend.

2 tablespoons all-purpose flour

Add the flour and pulse until the mixture is smooth, about 15 seconds.

Transfer the frangipane mixture to the chilled pastry shell and spread it out evenly with a rubber spatula.

ASSEMBLY

¾ to 1 pound fresh ripe apricots (7 to 10 medium), washed and dried

Using a sharp knife, slice the fruit in half along the seam and remove the stones. Rounded sides up, cut each half horizontally into ½-inch-thick slices, leaving them attached at one side. Place the halves around the outer edge of the tart, leaving about 2 inches of space between them. Gently press on the halves and they will fan out. Continue slicing and fanning the apricot halves, filling the center of the tart.

Bake the tart for 40 to 45 minutes, until the filling is puffed and light golden. Remove the tart from the oven and place on a cooling rack.

erator, or frozen, wrapped and labeled as above.

The frangipane filling can be made in advance and kept in a tightly covered plastic container in the refrigerator for up to 4 days before using.

The apricot glaze can be made in advance and kept in a tightly covered plastic container in the refrigerator up to 1 month before using. Warm it in a small saucepan over medium heat or in a microwave oven on medium power before using.

Making a Change
Replace the apricots with plums, peaches, or nectarines.

¼ cup apricot preserves
1 tablespoon amaretto,
    cognac, or water

Stir together the apricot preserves and liquid in a small saucepan. Bring to a boil over medium heat. Remove the pan from the heat and strain the glaze into a small bowl, pushing through as much of the pulp as possible.

Use a goose-feather pastry brush to lightly brush the top of the tart with the glaze. Don't apply a thick layer, which looks unappetizing. The purpose of the glaze is to keep the apricots from drying out and to make the top of the tart glisten.

Remove the sides of the tart pan (see page 42) before serving. Serve the tart warm or at room temperature.

Apricot Galette

A GALETTE is a rustic, free-form fruit tart, baked directly on a lined baking sheet rather than in a tart pan. Some galettes are made with puff pastry, others with yeast dough, and yet others with sweet tart or pastry dough. This galette is made with pastry dough and is chock full of sweet, fresh apricots. It's a perfect summertime dessert. **Makes one 9-inch tart, 8 to 10 servings**

PASTRY DOUGH

1½ cups all-purpose flour
2 teaspoons granulated
    sugar
¼ teaspoon salt

In the work bowl of a food processor fitted with the steel blade, combine the flour, sugar, and salt. Pulse briefly to blend.

4 ounces (8 tablespoons,
    1 stick) unsalted butter,
    chilled

Cut the butter into small pieces and add to the flour mixture. Pulse until the butter is cut into very tiny pieces, about 30 seconds. The texture should be sandy with very tiny lumps throughout.

2 teaspoons freshly
    squeezed lemon juice
2 to 3 tablespoons ice water
Zest of 1 large lemon

In a small bowl, combine the lemon juice, 2 tablespoons of water, and the lemon zest. With the food processor running, pour this mixture through the feed tube. Process until the dough begins to hold together. Turn off the food processor, remove the top, and feel the dough. If it holds together, it is done. If it is still crumbly, add the remaining tablespoon of ice water and process briefly, then check again.

Turn the pastry dough onto a large piece of plastic wrap. Shape into a flat disk and wrap tightly in a double layer of plastic wrap. Chill in

Essential Gear
• Food processor
• Baking sheet
• Parchment paper
• 1-inch natural-bristle pastry
  brush or a spoon
• Cooling rack

Keeping
Although the galette is best eaten the day it's made, it can last for up to 2 days. Store the galette tightly covered with aluminum foil at room temperature.

Making a Change
Replace the apricots with other stone fruit, such as plums, nectarines, and peaches.

Use a combination of fruit instead of a single type.

the refrigerator until firm before using, about 2 hours. Chilling the dough relaxes the gluten in the flour so it won't be too elastic and will roll out easily. It also firms up the butter in the dough so it will need less flour when rolled out. If the dough is too firm, it will splinter and break when rolled out. Let it stand at room temperature for 10 to 15 minutes before rolling to become more pliable.

Adding Style
Serve slices of the galette with vanilla ice cream.

APRICOT FILLING

1 pound fresh ripe apricots (8 to 10 medium), washed and dried	Using a sharp knife, slice the fruit in half along the seam. Remove the stone and cut the fruit into 1/2-inch-thick slices. You should have approximately 3 cups of sliced fruit.
2 tablespoons granulated sugar	Place the sliced apricots in a mixing bowl. Add the sugar and toss together to distribute evenly. Taste the fruit to see if it needs any more sugar.

ASSEMBLY

Center a rack in the oven and preheat it to 375°F.

On a smooth, flat surface, roll out the pastry dough between sheets of lightly floured waxed or parchment paper to a large circle 11 to 12 inches in diameter. Carefully peel the paper off the top of the dough. Brush excess flour off the dough, then loosely roll the pastry dough around the rolling pin without the bottom piece of paper. Place the lined baking sheet directly underneath the rolling pin and carefully unroll the pastry dough onto the baking sheet.

Mound the sliced apricots in the center of the dough circle, leaving a 2 1/2- to 3-inch border all around.

1 ounce (2 tablespoons) unsalted butter, chilled	Cut the butter into small pieces and distribute evenly over the sliced apricots.
	Fold the border up so that it partially covers the apricots. It will naturally form pleats as it is folded.
1 tablespoon heavy whipping cream **2 teaspoons granulated sugar**	Brush the dough border with the cream, being careful that it doesn't run down the sides and under the galette. If it does, wipe it up because it can cause the bottom of the galette to burn. Gently lift up the folds of the dough and brush under those areas with cream, then replace the folds. Evenly sprinkle the sugar over the dough border.

Bake the galette for 35 to 40 minutes, until light golden. Remove the pan from the oven and transfer to a rack to cool. Cut the galette into pie-shaped wedges to serve.

Apricot Streusel Pie

F RESH APRICOTS nestled in a classic pie dough shell are topped with a crumbly, crunchy topping full of toasted walnuts, light brown sugar, nutmeg, and chilled butter. This pie is perfect to bring to a picnic gathering. **Makes one 9-inch round pie, 12 to 14 servings**

Essential Gear
- Food processor
- Rolling pin
- 9-inch round pie pan
- Jelly-roll pan
- Cooling rack

PIE DOUGH

1½ cups all-purpose flour
1 teaspoon granulated sugar
¼ teaspoon salt

In the work bowl of a food processor fitted with the steel blade, combine the flour, sugar, and salt. Pulse briefly to blend.

4 ounces (8 tablespoons, 1 stick) unsalted butter, chilled

Cut the butter into small pieces and freeze for 20 minutes. Add the butter to the flour mixture. Pulse until the butter is cut into pea-sized pieces, 30 to 45 seconds. The texture should be sandy with very tiny lumps throughout.

3 to 4 tablespoons ice water

Remove the top of the food processor and sprinkle on 2 tablespoons of the ice water. Replace the top and pulse for 10 seconds. Squeeze a small amount of the dough in your hand. If it holds together, don't add any more water. If the dough is still very crumbly, add another tablespoon of water, pulse to blend, then check the dough again. It won't hold together unless you squeeze it, but that's the texture you want.

Turn the dough onto a smooth, flat work surface. Use the heel of your hand to push the dough a few times for a final blend. Don't mush all the butter into the dough, however. For a flaky crust, you want to see thin flecks of butter in the dough.

Shape the dough into a flat disk and wrap tightly in a double layer of plastic wrap. Chill in the refrigerator until firm before using, at least 2 hours. Chilling the dough relaxes the gluten in the flour so it won't be too elastic and will roll out easily. It also firms up the butter in the dough so it will need less flour when rolled out. If the dough is too firm, it will splinter and break when rolled out. Let it stand at room temperature for 10 to 15 minutes before rolling to become more pliable.

On a smooth, flat surface, roll out the pie dough between sheets of lightly floured waxed or parchment paper to a large circle about 12 inches in diameter. To tell if the dough will fit the pie pan, invert

Keeping
Store the pie loosely covered with waxed paper, then tightly wrapped with aluminum foil, at room temperature for up to 3 days.

Streamlining
The pie dough can be made in advance and kept in the refrigerator tightly wrapped in a double layer of plastic wrap for up to 4 days. To freeze for up to 3 months, wrap the dough snugly in several layers of plastic wrap and place it in a freezer bag. Use a large piece of masking tape and an indelible marker to label and date the contents. If frozen, defrost overnight in the refrigerator before using. The dough can also be fitted into the pie pan and frozen. Wrap as above and label.

The streusel topping can be made in advance and kept in the refrigerator in a tightly covered plastic container for up to 1 week.

Troubleshooting
Don't overprocess the pie dough or it will be tough and not flaky.

the pan over the dough. If there are 2 to 3 inches of dough that protrude beyond the sides of the pan, it will fit.

Carefully peel the paper off the top of the dough. Brush excess flour off the dough, then loosely roll the pastry dough around the rolling pin without the bottom piece of paper. Place the pie pan directly underneath the rolling pin and carefully unroll the pastry dough into the pan. Or loosely fold the dough in half. Carefully place it in half of the pie pan and gently unfold the dough. Gently lift up the sides and ease the pie dough into the bottom and sides of the pie pan. Trim off the excess pie dough at the top of the pan and crimp the sides (see page 40).

Transfer the pie pan to a baking sheet and chill in the freezer for 15 to 20 minutes. This helps prevent the pie dough from shrinking as it bakes and sets the butter in the dough to ensure flakiness.

Center a rack in the oven and preheat it to 350°F.

Making a Change
To make classic tender, flaky pie dough, replace half of the butter with lard or vegetable shortening.

EGG GLAZE

1 extra-large egg 2 teaspoons cool water	Using a fork, lightly beat the egg with the water in a small bowl. Using a pastry brush, brush the glaze over the inside of the pie shell. This will help prevent the shell from becoming soggy from the apricot juice.

APRICOT FILLING

1½ pounds fresh ripe apricots (14 to 16 medium), washed and dried	Using a sharp knife, slice the apricots in half along the seam. Remove the stone and cut the fruit into ½-inch-thick slices. Place the sliced apricots in a large bowl.
2 tablespoons light brown sugar	Add the sugar and toss together lightly to distribute evenly.
1 ounce (2 tablespoons) unsalted butter, cold	Transfer the apricots to the pie shell. Cut the butter into small pieces and distribute evenly over the sliced apricots. Refrigerate the pie while preparing the topping.

STREUSEL TOPPING

⅔ cup walnuts	Place the walnuts in a single layer in a cake or pie pan. Toast in the oven for 4 minutes. Shake the pan to stir the walnuts and toast for another 4 to 6 minutes, until lightly colored. Remove from the oven and cool.

⅓ cup all-purpose flour

⅓ cup firmly packed light brown sugar

¼ teaspoon freshly grated nutmeg

⅛ teaspoon salt

1½ ounces (3 tablespoons) unsalted butter, chilled

In the work bowl of a food processor fitted with the steel blade, combine the flour, sugar, nutmeg, and salt. Add the toasted walnuts and pulse until the walnuts are coarsely chopped, 20 to 30 seconds. Cut the butter into small pieces and add to the dry ingredients. Pulse until the butter is cut into very small pieces, 30 seconds to 1 minute.

Evenly sprinkle the topping over the apricots in the baking pan.

Bake the pie for 35 to 40 minutes, until the topping is light golden. Remove the pan from the oven and transfer to a rack to cool.

Cherry and Apricot Crisp

THIS IS AN EASY dessert to make and to eat. A crumbly topping of toasted oats is scattered over fresh cherries and apricots, mixed together in a square pan, and then baked. It's excellent eaten either warm or at room temperature. Be sure to use fresh, sweet fruit for the best flavor. The final garnish for this delicious dessert is a scoop of lightly whipped cream. To make it even better, add a scoop of vanilla ice cream to each serving. **Makes one 8-inch square crisp, 8 to 10 servings**

CHERRY AND APRICOT FILLING

½ pound fresh cherries, washed, dried, and stems removed

Use a cherry pitter or a small sharp knife to remove the pits from the cherries. Place the cherries in the baking pan.

1 pound fresh ripe apricots (about 10 medium), washed and dried

Using a sharp knife, slice the fruit in half along the seam. Remove the stone and cut each half into quarters. Place the cut apricots in the baking pan. Toss the cherries and apricots together lightly to mix evenly.

TOPPING

Center a rack in the oven and preheat it to 350°F.

⅔ cups rolled oats (not quick-cooking)

Place the oats in a single layer in a cake or pie pan. Toast in the oven for 15 minutes, until light golden. Remove from the oven and cool slightly.

Essential Gear
- Cherry pitter or small sharp knife
- 8-inch square baking pan
- Food processor
- Rubber spatula or wooden spoon
- Cooling rack

Keeping
Although the crisp is best eaten the day it's made, it can last for up to 2 days. Store the crisp tightly covered with aluminum foil in the refrigerator.

Streamlining
The topping can be made in advance. Store it in a tightly covered plastic container in the refrigerator for up to 4 days.

Making a Change
Use other types of stone fruit, such as nectarines and peaches.

½ cup firmly packed light brown sugar ¼ teaspoon cinnamon ¼ teaspoon freshly ground nutmeg ⅛ teaspoon salt	In the work bowl of a food processor fitted with the steel blade, combine the oats, sugar, cinnamon, nutmeg, and salt and pulse briefly to blend.	**Adding Style** Serve squares of the crisp with vanilla ice cream.
2 ounces (4 tablespoons, ½ stick) unsalted butter, chilled	Cut the butter into small pieces and add to the dry ingredients. Pulse until the butter is cut into very small pieces, 30 seconds to 1 minute. Evenly sprinkle the topping over the fruit in the baking pan.	
	Bake the crisp for 25 to 30 minutes, until the topping is light golden. Remove the pan from the oven and transfer to a rack to cool.	

GARNISH

1 cup heavy whipping cream	Place the cream in the bowl of an electric stand mixer or in a large mixing bowl. Use the wire whip attachment or a hand-held mixer to whip on medium speed until frothy.
2 tablespoons confectioners' sugar	Add the confectioners' sugar and continue whipping the cream until it holds soft peaks.
	Cut the crisp into squares, scooping up the fruit. Serve each square with a large dollop of whipped cream.

Cherry Clafouti

A *CLAFOUTI* is a classic, rustic dessert that originated in the Limousin region of France. It is a cross between a tart and a custard dessert, traditionally made with unpitted black cherries that are native to the region. This version uses pitted cherries, which makes the dessert much easier to eat. The cherries are placed in a deep pie dish and covered with a thick pancake-type batter that puffs up around the cherries as it bakes. **Makes one 10-inch clafouti, 8 to 10 servings**

Center a rack in the oven and preheat it to 375°F.

1 tablespoon unsalted butter, softened 1 tablespoon granulated sugar	Use your fingertips or a paper towel to butter the bottom and sides of the pie dish. Sprinkle the inside of the pan with sugar. Tilt and shake the dish so the sugar sticks to the butter. Turn the dish over and shake out any excess sugar over the sink.

Essential Gear
- 10-inch round deep pie dish
- Cherry pitter or small sharp knife
- Large mixing bowl
- Whisk, rubber spatula, or wooden spoon
- Large fine-mesh strainer
- Cooling rack

Keeping
Although the clafouti is best eaten the day it's made, it can last for up to 2 days.

CHERRY FILLING

3 cups fresh cherries,
washed, dried, and
stemmed

Use a cherry pitter or a small sharp knife to remove the pits from the cherries. Place the cherries in the pie dish.

BATTER

3 extra-large eggs

½ cup milk

½ cup heavy whipping cream

1½ ounces (3 tablespoons)
unsalted butter, melted
and cooled

1 tablespoon kirsch, cognac,
or rum

2 teaspoons pure vanilla
extract

In a large mixing bowl, combine the eggs, milk, cream, butter, kirsch, and vanilla. Stir together to blend.

⅔ cup all-purpose flour,
sifted

⅛ teaspoon salt

Add the flour and salt and whisk together until smooth.

Push the batter through a fine-mesh strainer to remove any lumps. Pour the batter evenly over the cherries in the pie dish.

Bake the clafouti for 40 to 45 minutes, until it is puffed and light golden. Remove the pan from the oven and transfer to a rack to cool.

GARNISH

2 tablespoons confectioners'
sugar

Dust the top of the clafouti evenly with confectioners' sugar. Cut into pie-shaped wedges and serve warm or at room temperature.

Store the clafouti tightly covered with plastic wrap in the refrigerator. Once the clafouti cools, it will fall slightly.

Making a Change
Use a couple of types of cherries, such as Bing and Rainier.

Replace the cherries with other stone fruit, such as plums and peaches, sliced ¼ inch thick.

Replace the cherries with berries, such as blueberries and raspberries. Replace the kirsch with cognac or rum.

Replace the cherries with pears or apples, cored and sliced ¼ inch thick or cut into cubes. Replace the kirsch with Armagnac or rum.

Adding Style
Serve slices of the clafouti with vanilla ice cream.

Cherry Pie

FRESH CHERRIES have a short season and this pie is one of the best ways to enjoy them. Sour cherries are the classic type used in this pie, but they can be hard to find. Bing cherries work equally well. The pie dough is made with a combination of unsalted butter and cream cheese, which gives it both a luscious flavor and a flaky texture. This is one of my favorite recipes for pie dough. **Makes One 10-inch round pie, 12 to 14 servings**

Essential Gear
- Food processor
- Rolling pin
- 10-inch round deep pie pan
- Baking sheet
- Cherry pitter or small sharp knife
- Cooling rack

PIE DOUGH

2 cups all-purpose flour
2 tablespoons granulated
sugar
½ teaspoon salt

In the work bowl of a food processor fitted with the steel blade, combine the flour, sugar, and salt. Pulse briefly to blend.

8 ounces (16 tablespoons,
2 sticks) unsalted butter,
chilled

Cut the butter into small pieces and freeze for 20 minutes.

8 ounces cream cheese,
chilled

Cut the cream cheese into small pieces and add to the dry ingredients in the food processor. Pulse to cut the cream cheese into very tiny pieces. The texture should be sandy with very tiny lumps throughout.

Add the butter to the flour mixture in the food processor. Pulse until the butter is cut into pea-sized pieces, 30 to 45 seconds.

3 to 4 tablespoons heavy
whipping cream

Remove the top of the food processor and sprinkle on 3 tablespoons of the cream. Replace the top and pulse for 10 seconds. Squeeze a small amount of the dough in your hand. If it holds together, don't add any more cream. If the dough is still very crumbly, add another tablespoon of cream, pulse to blend, then check the dough again. It won't hold together unless you squeeze it, but that's the texture you want.

Divide the dough in two equal pieces and shape each piece into a flat disk. Wrap each disk tightly in a double layer of plastic wrap. Chill in the refrigerator until firm before using, at least 2 hours. Chilling the dough relaxes the gluten in the flour so it won't be too elastic and will roll out easily. It also firms up the butter in the dough so it will need less flour when rolled out. If the dough is too firm it will splinter and break when rolled out. Let it stand at room temperature for 10 to 15 minutes before rolling to become more pliable.

On a smooth, flat surface, roll out one of the disks of pie dough between sheets of lightly floured waxed or parchment paper to a large circle about 12 inches in diameter. To tell if the dough will fit the pie pan, invert the pan over the dough. If there are 2 to 3 inches of dough that protrude beyond the sides of the pan, it will fit.

Carefully peel the paper off the top of the dough. Brush excess flour off the dough, then loosely roll the pastry dough around the rolling pin without the other piece of paper. Place the pie pan directly underneath the rolling pin and carefully unroll the pastry dough into the pan. Or loosely fold the dough in half. Carefully place it in half

Keeping

Store the pie loosely covered with waxed paper, then tightly wrapped with aluminum foil in the refrigerator for up to 3 days.

Streamlining

The pie dough can be made in advance and kept in the refrigerator, tightly wrapped in a double layer of plastic wrap, for up to 4 days. To freeze for up to 3 months, wrap the dough snugly in several layers of plastic wrap and place it in a freezer bag. Use a large piece of masking tape and an indelible marker to label and date the contents. If frozen, defrost overnight in the refrigerator before using. The dough can also be fitted into the pie pan and kept tightly covered in the refrigerator or frozen, wrapped and labeled as above.

Troubleshooting

Don't overprocess the pie dough or it will be tough and not flaky.

Making a Change

Replace the fresh cherries with drained canned cherries. Replace half of the cherries with peeled, diced rhubarb. Replace half of the cherries with blueberries and strawberries.

Adding Style

Serve slices of the pie with vanilla ice cream or whipped cream.

of the pie pan and gently unfold the dough. Gently lift up the sides and ease the pie dough into the bottom and sides of the pie pan. Trim off the excess pie dough at the top of the pan and crimp the sides (see page 40).

Transfer the pie pan to a baking sheet and chill in the freezer for 15 to 20 minutes. This helps prevent the pie dough from shrinking as it bakes and sets the butter in the dough to ensure flakiness.

CHERRY FILLING

5 cups fresh Bing cherries, washed, dried, and stemmed
¾ cup granulated sugar
¼ cup cornstarch, sifted
1 tablespoon freshly squeezed lemon juice
¼ teaspoon almond extract
⅛ teaspoon salt

Use a cherry pitter or a small sharp knife to remove the pits from the cherries. Place the cherries in a large bowl. Add the sugar, cornstarch, lemon juice, almond extract, and salt and stir together to coat the cherries completely. Cover the bowl with plastic wrap and let the mixture stand for at least 15 minutes or up to 2 hours in the refrigerator.

Transfer the cherry filling to the pie shell.

Adjust an oven rack to the lower third and preheat the oven to 425°F.

1 extra-large egg yolk, at room temperature
1 tablespoon heavy whipping cream

Use a fork to lightly beat the egg yolk and cream together in a small bowl. Use a pastry brush to brush the mixture on the edges of the bottom pastry shell to help the pastry and lattice topping stick together.

Roll out the remaining disk of pie dough on a smooth, flat surface between sheets of lightly floured waxed or parchment paper to a large circle about 12 inches in diameter. Peel off the top piece of paper. Use a ruler and a plain or fluted-edge pastry wheel to cut ½-inch-wide strips of dough. Form the strips into a lattice on top of the cherries (see page 41). Trim off the edges of both the lattice and the bottom pie shell evenly, leaving a ¾-inch overhang.

1 tablespoon granulated sugar

Fold the edges of the lattice over the bottom crust and press them to seal together. Crimp or flute the edges (see page 40). Brush the top of the lattice with the egg yolk/milk mixture and sprinkle sugar over the top of the dough.

Bake the pie for 40 to 45 minutes, until the crust is light golden and the filling is thickly bubbling inside. Remove the pie from the oven and cool on a rack. Serve warm or at room temperature.

Cherry-Rhubarb Lattice Pie

S OUR CHERRIES and naturally tart rhubarb create a delectable flavor combination in this pie. The leaves of rhubarb are not edible and are slightly toxic, so be sure to remove them completely before using the stalks. In this pie, I use my favorite pie dough made with both cream cheese and butter. Not only does it taste great, but it's the easiest pie dough to work with. The top of this pie has a lattice, which I prefer on pies because it allows the fruit to show through. **Makes one 10-inch round pie, 12 to 14 servings**

PIE DOUGH

2 cups all-purpose flour 2 tablespoons granulated sugar ½ teaspoon salt	In the work bowl of a food processor fitted with the steel blade, combine the flour, sugar, and salt. Pulse briefly to blend.
8 ounces (16 tablespoons, 2 sticks) unsalted butter, chilled	Cut the butter into small pieces and freeze for 20 minutes.
8 ounces cream cheese, chilled	Cut the cream cheese into small pieces and add to the dry ingredients in the food processor. Pulse to cut the cream cheese into very tiny pieces. The texture should be sandy with very tiny lumps throughout. Add the butter to the flour mixture in the food processor. Pulse until the butter is cut into pea-sized pieces, 30 to 45 seconds.
3 to 4 tablespoons heavy whipping cream	Remove the top of the food processor and sprinkle on 3 tablespoons of the cream. Replace the top and pulse for 10 seconds. Squeeze a small amount of the dough in your hand. If it holds together, don't add any more cream. If the dough is still very crumbly, add another tablespoon of cream, pulse to blend, then check the dough again. It won't hold together unless you squeeze it, but that's the texture you want. Divide the dough in two equal pieces and shape each piece into a flat disk. Wrap the disks tightly in a double layer of plastic wrap. Chill in the refrigerator until firm before using, at least 2 hours. Chilling the dough relaxes the gluten in the flour so it won't be too elastic and will roll out easily. It also firms up the butter in the dough so it will need less flour when rolled out. If the dough is too firm it will

Essential Gear
- Food processor
- Rolling pin
- 10-inch round deep pie pan
- Baking sheet
- Pastry brush
- Cooling rack

Keeping
Store the pie loosely covered with waxed paper, then tightly wrapped with aluminum foil at room temperature for up to 3 days.

Streamlining
The pie dough can be made in advance and kept in the refrigerator, tightly wrapped in a double layer of plastic wrap, for up to 4 days. To freeze for up to 3 months, wrap the dough snugly in several layers of plastic wrap and place it in a freezer bag. Use a large piece of masking tape and an indelible marker to label and date the contents. If frozen, defrost overnight in the refrigerator before using. The dough can also be fit into the pie pan and frozen. Wrap as above and label.

Troubleshooting
Don't overprocess the pie dough or it will be tough and not flaky.

Adding Style
Add 2 tablespoons finely grated or minced lemon zest

splinter and break when rolled out. Let it stand at room temperature for 10 to 15 minutes before rolling to become more pliable.

On a smooth, flat surface, roll out one of the disks of pie dough between sheets of lightly floured waxed or parchment paper to a large circle about 12 inches in diameter. To tell if the dough will fit the pie pan, invert the pan over the dough. If there are 2 to 3 inches of dough that protrude beyond the sides of the pan, it will fit.

Carefully peel the paper off the top of the dough. Brush excess flour off the dough, then loosely roll the pastry dough around the rolling pin without the bottom piece of paper. Place the pie pan directly underneath the rolling pin and carefully unroll the pastry dough into the pan. Or loosely fold the dough in half. Carefully place it in half of the pie pan and gently unfold the dough.. Gently lift up the sides and ease the pie dough into the bottom and sides of the pie pan. Trim off the excess pie dough at the top of the pan and crimp the sides (see page 40).

Transfer the pie pan to a baking sheet and chill in the freezer for 15 to 20 minutes. This helps prevent the pie dough from shrinking as it bakes and sets the butter in the dough to ensure flakiness.

to the pie dough before adding the butter.

Serve slices of the pie with vanilla ice cream or whipped cream.

CHERRY-RHUBARB FILLING

1 to 1¼ pounds (2½ cups) fresh sour cherries, washed, dried, stemmed, and pitted

1 pound fresh rhubarb, washed, dried, and cut into ½-inch pieces (about 3 cups)

⅔ cup granulated sugar

¼ cup firmly packed light brown sugar

¼ cup cornstarch, sifted

Finely grated zest of 2 large lemons

Place the cherries and rhubarb in a large bowl. Add the granulated sugar and brown sugar and toss to coat the fruit. Add the cornstarch and lemon zest and gently toss the fruit to coat with the ingredients.

Transfer this mixture to the chilled pie shell and spread it out evenly.

1 tablespoon unsalted butter, chilled

Cut the butter into tiny pieces and distribute them evenly over the fruit.

Adjust an oven rack to the lower third and preheat the oven to 425°F.

| 1 to 2 teaspoons water | Use a pastry brush to apply water to the edges of the bottom pastry shell to help the pastry and lattice topping stick together. |

Roll out the remaining disk of pie dough on a smooth, flat surface between sheets of lightly floured waxed or parchment paper to a large circle about 12 inches in diameter. Peel off the top piece of paper. Use a ruler and a plain or fluted-edge pastry wheel to cut $^1/_2$-inch-wide strips of dough. Form the strips into a lattice on top of the filling (see page 41). Trim off the edges of both the lattice and the bottom pie shell evenly, leaving a $^3/_4$-inch overhang. Fold the edges of the lattice over the bottom crust and press them to seal together. Crimp or flute the edges (see page 40).

Bake the pie for 15 minutes, then reduce the oven temperature to 350°F. Bake the pie another 40 to 50 minutes, until the crust is light golden and the fruit is thickly bubbling inside. Remove the pie from the oven and cool on a rack. Serve warm or at room temperature.

Cherry-Almond Cake

T HIS IS A RUSTIC-style cake that is baked in a glass pie plate and cut into pie-shaped wedges for serving. Fresh cherries are baked into a rich, buttery almond batter. A light dusting of confectioners' sugar is all this cake needs for decoration, but a scoop of vanilla ice cream or freshly whipped cream makes it a standout. I like to use fresh, sweet Bing cherries when they are in season, but any type of cherry works well. If you use canned cherries, be sure to drain off the liquid. **Makes one 9-inch cake, 8 to 10 servings**

Essential Gear
- 9-inch round pie pan
- Cherry pitter or small sharp knife
- Food processor
- Electric stand mixer with flat beater attachment or large mixing bowl and hand-held mixer
- Cooling rack

Keeping
Store the cake tightly covered with plastic wrap at room temperature for up to 4 days. The cake can be frozen for up to 3 months. Wrap it snugly in several layers of plastic wrap and aluminum foil. Use a large piece of masking tape and an indelible marker to label

Center a rack in the oven and preheat it to 400°F.

| 1 tablespoon unsalted butter, softened | Use your fingertips or a paper towel to butter the bottom and sides of the pan. |

| $^1/_2$ pound (1$^1/_4$ cups) fresh Bing cherries, washed, dried, and stemmed | Use a cherry pitter or a small sharp knife to remove the pits from the cherries. Place the cherries in a small bowl. |

| 2 tablespoons kirsch or amaretto | Add the liqueur, stir to coat all the cherries, and let them marinate while you prepare the cake batter. |

1 cup raw sliced or slivered almonds	Place the almonds and sugar in the work bowl of a food processor fitted with the steel blade. Pulse until finely ground, about 2 minutes.
1 tablespoon granulated sugar	
4 ounces (8 tablespoons, 1 stick) unsalted butter, softened	Place the butter in the bowl of an electric stand mixer or in a large mixing bowl. Use the flat beater attachment or a hand-held mixer to beat the butter on medium speed until it's fluffy, about 2 minutes.
½ cup granulated sugar	Add the sugar, and cream together well. Stop occasionally and scrape down the sides and bottom of the bowl with a spatula.
2 extra-large eggs, at room temperature	One at a time, add the eggs to the butter mixture, stopping to scrape down the bottom and sides of the bowl after each addition. At first the mixture may look curdled as the eggs are added, but as you stop and scrape down the bowl, the mixture will smooth out.
1 teaspoon pure vanilla extract	Add the vanilla and mix well.
⅓ cup all-purpose flour	Sift the flour and mix with the salt and the finely ground almonds. Add this mixture to the butter mixture. Blend together on low speed briefly until the ingredients are combined.
⅛ teaspoon salt	
	Remove the mixing bowl from the mixer and use a rubber spatula to fold in the cherries and liquid.
	Transfer the mixture to the pie pan. Use the rubber spatula to spread the mixture evenly in the pan.
	Bake the cake for 20 to 23 minutes, until it is set and light golden. Remove the pan from the oven and transfer to a rack to cool.

GARNISH

2 tablespoons confectioners' sugar	Dust the top of the cake evenly with confectioners' sugar. Cut into pie-shaped wedges and serve warm or at room temperature.

and date the contents. If frozen, defrost the cake overnight in the refrigerator.

Adding Style
Serve slices of the cake with vanilla ice cream or whipped cream.

Fresh Peach Buttercream Layer Cake

T HIS IS ONE OF my all-time favorite cakes because it is a symphony of flavors that work perfectly together. The cake layers are rich and dense, with the slight tangy flavor of sour cream. The buttercream is flavored with fresh peach puree and the cake is decorated with fresh peach slices and toasted sliced almonds. Although there are several steps involved in making this cake, most can be done in advance, making it easy to fit into your schedule. Assemble the cake a few hours before serving so the flavors and textures have time to marry together. **Makes one 9-inch round cake, 12 to 14 servings**

CAKE

Center a rack in the oven and preheat it to 325°F.

1 tablespoon unsalted butter, softened	Using a paper towel or your fingertips, generously butter the inside of the cake pans, coating them thoroughly
1 tablespoon all-purpose flour	Dust the inside of each pan with some of the flour. Shake and tilt the pans to evenly distribute the flour, then turn the pans over and shake out the excess over the sink.
	Cut a round of parchment paper to fit the bottom of each pan. Butter each parchment paper round and place in each pan, butter-side up.
12 ounces (24 tablespoons, 3 sticks) unsalted butter, softened	Place the butter in the bowl of an electric stand mixer or in a large mixing bowl. Use the flat beater attachment or hand-held mixer to beat the butter on medium speed until it's fluffy, about 2 minutes.
2¼ cups superfine sugar	Gradually add the sugar to the butter and cream together well. Stop occasionally and scrape down the bottom and sides of the bowl with a rubber spatula.
6 extra-large eggs, at room temperature	One at a time, add the eggs, stopping to scrape down the bottom and sides of the bowl after each addition. At first the mixture may look curdled as the eggs are added, but as you scrape down the bowl, the mixture will smooth out.
½ cup sour cream **2 teaspoons pure vanilla extract**	Add the sour cream and vanilla to the butter mixture and blend together well.

Essential Gear

- Two 9 × 2-inch round cake pans
- Scissors
- Parchment paper
- Electric stand mixer with flat beater attachment and wire whip attachment or large mixing bowl and hand-held mixer
- Two rubber spatulas
- Two cooling racks
- 10-inch flexible-blade icing spatula
- Goose-feather pastry brush
- Sugar thermometer

Keeping

Store the cake loosely covered with aluminum foil in the refrigerator for up to 2 days. Place several toothpicks in the top outer edges of the cake to hold the foil away from it so it won't mar the buttercream.

Streamlining

Bake the cake layers up to 2 days before assembling the cake and keep tightly covered with a double layer of plastic wrap at room temperature. To freeze the layers for up to 3 months, wrap them snugly in several layers of plastic wrap and place them in freezer bags. Use a large piece of masking tape and an indelible marker to label and date the contents. If frozen, defrost the layers overnight in the refrigerator.

3 cups cake flour
1 teaspoon baking powder
1/2 teaspoon baking soda
1/2 teaspoon salt

Over a large piece of waxed or parchment paper or a bowl, sift together the flour, baking powder, and baking soda. Add the salt and toss to blend well.

With the mixer on low speed, add the dry ingredients to the batter in 4 stages. Blend well after each addition and stop often to scrape down the bottom and sides of the bowl with a rubber spatula.

Divide the batter evenly between the two cake pans. Smooth the top of each pan with a rubber spatula.

Bake the cakes for 45 minutes, until they are golden and a cake tester inserted in the center comes out with no crumbs clinging to it.

Remove the cake pans from the oven and cool completely on racks. Invert the pans to remove the layers, then peel the parchment paper off the back of each layer. Re-invert the layers onto plates or cardboard cake circles.

PEACH BUTTERCREAM

1 pound fresh, ripe peaches (4 medium), washed

Bring water to a boil in a large saucepan or stockpot over high heat. Using a sharp knife, score a small X in the bottom of each peach. Add the peaches to the water and let them boil for 1 to 2 minutes. Use a slotted spoon or skimmer to remove the peaches from the boiling water. Place them in a bowl of cold water, which will stop them from further cooking.

Starting at the X, use a small sharp knife to gently peel the skin off the peaches. It should slip off easily. If the peaches are too hot, peel them under cold running water.

Cut 2 of the peaches in half and remove the pits. Place the peach halves in the work bowl of a food processor fitted with the steel blade or into the blender. Pulse until the peaches are pureed. You should have 1/3 to 1/2 cup peach puree.

Slice the remaining two peaches into 1/2-inch-thick slices. Place the slices on a plate and cover them with waxed paper to keep them from turning brown while you are assembling the cake.

2 extra-large eggs, at room temperature
2 extra-large egg yolks, at room temperature
1/4 cup granulated sugar

Place the eggs, egg yolks, and sugar in the bowl of an electric stand mixer or in a large mixing bowl. Use the wire whip attachment or a hand-held mixer and whip on medium speed until the mixture is very pale colored and holds a slowly dissolving ribbon as the beater is lifted, about 5 minutes.

The buttercream can be prepared up to 3 days in advance and kept in an airtight plastic container in the refrigerator or for up to 4 months in the freezer. If frozen, defrost overnight in the refrigerator. To reheat the buttercream, break it up into chunks and place in a mixing bowl. Place the bowl in a saucepan of warm water and let the buttercream begin to melt around the bottom. Wipe the bottom of the bowl dry and beat the buttercream with an electric mixer until it is fluffy and smooth.

Making a Change
Replace the sliced almonds with finely chopped walnuts or ground toasted hazelnuts.

Replace the peaches with apricots or nectarines.

Replace the peach preserves in the glaze with apricot, mango, or passion fruit preserves or orange marmalade.

Recovering from a Mishap
If one of the cake layers breaks during assembly, patch it together with some of the buttercream.

1¼ cups granulated sugar
½ cup water
¼ teaspoon cream of tartar

While the eggs are whipping, place the sugar, water, and cream of tartar in a 2-quart heavy-bottomed saucepan. Bring the mixture to a boil, without stirring. Place a wet pastry brush at the point where the sugar syrup meets the sides of the pan and sweep it around completely. Do this two times. Brushing down the sides of the pan while the sugar is cooking prevents sugar crystals from coming out of the mixture, which causes crystallization. This is a condition that creates a crust around the side of the pan. Once crystallization occurs, the sugar syrup won't come up to temperature correctly and has to be thrown away. Don't brush around the pan more than a few times. If you do, you're adding extra water to the sugar syrup, which takes more time to cook off and reach the desired temperature.

Cook over high heat until the mixture registers 242°F on a sugar thermometer (soft-ball stage). Immediately remove the thermometer and place it in a glass of warm water, then remove the pan from the heat so it won't continue to cook.

Adjust the mixer speed to low and pour the sugar syrup into the whipped eggs in a slow, steady stream. Aim the sugar syrup between the beater and the side of the bowl, so it doesn't get caught up in the beater or thrown against the sides of the bowl. Turn the mixer speed up to medium-high and whip until the bowl is cool to the touch, about 8 minutes.

Once the cooked sugar syrup is added to the whipped eggs, the mixture must whip until the bowl is completely cool to the touch before the butter is added, or the butter will melt. If this happens, the texture and consistency of the buttercream will be too soft and more butter needs to be added to bring it to the right point.

1 pound (2 cups, 4 sticks)
  unsalted butter, softened

Adjust the mixer speed to medium and add the butter, 2 tablespoons at a time. Continue to beat until the buttercream is thoroughly blended and fluffy.

Add the peach puree and beat until it is completely blended.

¼ cup peach preserves

With your fingertips, gently peel the skin off the top of each cake layer. Using a serrated knife, cut each cake layer in half horizontally (see page 34). Place the bottom of one cake layer on a serving plate. Use the flexible-blade spatula to spread the layer evenly with the peach preserves.

Place strips of waxed paper around the bottom edges of the cake to protect the plate while assembling the cake. With a clean, flexible-blade spatula, evenly spread some of the buttercream over the cake layer.

Position the second cake layer evenly over the buttercream and spread some of the buttercream over the layer. Repeat with the remaining 2 cake layers and buttercream.

Spread the remaining buttercream over the sides and top of the cake.

1 cup sliced almonds, lightly toasted

Press the toasted sliced almonds onto the sides of the cake just up to, but not over, the top edge.

Arrange the sliced peaches in a circle over the top outer edge of the cake. Arrange a second circle of sliced peaches inside of the outer circle and use any remaining slices to fill in the center of the top of the cake.

PEACH GLAZE

¼ cup peach preserves
1 tablespoon amaretto, cognac, or water

Combine the peach preserves and liquid in a small saucepan. Bring to a boil over medium heat. Remove the pan from the heat and strain the glaze into a small bowl, pushing through as much of the pulp as possible.

Use a goose-feather pastry brush to lightly brush the top of the sliced peaches with the glaze. Don't apply a thick glaze, which looks unappetizing. The purpose of the glaze is to keep the peaches from drying out and to make the top of the cake glisten.

Fresh Peach Coffee Cake

THERE'S NO COFFEE in this cake, but it does taste great with a cup of coffee or tea. It's baked in a quiche pan with fluted edges that give the cake an attractive design. A batter accented with lemon and orange zest and a little ground cinnamon bakes up to enclose fresh peach halves. For dessert, try serving this yummy cake with vanilla ice cream or whipped cream. You can eat this cake any time of day, even for breakfast. **Makes one 9½-inch cake, 8 to 10 servings**

Center a rack in the oven and preheat it to 400°F.

¾ to 1 pound fresh, ripe peaches (3 medium-large), washed

Bring water to a boil in a large saucepan or stockpot over high heat. Using a sharp knife, score a small X in the bottom of each peach. Add the peaches to the water and let them boil for 1 to 2 minutes. Use a slotted spoon or skimmer to remove the peaches from the

Essential Gear

- 4- or 5-quart saucepan or stockpot
- Small sharp knife
- Medium mixing bowl
- Rubber spatula or wooden spoon
- 9½-inch round, deep quiche pan with fluted edges and removable bottom
- Jelly-roll pan
- Cooling rack

boiling water. Place them in a bowl of cold water, which will stop them from further cooking.

Starting at the X, use a small sharp knife to gently peel the skin off the peaches. It should slip off easily. If the peaches are too hot, peel them under cold running water.

Cut the peaches in half and remove the pits. Place the peach halves on a plate and cover with waxed paper while preparing the cake.

1½ cups all-purpose flour
⅓ cup granulated sugar
¼ cup firmly packed light brown sugar
2 teaspoons baking powder
½ teaspoon ground cinnamon
¼ teaspoon salt

Place the flour, granulated sugar, brown sugar, baking powder, cinnamon, and salt in a medium mixing bowl. Use a rubber spatula or wooden spoon to stir together.

2 extra-large eggs
2 ounces (4 tablespoons, ½ stick) unsalted butter, melted
2 tablespoons heavy whipping cream
1 teaspoon pure vanilla extract
Finely grated zest of ½ small lemon
Finely grated zest of ½ small orange

Use a fork to lightly beat the eggs in a small mixing bowl. Add the butter, cream, vanilla, lemon zest, and orange zest and stir together until combined.

Add this mixture to the dry ingredients. Use a rubber spatula or wooden spoon to stir together until evenly blended.

Turn the mixture out into the quiche pan and spread it evenly.

Press the peach halves into the dough around the top of the cake. Place the quiche pan on a jelly-roll pan.

Bake the cake for 25 to 30 minutes, until puffed and golden colored, and a toothpick inserted into the center comes out clean.

Remove the pan from the oven and cool on a rack for 15 minutes. Carefully remove the sides of the quiche pan. Cut the cake into slices and serve warm.

Keeping

Store the cake tightly covered with aluminum foil at room temperature for up to 4 days. Warm it in a 350°F oven for 10 to 15 minutes before serving.

The cake can be frozen for up to 3 months. Wrap it snugly in several layers of plastic wrap and aluminum foil. Use a large piece of masking tape and an indelible marker to label and date the contents. If frozen, defrost the cake overnight in the refrigerator.

Adding Style

Serve slices of the cake with vanilla ice cream or whipped cream.

Making a Change

Replace the peaches with nectarines or apricots.

Peach Shortcakes with Honey Whipped Cream

PEACHES AND CREAM are a natural combination. When honey is added into the equation, the result is a subtle yet compelling flavor combination. Try using different types of honey to change the overall flavor of this dessert, but don't use a strongly flavored honey that will overpower the peaches and cream. These scrumptious shortcake biscuits are the perfect foil for peaches and honey whipped cream. **Makes ten 3¹/₄-inch round shortcakes**

Essential Gear
- Food processor
- 2³/₄-inch round, plain-edge biscuit cutter
- 1-inch natural-bristle pastry brush
- Baking sheet
- Parchment paper or non-stick liner
- Cooling rack
- Electric stand mixer with wire whip attachment or large mixing bowl and hand-held mixer
- Serrated knife

Center a rack in the oven and preheat it to 400°F. Line a baking sheet with parchment paper or a non-stick liner.

2 cups all-purpose flour ¼ cup firmly packed light brown sugar 2½ teaspoons baking powder ¼ teaspoon freshly grated nutmeg ⅛ teaspoon salt	In the work bowl of a food processor fitted with the steel blade, combine the flour, sugar, baking powder, nutmeg, and salt and pulse a few times to blend.
3 ounces (6 tablespoons, ¾ stick) unsalted butter, cold	Cut the butter into small pieces and chill in the freezer for 15 minutes. Add to the food processor and pulse until the butter is cut into pea-sized pieces, 30 to 45 seconds. The mixture should be crumbly. Don't cut the butter too small or the shortcakes will lose their flaky quality.
1 cup heavy whipping cream	With the food processor running, pour the cream through the feed tube and process until all the ingredients are combined and the dough is moist, about 30 seconds.

Turn the dough out onto a large piece of waxed or parchment paper lightly dusted with flour. Dust your hands with flour and shape the dough into a circle or rectangle about ¾ inch thick.

Use the biscuit cutter to cut out shortcakes. Cut straight down through the dough without twisting the cutter, which seals the edges of the dough and keeps the biscuits from rising in the oven. Place them on the lined baking sheet, leaving at least 2 inches of space between them so they have room to expand as they bake. Gather the scraps together and knead slightly. Pat them into a ¾-inch-thick circle or rectangle and proceed as above to get 10 shortcakes. Brush any excess flour off the shortcakes.

Keeping

Store the unassembled shortcakes in an airtight plastic container between layers of waxed paper at room temperature for up to 4 days. To freeze for up to 4 months, wrap the container tightly in several layers of plastic wrap and aluminum foil. Use a large piece of masking tape and an indelible marker to label and date the contents. If frozen, defrost overnight in the refrigerator and bring to room temperature before serving.

Making a Change

Replace the peaches with nectarines, plums, pluots, or pitted cherries. It's not necessary to blanch these fruits.

1 tablespoon heavy whipping cream	Brush the top of the shortcakes with cream, being careful that it doesn't run down the sides and underneath. If it does, wipe it up because it can cause the bottom of the shortcakes to burn.
1 tablespoon Demerara or crystal sugar	Lightly sprinkle the top of the shortcakes with sugar. Using these types of sugar adds extra texture to the shortcakes.
	Bake the shortcakes for 12 to15 minutes, until light golden.
	Remove the baking sheets from the oven and cool completely on racks.

ASSEMBLY

1¼ to 1½ pounds fresh ripe peaches (4 large), washed and dried	Bring water to a boil in a large saucepan or stockpot over high heat. Using a sharp knife, score a small X in the bottom of each peach. Add the peaches to the water and let them boil for 1 to 2 minutes. Use a slotted spoon or skimmer to remove the peaches from the boiling water. Place them in a bowl of cold water, which will stop them from cooking.
	Starting at the X, use a small sharp knife to gently peel the skin off the peaches. It should slip off easily. If the peaches are too hot, peel them under cold running water.
2 tablespoons light brown sugar **1 tablespoon amaretto (optional)**	Slice the blanched peaches into ½-inch-thick slices. Place the slices in a medium bowl. Add the sugar and amaretto, if using. Toss the peaches lightly to coat them completely. Cover the bowl tightly with plastic wrap and let the peaches marinate for 15 to 30 minutes.
1 cup heavy whipping cream	Place the cream in the chilled bowl of an electric stand mixer or a medium mixing bowl. Using the wire whip attachment or a hand-held mixer, whip the cream on medium speed until it is frothy.
3 tablespoons honey	Add the honey and continue to whip the cream on medium speed until it holds soft peaks.
	Slice each shortcake in half horizontally. Place the bottom of a shortcake on a serving plate and cover with a scoop of whipped cream. Place about 3 tablespoons of sliced peaches on top of the cream and cover the peaches with another small scoop of whipped cream. Lightly place the top of the shortcake on top of the peaches or arrange it at an angle to the bottom of the shortcake. Top with a dollop of whipped cream and scatter a few slices of peaches around the plate. Repeat with the remaining shortcakes. Serve immediately.

Spiced Fresh Peach Pie

A BLEND of cinnamon, ginger, and nutmeg brings out the best in fresh, ripe peaches nestled in a classic pie crust and covered with a lattice topping. This pie says "summer" to me. **Makes one 10-inch round pie, 12 to 14 servings**

PIE DOUGH

2 cups all-purpose flour

2 tablespoons granulated sugar

½ teaspoon salt

In the work bowl of a food processor fitted with the steel blade, combine the flour, sugar, and salt. Pulse briefly to blend.

8 ounces (16 tablespoons, 2 sticks) unsalted butter, chilled

Cut the butter into small pieces and freeze for 20 minutes.

8 ounces cream cheese, chilled

Cut the cream cheese into small pieces and add to the dry ingredients in the food processor. Pulse to cut the cream cheese into very tiny pieces. The texture should be sandy with very tiny lumps throughout.

Add the butter to the food processor. Pulse until the butter is cut into pea-sized pieces, 30 to 45 seconds.

3 to 4 tablespoons heavy whipping cream

Remove the top of the food processor and sprinkle on 3 tablespoons of the cream. Replace the top and pulse for 10 seconds. Squeeze a small amount of the dough in your hand. If it holds together, don't add any more cream. If the dough is still very crumbly, add another tablespoon of cream, pulse to blend, then check the dough again. It won't hold together unless you squeeze it, but that's the texture you want.

Divide the dough in 2 equal pieces and shape each piece into a flat disk. Wrap the disks tightly in a double layer of plastic wrap. Chill in the refrigerator until firm before using, at least 2 hours. Chilling the dough relaxes the gluten in the flour so it won't be too elastic and will roll out easily. It also firms up the butter in the dough so it will need less flour when rolled out. If the dough is too firm it will splinter and break when rolled out. Let it stand at room temperature for 10 to 15 minutes before rolling to become more pliable.

On a smooth, flat surface, roll out one of the disks of pie dough between sheets of lightly floured waxed or parchment paper to a large

Essential Gear

- Food processor
- Rolling pin
- 10-inch round deep pie pan
- Baking sheet
- Cooling rack
- Pastry brush

Keeping

Store the pie loosely covered with waxed paper, then tightly wrapped with aluminum foil in the refrigerator for up to 3 days.

Streamlining

The pie dough can be made in advance and kept in the refrigerator, tightly wrapped in a double layer of plastic wrap, for up to 4 days. To freeze for up to 3 months, wrap the dough snugly in several layers of plastic wrap and place it in a freezer bag. Use a large piece of masking tape and an indelible marker to label and date the contents. If frozen, defrost overnight in the refrigerator before using. The pie dough can also be fitted into the pie pan and kept tightly covered in the refrigerator or frozen, wrapped and labeled as above.

The assembled pie can be frozen for up to 3 months. To freeze the pie, cover it snugly in several layers of plastic wrap and place it in a freezer bag. Use a large piece of masking tape and circle about 12 inches in diameter. To tell if the dough will fit the pie pan, invert the pan over the dough. If there are 2 to 3 inches of dough that protrude beyond the sides of the pan, it will fit.

Carefully peel the paper off the top of the dough. Brush excess flour off the dough, then loosely roll the pastry dough around the rolling pin without the bottom piece of paper. Place the pie pan directly underneath the rolling pin and carefully unroll the pastry dough into the pan. Or loosely fold the dough in half. Carefully place it in half of the pie pan and gently unfold the dough. Gently lift up the sides and ease the pie dough into the bottom and sides of the pie pan.

Transfer the pie pan to a baking sheet and chill in the freezer for 15 to 20 minutes. This helps prevent the pie dough from shrinking as it bakes and sets the butter in the dough to ensure flakiness.

an indelible marker to label and date the contents. Do not defrost the pie to bake, but extend the baking time by 5 to 10 minutes.

Troubleshooting
Don't overprocess the pie dough or it will be tough and not flaky.

Making a Change
Replace the peaches with nectarines or apricots.

Adding Style
Serve slices of the pie with vanilla ice cream or whipped cream.

SPICED PEACH FILLING

2 pounds fresh ripe peaches (5 to 6 large), washed and dried

Cut the peaches in half and remove the stones. Cut each peach half into 4 slices. Place the sliced peaches in a 2-quart bowl.

½ cup firmly packed light brown sugar
¼ cup all-purpose flour
¼ teaspoon ground cinnamon
¼ teaspoon ground ginger
¼ teaspoon freshly grated nutmeg
⅛ teaspoon salt

Sprinkle the brown sugar, flour, cinnamon, ginger, nutmeg, and salt over the peaches. Using a rubber spatula, gently toss and stir to evenly distribute the dry ingredients and coat the peaches completely. Transfer the peach filling to the pie shell.

½ ounce (1 tablespoon) unsalted butter, chilled

Cut the butter into small pieces and place evenly over the top of the peaches.

Adjust an oven rack to the lower third and preheat the oven to 400°F.

1 extra-large egg yolk at room temperature
1 tablespoon heavy whipping cream

Use a fork to lightly beat the egg yolk and cream together in a small bowl. Use a pastry brush to brush the edges of the bottom pastry shell to help the shell and lattice topping stick together

Roll out the remaining disk of pie dough on a smooth, flat surface between sheets of lightly floured waxed or parchment paper to a large circle about 12 inches in diameter. Peel off the top piece of paper. Use a ruler and a plain or fluted-edge pastry wheel to cut ½-inch-wide strips of dough. Form the strips into a lattice on top of the sliced peaches (see page 41). Trim off the edges of both the lattice and the bottom pie shell evenly, leaving a ¾-inch overhang.

1 tablespoon granulated sugar

Fold the edges of the lattice over the bottom crust and press them to seal together. Crimp or flute the edges (see page 40). Brush the top of the lattice with the egg mixture and sprinkle sugar over the top of the dough.

Bake the pie for 50 to 60 minutes, until the crust is light golden and the filling is thickly bubbling inside.

Remove the pie from the oven and cool on a rack. Serve warm or at room temperature.

Nectarine and Almond Galette

THIS IS A FREE-FORM tart made with almond pastry dough that encloses a creamy frangipane filling and fresh nectarines. It's one of my very favorite summer fruit desserts. Be sure to use perfectly ripe fruit for the best flavor. **Makes one 9-inch tart, 8 to 10 servings**

PASTRY DOUGH

1 cup all-purpose flour
½ cup sliced or slivered almonds
2 teaspoons granulated sugar
¼ teaspoon salt

In the work bowl of a food processor, combine the flour, almonds, sugar, and salt. Pulse until the almonds are very finely ground, about 1 minute.

4 ounces (8 tablespoons, 1 stick) unsalted butter, chilled

Cut the butter into small pieces and add to the flour mixture. Pulse until the butter is cut into very tiny pieces, about 30 seconds. The texture should be sandy with very tiny lumps throughout.

2 teaspoons freshly squeezed lemon juice
2 to 3 tablespoons ice water
Finely grated zest of 1 large lemon

In a small bowl, combine the lemon juice, 2 tablespoons of water, and the lemon zest.

With the food processor running, pour the mixture through the feed tube. Process until the dough wraps itself around the blade, 30 sec-

Essential Gear
- Food processor
- Baking sheet
- Parchment paper
- Rolling pin
- 1-inch natural bristle pastry brush or a spoon
- Cooling rack

Keeping
Although the galette is best eaten the day it's made, it can last for up to 2 days. Store the galette tightly covered with aluminum foil at room temperature.

Making a Change
Replace the nectarines with other stone fruit, such as apricots, plums, pluots, or peaches.

Use a combination of fruit instead of a single type.

onds to 1 minute. If the dough seems dry, add the remaining table-spoon of water and process until the dough comes together.

Turn the pastry dough onto a large piece of plastic wrap. Shape into a flat disk and wrap tightly in a double layer of plastic wrap. Chill in the refrigerator until firm before using, about 2 hours. Chilling the dough relaxes the gluten in the flour so it won't be too elastic and will roll out easily. It also firms up the butter in the dough so it will need less flour when rolled out. If the dough is too firm it will splinter and break when rolled out. Let it stand at room temperature for 10 to 15 minutes before rolling to become more pliable.

Adding Style
Serve slices of the galette with vanilla ice cream.

NECTARINE FILLING

1 pound fresh ripe nectarines (4 medium), washed and dried

Using a sharp knife, slice the fruit in half along the seam. Remove the stone and cut the fruit into 1/2-inch-thick slices. You should have approximately 3 cups of sliced fruit.

2 tablespoons light brown sugar

Place the sliced nectarines in a mixing bowl. Add the sugar and toss together to distribute evenly. Taste the fruit to see if it needs any more sugar.

ASSEMBLY

Center a rack in the oven and preheat it to 375°F. Line a baking sheet with parchment paper.

On a smooth, flat surface, roll out the pastry dough between sheets of lightly floured waxed or parchment paper to a large circle 11 to 12 inches in diameter. Carefully peel the paper off the top of the dough. Brush excess flour off the dough, then loosely roll the pastry dough around the rolling pin, without the bottom piece of paper. Place the lined baking sheet directly underneath the rolling pin and carefully unroll the pastry dough onto the baking sheet.

1/3 cup frangipane filling (see Apricot Frangipane Tart, page 54)

Spread the filling over the center of the pastry dough, leaving a 3-inch border all around.

Mound the sliced nectarines in the center of the dough circle, leaving a 2 1/2- to 3-inch border all around.

1 tablespoon unsalted butter, chilled

Cut the butter into small pieces and distribute evenly over the sliced nectarines.

Fold the border up so that it partially covers the nectarines. It will naturally form pleats as it is folded.

1 tablespoon heavy whipping cream 2 teaspoons granulated sugar	With a pastry brush, apply cream to the dough border, being careful that it doesn't run down the sides and under the galette. If it does, wipe it up because it can cause the bottom of the galette to burn. Gently lift up the folds of the dough and brush under those areas with cream, then replace the folds. Evenly sprinkle the sugar over the dough border.

Bake the galette for 35 to 40 minutes, until light golden. Remove the pan from the oven and transfer to a rack to cool. Cut the galette into pie-shaped wedges to serve.

Nectarine Cobbler

SWEET, FRESH NECTARINES mixed with cinnamon are topped with a biscuit crust and baked to make this delectable cobbler. The name "cobbler" comes from the look of the biscuit topping of this dessert, which has a cobbled or broken appearance. This is a rustic dessert that's super easy to prepare and even easier to eat. I like to make this when nectarines are at their peak and full of flavor. **Makes one 8-inch square cobbler, 8 to 10 servings**

Essential Gear
- Chef's knife
- 8-inch square baking pan
- Food processor
- Rolling pin
- Cooling rack
- Pastry brush

Center a rack in the oven and preheat it to 375°F.

Keeping

Although the cobbler is best eaten the day it's made, it can last for up to 2 days. Store the cobbler tightly covered with aluminum foil in the refrigerator.

NECTARINE FILLING

1½ pounds fresh ripe nectarines (5 to 6 medium), washed and dried	Using a chef's knife, cut the nectarines in half and remove the stones. Cut each half into ½-inch-thick slices. You should have about 6 cups of sliced nectarines. Place the slices in the baking pan.
¼ cup firmly packed light brown sugar ¼ cup all-purpose flour 1 teaspoon ground cinnamon Finely grated zest of 1 large lemon 1 teaspoon freshly squeezed lemon juice	Add the sugar, flour, cinnamon, lemon zest, and lemon juice to the sliced nectarines and toss together to coat them completely.
2 ounces (4 tablespoons, ½ stick) unsalted butter, softened	Cut the butter into small pieces and distribute evenly over the sliced nectarines.

Making a Change

Use a mixture of other stone fruit, such as apricots and peaches.

BISCUIT DOUGH TOPPING

1 cup all-purpose flour
2 tablespoons granulated sugar
1 teaspoon ground cinnamon
1 teaspoon baking powder
¼ teaspoon salt
¼ teaspoon baking soda

In the work bowl of a food processor fitted with the steel blade, combine the flour, sugar, cinnamon, baking powder, salt, and baking soda. Pulse briefly to blend.

1½ ounces (3 tablespoons) unsalted butter, chilled

Cut the butter into small pieces and add to the dry ingredients. Pulse until the butter is cut into very tiny pieces, about 1 minute. The texture should feel sandy with tiny lumps throughout.

½ cup buttermilk
½ teaspoon pure vanilla extract or vanilla paste

Combine the buttermilk and vanilla in a liquid measuring cup. With the food processor running, pour this mixture through the feed tube. Process until the dough wraps itself around the blade, about 30 seconds.

Drop about 8 large spoonfuls of the dough over the top of the sliced nectarines, spacing them evenly.

1 tablespoon heavy whipping cream
1 tablespoon granulated sugar

Use a pastry brush to brush the top of the dough with cream, then sprinkle the top of the dough with the sugar.

Bake for 30 to 35 minutes, until the biscuit topping is set and a toothpick inserted into it comes out clean. Remove the pan from the oven and transfer to a rack to cool.

GARNISH

1 cup heavy whipping cream
2 tablespoons confectioners' sugar

Place the cream in the bowl of an electric stand mixer or in a large mixing bowl. Use the wire whip attachment or a hand-held mixer to whip on medium speed until frothy.

Add the confectioners' sugar and continue whipping the cream until it holds soft peaks.

Cut squares of the cobbler, scooping up the fruit. Serve each square with a large dollop of whipped cream.

Fresh Nectarine Pandowdy

A PANDOWDY is a classic American deep-dish fruit dessert that traces its heritage as far back as the Colonial period. It's a rustic dessert that is composed of fruit tossed with spices and topped with a biscuit-like crust. Partway through baking, the crust is broken up and pressed down into the fruit so it can absorb the juices. This technique is called "dowdying" and is where the dessert gets its name. After the crust is broken and baked, it becomes crispy. A pandowdy is traditionally served warm with heavy cream. **Makes one 9-inch square pandowdy, 8 to 10 servings**

PASTRY CRUST

1 cup all-purpose flour
1 tablespoon granulated sugar
¼ teaspoon salt

In the work bowl of a food processor fitted with the steel blade, combine the flour, sugar, and salt. Pulse briefly to blend.

4 ounces (8 tablespoons, 1 stick) unsalted butter, cold

Cut the butter into small pieces and add to the dry ingredients. Pulse until the butter is cut into very tiny pieces, about 30 seconds. The mixture should be sandy with very tiny lumps throughout.

3 tablespoons ice water
1 teaspoon freshly squeezed lemon juice

Combine the ice water and lemon juice in a liquid measuring cup. With the food processor running, pour this mixture through the feed tube. Process just until the dough begins to hold together.

Form the dough into a flat square and wrap tightly in plastic wrap. Chill in the refrigerator until firm before using, at least 1 hour. Chilling the dough relaxes the gluten in the flour so it won't be too elastic and will roll out easily.

Line a baking sheet with a sheet of parchment paper.

On a smooth, flat surface, roll out the dough between sheets of lightly floured waxed or parchment paper to a 10-inch square. While rolling the dough, give it a quarter turn often so it is always in a comfortable position for you to roll. Check to make sure that the waxed or parchment paper is not sticking to the dough by lifting it up often. Occasionally turn the dough package over and check the bottom piece of waxed or parchment paper to make sure it is not sticking. Sprinkle more flour on the dough as needed, to keep it from sticking.

Essential Gear
- Food processor
- Rolling pin
- Baking sheet
- Parchment paper
- 1-inch natural-bristle pastry brush
- 9-inch square baking pan
- Chef's knife
- Rubber spatula or wooden spoon
- Cooling rack

Keeping
Although the pandowdy is best eaten the day it's made, it can last for up to 2 days. Store the pandowdy tightly covered with aluminum foil in the refrigerator.

Troubleshooting
Don't overprocess the dough or it will be tough.

Making a Change
Use a mixture of other stone fruit, such as apricots and peaches.

Peel off the top piece of paper and brush off any excess flour. Holding the bottom piece of paper by the sides, turn the dough over and place it on the lined baking pan. Remove the paper and brush off any excess flour. Cover the dough with plastic wrap and chill 30 minutes.

Center a rack in the oven and preheat it to 400°F.

1 extra-large egg yolk, at room temperature
1 tablespoon heavy whipping cream
½ cup sliced almonds

Use a fork to lightly beat the egg yolk and cream together in a small bowl. Use a pastry brush to brush the top of the pastry crust with the mixture. Evenly sprinkle the almonds over the top of the crust.

Bake the pastry crust for 15 minutes, until it is set and lightly colored. Remove the baking pan from the oven and cool on a rack.

NECTARINE FILLING

1 tablespoon unsalted butter, softened

Using a paper towel or your fingertips, generously butter the inside of the pan.

3 pounds fresh, ripe nectarines (7 to 8 large), washed and dried

Using a chef's knife, cut the nectarines in half and remove the pits. Cut each nectarine half into ½-inch-thick slices. Place the slices in a 2-quart mixing bowl.

½ cup firmly packed light brown sugar
3 tablespoons cornstarch
1 tablespoon freshly squeezed lemon juice
¼ teaspoon salt
¼ teaspoon ground ginger
⅛ teaspoon freshly grated nutmeg
⅛ teaspoon ground allspice

Add the brown sugar, cornstarch, lemon juice, salt, ginger, nutmeg, and allspice to the nectarines and toss together with a rubber spatula or wooden spoon to coat them completely.

Transfer the nectarine mixture to the prepared baking pan.

Bake the pandowdy for 30 minutes. Lower the oven temperature to 350°F and bake for another 15 minutes. Remove the baking pan from the oven.

Using a large, flat spatula, transfer the pastry crust to the top of the fruit.

Return the baking pan to the oven and bake for 10 minutes. Use the back of a large spoon to gently press down on the pastry crust, break it into pieces, and press the pieces into the fruit. Bake for another 10 to 15 minutes, until the fruit is bubbling and the pastry crust is golden brown.

Remove the baking pan from the oven and cool on a rack.

GARNISH

1 cup heavy whipping cream	Place the cream in the bowl of an electric stand mixer or in a large mixing bowl. Use the wire whip attachment or a hand-held mixer to whip on medium speed until frothy.
2 tablespoons confectioners' sugar	Add the confectioners' sugar and continue whipping the cream until it holds soft peaks.

Cut squares of the pandowdy, scooping up the fruit. Serve each square with a large dollop of whipped cream.

Plum and Almond Cake

THIS CAKE is rich and satisfying without being too sweet. Almond paste adds flavor, texture, and moisture to the cake mixture. Fresh plums are cut in half and arranged over the top of the batter and sink to the bottom of the cake as it bakes. When the cake is cool, it's turned upside down and the plums adorn the top. Although it sounds like an upside-down cake, this is much richer and denser than the classic version. It is perfect served with afternoon coffee or tea, but is equally good for dessert or warmed up for breakfast. **Makes one 9-inch round cake, 12 to 14 servings**

Essential Gear
- 9 × 2-inch round cake pan
- Scissors
- Parchment paper
- Electric stand mixer with flat beater attachment or large mixing bowl and hand-held mixer
- Rubber spatula
- Cooling rack

Keeping
Store the cake loosely covered with waxed paper and tightly covered with aluminum foil at room temperature for up to 3 days.

CAKE

Position a rack in the center of the oven and preheat it to 325°F.

1 tablespoon unsalted butter, softened	Using a paper towel or your fingertips, generously butter the inside of the cake pan, coating it thoroughly.
2 teaspoons all-purpose flour	Dust the inside of the pan with some of the flour. Shake and tilt the pan to evenly distribute the flour, then turn the pan over and shake out the excess over the sink.

Cut a round of parchment paper to fit the bottom of the pan. Butter the parchment paper round and place in the pan, butter-side up.

Making a Change

Replace the walnuts with coarsely chopped, slivered almonds or finely ground, toasted hazelnuts.

Replace the plums with peaches, apricots, or nectarines.

1 cup (7½ ounces) almond paste, at room temperature 6 ounces (12 tablespoons, 1½ sticks) unsalted butter, softened	Place the almond paste and butter in the bowl of an electric stand mixer or in a large mixing bowl. Use the flat beater attachment or hand-held mixer to beat on medium speed until the mixture is fluffy, about 2 minutes.
1¼ cups superfine sugar	Gradually add the sugar to the butter mixture and cream together well. Stop occasionally and scrape down the bottom and sides of the bowl with a rubber spatula.
3 extra-large eggs, at room temperature	One at a time, add the eggs, stopping to scrape down the bottom and sides of the bowl after each addition. At first the mixture may look curdled as the eggs are added, but as you stop and scrape down the bowl, the mixture will smooth out.
3 tablespoons milk 2 teaspoons pure vanilla extract	Combine the milk and vanilla in a liquid measuring cup or a small bowl and add to the butter mixture. Blend together well.
1½ cups cake flour 2 teaspoon baking powder ½ teaspoon salt	Over a large piece of waxed or parchment paper or a bowl, sift together the flour and baking powder. Add the salt and toss to blend well.
	With the mixer on low speed, add the dry ingredients in 4 stages. Blend well after each addition and stop often to scrape down the bottom and sides of the bowl with a rubber spatula.
	Transfer the batter to the prepared cake pan. Smooth the top of the batter with a rubber spatula.
¾ pound ripe fresh plums (4 to 5 medium), washed and dried	Cut the plums in half and remove the stones. Place the plum halves around the outside edge of the cake, cut-side down, leaving about ½ inch of space between them. Arrange 2 plum halves in the center of the cake.
¼ cup walnuts, coarsely chopped	Scatter the chopped walnuts over the top of the cake batter and in between the plums.
	Bake the cake for 1 hour, until golden and a cake tester inserted in the center comes out with no crumbs clinging to it.

Remove the cake pan from the oven and cool on a rack for 15 minutes. Place a serving plate or 9-inch cardboard cake circle over the top of the cake pan. Invert the pan to remove the cake, then peel the parchment paper off the back of the cake. Let the cake cool to room temperature.

GARNISH

1 to 2 tablespoons confectioners' sugar

Dust the top of the cake with confectioners' sugar. Cut the cake into wedges to serve.

Fresh Plum Cobbler

R IPE, JUICY PLUMS, accented with cinnamon and nutmeg, are topped with a delectable biscuit crust. The biscuit topping has a cobbled or broken appearance, which is what gives this dessert its name. This is a very quick and easy dessert to prepare and it's so scrumptious that it's even easier to eat. **Makes one 8-inch square cobbler, 8 to 10 servings**

Center a rack in the oven and preheat it to 400°F.

PLUM FILLING

3 pounds fresh ripe plums (16 to 18 medium), washed and dried

Using a chef's knife, cut the plums in half and remove the stones. Cut each plum half into 1/2-inch-thick slices. Place the sliced plums in the baking pan.

1/3 cup firmly packed light brown sugar
1/4 cup granulated sugar
3 tablespoons cornstarch, sifted
1/2 teaspoon pure vanilla extract
1/4 teaspoon ground cinnamon
1/4 teaspoon freshly grated nutmeg

Add the brown sugar, granulated sugar, cornstarch, vanilla, cinnamon, and nutmeg to the sliced plums and toss together to coat them completely.

Bake the mixture for 15 minutes.

Essential Gear
- Chef's knife
- 8-inch square baking pan
- Food processor
- Pastry brush
- Cooling rack

Keeping
Although the cobbler is best eaten the day it's made, it can last for up to 2 days. Store the cobbler tightly covered with aluminum foil in the refrigerator.

Making a Change
Use a mixture of other stone fruit, such as apricots and peaches.

Serve the cobbler with vanilla ice cream instead of whipped cream

BISCUIT DOUGH TOPPING

1⅓ cups all-purpose flour 2 tablespoons granulated sugar 2 tablespoons light brown sugar 2 teaspoons baking powder ¼ teaspoon salt ¼ teaspoon freshly grated nutmeg	In the work bowl of a food processor fitted with the steel blade, combine the flour, granulated sugar, brown sugar, baking powder, salt, and nutmeg. Pulse briefly to blend.
3 ounces (6 tablespoons, ¾ stick) unsalted butter, chilled	Cut the butter into small pieces and add to the dry ingredients. Pulse until the butter is cut into very tiny pieces, about 1 minute. The texture should feel sandy with tiny lumps throughout.
½ cup heavy whipping cream 1 extra-large egg yolk	Combine the cream and egg yolk in a liquid measuring cup and use a fork to lightly blend the two together. With the food processor running, pour this mixture through the feed tube. Process until the dough wraps itself around the blade, about 30 seconds.
	Remove the baking pan from the oven. Stir the plum mixture, then drop about 8 large spoonfuls of the dough over the top of the mixture, spacing them evenly.
1 tablespoon heavy whipping cream 1 tablespoon granulated sugar	Use a pastry brush to brush the top of the dough with cream, then sprinkle the top of the dough with the sugar.
	Bake for 30 minutes, until the biscuit topping is set and the fruit is bubbling. Remove the pan from the oven and transfer to a rack to cool.

GARNISH

1 cup heavy whipping cream	Place the cream in the bowl of an electric stand mixer or in a large mixing bowl. Use the wire whip attachment or a hand-held mixer to whip on medium speed until frothy.
2 tablespoons confectioners' sugar	Add the confectioners' sugar and continue whipping the cream until it holds soft peaks.
	Cut squares of the cobbler, scooping up the fruit. Serve each square with a large dollop of whipped cream.

Plum Filo Triangles

I F YOU'VE EVER eaten spinach and feta cheese triangles, called *spanakopita* in Greek, you will recognize the shape of these pastries. But the filling in these is far different. It's made of fresh plums sautéed in butter with a dash of spices to enliven their flavor. The juice that the plums exude is cooked down to make a sauce for the finished triangles. These are great finger food for a buffet or any gathering. **Makes 12**

PLUM FILLING

2 pounds fresh ripe plums (10 to 12 medium), washed and dried	Cut the plums in half and remove the stones. Cut each plum half into 1/4-inch-thick slices.
1 ounce (2 tablespoons) unsalted butter	Cut the butter into small pieces and put it in a medium sauté or frying pan over medium heat.
	When the butter is completely melted, add the sliced plums. Cook, stirring occasionally, until the plums are soft but not mushy, 3 to 5 minutes.
1/3 cup firmly packed light brown sugar 1/2 teaspoon freshly grated nutmeg 1/4 teaspoon allspice	In a small bowl, mix together the brown sugar, nutmeg, and allspice. Add to the pan. Stir to coat the plums completely and cook until the sugar is melted.
1 tablespoon cognac or brandy	Add the cognac or brandy and stir to distribute evenly.
	Place the strainer over a medium bowl and pour the plum mixture into the strainer. Let the mixture drain off the liquid, about 5 minutes. Reserve the plums and liquid separately.
	Center a rack in the oven and preheat it to 375°F. Line a baking sheet with parchment paper or a non-stick liner.

FILO DOUGH TRIANGLES

1/2 pound 9 × 14-inch sheets frozen filo pastry dough, thawed	Place the filo dough on a smooth, flat surface and use a sharp serrated knife to cut it in half lengthwise into 4 1/2 × 14-inch sheets.

Essential Gear
- Chef's knife
- Medium sauté pan or frying pan
- Heat-resistant rubber spatula or wooden spoon
- Medium-size fine-mesh strainer
- 1-quart bowl
- Baking sheet
- Parchment paper or non-stick liner
- 1-inch natural-bristle pastry brush
- Cooling rack
- Small saucepan

Keeping
Store the baked triangles on a baking sheet, loosely covered with waxed paper and wrapped with aluminum foil, in the refrigerator for up to 4 days. Reheat them on a lined baking sheet in a 350°F oven for 10 to 15 minutes before serving.

Store the plum sauce in a tightly covered plastic container in the refrigerator for up to 4 days.

Streamlining
The plum filling can be made up to 2 days in advance. Keep it in a tightly covered plastic container in the refrigerator.

Making a Change
Instead of shaping the filo into triangles, shape it into

3 ounces (6 tablespoons, ¾ stick) unsalted butter, melted

Stack the filo sheets together. Keep them covered with plastic wrap and a damp kitchen towel to keep them from drying out.

Take 1 sheet of filo dough and lay it flat on the work surface. Brush it lightly all over with melted butter. Top with a second sheet of filo dough and brush it with melted butter. Repeat with one more filo dough sheet.

Place 1 to 2 tablespoons of the plum filling in the lower right-hand corner of the filo strip. Take the lower right-hand corner of the filo and fold it over to the left side to form a triangle. Take the bottom left corner and fold it up to make the next triangle, then take that triangle and fold it to the right side. Continue to fold the filo strips up and to opposite corners until the strip is finished. Brush the triangle all over with butter and fold any remaining piece of filo dough over the triangle. Place the triangle on the lined baking sheet.

Continue to form triangles with the remaining plum filling and filo dough. Leave about 2 inches of space between the triangles on the baking sheet.

2 tablespoons granulated sugar.

Sprinkle the top of each triangle lightly with sugar.

Bake the triangles for 20 to 25 minutes, until they are golden. Remove the baking sheet from the oven and use a wide, flat spatula to transfer the triangles to racks to cool completely.

PLUM SAUCE

Take the juice that drained from the plum filling and cook it in a small saucepan over medium heat until it is reduced by half the original amount, about 5 minutes.

Remove the plum sauce from the heat and cool.

GARNISH

Confectioners' sugar

Dust the top of each triangle with confectioners' sugar.

Place 1 tablespoon of the plum sauce on a serving plate and set a filo triangle on top of the sauce.

rolls. Place the filling at the bottom of the filo dough strip. Roll the strip up, folding both sides in to the center to contain the filling. Place the roll on the baking sheet seam-side down.

Replace the plums with pluots or stemmed and pitted cherries.

Plum Streusel Pie

F RESH, JUICY PLUMS are nestled inside of a classic pie crust and covered with a crumbly, crunchy, toasted walnut and brown sugar topping. For the best flavor, use very ripe plums. **Makes one 9-inch round pie, 12 to 14 servings**

PIE DOUGH

1½ cups all-purpose flour
1 teaspoon granulated sugar
¼ teaspoon salt

In the work bowl of a food processor fitted with the steel blade, combine the flour, sugar, and salt. Pulse briefly to blend.

4 ounces (8 tablespoons, 1 stick) unsalted butter, chilled

Cut the butter into small pieces and freeze for 20 minutes. Add the butter to the flour mixture. Pulse until the butter is cut into pea-sized pieces, 30 to 45 seconds. The texture should be sandy with very tiny lumps throughout.

1 tablespoon heavy whipping cream
2 to 3 tablespoons ice water

Remove the top of the food processor and sprinkle on the cream and 2 tablespoons of the ice water. Replace the top and pulse for 10 seconds. Squeeze a small amount of the dough in your hand. If it holds together, don't add any more water. If the dough is still very crumbly, add another tablespoon of water, pulse to blend, then check the dough again. It won't hold together unless you squeeze it, but that's the texture you want.

Turn the dough onto a smooth, flat work surface. Use the heel of your hand to push the dough a few times for a final blend. Don't mush all the butter into the dough, however. For a flaky crust, you want to see thin flecks of butter in the dough.

Shape the dough into a flat disk and wrap tightly in a double layer of plastic wrap. Chill in the refrigerator until firm before using, at least 2 hours. Chilling the dough relaxes the gluten in the flour so it won't be too elastic and will roll out easily. It also firms up the butter in the dough so it will need less flour when rolled out. If the dough is too firm it will splinter and break when rolled out. Let it stand at room temperature for 10 to 15 minutes before rolling to become more pliable.

On a smooth, flat surface, roll out the pie dough between sheets of lightly floured waxed or parchment paper to a large circle about 12 inches in diameter. To tell if the dough will fit the pie pan, invert the pan over the dough. If there are 2 to 3 inches of dough that protrude beyond the sides of the pan, it will fit.

Essential Gear
- Food processor
- Rolling pin
- 9-inch round pie pan
- Baking sheet
- Pastry brush
- Cooling rack

Keeping
Store the pie loosely covered with waxed paper, then tightly wrapped with aluminum foil, at room temperature for up to 3 days.

Streamlining
The pie dough can be made in advance and kept in the refrigerator tightly wrapped in a double layer of plastic wrap for up to 4 days. To freeze for up to 3 months, wrap the dough snugly in several layers of plastic wrap and place it in a freezer bag. Use a large piece of masking tape and an indelible marker to label and date the contents. If frozen, defrost overnight in the refrigerator before using. The dough can also be fitted into the pie pan and frozen. Wrap as above and label.

The streusel topping can be made in advance and kept in the refrigerator in a tightly covered plastic container for up to 1 week.

Carefully peel the paper off the top of the dough. Brush excess flour off the dough, then loosely roll the pastry dough around the rolling pin without the bottom piece of paper. Place the pie pan directly underneath the rolling pin and carefully unroll the pastry dough into the pan. Or loosely fold the dough in half. Carefully place it in half of the pie pan and gently unfold the dough. Gently lift up the sides and ease the pie dough into the bottom and sides of the pie pan. Trim off the excess pie dough at the top of the pan and crimp the sides (see page 40).

Transfer the pie pan to a baking sheet and chill in the freezer for 15 to 20 minutes. This helps prevent the pie dough from shrinking as it bakes and sets the butter in the dough to ensure flakiness.

Center a rack in the oven and preheat it to 350°F.

EGG GLAZE

1 extra-large egg
2 teaspoons cool water

Using a fork, lightly beat the egg with the water in a small bowl. Using a pastry brush, brush the glaze over the inside of the pie shell. This will help prevent the shell from becoming soggy from the plum juice.

PLUM FILLING

1½ pounds fresh ripe plums (7 to 8 medium), washed and dried

Using a sharp knife, slice the plums in half along the seam. Remove the stones and cut the plums into ½-inch-thick slices. Place the sliced plums in a large bowl.

¾ cup granulated sugar
¼ cup cornstarch, sifted
½ teaspoon ground cinnamon
½ teaspoon freshly grated nutmeg

Add the sugar, cornstarch, cinnamon, and nutmeg and toss together lightly to distribute evenly.

1 ounce (2 tablespoons) unsalted butter, cold

Transfer the plums to the pie shell. Cut the butter into small pieces and distribute evenly over the sliced plums. Refrigerate the pie while preparing the streusel topping.

STREUSEL TOPPING

Center a rack in the oven and preheat it to 350°F.

¾ cup walnuts

Place the walnuts in a single layer in a cake or pie pan. Toast in the oven for 4 minutes. Shake the pan to stir the walnuts and toast for another 4 to 6 minutes, until lightly colored. Remove from the oven and cool.

Troubleshooting

Don't overprocess the pie dough or it will be tough and not flaky.

Making a Change

To make classic tender, flaky pie dough, replace half of the butter with lard or vegetable shortening.

Replace the plums with pluots.

½ cup all-purpose flour

3 tablespoons light brown sugar

¼ teaspoon freshly grated nutmeg

⅛ teaspoon salt

1½ ounces (3 tablespoons) unsalted butter, chilled

In the work bowl of a food processor fitted with the steel blade, combine the flour, sugar, nutmeg, and salt. Add the toasted walnuts and pulse until the walnuts are coarsely chopped, 20 to 30 seconds. Cut the butter into small pieces and add to the dry ingredients. Pulse until the butter is cut into very tiny pieces, 30 seconds to 1 minute.

Evenly sprinkle the topping over the plums in the pie pan.

Bake the pie for 35 to 40 minutes, until the topping is light golden. Remove the pan from the oven and transfer to a rack to cool.

Pluot Custard Tart

THIS TART IS NOT baked in a tart pan, but in a springform pan, so it's deeper than a typical tart. When I worked in Switzerland, I made many tarts of this type. The sliced pluots sit on top of vanilla pastry cream nestled inside of sweet pastry dough. The tart is assembled, then baked all together, rather than being assembled in a pre-baked pastry shell. Be sure to make the pastry dough and the vanilla pastry cream at least several hours and up to a few days in advance of when you want to bake the tart, because they need time to chill. **Makes one 9½-inch round tart, 8 to 12 servings**

PASTRY DOUGH

2½ cups all-purpose flour

⅓ cup plus 1 tablespoon granulated sugar

¼ teaspoon salt

In the work bowl of a food processor fitted with the steel blade, combine the flour, sugar, and salt. Pulse briefly to blend.

8 ounces (16 tablespoons, 2 sticks) unsalted butter, chilled

Cut the butter into small pieces and add to the dry mixture. Pulse until the butter is cut into very tiny pieces, about 30 seconds. The texture should be sandy with very tiny lumps throughout.

1 extra-large egg yolk

1 teaspoon pure vanilla extract

1 teaspoon water

Use a fork to beat the egg yolk with the vanilla and water in a small bowl. With the food processor running, pour this mixture through the feed tube. Process until the dough wraps itself around the blade, 30 seconds to 1 minute. If the dough seems dry, add another teaspoon of water and process until the dough comes together.

Essential Gear

- Food processor
- Rolling pin
- 9½-inch round springform pan
- 3-quart heavy-duty saucepan
- Whisk, heat-resistant spatula, or wooden spoon
- Baking sheet
- Cooling rack

Keeping

The tart can last up to 3 days in the refrigerator. Place a piece of waxed paper over the top of the tart, then tightly cover it with aluminum foil.

Streamlining

The pastry dough can be made in advance and kept in the refrigerator, tightly wrapped in a double layer of plastic wrap, up to 4 days. To freeze up to 3 months, wrap the dough snugly in several

Turn the pastry dough onto a large piece of plastic wrap. Shape into a flat disk and wrap tightly in a double layer of plastic wrap. Chill in the refrigerator until firm before using, about 2 hours. Chilling the dough relaxes the gluten in the flour so it won't be too elastic and will roll out easily. It also firms up the butter in the dough so it will need less flour when rolled out. If the dough is too firm it will splinter and break when rolled out. Let it stand at room temperature for 10 to 15 minutes before rolling to become more pliable.

On a smooth, flat surface, roll out the pastry dough between sheets of lightly floured waxed or parchment paper to a large circle about 13 inches in diameter. Carefully peel the paper off the top of the dough. Brush excess flour off the dough, then loosely roll the pastry dough around the rolling pin without the bottom piece of paper. Place the springform pan directly underneath the rolling pin and carefully unroll the pastry dough onto it.

Gently lift up the sides and ease the pastry dough into the bottom and sides of the pan, pushing it lightly into the fluted edges. Use a small sharp knife to trim the pastry dough evenly to 1 inch below the top of the pan.

Place the tart pan on a baking sheet and chill for 15 minutes.

Center a rack in the oven and preheat it to 350°F.

layers of plastic wrap and place it in a freezer bag. Use a large piece of masking tape and an indelible marker to label and date the contents. If frozen, defrost overnight in the refrigerator before using. The pastry dough can also be fitted into the springform pan and kept tightly covered in the refrigerator or frozen, wrapped and labeled as above.

The vanilla pastry cream filling can be made in advance and kept in a tightly covered plastic container in the refrigerator up to 4 days before using.

Making a Change
Replace the pluots with plums, apricots, peaches, or nectarines.

VANILLA PASTRY CREAM

1 cup milk (whole, 2%, or 1%)
1 vanilla bean

Place the milk in a 3-quart heavy-duty saucepan. Use a small sharp knife to slice the vanilla bean open lengthwise. This exposes the tiny grains inside, which hold the essential vanilla flavor. Use the back of the knife to scrape out the vanilla seeds and add with the vanilla bean to the milk. Warm over medium heat until tiny bubbles begin to form around the edges of the pan, about 5 minutes

3 extra-large egg yolks, at room temperature
⅓ cup granulated sugar

Place the egg yolks in the bowl of an electric stand mixer. Using the wire whip attachment or a hand-held mixer, whip the egg yolks on medium-high speed until they are frothy. Add the sugar and whip together until the mixture is very thick and pale colored and holds a slowly dissolving ribbon as the beater is lifted, about 3 minutes.

2 tablespoons cornstarch, sifted

Turn the mixer speed to low and add the cornstarch. Use a rubber spatula to scrape down the bottom and sides of the bowl to encourage even mixing. Return the mixer speed to medium and whip until the cornstarch is thoroughly blended.

Again turn the mixer speed to low. Use a ladle to take about ¼ cup of the hot milk from the pan and slowly add it to the egg yolk mixture in the mixing bowl. Whip together to blend. This tempers the egg yolks so they won't curdle when they are added to the milk.

Transfer the egg yolk mixture into the milk in the saucepan. Stir the mixture constantly with a whisk, heat-resistant spatula, or wooden spoon, so it doesn't burn. Cook until the mixture starts to bubble and pop.

Remove the saucepan from the heat and immediately transfer the pastry cream to a bowl. Cover the top of the pastry cream with a piece of waxed paper to prevent a skin from forming on top. Cover the bowl with plastic wrap and place the bowl on a cooling rack. Leave the pastry cream to cool to room temperature, then refrigerate it until cold before using.

Use a whisk or rubber spatula to vigorously stir the cold pastry cream until it is smooth, about 30 seconds. Transfer the pastry cream to the pastry shell and spread it out evenly with a rubber spatula.

½ cup walnuts, lightly toasted

Finely chop the walnuts and evenly sprinkle them over the top of the pastry cream.

ASSEMBLY

¾ to 1 pound fresh ripe pluots (6 to 7 medium), washed and dried

Cut the pluots in half and remove the stones. Cut each half into ½-inch-thick slices, leaving the slices attached at the bottom. Place the halves around the outer edge of the tart (inside up), leaving about 1 inch of space between them. Gently press on the top of the halves and they will fan out. Continue slicing and fanning the pluot halves, filling the center of the tart.

1 tablespoon granulated sugar
1 teaspoon ground cinnamon

In a small bowl, combine the sugar and cinnamon until thoroughly mixed. Sprinkle this mixture evenly over the pluots.

Bake the tart for 40 to 45 minutes, until the crust is golden and the pluots are soft.

Remove the tart from the oven and place on a cooling rack

Remove the sides of the springform pan (see page 36) before serving. Serve the tart warm or at room temperature.

Pluot Upside-Down Cake

U PSIDE-DOWN CAKES are classic American desserts. The fruit is placed in the bottom of the pan and the cake batter goes on top. After the cake is baked and cooled briefly, it is inverted out of the pan and the fruit is on top. This recipe uses pluots, a delicious cross between plums and apricots, but you can use plums or apricots instead. I recommend blanching the pluots in boiling water to remove their skins, which can occasionally be bitter when baked. **Makes one 8-inch square cake, 8 to 10 servings**

Center a rack in the oven and preheat it to 350°F.

2 ounces (4 tablespoons, ½ stick) unsalted butter, melted ½ cup firmly packed light brown sugar	Pour the butter into the bottom of the baking pan. Sprinkle the brown sugar over the butter. Stir together with a rubber spatula until smooth.
1 pound fresh ripe pluots (7 to 8 medium), washed	Bring water to a boil in a large saucepan or stockpot over high heat. Add the pluots and let them boil for 1 to 2 minutes. Use a slotted spoon or skimmer to remove the pluots from the boiling water. Place them in a bowl of cold water, which will stop them from cooking. Use a small sharp knife to gently peel the skin off the pluots. It should slip off easily. If the pluots are too hot, peel them under cold running water. Using a chef's knife, cut the skinned pluots into ½-inch-thick slices. Arrange the slices in overlapping rows, completely covering the bottom of the baking pan.
¼ teaspoon freshly grated nutmeg	Sprinkle nutmeg evenly over the pluots.
4 ounces (8 tablespoons, 1 stick) unsalted butter, softened	Place the butter in the bowl of an electric stand mixer or in a large mixing bowl. Use the flat beater attachment or hand-held mixer to beat the butter on medium speed until it's fluffy, about 2 minutes.
1 cup granulated sugar	Add the sugar, and cream together well. Stop occasionally and scrape down the sides and bottom of the bowl with a spatula.
2 extra-large eggs, at room temperature	One at a time, add the eggs to the butter mixture, stopping to scrape down the bottom and sides of the bowl after each addition. At first

the mixture may look curdled as the eggs are added, but as you stop and scrape down the bowl, the mixture will smooth out.

½ **cup milk** **1 teaspoon pure vanilla** **extract**	In a liquid measuring cup or a bowl, combine the milk and vanilla.
1⅓ **cups cake flour** 1½ **teaspoons baking** **powder** ¼ **teaspoon salt**	Over a large piece of waxed or parchment paper or a bowl, sift together the flour and baking powder. Add the salt and toss to blend well. Add this mixture to the butter mixture, alternately with the milk and vanilla mixture. Start and end with the dry ingredients. Stop often and scrape down the bottom and sides of the bowl with a rubber spatula to encourage even mixing.
	Transfer the batter to the baking pan. Use the rubber spatula to spread the batter evenly over the fruit. Bake the cake for 45 to 50 minutes, until it is set and light golden, and a toothpick inserted in the center comes out clean. Remove the pan from the oven and transfer to a rack to cool for 10 minutes.
	Place a serving plate over the top of the baking pan and invert the pan onto the plate. The cake should easily slip out of the baking pan. Cut the cake into squares and serve warm.

APPLES, PEARS,

AND QUINCES

AMERICANS LIKE just about anything baked with apples, and pears are a close second. Quinces are similar to apples and pears in texture and look, but have their own distinct flavor. What I have the fondest memories of is the smell of freshly baked apple pie. I had a realtor tell me once, "If you want a quick sale of your house when showing it, have an apple pie baking in the oven." You will find a large variety of great recipes in this chapter. I encourage you to try them all, especially those that use quinces.

Apples, pears, and quinces are most widely available in the fall and winter. Apples, because they ship well, can usually be found anytime of the year. This is not true for pears or quinces. Apples, pears, and quinces are found in the produce section of most supermarkets, at specialty produce stores, and at farmer's markets.

TIPS AND TECHNIQUES

Many different types of apples can be used for baking. Your selection should be based on the flavor and texture you desire. I use both sweet and tart apples for baking. Apples that are juicier, such as Golden Delicious, are not the best for baking because they become too soft and mushy. Select apples that are firm, without bruises and blemishes, and that have good color. Pears should also have good, even color but they don't need to be as firm as apples. Quinces should be firm with minimal marks on their skin and also have good color.

All of these fruits are usually picked before they are fully ripe, so you may need to ripen them at home. Placing them in a large bowl at room temperature with plenty of air and light is the best way to do this. Rotate them occasionally so they are evenly exposed to the air and light.

Pears need to be handled a little more gently than apples and quinces. As they ripen, they soften and bruise easily. None of these fruits has a strong aroma when ripening, so that's not the best test of ripeness for them. For apples and pears, you need to cut a slice and taste it. For quinces, your best bet is to allow them to sit for a few days after buying. Taking into account transportation to the market and with those few days, the quinces should be ready to use.

Apples, pears, and quinces all should be skinned and cored before being used in baking. There are some exceptions for peeling apples and pears, but the skin of quinces is never eaten. Unlike apples and pears, quinces are never eaten raw. They must be cooked, which softens them. When cooked, the flesh of quinces turns a beautiful rose-pink color.

For peeling, it's best to use a sharp vegetable peeler, while a melon baller or a small sharp knife works well for coring. Apples and pears do not need to be poached, unless the recipe specifically calls for it. Before using any of these for baking, you need to slice or cut them into chunks with a sharp knife. The recipe you use will determine the size of the slices or chunks.

Apple and Dried Cherry Crisp

A COMBINATION of apples and dried cherries gives this crisp a lot of flavor. I like to use Braeburn and Gala apples, because they don't become mushy when they're baked and they taste very good. But Granny Smith or Pippin apples work well, too. This is a great dessert to make on short notice because it's very quick to assemble. It's excellent served warm with whipped cream or vanilla ice cream. This is one of my favorite fall desserts. **Makes one 8-inch square crisp, 8 to 10 servings**

Essential Gear
- Knife or vegetable peeler
- Chef's knife
- 2-quart bowl
- 8-inch square baking pan
- Food processor
- Rubber spatula or wooden spoon
- Cooling rack

APPLE AND DRIED CHERRY FILLING

2½ pounds apples (6 to 7 medium)

Use a vegetable peeler or a knife to peel the apples. Use a chef's knife to cut the apples into quarters, then use a small sharp knife to remove the core and seeds. Slice the apples into ½-inch slices and place them in a 2-quart mixing bowl.

1 cup dried cherries
⅔ cup firmly packed light brown sugar
½ cup granulated sugar
3 tablespoons freshly squeezed orange juice
Finely grated zest of 1 large orange
½ teaspoon freshly ground nutmeg
⅛ teaspoon salt

Add the cherries, brown sugar, granulated sugar, juice, zest, nutmeg, and salt to the sliced apples and toss to blend together well.

Keeping
Although the crisp is best eaten the day it's made, it can last for up to 2 days. Store the crisp tightly covered with aluminum foil in the refrigerator.

Streamlining
The topping can be made in advance. Store it in a tightly covered plastic container in the refrigerator up to 4 days.

Making a Change
Use other types of apples or a combination of apples.

Use different types of dried fruit or nuts.

Transfer the filling to the baking dish.

TOPPING

Center a rack in the oven and preheat it to 375°F.

¾ cup all-purpose flour
½ cup whole, unblanched almonds
⅓ cup firmly packed light brown sugar
2 tablespoons granulated sugar
½ teaspoon freshly grated nutmeg
⅛ teaspoon salt

In the work bowl of a food processor fitted with the steel blade, combine the flour, almonds, brown sugar, granulated sugar, nutmeg, and salt. Pulse until the almonds are finely chopped, 30 seconds to 1 minute.

Adding Style
Serve squares of the crisp with vanilla ice cream.

4 ounces (8 tablespoons, 1 stick) unsalted butter, chilled	Cut the butter into small pieces and add it to the dry ingredients. Pulse until the butter is cut into very small pieces, about 30 seconds.
	Evenly sprinkle the topping over the sliced apples in the baking pan.
	Bake the crisp for 1 hour, until the topping is light golden. Remove the pan from the oven and transfer to a rack to cool.

GARNISH

1 cup heavy whipping cream	Place the cream in the bowl of an electric stand mixer or in a large mixing bowl. Use the wire whip attachment or a hand-held mixer to whip on medium speed until frothy.
2 tablespoons confectioners' sugar	Add the confectioners' sugar and continue whipping the cream until it holds soft peaks.
	Cut squares of the crisp, scooping up the fruit. Serve each square with a large dollop of whipped cream.

Apple Custard Tart with Dried Apricots and Almonds

THINLY SLICED apples are sprinkled with sugar and cooked in butter until they caramelize. Once the cooked apples are cool, they are fanned out in a partially baked pastry shell with chunks of dried apricots. An almond custard filling is poured over the apples, then the tart is baked until the custard is set. After it's baked, the top of the warm tart is brushed with apricot glaze to keep the apples moist and to make them shine. Although this tart has several steps and takes a bit of time to prepare, it's well worth the effort. **Makes one 11-inch round tart, 12 to 14 servings**

Essential Gear
- Food processor
- Rolling pin
- 11-inch round fluted-edge tart pan with removable bottom
- Baking sheet
- Cooling rack
- 2-cup saucepan
- Medium-size fine-mesh strainer
- Goose-feather pastry brush
- Pie weights
- Knife or vegetable peeler
- Chef's knife

Keeping
The tart can last for up to 3 days in the refrigerator.

PASTRY DOUGH

1¼ cups all-purpose flour **2 teaspoons granulated sugar** **⅛ teaspoon salt**	In the work bowl of a food processor fitted with the steel blade, combine the flour, sugar, and salt. Pulse briefly to blend together.
3½ ounces (7 tablespoons) unsalted butter, chilled	Cut the butter into small pieces and add. Pulse until the butter is cut into very tiny pieces, about 30 seconds. The texture should be sandy with very tiny lumps throughout.

3 tablespoons ice water

With the food processor running, pour the water through the feed tube. Process until the dough wraps itself around the blade, 30 seconds to 1 minute

Turn the pastry dough onto a large piece of plastic wrap. Shape into a flat disk and wrap tightly in a double layer of plastic wrap. Chill in the refrigerator until firm before using, about 2 hours. Chilling the dough relaxes the gluten in the flour so it won't be too elastic and will roll out easily. It also firms up the butter in the dough so it will need less flour when rolled out. If the dough is too firm it will splinter and break when rolled out. Let it stand at room temperature for 10 to 15 minutes before rolling to become more pliable.

Center a rack in the oven and preheat it to 400°F.

On a smooth, flat surface, roll out the pastry dough between sheets of lightly floured waxed or parchment paper to a large circle about 12 inches in diameter. Carefully peel the paper off the top of the dough. Brush excess flour off the dough, then loosely roll the pastry dough around the rolling pin without the bottom piece of paper. Place the tart pan directly underneath the rolling pin and carefully unroll the pastry dough onto it

Gently lift up the sides and ease the pastry dough into the bottom and sides of the tart pan, pushing it lightly into the fluted edges. Trim off the excess pastry dough at the top of the pan by running the rolling pin over the top. Or use your fingers to press against the top of the pan to remove the excess pastry dough. Pierce the bottom of the shell in several places with a fork or sharp knife. Place the tart pan on a baking sheet.

Line the pastry shell with a large piece of aluminum foil that fits well against the bottom and sides. Fill with pie weights and bake for 10 minutes. Remove from the oven and cool on a rack, then remove the foil and weights.

APPLE AND APRICOT FILLING

1 cup dried apricot halves, quartered
1 tablespoon granulated sugar

Place the apricots in a 1-quart bowl and cover with water. Let them soak for 20 minutes, then drain and pat dry on paper towels. Sprinkle the apricots with the sugar.

1½ pounds tart cooking apples, such as Granny Smith (4 to 5 medium)

Use a vegetable peeler or a knife to peel the apples. Use a sharp chef's knife to cut the apples lengthwise in half, then cut them in half again. Remove the core from each quarter and cut the quarters lengthwise into ¼-inch-thick slices.

Place a piece of waxed paper over the top of the tart, then tightly cover it with aluminum foil.

Streamlining
The pastry dough can be made in advance and kept in the refrigerator, tightly wrapped in a double layer of plastic wrap, for up to 4 days. To freeze for up to 3 months, wrap the dough snugly in several layers of plastic wrap and place it in a freezer bag. Use a large piece of masking tape and an indelible marker to label and date the contents. If frozen, defrost overnight in the refrigerator before using. The dough can also be fitted into the pan and kept tightly covered in the refrigerator or frozen, wrapped and labeled as above.

The apricot glaze can be made in advance and kept in a tightly covered plastic container in the refrigerator up to 1 month before using. Warm it in a small saucepan over medium heat or in a microwave oven on medium power before using.

Making a Change
Replace the dried apricots with dried pears.

½ cup granulated sugar	Place the apple slices in a medium mixing bowl and sprinkle with the sugar. Toss them gently to coat with the sugar.
2 ounces (4 tablespoons, ½ stick) unsalted butter	Melt 3 tablespoons of the butter in a large heavy-duty sauté pan over medium-high heat. When the butter is bubbling, add the apple slices. Cook, stirring frequently, until the sugar caramelizes, about 15 minutes. Remove the slices and place them on a lined baking sheet to cool.
	Melt the remaining tablespoon of butter in the sauté pan and cook the apricots until they begin to caramelize. Remove from the pan and cool.

ASSEMBLY

Arrange the apple slices in a slightly overlapping circle inside the tart shell. Make a second circle of the dried apricots and fill in the center of the tart with the remaining apple slices.

CUSTARD FILLING

½ cup heavy whipping cream 1 extra-large egg, at room temperature 1 extra-large egg yolk, at room temperature 3 tablespoons finely ground almonds 2 tablespoons granulated sugar 1 teaspoon orange liqueur or almond extract	Lightly beat the cream, egg, and egg yolk together in a small bowl. Add the ground almonds, sugar, and liqueur or extract and blend together well. Pour the custard over the filling in the tart shell.

Bake the tart for 35 to 38 minutes, until the filling is puffed and light golden.

Remove the tart from the oven and place on a cooling rack.

APRICOT GLAZE

¼ cup apricot preserves 1 tablespoon orange liqueur, cognac, or water	Combine the apricot preserves and liquid in a small saucepan. Bring to a boil over medium heat. Remove the pan from the heat and strain the glaze into a small bowl, pushing through as much of the pulp as possible.

Use a goose-feather pastry brush to lightly brush the top of the tart with the glaze. Don't apply a thick glaze, which looks unappetizing. The purpose of the glaze is to keep the fruit from drying out and to make the top of the tart glisten.

Remove the sides of the tart pan (see page 42) before serving. Cut the tart into slices and serve warm or at room temperature.

Apple Pie with Sour Cream

THIS PIE is a wonderful way to showcase apples. Not only does it look and taste good, but the aroma is so tantalizing that anyone who walks near this pie won't be able to resist eating a piece. The pie dough is made with a combination of cream cheese and butter, which is my favorite because it's easy to work with, has a great flaky texture, and is very tasty. **Makes one 10-inch round pie, 12 to 14 servings**

PIE DOUGH

1¼ cups all-purpose flour 1 tablespoon granulated sugar ¼ teaspoon salt	In the work bowl of a food processor fitted with the steel blade, combine the flour, sugar, and salt. Pulse briefly to blend.

4 ounces (8 tablespoons,
    1 stick) unsalted butter,
    chilled
	Cut the butter into small pieces and freeze for 20 minutes.

4 ounces cream cheese, chilled	Cut the cream cheese into small pieces and add to the food processor. Pulse to cut the cream cheese into very tiny pieces. The texture should be sandy with very tiny lumps throughout. Add the butter to the food processor. Pulse until the butter is cut into pea-sized pieces, 30 to 45 seconds.
2 to 3 tablespoons heavy whipping cream	Remove the top of the food processor and sprinkle on 2 tablespoons of the cream. Replace the top and pulse for 10 seconds. Squeeze a small amount of the dough in your hand. If it holds together, don't add any more cream. If the dough is still very crumbly, add another tablespoon of cream, pulse to blend, then check the dough again. It won't hold together unless you squeeze it, but that's the texture you want.

Essential Gear
- Knife or vegetable peeler
- Chef's knife
- Food processor
- Rolling pin
- 10-inch round deep pie pan
- Baking sheet
- Cooling rack

Keeping
Store the pie loosely covered with waxed paper, then tightly wrapped with aluminum foil at room temperature up to 3 days.

Streamlining
The pie dough can be made in advance and kept in the refrigerator, tightly wrapped in a double layer of plastic wrap, up to 4 days. To freeze for up to 3 months, wrap the dough snugly in several layers of plastic wrap and place it in a freezer bag. Use a large piece of masking tape and an indelible marker to label and date the contents. If frozen, defrost overnight in the refrigerator before using. The pie dough can also be fit into the pie pan and frozen. Wrap as above and label.

Shape the dough piece into a flat disk and wrap tightly in a double layer of plastic wrap. Chill in the refrigerator until firm before using, about 2 hours. Chilling the dough relaxes the gluten in the flour so it won't be too elastic and will roll out easily. It also firms up the butter in the dough so it will need less flour when rolled out. If the dough is too firm it will splinter and break when rolled out. Let it stand at room temperature for 10 to 15 minutes before rolling to become more pliable.

On a smooth, flat surface, roll out the pie dough between sheets of lightly floured waxed or parchment paper to a large circle about 12 inches in diameter. To tell if the dough will fit the pie pan, invert the pan over the dough. If there are 2 to 3 inches of dough that protrude beyond the sides of the pan, it will fit.

Carefully peel the paper off the top of the dough. Brush excess flour off the dough, then loosely roll the pastry dough around the rolling pin without the bottom piece of paper. Place the pie pan directly underneath the rolling pin and carefully unroll the pastry dough into the pan. Or loosely fold the dough in half. Carefully place it in half of the pie pan and gently unfold the dough. Gently lift up the sides and ease the pie dough into the bottom and sides of the pie pan. Trim off the excess pie dough at the top of the pan and crimp the sides (see page 40).

Transfer the pie pan to a baking sheet and chill in the freezer for 15 to 20 minutes. This helps prevent the pie dough from shrinking as it bakes and sets the butter in the dough, which helps to ensure flakiness.

Troubleshooting

Don't overprocess the pie dough or it will be tough and not flaky.

Making a Change

Replace ½ cup of flour in the pie dough with chopped walnuts. Pulse with the remaining flour in the recipe until the walnuts are very finely chopped.

Replace the walnuts in the topping with pecans, almonds, or hazelnuts.

Adding Style

Add 2 tablespoons finely grated or minced lemon zest to the pie dough before adding the butter.

Serve slices of the pie with vanilla ice cream or whipped cream.

APPLE FILLING

Adjust an oven rack to the lower third and preheat it to 350°F.

2 pounds tart apples, such as Pippin or Granny Smith (7 to 8 small or 5 to 6 medium)

⅓ cup granulated sugar

3 tablespoons all-purpose flour

⅛ teaspoon salt

Use a vegetable peeler or a knife to peel the apples, then cut them into quarters. Use a small sharp knife to remove the core from each quarter. Use a chef's knife to cut the apple quarters lengthwise into ½-inch-thick slices. Place the sliced apples in a 2-quart mixing bowl. Add the sugar, flour, and salt and toss to coat the apples.

⅔ cup sour cream

1 extra-large egg, at room temperature, lightly beaten

In a small bowl, stir together the sour cream, egg, and vanilla. Add this mixture to the apples and gently toss to coat them thoroughly.

| 1 teaspoon pure vanilla extract | Transfer the apple filling to the chilled pie shell and spread it out evenly. |

WALNUT TOPPING

| 1 cup walnuts, finely chopped
3 tablespoons light brown sugar
3 tablespoons granulated sugar
1 teaspoon ground cinnamon | Combine the walnuts, brown sugar, granulated sugar, and cinnamon in a small bowl and stir together until well blended. Sprinkle this mixture evenly over the top of the apples in the pie pan. |

Bake the pie for 1 hour, until light golden and the apples give easily when a cake tester is inserted into them.

Remove the pie from the oven and cool on a rack. Serve warm or at room temperature.

Streusel Apple Pie

A CRUMBLY, crunchy topping sets off the crisp apples mixed with sour cream in this classic pie. It's a winner! **Makes one 9-inch round pie, 12 to 14 servings**

PIE DOUGH

1½ cups all-purpose flour 1 teaspoon granulated sugar ¼ teaspoon salt	In the work bowl of a food processor fitted with the steel blade, combine the flour, sugar, and salt. Pulse briefly to blend.
4½ ounces (9 tablespoons, 1 stick plus 1 tablespoon) unsalted butter, chilled	Cut the butter into small pieces and freeze for 20 minutes. Add the butter to the flour mixture in the food processor. Pulse until the butter is cut into pea-sized pieces, 30 to 45 seconds.
4 to 5 tablespoons ice water	Remove the top of the food processor and sprinkle on 4 tablespoons of the ice water. Replace the top and pulse for 10 seconds. Squeeze a small amount of the dough in your hand. If it holds together, don't add any more water. If the dough is still very crumbly, add another tablespoon of water, pulse to blend, then check the dough again. It won't hold together unless you squeeze it, but that's the texture you want.

Essential Gear

- Food processor
- Rolling pin
- 9-inch round pie pan
- Baking sheet
- Cooling rack
- Pastry brush
- Knife or vegetable peeler
- Chef's knife

Keeping

Store the pie loosely covered with waxed paper, then tightly wrapped with aluminum foil, at room temperature for up to 3 days.

Streamlining

The pie dough can be made in advance and kept in the refrigerator, tightly wrapped in a double layer of plastic

Turn the dough onto a smooth, flat work surface. Use the heel of your hand to push the dough a few times for a final blend. Don't mush all the butter into the dough, however. For a flaky crust, you want to see thin flecks of butter in the dough.

Shape the dough into a flat disk and wrap tightly in a double layer of plastic wrap. Chill in the refrigerator until firm before using, at least 2 hours. Chilling the dough relaxes the gluten in the flour so it won't be too elastic and will roll out easily. It also firms up the butter in the dough so it will need less flour when rolled out. If the dough is too firm it will splinter and break when rolled out. Let it stand at room temperature for 10 to 15 minutes before rolling to become more pliable.

On a smooth, flat surface, roll out the pie dough between sheets of lightly floured waxed or parchment paper to a large circle about 12 inches in diameter. To tell if the dough will fit the pie pan, invert the pan over the dough. If there are 2 to 3 inches of dough that protrude beyond the sides of the pan, it will fit.

Carefully peel the paper off the top of the dough. Brush excess flour off the dough, then loosely roll the pastry dough around the rolling pin without the bottom piece of paper. Place the pie pan directly underneath the rolling pin and carefully unroll the pastry dough into the pan. Or loosely fold the dough in half. Carefully place it in half of the pie pan and gently unfold the dough. Gently lift up the sides and ease the pie dough into the bottom and sides of the pie pan. Trim off the excess pie dough at the top of the pan and crimp the sides (see page 40).

Transfer the pie pan to a baking sheet and chill in the freezer for 15 to 20 minutes. This helps prevent the pie dough from shrinking as it bakes and sets the butter in the dough to ensure flakiness.

wrap, for up to 4 days. To freeze for up to 3 months, wrap the dough snugly in several layers of plastic wrap and place it in a freezer bag. Use a large piece of masking tape and an indelible marker to label and date the contents. If frozen, defrost overnight in the refrigerator before using. The pie dough can also be fitted into the pie pan and frozen. Wrap as above and label.

The streusel topping can be made in advance and kept in the refrigerator in a tightly covered plastic container for up to 1 week.

Troubleshooting

Don't overprocess the pie dough or it will be tough and not flaky.

Making a Change

To make classic tender, flaky pie dough, replace half of the butter with lard or vegetable shortening.

EGG GLAZE

1 extra-large egg, at room temperature
2 teaspoons cool water

Using a fork, lightly beat the egg with the water in a small bowl. Using a pastry brush, brush the glaze over the inside of the pie shell. This will help prevent the shell from becoming soggy from the juice the apples release as they bake.

APPLE FILLING

2 pounds tart apples, such as Granny Smith or Pippin (6 to 7 medium)
1/2 cup sour cream

Using a vegetable peeler or a knife, peel the apples. Use a sharp knife to cut the apples into quarters and remove the core. Slice the apples lengthwise into 1/2-inch-thick slices. Place the sliced apples in a large bowl and toss with the sour cream.

THE ESSENTIAL BAKER

**2 tablespoons all-purpose
flour**
**¼ cup firmly packed light
brown sugar**
½ teaspoon ground cinnamon
**½ teaspoon freshly grated
nutmeg**

Add the flour, sugar, cinnamon, and nutmeg to the sliced apples and toss together lightly to distribute evenly.

Transfer the filling to the pie shell.

STREUSEL TOPPING

Center a rack in the oven and preheat it to 350°F.

½ cup all-purpose flour
**½ cup firmly packed light
brown sugar**
**¼ teaspoon ground
cinnamon**
**2½ ounces (5 tablespoons)
unsalted butter, chilled**

Combine the flour, brown sugar, and cinnamon in the work bowl of a food processor fitted with the steel blade. Cut the butter into small pieces and add to the dry ingredients. Pulse until the butter is cut into very small pieces, 30 seconds to 1 minute.

Evenly sprinkle the topping over the apples in the baking pan. Place the pie pan on a baking sheet.

Bake the pie for 45 to 50 minutes, until the topping is light golden and the apples are tender. Remove the pan from the oven and transfer to a rack to cool.

Tarte Tatin

ARTE TATIN is a classic French upside-down, caramelized apple tart that takes its name from two sisters in the Loire region of France who served it at their hotel in the late nineteenth and early twentieth centuries. This tarte takes a bit of work to make, but it is well worth it. In this recipe, I use a pastry dough that is similar to pie dough, but you can also use puff pastry. **Makes one 10-inch round tart, 10 to 12 servings**

PASTRY DOUGH

1 cup all-purpose flour
**¼ teaspoon granulated
sugar**
⅛ teaspoon salt

In the work bowl of a food processor fitted with the steel blade, combine the flour, sugar, and salt. Pulse briefly to blend.

Essential Gear
- Food processor
- Vegetable peeler
- Chef's knife
- 2-cup heavy-bottomed
  saucepan
- 10-inch sauté pan or
  frying pan
- Rolling pin
- 10-inch round pie pan
- Cooling rack

Keeping
Although the tarte is best eaten the day it's made, it

3 ounces (6 tablespoons, ¾ stick) unsalted butter, chilled	Cut the butter into small pieces and add to the dry ingredients. Pulse the food processor several times until the butter is cut into very tiny pieces. The mixture should feel sandy with tiny lumps throughout.
3 tablespoons cold water	With the food processor running, add the cold water through the feed tube. Process until the dough wraps itself around the blade, 30 seconds to 1 minute.

Turn the pastry dough onto a large piece of plastic wrap. Shape into a flat disk and wrap tightly in a double layer of plastic wrap. Chill in the refrigerator until firm before using, about 2 hours. Chilling the dough relaxes the gluten in the flour so it won't be too elastic and will roll out easily. It also firms up the butter in the dough so it will need less flour when rolled out. If the dough is too firm it will splinter and break when rolled out. Let it stand at room temperature for 10 to 15 minutes before rolling to become more pliable.

can last for up to 2 days. Store the tarte loosely covered with waxed paper, then tightly wrapped with aluminum foil in the refrigerator.

Streamlining

The pastry dough can be rolled out in advance and kept in the refrigerator, tightly wrapped in a double layer of plastic wrap, for up to 3 days.

APPLE FILLING

½ cup granulated sugar **½ cup water** **⅛ teaspoon cream of tartar**	Place the sugar, water, and cream of tartar in the saucepan. Bring the mixture to a boil over medium-high heat, without stirring. Place a wet pastry brush at the point where the sugar syrup meets the sides of the pan and sweep it around completely. Do this two times. This prevents the sugar from crystallizing by brushing any stray crystals back into the mixture. Cook the mixture over high heat until it turns medium caramel color.

Immediately remove the saucepan from the heat and pour the caramel into the bottom of the pie pan. Swirl the pan to completely coat the bottom with the caramel.

2 pounds Granny Smith or other tart apples (6 to 7 medium)	Use a vegetable peeler or a knife to peel the apples, then cut them into quarters. Remove the core from each quarter and cut them lengthwise into ½-inch-thick slices with a chef's knife.
2 ounces (4 tablespoons, ¼ stick) unsalted butter **⅓ cup granulated sugar** **Finely grated zest of 1 large lemon**	Heat the butter in the sauté pan or frying pan over medium heat until it is foamy. Add the sliced apples and sprinkle them with the sugar and lemon zest. Stir the apples to coat them with the sugar. Cook the apples over medium heat until they are golden and soft, stirring often with a wooden spoon or heat-resistant spatula, about 15 minutes. Transfer the cooked apples to a parchment paper–lined baking sheet to cool.

ASSEMBLY

Adjust the oven rack to the lower third and preheat it to 400°F.

On a smooth, flat work surface, roll out the pastry dough between sheets of lightly floured waxed or parchment paper to a circle 12-inches in diameter. Carefully peel the paper off the top of the dough. Brush excess flour off the dough,

Arrange the cooled, cooked apple slices in tight concentric circles over the caramel in the pie pan.

Loosely roll the pastry dough around the rolling pin without the bottom piece of paper and unroll over the apples. Or loosely fold the pastry dough in half, place on top of the apples, and unfold. Tuck the pastry dough inside the edges of the pan so that the apples are completely covered. Pierce the pastry dough in several places to release steam while it bakes.

Bake the tarte for 45 minutes, until the pastry is golden and puffed. Remove the tarte from the oven and cool on a rack for 15 minutes.

Place a serving plate over the pan and carefully invert the tarte onto the plate. Gently lift the pan off of the tarte. If any apple slices stick to the pan, use a spatula to carefully remove them and any remaining caramel sauce, and arrange on top of the tarte.

Serve the tart warm or at room temperature with vanilla ice cream or lightly sweetened whipped cream.

Apple Puff Pastry Tartlets

INDIVIDUAL CIRCLES of puff pastry hold a yummy filling of sliced apples drizzled with honey. After baking, the tartlets are brushed with apricot glaze, making them shiny. These are classic apple tartlets found in pastry shops throughout France. Although they look like a professional made them, they are very easy to assemble. You can choose to make your own puff pastry or you can use store bought. Either way, these tartlets are hard to resist. **Makes eight 5^1/$_2$-inch round tartlets**

Essential Gear
- Rolling pin
- Chef's knife
- Two baking sheets
- Two parchment paper sheets
- Two cooling racks
- Goose-feather pastry brush

Keeping
Although the tartlets are best eaten the day they're made, they can last for up to 2 days. Store the tartlets loosely covered with waxed

PUFF PASTRY DOUGH

1 pound Quick Puff Pastry (page 196) or store-bought puff pastry

If the puff pastry is frozen, defrost it in the refrigerator before rolling out. Divide the puff pastry into two equal pieces and roll each piece out between sheets of lightly floured waxed or parchment paper to a 9-inch square.

Use a ruler to cut each square into equal-sized quarters, making a total of eight 4½-inch squares.

On a smooth, flat work surface between sheets of lightly floured waxed or parchment paper, roll out each puff pastry piece to a circle about 5½-inches in diameter. Use a 5½-inch round plate or other shape to place gently on top of the puff pastry as a guide and trim off the excess puff pastry.

Use a 4½-inch round plate or other shape to place gently on top of the puff pastry as a guide and, using a sharp knife, draw an inner circle in each puff pastry circle, but don't cut all the way through the puff pastry. Remove the guide and fold the pastry edges in to the center to form a lip, pressing on them gently so they will stick.

Line two baking sheets with parchment paper sheets or non-stick liners and place 4 puff pastry circles on each baking sheet, leaving at least 3 inches of space between them.

2 tablespoons heavy whipping cream
2 tablespoons granulated sugar
Finely grated zest of 1 lemon

Using a small pastry brush or a spoon, brush the center of each puff pastry circle lightly with the cream. Then sprinkle sugar and lemon zest over the cream in the center of each circle.

Place the baking sheets in the freezer for 20 minutes.

Adjust the oven racks to the upper and lower thirds and preheat it to 450°F.

ASSEMBLY

¾ pound apples, such as Granny Smith, Braeburn, or Delicious (2 to 3 medium)
½ cup freshly squeezed orange juice

Use a vegetable peeler to peel the apples. Cut them into quarters and remove the core from each quarter. Then cut the quarters lengthwise into ½-inch-thick slices. Place the slices in a medium mixing bowl and cover with the orange juice. Let the apple slices soak for 10 minutes, then pat them dry on paper towels.

Arrange the apple slices in concentric circles on each puff pastry circle, overlapping them to fill in the center of each circle.

2 tablespoons honey

Drizzle a little honey over the apple slices.

Place the baking sheets in the oven and reduce the oven temperature to 425°F.

paper, then tightly wrapped with aluminum foil in the refrigerator.

Streamlining
The puff pastry dough can be rolled out in advance and kept in the refrigerator, tightly wrapped in a double layer of plastic wrap, for up to 3 days. The apples can be sliced and kept in the bowl of orange juice in the refrigerator, tightly covered with plastic wrap, up to 1 day.

The apricot glaze can be made in advance and kept in a tightly covered plastic container in the refrigerator up to 1 month before using. Warm it in a small saucepan over medium heat or in a microwave oven on medium power before using.

Bake the tartlets for 10 minutes. Then switch the baking sheets and bake another 8 to 10 minutes, until the pastry is golden and the apples give easily when a cake tester is inserted into them

Remove the baking sheets from the oven and cool on racks.

APRICOT GLAZE

¼ cup apricot preserves
2 teaspoons freshly squeezed lemon juice
1 teaspoon amaretto, cognac, or water

Combine the apricot preserves, juice, and liqueur in a small saucepan. Bring to a boil over medium heat. Remove the pan from the heat and strain the glaze into a small bowl, pushing through as much of the pulp as possible.

Use a goose-feather pastry brush to lightly brush the top of the tartlets with the glaze. Don't apply a thick glaze, which looks unappetizing. The purpose of the glaze is to keep the apples from drying out and to make the top of the tartlets glisten.

Serve the tartlets warm or at room temperature with vanilla ice cream or lightly sweetened whipped cream.

Apple Turnovers

TURNOVERS ARE GREAT for dessert, for afternoon tea, and warmed up for breakfast. These are prepared with puff pastry, making them flaky and succulent. The turnovers are sprinkled with pearl sugar before baking, giving them a crisp topping. Pearl sugar is processed into small, round balls that are four to six times larger than regular grains of sugar, resembling pearls. Pearl sugar is not used as a sweetener, but as a garnish because it doesn't melt in the heat of the oven. **Makes eight 6-inch turnovers**

PUFF PASTRY DOUGH

1 pound Quick Puff Pastry (page 196) or store-bought puff pastry

If the puff pastry is frozen, defrost it in the refrigerator before rolling out. Divide the puff pastry into two equal pieces and roll each piece out between sheets of lightly floured waxed or parchment paper to a 12-inch square.

Use a ruler to cut each square into equal quarters, making a total of eight 6-inch squares. Line two baking sheets with parchment paper and place the squares on the sheets; chill while preparing the filling.

Essential Gear
- Rolling pin
- Two baking sheets
- Two parchment paper sheets
- Vegetable peeler or knife
- 10-inch sauté or frying pan
- 1-inch natural-bristle pastry brush or spoon
- Two cooling racks

Keeping
Store the turnovers loosely covered with waxed paper, then tightly wrapped with aluminum foil, at room temperature for up to 2 days.

APPLE FILLING

3 pounds tart apples, such as Granny Smith or Pippins (8 to 10 medium)

Use a vegetable peeler or knife to peel the apples. Cut them into quarters and remove the cores. Cut each apple quarter into 1-inch chunks.

3 ounces (6 tablespoons, ¾ stick) unsalted butter, cut into small pieces

Melt the butter in a 10-inch sauté pan or frying pan over medium heat. When the butter begins to bubble, add the apple chunks.

⅔ cup superfine sugar
1 teaspoon freshly grated nutmeg
1 teaspoon ground cloves
1 teaspoon ground cinnamon

Sprinkle the sugar, nutmeg, cloves, and cinnamon over the apples and stir until the apples are evenly coated. Cook the apples, stirring often, until they are soft, but not limp, about 10 minutes. Transfer the apples to a plate to cool slightly.

Adjust the oven racks to the upper and lower thirds and preheat it to 425°F.

ASSEMBLY

1 extra-large egg, at room temperature

Lightly beat the egg in a small bowl. Use a pastry brush to brush the top edges of each pastry-dough square with beaten egg. Be sure to brush only the inner part of the dough, not the outside. This will help the pastry dough stick together when the turnovers are formed.

Place 2 heaping tablespoons of the apple filling in the center of each square. Bring opposite corners of the square together and fold each pastry square in half diagonally, lining up all the edges and points, making a triangle. Pinch the edges together firmly, then crimp with a fork or roll the edges in slightly to give them a finished look (see page 40).

Place the turnovers on the lined baking sheet, leaving at least 1 inch of space between them.

Brush the top of each turnover with the beaten egg. Be careful that the egg doesn't run down the sides and underneath the turnovers. If it does, wipe it up because it can cause the bottom of the turnovers to burn.

3 tablespoons pearl sugar

Sprinkle the top of each turnover evenly with pearl sugar.

Bake the turnovers for 8 minutes, then switch the baking sheets and bake another 7 minutes. Switch the sheets again and bake another

Making a Change
Replace the apples with pears.

8 to 12 minutes, until the turnovers are golden and crisp. Remove the pans from the oven and cool on a rack for 15 minutes. Serve the turnovers warm or at room temperature.

The turnovers can be rewarmed at 350°F for 10 to 15 minutes. To do this, place them in a single layer on a baking sheet lined with parchment paper.

Granny Smith Apple and Raisin Crisp

THIS IS A RUSTIC dessert that is very easy to make. A crumbly topping of flour, light brown sugar, pecans, and butter is scattered over sliced Granny Smith apples and raisins. I like to use Granny Smith apples because they are my favorite eating apples and they don't become mushy when baked, but you can use any type of apples. I use plump Monukka raisins to add extra flavor. These are large, dark, seedless raisins that are usually found in bulk bins in health or natural food stores. I like to eat this dessert warm, but it is equally yummy at room temperature. Although good on its own, try serving the crisp with vanilla ice cream or lightly sweetened whipped cream. **Makes one 8-inch square crisp, 8 to 10 servings**

Essential Gear

- Vegetable peeler or knife
- Chef's knife
- 2-quart bowl
- 8-inch square baking pan
- Food processor
- Rubber spatula or wooden spoon
- Cooling rack

Keeping

Although the crisp is best eaten the day it's made, it can last for up to 2 days. Store the crisp tightly covered with aluminum foil in the refrigerator.

Streamlining

The topping can be made in advance. Store it in a tightly covered plastic container in the refrigerator up to 4 days.

Making a Change

Use other types of apples or a combination of apples.

Adding Style

Serve squares of the crisp with vanilla ice cream.

APPLE AND RAISIN FILLING

2 pounds Granny Smith apples (8 small or 5 to 6 medium)

²/₃ cup dark raisins
¼ cup firmly packed light brown sugar
¼ cup apple juice
1 teaspoon ground cinnamon
½ teaspoon freshly ground nutmeg

Use a vegetable peeler or knife to peel the apples. Use a chef's knife to cut the apples into quarters, then use a small sharp knife to remove the core and seeds. Slice the apples into ½-inch-thick lengthwise slices and place them in a 2-quart mixing bowl.

Add the raisins, brown sugar, apple juice, cinnamon, and nutmeg to the sliced apples and toss to blend together well.

Transfer the filling to the baking pan.

TOPPING

Center a rack in the oven and preheat it to 375°F.

¾ cup all-purpose flour	Combine the flour, pecans, brown sugar, baking powder, and salt in the work bowl of a food processor fitted with the steel blade. Pulse until the pecans are finely chopped, 30 seconds to 1 minute.
½ cup pecans	
⅓ cup firmly packed light brown sugar	
½ teaspoon baking powder	
⅛ teaspoon salt	
4 ounces (8 tablespoons, 1 stick) unsalted butter, chilled	Cut the butter into small pieces and add to the dry ingredients. Pulse until the butter is cut into very small pieces, about 30 seconds.
	Evenly sprinkle the topping over the fruit in the baking pan.
	Bake the crisp for 45 minutes, until the topping is light golden. Remove the pan from the oven and transfer to a rack to cool.

GARNISH

1 cup heavy whipping cream	Place the cream in the bowl of an electric stand mixer or in a large mixing bowl. Use the wire whip attachment or a hand-held mixer to whip on medium speed until frothy.
2 tablespoons confectioners' sugar	Add the confectioners' sugar and continue whipping the cream until it holds soft peaks.
	Cut squares of the crisp, scooping up the fruit. Serve each square with a large dollop of whipped cream.

Grated Apple and Raisin Tart

I LEARNED TO MAKE this classic Eastern European tart when I worked in Switzerland. It's unusual because the apples for the filling are grated rather than sliced, creating a unique texture. Tart apples such as Granny Smiths or Pippins are the type traditionally used in this tart. Like many Eastern European pastries, this one is not heavily sweetened. **Makes one 9-inch round tart, 12 to 14 servings**

Essential Gear
- Food processor
- Rolling pin
- 9-inch round, deep fluted-edge tart or quiche pan with removable bottom
- Vegetable peeler or knife
- Chef's knife
- Baking sheet
- Cooling rack

PASTRY DOUGH

1¼ cups all-purpose flour	In the work bowl of a food processor fitted with the steel blade, combine the flour, sugar, and salt. Pulse briefly to blend together.
2 tablespoons granulated sugar	
⅛ teaspoon salt	

4 ounces (8 tablespoons, 1 stick) unsalted butter, chilled	Cut the butter into small pieces and add. Pulse until the butter is cut into very tiny pieces, about 30 seconds. The texture should be sandy with very tiny lumps throughout.
1 extra-large egg yolk, at room temperature ½ teaspoon pure vanilla extract	In a small bowl, whisk the egg yolk and vanilla together. With the food processor running, pour this mixture through the feed tube. Process until the dough wraps itself around the blade, 30 seconds to 1 minute

Turn the pastry dough onto a large piece of plastic wrap. Shape into a flat disk and wrap tightly in a double layer of plastic wrap. Chill in the refrigerator until firm before using, about 2 hours. Chilling the dough relaxes the gluten in the flour so it won't be too elastic and will roll out easily. It also firms up the butter in the dough so it will need less flour when rolled out. If the dough is too firm it will splinter and break when rolled out. Let it stand at room temperature for 10 to 15 minutes before rolling to become more pliable.

Center a rack in the oven and preheat it to 375°F.

On a smooth, flat surface, roll out the pastry dough between sheets of lightly floured waxed or parchment paper to a large square about 11 inches wide. Carefully peel the paper off the top of the dough. Brush excess flour off the dough, then loosely roll the pastry dough around the rolling pin without the bottom piece of paper. Place the tart pan directly underneath the rolling pin and carefully unroll the pastry dough onto it.

Gently lift up the sides and ease the pastry dough into the bottom and sides of the tart pan, pushing it lightly into the fluted edges. Trim off the excess pastry dough at the top of the pan by running the rolling pin over the top. Or use your fingers to press against the top of the pan to remove the excess pastry dough. Place the tart pan on a baking sheet.

FILLING

⅓ cup hazelnuts, toasted and skinned 1 tablespoon granulated sugar	Place the hazelnuts and sugar in the work bowl of a food processor fitted with the steel blade. Pulse until the hazelnuts are very finely ground, about 1 minute.
	Sprinkle the bottom of the tart shell with the ground hazelnuts.
1¼ pounds tart green apples, such as Granny Smith or Pippin (4 to 5 medium)	Use a vegetable peeler or knife to peel the apples. Use a sharp chef's knife to cut the apples lengthwise in half, then cut them in half again. Remove the core from each quarter and grate the apples finely

Keeping
The tart can last for up to 3 days in the refrigerator. Place a piece of waxed paper over the top of the tart, then tightly cover it with aluminum foil.

Streamlining
The pastry dough can be made in advance and kept in the refrigerator, tightly wrapped in a double layer of plastic wrap, for up to 4 days. To freeze for up to 3 months, wrap the dough snugly in several layers of plastic wrap and place it in a freezer bag. Use a large piece of masking tape and an indelible marker to label and date the contents. If frozen, defrost overnight in the refrigerator before using.

Making a Change
Replace the finely ground hazelnuts with finely chopped walnuts.

Add ½ cup finely chopped walnuts to the grated apples and raisins before adding the custard.

⅓ cup dark raisins	over a medium mixing bowl. Add the raisins and toss together to blend well. Transfer to the tart shell and spread out evenly.
1 cup heavy whipping cream **1 extra-large egg, at room temperature** **2 tablespoons granulated sugar** **1 tablespoon plus 2 teaspoons all-purpose flour** **½ teaspoon freshly grated nutmeg**	Lightly beat the cream and egg together in a small bowl. Add the sugar, flour, and nutmeg and blend together well. Pour the custard over the apples and raisins in the tart shell.
	Bake the tart for 40 to 45 minutes, until the filling is puffed, set, and light golden. Remove the tart from the oven and place on a cooling rack
	Remove the sides of the tart pan (see page 42) before serving. Cut the tart into slices and serve warm or at room temperature.

Baked Pears with Honey Whipped Cream

THIS IS ONE OF my favorite ways to prepare the bounty of fall pears for dessert. I like to use Bosc pears because they are my favorite eating pears, but you can use any type of pears in this recipe. Cinnamon and nutmeg add spicy warmth to the flavor and honey adds a bit of extra sweetness. The honey whipped cream as a garnish is rich and flavorful. **Makes 8 servings**

Center an oven rack and preheat it to 350°F.

1 pound ripe pears (3 to 4 medium)	Use a vegetable peeler or a knife to peel the pears. Cut the pears in half lengthwise and scoop out the seeds and stems.
½ cup firmly packed light brown sugar	Sprinkle the bottom of the baking pan with 2 tablespoons of the sugar. Arrange the pear halves on top of the sugar, with the cut sides up.
Finely grated zest of 1 lemon **1 teaspoon ground cinnamon** **¼ teaspoon freshly grated nutmeg** **¼ teaspoon salt**	Place the rest of the sugar in a small bowl and add the lemon zest, cinnamon, nutmeg, and salt. Toss together to blend well. Sprinkle this mixture over the top of the pear halves.

Essential Gear

- Vegetable peeler or knife
- 8-inch square baking pan
- Cooling rack
- Electric stand mixer with wire whip attachment or large mixing bowl and hand-held mixer
- Rubber spatula

Keeping

The pears are best eaten the same day they are baked.

Making a Change

Sprinkle ½ cup chopped pecans, walnuts, or almonds on top of the pears before baking.

1 tablespoon honey 1 ounce (2 tablespoons) unsalted butter, softened	Drizzle the honey over the pears, then dot them evenly with the butter.
	Bake the pears for 45 minutes to 1 hour, until they are soft. Test them with the tip of a knife to see if they give easily. Remove the baking pan from the oven and place on a cooling rack.

Adding Style

Serve the pear halves with vanilla ice cream.

HONEY WHIPPED CREAM

½ cup heavy whipping cream 2 tablespoons honey	Place the cream in the bowl of an electric stand mixer or in a large mixing bowl. Use the wire whip attachment or a hand-held mixer to whip the cream on medium speed until frothy. Drizzle on the honey and continue to whip the cream until it holds soft peaks.
	Place a warm baked pear half on a serving plate and serve with a large scoop of honey whipped cream.

Fall Pear Cake with Cream Cheese Icing

THIS CAKE, perfect for any casual fall or winter gathering, is composed of two layers of rich, dense pear cake with cream cheese icing and chopped toasted pecans on the sides. All of these flavors blend together well and enhance each other. The cake itself can be baked a couple of days in advance and can be assembled with the icing and decoration shortly before serving. I like to use Bosc or Comice pears when I make this cake because they are my favorite types of eating pears. **Makes one 9-inch round cake, 12 to 14 servings**

PEAR CAKE

Center a rack in the oven and preheat it to 350°F.

1 tablespoon unsalted butter, softened	Use your fingertips or a paper towel to butter the bottom and sides of the cake pan, coating it thoroughly.
2 teaspoons all-purpose flour	Dust the inside of the pan with the flour. Shake and tilt the pan to evenly distribute the flour, then turn the pan over and shake out the excess over the sink.
	Cut a round of parchment paper to fit the bottom of the pan. Butter the parchment paper round and place in the pan, butter-side up.

Essential Gear

- One 9 × 2-inch round cake pan
- Scissors
- Parchment paper
- Electric stand mixer with flat beater attachment and wire whip attachment, or large mixing bowl and hand-held mixer
- Vegetable peeler or knife
- Two rubber spatulas
- Cooling rack
- 10-inch flexible-blade icing spatula

Keeping

Store the cake loosely covered with aluminum foil in the refrigerator for up to 3 days. Place several toothpicks in the top outer edges of the cake to hold the foil

4 ounces (8 tablespoons, 1 stick) unsalted butter, softened	Place the butter in the bowl of an electric stand mixer or in a large mixing bowl. Use the flat beater attachment or hand-held mixer to beat the butter on medium speed until it's fluffy, about 2 minutes.
1 cup firmly packed light brown sugar	Add the sugar to the butter and cream together well. Stop occasionally and scrape down the bottom and sides of the bowl with a rubber spatula.
2 extra-large eggs, at room temperature	One at a time, add the eggs to the butter mixture, stopping to scrape down the bottom and sides of the bowl after each addition. At first the mixture may look curdled as the eggs are added, but as you stop and scrape down the bowl, the mixture will smooth out.
2 cups all-purpose flour 1 teaspoon baking powder 1 teaspoon baking soda 1 teaspoon ground cinnamon ½ teaspoon ground ginger ½ teaspoon freshly grated nutmeg ½ teaspoon salt	Over a large piece of waxed or parchment paper or a bowl, sift together the flour, baking powder, baking soda, cinnamon, and ginger. Add the nutmeg and salt and toss to blend well. With the mixer on low speed, add the dry ingredients in 3 stages. Blend well after each addition and stop often to scrape down the bottom and sides of the bowl with a rubber spatula to ensure even mixing.
½ cup heavy whipping cream ¼ cup sour cream	Add the cream and sour cream to the mixture and blend thoroughly.
1 pound ripe pears (2 large or 3 to 4 medium)	Use a vegetable peeler or knife to peel the pears. Cut the pears in half lengthwise, then in half again. Remove the core from each pear quarter and cut the pears crosswise into 1-inch chunks. Place the pear chunks in the work bowl of a food processor or a blender and pulse until they are finely chopped.
1 cup raisins 1 teaspoon pure vanilla extract	Add the chopped pears, raisins, and vanilla to the cake mixture and blend together well.
	Transfer the cake batter to the cake pan. Smooth the top of the pan with a rubber spatula. Bake the cake for 35 to 40 minutes, until golden and a cake tester inserted in the center comes out with no crumbs clinging to it. Remove the cake pan from the oven and cool completely on a rack. Invert the pan to remove the cake, then peel the parchment paper off the cake. Re-invert the cake onto a cardboard cake circle.

away from it so it won't mar the icing.

Streamlining
Bake the cake up to 2 days before assembling and keep tightly covered with a double layer of plastic wrap, at room temperature or in the refrigerator, for up to 4 days. To freeze the cake up to 3 months, wrap it snugly in several layers of plastic wrap and place in a freezer bag. Use a large piece of masking tape and an indelible marker to label and date the contents. If frozen, defrost the layers overnight in the refrigerator.

Adding Style
Add ½ cup finely chopped pecans to the cake. Add the nuts with the dry ingredients when mixing the cake batter.

Recovering from a Mishap
If one of the cake layers breaks during assembly, patch it together with some of the icing.

CREAM CHEESE ICING

12 ounces cream cheese, softened

Place the cream cheese in the bowl of an electric stand mixer or in a large mixing bowl. Use the flat beater attachment or a hand-held mixer and beat the cream cheese until it is fluffy, about 3 minutes.

¾ cup confectioners' sugar, sifted
2 tablespoons heavy whipping cream
2 teaspoons freshly squeezed lemon juice

Add the confectioners' sugar, cream, and lemon juice to the cream cheese and beat together well.

ASSEMBLY

Using a serrated knife, cut the cake in half horizontally (see page 34). Place one cake layer on a serving plate. Place strips of waxed paper around the bottom edges of the cake to protect the plate while assembling the cake. Use the flexible-blade spatula to spread the layer evenly with ⅓ of the icing.

Position the top layer of the cake over the icing and spread the remaining icing over the sides and top of the cake.

1 cup lightly toasted, finely chopped pecans

Press the toasted, chopped pecans into the sides of the cake just up to the top edge.

Let the cake chill for at least 2 hours before serving so it has time to set and will be easier to cut. Serve the cake at room temperature.

Pear and Dried Cranberry Cobbler

THIS COBBLER is perfect for fall, when pears come into season. My favorite pears are Bosc because I like their flavor best, but use any that you like or use a variety of types of pears. Cobblers are a rustic style of dessert whose name comes from the cobbled or broken appearance of the biscuit topping. **Makes one 8-inch square cobbler, 8 to 10 servings**

Center a rack in the oven and preheat it to 350°F.

Essential Gear
- Vegetable peeler or knife
- Chef's knife
- 2-quart bowl
- 8-inch square baking pan
- Food processor
- Cooling rack
- Electric stand mixer with wire whip attachment, or

PEAR AND DRIED CRANBERRY FILLING

2¼ pounds firm but ripe
  pears, such as Bosc,
  Comice, or Anjou (6 to
  7 medium)

½ cup dried cranberries
⅓ cup firmly packed light
  brown sugar
2 tablespoons finely chopped
  crystallized ginger
2 tablespoons freshly
  squeezed lemon juice
Finely grated zest of 1 lemon
¼ teaspoon freshly grated
  nutmeg

Using a vegetable peeler or knife, peel the pears. Using a chef's knife, cut the pears in half lengthwise, then in half again. Cut out the core and cut each pear quarter into 1-inch-thick pieces. Place the cut pears in a 2-quart mixing bowl.

Add the dried cranberries, brown sugar, crystallized ginger, lemon juice, lemon zest, and nutmeg to the pears and toss together to coat them completely.

Transfer the mixture to the baking pan and spread it out evenly.

BISCUIT DOUGH TOPPING

1¼ cups all-purpose flour
½ cup sliced almonds
¼ cup granulated sugar
2 tablespoons crystallized
  ginger
½ teaspoon baking soda
¼ teaspoon salt

Combine the flour, almonds, sugar, crystallized ginger, baking soda, and salt in the work bowl of a food processor fitted with the steel blade. Pulse until the almonds are finely ground, about 30 seconds.

3 ounces (6 tablespoons,
  ¾ stick) unsalted butter,
  chilled

Cut the butter into small pieces and add to the dry ingredients. Pulse until the butter is cut into very tiny pieces, about 1 minute. The texture should feel sandy with tiny lumps throughout.

⅓ cup buttermilk

With the food processor running, pour the buttermilk through the feed tube. Process until the dough wraps itself around the blade, about 30 seconds.

Drop about 8 large spoonfuls of the dough over the top of the mixture, spacing them evenly.

1 tablespoon granulated
  sugar

Sprinkle the top of the dough with the sugar.

Bake for 35 minutes, until the biscuit topping is set and the fruit is bubbling. Remove the pan from the oven and transfer to a rack to cool.

large mixing bowl and
hand-held mixer

Keeping
Although the cobbler is best eaten the day it's made, it can last for up to 2 days. Store the cobbler tightly covered with aluminum foil in the refrigerator.

Making a Change
Replace the dried cranberries with dried cherries or dried blueberries.

GARNISH

1 cup heavy whipping cream	Place the cream in the bowl of an electric stand mixer or in a large mixing bowl. Use the wire whip attachment or a hand-held mixer to whip on medium speed until frothy.
2 tablespoons confectioners' sugar	Add the confectioners' sugar and continue whipping the cream until it holds soft peaks.

Cut squares of the cobbler, scooping up the fruit. Serve each square with a large dollop of whipped cream.

Pear and Walnut Layer Cake with Maple–Cream Cheese Icing

THREE LAYERS of luscious cake packed with pears, walnuts, and crystallized ginger are alternated with maple–cream cheese icing to create a scrumptious dessert. This is an easy cake to make and it's a great way to use pears during their season. The maple syrup adds just the right touch of sweetness to the cream cheese and is a terrific complement to the other flavors of the cake. **Makes one 10-inch round cake, 12 to 14 servings**

PEAR AND WALNUT CAKE

Center a rack in the oven and preheat it to 350°F.

1 tablespoon unsalted butter, softened	Use your fingertips or a paper towel to butter the bottom and sides of the springform pan, coating it thoroughly.
1 tablespoon all-purpose flour	Dust the inside of the pan with the flour. Shake and tilt the pan to evenly distribute the flour, then turn the pan over and shake out the excess over the sink.
	Cut a round of parchment paper to fit the bottom of the pan. Butter the parchment paper round and place in the pan, butter-side up.
5 ounces (10 tablespoons, 1¼ sticks) unsalted butter, softened	Place the butter in the bowl of an electric stand mixer or in a large mixing bowl. Use the flat beater attachment or hand-held mixer to beat the butter on medium speed until it's fluffy, about 2 minutes.

Essential Gear

- 10-inch round spring-form pan
- Scissors
- Parchment paper
- Vegetable peeler or knife
- Two rubber spatulas
- Electric stand mixer with flat beater attachment and wire whip attachment, or large mixing bowl and hand-held mixer
- Cooling rack
- 10-inch cardboard cake circle or serving plate
- 10-inch flexible-blade icing spatula

Keeping

Store the cake loosely covered with aluminum foil in the refrigerator for up to 3 days. Place several toothpicks in the top outer edges of the cake to hold the foil

1 cup granulated sugar ²/₃ cup firmly packed light brown sugar	Add the granulated sugar and brown sugar to the butter, and cream together well. Stop occasionally and scrape down the bottom and sides of the bowl with a rubber spatula to ensure even mixing.
3 extra-large eggs, at room temperature	One at a time, add the eggs to the butter mixture, stopping to scrape down the bottom and sides of the bowl after each addition. At first the mixture may look curdled as the eggs are added, but as you stop and scrape down the bowl, the mixture will smooth out.
1¾ cups all-purpose flour 1 teaspoon baking powder 1 teaspoon baking soda 1 teaspoon ground cinnamon ½ teaspoon ground cloves ½ teaspoon freshly grated nutmeg ¼ teaspoon salt ⅓ cup buttermilk	Over a large piece of waxed or parchment paper or a bowl, sift together the flour, baking powder, baking soda, cinnamon, and cloves. Add the nutmeg and salt and toss to blend well. With the mixer on low speed, add the dry ingredients alternately with the buttermilk in 3 stages. Blend well after each addition and stop often to scrape down the bottom and sides of the bowl with a rubber spatula to ensure even mixing.
1 pound ripe pears (3 to 4 medium)	Use a vegetable peeler or a knife to peel the pears. Cut the pears in half lengthwise, then in half again. Remove the stem and core from each pear quarter and dice the pears. You should have 2 cups of pears.

¾ cup walnuts, finely
  chopped
⅓ cup finely chopped
  crystallized ginger
1 teaspoon pure vanilla
  extract
	Add the pears, walnuts, ginger, and vanilla to the mixture and blend together well.

	Transfer the cake batter to the prepared pan. Smooth the top of the cake with a rubber spatula. Bake the cake for 55 minutes to 1 hour, until a cake tester inserted in the center comes out with no crumbs clinging to it. Remove the cake pan from the oven and cool completely on a rack. Remove the sides of the springform pan to release the cake. Using a flexible-blade spatula to release the bottom of the cake from the pan, transfer the cake to a cardboard cake circle.

CREAM CHEESE ICING

1½ pounds cream cheese, softened	Place the cream cheese in the bowl of an electric stand mixer or in a large mixing bowl. Use the flat beater attachment or a hand-held mixer and beat the cream cheese until it is fluffy, about 3 minutes.

away from it so it won't mar the icing.

Streamlining
Bake the cake up to 2 days before assembling and keep it tightly covered with a double layer of plastic wrap, at room temperature or in the refrigerator, for up to 4 days. To freeze the cake up to 3 months, wrap it snugly in several layers of plastic wrap and place in a freezer bag. Use a large piece of masking tape and an indelible marker to label and date the contents. If frozen, defrost the layers overnight in the refrigerator.

Making a Change
Replace the pears with apples.

Replace the walnuts with pecans both inside and outside the cake.

Recovering from a Mishap
If one of the cake layers breaks during assembly, patch it together with some of the icing.

⅓ **cup pure maple syrup**	Add the maple syrup to the cream cheese and beat together well.

ASSEMBLY

Using a serrated knife, cut the cake in 3 layers horizontally (see page 34). Place the bottom layer of cake on a serving plate. Place waxed paper strips around the base of the cake to keep the plate clean while icing the cake. Use the flexible-blade spatula to spread the layer evenly with ¼ of the icing. Position the second layer of cake over the icing and spread evenly with another ¼ of the icing.

Position the top layer of the cake over the icing. Spread the remaining icing over the sides and top of the cake.

12 walnut halves **1 cup finely chopped** **walnuts**	Visually divide the cake into 12 serving pieces and press a walnut half at the outer center edge of each piece. Press the toasted, chopped walnuts into the sides of the cake just up to the top edge.

Let the cake chill for at least 2 hours before serving so it has time to set and will be easier to cut. Serve the cake at room temperature.

Pear Frangipane Tart

PEARS POACHED in a sugar and water mixture accented with cinnamon, cloves, and lemon juice are nestled into a creamy almond filling inside an almond pastry shell. After the tart is baked, it's brushed lightly with apricot glaze to make it glisten. This is a classic tart found in many pastry shops throughout France. I ate this tart on my first trip to Europe soon after graduating from college. Every time I eat a piece of this tart it takes me back to that first European experience and puts a smile on my face. **Makes one 9½-inch round tart, 12 to 14 servings**

PASTRY DOUGH

1 cup all-purpose flour **½ cup sliced or slivered** **almonds** **2 teaspoons granulated sugar** **¼ teaspoon salt**	In the work bowl of a food processor fitted with the steel blade, combine the flour, almonds, sugar, and salt. Pulse until the almonds are very finely ground, about 1 minute.

4 ounces (8 tablespoons,
    1 stick) unsalted butter,
    chilled
	Cut the butter into small pieces and add. Pulse until the butter is cut into very tiny pieces, about 30 seconds. The texture should be sandy with very tiny lumps throughout.

Essential Gear
- Food processor
- Rolling pin
- 9½-inch round, fluted-edge tart pan with removable bottom
- Vegetable peeler or knife
- Chef's knife
- 4-quart heavy-bottomed saucepan
- Cooling rack
- Baking sheet
- Rubber spatula
- Small saucepan
- Medium-size fine-mesh strainer
- Goose-feather pastry brush

Keeping
The tart can last for up to 3 days in the refrigerator.

**2 teaspoons freshly
squeezed lemon juice
2 to 3 tablespoons ice water**

In a small bowl, combine the lemon juice and 2 tablespoons of water. With the food processor running, pour this mixture through the feed tube. Process until the dough wraps itself around the blade, 30 seconds to 1 minute. If the dough seems dry, add the remaining tablespoon of water and process until the dough comes together.

Turn the pastry dough onto a large piece of plastic wrap. Shape into a flat disk and wrap tightly in a double layer of plastic wrap. Chill in the refrigerator until firm before using, about 2 hours. Chilling the dough relaxes the gluten in the flour so it won't be too elastic and will roll out easily. It also firms up the butter in the dough so it will need less flour when rolled out. If the dough is too firm it will splinter and break when rolled out. Let it stand at room temperature for 10 to 15 minutes before rolling to become more pliable.

POACHED PEARS

**4 cups water
2 cups sugar
Juice of 1 large lemon
2 cinnamon sticks
2 whole cloves**

Combine the water, sugar, lemon juice, cinnamon sticks, and cloves in the saucepan and bring to a boil over medium-high heat.

**1¼ pounds ripe but firm
pears (4 medium)**

Use a vegetable peeler or a knife to peel the pears. Use a sharp chef's knife to cut the pears lengthwise in half, then remove the stems and seeds. Place the pears in the sugar syrup and cook, simmering, until they are soft, but not mushy, about 1 hour.

Transfer the pears to a bowl of cold water to stop them from cooking. Drain them and pat dry with a towel before using. The pears can be kept in a tightly covered bowl or container in the refrigerator in their poaching liquid for up to 2 weeks.

Center a rack in the oven and preheat it to 375°F.

On a smooth, flat surface, roll out the pastry dough between sheets of lightly floured waxed or parchment paper to a large circle about 11 inches in diameter. Carefully peel the paper off the top of the dough. Brush excess flour off the dough, then loosely roll the pastry dough around the rolling pin without the bottom piece of paper. Place the tart pan directly underneath the rolling pin and carefully unroll the pastry dough onto it

Gently lift up the sides and ease the pastry dough into the bottom and sides of the tart pan, pushing it lightly into the fluted edges. Trim off the excess pastry dough at the top of the pan by running the

Place a piece of waxed paper over the top of the tart, then tightly cover it with aluminum foil.

Streamlining
The pastry dough can be made in advance and kept in the refrigerator, tightly wrapped in a double layer of plastic wrap, for up to 4 days. To freeze for up to 3 months, wrap the dough snugly in several layers of plastic wrap and place it in a freezer bag. Use a large piece of masking tape and an indelible marker to label and date the contents. If frozen, defrost overnight in the refrigerator before using. The tart dough can also be fitted into the tart pan and kept tightly covered in the refrigerator or frozen, wrapped and labeled as above.

The frangipane filling can be made in advance and kept in a tightly covered plastic container in the refrigerator up to 4 days before using.

The apricot glaze can be made in advance and kept in a tightly covered plastic container in the refrigerator up to 1 month before using. Warm it in a small saucepan over medium heat or in a microwave oven on medium power before using.

rolling pin over the top. Or use your fingers to press against the top of the pan to remove the excess pastry dough.

Place the tart pan on a baking sheet and chill while preparing the filling.

FRANGIPANE FILLING

1 cup sliced almonds
½ cup granulated sugar

Place the almonds and sugar in the work bowl of a food processor fitted with the steel blade. Pulse until the almonds are very finely ground, about 1 minute.

1 extra-large egg, at room temperature
½ teaspoon pure vanilla extract
½ teaspoon almond extract

Add the egg, vanilla, and almond extract and pulse several times to blend together well.

2½ ounces (5 tablespoons) unsalted butter, softened

Cut the butter into small pieces and add to the mixture. Pulse several times to blend.

2 tablespoons all-purpose flour

Add the flour and pulse until the mixture is smooth, about 15 seconds.

Transfer the mixture to the pastry shell and spread it out evenly with a rubber spatula.

ASSEMBLY

Thinly slice each pear half crosswise, keeping the slices attached at one side. Place a pear half on top of the frangipane filling toward the outer edge of the tart pan, with the stem end pointing inward, fanning out the pear as you press it down lightly into the frangipane. Repeat with the remaining pear halves, arranging them to fill the top of the tart.

Bake the tart for 35 to 40 minutes, until the filling is puffed and light golden.

Remove the tart from the oven and place on a cooling rack.

APRICOT GLAZE

¼ cup apricot preserves
1 tablespoon amaretto, cognac, or water

Combine the apricot preserves and liquid in a small saucepan. Bring to a boil over medium heat. Remove the pan from the heat and strain the glaze into a small bowl, pushing through as much of the pulp as possible.

Use a goose-feather pastry brush to lightly brush the top of the tart with the glaze. Don't apply a thick glaze, which looks unappetizing. The purpose of the glaze is to keep the pears from drying out and to make the top of the tart glisten.

Remove the sides of the tart pan (see page 42) before serving. Cut the tart into wedges and serve warm or at room temperature.

Quince and Apple Pie

POACHED QUINCES and crisp apples are a fabulous combination in this classic pie. It's a perfect pie to make in early fall, when apples are first making their appearance. Many people are astounded the first time they eat anything made with quinces because the fruit is so luscious. This is one of my favorite pies. Try serving each slice with a dollop of freshly whipped cream or vanilla ice cream. **Makes one 10-inch round pie, 12 to 14 servings**

Essential Gear

- 4-quart heavy-bottomed saucepan
- Vegetable peeler or knife
- Chef's knife
- Rubber spatula
- Pastry brush
- Food processor
- Rolling pin
- 10-inch round deep pie pan
- Baking sheet
- Cooling rack

Keeping

Store the pie loosely covered with waxed paper, then tightly wrapped with aluminum foil, in the refrigerator for up to 3 days.

Streamlining

The pie dough can be made in advance and kept in the refrigerator, tightly wrapped in a double layer of plastic wrap, for up to 4 days. To freeze for up to 3 months, wrap the dough snugly in several layers of plastic wrap and place it in a freezer bag. Use a large piece of masking tape and an indelible marker to label and date the contents. If frozen, defrost

POACHED QUINCES

1½ cups sugar
3 cups water
1 vanilla bean, split down the center
Finely grated zest of 1 large lemon

Combine the sugar and water in the saucepan. Bring to a boil over medium-high heat. Add the vanilla bean and lemon zest. Reduce the heat to low.

1 pound ripe quinces (3 medium or 2 large)

Use a vegetable peeler to peel the quinces. Use a sharp chef's knife to cut the quinces into quarters and remove the core and seeds. Place the quince quarters in the sugar syrup and cook, simmering, until the quinces are soft and turn a light rose color, 1½ to 2 hours.

Remove the pan from the heat and transfer the quinces and their cooking liquid to a large bowl. Cover with plastic wrap and cool in their liquid. The quinces can be kept in a tightly covered bowl or container in their cooking liquid, in the refrigerator for up to 2 weeks.

PIE DOUGH

2 cups all-purpose flour
2 tablespoons granulated sugar
½ teaspoon salt

Place the flour, sugar, and salt in the work bowl of a food processor fitted with the steel blade. Pulse briefly to blend.

8 ounces (16 tablespoons, 2 sticks) unsalted butter, chilled	Cut the butter into small pieces and freeze for 20 minutes.
8 ounces cream cheese, chilled	Cut the cream cheese into small pieces and add to the food processor. Pulse to cut the cream cheese into very tiny pieces. The texture should be sandy with very tiny lumps throughout.
	Add the butter to the food processor. Pulse until the butter is cut into pea-sized pieces, 30 to 45 seconds.
3 to 4 tablespoons heavy whipping cream	Remove the top of the food processor and sprinkle on 3 tablespoons of the cream. Replace the top and pulse for 10 seconds. Squeeze a small amount of the dough in your hand. If it holds together, don't add any more water. If the dough is still very crumbly, add another tablespoon of cream, pulse to blend, then check the dough again. It won't hold together unless you squeeze it, but that's the texture you want.
	Divide the dough in two equal pieces and shape each piece into a flat disk. Wrap the disks tightly in a double layer of plastic wrap. Chill in the refrigerator until firm before using, at least 2 hours. Chilling the dough relaxes the gluten in the flour so it won't be too elastic and will roll out easily. It also firms up the butter in the dough so it will need less flour when rolled out. If the dough is too firm it will splinter and break when rolled out. Let it stand at room temperature for 10 to 15 minutes before rolling to become more pliable.

On a smooth, flat surface, roll out one of the disks of pie dough between sheets of lightly floured waxed or parchment paper to a large circle about 12 inches in diameter. To tell if the dough will fit the pie pan, invert the pan over the dough. If there are 2 to 3 inches of dough that protrude beyond the sides of the pan, it will fit.

Carefully peel the paper off the top of the dough. Brush excess flour off the dough, then loosely roll the pastry dough around the rolling pin without the bottom piece of paper. Place the pie pan directly underneath the rolling pin and carefully unroll the pastry dough into the pan. Or loosely fold the dough in half. Carefully place it in half of the pie pan and gently unfold the dough. Gently lift up the sides and ease the pie dough into the bottom and sides of the pie pan. Trim off the excess pie dough at the top of the pan and crimp the sides (see page 40).

Transfer the pie pan to a baking sheet and chill in the freezer for 15 to 20 minutes. This helps prevent the pie dough from shrinking as it bakes and sets the butter in the dough to ensure flakiness.

overnight in the refrigerator before using. The pie dough can also be fitted into the pie pan and kept tightly covered in the refrigerator or frozen, wrapped and labeled as above.

The assembled unbaked pie can be frozen for up to 3 months. To freeze the pie, cover it snugly in several layers of plastic wrap and place it in a freezer bag. Use a large piece of masking tape and an indelible marker to label and date the contents. Do not defrost the pie to bake, but extend the baking time by 5 to 10 minutes.

Troubleshooting

Don't overprocess the pie dough or it will be tough and not flaky.

Making a Change

To make Classic Apple Pie, replace the quinces with 1 pound of apples.

To make Quince Pie, replace the apples with 3 poached quinces.

Adding Style

Serve slices of the pie with vanilla ice cream or whipped cream.

1½ pounds Granny Smith apples (4 to 5 medium)

Use a vegetable peeler or a knife to peel the apples. Cut each apple in half, then in half again. Use a small sharp knife to remove the core of each quarter and slice them lengthwise into ½-inch-thick slices. Place the apple slices in a large mixing bowl.

¼ cup firmly packed light brown sugar
2 teaspoons freshly squeezed lemon juice
¼ teaspoon freshly grated nutmeg
¼ teaspoon ground cinnamon
⅛ teaspoon salt

Sprinkle the brown sugar, lemon juice, nutmeg, cinnamon, and salt over the apples. Using a rubber spatula, gently toss and stir the apples to evenly distribute the dry ingredients and coat the apples completely.

Dry the poached quinces on paper towels and slice each quarter into ½-inch-thick slices. Add the quince slices to the apples in the bowl and toss together gently.

Transfer the mixture to the pie shell.

Adjust an oven rack to the lower third and preheat the oven to 425°F.

Roll out the remaining disk of pie dough on a smooth, flat surface between sheets of lightly floured waxed or parchment paper to a large circle about 12 inches in diameter. Peel off the top piece of paper. Brush excess flour off the dough, then loosely roll the pastry dough around the rolling pin without the bottom piece of paper. Place the pie pan directly underneath the rolling pin and carefully unroll the pastry dough onto the filling. Or loosely fold the dough in half. Carefully place it on half of the filling and gently unfold the dough. Trim off the edges of both the top and the bottom pie shell evenly, leaving a ¾-inch overhang.

1 extra-large egg yolk, at room temperature
1 tablespoon heavy whipping cream

1 tablespoon granulated sugar

Use a fork to lightly beat the egg yolk and cream together in a small bowl. Use a pastry brush to brush the edges of the bottom pastry shell with the mixture to help the two layers of pastry dough stick together. Fold the edges of the top crust over the bottom crust and press them to seal together. Crimp or flute the edges (see page 40). Brush the top of the pie with the egg mixture and sprinkle sugar over the top of the dough. Use a small sharp knife to cut several slits in the top of the pie to allow steam to escape as it bakes.

Bake the pie for 10 minutes, then lower the oven temperature to 350°F. Bake for another 40 to 45 minutes, until the crust is light golden and the filling is thickly bubbling inside.

Remove the pie from the oven and cool on a rack. Serve warm or at room temperature.

Quince Frangipane Tart

QUINCE AND ALMOND are a scrumptious flavor combination. Each flavor complements the other very well in this yummy tart. Quinces are first poached in vanilla sugar syrup to soften them, then they are baked into a classic frangipane filling in an almond pastry shell. After baking, the top of the warm tart is brushed with apricot glaze to keep the quinces moist and to make them shine. **Makes one 8-inch square tart, 9 servings**

PASTRY DOUGH

1 cup all-purpose flour
½ cup sliced or slivered almonds
2 teaspoons granulated sugar
¼ teaspoon salt

In the work bowl of a food processor fitted with the steel blade, combine the flour, almonds, sugar, and salt. Pulse until the almonds are very finely ground, about 1 minute.

4 ounces (8 tablespoons, 1 stick) unsalted butter, chilled

Cut the butter into small pieces and add. Pulse until the butter is cut into very tiny pieces, about 30 seconds. The texture should be sandy with very tiny lumps throughout.

2 teaspoons freshly squeezed lemon juice
2 to 3 tablespoons ice water

In a small bowl, combine the lemon juice and 2 tablespoons of water. With the food processor running, pour this mixture through the feed tube. Process until the dough wraps itself around the blade, 30 seconds to 1 minute. If the dough seems dry, add the remaining tablespoon of water and process until the dough comes together.

Turn the pastry dough onto a large piece of plastic wrap. Shape into a flat disk and wrap tightly in a double layer of plastic wrap. Chill in the refrigerator until firm before using, about 2 hours. Chilling the dough relaxes the gluten in the flour so it won't be too elastic and will roll out easily. It also firms up the butter in the dough so it will need less flour when rolled out. If the dough is too firm it will splinter and break when rolled out. Let it stand at room

Essential Gear

- Food processor
- Rolling pin
- 8-inch square, fluted-edge tart pan with removable bottom
- Baking sheet
- Cooling rack
- 4-quart heavy-bottomed saucepan
- Medium-size fine-mesh strainer
- Goose-feather pastry brush

Keeping
The tart can last for up to 3 days in the refrigerator. Place a piece of waxed paper over the top of the tart, then tightly cover it with aluminum foil.

Streamlining
The pastry dough can be made in advance and kept in the refrigerator, tightly wrapped in a double layer of plastic wrap, for up to 4 days. To freeze for up to 3 months, wrap the dough snugly in several layers of plastic wrap and place it in a freezer bag. Use a large piece of masking tape and

temperature for 10 to 15 minutes before rolling to become more pliable.

POACHED QUINCES

3 cups water
1½ cups sugar
1 vanilla bean, split down
  the center
Finely grated zest of 1 large
  lemon

Combine the sugar and water in the saucepan. Bring to a boil over medium-high heat. Add the vanilla bean and lemon zest. Reduce the heat to low.

1 pound ripe quinces
  (3 medium or 2 large)

Use a vegetable peeler to peel the quinces. Use a sharp chef's knife to cut the quinces into quarters and remove the core and seeds. Place the quince quarters in the sugar syrup and cook, simmering, until the quinces are soft and turn a light rose color, 1½ to 2 hours.

Remove the pan from the heat and transfer the quinces and their cooking liquid to a large bowl. Cover with plastic wrap and cool in their liquid. The quinces can be kept in a tightly covered bowl or container in their cooking liquid, in the refrigerator for up to 2 weeks.

Center a rack in the oven and preheat it to 375°F.

On a smooth, flat surface, roll out the pastry dough between sheets of lightly floured waxed or parchment paper to a large square about 10 inches wide. Carefully peel the paper off the top of the dough. Brush excess flour off the dough, then loosely roll the pastry dough around the rolling pin without the bottom piece of paper. Place the tart pan directly underneath the rolling pin and carefully unroll the pastry dough onto it.

Gently lift up the sides and ease the pastry dough into the bottom and sides of the tart pan, pushing it lightly into the corners and the fluted edges. Trim off the excess pastry dough at the top of the pan by running the rolling pin over the top. Or use your fingers to press against the top of the pan to remove the excess pastry dough.

Place the tart pan on a baking sheet and chill while preparing the filling.

FRANGIPANE FILLING

1 cup sliced almonds
½ cup granulated sugar

Place the almonds and sugar in the work bowl of a food processor fitted with the steel blade. Pulse until the almonds are very finely ground, about 1 minute.

an indelible marker to label and date the contents. If frozen, defrost overnight in the refrigerator before using. The tart dough can also be fitted into the tart pan and kept tightly covered in the refrigerator or frozen, wrapped and labeled as above.

The frangipane filling can be made in advance and kept in a tightly covered plastic container in the refrigerator up to 4 days before using.

The apricot glaze can be made in advance and kept in a tightly covered plastic container in the refrigerator up to 1 month before using. Warm it in a small saucepan over medium heat or in a microwave oven on medium power before using.

1 extra-large egg, at room temperature	Add the egg, vanilla, and almond extract, and pulse several times to blend together well.
1/2 teaspoon pure vanilla extract	
1/2 teaspoon almond extract	
2 1/2 ounces (5 tablespoons) unsalted butter, softened	Cut the butter into small pieces and add to the mixture. Pulse several times to blend.
2 tablespoons all-purpose flour	Add the flour and pulse until the mixture is smooth, about 15 seconds. Transfer the mixture to the pastry shell and spread it out evenly with a rubber spatula.

ASSEMBLY

Cut each quince quarter into 1/2-inch-thick slices, leaving them attached at the top. Place a quince quarter on top of the frangipane filling, in a corner of the tart pan, fanning out the quince as you press it down lightly into the frangipane. Repeat with the remaining quince quarters, arranging them to fill the top of the tart.

Bake the tart for 40 to 45 minutes, until the filling is puffed and light golden.

Remove the tart from the oven and place on a cooling rack.

APRICOT GLAZE

1/4 cup apricot preserves	Combine the apricot preserves and liquid in a small saucepan. Bring to a boil over medium heat. Remove the pan from the heat and strain the glaze into a small bowl, pushing through as much of the pulp as possible.
1 tablespoon amaretto, cognac, or water	

Use a goose-feather pastry brush to lightly brush the top of the tart with the glaze. Don't apply a thick glaze, which looks unappetizing. The purpose of the glaze is to keep the quinces from drying out and to make the top of the tart glisten.

Remove the sides of the tart pan (see page 42) before serving. Cut the tart into squares and serve warm or at room temperature.

Quince Galette

THIS IS A FREE-form, rustic tart made with pie dough filled with sautéed quinces. It's an easy dessert to make and one of my favorite ways to use quinces. This is perfect for an early fall dessert, when quinces first come into season. Try serving it with vanilla ice cream or whipped cream. **Makes one 9-inch galette, 8 to 10 servings**

PASTRY DOUGH

1½ cups all-purpose flour
2 teaspoons granulated
  sugar
¼ teaspoon salt

In the work bowl of a food processor fitted with the steel blade, combine the flour, sugar, and salt. Pulse briefly to blend.

4 ounces (8 tablespoons,
  1 stick) unsalted butter,
  softened

Cut the butter into small pieces and add. Pulse until the butter is cut into very tiny pieces, about 30 seconds. The texture should be sandy with very tiny lumps throughout.

Zest of 1 large lemon
2 teaspoons freshly
  squeezed lemon juice
2 to 3 tablespoons ice water

Add the lemon zest to the mixture. In a small bowl, combine the lemon juice and 2 tablespoons of water. With the food processor running, pour this mixture through the feed tube. Process until the dough begins to hold together, 30 seconds to 1 minute. Turn off the food processor, remove the top, and feel the dough. If it holds together, it is done. If it is still crumbly, add the remaining tablespoon of ice water and process briefly, then check again.

Turn the pastry dough onto a large piece of plastic wrap. Shape into a flat disk and wrap tightly in a double layer of plastic wrap. Chill in the refrigerator until firm before using, about 2 hours. Chilling the dough relaxes the gluten in the flour so it won't be too elastic and will roll out easily. It also firms up the butter in the dough so it will need less flour when rolled out. If the dough is too firm it will splinter and break when rolled out. Let it stand at room temperature for 10 to 15 minutes before rolling to become more pliable.

QUINCE FILLING

2½ pounds ripe quinces
  (7 medium or 5 large)

Using a vegetable peeler, peel the quinces. Using a sharp chef's knife, cut the quinces into thick chunks, removing the core and seeds as you cut. Transfer the chunks to a bowl.

Essential Gear

- Food processor
- Vegetable peeler
- Chef's knife
- Large sauté pan
- Non-stick spatula or wooden spoon
- Baking sheet
- Parchment paper
- Rolling pin
- 1-inch natural-bristle pastry brush or a spoon
- Cooling rack

Keeping

Although the galette is best eaten the day it's made, it can last for up to 2 days. Store the galette tightly covered with aluminum foil at room temperature.

Making a Change

Replace half of the quinces with apples.

Adding Style

Serve slices of the galette with vanilla ice cream or lightly sweetened whipped cream.

4 ounces (8 tablespoons, 1 stick) unsalted butter, cut into small pieces.
½ cup granulated sugar
½ teaspoon ground cinnamon

Melt the butter in a large sauté pan over medium heat. Add the quince chunks. Sprinkle on the sugar and cinnamon and stir the quinces until they are coated. Cook the quinces over medium heat, stirring often, until they are soft, about 25 minutes.

Remove the pan from the heat and let the quinces cool for 15 minutes.

ASSEMBLY

Center a rack in the oven and preheat it to 375°F. Line the baking sheet with parchment paper.

On a smooth, flat surface, roll out the pastry dough between sheets of lightly floured waxed or parchment paper to a large circle 11 to 12 inches in diameter. Carefully peel the paper off the top of the dough. Brush excess flour off the dough, then loosely roll the pastry dough around the rolling pin without the bottom piece of paper. Place the lined baking sheet directly underneath the rolling pin and carefully unroll the pastry dough onto the baking sheet

Use a slotted spoon to remove the quinces from their cooking liquid. Mound them in the center of the dough circle, leaving a 2½- to 3-inch border all around.

Use a spoon to sprinkle the quinces with 2 to 3 tablespoons of their cooking liquid.

Fold the border up so that it partially covers the quinces. It will naturally form pleats as it is folded.

1 tablespoon heavy whipping cream
2 teaspoons granulated sugar

Brush the dough border with the cream, being careful that it doesn't run down the sides and under the galette. If it does, wipe it up because it can cause the bottom of the galette to burn. Gently lift up the folds of the dough and brush under those areas with cream, then replace the folds. Evenly sprinkle the sugar over the dough border.

Bake the galette for 35 to 40 minutes, until light golden. Remove the pan from the oven and transfer to a rack to cool.

Cut the galette into pie-shaped wedges to serve.

CITRUS FRUIT

WHO DOESN'T like the flavor of oranges—and lemons or limes for that matter? No one I know. What makes citrus fruit so perfect to use is that it imparts a mildly sweet flavor that is just a little tart, but never overpowering. To me, citrus has what I call a "fresh flavor," and I truly love the aroma. If I'm not sure what to bake when I have people over, citrus is one of my first choices, so I always keep a good supply of citrus fruit on hand. The lemon, lime, and orange recipes in this chapter are guaranteed to add some "zest" to your baked desserts.

You can find lemons, limes, and oranges year-round. The primary season for oranges is during the cooler months of the year—late fall and winter. Lemons and limes are more readily available during late spring and summer. July and August are the best times to find Key limes, my favorite because they are so juicy, and they have a complex sweet-tart flavor and an incredible aroma. Citrus fruit is available in most supermarkets, produce stores, and farmer's markets.

TIPS AND TECHNIQUES

When selecting lemons, limes, and oranges, make sure they have good consistent color without bruises or soft spots. Bring them up to your nose and smell them for their unique scent. Overripe citrus fruit takes on a wrinkled look and the skins become dry. Because citrus fruit is ripe when picked, it can be used straight out of the market. But if you don't need to use the fruit right away, they keep at room temperature up to two weeks. In any of the recipes that call for Key limes, Meyer lemons, and blood oranges, you can use other limes, lemons, and oranges.

To extract the most juice from lemons and limes, roll them on a flat surface while pressing down with your hand. Lemons and limes release more juice when they are at room temperature than when they are cold. Squeeze the juice from the fruit by hand, with a juicer, or with a citrus reamer. Citrus juice can be frozen for up to one year. Freeze it in small containers or in ice cube trays. Once they're frozen, transfer the cubes to a container. Be sure to label and date the containers so you know how long they've been there. The juice of navel oranges turns bitter if left to stand for any amount of time, so juice those as needed.

Both the outer rind, called the zest, and the juice of citrus fruit are used in baking. Always zest citrus fruit right before the zest is to be used. To remove the zest, use a fine grater or a zester, a tool developed for this purpose. Re-move only the colored part, not the white pith underneath, which is bitter. Be sure to scrub the skins with soap and water before zesting. Note that Key limes are not good for zesting because they have a thin, fine-grained skin.

With any of the recipes in this chapter, you can always decorate them with either segments of the fruit or the zest. This also shows off the vibrant colors of these fruits.

Blood Orange and Brown Sugar Chiffon Cake

T HIS CHIFFON CAKE is flavored with blood oranges and brown sugar, which give the cake an orange-tan color and deep, rich flavor. Dust the cake lightly on top with confectioners' sugar for decoration or serve each slice with a scoop of whipped cream and a few segments of blood orange for a wonderful color contrast. I love the lightness of this cake and enjoy serving it anytime. **Makes one 10-inch round cake, 12 to 14 servings**

Center a rack in the oven and preheat it to 325°F.

Cut a round of parchment paper to fit the bottom of the tube pan and cut out a hole in the middle to fit the center tube of the pan. This cake is baked in an ungreased pan because greasing the pan would keep the batter from rising and gripping the sides of the pan as the cake bakes.

2 medium blood oranges

Over a piece of waxed or parchment paper, finely grate the zest from the oranges. Cut the oranges in half and squeeze out the juice; strain it to remove any seeds.

Place the juice in a small saucepan. Bring to a boil over medium heat, swirling the pan a couple of times, and cook the juice until it is reduced by half, to about 2 tablespoons. The juice will become thicker as it cooks down. Watch it carefully as it cooks so it doesn't cook down completely. Pour the juice into a small bowl

½ cup water
½ cup unflavored vegetable oil (canola or safflower)
1 teaspoon pure vanilla extract

In a 2-cup liquid measure, combine the water, vegetable oil, vanilla, orange zest, and the reduced orange juice.

2¼ cups cake flour
1 tablespoon baking powder
⅔ cup firmly packed light brown sugar
½ cup superfine sugar
¼ teaspoon salt

Sift together the cake flour and baking powder into a large mixing bowl. Add the light brown sugar, superfine sugar, and salt and stir together.

6 extra-large eggs yolks, at room temperature

Make a well in the center of the mixture by pushing the dry ingredients toward the sides of the bowl. Add the water mixture and the egg yolks. Using a rubber spatula or a whisk, stir together until thoroughly combined.

Essential Gear

- Electric stand mixer with wire whip attachment, or large mixing bowl and hand-held mixer
- 10 × 4-inch tube pan with removable bottom
- Rubber spatula
- Cooling rack
- Thin-bladed knife
- Sugar dredger or fine-mesh strainer
- Parchment paper
- Small saucepan

Keeping

Store the cake tightly wrapped in plastic for up to 3 days at room temperature. To freeze for up to 4 months, tightly wrap the cake in several layers of plastic wrap and aluminum foil. Use a large piece of masking tape and an indelible marker to label and date the contents. If frozen, defrost overnight in the refrigerator and bring to room temperature before serving.

Making a Change

Add 1½ cups coarsely chopped nuts to the dry ingredients.

Add 1½ cups finely chopped dried apricots or dried peaches to the dry ingredients.

6 extra-large egg whites, at room temperature **1/2 teaspoon cream of tartar**	Place the egg whites in the grease-free bowl of an electric stand mixer or a large grease-free mixing bowl. Using the wire whip attachment or a hand-held mixer, whip the egg whites on medium speed until they are frothy. Add the cream of tartar and continue to whip.
1/2 cup firmly packed light brown sugar	Slowly sprinkle on the brown sugar and continue whipping until the egg whites hold glossy and firm, but not stiff, peaks, about 5 minutes.
	Fold the egg whites into the cake batter in 3 or 4 stages, blending well after each addition.

Transfer the mixture to the tube pan. Use the rubber spatula to smooth and even the top. Bake for 1 hour, until a cake tester inserted in the center of the cake comes out clean.

Remove the pan from the oven and invert it over a cooling rack onto its feet or over a funnel or a thin-necked bottle. Let the cake hang to cool completely. Don't set the pan on a cooling rack on its base. This will cause the cake to collapse onto itself.

Don't shake the cake out of the pan before it is cool. Once it is cool, use a thin-bladed knife or flexible-blade spatula to run around the outer edge and the inside tube to help release the cake from the pan. Invert the cake onto a rack, then re-invert onto a serving plate.

GARNISH

1 tablespoon confectioners' sugar	Dust the top of the cake lightly with confectioners' sugar.
1 cup heavy whipping cream **2 tablespoons light brown sugar**	Place the cream in the bowl of an electric stand mixer or in a large mixing bowl. Use the wire whip attachment or a hand-held mixer to whip the cream until it is frothy. Gradually sprinkle on the brown sugar and continue to whip until the cream holds soft peaks.
3 to 4 medium blood oranges	Over a piece of waxed or parchment paper or a bowl, finely grate the zest of the oranges. Separate the orange segments.
	Serve each slice of cake with a scoop of whipped cream topped with freshly grated blood orange zest and 4 to 5 segments of a blood orange.

Individual Blood Orange Crème Caramels

BLOOD ORANGES give this classic creamy custard a tart, yet sweet, citrus flavor. After the custard is baked and turned out of the molds, it is decorated with blood orange zest and segments of the oranges, which add their beautiful orange-red color. **Makes eight ¹/₂-cup servings**

Center a rack in the oven and preheat it to 350°F. Place the custard cups in the baking dish or roasting pan.

CARAMEL

¹/₂ cup granulated sugar
¹/₄ cup water
¹/₈ teaspoon cream of tartar

Combine the sugar, water, and cream of tartar in the 1-quart saucepan over medium-high heat. Bring the mixture to a boil and stir to dissolve the sugar. Cook the mixture without stirring until it turns a rich golden brown, about 8 minutes.

2 tablespoons water

Remove the pan from the heat and stir in the water. Be careful because the mixture may bubble and foam up. Return the pan to the heat and stir with a wooden spoon or a heat-resistant spatula to dissolve any lumps.

Divide the caramel evenly among the custard cups. Tilt and rotate each cup so the caramel completely covers the bottom.

BLOOD ORANGE CUSTARD

2 medium blood oranges

Over a piece of waxed or parchment paper or a bowl, finely grate the zest from the oranges. Cut the oranges in half, squeeze out the juice; strain it to remove any seeds, and place it in a small saucepan. Bring to a boil over medium heat, swirling the pan a couple of times, and cook the juice until it is reduced by half, to about 2 tablespoons. The juice will become thicker as it cooks down. Watch it carefully as it cooks so it doesn't cook down completely. Pour the juice into a small bowl and let it stand while preparing the custard.

2¹/₂ cups milk

Place the milk in the 2-quart saucepan. Warm it over medium heat until tiny bubbles become visible at the edges. Add the orange zest. Remove the pan from the heat, cover it, and let the milk infuse.

3 extra-large eggs, at room
  temperature
3 extra-large egg yolks, at
  room temperature

Place the eggs and egg yolks in the bowl of an electric stand mixer or in a large mixing bowl. Use the wire whip attachment or a hand-held mixer to whisk together until they are frothy.

Essential Gear

- Eight ¹/₂-cup custard cups or shallow bowls
- 1-quart heavy-bottomed saucepan
- Wooden spoon or heat-resistant spatula
- 2-quart heavy-bottomed saucepan
- Electric stand mixer with wire whip attachment, or a large mixing bowl and hand-held mixer
- Large liquid measuring cup (2- or 4-cup capacity)
- 3-quart baking dish or roasting pan
- Cooling rack
- Microplane grater or citrus zester

Keeping

Store the baked custard in the custard cups, tightly covered with a double layer of plastic wrap, in the refrigerator for up to 3 days.

Adding Style

Sprinkle a few dried lavender flowers over the top of each custard and around each plate.

½ **cup granulated sugar**	With the mixer on medium speed, slowly sprinkle on the sugar.
	In a steady stream, pour in the warm milk and mix thoroughly.
	Add the reduced orange juice and mix completely.
	Pour the custard into a large measuring cup, then divide it evenly among the custard cups. Place the custard cups in the baking dish.
1 quart boiling water	Place the baking dish or roasting pan on the oven rack. Carefully pour the water into the baking dish until it reaches halfway up the sides of the cups or bowls.
	Reduce the oven temperature to 325°F.
	Bake the custards for 40 minutes, until a toothpick or cake tester inserted in the center comes out clean or with only a tiny amount of custard clinging to it and the centers of the custards jiggle slightly. Remove the roasting pan from the oven and transfer the custard cups to a rack to cool.
	To unmold the custards, run a thin-bladed knife around the edges of the custard cups. Place a serving plate over the top of each custard cup and invert the custard onto the plate.
	Serve the custards immediately or refrigerate until ready to serve.

GARNISH

2 medium blood oranges	Over a piece of waxed or parchment paper or a bowl, finely grate the zest of the oranges. Separate the orange segments.
	Decorate each custard with a sprinkling of blood orange zest on top and arrange a few of the orange segments around the plate.

Double Lemon Layer Cake

LEMON FLAVORS both the cake layers and the filling in this scrumptious layer cake—a real treat for lemon lovers. Lemon curd, a soft, spreadable cooked cream, is blended with whipped cream for the filling. Because it needs time to cool and chill before it's used, lemon curd can be made up to one month in advance. Although there are several steps involved in making this cake, many can be done in advance, making it easy to fit into your schedule. It's

Essential Gear
- Fine grater or zester
- Double boiler
- Medium-size fine-mesh strainer
- Heat-resistant spatula or wooden spoon

best to assemble the cake no more than four hours before serving because there is whipped cream in the filling, which starts to lose its body if it stands too long. **Makes one 9-inch round cake, 12 to 14 servings**

LEMON CURD

2 large lemons	Use a fine grater to remove the outer rind of the lemons. Take care not to grate the inner white pith, which is very bitter. Or use a zester to remove the lemon zest and chop it very finely with a chef's knife.
	Cut the lemons in half, squeeze out the juice, and strain it to remove any seeds.
5 extra-large egg yolks, at room temperature ½ cup granulated sugar	Place the egg yolks and sugar in the top pan of a double boiler over simmering water. Stir together to dissolve the sugar, about 3 minutes.
2 ounces (4 tablespoons, ½ stick) unsalted butter, melted	Add the lemon zest, lemon juice, and butter. Stir the mixture constantly with a heat-resistant spatula or wooden spoon until it thickens, about 12 minutes.
	A good test to see if the mixture is at the right consistency is to dip the spatula or spoon into it. Lift the spatula or spoon from the mixture and hold it with the width of the spatula blade or spoon parallel to the top of the pan. With your finger, draw a parallel line across the middle of the spatula or spoon. If the mixture does not run over the line, it's thick enough. The mixture will thicken more as it cools and chills.
	Remove the top pan of the double boiler and wipe the bottom and sides dry.
	Transfer the lemon curd to a bowl or plastic container. Cover tightly with plastic wrap or the container lid. Cool to room temperature, then place in the refrigerator until thoroughly chilled.

CAKE

	Center a rack in the oven and preheat it to 350°F.
1 tablespoon unsalted butter, softened	Using a paper towel or your fingertips, generously butter the inside of the cake pans, coating them thoroughly.
1 tablespoon all-purpose flour	Dust the inside of each pan with some of the flour. Shake and tilt the pans to evenly distribute the flour, then turn the pans over and shake out the excess over the sink.

- Two 9 × 2-inch round cake pans
- Scissors
- Parchment paper
- Two rubber spatulas
- Electric stand mixer with flat beater attachment and wire whip attachment, or large mixing bowl and hand-held mixer
- Two cooling racks
- 10-inch flexible-blade icing spatula
- 12-inch pastry bag and large pastry tube with star opening

Keeping

Store the cake loosely covered with aluminum foil in the refrigerator for up to 2 days. Place several toothpicks in the top outer edges of the cake to hold the foil away from it so it won't mar the icing.

Streamlining

Bake the cake layers up to 2 days before assembling the cake and keep tightly covered with a double layer of plastic wrap at room temperature. To freeze the layers up to 3 months, wrap them snugly in several layers of plastic wrap and place them in freezer bags. Use a large piece of masking tape and an indelible marker to label and date the contents. If frozen, defrost the layers overnight in the refrigerator.

Make the lemon curd up to 1 month in advance. Store it

Cut a round of parchment paper to fit the bottom of each pan. Butter each parchment paper round and place in each pan, butter-side up.

6 ounces (12 tablespoons, 1½ sticks) unsalted butter, softened	Place the butter in the bowl of an electric stand mixer or in a large mixing bowl. Use the flat beater attachment or a hand-held mixer to beat the butter on medium speed until it's fluffy, about 2 minutes.
1¾ cups granulated sugar	Add the sugar to the butter and cream together well. Stop occasionally and scrape down the bottom and sides of the bowl with a rubber spatula.
2 extra-large eggs, at room temperature	One at a time, add the eggs to the butter mixture, stopping to scrape down the bottom and sides of the bowl after each addition. At first the mixture may look curdled as the eggs are added, but as you stop and scrape down the bowl, the mixture will smooth out.
1 teaspoon pure vanilla extract **Finely grated or minced zest of 2 large lemons**	Add the vanilla and lemon zest to the mixture and blend together well.
2¾ cups cake flour **2 teaspoons baking powder** **¼ teaspoon baking soda** **¼ teaspoon salt**	Over a large piece of waxed or parchment paper or a bowl, sift together the flour, baking powder, and baking soda. Add the salt and toss to blend well.
1¼ cups buttermilk	With the mixer on low speed, add the dry ingredients in 3 stages, alternating with the buttermilk. Blend well after each addition and stop often to scrape down the bottom and sides of the bowl with a rubber spatula to ensure even mixing.

Divide the batter evenly between the two cake pans. Smooth the top of each pan with a rubber spatula.

Bake the layers for 30 minutes, until a cake tester inserted in the center comes out with no crumbs clinging to it.

Remove the cake pans from the oven and cool completely on racks. Invert the pans to remove the layers, then peel the parchment paper off the back of each layer. Re-invert the layers onto plates or cardboard cake circles.

FILLING AND FROSTING

Whisk the lemon curd until smooth and creamy, about 1 minute.

in a tightly covered plastic container in the refrigerator.

Making a Change
Replace the sliced almonds with finely chopped walnuts or ground, toasted hazelnuts.

Replace the apricot preserves with mango or passion fruit preserves or orange marmalade.

Recovering from a Mishap
If one of the cake layers breaks during assembly, patch it together with some of the filling and frosting.

2 cups heavy whipping cream	Place the cream in the chilled bowl of an electric stand mixer or a large mixing bowl. Use the wire whip attachment or a hand-held mixer to whip the cream on medium speed until frothy.
3 tablespoons confectioners' sugar, sifted	Add the confectioners' sugar and whip on medium-high speed until the cream holds soft peaks.
	Stir about ½ cup of the whipped cream into the lemon curd and blend together well. Add this mixture to the bowl of whipped cream and fold together until completely incorporated.

ASSEMBLY

⅓ cup apricot preserves	Using a serrated knife, cut each cake layer in half horizontally (see page 34). Place one cake layer on a serving plate. Use the flexible-blade spatula to spread the layer evenly with the apricot preserves.
	Place strips of waxed paper around the bottom edges of the cake to protect the plate while assembling the cake. With a clean flexible-blade spatula, evenly spread some of the lemon whipped cream filling over the cake layer.
	Position the second cake layer evenly over the filling and use the flexible-blade spatula to spread some of the filling over the layer. Repeat with the remaining two cake layers and filling.
	Reserve ½ cup of the filling for decoration and spread the remaining filling over the sides and top of the cake.
1 cup sliced almonds, lightly toasted	Press the toasted sliced almonds onto the sides of the cake just up to, but not over, the top edge.
	Fit the pastry bag with the star tube. Pipe a border of shells around the top outer edge of the cake (see page 44).
	Let the cake chill for at least 2 hours before serving so it has time to set and will be easier to cut.

Meyer Lemon Soufflés

MEYER LEMONS give these individual soufflés their delectable, slightly tart flavor. Individual soufflés are very impressive, but they are fragile and must be eaten as soon as they come out of the oven so they don't collapse. Whipped egg whites in the batter are what allow the soufflés to rise as they bake. **Makes 6 servings**

Position a rack in the lower third of the oven and preheat it to 400°F.

1 tablespoon unsalted butter, softened
1 tablespoon granulated sugar

Use a paper towel or your fingertips to butter the inside of the soufflé ramekins or bowls, then sprinkle the inside of each with sugar. Tilt the dishes so the sugar sticks to the butter. Set aside while preparing the soufflé batter.

½ cup milk

Place the milk in the saucepan and bring to a boil over medium-high heat.

3 extra-large egg yolks, at room temperature
¼ cup granulated sugar
2 tablespoons all-purpose flour

Place the egg yolks in a medium mixing bowl. Add the sugar and whisk or stir together until thoroughly blended. Then add the flour and whisk or stir to blend well.

Add the hot milk to the egg yolk mixture and whisk constantly until thoroughly combined to temper the eggs and keep them from cooking. Transfer this mixture to the saucepan and stir constantly over medium heat until the mixture thickens and begins to boil around the edges. Remove the pan from the heat and set aside briefly.

3 medium Meyer lemons

Finely grate the zest of the lemons, taking care not to grate the white pith under the zest, which is bitter. Cut the lemons in half and squeeze out their juice, straining it to remove any seeds. There should be about ⅓ cup of juice. Add the zest and the juice to the soufflé mixture and stir together until thoroughly blended.

4 extra-large egg whites, at room temperature
½ teaspoon cream of tartar
1 tablespoon granulated sugar

Place the egg whites in the grease-free bowl of an electric stand mixer or in a large grease-free mixing bowl. Using the wire whip attachment or a hand-held mixer, whip the egg whites on medium-high speed until they are frothy. Add the cream of tartar and continue to whip. When soft peaks form, gradually sprinkle on the sugar and continue to whip until the egg whites hold glossy and firm, but not stiff, peaks.

Essential Gear

- Six 1-cup soufflé ramekins or straight-sided custard cups or bowls
- 2-quart heavy-bottomed saucepan
- Microplane grater or citrus zester
- Whisk or heat-resistant spatula
- Electric stand mixer with wire whip attachment or large mixing bowl and hand-held mixer
- Rubber spatula

Keeping

Store the raspberry sauce in a tightly covered plastic container in the refrigerator up to 1 week. To freeze up to 3 months, wrap the container tightly in several layers of plastic wrap and place in a freezer bag. Defrost overnight in the refrigerator before using.

Making a Change

Use regular lemons in place of Meyer lemons.

Use oranges in place of Meyer lemons and add ¼ cup Grand Marnier or other orange liqueur in place of the lemon juice.

Gently fold the whipped egg whites into the yolk mixture in 4 stages, blending thoroughly. Be careful not to mix so vigorously that you deflate the air beaten into the egg whites, which is what makes the soufflés rise as they bake.

Divide the soufflé mixture evenly among the prepared ramekins or bowls. Use a rubber spatula to smooth and even the tops. Place the ramekins or bowls on a baking sheet. Bake for 10 to 12 minutes, until the soufflés are puffed over the top of the dishes and look set, and the center wiggles only a little. You can also test for doneness with a cake tester inserted into the center of a soufflé. It should come out moist, but not runny.

2 tablespoons confectioners' sugar

Remove the baking sheet from the oven, sprinkle the top of each soufflé with confectioners' sugar, and serve immediately.

RASPBERRY SAUCE

2 cups fresh or frozen raspberries, defrosted

Place the raspberries in the work bowl of a food processor fitted with the steel blade or in a blender. Pulse until the berries are pureed into liquid, about 1 minute.

Using a rubber spatula or wooden spoon and a fine-mesh strainer, strain the raspberry puree into a medium mixing bowl. Push through the strainer as much of the liquid as possible, without the seeds.

3 tablespoons superfine sugar
2 teaspoons freshly squeezed lemon juice
2 tablespoons framboise, Chambord, kirsch, or Grand Marnier

Add the sugar, lemon juice, and liqueur to the raspberry puree and blend together thoroughly.

Serve the sauce in a separate bowl or pour a tablespoon of sauce over the top of each soufflé right before serving.

Lemon-Cornmeal Muffins

L EMON PROVIDES its tart, bright flavor and cornmeal adds chewy texture to these muffins. They're not too sweet and are yummy anytime of day—for breakfast, at afternoon tea, as a snack, or for dessert. Although they are great on their own, I like them best warm, served with jam or honey. **Makes 12 muffins**

Essential Gear
- 12-cavity 3-inch muffin pan
- 3-inch pleated paper muffin cups
- Electric stand mixer and flat beater, or hand-held

	Center a rack in the oven and preheat it to 325°F. Line each cavity of the muffin pan with a paper muffin cup.	mixer and large mixing bowl

Center a rack in the oven and preheat it to 325°F. Line each cavity of the muffin pan with a paper muffin cup.

- mixer and large mixing bowl
- Rubber spatula or wooden spoon
- Microplane grater or citrus zester
- Cooling rack

6 ounces (12 tablespoons, 1½ sticks) unsalted butter, softened

Place the butter in the bowl of an electric stand mixer or in a large mixing bowl. Use the flat beater attachment or hand-held mixer to beat the butter on medium speed until it's fluffy, about 2 minutes.

1½ cups granulated sugar

Add the sugar to the butter and cream together well. Stop occasionally and scrape down the sides and bottom of the bowl with a rubber spatula.

Keeping

Store the muffins in an airtight plastic container between layers of waxed paper at room temperature for up to 3 days. To freeze for up to 2 months, wrap the container tightly in several layers of plastic wrap and aluminum foil. Use a large piece of masking tape and an indelible marker to label and date the contents. If frozen, defrost overnight in the refrigerator and bring to room temperature before serving.

3 extra-large eggs, at room temperature

One at a time, add the eggs to the butter mixture, stopping to scrape down the bottom and sides of the bowl after each addition. At first the mixture may look curdled as the eggs are added, but as you stop and scrape down the bowl, the mixture will smooth out.

Finely grated zest of 2 large lemons

Add the lemon zest to the butter mixture and blend together well.

**1¾ cups all-purpose flour
2¼ teaspoons baking powder
½ cup stone-ground fine yellow cornmeal
¼ teaspoon salt**

Over a large piece of waxed or parchment paper or a bowl, sift together the flour and baking powder. Add the cornmeal and salt and toss to blend well.

Add the dry ingredients to the butter mixture in 3 stages, stopping to scrape down the sides and bottom of the bowl with a rubber spatula after each addition.

**½ cup milk
3 tablespoons freshly squeezed lemon juice**

Add the milk and lemon juice to the batter and blend thoroughly.

Use a spoon to divide the batter evenly among the 12 muffin cups, filling them to the top.

Bake the muffins for about 30 minutes, until they have risen and set and a tester inserted in the center comes out clean. Remove the pan from the oven and cool on a rack. When the muffins are cool, gently pry them out of the pan. Serve warm or at room temperature.

To rewarm the muffins, place them in a 325°F oven for 8 to 10 minutes.

Lemon-Cornmeal Pound Cake with Blueberry Compote

T HIS IS ONE OF my favorite cakes because of the flavor and texture combinations. Cornmeal adds texture to the cake, but it still retains a delicate crumb. Lemon adds lots of zesty flavor and the blueberry compote is a perfect complement. This is a great cake to serve for afternoon tea. It's also delicious lightly toasted for breakfast or anytime. **Makes one $8^{1}/_2 \times 4^{1}/_2 \times 2^{1}/_2$-inch loaf cake, 12 servings**

Essential Gear

- Electric stand mixer with flat beater attachment, or large mixing bowl and hand-held mixer
- Rubber spatula
- Microplane grater or citrus zester
- Aluminum foil
- Heat-resistant rubber spatula or wooden spoon
- $8^{1}/_2 \times 4^{1}/_2 \times 2^{1}/_2$-inch loaf pan
- Cooling rack
- 1-quart heavy-bottomed saucepan

CAKE

1 tablespoon unsalted butter, softened	Center a rack in the oven and preheat it to 350°F. Line the loaf pan with aluminum foil that extends over the sides. Use a paper towel or your fingertips to butter the foil inside the pan.
6 ounces (12 tablespoons, 1½ sticks) unsalted butter, softened	Place the butter in the bowl of an electric stand mixer or in a large mixing bowl. Use the flat beater attachment or a hand-held mixer to beat the butter on medium speed until it's fluffy, about 2 minutes.
¾ cup granulated sugar	Add the sugar to the butter and cream together well. Stop occasionally and scrape down the bottom and sides of the bowl with a rubber spatula.
3 extra-large eggs, at room temperature	One at a time, add the eggs to the butter mixture, stopping to scrape down the bottom and sides of the bowl after each addition. At first the mixture may look curdled as the eggs are added, but as you stop and scrape down the bowl, the mixture will smooth out.
1¼ cups cake flour 2 teaspoon baking powder	Over a large piece of waxed or parchment paper or a bowl, sift together the cake flour and baking powder.
½ cup stone-ground fine yellow cornmeal ¼ teaspoon salt	Add the cornmeal and salt and stir to blend well.
	Add the dry ingredients to the butter mixture in 3 stages, blending well after each.
Finely grated or minced zest of 2 large lemons 2 teaspoons freshly squeezed lemon juice	Add the lemon zest and lemon juice to the batter and blend well.

Keeping

Store the cake, tightly wrapped in aluminum foil, at room temperature for up to 4 days. To freeze for up to 3 months, wrap the cake tightly in several layers of plastic wrap and aluminum foil. Use a large piece of masking tape and an indelible marker to label and date the contents. If frozen, defrost overnight in the refrigerator and bring to room temperature before serving.

Store the blueberry compote in an airtight plastic container in the refrigerator for up to 1 week. Rewarm in a microwave oven on low power for 1 minute or in a small saucepan over low heat before serving.

Transfer the batter to the prepared loaf pan. The batter is very thick, so use a rubber spatula to spread it evenly into the pan.

Bake for 45 minutes, until the cake is light golden on top and a cake tester inserted into the center comes out slightly moist.

Remove the pan from the oven and cool completely on a rack.

Making a Change
Replace the blueberries with fresh or frozen raspberries.

BLUEBERRY COMPOTE

¼ **cup granulated sugar**
1 cup water

Combine the sugar and water in the saucepan. Bring to a boil, without stirring, over high heat.

½ **cup dried or 1 cup fresh**
  blueberries
5 strips lemon zest

Lower the heat to medium. Add the blueberries and lemon zest. Cook until the fruit is soft, about 15 minutes. If using fresh berries, they will pop. Use a heat-resistant spatula or wooden spoon to stir the berries occasionally.

Remove the saucepan from the heat and transfer the compote to a bowl, so it stops cooking. Cool the compote to room temperature before serving.

Lift the cake from the pan by holding onto the foil. Peel the foil away and slice the cake into serving pieces, about ¾ inch thick. Place a slice on a serving plate and top with a large spoonful of blueberry compote.

Lemon Mascarpone Tart

A SMOOTH CUSTARD filling flavored with mascarpone and lemon is enclosed in a lemon-accented, sweet pastry crust. Mascarpone is a soft Italian cheese with a tangy flavor. It is sometimes compared to cream cheese, but mascarpone is really in a category of its own. You can find it in markets that sell Italian ingredients and in specialty food shops. Since this large tart serves many, it's a good choice for a party. **Makes one 11-inch round tart, 16 to 20 servings**

PASTRY DOUGH

2 cups all-purpose flour
1¼ cups granulated sugar
¼ **teaspoon salt**

In the work bowl of a food processor fitted with the steel blade, combine the flour, sugar, and salt. Pulse briefly to blend.

Essential Gear
- Food processor
- Microplane grater or citrus zester
- Rolling pin
- 11-inch round, fluted-edge tart pan with removable bottom
- Jelly-roll pan
- Electric stand mixer with flat beater attachment, or large mixing bowl and hand-held mixer
- Cooling rack

Finely grated or minced zest of 2 large lemons	Add the lemon zest and pulse briefly to blend.
5 ounces (10 tablespoons, 1¼ sticks) unsalted butter, chilled	Cut the butter into small pieces and add to the flour. Pulse until the butter is cut into very tiny pieces, about 30 seconds. The texture will be sandy with very tiny lumps throughout.
3 tablespoons heavy whipping cream	With the food processor running, pour the cream through the feed tube. Process the dough until the mixture wraps itself around the blade, about 1 minute.

Turn the pastry dough onto a large piece of plastic wrap. Shape into a flat disk and wrap tightly in a double layer of plastic wrap. Chill in the refrigerator until firm before using, at least 2 hours. Chilling the dough relaxes the gluten in the flour so it won't be too elastic and will roll out easily. It also firms up the butter in the dough so it will need less flour when rolled out. If the dough is too firm, it will splinter and break when rolled out. Let it stand at room temperature for 10 to 15 minutes before rolling to become more pliable.

On a smooth, flat surface, roll out the pastry dough between sheets of lightly floured waxed or parchment paper to a large circle about 13 inches in diameter. To tell if the dough will fit the tart pan, hold the pan above the dough. If there are 2 or 3 inches of dough that protrude beyond the sides of the pan, it will fit.

Carefully peel the paper off the top of the dough. Brush excess flour off the dough, then loosely roll the pastry dough around the rolling pin without the bottom piece of paper. Place the tart pan directly underneath the rolling pin and carefully unroll the pastry dough into the tart pan.

Gently lift up the sides and ease the pastry dough into the bottom and sides of the tart pan. Trim off the excess pastry dough at the top of the pan. Transfer the tart pan to a jelly-roll pan and chill in the freezer for 15 minutes.

Center a rack in the oven and preheat it to 350°F.

MASCARPONE-LEMON FILLING

1 pound mascarpone, softened	Place the mascarpone in the bowl of an electric stand mixer or a large mixing bowl. Use the flat beater attachment or a hand-held mixer to beat the mascarpone on medium speed until it is fluffy, about 2 minutes.

Keeping

Store the tart, loosely covered with waxed paper and tightly wrapped with aluminum foil, in the refrigerator up to 5 days.

Streamlining

The pastry dough can be made in advance and kept in the refrigerator, tightly wrapped in a double layer of plastic wrap, up to 4 days. To freeze up to 3 months, wrap the dough snugly in several layers of plastic wrap and place it in a freezer bag. Use a large piece of masking tape and an indelible marker to label and date the contents. If frozen, defrost overnight in the refrigerator before using.

Troubleshooting

Don't roll out the pastry dough before it is chilled. The dough will be too soft and it will require a lot of flour to roll out, which results in a tough dough.

Once the pastry dough is unrolled into the tart pan, don't push it down forcefully. This will stretch the dough, which will shrink as it bakes, making it flat instead of taking the shape of the tart pan.

Adding Style

Instead of topping the tart with confectioners' sugar, serve each slice with a

1/3 **cup granulated sugar**	Add the sugar and blend with the mascarpone thoroughly. Stop and scrape down the bottom and sides of the bowl with a rubber spatula.
4 large lemons	Use a fine grater to remove the outer rind of the lemons. Take care not to grate the inner white pith, which is very bitter. Or use a zester to remove the lemon zest and chop it very finely with a chef's knife. Add the lemon zest to the mascarpone mixture.
2 teaspoons freshly squeezed lemon juice.	Strain the juice to remove any seeds and add it to the mascarpone mixture. Blend very well.
5 extra-large eggs, at room temperature	One at a time, add the eggs to the mascarpone mixture, stopping to scrape down the bottom and sides of the bowl after each addition. At first the mixture may look curdled as the eggs are added, but as you stop and scrape down the bowl, the mixture will smooth out.
	Pour the filling evenly into the tart shell. Gently shake the tart pan from side to side to smooth out the filling and eliminate any air bubbles.
1/2 **cup pine nuts, lightly toasted**	Bake the tart for 8 minutes. Open the oven door and pull the rack out partway. Evenly sprinkle the pine nuts over the top of the tart.
	Continue to bake the tart for 30 to 35 minutes, until the filling is light golden and set.
	Remove the pan from the oven and cool on a rack. Carefully remove the side of the tart pan.
1 tablespoon confectioners' sugar	Lightly dust the top of the tart with confectioners' sugar and serve at room temperature.

dollop of whipped cream and decorate the top of the cream with a few strands of lemon zest.

Lemon Meringue Pie

MOST OF US grew up eating lemon meringue pie and have fond memories of doing so, and many of us spent hours in the kitchen watching our mothers prepare this classic. Although traditional pie dough is made with lard or shortening, I prefer to use a dough made with all butter for this pie because it has the best flavor. I've learned to make it with a flaky texture that is the hallmark of classic pie dough. The key to success with this pie is to pour the hot filling into a pre-baked pie shell and keep it hot while

Essential Gear
- 10-inch round pie pan
- Food processor
- Rolling pin
- Baking sheet
- Aluminum foil
- Pie weights
- Cooling rack

making the meringue. Also, to prevent shrinkage of the meringue when the pie bakes, make sure it's securely attached to the edges of the pie shell. **Makes one 10-inch round pie, 12 to 14 servings**

PIE DOUGH

1½ cups all-purpose flour ¼ teaspoon salt	In the work bowl of a food processor fitted with the steel blade, combine the flour and salt. Pulse briefly to blend.
4 ounces (8 tablespoons, 1 stick) unsalted butter, chilled	Cut the butter into small pieces and freeze for 20 minutes. Add the butter to the flour mixture. Pulse until the butter is cut into pea-sized pieces, 30 to 45 seconds. The texture should be sandy with very tiny lumps throughout.
3 to 4 tablespoons ice water	Remove the top of the food processor and sprinkle on 2 tablespoons of the ice water. Replace the top and pulse for 10 seconds. Squeeze a small amount of the dough in your hand. If it holds together, don't add any more water. If the dough is still very crumbly, add another tablespoon of water, pulse to blend, then check the dough again. It won't hold together unless you squeeze it, but that's the texture you want. Turn the dough onto a smooth, flat work surface. Use the heel of your hand to push the dough a few times for a final blend. Don't mush all the butter into the dough, however. For a flaky crust, you want to see thin flecks of butter in the dough. Shape the dough into a flat disk and wrap tightly in a double layer of plastic wrap. Chill in the refrigerator until firm before using, at least 2 hours. Chilling the dough relaxes the gluten in the flour so it won't be too elastic and will roll out easily. It also firms up the butter in the dough so it will need less flour when rolled out. If the dough is too firm it will splinter and break when rolled out. Let it stand at room temperature for 10 to 15 minutes before rolling to become more pliable.

On a smooth, flat surface, roll out the pie dough between sheets of lightly floured waxed or parchment paper to a large circle about 12 inches in diameter. To tell if the dough will fit the pie pan, invert the pan over the dough. If there are 2 to 3 inches of dough that protrude beyond the sides of the pan, it will fit.

Carefully peel the paper off the top of the dough. Brush excess flour off the dough, then loosely roll the pastry dough around the rolling pin without the bottom piece of paper. Place the pie pan directly underneath the rolling pin and carefully unroll the pastry dough into

- Whisk or rubber spatula
- Medium heavy-bottomed saucepan
- Instant-read thermometer
- Heat-resistant rubber spatula or wooden spoon

Keeping
Store the pie, loosely covered with waxed paper and tightly wrapped with aluminum foil, in the refrigerator for up to 3 days.

Streamlining
The pie dough can be made in advance and kept in the refrigerator, tightly wrapped in a double layer of plastic wrap, for up to 4 days. To freeze up to 3 months, wrap the dough snugly in several layers of plastic wrap and place it in a freezer bag. Use a large piece of masking tape and an indelible marker to label and date the contents. If frozen, defrost overnight in the refrigerator before using. The pie dough can also be fitted into the pie pan and frozen. Wrap as above and label.

Troubleshooting
Don't overprocess the pie dough or it will be tough and not flaky.

Making a Change
To make classic tender, flaky pie dough, replace half of the butter with lard or vegetable shortening.

To make a Lime Meringue Pie, replace the lemon zest

the pan. Or loosely fold the dough in half. Carefully place it in half of the pie pan and gently unfold the dough. Gently lift up the sides and ease the pie dough into the bottom and sides of the pie pan. Trim off the excess pie dough at the top of the pan and crimp the sides (see page 40).

Use a fork to lightly pierce the bottom of the pie crust all over. Transfer the pie pan to a baking sheet and chill in the freezer for 15 to 20 minutes. This helps prevent the pie dough from shrinking as it bakes and sets the butter in the dough to ensure flakiness.

Center a rack in the oven and preheat it to 400°F. Line the pie shell with a large piece of aluminum foil that fits well against the bottom and sides. Fill with pie weights or a mixture of rice and beans. Bake for 15 minutes. Remove the foil and weights and bake another 10 to 12 minutes, until light golden and set. Remove the pan from the oven and transfer to a rack while you prepare the filling.

and juice with lime zest and juice.

To make an Orange Meringue Pie, replace the lemon zest and juice with orange zest and juice.

Adding Style

Add 2 tablespoons finely grated or minced lemon zest to the pie dough before adding the butter.

LEMON FILLING

6 extra-large yolks, at room temperature (set aside the egg whites for the meringue)

Place the egg yolks in a medium mixing bowl and whisk together lightly.

2 cups water
1½ cups granulated sugar
½ cup cornstarch, sifted

Place the water, sugar, and cornstarch in the saucepan. Stir constantly over medium heat until the mixture is thick, shiny, and translucent, about 7 minutes. Remove the saucepan from the heat.

Take about ½ cup of this mixture and stir it into the egg yolks to temper them. Add the egg yolks to the cornstarch mixture, stirring constantly. Return the saucepan to the heat and cook over medium heat, stirring constantly, until the mixture comes to a boil and registers 170°F on an instant-read thermometer, about 7 minutes.

½ cup freshly squeezed lemon juice
1½ ounces (3 tablespoons) unsalted butter, softened, cut into small pieces
2 tablespoons finely grated or minced lemon zest
¼ teaspoon salt

Remove the saucepan from the heat and blend in the lemon juice, butter, lemon zest, and salt. Stir to blend completely and to melt the butter.

2 tablespoons fine dry cake crumbs

Pour the filling evenly into the pie shell. Evenly sprinkle the cake crumbs over the filling, then place a large piece of plastic wrap directly on top of the filling to keep it hot while preparing the meringue.

**6 extra-large egg whites, at
room temperature**
¾ cup granulated sugar
¾ teaspoon cream of tartar

Place the egg whites, sugar, and cream of tartar in the bowl of an electric stand mixer or a large mixing bowl. Place the mixing bowl over a pan of simmering water and whisk constantly to keep the egg whites from cooking. Whisk the mixture until the temperature registers 160°F on an instant-read thermometer, about 7 minutes. It will look thick and foamy at this point. Immediately place the bowl on the mixer and use the wire whip attachment, or use a hand-held mixer, to whip the egg whites on high speed until they hold stiff, shiny peaks.

Heating the egg whites to 160°F is recommended by the American Egg Board to kill any salmonella bacteria. It's very important to keep the egg whites from coagulating while they are warming over simmering water. Adding water and sugar to the egg whites helps prevent this, but they must also be stirred constantly. As soon as the egg whites reach 160°F, they must be whipped immediately.

Remove the plastic wrap from the top of the lemon filling. Use a rubber spatula to spread some of the meringue in an even layer around the rim of the pie plate, making sure it adheres to the pie crust. This helps prevent the meringue from shrinking as it bakes. Spread the rest of the meringue over the top of the pie, mounding it slightly in the center. Use the spatula to form swirls and peaks randomly over the meringue.

Bake the pie for 8 to 10 minutes, until the meringue is lightly browned. Or use a propane kitchen torch to brown the top of the meringue.

Remove the pie from the oven and cool on a rack. Serve the pie at room temperature or cold.

Lemon Shortbread Coins

LIKE CLASSIC SHORTBREAD, these lemony cookies are made with few ingredients, so the lemon flavor shines through. I like to add light brown sugar because it enhances the flavor. These are also typical refrigerator cookies because, after the dough is made, these are formed into logs, wrapped tightly, and chilled. When you're ready to bake them, simply slice the logs into pieces. **Makes 7 dozen cookies**

Essential Gear
• Electric stand mixer with flat beater attachment, or large mixing bowl and hand-held mixer
• Rubber spatula
• Two baking sheets

8 ounces (16 tablespoons, 2 sticks) unsalted butter, softened	Place the butter in the bowl of an electric stand mixer or in a large mixing bowl. Using the flat beater attachment or a hand-held mixer, beat the butter on medium speed until light and fluffy, about 2 minutes.
¼ cup granulated sugar ¼ cup firmly packed light brown sugar	Add the granulated sugar and brown sugar and beat together until thoroughly blended, about 2 minutes. Stop occasionally and scrape down the bottom and sides of the bowl with a rubber spatula.
2 cups all-purpose flour ¼ teaspoon salt	Combine the flour and salt and add this mixture to the butter mixture in 4 stages, blending well after each addition. Stop and scrape down the bottom and sides of the bowl with a rubber spatula to help mix evenly.
Finely grated or minced zest of 2 large lemons	Add the lemon zest to the dough and blend well.
	Divide the dough in half. Working on a smooth, flat surface, form each half into a ball. Use the waxed paper to shape and roll the dough ball into a cylinder about 1½ inches thick and 12 inches long. Repeat with the other half of the dough.
4 tablespoons superfine sugar	Lay out a large piece of waxed or parchment paper on a smooth, flat work surface. Place 2 tablespoons of the sugar in a horizontal line across the center of the paper. Roll the cylinder of shortbread dough in the sugar, coating the outside completely. Repeat with the other dough cylinder.
	Wrap each dough cylinder tightly in the waxed paper, twisting it at both ends to seal, then tightly wrap in plastic wrap and chill the dough for at least 1 hour.
	Line the baking sheets with parchment paper or non-stick liners. Unwrap one of the dough cylinders. Using a chef's knife, cut the cylinder into slices ¼ to ⅜ inch thick. Cut straight down and roll the cylinder a quarter turn after every 6 slices so it will keep its round shape. If the dough becomes soft while you're working with it, rewrap it and chill for another 10 to 15 minutes, then continue slicing.
	Transfer the coins to the baking sheets, leaving at least 1 inch of space between them. Chill the coins for 15 minutes before baking.
	Position the oven racks to the upper and lower thirds and preheat the oven to 300°F.
	Bake the shortbread coins for 12 minutes, then switch the baking sheets and bake another 12 to 14 minutes, until the coins are set and very light golden. Remove the baking sheets and transfer them to racks to cool completely.

- Microplane grated or citrus zester
- Two parchment paper sheets or nonstick liners
- Two cooling racks

Keeping

Store the shortbread coins in an airtight plastic container between layers of waxed paper at room temperature for up to 1 week.

Streamlining

The shortbread dough can be made up to 3 days in advance and kept tightly wrapped in a double layer of plastic wrap in the refrigerator. To freeze up to 3 months, wrap the cylinders snugly in several layers of plastic wrap and place in a freezer bag. Use a large piece of masking tape and an indelible marker to label and date the contents. If frozen, defrost in the refrigerator.

Making a Change

Roll the shortbread cylinders in organic evaporated cane juice or Demerara sugar for a different flavor and texture.

Adding Style

Make shortbread sandwich cookies by spreading a thin layer of lemon curd (see page 140) or raspberry or apricot jam on the flat side of one shortbread coin and topping it with the flat side of another coin.

Perfect Lemon Tart

THIS IS WHAT I dream about when I think of lemon. It has just the right balance of textures, with a silky smooth and very tart lemon filling enclosed in a delicate cookie crust. A light dusting of confectioners' sugar on top is all the decoration it needs. Serve this to your lemon-loving friends and family and watch their eyes light up. **Makes one 9¹/₂-inch round tart, 12 to 14 servings**

PASTRY DOUGH

1¹/₄ cups all-purpose flour
¹/₄ cup granulated sugar
¹/₈ teaspoon salt

In the work bowl of a food processor fitted with the steel blade, combine the flour, sugar, and salt. Pulse briefly to blend.

4 ounces (8 tablespoons, 1 stick) unsalted butter, chilled

Cut the butter into small pieces and add to the flour mixture. Pulse until the butter is cut into very tiny pieces, about 30 seconds.

1 extra-large egg yolk, at room temperature

With the food processor running, pour the egg yolk through the feed tube. Process the dough until the mixture wraps itself around the blade, about 1 minute.

Turn the pastry dough onto a large piece of plastic wrap. Shape into a flat disk and wrap tightly in a double layer of plastic wrap. Chill in the refrigerator until firm before using, at least 2 hours. Chilling the dough relaxes the gluten in the flour so it won't be too elastic and will roll out easily. It also firms up the butter in the dough so it will need less flour when rolled out. If the dough is too firm it will splinter and break when rolled out. Let it stand at room temperature for 10 to 15 minutes before rolling to become more pliable.

On a smooth, flat surface, roll out the pastry dough between sheets of lightly floured waxed or parchment paper to a large circle about 11 inches in diameter. To tell if the dough will fit the tart pan, hold the pan above the dough. If there are about 2 inches of dough that protrude beyond the sides of the pan, it will fit.

Carefully peel the paper off the top of the dough. Brush excess flour off of the dough, then loosely roll the pastry dough around the rolling pin without the bottom piece of paper. Place the tart pan directly underneath the rolling pin and carefully unroll the pastry dough into the tart pan. Gently lift up the sides and ease the pastry dough into the bottom and sides of the tart pan.

Essential Gear
- Food processor
- Rolling pin
- 9¹/₂-inch round, fluted-edge tart pan with removable bottom
- Microplane grated or citrus zester
- Baking sheet
- Pie weights
- Cooling rack
- Whisk or rubber spatula
- Double boiler
- Medium-size fine-mesh strainer

Keeping
Although the tart is best eaten the day it's made, it can last up to 3 days. Store the tart, loosely covered with waxed paper and tightly wrapped with aluminum foil, in the refrigerator.

Streamlining
The pastry dough can be made in advance and kept in the refrigerator, tightly wrapped in a double layer of plastic wrap, for up to 4 days. To freeze up to 3 months, wrap the dough snugly in several layers of plastic wrap and place it in a freezer bag. Use a large piece of masking tape and an indelible marker to label and date the contents. If frozen, defrost overnight in the refrigerator before using.

Trim off the excess pastry dough at the top of the pan. Transfer the tart pan to a baking sheet and chill in the freezer for 15 minutes.

Center a rack in the oven and preheat it to 375°F.

Line the pastry shell with a large piece of aluminum foil that fits against the bottom and sides. Fill with pie weights or a mixture of rice and beans. Bake for 10 minutes. Remove the foil and weights. If the bottom of the pastry shell puffs up, gently pierce it in several places with a fork to release the air. Bake the pastry shell another 10 to 12 minutes, until light golden and set. Remove the pan from the oven and transfer to a rack to cool while you prepare the filling.

FILLING

4 large lemons

Use a fine grater to remove the outer rind of the lemons. Take care not to grate the inner white pith, which is very bitter. Or use a zester to remove the lemon zest and chop it very finely with a chef's knife.

Cut the lemons in half, squeeze out the juice, and strain it to remove any seeds. Juice another lemon or two, if necessary, to measure $2/3$ cup.

4 extra-large egg yolks, at room temperature
1 extra-large egg, at room temperature
$3/4$ cup granulated sugar

Place the egg yolks, egg, and sugar in the top pan of a double boiler over simmering water. Stir together to dissolve the sugar, about 3 minutes.

2 ounces (4 tablespoons, $1/2$ stick) unsalted butter, melted

Add the lemon zest, lemon juice, and butter. Stir the mixture constantly with a heat-resistant spatula or wooden spoon until it thickens, about 12 minutes.

A good test to see if the mixture is at the right consistency is to dip the spatula or spoon into it. Lift the spatula or spoon from the mixture and hold it with the width of the spatula blade or spoon parallel to the top of the pan. With your finger, draw a parallel line across the middle of the spatula or spoon. If the mixture does not run over the line, it's thick enough.

Remove the top pan of the double boiler and strain the mixture into a medium bowl.

2 tablespoons heavy whipping cream

Add the cream to the lemon mixture and stir to blend well.

Troubleshooting
Don't roll out the pastry dough before it is chilled. The dough will be too soft and it will require a lot of flour to roll out, which results in a tough dough.

Once the pastry dough is unrolled into the tart pan, don't push it down forcefully. This will stretch the dough, which will shrink as it bakes, making it flat instead of taking the shape of the tart pan.

Making a Change
Instead of topping the tart with confectioners' sugar, arrange concentric circles of fresh berries over the tart.

Recovering from a Mishap
The tart dough is delicate and needs to be handled gently. If the dough breaks while you're working with it, it's easy to patch by pressing two pieces of dough together.

Adding Style
If you top the tart with berries, serve each slice of tart in a small pool of raspberry sauce (see sauce recipe in Meyer Lemon Soufflés, page 143).

	Pour the filling evenly into the tart shell. Bake 12 to 14 minutes, until the filling is set but jiggles slightly when the pan is shaken. Remove the pan from the oven and cool on a rack. Carefully remove the side of the tart pan (see page 42).
1 tablespoon confectioners' sugar	Lightly dust the top of the tart with confectioners' sugar and serve at room temperature.

The World's Best Lemon Bars

THESE ARE the quintessential lemon bars. They have a tangy lemon topping that sits on a crisp pastry dough base. The pastry dough is partially baked, the topping is added, and then the cookies are baked. After the cookies cool, they are cut into bars and garnished with confectioners' sugar and sliced almonds. **Makes twenty $1^1/_2 \times$ 3-inch bars**

1 tablespoon unsalted butter, softened	Center a rack in the oven and preheat it to 350°F. Line the baking pan with a large piece of aluminum foil that extends over the sides. Press the foil over the sides of the pan. Use a paper towel or your fingertips to butter the foil evenly.

PASTRY DOUGH

2 cups all-purpose flour **$^2/_3$ cup confectioners' sugar** **$^1/_4$ teaspoon salt**	In the work bowl of a food processor fitted with the steel blade, combine the flour, confectioners' sugar, and salt. Pulse briefly to blend.
8 ounces (16 tablespoons, 2 sticks) unsalted butter, chilled **Finely grated or minced zest of 1 large lemon**	Cut the butter into small pieces and add to the flour mixture. Add the lemon zest and pulse until the butter is cut into very tiny pieces. Process until the dough wraps itself around the blade, about 1 minute.
	Turn the pastry dough into the foil-lined baking pan. Dust your hands with flour and press the dough evenly into the pan.
	Bake the dough for 25 minutes, until light golden on the edges. Remove the baking pan from the oven and cool on a rack while preparing the filling.
	Reduce the oven temperature to 325°F.

Essential Gear

- 9 × 13-inch baking pan
- Food processor
- Microplane grater or citrus zester
- Cooling rack
- Electric stand mixer with wire whip attachment, or large mixing bowl and hand-held mixer
- Rubber spatula
- Ruler
- Chef's knife
- Sugar dredger or medium-size fine-mesh strainer
- Aluminum foil

Keeping

Store the bars in a single layer between pieces of waxed paper in an airtight container at room temperature up to 5 days.

Streamlining

The pastry dough can be made in advance and kept in the refrigerator, tightly wrapped in a double layer of plastic wrap, for up to 4 days. To freeze up to 3 months, wrap the dough snugly in several layers of

FILLING

4 extra-large eggs, at room temperature

Place the eggs in the bowl of an electric stand mixer or in a large mixing bowl. Use the wire whip attachment or a hand-held mixer to whip the eggs on medium-high speed until they thicken, about 2 minutes.

1½ cups granulated sugar

Slowly sprinkle on the sugar and continue to whip on medium-high speed until the mixture is very thick and pale colored and holds a slowly dissolving ribbon as the beater is lifted, about 5 minutes.

¼ cup all-purpose flour
½ teaspoon baking powder

In a small bowl, combine the flour and baking powder and stir together to blend well. Add to the egg mixture and blend together well on medium speed. Stop and scrape down the sides and bottom of the mixing bowl with a rubber spatula.

⅔ cup freshly squeezed, strained lemon juice
Finely grated or minced zest of 1 large lemon

Add the lemon juice and lemon zest to the mixture and blend well.

Pour the filling over the top of the crust in the baking pan. Bake for 30 minutes, until the top is set and light golden, and a cake tester inserted in the center comes out clean or only slightly damp. Remove the baking pan from the oven and cool completely on a rack.

Use the foil to lift the bars from the baking pan and place on a cutting board. Peel the foil away from the sides of the bars. Use a ruler to mark where to cut the cookies, measuring 1½ inches wide and 3 inches long. Use a chef's knife to cut the cookies into bars.

GARNISH

3 tablespoons confectioners' sugar

Place the confectioners' sugar in a dredger or a fine-mesh strainer and heavily dust the tops of the lemon bars.

2 tablespoons sliced almonds, lightly toasted

Decorate the top of each lemon bar with 3 or 4 sliced almonds in the center.

plastic wrap and place it in a freezer bag. Use a large piece of masking tape and an indelible marker to label and date the contents. If frozen, defrost overnight in the refrigerator before using. If the dough is too firm to press into the pan, let it stand to warm up to room temperature.

Making a Change
Use Meyer lemons to make the lemon filling.

Adding Style
Decorate the top of each lemon bar with 3 fresh raspberries.

Make a small heart-shaped stencil and place it in the center of the top of each lemon bar before dusting with confectioners' sugar. Lift off the stencil and there will be a heart in the center of each bar.

Lemon Tea Cake with Pecans

L EMON AND PECANS complement each other perfectly. They both add lots of flavor, and sour cream adds its own special tang to this cake. It's a great cake to serve for afternoon tea and is also scrumptious lightly toasted for breakfast. **Makes one 10 × 4-inch tube cake, 12 to 14 servings**

CAKE

1 tablespoon unsalted butter, softened	Center a rack in the oven and preheat it to 325°F. Use a paper towel or your fingertips to generously butter the inside of the tube pan.
1 tablespoon all-purpose flour	Dust the inside of the pan with the flour. Shake and tilt the pan to coat it with flour. Turn the pan over the sink and tap out the excess flour.
8 ounces (16 tablespoons, 2 sticks) unsalted butter, softened	Place the butter in the bowl of an electric stand mixer or in a large mixing bowl. Use the flat beater attachment or hand-held mixer to beat the butter on medium speed until it's fluffy, about 2 minutes.
1½ cups granulated sugar 1 cup firmly packed light brown sugar	Add the granulated sugar and brown sugar to the butter, and cream together well. Stop occasionally and scrape down the bottom and sides of the bowl with a rubber spatula.
6 extra-large eggs, at room temperature	One at a time, add the eggs to the butter mixture, stopping to scrape down the bottom and sides of the bowl after each addition. At first the mixture may look curdled as the eggs are added, but as you stop and scrape down the bowl, the mixture will smooth out.
3 cups cake flour ½ teaspoon baking soda ¼ teaspoon salt ¼ teaspoon freshly grated nutmeg	Over a large piece of waxed or parchment paper or a bowl, sift together the flour and baking soda. Add the salt and nutmeg and toss together to blend well.
1 cup pecans, finely chopped	Take 2 tablespoons of the dry ingredients and toss with the pecans. Add the dry ingredients to the butter mixture in 3 stages, blending well after each.
Finely grated or minced zest of 2 large lemons ½ teaspoon pure vanilla extract	Add the lemon zest and vanilla to the batter and blend well.

Essential Gear

- Electric stand mixer with flat beater attachment, or large mixing bowl and hand-held mixer
- Rubber spatula
- 10 × 4-inch round tube pan or Bundt pan
- Microplane grater or citrus zester
- Cooling rack

Keeping

Store the cake, tightly wrapped in aluminum foil, at room temperature for up to 4 days. To freeze for up to 3 months, wrap the cake tightly in several layers of plastic wrap and aluminum foil. Use a large piece of masking tape and an indelible marker to label and date the contents. If frozen, defrost overnight in the refrigerator and bring to room temperature before serving.

Making a Change

Replace the pecans with walnuts or macadamia nuts.

1 cup sour cream	Stir in the sour cream and blend well. Then add the chopped pecans and stir to blend thoroughly.
	Transfer the batter to the prepared pan. The batter is very thick, so use a rubber spatula to spread it evenly into the pan.
	Bake for 1 hour and 20 minutes, until the cake is light golden on top and a cake tester inserted into the center comes out slightly moist.
	Remove the pan from the oven and cool completely on a rack.
	Invert the cake onto a serving plate.
Confectioners' sugar	Lightly dust the top of the cake with confectioners' sugar before serving.

Key Lime and Coconut Cake

LAYERS OF A LUSCIOUS butter cake are filled and frosted with Key lime and white chocolate icing, and shredded coconut adorns the sides and top of the cake. Although there are several steps involved in making this cake, most can be done in advance, so it's easy to assemble the day you want to serve it. This is the perfect cake for a spring or summer gathering because its fresh flavors remind me of a tropical island, but it's great to make any time of year. If you can't find Key limes, use bottled Key lime juice. **Makes one 9-inch round cake, 12 to 14 servings**

CAKE

Center a rack in the oven and preheat it to 350°F.

1 tablespoon unsalted butter, softened	Using a paper towel or your fingertips, generously butter the inside of the cake pans, coating them thoroughly.
1 tablespoon all-purpose flour	Dust the inside of each pan with some of the flour. Shake and tilt the pans to evenly distribute the flour, then turn the pans over and shake out the excess over the sink.
	Cut a round of parchment paper to fit the bottom of each pan. Butter each parchment paper round and place in each pan, butter-side up.

Essential Gear

- Two 9 × 2-inch round cake pans
- Scissors
- Parchment paper
- Two rubber spatulas
- Electric stand mixer with flat beater attachment and wire whip attachment or large mixing bowl and hand-held mixer
- Two cooling racks
- Small saucepan
- Double boiler
- 10-inch flexible-blade icing spatula
- 12-inch pastry bag and large pastry tube with star opening

Keeping

Store the cake, loosely covered with waxed paper and tightly covered with alumi-

6 ounces (12 tablespoons, 1½ sticks) unsalted butter, softened	Place the butter in the bowl of an electric stand mixer or in a large mixing bowl. Use the flat beater attachment or a hand-held mixer to beat the butter on medium speed until it's fluffy, about 2 minutes.
1 cup granulated sugar **⅔ cup firmly packed light brown sugar**	Add the granulated sugar and the light brown sugar to the butter and cream together well. Stop occasionally and scrape down the bottom and sides of the bowl with a rubber spatula.
4 extra-large eggs, at room temperature	One at a time, add the eggs to the butter mixture, stopping to scrape down the bottom and sides of the bowl after each addition. At first the mixture may look curdled as the eggs are added, but as you stop and scrape down the bowl, the mixture will smooth out.
1 tablespoon freshly squeezed or bottled Key lime juice **Finely grated or minced zest of 4 (regular) large limes**	Add the juice and lime zest to the butter mixture and blend together well.
2½ cups cake flour **½ teaspoon baking soda** **½ cup sweetened shredded coconut** **½ teaspoon salt**	Over a large piece of waxed or parchment paper or a bowl, sift together the flour and baking soda. Add the coconut and salt and toss to blend well.
1 cup buttermilk	With the mixer on low speed, add the dry ingredients in 3 stages, alternating with the buttermilk. Blend well after each addition and stop often to scrape down the bottom and sides of the bowl with a rubber spatula.
	Divide the batter evenly between the two cake pans. Smooth the top of each pan with a rubber spatula.
	Bake the layers for 30 minutes, until a cake tester inserted in the center comes out with no crumbs clinging to it.
	Remove the cake pans from the oven and cool completely on racks. Invert the pans to remove the layers, then peel the parchment paper off the back of each layer. Re-invert the layers onto plates or cardboard cake circles.

SUGAR SYRUP

3 tablespoons granulated sugar **⅓ cup water** **Finely grated zest of 2 large limes**	Combine the sugar and water in a small saucepan. Bring to a boil over high heat to dissolve the sugar. Add the lime zest to the sugar syrup. Cover the pan and let steep for 15 minutes. Strain the sugar syrup to remove the zest.

num foil, in the refrigerator for up to 4 days. Place several toothpicks in the top outer edges of the cake to hold the foil away from it so it won't mar the icing. To freeze, place the cake in a cake box and wrap with several layers of plastic wrap and aluminum foil. Or place the cake on a lined baking sheet in the freezer and let it freeze (about 3 hours). Loosely wrap the frozen cake in layers of plastic wrap and aluminum foil. If frozen, defrost overnight in the refrigerator. Bring the cake to room temperature at least 30 minutes before serving.

Streamlining
Bake the cake layers up to 2 days before assembling the cake and keep tightly covered with a double layer of plastic wrap at room temperature. To freeze the layers for up to 3 months, wrap them snugly in several layers of plastic wrap and place them in freezer bags. Use a large piece of masking tape and an indelible marker to label and date the contents. If frozen, defrost the layers overnight in the refrigerator.

Recovering from a Mishap
If one of the cake layers breaks during assembly, patch it together with some of the filling and frosting.

½ cup freshly squeezed or bottled Key lime juice (from 8 to 12 Key limes)	Place the lime juice in a small saucepan and bring to a boil over medium heat. Cook the juice until it is reduced by half, to ¼ cup. This greatly concentrates the flavor, which allows deep flavor to be blended into the white chocolate filling and frosting. Remove the saucepan from the heat and cool the juice while preparing the filling and frosting.
1 pound plus 3 ounces white chocolate, finely chopped	Place the white chocolate in the top of a double boiler over low heat. Stir often with a rubber spatula to help melt evenly. Remove the top pan of the double boiler and wipe the bottom and sides very dry. Or place the chocolate in a microwave-safe bowl and melt on low power for 30-second bursts. Stir with a rubber spatula after each burst.
14 ounces (28 tablespoons, 1¾ sticks) unsalted butter, softened	Place the butter in the bowl of an electric stand mixer or in a large mixing bowl. Use the flat beater attachment or a hand-held mixer to beat the butter on medium speed until it's fluffy, about 2 minutes.
2 cups confectioners' sugar, sifted	Add the confectioners' sugar to the butter, and cream together well. Stop occasionally and scrape down the sides and bottom of the bowl with a rubber spatula.
	Add the white chocolate to the mixture and blend together well. Add the cooled lime juice to the mixture and blend thoroughly. If the icing seems too soft, place the bowl in the freezer for 10 minutes, then beat vigorously until the mixture holds soft peaks.

ASSEMBLY

Using a serrated knife, cut each cake layer in half horizontally (see page 34). Place one cake layer on a serving plate. Brush the layer generously with the sugar syrup.

Place strips of waxed paper around the bottom edges of the cake to protect the plate while assembling the cake. With a flexible-blade spatula, evenly spread about ¼ of the key lime–white chocolate icing over the cake layer.

Position the second cake layer evenly over the icing. Brush the layer generously with some of the sugar syrup. Use the flexible-blade spatula to spread some of the filling over the layer. Repeat with the remaining two cake layers and filling.

Spread the remaining filling over the sides and top of the cake. Run the flexible-blade spatula under hot water and dry it, then use it to smooth and even the top of the cake.

1 cup sweetened shredded or flaked coconut

Press the coconut onto the sides of the cake up to, but not above, the top edge. Sprinkle any remaining coconut lightly on top of the cake.

Let the cake chill for at least 2 hours before serving.

Key Lime Pie

THE LIMES are what makes this pie special. Key limes are much smaller than regular limes and have a lot more flavor, and their juice is actually yellow rather than green. Key limes come from Key West, Florida, but these days they are also grown in Mexico and can be found in many specialty food shops and produce markets. The juice is also sold in some cookware shops and supermarkets. The juice can be frozen for up to one year, so you can squeeze it from the limes and have it on hand to make Key lime pie whenever you want. The filling for this pie thickens without cooking on the stovetop because the high acidity of the limes causes the proteins in the sweetened condensed milk and the egg yolks to bond together in the same way as they do when heated. Because the skin of Key limes is so thin, it's not possible to zest them, so use regular limes for the zest. A graham cracker crust is the traditional one for this pie, but I also like to use a crust made with ground almonds. **Makes one 9-inch round pie, 12 to 14 servings**

GRAHAM CRACKER CRUST

9 graham crackers (1 cellophane-wrapped package, 1/3 of a box), broken into pieces
2 tablespoons granulated sugar
1/4 teaspoon ground cinnamon

Place the graham crackers, sugar, and cinnamon in the work bowl of a food processor fitted with the steel blade. Pulse until the graham crackers are very finely ground, about 2 minutes. You should have 1 1/2 cups of crumbs.

3 ounces (6 tablespoons, 3/4 stick) unsalted butter, melted

With the food processor on, pour the melted butter through the feed tube. Process until the mixture begins to hold together, about 30 seconds.

Essential Gear

- 9-inch round pie pan
- Food processor
- Microplane grater or citrus zester
- Baking sheet
- Cooling rack
- Whisk
- Rubber spatula
- Electric stand mixer with wire whip attachment, or large mixing bowl and hand-held mixer

Keeping

Store the pie, without the whipped cream garnish, loosely covered with waxed paper sprayed with non-stick cooking spray, then tightly wrapped with aluminum foil, in the refrigerator for up to 3 days.

Streamlining

The pie crust can be made in advance and kept in the pie pan in the refrigerator, tightly wrapped in a double layer of plastic wrap, for up to 4 days. To freeze for up to

Transfer the crust to the pie pan. Use your fingertips, the back of a spoon, or the flat bottom of a cup or small bowl to press the crust evenly into the bottom and up the sides of the pie pan.

To make a straight-edged crust around the rim of the pie pan, press the crumbs between your index fingers horizontally at the top of the pan.

Transfer the pie pan to a baking sheet and chill in the freezer for 20 minutes. This keeps the pie crust from sliding down the sides of the pan as it bakes.

Adjust an oven rack to the lower third and preheat the oven to 350°F.

Bake the pie crust for 8 to 10 minutes, until lightly colored and set.

Remove the pan from the oven and cool on a rack while preparing the filling. Lower the oven heat to 325°F.

KEY LIME FILLING

4 extra-large egg yolks, at room temperature

Place the egg yolks in a medium mixing bowl and whisk together lightly.

One 14-ounce can sweetened condensed milk
½ cup freshly squeezed or bottled Key lime juice
Finely grated zest of 2 (regular) medium limes

Add the sweetened condensed milk to the egg yolks and whisk together thoroughly. Add the lime juice and zest and whisk together until smooth, about 1 minute. Let the mixture stand for 1 to 2 minutes and it will begin to thicken.

Transfer the filling to the pie crust and spread it out smoothly and evenly with a rubber spatula.

Bake the pie until the filling is set and doesn't jiggle when the pan is shaken, 12 to 15 minutes.

Remove the pan from the oven and cool completely on a rack. Chill the pie in the refrigerator for at least 1 hour. To hold the pie longer than an hour and prevent a crust from forming on top of the filling, spray a large piece of waxed paper with non-stick cooking spray and place it directly on top of the pie. Then tightly cover the pie with a double layer of plastic wrap.

3 months, wrap the pie pan snugly in several layers of plastic wrap and place it in a freezer bag. Use a large piece of masking tape and an indelible marker to label and date the contents. If frozen, defrost overnight in the refrigerator before using.

The pie crust can be baked in advance and kept tightly covered with aluminum foil at room temperature for up to 2 days before filling.

Making a Change
To make an almond nut crust, replace the graham crackers with 1¾ cups sliced or slivered almonds or 1½ cups almond meal.

Adding Style
Add 2 tablespoons finely grated or minced lime zest to the pie crust before adding the butter.

¾ cup heavy whipping
cream

Place the cream in the chilled bowl of an electric stand mixer or a chilled large mixing bowl. Use a chilled wire whip attachment or a hand-held mixer to whip the cream on medium speed until frothy.

¼ cup confectioners' sugar,
sifted
1 teaspoon pure vanilla
extract

Add the confectioners' sugar and vanilla and continue to whip until the cream holds soft peaks.

Remove the pie from the refrigerator and remove the plastic wrap and waxed paper. Transfer the whipped cream to the top of the chilled pie. Use a rubber spatula to spread it evenly over the top of the pie.

Finely grated zest of
2 (regular) medium limes

Sprinkle the lime zest evenly over the top of the pie. Cut the pie into wedges and serve.

Key Lime Squares

THESE ARE SIMILAR to lemon bars, but more exotic, and taste like the tropics to me. They have a flavorful Key lime topping that sits on a pastry dough base made with coconut and macadamia nuts. The topping is added to the partially baked pastry dough and then the cookies are baked through. After the cookies cool, they are cut into squares and dusted with confectioners' sugar. **Makes sixteen 2-inch squares**

Essential Gear

- 9-inch square baking pan
- Food processor
- Microplane grater or citrus zester
- Cooling rack
- Electric stand mixer with wire whip attachment, or large mixing bowl and hand-held mixer
- Rubber spatula
- Ruler
- Chef's knife
- Sugar dredger or medium-size fine-mesh strainer

Keeping

Store the squares in a single layer between pieces of waxed paper in an airtight container at room temperature for up to 5 days.

1 tablespoon unsalted butter,
softened

Center a rack in the oven and preheat it to 350°F. Line the baking pan with a large piece of aluminum foil that extends over the sides. Press the foil under the sides of the pan. Use a paper towel or your fingertips to butter the foil evenly.

PASTRY DOUGH

1½ cups all-purpose flour
¾ cup unsweetened
shredded coconut
⅓ cup confectioners' sugar
⅓ cup toasted, unsalted
macadamia nuts
⅛ teaspoon salt

In the work bowl of a food processor fitted with the steel blade, combine the flour, coconut, confectioners' sugar, macadamia nuts, and salt. Pulse until the nuts are very finely ground, about 2 minutes.

6 ounces (12 tablespoons, 1½ sticks) unsalted butter, chilled	Cut the butter into small pieces and add to the flour mixture. Pulse until the butter is cut into very tiny pieces, then process until the dough wraps itself around the blade, about 1 minute.
	Turn the pastry dough onto the foil-lined baking pan. Dust your hands with flour and press the dough evenly into the pan.
	Bake the dough for 20 to 23 minutes, until light golden on the edges. Remove the baking pan from the oven and cool on a rack while preparing the filling.

KEY LIME FILLING

3 extra-large eggs, at room temperature	Place the eggs in the bowl of an electric stand mixer or in a large mixing bowl. Use the wire whip attachment or a hand-held mixer to whip the eggs on medium-high speed until they thicken, about 2 minutes.
1¼ cups granulated sugar	Slowly sprinkle on the sugar and continue to whip on medium-high speed until the mixture is very thick and pale colored and holds a slowly dissolving ribbon as the beater is lifted, about 5 minutes.
3 tablespoons all-purpose flour ¾ teaspoon baking powder	In a small bowl, combine the flour and baking powder and stir together to blend well. Add to the egg mixture and blend together well on medium speed. Stop and scrape down the sides and bottom of the mixing bowl with a rubber spatula.
⅓ cup freshly squeezed or bottled Key lime juice (from 10 to 12 Key limes) Finely grated or minced zest of 2 (regular) limes	Add the lime juice and lime zest to the mixture and blend well.
	Pour the filling over the top of the crust in the baking pan. Bake for 30 to 35 minutes, until the top is set and light golden, and a cake tester inserted in the center comes out clean or only slightly damp. Remove the baking pan from the oven and cool completely on a rack.
	Use the foil to lift the baked uncut cake from the baking pan and place on a cutting board. Peel the foil away from the sides. Use a ruler to mark where to cut the bars, measuring 2 inches square, then use a chef's knife to cut the squares.

GARNISH

3 tablespoons confectioners' sugar	Place the confectioners' sugar in a dredger or a fine-mesh strainer and heavily dust the tops of the lime squares.

Streamlining

The pastry dough can be made in advance and kept in the refrigerator, tightly wrapped in a double layer of plastic wrap, for up to 4 days. To freeze for up to 3 months, wrap the dough snugly in several layers of plastic wrap and place it in a freezer bag. Use a large piece of masking tape and an indelible marker to label and date the contents. If frozen, defrost overnight in the refrigerator before using. If the dough is too firm to press into the pan, let it stand to warm up to room temperature.

Making a Change

Replace the Key lime juice with regular lime juice.

Adding Style

Decorate the top of each lime square with 1 teaspoon of finely chopped, toasted, unsalted macadamia nuts.

Lime and Macadamia Nut Tart

THE LIME and macadamia nut custard filling of this tart is surrounded by a delicate tart dough accented with ground macadamia nuts. A little whipped cream for decoration, with lime zest and a scattering of chopped, toasted macadamia nuts, sets off this tart beautifully. **Makes one 9-inch square tart, 9 servings**

MACADAMIA NUT PASTRY DOUGH

1½ cups all-purpose flour
½ cup toasted, unsalted macadamia nuts
1 tablespoon granulated sugar
⅛ teaspoon salt

In the work bowl of a food processor fitted with the steel blade, combine the flour, macadamia nuts, sugar, and salt. Pulse until the nuts are finely ground, 30 seconds to 1 minute.

4 ounces (8 tablespoons, 1 stick) unsalted butter, chilled

Cut the butter into small pieces and add to the flour. Pulse until the butter is cut into very tiny pieces, about 30 seconds. The texture will be sandy with very tiny lumps throughout.

1 extra-large egg yolk, at room temperature
½ teaspoon pure vanilla extract
2 to 3 tablespoons cold water

In a small bowl, use a fork to lightly beat the egg yolk with the vanilla. Add the water and stir together.

With the food processor running, pour the egg yolk mixture through the feed tube. Process the dough until the mixture wraps itself around the blade, about 1 minute. If the dough is dry, add another tablespoon of water.

Turn the pastry dough onto a large piece of plastic wrap. Shape into a flat disk and wrap tightly in a double layer of plastic wrap. Chill in the refrigerator until firm before using, at least 2 hours. Chilling the dough relaxes the gluten in the flour so it won't be too elastic and will roll out easily. It also firms up the butter in the dough so it will need less flour when rolled out. If the dough is too firm it will splinter and break when rolled out. Let it stand at room temperature for 10 to 15 minutes before rolling to become more pliable.

On a smooth, flat surface, roll out the pastry dough between sheets of lightly floured waxed or parchment paper to a large square about

Essential Gear

- Food processor
- Rolling pin
- 9-inch square, fluted-edge tart pan with removable bottom
- Baking sheet
- Aluminum foil
- Pie weights
- Whisk or rubber spatula
- Fine grater or citrus zester
- Cooling rack
- 12- to 14-inch pastry bag with large open star tube
- Electric stand mixer with wire whip attachment, or hand-held mixer and medium mixing bowl

Keeping

Although the tart is best eaten the day it is made, it can last up to 3 days. Store the tart on a jelly-roll pan, loosely covered with waxed paper and then tightly wrapped with aluminum foil, in the refrigerator.

Streamlining

The pastry dough can be made in advance and kept in the refrigerator, tightly wrapped in a double layer of plastic wrap, for up to 4 days. To freeze up to 3 months, wrap the dough snugly in several layers of plastic wrap and place it in a freezer bag. Use a large piece of masking tape and an indelible marker to label and date the contents. If

11 inches wide. To tell if the dough will fit the tart pan, hold the pan above the dough. If there are about 2 inches of dough that protrude beyond the sides of the pan, it will fit.

Carefully peel the paper off the top of the dough. Brush excess flour off the dough, then loosely roll the pastry dough around the rolling pin without the bottom piece of paper. Place the tart pan directly underneath the rolling pin and carefully unroll the pastry dough into the tart pan. Gently lift up the sides and ease the pastry dough into the bottom and sides of the tart pan. Trim off the excess pastry dough at the top of the pan. Transfer the tart pan to a baking sheet and chill in the freezer for 15 minutes. This helps prevent the dough from shrinking as it bakes.

Center a rack in the oven and preheat it to 400°F.

Line the pastry shell with a large piece of aluminum foil that fits well against the bottom and sides. Fill with pie weights or a mixture of rice and beans. Bake for 15 minutes. Remove the foil and weights. If the bottom of the pastry shell puffs up, gently pierce it in several places with a fork to release the air. Remove the pan from the oven and transfer to a rack to cool while preparing the filling.

LIME AND MACADAMIA NUT FILLING

2 large limes

Use a fine grater to remove the outer rind of the limes. Take care not to grate the inner white pith, which is very bitter. Or use a zester to remove the lime zest and chop it very finely with a chef's knife.

Cut the limes in half, squeeze out the juice, and strain it to remove any seeds.

½ cup granulated sugar
½ cup toasted, unsalted macadamia nuts, finely ground
2 extra-large eggs, at room temperature
3 ounces (6 tablespoons, ¾ stick) unsalted butter, melted and cooled

In the work bowl of a food processor fitted with the steel blade, combine the lime zest, sugar, macadamia nuts, and eggs. Pulse briefly to blend. Add the lime juice and butter and process about 15 seconds to blend thoroughly.

Pour the filling into the tart shell. Bake for 30 minutes, until firm and lightly browned on top.

Remove the pan from the oven and cool completely on a rack.

frozen, defrost overnight in the refrigerator before using.

Troubleshooting

Don't roll out the pastry dough before it is chilled. The dough will be too soft and it will require a lot of flour to roll out, which results in a tough dough.

Once the pastry dough is unrolled into the tart pan, don't push it down forcefully. This will stretch the dough, which will shrink as it bakes, making it flat instead of taking the shape of the tart pan.

Making a Change

Replace the limes with lemons.

Replace the macadamia nuts with pecans or pistachio nuts.

⅓ cup heavy whipping
cream

Place the cream in the chilled bowl of an electric stand mixer or a medium mixing bowl. Using the wire whip attachment or a hand-held mixer, whip the cream on medium speed until it is frothy.

2 teaspoons confectioners'
sugar

Add the confectioners' sugar and continue to whip the cream on medium speed until it holds soft peaks.

Fit the pastry bag with the star tip and fill partway with the whipped cream. Holding the pastry bag about 1 inch above the tart, pipe a row of shells from the center, diagonally across to one of the corners (see page 44). Repeat this design over the top of the tart.

Finely grated zest of
1 large lime
¼ cup finely chopped
toasted, unsalted
macadamia nuts

Scatter the lime zest and macadamia nuts over the top of the tart.

Orange Cheesecake with Candied Orange Slices

THIS DENSE and creamy cheesecake has a crust made of ground walnuts. The top of the cake is decorated with candied orange slices that not only look good, but taste good too. Be sure to make the cheesecake in advance of serving because it needs hours to cool and chill. It freezes very well, but it's best to freeze it without the candied orange slices. Although this cheesecake is not cooked in a water bath like many other cheesecakes, it still has a creamy texture. **Makes one 9½-inch round cake, 12 to 14 servings**

Center a rack in the oven and preheat it to 375°F.

WALNUT CRUST

2 cups walnuts
2 tablespoons light brown
sugar
¼ teaspoon ground
cinnamon
2 ounces (4 tablespoons,
½ stick) unsalted butter,
melted and cooled

In the work bowl of a food processor fitted with the steel blade, combine the walnuts, brown sugar, and cinnamon. Pulse until the walnuts are finely ground, about 1 minute. Add the butter and pulse briefly to blend.

Essential Gear
- Food processor or rolling pin
- 9½-inch round spring-form pan
- Electric stand mixer with flat beater attachment, or hand-held mixer and 3-quart mixing bowl
- Cooling rack
- 2-quart heavy-bottomed saucepan
- Microplane grater or citrus zester
- Rubber spatula

Keeping
Store the cheesecake, tented with aluminum foil, in the refrigerator up to 4 days. To freeze up to 2 months with-

Transfer the mixture to the springform pan and use your fingers to press the mixture evenly into the bottom of the pan Chill the crust while preparing the cheesecake batter.

CHEESECAKE

1½ pounds cream cheese, softened	Place the cream cheese in the bowl of an electric stand mixer or in a large mixing bowl. Use the flat beater attachment or hand-held mixer to beat the cream cheese on medium speed until it's fluffy, about 2 minutes.
¾ cup granulated sugar **½ cup firmly packed light brown sugar**	Add the granulated sugar and brown sugar to the cream cheese and mix thoroughly. Stop occasionally and scrape down the sides and bottom of the bowl with a rubber spatula.
3 extra-large eggs, at room temperature	One at a time, add the eggs to the cream cheese, beating well after each addition. The eggs will sit on top of the cream cheese, so stop frequently and scrape down the bottom and sides of the bowl with a rubber spatula to help mix evenly.
2 teaspoons pure vanilla extract **½ teaspoon salt**	Add the vanilla and salt to the cream cheese and blend well.
2 cups sour cream **Finely grated zest of 3 large oranges**	Add the sour cream to the cream cheese and blend thoroughly. Then add the orange zest and blend well. Turn the batter into the crust in the springform pan. Use a rubber spatula to smooth and even the top. Place the springform pan on a baking sheet.
	Bake the cake for 50 to 60 minutes, until the top is light golden and set, but still jiggles slightly. Remove the pan from the oven and cool the cheesecake on a rack. Cover the top of the cheesecake with waxed paper and wrap tightly in aluminum foil. Refrigerate the cake for at least 6 hours before serving. To unmold the cheesecake, dip a thin-bladed knife in hot water and dry it, then run it around the inner edge of the pan, release the clip on the rim of the pan, and gently lift it off the cake.

CANDIED ORANGE SLICES

4 cups granulated sugar **2 cups water**	Combine the sugar and water in the saucepan. Bring to a boil over medium-high heat to dissolve the sugar.

out the candied orange slices, wrap the cake tightly in several layers of plastic wrap and aluminum foil. Use a large piece of masking tape and an indelible marker to label and date the contents. If frozen, defrost overnight in the refrigerator and bring to room temperature before serving.

Store the candied orange slices in the sugar syrup in an airtight container in the refrigerator for up to 3 weeks.

Making a Change
Replace the walnuts with macadamia nuts or pecans.

2 large oranges	Slice each end off of the oranges, then slice the oranges into ¼-inch-thick slices. Add the oranges to the sugar syrup and simmer for 30 minutes. Remove the pan from the heat and cool the orange slices in the sugar syrup, about 4 hours.
	Arrange the candied orange slices on top of the cheesecake in circles, slightly overlapping each other, and covering the top completely.

Orange Muffins with Dried Cherries

DRIED CHERRIES soaked in orange juice add moisture and lots of flavor to these yummy muffins. These are great for breakfast, for afternoon tea, as a snack, or for dessert. Try them warmed up and served with jam. **Makes 12 muffins**

Center a rack in the oven and preheat it to 400°F. Line each cavity of the muffin pan with a paper muffin cup.

1 cup dried cherries **Juice of 1 large orange** **(about ⅓ cup)**	Place the dried cherries in a small bowl and cover with the orange juice. Tightly cover the bowl with plastic wrap and let the cherries soak for at least 15 minutes.
4 ounces (8 tablespoons, **1 stick) unsalted butter,** **softened**	Place the butter in the bowl of an electric stand mixer or in a large mixing bowl. Use the flat beater attachment or hand-held mixer to beat the butter on medium speed until it's fluffy, about 2 minutes.
½ cup granulated sugar	Add the sugar to the butter, and cream together well. Stop occasionally and scrape down the sides and bottom of the bowl with a rubber spatula.
1 extra-large egg, at room **temperature** **½ teaspoon pure vanilla** **extract**	Lightly beat the egg and vanilla together in a small bowl and add to the butter mixture. The egg will sit on top, so scrape down the sides and bottom of the bowl with a rubber spatula to help mix evenly. The mixture may look curdled as the eggs are added, but as you stop and scrape down the bowl, the mixture will smooth out.
Finely grated zest of 2 large **oranges**	Add the orange zest to the butter mixture and blend together well.
1⅔ cups all-purpose flour **1 teaspoon baking powder** **1 teaspoon baking soda** **¼ teaspoon salt**	Over a large piece of waxed or parchment paper or a bowl, sift together the flour, baking powder, and baking soda. Add the salt and toss to blend well.

Essential Gear

- 12-cavity 3-inch muffin pan
- 3-inch pleated paper muffin cups
- Electric stand mixer and flat beater, or hand-held mixer and large mixing bowl
- Rubber spatula or wooden spoon
- Cooling rack
- Microplane grater or citrus zester

Keeping

Store the muffins in an airtight plastic container between layers of waxed paper at room temperature up to 3 days. To freeze up to 2 months, wrap the container tightly in several layers of plastic wrap and aluminum foil. Use a large piece of masking tape and an indelible marker to label and date the contents. If frozen, defrost overnight in the refrigerator and bring to room temperature before serving.

Add the dry ingredients to the butter mixture in 3 stages, stopping to scrape down the sides and bottom of the bowl with a rubber spatula between each addition.

½ cup buttermilk

Add the buttermilk to the batter and blend thoroughly.

Add the dried cherries and orange juice and blend until smooth.

Use a spoon to divide the batter evenly among the 12 muffin cups, filling them to the top.

Bake the muffins for 18 to 20 minutes, until they have risen and set and a tester inserted in the center comes out clean. Remove the pan from the oven and cool on a rack. When the muffins are cool, gently pry them out of the pan. Serve warm or at room temperature.

To rewarm the muffins, place them in a 325°F oven for 8 to 10 minutes.

Candied Orange Peel

HOMEMADE CANDIED orange peel is one of my all-time favorite confections. It is a completely different animal than the store-bought version, unless you are lucky enough to live near a fabulous pastry shop. This is divine to eat on its own and even better when dipped in chocolate. It also is an extraordinary ingredient to add to a variety of cakes and other desserts. This recipe makes a large quantity, but it keeps for several months in a tightly sealed container in the refrigerator. When you have this on hand, you will devise ways to use it because it tastes so good. Once you make this, you will be a convert! **Makes 6 cups**

6 to 8 large, thick-skinned oranges

Using a chef's knife, slice the ends off the oranges, then cut the oranges into quarters. Cut off most of the pulp, but leave some attached. This keeps the orange peel from becoming bitter as it cooks.

Cut the orange quarters lengthwise into thin slices.

Place the orange slices in the saucepan and cover with cold water. Bring the water to a boil over medium-high heat and cook for 5 minutes.

Essential Gear

- Chef's knife
- Very large saucepan
- Colander or strainer
- Heat-resistant spatula or wooden spoon
- Two or three baking sheets

To Keep

Store the candied orange peel in an airtight container in the refrigerator up to 4 months.

Making a Change

Replace the oranges with 12 large lemons, 14 limes, 12 tangerines, or 4 grapefruits.

Drain the oranges and cover with fresh cold water. Bring the water to a boil over medium-high heat and cook for 5 minutes.

Once again, drain the oranges and repeat the process with fresh cold water.

Drain the oranges and rinse them in cold water. Using your fingers, remove any remaining pulp that is still attached to the orange slices.

3 cups granulated sugar
¼ cup orange liqueur

Replace the orange slices in the saucepan. Add the sugar and orange liqueur. Cook over low heat, stirring frequently, until the sugar is dissolved, about 5 minutes.

Cook the mixture at a simmer over very low heat for $1\frac{1}{2}$ hours, stirring frequently. Most of the sugar will be absorbed by the orange peel as it cooks.

Remove the saucepan from the heat.

Cover 2 or 3 baking sheets with waxed or parchment paper.

3 cups granulated sugar

Mound the sugar in the center of a large sheet of waxed or parchment paper.

Take large spoonfuls of the orange peel and place them in the sugar. Roll them in the sugar, separating the slices, then transfer them to the lined baking sheets and let them air dry for 20 to 30 minutes. Repeat until all the orange slices are coated in sugar.

4

BERRIES AND

GRAPES

SELDOM DO ALL the berries that I buy at the store make it home. When I get to my car, I always open up one of the little cartons and start eating them. I love all berries, but I have to admit raspberries and blueberries are my favorites. Berries by themselves are great, but baking with berries, either by baking them into something or putting fresh berries on top or garnishing with them, can bring about the ultimate results when it comes to baked goods. You get the great taste of the berries combined with many other wonderful flavors and textures. You can't go wrong with berries, as you will see with the recipes that I have included in this chapter.

Berries are a summer fruit—except for cranberries, which are in season in the fall. Another exception is strawberries, which are avail-able in mid- to late winter where I live in southern California. Also, I have noticed that during the winter and spring months, a limited amount of all berries show up in the market that are grown inside environmentally controlled nurseries or shipped in from other parts of the world.

Although this isn't commonly known, grapes are related to berries. Like berries, they grow in bunches on vines. Also like berries, seldom do the grapes I buy make it home without me personally tasting them. But unlike berries, grapes are available year-round and, as you may know, there is a very large variety of them.

Berries and grapes are found in the produce section of supermarkets, produce stores, farmer's markets, and the roadside stands in the berry fields near my home, where I like to buy my berries.

Berries are the most perishable of all fruits.

TIPS AND TECHNIQUES

Berries should be bought when they are ripe and must be used quickly. One or two days in the refrigerator is usually okay. Berries are the most perishable of all fruits. They should have good consistent color and, of course, be the right color for that berry. Also, berries should be plump and have good form. Watch out for smashed berries, which can easily happen if they have been mishandled or too many berries have been stacked on each other. Usually berries are packaged in shallow containers to avoid being smashed. And make sure that your berries do not have mold. This can look like a grayish coating or small black spots, and any discoloring can be a sign that the berries are going bad. Do look closely because sometimes the packaging over the berries can camouflage their appearance. Turn over the container and check the bottom to make sure there is no juice, which is an indication that the berries are overripe. Bring the berries close to your nose so you can smell their luscious aroma.

Several recipes in this chapter state that fresh-frozen berries can be used if fresh berries are not available. Here I am referring to berries that have been packaged without added sugar syrup. It's not necessary to defrost the frozen berries, but most recipes will need to bake a few minutes longer. Follow the instructions in each recipe.

Grapes are commonly bought in bunches that are packaged in premeasured plastic bags. These bags have holes in them so the grapes can breathe. Grapes should look plump and have good color and a slight fragrance. If possible, taste them for sweetness before buying.

Limit the handling of berries because they are so delicate. Rinse them with cold water and dry on paper towels right before using. Strawberries should be hulled before use but after they are washed. There are small tools called strawberry hullers that look like a fat pair of tweezers. These are used to pinch the green caps off of the berries.

To prevent batters from turning blue when using blueberries, fold the berries in at the last minute. Because cranberries are so tart, they need to be added to the batter of muffins or cakes that have a good amount of sugar. Fresh cranberries come in 12-ounce plastic bags and last up to four months in the refrigerator and up to a year in the freezer.

Grapes keep at room temperature for a few days and in the refrigerator for one week or longer. Rinse grapes in cold water right before using and dry thoroughly with paper towels.

Bagatelle

ABAGATELLE is a stunning classic French strawberry cake. The cake is made with génoise, which is a light and airy butter sponge cake that is mainly used as the base for multi-layered cakes and desserts. The génoise is cut in half horizontally and spread with a mixture of vanilla pastry cream and whipped cream firmed up with gelatin. A layer of fresh strawberries covers the cream filling, and vertically cut strawberries show around the outside edges of the cake. The top of the cake is decorated with a thin circle of marzipan and a twisted marzipan rope. This cake has several component parts and many of them can be prepared in advance for later assembly. It's a beautiful and luscious cake that can take center stage at any spring or summer gathering. **Makes one 9-inch round cake, 12 to 14 servings**

GÉNOISE

Center a rack in the oven and preheat it to 300°F.

2 teaspoons unsalted butter, softened	Using a paper towel or your fingertips, generously butter the inside of the cake pan, coating it thoroughly.
2 teaspoons all-purpose flour	Dust the inside of the pan with the flour. Shake and tilt the pan to evenly distribute the flour, then turn the pan over and shake out the excess over the sink.
	Cut a round of parchment paper to fit the bottom of the pan. Butter the parchment paper round and place in the pan, butter-side up.
3 extra-large eggs, at room temperature **3 extra-large egg yolks, at room temperature**	Place the eggs and egg yolks in the bowl of an electric stand mixer or in a large mixing bowl. Use the wire whip attachment or a hand held mixer to blend together at low speed.
½ cup granulated sugar	Add the sugar and increase the mixer speed to medium. Whip the eggs, yolks, and sugar together until the mixture is very thick and pale colored and holds a slowly dissolving ribbon as the beater is lifted, about 5 minutes
¼ cup all-purpose flour **¼ cup cornstarch**	Over a piece of waxed or parchment paper or a bowl, sift together the flour and cornstarch. Using a rubber spatula, fold this mixture into the whipped egg mixture in 3 stages, blending thoroughly after each addition.

Essential Gear

- One 9 × 2-inch round cake pan
- Scissors
- Parchment paper
- Two rubber spatulas
- Electric stand mixer with flat beater attachment, and wire whip attachment or large mixing bowl and hand-held mixer
- Cooling rack
- Two 9-inch cardboard cake circles
- 2-cup heavy-bottomed saucepan
- Serrated knife
- 1-inch natural-bristle pastry brush
- 10-inch flexible-blade icing spatula
- Strainer
- Rolling pin
- Offset spatula

Keeping

Store the cake, loosely covered with waxed paper and tightly covered with aluminum foil, in the refrigerator for up to 2 days. If the marzipan forms condensation, use a paper towel to blot it off and dust the area lightly with confectioners' sugar.

Streamlining

Bake the génoise up to 2 days before assembling the cake and keep it tightly covered with a double layer of plastic wrap in the refrigerator. To freeze the

1 tablespoon unsalted butter, melted	Using a rubber spatula, fold the butter into the egg mixture in 2 stages, blending well. The butter has a tendency to fall straight to the bottom of the bowl, so be sure to scrape the bottom of the bowl with the rubber spatula as you fold the mixture.

Transfer the cake mixture to the prepared cake pan and use the rubber spatula to smooth the top.

Bake the cake for 45 to 50 minutes, until golden and the top springs back when lightly touched.

Remove the cake pan from the oven and cool on a rack.

Place the cake circle or a plate over the top of the cake pan and invert the cake. Lift off the cake pan and carefully peel the parchment paper off of the bottom. Re-invert the cake onto the cardboard cake circle or plate. Let the cake cool completely on a rack.

SUGAR SYRUP

2 tablespoons granulated sugar **¼ cup water**	Combine the sugar and water in the saucepan. Bring to a boil over medium heat to dissolve the sugar. Remove the saucepan from the heat and cool the sugar syrup.

CREAM FILLING

¾ cup heavy whipping cream	Place the cream in the chilled bowl of an electric stand mixer or in a chilled large mixing bowl. Use the wire whip attachment or a hand-held mixer to whip the cream on medium speed until it holds firm peaks.
¾ cup Vanilla Pastry Cream (see Pluot Custard Tart, page 92)	Whisk or stir the pastry cream vigorously to remove any lumps. Using a rubber spatula, fold the whipped cream into the pastry cream, blending well. Cover the bowl with plastic wrap and refrigerate the cream mixture while preparing the gelatin.
1 envelope (2¼ teaspoons) powdered gelatin or 4 leaves gelatin	If using powdered gelatin, sprinkle it over 2 tablespoons cold water in a small bowl and let it stand for 5 minutes. Then transfer the mixture to the top of a double boiler and melt over low heat, stirring occasionally.

If using gelatin leaves, which are very brittle, soak them in cold water to soften for 10 minutes until they are soft and very pliable. Squeeze out the excess liquid and melt the gelatin in a small saucepan over very low heat.

genoise up to 3 months, wrap it snugly in several layers of plastic wrap and place in a freezer bag. Use a large piece of masking tape and an indelible marker to label and date the contents. If frozen, defrost the cake overnight in the refrigerator.

The sugar syrup can be made in advance and kept in a tightly covered plastic container in the refrigerator for up to 2 weeks.

The marzipan can be colored and cut into a circle, and the rope shaped in advance. Store the marzipan on a waxed paper–lined baking sheet, tightly covered with plastic wrap to keep it from drying out, at room temperature for up to 3 days.

Remove the bowl with the cream filling from the refrigerator and remove the plastic wrap. Pour the liquid gelatin into the cream mixture in a steady stream, whisking by hand constantly and thoroughly until well blended. The gelatin may clump in the bottom of the bowl, so it's very important to whisk continuously while pouring it into the cream mixture.

ASSEMBLY

2 pints fresh strawberries, washed, dried, hulled, and cut in half vertically

Using a serrated knife, cut the génoise in half horizontally (see page 34). Place the bottom layer back on the cake circle or a serving plate. With your fingertips, gently peel the skin off of the top of the cake.

Place strips of waxed paper around the bottom edges of the cake to protect the plate while assembling the cake. Use the pastry brush to brush the bottom layer with half of the cooled sugar syrup to moisten it.

Using a flexible-blade spatula, spread half of the cream filling over the bottom cake layer. Spread the filling just to the outer edges but not over them.

Make a tight circle of cut strawberries around the edge of the génoise, standing the berries on their stem ends, with the cut sides facing out. Choose berries that are the same height so the cake won't look lopsided.

Cover the cream with the remaining strawberries, cut sides down, close together.

Using a flexible-blade spatula, spread the remaining cream filling over the berries, leaving the tops of the outer row of berries clean.

Place the top layer of génoise on top of the cream, lining up the edges so it sits straight on top of the berries and cream. Brush the top of the cake layer with the remaining cooled sugar syrup.

APRICOT GLAZE

¼ cup apricot preserves
1 tablespoon amaretto, cognac, or water

Combine the apricot preserves and liquid in a small saucepan. Bring to a boil over medium heat. Remove the pan from the heat and strain the glaze into a small bowl, pushing through as much of the pulp as possible.

Brush the top of the cake with the apricot glaze.

MARZIPAN DECORATION

1½ rolls (10 ounces) marzipan

Divide the marzipan into two pieces, the smaller being ⅓ of the total amount.

Red paste food coloring
Confectioners' sugar

Take the smaller piece of marzipan and use a toothpick to dab 2 or 3 drops of red paste food coloring into it. Sprinkle a smooth flat work surface with confectioners' sugar. Knead the marzipan (see page 47) to evenly distribute the coloring until it is smooth. Use more confectioners' sugar as needed to keep the marzipan from sticking to the work surface. Cover the marzipan with plastic wrap to keep it from drying out.

Green paste food coloring
Confectioners' sugar

Take the remaining piece of marzipan and color it with green paste food coloring in the same way as above, using confectioners' sugar to keep it from sticking to the work surface.

Set aside ⅓ of the green marzipan, keeping it covered with plastic wrap so it doesn't dry out. On a smooth, flat work surface dusted with confectioners' sugar, roll out the remaining green marzipan to a thickness of ⅛ inch. Using a 9-inch cardboard cake circle as a guide, cut a circle out of the marzipan. Use an offset spatula to slide under the marzipan circle to make sure it's not sticking to the work surface. Use the spatula to help move the marzipan circle to the top of the cake. Press lightly on the marzipan so it sticks to the apricot glaze on the cake. If necessary, use scissors to trim the outer edge of the marzipan circle so it is even with the edge of the cake. Lightly brush the outer top edge of the marzipan circle with water.

Roll the remaining green marzipan into a thin rope about 14 inches long. Repeat this with the pink marzipan. Lay both marzipan ropes next to each other and wind them together to form a twisted rope by holding one hand palm-side down at one end of the ropes and pushing it away from you while using your other hand at the opposite end to twist toward yourself.

Place the rope around the outside top edge of the cake, tucking in the ends, or trimming them off if necessary.

Confectioners' sugar

Lightly dust the top of the cake with confectioners' sugar.

Serve immediately, cutting the cake into wedges, or refrigerate for up to 6 hours, covered with waxed paper.

Berry Tartlets

C LASSIC PÂTE SUCRÉE (pronounced pot sue *cray*) pastry dough baked into individual tartlets holds a filling of velvety vanilla pastry cream. Fresh berries sit on top of the pastry cream and are brushed with apricot glaze. These tartlets look like little jewels on a serving platter. You can create a diverse assortment by changing the shape of the tartlets and the berries on top. Be sure to make the pastry dough in advance of when you plan to assemble these so it has time to rest, and the pastry cream should also be made ahead so it has time to cool and thicken. **Makes eighteen 2¹/₂-inch round tartlets, twelve 5 × 1³/₄ × ³/₄-inch boat-shaped tartlets, or four 4¹/₄ × ³/₄-inch round tartlets**

PASTRY DOUGH

1¹/₄ **cups all-purpose flour**
3 **tablespoons granulated sugar**
¹/₈ **teaspoon salt**

In the work bowl of a food processor fitted with the steel blade, combine the flour, sugar, and salt. Pulse briefly to blend.

4 **ounces (8 tablespoons, 1 stick) unsalted butter, chilled**

Cut the butter into small pieces and add to the flour mixture. Pulse until the butter is cut into very tiny pieces, about 30 seconds. The texture will be sandy with very tiny lumps throughout.

1 **extra-large egg yolk, at room temperature**
¹/₂ **teaspoon pure vanilla extract**

In a small bowl, use a fork to lightly beat the egg yolk with the vanilla. With the food processor running, pour this mixture through the feed tube. Process the dough until the mixture wraps itself around the blade, about 1 minute.

Turn the pastry dough onto a large piece of plastic wrap. Shape into a flat disk and wrap tightly. Chill in the refrigerator until firm before using, at least 2 hours. Chilling the dough relaxes the gluten in the flour so it won't be too elastic and will roll out easily. It also firms up the butter in the dough so it will need less flour when rolled out. If the dough is too firm it will splinter and break when rolled out. Let it stand at room temperature for 10 to 15 minutes before rolling to become more pliable.

Center a rack in the oven and preheat it to 375°F.

On a smooth, flat surface, roll out the pastry dough between sheets of lightly floured waxed or parchment paper to a large rectangle about 16 × 12 inches. Carefully peel the paper off the top of the

Essential Gear

- Food processor
- Rolling pin
- 3¹/₄-inch plain round cutter
- Thirty-six 2¹/₂-inch round, fluted-edge tartlet pans or twenty-four 5 × 1³/₄ × ³/₄-inch boat-shaped, fluted-edge tartlet pans or six 4¹/₂-inch fluted-edge tartlet pans with removable bottoms
- Pie weights (for 4¹/₂-inch tartlets)
- Baking sheet
- Cooling rack
- 1-inch natural-bristle-pastry brush or a spoon
- Goose-feather pastry brush
- Strainer

Keeping

Store the tartlets in a single layer on a jelly-roll pan. Cover the top of the tartlets with a large piece of waxed paper to keep the surface from becoming marred. Tightly wrap the pan with plastic wrap and keep in the refrigerator up to 3 days.

Streamlining

The pastry dough can be made in advance and kept in the refrigerator, tightly wrapped in a double layer of plastic wrap, up to 4 days before using. To freeze up to 4 months, wrap it in a double layer of plastic wrap and place it inside a freezer bag. Use a large piece of masking

dough. Brush excess flour off the dough. Use the round cutter or a small bowl measuring 3¼ inches and cut out circles of the pastry dough. Carefully peel the circles off the bottom piece of paper. Gather together the dough scraps, reroll, and cut out any remaining circles. For the boat-shaped tartlets, use a small knife to cut out shapes slightly larger than the tartlet pans.

For the 4½-inch round tartlets, roll out the dough to a large rectangle about 16 × 12 inches. Carefully peel the paper off the top of the dough and brush off excess flour. Cut the dough in half horizontally, then vertically into 6 equal pieces. Carefully peel the squares off the bottom piece of paper.

Gently place each circle or square in the tartlet pans you are using. Carefully lift up the sides of the pastry dough and ease the dough into the bottom and sides of each tart pan. Trim off the excess pastry dough at the top of the pan with your fingertips. Transfer the tart pans to a baking sheet and chill for at least 15 minutes to set.

If using the 2½-inch round or the boat-shaped tartlets pan, top each with another tartlet pan the same size to act as weights while they bake. If using the 4½-inch round tartlet pans, line each pastry shell with a large piece of aluminum foil that fits well against the bottom and sides. Fill each pastry shell with pie weights or a mixture of rice and beans.

Bake the tartlet shells for 8 minutes for the smaller pans and 10 minutes for the larger pans, then remove the top tartlet pan or the foil and weights. If the bottom of the pastry shell puffs up, gently pierce it in a few places with a fork or the point of a knife to release the air. Bake another 10 minutes for the smaller pans and 12 to 14 minutes for the larger pans, until light golden and set. Remove the baking pan from the oven and transfer the tartlets to racks to cool completely.

To remove the tartlet shells from their pans, gently tap each pan on the countertop. The tartlet shell should slip out of the pan easily. If using the larger tartlet pans, set each pan on top of an upside-down bowl or cup that is smaller than the pan and the sides will fall away. Gently lift the tartlet shell off of the bottom of the pan.

ASSEMBLY

1 recipe Vanilla Pastry Cream (see Pluot Custard Tart, page 92)

Stir the pastry cream vigorously with a whisk or rubber spatula to eliminate any lumps. Using a spoon, spread pastry cream into each tartlet shell, filling it ¾ full.

tape and an indelible marker to label and date the contents. If frozen, defrost in the refrigerator overnight before using. If the dough is too cold to roll out, let it stand at room temperature to become pliable.

The tartlet shells can be baked and held at room temperature for up to 2 days before filling. After they are completely cool, place them on a jelly-roll pan between layers of waxed or parchment paper and tightly wrap the pan in aluminum foil.

The apricot glaze can be made in advance and kept in a tightly covered plastic container in the refrigerator up to 1 month before using. Warm it in a small saucepan over medium heat or in a microwave oven on medium power before using.

Making a Change

Replace the vanilla pastry cream filling with lemon curd (page 140) or 1 cup mascarpone plus 2 tablespoons superfine sugar whipped to soft peaks.

Troubleshooting

Don't roll out the pastry dough before it is chilled. The dough will be too soft and it will require a lot of flour to roll out, which will make the dough tough.

**1 cup fresh strawberries,
washed, dried, and hulled**

**1 cup fresh raspberries,
blackberries, and/or
blueberries**

Arrange berries on top of the pastry cream in each tartlet shell. Here are some arrangement ideas:

- Place a strawberry in the center and arrange vertically cut strawberry halves around it
- Place a strawberry in the center and arrange blueberries or blackberries around it.
- Place a raspberry in the center and arrange blueberries around it.
- Place a raspberry in the center and arrange raspberries around it.
- Place a blackberry in the center and arrange raspberries around it.

APRICOT GLAZE

⅓ cup apricot preserves

**1 tablespoon plus
2 teaspoons amaretto,
cognac, or water**

Combine the apricot preserves and liquid in a small saucepan. Bring to a boil over medium heat. Remove the pan from the heat and strain the glaze into a small bowl, pushing through as much of the pulp as possible.

Use a goose-feather pastry brush to lightly brush the top of each tartlet with the glaze. Don't apply a thick glaze, which looks unappetizing. The purpose of the glaze is to keep the berries from drying out and to make the top of each tartlet glisten.

The tartlets are best served within a few hours of assembly because the pastry cream will start to soften the tartlet shells. Refrigerate them until ready to serve.

Fresh Blackberry Cobbler

FRESH BLACKBERRIES take center stage in this cobbler. I have fond memories of picking wild blackberries with my brothers in the Berkeley hills when we lived there during and after college. We would pick gallons of berries and spent many days not only eating them fresh, but baking them into pies, cobblers, scones, and cakes and making delicious blackberry ice cream. This recipe is one of my favorites. You can replace the blackberries with other berries, like blueberries, raspberries, and boysenberries, or make a mixed berry cobbler. **Makes one 8-inch square cobbler, 8 to 10 servings**

Essential Gear

- 8-inch square baking pan
- Food processor
- Rolling pin
- Cooling rack
- Electric stand mixer with flat beater attachment and wire whip attachment, or large mixing bowl and hand-held mixer

Center a rack in the oven and preheat it to 400°F.

BLACKBERRY FILLING

7 cups fresh blackberries

Place the blackberries in the baking pan.

¾ cup granulated sugar
⅓ cup all-purpose flour
Finely grated or minced zest
of 1 large lemon
2 tablespoons freshly
squeezed lemon juice

Add the sugar, flour, lemon zest, and lemon juice to the berries and gently toss together to coat them completely.

2 ounces (4 tablespoons,
½ stick) unsalted butter,
softened

Cut the butter into small pieces and distribute evenly over the berries.

BISCUIT DOUGH TOPPING

1 cup all-purpose flour
2 tablespoons granulated
sugar
2 teaspoons baking powder
¼ teaspoon salt

In the work bowl of a food processor fitted with the steel blade, combine the flour, sugar, baking powder, and salt. Pulse briefly to blend.

2 ounces (4 tablespoons,
½ stick) unsalted butter,
chilled

Cut the butter into small pieces and add to the dry ingredients. Pulse until the butter is cut into very tiny pieces, about 1 minute. The texture should feel sandy with tiny lumps throughout.

⅓ cup heavy whipping
cream

With the food processor running, pour the cream through the feed tube. Process until the dough wraps itself around the blade, about 30 seconds.

On a smooth, flat surface, roll out the pastry dough between sheets of lightly floured waxed or parchment paper to a 9-inch square.

Carefully peel the waxed or parchment paper off the top of the dough. Brush excess flour off the dough, then loosely roll the pastry dough around the rolling pin without the bottom piece of paper. Place the baking pan directly underneath the rolling pin and carefully unroll the pastry dough into the pan. Roll the edges under and tuck them around the inside edges of the pan.

1 ounce (2 tablespoons)
unsalted butter, melted
1 tablespoon granulated
sugar

Pour the butter evenly over the top of the biscuit dough, then sprinkle with the sugar.

Keeping
Although the cobbler is best eaten the day it's made, it can last for up to 2 days. Store the cobbler, tightly covered with aluminum foil, in the refrigerator.

Streamlining
The biscuit dough can be made in advance. Shape it into a disk and keep in the refrigerator, tightly wrapped in a double layer of plastic wrap, up to 4 days. To freeze up to 3 months, wrap the dough snugly in several layers of plastic wrap and place it in a freezer bag. Use a large piece of masking tape and an indelible marker to label and date the contents. If frozen, defrost overnight in the refrigerator before using.

Making a Change
Use a mixture of fresh berries such as raspberries, blueberries, or boysenberries. If using mixed berries, eliminate the flour in the filling.

Use fresh-frozen berries if fresh berries are not available. It's not necessary to defrost the fresh-frozen berries before using, but bake the cobbler about 3 minutes longer.

Bake for 20 minutes, until the biscuit topping is light golden and set. Remove the pan from the oven and transfer to a rack to cool.

GARNISH

1 cup heavy whipping cream

Place the cream in the chilled bowl of an electric stand mixer or in a large mixing bowl. Use the wire whip attachment or a hand-held mixer to whip on medium speed until frothy.

2 tablespoons confectioners' sugar

Add the sugar and continue whipping the cream until it holds soft peaks.

Cut squares of the cobbler, scooping up the fruit. Serve each square with a large dollop of whipped cream.

Fresh Blueberry Coffee Cake

THERE IS NO COFFEE in this cake, but it's delicious eaten with coffee, or tea for that matter, at any time of day. This cake is especially good when warm. It's quick and easy to assemble and is perfect for spur-of-the-moment baking. **Makes one 8-inch square cake, 8 to 10 servings**

Center a rack in the oven and preheat it to 350°F.

1 tablespoon unsalted butter, softened

Use your fingertips or a paper towel to butter the inside of the baking pan.

CAKE

6 ounces (12 tablespoons, 1½ sticks) unsalted butter, softened

Place the butter in the bowl of an electric stand mixer or in a large mixing bowl. Use the flat beater attachment or hand-held mixer to beat the butter on medium speed until it's fluffy, about 2 minutes.

¾ cup granulated sugar

Add the sugar to the butter and cream together well. Stop occasionally and scrape down the sides and bottom of the bowl with a rubber spatula.

2 extra-large eggs, at room temperature

One at a time, add the eggs to the butter mixture, stopping to scrape down the bottom and sides of the bowl after each addition. At first

Essential Gear
- 8-inch square baking pan
- Rubber spatula or wooden spoon
- Electric stand mixer with flat beater attachment, or large mixing bowl and hand-held mixer
- Cooling rack
- Microplane grater or citrus zester

Keeping
Store the coffee cake, tightly covered with aluminum foil, at room temperature up to 4 days. To serve the cake warm, heat it in a 350°F oven for 12 minutes before serving.

Streamlining
The topping can be made in advance. Store it in a

the mixture may look curdled as the eggs are added, but as you stop and scrape down the bowl, the mixture will smooth out.

½ teaspoon pure vanilla extract

Finely grated zest of 1 large lemon

Add the vanilla and lemon zest and blend together well.

1¾ cups all-purpose flour
2 teaspoons baking powder
½ teaspoon freshly grated nutmeg
¼ teaspoon baking soda
¼ teaspoon salt
½ cup plain yogurt

In a medium bowl, combine the flour, baking powder, nutmeg, baking soda, and salt. Stir together to combine. In 3 stages, add to the butter mixture, alternately with the yogurt, starting with the dry ingredients. Stop and scrape down the bottom and sides of the bowl after each addition to encourage even mixing.

Transfer the cake batter to the prepared baking pan. Use a rubber spatula to spread the batter evenly into the pan and the corners.

2 cups fresh blueberries

Sprinkle the blueberries evenly over the cake batter.

TOPPING

½ cup all-purpose flour
½ cup firmly packed light brown sugar
½ teaspoon ground cinnamon

Combine the flour, brown sugar, and cinnamon in a small mixing bowl. Toss together to mix well.

3 ounces (6 tablespoons, ¾ stick) unsalted butter, chilled

Cut the butter into small pieces and add to the dry ingredients. Use your fingertips to quickly work the butter into the mixture until it is the size of small peas. If your fingertips are warm, run them under cold water and dry them before handling the butter to keep it from melting.

Evenly sprinkle this topping over the fruit in the baking pan.

Bake the cake for 40 to 45 minutes, until the topping is light golden and a cake tester inserted into the center comes out clean. Remove the pan from the oven and transfer to a rack to cool slightly.

Cut the cake into squares to serve.

tightly covered plastic container in the refrigerator up to 4 days.

Making a Change
Use wild blueberries if they are available, because they have an intensely sweet flavor.

Use fresh-frozen blueberries if fresh berries are not available. It's not necessary to defrost the fresh-frozen berries, but bake the coffee cake about 3 minutes longer.

Replace half of the blueberries with raspberries.

Adding Style
Serve squares of the coffee cake with vanilla ice cream.

Blueberry-Raspberry Buckle

A BUCKLE is an easy-to-make, classic, deep-dish American dessert. A rich cake batter is spread into a square baking pan, the berries are strewn over the batter, and a streusel topping is sprinkled over the berries. As the cake batter puffs up, it encloses the berries while their juices mix with the streusel topping to form a crisp top crust. This dessert is delicious served warm with whipped cream or vanilla ice cream. **Makes one 8-inch square buckle, 8 to 10 servings**

CAKE

Center a rack in the oven and preheat it to 350°F.

1 tablespoon unsalted butter, softened	Using a paper towel or your fingertips, generously butter the inside of the baking pan.
2 cups all-purpose flour **2½ teaspoons baking powder** **¼ teaspoon salt**	Over a large piece of waxed or parchment paper or a bowl, sift together the flour and baking powder. Add the salt and toss to blend well.
2 ounces (4 tablespoons, ½ stick) unsalted butter, softened	Place the butter in the bowl of an electric stand mixer or in a large mixing bowl. Use the flat beater attachment or a hand-held mixer to beat the butter on medium speed until it's fluffy, about 2 minutes.
½ cup firmly packed light brown sugar	Add the sugar to the butter, and cream together well. Stop occasionally and scrape down the sides and bottom of the bowl with a rubber spatula.
2 extra-large eggs, at room temperature	One at a time, add the eggs to the butter mixture, stopping to scrape down the bottom and sides of the bowl with a rubber spatula after each addition. At first the mixture may look curdled as the eggs are added, but as you stop and scrape down the bowl, the mixture will smooth out.
½ cup milk **1½ teaspoons pure vanilla extract**	In a liquid measuring cup, combine the milk and vanilla. With the mixer on low speed, alternately add the dry ingredients and the milk to the butter mixture in 3 stages. Stop after each addition and scrape down the bottom and sides of the bowl with a rubber spatula to help the ingredients mix evenly. The batter will be very thick. Remove the bowl from the mixer.
1 cup fresh blueberries **1 cup fresh raspberries**	Combine the blueberries and raspberries in a small bowl and toss together. Add half of the berry combination to the batter and

Essential Gear
- 8-inch square baking pan
- Electric stand mixer with flat beater attachment and wire whip attachment, or large mixing bowl and hand-held mixer
- Rubber spatula or wooden spoon
- Cooling rack

Keeping
The buckle will keep up to 4 days. Store it tightly covered with aluminum foil at room temperature.

Streamlining
The streusel topping can be made in advance. Store it in a tightly covered plastic container in the refrigerator up to 4 days.

Making a Change
Use one type of berry instead of a blend.

Add other berries to the blend, such as blackberries.

Use fresh-frozen berries if fresh berries are not available. It's not necessary to defrost the fresh-frozen berries before using, but bake the buckle about 3 minutes longer.

Replace the milk with buttermilk and replace the baking powder with ¾ teaspoon baking soda.

use a rubber spatula or wooden spoon to gently blend them into the batter.

Transfer the batter to the prepared pan.

Evenly sprinkle the remaining cup of mixed berries over the top of the batter in the baking pan.

¼ cup firmly packed light
    brown sugar
¼ cup all-purpose flour
½ teaspoon ground
    cinnamon
¼ teaspoon ground ginger
¼ teaspoon freshly grated
    nutmeg
1½ ounces (3 tablespoons)
    unsalted butter, chilled

Place the sugar, flour, cinnamon, ginger, and nutmeg in a small bowl and stir to blend together. Cut the butter into small pieces and toss together with the dry ingredients.

Evenly sprinkle the topping over the berries in the baking pan.

Bake the buckle 55 to 60 minutes, until golden and a cake tester inserted in the center comes out clean.

Remove the baking pan from the oven and cool on a rack.

GARNISH

1 cup heavy whipping cream

Place the cream in the bowl of an electric stand mixer or in a large mixing bowl. Use the wire whip attachment or a hand-held mixer to whip on medium speed until frothy.

2 tablespoons confectioners'
    sugar

Add the confectioners' sugar and continue whipping the cream until it holds soft peaks.

Cut squares of the warm buckle and serve each with a large dollop of whipped cream.

Adding Style
Serve squares of the buckle with vanilla ice cream.

Cranberry Nut Tea Loaf

U SE EITHER fresh or frozen cranberries to make this cake. If using frozen berries, don't defrost them because they become mushy. The red berries look bright and lively against the paleness of the cake. **Makes one 8¹/₂ × 4¹/₂ × 2¹/₂-inch loaf cake, 12 servings**

CAKE

Center a rack in the oven and preheat it to 375°F.

1 tablespoon unsalted butter, softened	Use your fingertips or a paper towel to butter the inside of the pan. Or spray the inside of the pan with non-stick baking spray.
²/₃ cup pecans, coarsely chopped	Place the pecans in a single layer in a cake or pie pan. Toast them in the oven for 6 to 8 minutes. Remove the pan from the oven and cool.
2 cups all-purpose flour **1 cup granulated sugar** **1¹/₄ teaspoons baking powder** **¹/₄ teaspoon baking soda** **¹/₂ teaspoon salt**	Over a large bowl, sift together the flour, sugar, baking powder, and baking soda. Add the salt and toss to blend together well.
1 extra-large egg, at room temperature **²/₃ cup plain yogurt** **¹/₃ cup freshly squeezed orange juice** **3 ounces (6 tablespoons, ³/₄ stick) unsalted butter, melted and cooled** **Finely grated zest of 1 large orange**	In a medium mixing bowl, lightly beat the egg with a fork. Add the yogurt, orange juice, butter, and orange zest and stir together until well blended and smooth.
2 cups cranberries	Place the cranberries in the work bowl of a food processor fitted with the steel blade. Pulse briefly until the cranberries are roughly chopped.
	Add the liquid ingredients to the dry ingredients and stir together just until the dry ingredients are moistened.

Essential Gear

- 8¹/₂ × 4¹/₂ × 2¹/₂-inch loaf pan
- 2-quart mixing bowl
- Rubber spatula
- Microplane grater or citrus zester
- Food processor
- Cooling rack

Keeping

Store the cake, tightly wrapped in aluminum foil, at room temperature up to 4 days. To freeze up to 3 months, wrap the cake tightly in several layers of plastic wrap and aluminum foil. Use a large piece of masking tape and an indelible marker to label and date the contents. If frozen, defrost overnight in the refrigerator and bring to room temperature before serving.

Making a Change

Replace the pecans with walnuts or whole, unblanched almonds.

Add the chopped cranberries and the toasted, chopped pecans. Stir to distribute evenly. The batter will be very thick.

Transfer the batter to the prepared loaf pan. Use a rubber spatula to spread it evenly into the pan.

Bake for 20 minutes, then reduce the oven temperature to 350°F and bake another 40 minutes, until the cake is golden on top and a cake tester inserted into the center comes out clean.

Remove the pan from the oven and cool completely on a rack. When the loaf cake is cool, turn it out of the pan.

Cut the loaf cake crosswise into 1/2-inch-thick slices.

Cranberry Walnut Scones

FRESH CRANBERRIES add tartness to these scones. It is fine to use frozen cranberries, just don't defrost them before adding to the mixture or they will become mushy. These scones are delicious any time of year and are a festive addition to the winter holiday season. **Makes twelve 3-inch scones**

Adjust the oven racks to the upper and lower thirds and preheat the oven to 425°F. Line two baking sheets with parchment paper or non-stick pan liners.

2½ cups all-purpose flour
3 tablespoons granulated sugar
1 tablespoon plus 1 teaspoon baking powder
¼ teaspoon salt

In the work bowl of a food processor fitted with the steel blade, combine the flour, sugar, baking powder, and salt. Pulse a few times to blend.

4 ounces (8 tablespoons, 1 stick) unsalted butter, chilled

Cut the butter into small pieces and add to the mixture in the food processor. Pulse until the butter is cut into very tiny pieces, about 30 seconds. The mixture should feel sandy with tiny lumps throughout.

⅔ cup chopped walnuts
1 cup whole fresh (or fresh-frozen) cranberries

Add the walnuts and cranberries to the food processor and pulse briefly to chop them and blend into the mixture.

Essential Gear

- Two baking sheets
- Two parchment paper sheets or non-stick pan liners
- Food processor
- 1-inch natural-bristle pastry brush
- Chef's knife
- Two cooling racks

Keeping

Store the scones in an airtight plastic container between layers of waxed paper at room temperature up to 4 days. To freeze up to 4 months, wrap the container tightly in several layers of plastic wrap and aluminum foil. Use a large piece of masking tape and an indelible marker to label and date the contents. If frozen, defrost overnight in

2/3 cup heavy whipping
    cream
2 extra-large eggs, at room
    temperature

Pour the cream into a liquid measuring cup and add the eggs. Use a fork to lightly beat the mixture to break up the eggs. With the food processor running, pour this mixture through the feed tube and process until the dough wraps itself around the blade, about 30 seconds.

Divide the dough in half. Turn one piece of the dough out onto a large piece of waxed or parchment paper dusted with flour. Dust your hands with flour and shape the dough into a circle about 1 inch thick and 6 inches in diameter.

Use a chef's knife to cut the circle in half, then cut each half into 3 equal triangles. Separate the scones and place them on the lined baking sheets, leaving at least 1 inch of space between them. Repeat with the other half of the dough. Brush any excess flour off the scones.

GARNISH

1 tablespoon heavy whipping
    cream

Brush the top of each scone with cream, being careful that it doesn't run down the sides and underneath. If it does, wipe it up because it can cause the bottom of the scones to burn.

2 tablespoons granulated
    sugar

Lightly sprinkle the top of each scone with sugar.

Bake the scones for 8 minutes, then switch the baking sheets. Bake another 5 to 7 minutes, until the scones are light golden.

Remove the baking sheets from the oven and cool completely on racks.

the refrigerator and bring to room temperature before serving.

Streamlining
The unbaked scones can be frozen for up to 3 months, wrapped as above. It's not necessary to defrost the scones, but bake them 5 to 6 minutes longer.

Making a Change
Replace the walnuts with pecans.

Adding Style
Use a 2-inch round, plain-edge cutter to cut the scones into circles instead of cutting them into triangles.

Four-Berry Turnovers

THE DOUGH for these turnovers is my favorite pie dough, made with a combination of cream cheese and butter. It's very tasty and very easy to work with. But these turnovers are also scrumptious made with puff pastry. Turnovers are great for dessert, for afternoon tea, and warmed up for breakfast. **Makes six 6-inch turnovers**

Essential Gear
• Food processor
• Rolling pin
• Baking sheet
• Parchment paper or non-stick pan liner
• Ruler
• Sharp knife
• Microplane grater or citrus zester

DOUGH

1⅓ cups all-purpose flour
1 tablespoon plus 1 teaspoon granulated sugar
¼ teaspoon salt

In the work bowl of a food processor fitted with the steel blade, combine the flour, sugar, and salt. Pulse briefly to blend.

5½ ounces (11 tablespoons) unsalted butter, chilled

Cut the butter into small pieces and freeze for 20 minutes.

5½ ounces cream cheese, chilled

Cut the cream cheese into small pieces and add to the dry ingredients. Pulse to cut the cream cheese into very tiny pieces. The texture should be sandy with very tiny lumps throughout.

Add the butter to the flour mixture. Pulse until the butter is cut into pea-sized pieces, 30 to 45 seconds.

2 tablespoons heavy whipping cream

Remove the top of the food processor and sprinkle on the cream. Replace the top and pulse for 10 seconds. Pulse until the dough begins to hold together, about 30 seconds.

Shape the dough into a flat disk and wrap it tightly in a double layer of plastic wrap. Chill in the refrigerator until firm before using, about 2 hours. Chilling the dough relaxes the gluten in the flour so it won't be too elastic and will roll out easily. It also firms up the butter in the dough so it will need less flour when rolled out. If the dough is too firm it will splinter and break when rolled out. Let it stand at room temperature for 10 to 15 minutes before rolling to become more pliable.

On a smooth, flat surface, roll out the dough between sheets of lightly floured waxed or parchment paper to a large rectangle measuring 12 by 18 inches.

Carefully peel the waxed or parchment paper off the top of the dough and brush excess flour off the dough. Use a sharp knife or pastry wheel to trim off any rough edges. Cut the dough in half horizontally. Use a ruler to mark 6-inch pieces along the horizontal line and cut each half into three 6-inch squares. Carefully peel the squares off the bottom piece of paper.

Adjust an oven rack to the lower third and preheat the oven to 400°F.

Line a baking sheet with parchment paper.

- 1-inch natural-bristle pastry brush or spoon
- Cooling rack

Keeping
Store the turnovers, loosely covered with waxed paper and then tightly wrapped with aluminum foil, at room temperature up to 2 days.

Streamlining
The dough can be made in advance and kept in the refrigerator, tightly wrapped in a double layer of plastic wrap, up to 4 days. To freeze up to 3 months, wrap the dough snugly in several layers of plastic wrap and place it in a freezer bag. Use a large piece of masking tape and an indelible marker to label and date the contents. If frozen, defrost overnight in the refrigerator before using.

Troubleshooting
Don't overprocess the dough or it will be tough and not flaky.

Making a Change
Replace ½ cup of flour in the dough with sliced or slivered almonds. Pulse with the remaining flour in the recipe until the almonds are very finely ground.

Replace the pastry dough with 12 ounces (⅓ recipe) Quick Puff Pastry (page 196) or use store-bought puff pastry.

FOUR-BERRY FILLING

1 cup fresh strawberries,
   washed, dried, and sliced
   in quarters lengthwise
2 cups mixed blueberries,
   raspberries, and
   blackberries
3 tablespoons light brown
   sugar
2 tablespoons cornstarch,
   sifted
Finely grated zest of
   1 medium lemon

Place the strawberries, blueberries, raspberries, and blackberries in a large bowl. Add the brown sugar and toss to coat the fruit. Add the cornstarch and lemon zest and gently toss the fruit to coat with the ingredients. Divide this mixture evenly among the 6 dough squares, placing it in the center.

Use one type of berry instead of a mixture.

Use other berries, if they are available.

Adding Style
Add 2 tablespoons finely grated or minced lemon zest to the dough before adding the butter.

1 to 2 teaspoons water

Use a pastry brush to brush the outer edges of each square with water. Be sure to brush only the inner part of the dough, not the outside. This will help the pastry dough stick together when the turnovers are formed.

Bring opposite corners together and fold each pastry square diagonally in half, lining up all the edges and points, making a triangle. Pinch the edges together firmly, then crimp or roll (see page 40).

Place the turnovers on the lined baking sheet, leaving at least 1 inch of space between them.

EGG WASH

1 extra-large egg yolk
1 tablespoon heavy whipping
   cream

Use a fork to lightly beat the egg yolk and cream together in a small bowl. Brush the top of each turnover with the egg wash. Be careful that the egg wash doesn't run down the sides and underneath the turnovers. If it does, wipe it up because it can cause the bottom of the turnovers to burn.

Bake the turnovers for about 25 minutes, until light golden and the fruit is thickly bubbling inside. Remove the pan from the oven and cool on a rack for 10 minutes. Serve the turnovers warm or at room temperature.

They can be re-warmed at 350°F for 10 to 15 minutes. To do this, place them in a single layer on a baking sheet lined with parchment paper.

Fresh Blueberry Muffins

THESE MUFFINS are delicious for breakfast, for afternoon tea, as a snack, or for dessert. They are plump with fresh blueberries. For a variation, I like to replace some of the blueberries with fresh raspberries. These are quick and easy to prepare and freeze very well. **Makes 12 muffins**

Center a rack in the oven and preheat it to 375°F. Line each cavity of the muffin pan with a paper muffin cup.

2 cups all-purpose flour
⅓ cup granulated sugar
¼ cup firmly packed light brown sugar
1 tablespoon baking powder
¼ teaspoon salt

Combine the flour, granulated sugar, brown sugar, baking powder, and salt in a large mixing bowl. Use a rubber spatula or wooden spoon to stir together well.

1 cup milk
4 ounces (8 tablespoons, 1 stick) unsalted butter, melted and cooled
1 extra-large egg, at room temperature, lightly beaten with a fork

In a liquid measuring cup or small bowl, combine the milk, butter, and egg. Add to the dry ingredients and stir together just until combined. This batter should be a little lumpy. If the batter is overmixed, the muffins may crumble instead of rising as they bake.

1 cup fresh blueberries
Finely grated zest of 1 large lemon

Fold the blueberries and lemon zest into the batter.

Use a spoon to divide the batter evenly among the 12 muffin cups, filling them to the top.

Bake the muffins about 20 minutes, until they are light golden brown and a tester inserted in the center comes out clean. Remove the pan from the oven and cool on a rack. Serve warm or at room temperature.

To rewarm the muffins, place them in a 350°F oven for 8 to 10 minutes.

Essential Gear
- 12-cavity 3-inch muffin pan
- 3-inch pleated paper muffin cups
- Microplane grater or citrus zester
- Large mixing bowl
- Rubber spatula or wooden spoon
- Cooling rack

Keeping
Store the muffins in an airtight plastic container between layers of waxed paper at room temperature up to 3 days. To freeze up to 2 months, wrap the container tightly in several layers of plastic wrap and aluminum foil. Use a large piece of masking tape and an indelible marker to label and date the contents. If frozen, defrost overnight in the refrigerator and bring to room temperature before serving.

Making a Change
Replace some of the blueberries with other berries, such as raspberries or blackberries.

Use fresh-frozen blueberries if fresh berries are not available. It's not necessary to defrost the fresh-frozen berries before using, but bake the muffins about 3 minutes longer.

Fresh Blueberry Scones

THESE TENDER, delicate scones are great for afternoon tea or breakfast. The flavor of the sliced almonds in this recipe combines very well with fresh blueberries. **Makes eight 3-inch scones**

Center a rack in the oven and preheat it to 425°F. Line a baking sheet with parchment paper or a non-stick liner.

2¹/₂ cups all-purpose flour
2 tablespoons granulated sugar
2¹/₂ teaspoons baking powder
¹/₂ teaspoon baking soda
¹/₂ teaspoon freshly grated nutmeg
¹/₄ teaspoon salt

In the work bowl of a food processor fitted with the steel blade, combine the flour, sugar, baking powder, baking soda, nutmeg, and salt. Pulse a few times to blend.

2 ounces (4 tablespoons, ¹/₂ stick) unsalted butter, chilled

Cut the butter into small pieces and add to the mixture in the food processor. Pulse until the butter is cut into very tiny pieces, about 30 seconds. The mixture should feel sandy with tiny lumps throughout.

1 cup sliced almonds

Add the almonds and pulse briefly to blend them into the mixture.

2/3 cup buttermilk
1 extra-large egg, at room temperature

Pour the buttermilk into a liquid measuring cup and add the egg. Use a fork to lightly beat the mixture to break up the egg. With the food processor running, pour this mixture through the feed tube and process until the dough wraps itself around the blade, about 30 seconds.

1 cup fresh blueberries, rinsed and dried

Add the blueberries to the dough in the work bowl and gently stir by hand to blend them in.

Turn the dough out onto a large piece of waxed or parchment paper dusted with flour. Dust your hands with flour and shape the dough into a large circle, about ¹/₂ inch thick and 9 to 10 inches in diameter.

Use a chef's knife to cut the circle into quarters, then cut each quarter in half, forming 8 scones, or into thirds to form 12 scones. Separate the scones and place them on the lined baking sheet, leaving at least 1 inch of space between them. Brush any excess flour off of the scones.

Essential Gear
- Baking sheet
- Parchment paper or non-stick liner
- Food processor
- Chef's knife
- 1-inch natural-bristle pastry brush
- Cooling rack

Keeping
Store the scones in an airtight plastic container between layers of waxed paper at room temperature up to 4 days. To freeze up to 4 months, wrap the container tightly in several layers of plastic wrap and aluminum foil. Use a large piece of masking tape and an indelible marker to label and date the contents. If frozen, defrost overnight in the refrigerator and bring to room temperature before serving.

Streamlining
The unbaked scones can be frozen for up to 3 months, wrapped as above. It's not necessary to defrost the scones, but bake them 5 to 6 minutes longer.

Making a Change
Replace the almonds with walnuts or macadamia nuts.

Replace the fresh blueberries with fresh-frozen blueberries. It's not necessary to defrost the fresh-frozen blueberries

1 tablespoon heavy whipping cream	Brush the top of each scone with cream, being careful that it doesn't run down the sides and underneath. If it does, wipe it up because it can cause the bottom of the scones to burn.
2 tablespoons crystal sugar	Lightly sprinkle the top of each scone with crystal sugar.

Bake the scones for 15 minutes, until light golden.

Remove the baking sheet from the oven and cool completely on a rack.

before using, but bake the scones about 3 minutes longer.

Adding Style

Use a 2-inch round, plain-edge cutter to cut the scones instead of cutting them into triangles.

Fresh Strawberry Tart

THIS IS A CLASSIC summer dessert composed of pâte sucrée (pronounced pot sue *cray*) pastry dough baked into a tart shell that holds a filling of velvety vanilla pastry cream. Fresh sweet strawberries cover the top of the pastry cream. This tart is easy to prepare because you need to make both the pastry dough and pastry cream in advance of when you plan to assemble it so they have time to rest and cool. **Makes one 9¹⁄₂-inch round tart, 12 to 14 servings**

Essential Gear

- Food processor
- Rolling pin
- 9½-inch round, fluted-edge tart pan with removable bottom
- Baking sheet
- Pie weights
- Cooling rack
- Aluminum foil
- Whisk or rubber spatula
- Small saucepan
- Medium-size fine-mesh strainer
- Goose-feather pastry brush

PASTRY DOUGH

1¼ cups all-purpose flour 3 tablespoons granulated sugar 1⁄8 teaspoon salt	In the work bowl of a food processor fitted with the steel blade, combine the flour, sugar, and salt. Pulse briefly to blend.
4 ounces (8 tablespoons, 1 stick) unsalted butter, chilled	Cut the butter into small pieces and add to the flour mixture. Pulse until the butter is cut into very tiny pieces, about 30 seconds. The texture will be sandy with very tiny lumps throughout.
1 extra-large egg yolk, at room temperature 1⁄2 teaspoon pure vanilla extract	In a small bowl, use a fork to lightly beat the egg yolk with the vanilla. With the food processor running, pour the egg yolk through the feed tube. Process the dough until the mixture wraps itself around the blade, about 1 minute.

Turn the pastry dough onto a large piece of plastic wrap. Shape into a flat disk and wrap tightly in a double layer of plastic wrap. Chill in

Keeping

Although the tart is best eaten the day it's made, it can last up to 3 days. Store the tart, loosely covered with waxed paper and then tightly wrapped with aluminum foil, in the refrigerator.

Streamlining

The pastry dough can be made in advance and kept

the refrigerator until firm before using, at least 2 hours. Chilling the dough relaxes the gluten in the flour so it won't be too elastic and will roll out easily. It also firms up the butter in the dough so it will need less flour when rolled out. If the dough is too firm it will splinter and break when rolled out. Let it stand at room temperature for 10 to 15 minutes before rolling to become more pliable.

Center a rack in the oven and preheat it to 375°F.

On a smooth, flat surface, roll out the pastry dough between sheets of lightly floured waxed or parchment paper to a large circle about 11 inches in diameter. To tell if the dough will fit the tart pan, hold the pan above the dough. If there are about 2 inches of dough that protrude beyond the sides of the pan, it will fit.

Carefully peel the paper off the top of the dough. Brush excess flour off the dough, then loosely roll the pastry dough around the rolling pin without the bottom piece of paper. Place the tart pan directly underneath the rolling pin and carefully unroll the pastry dough into the tart pan.

Gently lift up the sides and ease the pastry dough into the bottom and sides of the tart pan. Trim off the excess pastry dough at the top of the pan. Transfer the tart pan to a baking sheet and chill in the freezer for 15 minutes.

Line the pastry shell with a large piece of aluminum foil that fits well against the bottom and sides. Fill with pie weights or a mixture of rice and beans. Bake for 10 minutes. If the bottom of the pastry shell puffs up, gently pierce it in several places with a fork to release the air. Remove the foil and weights and bake another 10 to 12 minutes, until light golden and set. Remove the pan from the oven and transfer to a rack to cool completely.

Remove the sides of the tart pan by placing it on top of an upside-down bowl that is smaller than the pan. The sides should fall away. Transfer the pastry shell to a serving plate.

ASSEMBLY

2 recipes Vanilla Pastry Cream (see Pluot Custard Tart, page 92)

Stir the pastry cream vigorously with a whisk or rubber spatula to eliminate any lumps. Use a spoon or rubber spatula to spread pastry cream into the tart shell, filling it ¾ full.

3 cups fresh strawberries, washed, dried, and hulled

Place one whole strawberry in the center of the tart. Cut the rest of the strawberries in half vertically. Arrange them in circles, on their sides, around the center strawberry so they overlap slightly.

in the refrigerator, tightly wrapped in a double layer of plastic wrap, up to 4 days. To freeze up to 3 months, wrap the dough snugly in several layers of plastic wrap and place it in a freezer bag. Use a large piece of masking tape and an indelible marker to label and date the contents. If frozen, defrost overnight in the refrigerator before using.

The tartlet shells can be baked and held at room temperature up to 2 days before filling. After they are completely cool, place them on a baking sheet between layers of waxed or parchment paper and tightly wrap the pan in aluminum foil.

The apricot glaze can be made in advance and kept in a tightly covered plastic container in the refrigerator up to 1 month before using. Warm it in a small saucepan over medium heat or in a microwave oven on medium power before using.

Troubleshooting

Don't roll out the pastry dough before it is chilled. The dough will be too soft and it will require a lot of flour to roll out, which results in a tough dough.

Once the pastry dough is unrolled into the tart pan, don't push it down forcefully. This will stretch the dough, which will shrink as it bakes,

APRICOT GLAZE

¼ cup apricot preserves
1 tablespoon amaretto,
    cognac, or water

Combine the apricot preserves and liquid in a small saucepan. Bring to a boil over medium heat. Remove the pan from the heat and strain the glaze into a small bowl, pushing through as much of the pulp as possible.

Use a goose-feather pastry brush to lightly brush the top of each tart-let with the glaze. Don't apply a thick glaze, which looks unappetiz-ing. The purpose of the glaze is to keep the berries from drying out and to make the top of each tartlet glisten.

The tart is best served within a few hours of assembly because the pastry cream will start to soften the pastry shell. Refrigerate until ready to serve, then cut into wedges.

Making a Change

Use a variety of mixed berries or any other single berry, such as raspberries, blackberries, or blueberries.

Replace the vanilla pastry cream filling with Lemon Curd (see Double Lemon Layer Cake, page 139) or ½ of the mascarpone cream filling used in Red, White, and Blue Berry Pizza (page 201).

Mixed Berry Puff Pastry Rectangle Tart

P UFF PASTRY is famous for its flaky layers that rise in the heat of the oven. It's made by rolling and folding dough and but-ter together several times to create the many airy layers. It can be a daunting process to make puff pastry from scratch, especially for novice bakers. I've devised a method for making puff pastry that's not only very quick, but also puffs as well as classic puff pastry. With this in the refrigerator or freezer, you'll always be prepared to make an elegant and delectable dessert on a moment's notice. This tart is shaped into a traditional rectangle. The pastry shell is baked, then filled with vanilla pastry cream and topped with a mixture of sea-sonal fresh berries. **Makes one 5 × 12-inch tart, 12 to 14 servings**

Essential Gear

- Food processor
- Rolling pin
- Baking sheet
- Parchment paper
- Chef's knife
- 1-inch natural-bristle pastry brush
- Cooling rack
- Rubber spatula
- Small saucepan
- Medium-size fine-mesh strainer
- Goose-feather pastry brush

QUICK PUFF PASTRY

10 ounces (20 tablespoons
2½ sticks) unsalted butter,
chilled

Cut the butter into ½-inch cubes and place on a waxed paper–covered plate in the freezer for 10 minutes.

3 cups all-purpose flour
1 teaspoon salt

Place the flour and salt in the work bowl of a food processor fitted with the steel blade. Pulse briefly to blend.

2 ounces (4 tablespoons,
½ stick) unsalted butter,
chilled

Cut the butter into small pieces and add to the flour mixture. Pulse until the butter is cut into pieces the size of a dime, about 10 seconds.

Add the 10 ounces of chilled butter and pulse 6 to 8 times.

Keeping

Although the tart is best eaten the day it's made, it can last up to 2 days. Store the tart, loosely covered with waxed paper and then tightly wrapped with aluminum foil, in the refrigerator.

¾ cup ice water
1 teaspoon freshly squeezed
    lemon juice

Combine the water and lemon juice in a liquid measuring cup. Turn on the food processor and pour the liquid through the feed tube. Process the dough until the mixture forms a rough ball, about 10 seconds. Do not overprocess the dough or it will become tough.

Turn the pastry dough onto a large piece of lightly floured waxed or parchment paper. Form the pastry dough into a rectangle, lightly flour the top of the dough, and cover it with another piece of waxed or parchment paper.

Roll the pastry dough out to a large rectangle measuring 12 × 18 inches. Turn the dough a quarter turn frequently as you roll it. This makes it easier to roll the dough and ensures that it rolls evenly. Several times, lift off the top piece of paper and lightly flour the dough if needed. Turn the dough package over and lift off the other piece of paper. If the dough becomes too soft as you are working with it, transfer it to a baking sheet and chill in the refrigerator for 30 minutes to firm the butter, then roll again.

Peel off the top piece of paper and brush off excess flour. With a long side of the dough positioned toward you, fold the dough in thirds, bringing the top edge down and the bottom edge up. Then starting from the narrow end, roll the dough up loosely onto itself, forming a rectangle. Press down on the dough lightly to form a square, wrap the dough in a double layer of plastic wrap, and chill in the refrigerator for 30 minutes.

Repeat the rolling, folding, and rolling again. Wrap tightly in a double layer of plastic wrap and chill for at least 1 hour before shaping into the tart shell.

12 ounces (⅓ batch) puff
    pastry or store-bought,
    thawed in the refrigerator

Cut off the amount of dough you need, wrap the rest tightly, and chill for another use.

Roll out the pastry dough between sheets of lightly floured waxed or parchment paper on a smooth, flat work surface to a large rectangle measuring 8 × 16 inches, about ⅛ inch thick. Turn the dough a quarter turn frequently as you roll it. This makes it easier to roll the dough and ensures that it rolls evenly. Several times, lift off the top piece of paper and lightly flour the dough if needed. Turn the dough package over and lift off the other piece of paper. If the dough becomes too soft as you are working with it, transfer it to a baking sheet and chill for 30 minutes in the refrigerator to firm the butter, then roll again.

Streamlining

The puff pastry can be made in advance and kept in the refrigerator, tightly wrapped in a double layer of plastic wrap, up to 3 days. To freeze up to 3 months, wrap the dough snugly in several layers of plastic wrap and place it in a freezer bag. Use a large piece of masking tape and an indelible marker to label and date the contents. If frozen, defrost overnight in the refrigerator before using.

The tart shell can be baked and held at room temperature up to 2 days before filling. After it is completely cool, place it on a baking sheet between layers of waxed or parchment paper and tightly wrap the pan in aluminum foil.

The apricot glaze can be made in advance and kept in a tightly covered container in the refrigerator up to a month. Warm it in a small saucepan over medium heat or in a microwave oven on medium power before using.

Making a Change

Use any single type of berry instead of a combination. If using strawberries, cut them in half vertically and arrange them so they slightly overlap each other in lengthwise rows.

Replace the vanilla pastry cream filling with Lemon Curd (see Double Lemon Layer Cake, page 139) or

Transfer the pastry rectangle to a parchment paper–lined baking sheet. Use a sharp knife to trim off the uneven ends. Cut straight down through the dough so it will rise evenly as it bakes. A sawing motion will seal the edges of the dough, making it difficult for it to rise.

Use a damp pastry brush to brush around the edges of the rectangle, making a border about 1 1/2 inches wide. Fold the long ends in 1 1/4 inches, then brush the short ends and fold those over 1 1/4 inches. Use a sharp knife to cut a narrow slice off all of the ends, so they can rise well as they bake.

With the back of the knife, make short slanted notches or crosshatch marks around the border. Prick the inside of the pastry shell all over with a fork to prevent it from rising as it bakes. Freeze the pastry rectangle for 30 minutes.

Position a rack to the lower third of the oven and preheat it to 400°F.

1/4 of the mascarpone cream filling used in Red, White, and Blue Berry Pizza (page 201).

EGG WASH

1 extra-large egg yolk, at
room temperature
1 teaspoon heavy whipping
cream

Use a fork to lightly beat the egg yolk and cream in a small bowl.

Brush the top of the pastry dough border with the egg wash. Be careful that the egg wash doesn't run down the sides and underneath the pastry shell, which will cause it to burn. If any of the egg wash does run down, wipe it up.

Bake the tart shell 30 to 35 minutes, until puffed and golden.

Remove the baking pan from the oven and cool completely on a rack.

ASSEMBLY

1 recipe Vanilla Pastry
Cream (see Pluot Custard
Tart, page 92)

Stir the pastry cream vigorously with a whisk or rubber spatula to eliminate any lumps. Use a spoon or rubber spatula to evenly spread pastry cream into the tart shell.

2 cups mixed fresh berries,
washed and dried (blue-
berries, raspberries,
blackberries, or straw-
berries, hulled and cut in
half vertically)

Starting at one corner, arrange the berries in alternating diagonal rows across the top of the pastry cream, filling the pastry shell.

¼ cup apricot preserves
1 tablespoon amaretto,
  cognac, or water

Combine the apricot preserves and liquid in a small saucepan. Bring to a boil over medium heat. Remove the pan from the heat and strain the glaze into a small bowl, pushing through as much of the pulp as possible.

Use the goose-feather pastry brush to lightly brush the top of the fruit with the glaze. Don't apply a thick glaze, which looks unappetizing. The purpose of the glaze is to keep the fruit from drying out and to make it glisten. The tart is best served within a few hours of assembly because the pastry cream will start to soften the pastry shell. Refrigerate until ready to serve, then cut across the width into slices.

Raspberry-Blueberry Galette

THIS IS A FREE-FORM tart that is baked on a lined baking sheet rather than in a tart pan. It's bursting with fresh raspberries and blueberries. I love to make this as dessert for a casual late spring or summer dinner. I assemble it and bake it while we're eating dinner so it can be served warm and juicy. But it's also delicious eaten at room temperature. **Makes one 9-inch galette, 8 to 10 servings**

Essential Gear
- Food processor
- Baking sheet
- Parchment paper
- 1-inch natural-bristle pastry brush or a spoon
- Cooling rack

Keeping
Although the galette is best eaten the day it's made, it can last up to 2 days. Store the galette, tightly covered with aluminum foil, at room temperature.

Streamlining
The pastry dough can be made in advance and kept tightly wrapped in a double layer of plastic wrap in the refrigerator up to 4 days. To freeze up to 3 months, wrap the dough snugly in several layers of plastic wrap and place it in a freezer bag. Use a large piece of masking

PASTRY DOUGH

1¼ cups all-purpose flour
¼ cup stone-ground fine yellow cornmeal
2 teaspoons granulated sugar
¼ teaspoon salt

In the work bowl of a food processor fitted with the steel blade, combine the flour, cornmeal, sugar, and salt. Pulse briefly to blend.

4 ounces (8 tablespoons, 1 stick) unsalted butter, softened

Cut the butter into small pieces and add to the flour mixture. Pulse until the butter is cut into very tiny pieces, about 30 seconds. The texture should be sandy with very tiny lumps throughout.

1 tablespoon heavy whipping cream
2 to 3 tablespoons ice water

With the food processor running, pour the cream and 2 tablespoons of the ice water through the feed tube. Process until the dough begins to hold together. Turn off the food processor, remove the top, and feel the dough. If it holds together, it is done. If it is still crumbly, add the remaining tablespoon of ice water and process briefly, then check again.

Turn the pastry dough onto a large piece of plastic wrap. Shape into a flat disk and wrap tightly in a double layer of plastic wrap. Chill in the refrigerator until firm before using, about 2 hours. Chilling the dough relaxes the gluten in the flour so it won't be too elastic and will roll out easily. It also firms up the butter in the dough so it will need less flour when rolled out. If the dough is too firm it will splinter and break when rolled out. Let it stand at room temperature for 10 to 15 minutes before rolling to become more pliable.

RASPBERRY-BLUEBERRY FILLING

1½ cups fresh raspberries, rinsed and dried
1½ cups fresh blueberries, washed and dried
2 tablespoons granulated sugar

Place the raspberries and blueberries in a mixing bowl. Add the sugar and toss together to distribute evenly. Taste the fruit to see if it needs any more sugar.

ASSEMBLY

Center a rack in the oven and preheat it to 375°F.

On a smooth, flat surface, roll out the pastry dough between sheets of lightly floured waxed or parchment paper to a large circle 11 to 12 inches in diameter. Carefully peel the paper off the top of the dough. Brush excess flour off the dough, then loosely roll the pastry dough around the rolling pin without the bottom piece of paper. Place the lined baking sheet directly underneath the rolling pin and carefully unroll the pastry dough onto the baking sheet.

Mound the sliced berries in the center of the dough circle, leaving a 2½- to 3-inch border all around.

1 ounce (2 tablespoons) unsalted butter, chilled

Cut the butter into small pieces and distribute evenly over the berries.

Fold the border up so that it partially covers the berries. It will naturally form pleats as it is folded.

1 tablespoon heavy whipping cream
2 teaspoons granulated sugar

Brush the dough border with cream, being careful that it doesn't run down the sides and under the galette. If it does, wipe it up because it can cause the bottom of the galette to burn. Gently lift up the folds of the dough and brush under those areas with cream, then replace the folds. Evenly sprinkle the sugar over the dough border.

Bake the galette for 30 to 35 minutes, until light golden. Remove the pan from the oven and transfer to a rack to cool. Cut the galette into pie-shaped wedges to serve.

tape and an indelible marker to label and date the contents. If frozen, defrost overnight in the refrigerator before using.

Making a Change
Replace the raspberries and blueberries with other berries or use a single type of berry instead of a combination.

Use fresh-frozen berries if fresh berries are not available. It's not necessary to defrost the fresh-frozen berries before using, but bake the galette about 3 minutes longer.

Adding Style
Serve slices of the galette with vanilla ice cream.

Red, White, and Blue Berry Pizza

T HIS IS A DELECTABLE berry tart shaped like a pizza. An almond cookie crust is the base for a smooth filling of mascarpone and whipping cream. Concentric circles of strawberries, blueberries, and raspberries top the filling and are lightly glazed with apricot preserves. This is the perfect dessert to serve for Memorial Day and the Fourth of July, but don't feel you have to wait for those holidays to share this with family and friends. It's a great way to showcase seasonal fresh berries. **Makes 16 to 20 servings**

PASTRY DOUGH

1¾ cups all-purpose flour
½ cup sliced or slivered almonds
¾ cup confectioners' sugar
⅛ teaspoon salt

In the work bowl of a food processor fitted with the steel blade, combine the flour, almonds, sugar, and salt. Pulse until the almonds are very finely ground, about 2 minutes.

7 ounces (14 tablespoons, 1¾ sticks) unsalted butter, chilled

Cut the butter into small pieces and add. Pulse until the butter is cut into very tiny pieces, about 30 seconds. The texture should be sandy with very tiny lumps throughout.

2 extra-large egg yolks
1 teaspoon pure vanilla extract

Use a fork to lightly beat together the egg yolks and vanilla in a small bowl.

With the food processor running, pour this mixture through the feed tube. Process until the dough wraps itself around the blade, 30 seconds to 1 minute.

Turn the pastry dough onto a large piece of plastic wrap. Shape into a flat disk and wrap tightly in a double layer of plastic wrap. Chill in the refrigerator until firm before using, about 2 hours. Chilling the dough relaxes the gluten in the flour so it won't be too elastic and will roll out easily. It also firms up the butter in the dough so it will need less flour when rolled out. If the dough is too firm it will splinter and break when rolled out. Let it stand at room temperature for 10 to 15 minutes before rolling to become more pliable.

Center a rack in the oven and preheat it to 375°F.

On a smooth, flat surface, roll out the pastry dough between sheets of lightly floured waxed or parchment paper to a large circle about 14 inches in diameter. Carefully peel the paper off the top of the dough. Brush excess flour off the dough, then loosely roll the pas-

Essential Gear

- Food processor
- Rolling pin
- 14-inch round metal pizza pan
- Pie weights
- Cooling rack
- Aluminum foil
- Electric stand mixer and wire whip attachment, or large mixing bowl and hand-held mixer
- Small saucepan
- Medium-size fine-mesh strainer
- Goose-feather pastry brush

Keeping

The pizza can last up to 2 days in the refrigerator. Place a piece of waxed paper over the top, then tightly cover with aluminum foil.

Streamlining

The pizza dough can be made in advance and kept in the refrigerator, tightly wrapped in a double layer of plastic wrap, up to 4 days. To freeze for up to 3 months, wrap the dough snugly in several layers of plastic wrap and place it in a freezer bag. Use a large piece of masking tape and an indelible marker to label and date the contents. If frozen, defrost overnight in the refrigerator before using. The pizza dough can also be fitted into the pizza pan and kept

try dough around the rolling pin without the bottom piece of paper. Place the pizza pan directly underneath the rolling pin and carefully unroll the pastry dough onto it.

Trim any rough edges of the dough so it fits evenly into the pan. Press the tines of a fork all around the outer edge of the dough to form a design and create the outer border. Freeze for 15 minutes to set the dough.

Place a large piece of aluminum foil on top of the dough and cover with pie weights or a mixture of rice and beans. Bake the pastry for 10 minutes. Remove the foil and weights and bake for another 8 to 10 minutes, until set and light golden. Remove the pan from the oven and cool completely on a rack.

tightly covered in the refrigerator or frozen, wrapped and labeled as above.

Making a Change

Use only one type of berry instead of a combination or use other berries, such as blackberries and golden raspberries.

Replace the almonds in the pastry dough with the same amount of flour.

MASCARPONE CREAM FILLING

1 pound mascarpone, softened

1½ cups heavy whipping cream

Place the mascarpone and cream in the bowl of an electric stand mixer or a large mixing bowl. Use the wire whip attachment or a hand-held mixer to whip on medium speed until the mixture is frothy. Stop a few times and scrape down the bottom and sides of the bowl with a rubber spatula to encourage even mixing.

½ cup confectioners' sugar, sifted

1½ teaspoons pure vanilla extract

Add the sugar and vanilla and continue to whip until the mixture holds soft peaks.

Transfer the mixture to the cooled pizza shell and spread it out evenly with a rubber spatula or small offset spatula, leaving a 1-inch border all around.

ASSEMBLY

3 cups fresh strawberries, washed, dried, and hulled

Place a whole strawberry, pointed end up, in the center of the filling. Slice the rest of the strawberries in half vertically and use about ⅓ of them to form an overlapping circle (the tip of one half should balance on the bottom of another) around the center berry.

1½ cups fresh blueberries, washed and dried

1 cup fresh raspberries

Using blueberries, form a double row around the ring of strawberries. Using raspberries, form a double row around the ring of blueberries. Using blueberries, form a single row around the ring of raspberries.

Use the remaining cut strawberries to form a ring around the raspberries. If there is any room left on the filling, make another row of blueberries, then one of raspberries.

¼ cup apricot preserves
1 tablespoon amaretto,
    cognac, or water

Combine the apricot preserves and liquid in a small saucepan. Bring to a boil over medium heat. Remove the pan from the heat and strain the glaze into a small bowl, pushing through as much of the pulp as possible.

Use a goose-feather pastry brush to lightly brush the top of the fruit with the glaze. Don't apply a thick glaze, which looks unappetizing. The purpose of the glaze is to keep the fruit from drying out and to make it glisten.

The tart is best served within a few hours of assembly because the filling will start to soften the pastry shell. Refrigerate until ready to serve, then cut into wedges.

Strawberry-Rhubarb Lattice Pie

MANY PEOPLE THINK they don't like rhubarb, until they taste this pie. The sweetness of the strawberries subtly balances the natural tartness of rhubarb. Be sure to remove any leaves from the rhubarb stalks because they are slightly toxic. The pie dough is made with a combination of cream cheese and butter, which is my favorite. It's easy to work with and delicious. I love the look of a lattice top on pies because it allows the fruit to show through. **Makes one 10-inch round pie, 12 to 14 servings**

PIE DOUGH

2 cups all-purpose flour
2 tablespoons granulated
    sugar
½ teaspoon salt

In the work bowl of a food processor fitted with the steel blade, combine the flour, sugar, and salt. Pulse briefly to blend.

8 ounces (16 tablespoons,
    2 sticks) unsalted butter,
    chilled

Cut the butter into small pieces and freeze for 20 minutes.

8 ounces cream cheese,
    chilled

Cut the cream cheese into small pieces and add to the dry ingredients. Pulse to cut the cream cheese into very tiny pieces. The texture should be sandy with very tiny lumps throughout.

Essential Gear
- Food processor
- Rolling pin
- 10-inch round deep pie pan
- Jelly-roll pan
- 1-inch natural-bristle pastry brush
- Cooling rack
- Microplane grater or citrus zester
- Pastry wheel

Keeping
Store the pie, loosely covered with waxed paper and then tightly wrapped with aluminum foil, at room temperature up to 3 days.

Streamlining
The pie dough can be made in advance and kept in the refrigerator, tightly wrapped in a double layer of plastic

Add the butter to the flour mixture. Pulse until the butter is cut into pea-sized pieces, 30 to 45 seconds.

3 to 4 tablespoons heavy whipping cream

Remove the top of the food processor and sprinkle on 3 tablespoons of the cream. Replace the top and pulse for 10 seconds. Squeeze a small amount of the dough in your hand. If it holds together, don't add any more water. If the dough is still very crumbly, add another tablespoon of cream, pulse to blend, then check the dough again. It won't hold together unless you squeeze it, but that's the texture you want.

Divide the dough in two equal pieces and shape each piece into a flat disk. Wrap the disks tightly in a double layer of plastic wrap. Chill in the refrigerator until firm before using, about 2 hours. Chilling the dough relaxes the gluten in the flour so it won't be too elastic and will roll out easily. It also firms up the butter in the dough so it will need less flour when rolled out. If the dough is too firm it will splinter and break when rolled out. Let it stand at room temperature for 10 to 15 minutes before rolling to become more pliable.

On a smooth, flat surface, roll out one of the disks of pie dough between sheets of lightly floured waxed or parchment paper to a large circle about 12 inches in diameter. To tell if the dough will fit the pie pan, invert the pan over the dough. If there are 2 to 3 inches of dough that protrude beyond the sides of the pan, it will fit.

Carefully peel the paper off the top of the dough. Brush excess flour off the dough, then loosely roll the pastry dough around the rolling pin without the bottom piece of paper. Place the pie pan directly underneath the rolling pin and carefully unroll the pastry dough into the pan. Or loosely fold the dough in half. Carefully place it in half of the pie pan and gently unfold the dough. Gently lift up the sides and ease the pie dough into the bottom and sides of the pie pan. Trim off the excess pie dough at the top of the pan and crimp the sides (see page 40).

Transfer the pie pan to a jelly-roll pan and chill in the freezer for 15 to 20 minutes. This helps prevent the pie dough from shrinking as it bakes and sets the butter in the dough to ensure flakiness.

wrap, up to 4 days. To freeze up to 3 months, wrap the dough snugly in several layers of plastic wrap and place it in a freezer bag. Use a large piece of masking tape and an indelible marker to label and date the contents. If frozen, defrost overnight in the refrigerator before using. The pie dough can also be fitted into the pie pan and frozen. Wrap as above and label.

Troubleshooting

Don't overprocess the pie dough or it will be tough and not flaky.

Making a Change

Replace ½ cup of flour in the pie dough with sliced or slivered almonds. Pulse with the remaining flour in the recipe until the almonds are very finely ground.

Adding Style

Add 2 tablespoons finely grated or minced lemon zest to the pie dough before adding the butter.

Serve slices of the pie with vanilla ice cream or whipped cream.

STRAWBERRY RHUBARB FILLING

3 cups fresh strawberries, washed, dried, and sliced in half lengthwise

Place the strawberries and rhubarb in a large bowl. Add the granulated sugar and brown sugar and toss to coat the fruit. Add the corn-

1 pound fresh rhubarb, cut into ½-inch pieces (about 3 cups) **⅔ cup granulated sugar** **¼ cup firmly packed light brown sugar** **¼ cup cornstarch, sifted** **Finely grated zest of 2 large lemons**	starch and lemon zest and gently toss the fruit to coat with the ingredients. Transfer this mixture to the chilled pie shell and spread it out evenly.
1 tablespoon unsalted butter, chilled	Cut the butter into tiny pieces and distribute them evenly over the fruit.
	Adjust an oven rack to the lower third and preheat the oven to 425°F.
1 to 2 teaspoons water	Brush the edges of the bottom pastry shell to help the pastry and lattice topping stick together.

Roll out the remaining disk of pie dough on a smooth, flat surface between sheets of lightly floured waxed or parchment paper to a large circle about 12 inches in diameter. Peel off the top piece of paper. Use a ruler and a plain or fluted-edge pastry wheel to cut ½-inch-wide strips of dough. Carefully peel the strips off the other piece of paper. Form the strips into a lattice on top of the fruit (see page 41). Trim off the edges of both the lattice and the bottom pie shell evenly, leaving a ¾-inch overhang. Fold the edges of the lattice over the bottom crust and press them to seal together. Crimp or flute the edges (see page 40).

Bake the pie for 15 minutes, then reduce the oven temperature to 350°F. Bake the pie another 40 to 50 minutes, until light golden and the fruit is thickly bubbling inside.

Remove the pie from the oven and cool on a rack. Serve warm or at room temperature.

Strawberry Shortcakes

N OTHING SAYS SUMMER quite like strawberry shortcake. These tender shortcake biscuits are the perfect accompaniment for fresh berries and whipped cream. **Makes ten 2¾-inch round shortcakes**

Essential Gear
- Baking sheet
- Parchment paper or non-stick liner
- Food processor

Center a rack in the oven and preheat it to 400°F. Line a baking sheet with parchment paper or a non-stick liner.

2 cups all-purpose flour **2 tablespoons light brown sugar** **4 teaspoons baking powder** **½ teaspoon baking soda** **¼ teaspoon salt** **¼ teaspoon freshly grated nutmeg**	In the work bowl of a food processor fitted with the steel blade, combine the flour, sugar, baking powder, baking soda, salt, and nutmeg. Pulse a few times to blend.
3 ounces (6 tablespoons, ¾ stick) unsalted butter, chilled	Cut the butter into small pieces and add to the food processor. Pulse until the butter is cut into pea-sized pieces, about 30 seconds. The mixture should be crumbly. Don't cut the butter too small or the shortcakes will lose their flaky quality.
¾ cup buttermilk **1 teaspoon pure vanilla extract**	Pour the milk into a liquid measuring cup and add the vanilla. Use a fork to lightly beat the mixture together. With the food processor running, pour this mixture through the feed tube and process until all the ingredients are combined and the dough is moist, about 30 seconds.

Turn the dough out onto a large piece of waxed or parchment paper dusted with flour. Dust your hands with flour and shape the dough into a circle or rectangle about ¾ inch thick.

Use the biscuit cutter to cut out shortcakes. Cut straight down through the dough without twisting the cutter, which seals the edges of the dough and keeps the biscuits from rising in the oven. Place them on the lined baking sheet, leaving at least 2 inches of space between them so they have room to expand as they bake. Gather the scraps together and knead slightly. Pat them into a ¾-inch-thick circle or rectangle and proceed as above to get 10 shortcakes. Brush any excess flour off the shortcakes.

GARNISH

1 tablespoon heavy whipping cream	Brush the top of each shortcake with cream, being careful that it doesn't run down the sides and underneath. If it does, wipe it up because it can cause the bottom of the shortcakes to burn.
1 tablespoon Demerara or crystal sugar	Lightly sprinkle the top of each shortcake with sugar. Using these types of sugar adds extra texture to the shortcakes.

Bake the shortcakes for 12 to 15 minutes, until light golden.

- 2¾-inch round, plain-edge biscuit cutter
- 1-inch natural-bristle pastry brush
- Cooling rack
- Electric stand mixer with wire whip attachment, or large mixing bowl and hand-held mixer
- Serrated knife

Keeping
Store the unassembled shortcakes in an airtight plastic container between layers of waxed paper or on a baking sheet, tightly covered with aluminum foil, at room temperature up to 4 days. To freeze for up to 4 months, wrap the container tightly in several layers of plastic wrap and aluminum foil. Use a large piece of masking tape and an indelible marker to label and date the contents. If frozen, defrost overnight in the refrigerator and bring to room temperature before serving.

Making a Change
Replace the strawberries with blueberries, raspberries, or blackberries, or a combination of berries.

Remove the baking sheet from the oven and cool completely on a rack.

ASSEMBLY

1 cup heavy whipping cream

Place the cream in the chilled bowl of an electric stand mixer or a medium mixing bowl. Using the wire whip attachment or a hand-held mixer, whip the cream on medium speed until it is frothy.

2 teaspoons confectioners' sugar

Add the confectioners' sugar and continue to whip the cream on medium speed until it holds soft peaks.

4 cups fresh strawberries, washed, dried, and hulled
2 tablespoons superfine sugar (optional)

Slice the berries thinly from top to bottom. If they are tart, toss them lightly with the sugar to coat completely.

Slice each shortcake in half horizontally. Place the bottom of a short-cake on a serving plate and cover with a scoop of whipped cream. Place about 2 tablespoons of sliced berries on top of the cream and cover the berries with another small scoop of whipped cream. Lightly place the top of the shortcake on top of the berries or arrange it at an angle to the bottom of the shortcake. Scatter a few slices of berries around the plate. Repeat with the remaining shortcakes. Serve immediately.

Triple Berry Pie

T HIS PIE showcases fresh berries at their peak. I like to use a combination of raspberries, blueberries, and strawberries, but sometimes I add blackberries. Use any combination of berries you like; just be sure they are sweet and flavorful. **Makes one 10-inch round pie, 12 to 14 servings**

Essential Gear
- Food processor
- Rolling pin
- 10-inch round deep pie pan
- Baking sheet
- Cooling rack
- 1-inch natural-bristle pastry brush
- Ruler
- Pastry wheel

PIE DOUGH

3 cups all-purpose flour
½ teaspoon salt

In the work bowl of a food processor fitted with the steel blade, combine the flour and salt. Pulse briefly to blend.

8 ounces (16 tablespoons, 2 sticks) unsalted butter, chilled

Cut the butter into small pieces and freeze for 20 minutes.

Add the butter to the flour mixture. Pulse until the butter is cut into pea-sized pieces, 30 to 45 seconds.

Keeping
Store the pie, loosely covered with waxed paper and then tightly wrapped with alu-

4 to 6 tablespoons ice water

Remove the top of the food processor and sprinkle on 4 tablespoons of the ice water. Replace the top and pulse for 10 seconds. Squeeze a small amount of the dough in your hand. If it holds together, don't add any more water. If the dough is still very crumbly, add another tablespoon of water, pulse to blend, then check the dough, again. It won't hold together unless you squeeze it, but that's the texture you want.

Turn the dough onto a smooth, flat work surface. Use the heel of your hand to push the dough a few times for a final blend. Don't mush all the butter into the dough, however. For a flaky crust, you want to see thin flecks of butter in the dough.

Divide the dough in two equal pieces and shape each piece into a flat disk. Wrap the disks tightly in a double layer of plastic wrap. Chill in the refrigerator until firm before using, at least 2 hours. Chilling the dough relaxes the gluten in the flour so it won't be too elastic and will roll out easily. It also firms up the butter in the dough so it will need less flour when rolled out. If the dough is too firm it will splinter and break when rolled out. Let it stand at room temperature for 10 to 15 minutes before rolling to become more pliable.

On a smooth, flat surface, roll out one of the disks of pie dough between sheets of lightly floured waxed or parchment paper to a large circle about 12 inches in diameter. To tell if the dough will fit the pie pan, invert the pan over the dough. If there are 2 to 3 inches of dough that protrude beyond the sides of the pan, it will fit.

Carefully peel the paper off the top of the dough. Brush excess flour off the dough, then loosely roll the pastry dough around the rolling pin without the bottom piece of paper. Place the pie pan directly underneath the rolling pin and carefully unroll the pastry dough into the pan. Or loosely fold the dough in half. Carefully place it in half of the pie pan and gently unfold the dough. Gently lift up the sides and ease the pie dough into the bottom and sides of the pie pan. Trim off the excess pie dough at the top of the pan and crimp the sides (see page 40).

Transfer the pie pan to a baking sheet and chill in the freezer for 15 to 20 minutes. This helps prevent the pie dough from shrinking as it bakes and sets the butter in the dough to ensure flakiness.

BERRY FILLING

6 cups mixed fresh berries, washed and dried (raspberries, blueberries, and strawberries, quartered)

Place the berries in a large bowl. Add $1/2$ cup sugar and toss to coat the berries. Taste to see if the berries need more sugar. If they are sweet, don't add more sugar; if they are still tart, add the remaining

minum foil, at room temperature up to 3 days.

Streamlining
The pie dough can be made in advance and kept in the refrigerator, tightly wrapped in a double layer of plastic wrap, up to 4 days. To freeze up to 3 months, wrap the dough snugly in several layers of plastic wrap and place it in a freezer bag. Use a large piece of masking tape and an indelible marker to label and date the contents. If frozen, defrost overnight in the refrigerator before using. The pie dough can also be fitted into the pie pan and frozen. Wrap as above and label.

Troubleshooting
Don't overprocess the pie dough or it will be tough and not flaky.

Making a Change
To make classic tender, flaky pie dough, replace half of the butter with lard or vegetable shortening.

Replace $1/2$ cup of flour in the pie dough with sliced or slivered almonds. Pulse with the remaining flour in the recipe until the almonds are very finely ground.

Use fresh-frozen berries if fresh berries are not available. It's not necessary to defrost the fresh-frozen berries before using, but bake the pie about 3 minutes longer.

½ to ¾ cup granulated sugar
¼ cup cornstarch, sifted
2 teaspoons freshly
   squeezed lemon juice
½ teaspoon freshly grated
   nutmeg
¼ teaspoon ground
   cinnamon

¼ cup sugar. Add the cornstarch, lemon juice, nutmeg, and cinnamon and gently toss the berries to coat them with the ingredients.

Adding Style
Add 2 tablespoons finely grated or minced lemon zest to the pie dough before adding the butter.

Serve slices of the pie with vanilla ice cream or whipped cream.

1 tablespoon unsalted butter,
   chilled

Transfer the berry mixture to the chilled pie shell and spread them out evenly. Cut the butter into tiny pieces and distribute them evenly over the berries.

Adjust an oven rack to the lower third and preheat the oven to 425°F.

1 extra-large egg yolk, at
   room temperature
1 tablespoon milk

Use a fork to lightly beat the egg yolk and milk together in a small bowl. Brush the edges of the bottom pastry shell to help the shell and lattice topping stick together.

Roll out the remaining disk of pie dough on a smooth, flat surface between sheets of lightly floured waxed or parchment paper to a large circle about 12 inches in diameter. Peel off the top piece of paper. Use a ruler and a plain or fluted-edge pastry wheel to cut ½-inch-wide strips of dough. Carefully peel the strips off the other piece of paper. Form the strips into a lattice on top of the berries (see page 41). Trim off the edges of both the lattice and the bottom pie shell evenly, leaving a ¾-inch overhang.

1 tablespoon granulated
   sugar

Fold the edges of the lattice over the bottom crust and press them to seal together. Crimp or flute the edges (see page 40). Brush the top of the lattice with the egg mixture and sprinkle sugar over the top of the dough.

Bake the pie for 15 minutes, then reduce the oven temperature to 375°F. Bake the pie another 25 to 30 minutes, until light golden and the berries are bubbling inside.

Remove the pie from the oven and cool on a rack. Serve warm or at room temperature.

Triple Berry Upside-Down Cake

FRESH BLUEBERRIES, blackberries, and raspberries are topped with a delicate crumb cake. This is a great cake to make for any casual gathering. It's easy to prepare by simply combining the berries with a mixture of butter and sugar and topping them with the cake mixture, all in the same baking pan. This is delicious served warm, but is equally good at room temperature. **Makes one 8-inch square cake, 8 to 10 servings**

Essential Gear
- 8-inch square baking pan
- 1-quart heavy-bottomed saucepan
- Electric stand mixer with flat beater attachment, or large mixing bowl and hand-held mixer
- Rubber spatula
- Cooling rack

1 tablespoon unsalted butter, softened

Center a rack in the oven and preheat it to 350°F. Use your fingertips or a paper towel to butter the inside of the baking pan.

Keeping

Although the cake is best eaten the day it's made, it can last up to 2 days. Store the cake, tightly covered with aluminum foil, at room temperature.

BERRY TOPPING

2 ounces (4 tablespoons, ½ stick) unsalted butter
½ cup granulated sugar

Cut the butter into small pieces and place in the saucepan over low heat. When the butter is melted, add the sugar and stir together for 2 minutes, until well combined. Transfer this mixture to the prepared baking pan.

Making a Change

Use a single type of berry instead of a blend.

1 cup fresh blackberries
1½ cups fresh raspberries
1½ cups fresh blueberries

Combine the berries in a medium bowl and gently toss together. Transfer the berries to the baking pan and arrange them evenly over the butter/sugar mixture.

Use fresh-frozen berries if fresh berries are not available. It's not necessary to defrost them before using, but bake the cake about 3 minutes longer.

CAKE

3 ounces (6 tablespoons, ¾ stick) unsalted butter, softened

Place the butter in the bowl of an electric stand mixer or in a large mixing bowl. Use the flat beater attachment or hand-held mixer to beat the butter on medium speed until it's fluffy, about 2 minutes.

½ cup granulated sugar
¼ cup firmly packed light brown sugar

Add the granulated sugar and brown sugar to the butter, and cream together well. Stop occasionally and scrape down the sides and bottom of the bowl with a rubber spatula.

1 extra-large egg, at room temperature
1 teaspoon pure vanilla extract

Using a fork, lightly beat the egg with the vanilla in a small bowl. Add to the butter mixture. Blend well, stopping to scrape down the sides and bottom of the mixing bowl. At first the mixture may look curdled as the egg is added, but as you stop and scrape down the bowl, the mixture will smooth out.

1⅓ cups all-purpose flour
2 teaspoons baking powder
¼ teaspoon salt

Over a large piece of waxed or parchment paper or a bowl, sift together the flour and baking powder. Add the salt and toss to blend well.

¹⁄₃ cup milk

Add the dry ingredients to the butter mixture in 3 stages, alternating with the milk. Stop after each addition and scrape down the bottom and sides of the bowl with a rubber spatula. The batter should be smooth and creamy.

Transfer the batter to the baking pan. Use a rubber spatula or small offset spatula to spread it evenly over the top of the berries and into the corners of the pan.

Bake the cake for 45 minutes, until a tester inserted in the center comes out with a few moist crumbs clinging to it. Remove the pan from the oven and cool on a rack for 10 minutes.

Cut squares of the cake, scooping up the berries. Turn the cake out onto serving plates with the fruit on top.

GARNISH

¹⁄₂ cup heavy whipping cream
2 tablespoons confectioners' sugar, sifted
¹⁄₂ teaspoon pure vanilla extract

Place the cream in the chilled bowl of an electric stand mixer. Use the wire whip attachment or a hand-held mixer to whip the cream on medium speed until frothy. Add the confectioners' sugar and vanilla and continue to whip the cream on medium-high speed until it holds soft peaks.

Serve each square of cake with a large dollop of whipped cream.

Champagne Grape Tartlets

TINY CHAMPAGNE GRAPES that look like little glistening jewels sit on top of a classic vanilla pastry cream filling, nestled in toasted coconut tart shells. There is a variety of textures in these tartlets, and they are both beautiful to see and scrumptious to eat. These are easy to make because you can prepare the pastry dough and the vanilla pastry cream in advance and assemble them shortly before serving. **Makes six 4¹⁄₂-inch tartlets**

PASTRY DOUGH

Center a rack in the oven and preheat it to 350°F.

³⁄₄ cup sweetened, shredded coconut

Place the coconut in a shallow cake or pie pan and toast for 12 to 15 minutes, until light golden. Every 5 minutes, shake the pan to stir

Essential Gear

- Shallow cake pan
- Food processor
- Rolling pin
- Six 4¹⁄₂-inch round fluted-edge tartlet pans with removable bottoms
- Baking sheet
- Pie weights
- Two cooling racks
- Goose-feather pastry brush
- Aluminum foil
- Rubber spatula
- Medium-size fine-mesh strainer

the coconut to keep it from burning. Remove the pan from the oven and cool the coconut completely.

1½ cups all-purpose flour ¼ cup granulated sugar ⅛ teaspoon salt	In the work bowl of a food processor fitted with the steel blade, combine the toasted coconut, flour, sugar, and salt. Pulse briefly to blend.
6 ounces (12 tablespoons, 1½ sticks) unsalted butter, chilled	Cut the butter into small pieces and add to the flour mixture. Pulse until the butter is cut into very tiny pieces, about 30 seconds. The texture will be sandy with very tiny lumps throughout.
1 extra-large egg, at room temperature 1 tablespoon heavy whipping cream 1 teaspoon pure vanilla extract	In a small bowl, use a fork to lightly beat the egg with the cream and vanilla.

With the food processor running, pour this mixture through the feed tube. Process the dough until the mixture wraps itself around the blade, about 1 minute.

Turn the pastry dough onto a large piece of plastic wrap. Shape into a flat disk and wrap tightly. Chill in the refrigerator until firm before using, at least 2 hours. Chilling the dough relaxes the gluten in the flour so it won't be too elastic and will roll out easily. It also firms up the butter in the dough so it will need less flour when rolled out. If the dough is too firm, it will splinter and break when rolled out. Let it stand at room temperature for 10 to 15 minutes before rolling to become more pliable.

Increase the oven temperature to 375°F.

On a smooth, flat surface, roll out the pastry dough between sheets of lightly floured waxed or parchment paper to a large rectangle about 16 by 12 inches. Carefully peel the paper off the top of the dough. Brush excess flour off the dough, Cut the dough in half horizontally, then into 3 equal sections vertically, making 6 large squares. Carefully peel the pieces off the bottom piece of paper.

Gently place each square into a tart pan. Carefully lift up the sides of the pastry dough and ease the dough into the bottom and sides of each tart pan. Trim off the excess pastry dough at the top of the pan. Transfer the tart pans to a baking sheet and chill for at least 15 minutes to set.

Keeping

Store the tartlets in a single layer on a baking sheet. Cover the top of the tartlets with a large piece of waxed paper to keep the surface from becoming marred. Tightly wrap the pan with plastic wrap and keep in the refrigerator for up to 3 days.

Streamlining

The pastry dough can be made in advance and kept in the refrigerator, tightly wrapped in a double layer of plastic wrap, up to 4 days before using. To freeze up to 4 months, wrap it in a double layer of plastic wrap and place it inside a freezer bag. Use a large piece of masking tape and an indelible marker to label and date the contents. If frozen, defrost in the refrigerator overnight before using. If the dough is too cold to roll out, let it stand at room temperature to become pliable.

The tartlet shells can be baked and held at room temperature up to 2 days before filling. After they are completely cool, place them on a jelly-roll pan between layers of waxed or parchment paper and tightly wrap the pan in aluminum foil.

The vanilla pastry cream can be made up to 4 days in advance and kept in the refrigerator in a tightly sealed plastic container.

Line each pastry shell with a large piece of aluminum foil that fits well against the bottom and sides. Fill each pastry shell with pie weights or a mixture of rice and beans. Bake for 10 minutes, then remove the foil and weights. If the bottom of the pastry shell puffs up, gently pierce it in a few places with a fork or the point of a knife to release the air. Bake another 12 to 14 minutes, until light golden and set. Remove the pan from the oven and transfer the tartlets to racks to cool completely.

ASSEMBLY

1 recipe Vanilla Pastry Cream (see Pluot Custard Tart, page 92)

Whisk the pastry cream vigorously to remove any lumps. Using a rubber spatula, spread the inside of each tartlet shell with pastry cream, filling it ¾ full. Use the rubber spatula to smooth the top of the pastry cream.

1 pound champagne grapes, washed, dried, and stemmed

Arrange the grapes on top of the vanilla pastry cream, covering it completely, and slightly stacking the grapes.

APRICOT GLAZE

¼ cup apricot preserves
1 tablespoon amaretto, cognac, or water

Combine the apricot preserves and liquid in a small saucepan. Bring to a boil over medium heat. Remove the pan from the heat and strain the glaze into a small bowl, pushing through as much of the pulp as possible.

Use a goose-feather pastry brush to lightly brush the top of the tartlets with the glaze. Don't apply a thick glaze, which looks unappetizing. The purpose of the glaze is to keep the grapes from drying out and to make the top of the tart glisten.

The tartlets are best served within a few hours of assembly because the pastry cream will start to soften the tartlet shells. Keep them in the refrigerator until ready to serve, and serve each tartlet on its own plate.

Troubleshooting

Don't roll out the pastry dough before it is chilled. The dough will be too soft and it will require a lot of flour to roll out, which will make the dough tough.

Making a Change

Use the same amount of Concord grapes in place of champagne grapes.

Concord Grape Pie

CONCORD GRAPES have their own special sweet/tart flavor that I love. They bake up beautifully in this pie, which always signals to me that it's the end of summer because that's when these grapes are available. The grapes are cooked in a saucepan without their skins but with their stems to make the filling for this pie; then the stems are strained out and the skins are added before the

Essential Gear
- Food processor
- Rolling pin
- 10-inch round deep pie pan
- Baking sheet
- Large saucepan

filling goes into the pie shell. I like to use a lattice top crust for this pie, to show off the beauty of the deeply colored, plump purple grapes. **Makes one 10-inch round pie, 12 to 14 servings**

PIE DOUGH

2 cups all-purpose flour 2 tablespoons granulated sugar 1/2 teaspoon salt	In the work bowl of a food processor fitted with the steel blade, combine the flour, sugar, and salt. Pulse briefly to blend.

8 ounces (16 tablespoons,
  2 sticks) unsalted butter,
  chilled
	Cut the butter into small pieces and freeze for 20 minutes.

8 ounces cream cheese, chilled	Cut the cream cheese into small pieces and add to the dry ingredients. Pulse to cut the cream cheese into very tiny pieces. The texture should be sandy with very tiny lumps throughout. Add the butter to the flour mixture. Pulse until the butter is cut into pea-sized pieces, 30 to 45 seconds.
3 to 4 tablespoons heavy whipping cream	Remove the top of the food processor and sprinkle on 3 tablespoons of the cream. Replace the top and pulse for 10 seconds. Squeeze a small amount of the dough in your hand. If it holds together, don't add any more water. If the dough is still very crumbly, add another tablespoon of cream, pulse to blend, then check the dough again. It won't hold together unless you squeeze it, but that's the texture you want.

Divide the dough in two equal pieces and shape each piece into a flat disk. Wrap the disks tightly in a double layer of plastic wrap. Chill in the refrigerator until firm before using, about 2 hours. Chilling the dough relaxes the gluten in the flour so it won't be too elastic and will roll out easily. It also firms up the butter in the dough so it will need less flour when rolled out. If the dough is too firm it will splinter and break when rolled out. Let it stand at room temperature for 10 to 15 minutes before rolling to become more pliable.

On a smooth, flat surface, roll out one of the disks of pie dough between sheets of lightly floured waxed or parchment paper to a large circle about 12 inches in diameter. To tell if the dough will fit the pie pan, invert the pan over the dough. If there are 2 to 3 inches of dough that protrude beyond the sides of the pan, it will fit.

Carefully peel the paper off the top of the dough. Brush excess flour off the dough, then loosely roll the pastry dough around the rolling

- 1-inch natural-bristle pastry brush
- Cooling rack
- Ruler
- Pastry wheel
- Microplane grater or citrus zester
- Medium-size fine-mesh strainer

Keeping
Store the pie, loosely covered with waxed paper and then tightly wrapped with aluminum foil, at room temperature up to 3 days.

Streamlining
The pie dough can be made in advance and kept in the refrigerator, tightly wrapped in a double layer of plastic wrap, up to 4 days. To freeze up to 3 months, wrap the dough snugly in several layers of plastic wrap and place it in a freezer bag. Use a large piece of masking tape and an indelible marker to label and date the contents. If frozen, defrost overnight in the refrigerator before using. The pie dough can also be fitted into the pie pan and frozen. Wrap as above and label.

Troubleshooting
Don't overprocess the pie dough or it will be tough and not flaky.

Making a Change
Replace 1/2 cup of flour in the pie dough with sliced or slivered almonds. Pulse with

pin without the bottom piece of paper. Place the pie pan directly underneath the rolling pin and carefully unroll the pastry dough into the pan. Or loosely fold the dough in half. Carefully place it in half of the pie pan and gently unfold the dough. Gently lift up the sides and ease the pie dough into the bottom and sides of the pie pan. Trim off the excess pie dough at the top of the pan and crimp the sides (see page 40).

Transfer the pie pan to a jelly-roll pan and chill in the freezer for 15 to 20 minutes. This helps prevent the pie dough from shrinking as it bakes and sets the butter in the dough to ensure flakiness.

the remaining flour in the recipe until the almonds are very finely ground.

Adding Style

Add 2 tablespoons finely grated or minced orange zest to the pie dough before adding the butter.

Serve slices of the pie with vanilla ice cream or whipped cream.

CONCORD GRAPE FILLING

2 pounds (about 4 cups) Concord grapes, washed and dried

Remove the stems from the grapes and place the stems in the saucepan. Remove the skins from the grapes by pinching them between your thumb and forefinger. They will pop out. Place the skins in a separate bowl and add the grapes to the stems in the saucepan.

Cover the saucepan and bring the grapes and stems to a boil over medium heat. Simmer them for 5 minutes, then remove the saucepan from the heat. Strain the mixture to remove the stems and seeds.

³/₄ cup granulated sugar
3¹/₂ tablespoons cornstarch, sifted
Finely grated zest of 1 large orange
1 tablespoon plus 1 teaspoon freshly squeezed orange juice

Add the sugar, cornstarch, orange zest and orange juice, and the reserved grape skins. Stir together to blend well.

Transfer this mixture to the chilled pie shell and spread it out evenly.

Adjust an oven rack to the lower third and preheat it to 425°F.

1 to 2 teaspoons water

Use a pastry brush to brush the edges of the bottom pastry shell with water to help the pastry and lattice topping stick together.

Roll out the remaining disk of pie dough on a smooth, flat surface between sheets of lightly floured waxed or parchment paper to a large circle about 12 inches in diameter. Peel off the top piece of paper. Use a ruler and a plain or fluted-edge pastry wheel to cut ¹/₂-inch-wide strips of dough. Carefully peel the strips off the other piece of paper. Form the strips into a lattice on top of the fruit (see page 41). Trim off the edges of both the lattice and the bottom pie shell evenly, leaving a ³/₄-inch overhang. Fold the edges of the top crust over the bottom crust and press them to seal together. Crimp or flute the edges (see page 40).

Bake the pie for 30 minutes, then reduce the oven temperature to 375°F. Bake the pie another 10 to 15 minutes, until light golden and the fruit is thickly bubbling inside.

Remove the pie from the oven and cool on a rack. Serve warm or at room temperature.

Fresh Grape Tart with Lemon Cream Filling and Hazelnut Crust

FRESH GRAPES are nestled on top of a light and airy lemon cream filling that sits in a hazelnut pastry crust. It's a wonderful blend of flavors and textures. Be sure to use seedless grapes so no one has to worry about the pits. I like to use Red Globe and Concord grapes for this tart, but any table grape works well. Both the pastry dough and the lemon curd for the filling can be made in advance, which makes preparing this tart easy to fit into a busy schedule. **Makes one 9¹/₂-inch round tart, 8 to 12 servings**

PASTRY DOUGH

1 cup all-purpose flour
¹/₃ cup hazelnuts, toasted and skinned (see page 330)
3 tablespoons granulated sugar
Finely grated zest of 1 large lemon

In the work bowl of a food processor fitted with the steel blade, combine the flour, hazelnuts, sugar, and lemon zest. Pulse until the hazelnuts are very finely ground, about 2 minutes.

4 ounces (8 tablespoons, 1 stick) unsalted butter, chilled

Cut the butter into small pieces and add. Pulse until the butter is cut into very tiny pieces, about 30 seconds. The texture should be sandy with very tiny lumps throughout.

1 extra-large egg yolk, at room temperature
¹/₂ teaspoon pure vanilla extract

Use a fork to lightly beat the egg yolk and vanilla together in a small bowl. With the food processor running, pour this mixture through the feed tube. Process until the dough wraps itself around the blade, 30 seconds to 1 minute.

Essential Gear
- Food processor
- Rolling pin
- 9¹/₂-inch round, fluted-edge tart pan with removable bottom
- Pie weights
- Microplane grater or citrus zester
- Aluminum foil
- Cooling rack
- Electric stand mixer with flat beater attachment, and wire whip attachment or large mixing bowl and hand-held mixer
- Whisk or rubber spatula
- Small saucepan
- Medium-size fine-mesh strainer
- Goose-feather pastry brush

Keeping
The tart can last up to 3 days in the refrigerator. Place a piece of waxed paper over the top of the tart, then tightly cover it with aluminum foil.

Turn the pastry dough onto a large piece of plastic wrap. Shape into a flat disk and wrap tightly in a double layer of plastic wrap. Chill in the refrigerator until firm before using, about 2 hours. Chilling the dough relaxes the gluten in the flour so it won't be too elastic and will roll out easily. It also firms up the butter in the dough so it will need less flour when rolled out. If the dough is too firm it will splinter and break when rolled out. Let it stand at room temperature for 10 to 15 minutes before rolling to become more pliable.

Center a rack in the oven and preheat it to 375°F.

On a smooth, flat surface, roll out the pastry dough between sheets of lightly floured waxed or parchment paper to a large circle about 11 inches in diameter. To tell if the dough will fit the tart pan, hold the pan above the dough. If there are 2 or 3 inches of dough that protrude beyond the sides of the pan, it will fit.

Carefully peel the paper off the top of the dough. Brush excess flour off the dough, then loosely roll the pastry dough around the rolling pin without the bottom piece of paper. Place the tart pan directly underneath the rolling pin and carefully unroll the pastry dough onto it. Gently lift up the sides and ease the pastry dough into the bottom and sides of the tart pan, pushing it lightly into the fluted edges. Trim off the excess pastry dough at the top of the pan by running the rolling pin over the top. Or use your fingers to press against the top of the pan to remove the excess pastry dough.

Line the pastry shell with a large piece of aluminum foil that fits well against the bottom and sides. Fill with pie weights or a mixture of rice and beans. Bake for 10 minutes, then remove the foil and weights. If the bottom of the pastry shell puffs up, gently pierce it in several places with a fork or a sharp knife to release the air. Bake another 12 to 14 minutes, until light golden and set. Remove the pan from the oven and transfer to a rack while preparing the filling.

LEMON CREAM FILLING

½ cup heavy whipping cream

2 teaspoons confectioners' sugar, sifted

1 recipe Lemon Curd (see Double Lemon Layer Cake, page 139)

Place the whipping cream in the chilled bowl of an electric stand mixer or a large mixing bowl. Use the wire whip attachment or a handheld mixer to whip on medium speed until frothy. Add the confectioners' sugar and continue to whip until the cream holds soft peaks.

Use a whisk or rubber spatula to vigorously stir the lemon curd until it is smooth.

Using a rubber spatula, fold the whipped cream into the lemon curd in 2 stages until completely blended.

Streamlining

The pastry dough can be made in advance and kept in the refrigerator, tightly wrapped in a double layer of plastic wrap, up to 4 days. To freeze up to 3 months, wrap the dough snugly in several layers of plastic wrap and place it in a freezer bag. Use a large piece of masking tape and an indelible marker to label and date the contents. If frozen, defrost overnight in the refrigerator before using. The dough can also be fitted into the pan and kept tightly covered in the refrigerator or frozen, wrapped and labeled as above.

The lemon curd filling can be made in advance and kept in a tightly covered plastic container in the refrigerator up to 5 days before using.

The apricot glaze can be made in advance and kept in a tightly covered plastic container in the refrigerator up to 1 month before using. Warm it in a small saucepan over medium heat or in a microwave oven on medium power before using.

ASSEMBLY

Transfer the filling to the cooled tart shell and spread it out evenly using a rubber spatula.

10 ounces (2 to 2½ cups) fresh seedless medium grapes, washed, dried, and stemmed

Cover the top of the filling with grapes, stem ends down, placed very close together.

APRICOT GLAZE

¼ cup apricot preserves
1 tablespoon amaretto, cognac, or water

Combine the apricot preserves and liquid in a small saucepan. Bring to a boil over medium heat. Remove the pan from the heat and strain the glaze into a small bowl, pushing through as much of the pulp as possible.

Use a goose-feather pastry brush to lightly brush the top of the grapes with the glaze. Don't apply a thick glaze, which looks unappetizing. The purpose of the glaze is to keep the grapes from drying out and to make the top of the tart glisten.

Remove the sides of the tart pan (see page 42) before serving. Serve the tart chilled or at room temperature.

5

TROPICAL AND

EXOTIC FRUIT

MANY OF MY favorite fruits to use in baking fit into the category of tropical and exotic fruit. Some of these are commonly used, which may be because they are more readily available. For example, bananas, coconut, kiwifruit, and pineapples can be found in most supermarkets, whereas figs, mangoes, papayas, passion fruit, persimmons, and pomegranates are a little harder to find. Also, some of these fruits impart a flavor that you may not be acquainted with, but I can assure you that the recipes in this chapter will excite your taste buds and leave you wanting more.

Whether or not the particular fruit you're using is available will determine when you can make some of the recipes in this chapter. Using bananas is no problem because they are available throughout all seasons. Kiwis can also be found year-round, primarily because they are imported. Like kiwis, pineapples are usually in supermarkets all year, but are more common in late spring. Because coconuts are imported, they are generally available all year with their peak season in fall and winter. For the same reason, papayas, mangoes, and passion fruit can also be obtained year-round. Late spring, summer, and fall are the main seasons for figs. Pomegranates are found from August through December, and persimmons are available October through December. All of these tropical and exotic fruits can be found in most large supermarkets. Often tropical and exotic fruits are in a special produce section. Passion fruit can be a little harder to find, requiring a specialty purveyor.

TIPS AND TECHNIQUES

Bananas are often bought when their skin is green. The problem here is that if they are too green, they may not ripen properly to a bright yellow color. It's best to select bananas when they have some yellow on their skins. They may be overripe if they have too many brown spots. You can ripen bananas at room temperature for several days, but do not put them in the refrigerator because they will turn black.

Use bananas before they shrivel and become mushy. Cut them right before using or they will turn brown from exposure to air. To prevent this, soak cut bananas in orange or lemon juice.

For the recipes in this book, I advise you to use store-bought, sweetened, shredded or flaked coconut. It's just too much work to obtain the flesh from fresh coconut. Coconut can be kept in the refrigerator for a month or longer in a tightly sealed plastic bag or container.

Figs come in a lot of different colors and can be a little tricky to select. This is because they are often packaged. Look them over closely to make sure they have good form and are plump. The blossom end of the fruit should not be dried out. They should have good color; for example, Mission figs will have dark purple skins. Try to smell the figs for their sweet scent. Watch out for overripe figs, which have split skins and are oozing. Figs can be kept at room temperature for a couple of days. Wash them under cold water and dry gently before using. Figs are used either peeled or unpeeled. To peel them, use a sharp paring knife.

Kiwis are easy to select. They should be uniformly firm but not rock hard, without any blemishes or tears in their skin. Kiwis that are too soft are overripe and should not be bought. Ripen kiwis at room temperature. When they are ripe, they should give to slight pressure. Peel off the outer skin with a sharp paring knife.

Mangoes often come to the market unripe and need a few days for ripening at room temperature. Their skin is multicolored orange-red. Like all other fruits, the skin of mangoes should not be bruised or have blemishes. You should smell mangoes for their sweet perfume, which

can be very pronounced. The skin should be removed using a sharp paring knife or a vegetable peeler.

When a passion fruit is ripe, its skin is dry and bumpy, similar to a golf ball. If it is overripe, the skin will start to split. Of all the fruits on the market, passion fruit probably has the strongest fragrance, and as it ripens this fragrance becomes even more pronounced. Passion fruit takes several days to ripen at room temperature. To use passion fruit, cut it in half and scoop out the pulp and seeds into a strainer. Use a spoon to push the pulp through the strainer, leaving the seeds behind.

Pineapples are normally bought when they are slightly on the green side. This is fine because they will ripen on their own within a few days at room temperature. If you want to buy a fully ripe pineapple, look for one that is yellow with fresh, dark green leaves. Pull a leaf from the center of the crown, which should come out easily. Also, the bottom of a ripe pineapple should be slightly soft. Watch out for bruised areas on pineapples, which indicate that decay has set in. A fully ripe pineapple will have a nice, sweet scent.

Once ripe, pineapple can be stored in the refrigerator, but it's best to cut the pineapple and store the cut pieces in a tightly sealed container for no more than three days. Pineapple can ferment easily. Raw pineapple contains an enzyme that prevents gelatin from setting. To use it with gelatin, the pineapple must be cooked first.

Cut the top and bottom off the pineapple using a chef's knife or one with a serrated edge. Then cut off the skin from top to bottom, making sure to remove all the eyes. Cut the pineapple into quarters, cut out the core, and slice into pieces. The core is not edible. South African baby pineapples are small, about 5×3 inches. The core is edible on these and has a crunchy texture.

Papayas come in a variety of sizes and, when ripe, their skin turns from green to yellow. Great

When a passion fruit is ripe, its skin is dry and bumpy...

caution has to be exercised when selecting papayas. Their thin skin makes them vulnerable to bruises and tears. Select papayas that have smooth, unblemished skins and are slightly firm. Also, a ripe papaya will have a mildly sweet aroma. Generally the flesh of a ripe papaya is bright salmon colored. Cut papayas in half lengthwise and scoop out the seeds, then use a paring knife or vegetable peeler to remove their skin.

There are two main types of persimmons, Fuyu and Hachiya. Fuyu persimmons are short and squat and look like a large tomato. They are a firmer variety and can be eaten like an apple. The Hachiya variety is acorn shaped and soft when ripe. Both of these varieties have smooth, shiny orange to red skins. Their skins should be slightly glossy without any cracks. Watch out for persimmons that have yellow spots; this is an indication that they are not yet ripe. Leave persimmons at room temperature to ripen. There are two options for using persimmons: with or without their skin. I prefer to remove the skins. Use a sharp paring knife to remove the top leaves and to peel them. Then cut them in half and remove the core. If the persimmon is very ripe, it's easier to use a spoon to scoop out the core.

Select pomegranates that are bright in color and shiny. The color of the skin of a pomegranate is crimson and it feels a bit leathery. Pomegranates that have a shriveled look are overripe and should be avoided. Also watch out for cracks in the skin. The seeds or juice of pomegranates are used for baking. There is no easy way to remove the seeds. Soak the whole pomegranate in a bowl of cold water for a short while, then score it into quarters. Peel back the outer skin, pull the seeds away from the inner white membrane with your fingers, and place the seeds in a bowl. This keeps the seeds and juice from staining your hands brown. Use the seeds whole or strain them to remove the juice. It's best to use glass bowls because aluminum bowls can cause the juice to turn bitter. Some specialty markets now sell pomegranate seeds in containers.

Banana-Almond Muffins

WHEN ONE OF MY friends ate these muffins, she said it was like eating a full brunch because these are hearty. They are full of bananas and almonds, with delicious accents of sour cream and a blend of spices. **Makes 12 muffins**

Center a rack in the oven and preheat it to 375°F. Line each cavity of the muffin pan with a paper muffin cup.

4 ounces (8 tablespoons, 1 stick) unsalted butter, softened	Place the butter in the bowl of an electric stand mixer or a large mixing bowl. Use the flat beater attachment or a hand-held mixer to beat the butter until light and fluffy, about 2 minutes.
½ cup firmly packed light brown sugar **⅓ cup granulated sugar**	Add the brown sugar and granulated sugar to the butter, and cream together well.
2 extra-large eggs, at room temperature	One at a time, add the eggs to the butter mixture, stopping to scrape down the bottom and sides of the bowl after each addition. At first the mixture may look curdled as the eggs are added, but as you stop and scrape down the bowl, the mixture will smooth out.
3 medium, ripe bananas **¼ cup sour cream** **1 teaspoon pure vanilla extract**	Use a fork to mash the bananas in a bowl. Add the sour cream and vanilla and mix together well. Add to the butter mixture and blend thoroughly.
1½ cups all-purpose flour **½ cup whole wheat flour** **2 teaspoons baking powder** **½ teaspoon baking soda** **½ teaspoon ground cinnamon** **¼ teaspoon salt** **¼ teaspoon freshly grated nutmeg** **¼ teaspoon ground cardamom**	Over a large piece of waxed or parchment paper or a bowl, sift together the flour, whole wheat flour, baking powder, and baking soda. Add the cinnamon, salt, nutmeg, and cardamom and toss to blend together. Add to the banana mixture in 3 stages, stopping after each addition to scrape down the bottom and sides of the bowl to promote even blending.
¾ cup coarsely chopped whole unblanched almonds	Add the chopped almonds to the batter and stir to distribute evenly.

Essential Gear

- 12-cavity 3-inch muffin pan
- 3-inch pleated paper muffin cups
- Electric stand mixer with flat beater attachment, or large mixing bowl and hand-held mixer
- Rubber spatula
- Cooling rack

Keeping

Store the muffins in an airtight plastic container between layers of waxed paper at room temperature up to 3 days. To freeze up to 2 months, wrap the container tightly in several layers of plastic wrap and aluminum foil. Use a large piece of masking tape and an indelible marker to label and date the contents. If frozen, defrost overnight in the refrigerator and bring to room temperature before serving.

Making a Change

Replace the almonds with walnuts, pecans, or toasted hazelnuts.

Adding Style

Drizzle the tops of the cooled muffins with thin lines of white, milk, or dark chocolate. Let the chocolate set for 15 minutes in the refrigerator before serving or storing.

Use a spoon to divide the batter evenly among the 12 muffin cups, filling them to the top.

Bake the muffins 25 to 30 minutes, until they are light golden brown and a tester inserted in the center comes out clean. Remove the pan from the oven and cool on a rack.

Banana and Coconut Layer Cake

THIS CAKE is composed of three alternating layers of rich, dense banana cake and cream cheese icing sprinkled with coconut. Shredded coconut decorates the sides and top of the cake. The flavors of banana, coconut, and cream cheese blend very well together and create a unique tropical flavor. This cake is perfect for any gathering because bananas and coconut are available year-round. Most of the steps involved in making this cake can be done in advance, so it's easy to assemble it a few hours to a day before serving. **Makes one 9-inch round cake, 12 to 14 servings**

BANANA CAKE

Center a rack in the oven and preheat it to 350°F.

1 tablespoon unsalted butter, softened	Using a paper towel or your fingertips, generously butter the inside of the cake pan, coating it thoroughly
2 teaspoons all-purpose flour	Dust the inside of the pan with the flour. Shake and tilt the pan to evenly distribute the flour, then turn the pan over and shake out the excess over the sink.
	Cut a round of parchment paper to fit the bottom of the pan. Butter the parchment paper round and place in the pan, butter-side up.
6 ounces (12 tablespoons, 1½ sticks) unsalted butter, softened	Place the butter in the bowl of an electric stand mixer or in a large mixing bowl. Use the flat beater attachment or hand-held mixer to beat the butter on medium speed until it's fluffy, about 2 minutes.
2 cups granulated sugar	Gradually add the sugar to the butter, and cream together well. Stop occasionally and scrape down the bottom and sides of the bowl with a rubber spatula.
3 extra-large eggs, at room temperature	One at a time, add the eggs, stopping to scrape down the bottom and sides of the bowl after each addition. At first the mixture may look

Essential Gear

- One 9 × 2-inch round cake pan
- Scissors
- Parchment paper
- Electric stand mixer with flat beater attachment and wire whip attachment, or large mixing bowl and hand-held mixer
- Two rubber spatulas
- Cooling rack
- Sifter
- 9-inch cardboard cake circle
- 10-inch flexible-blade icing spatula

Keeping

Store the cake loosely covered with aluminum foil in the refrigerator up to 3 days. Place several toothpicks in the top outer edges of the cake to hold the foil away from it so it won't mar the icing.

Streamlining

Bake the cake up to 2 days before assembling and keep tightly covered with a double layer of plastic wrap, at room temperature or in the

curdled as the eggs are added, but as you stop and scrape down the bowl, the mixture will smooth out.

2½ cups cake flour
1 teaspoon baking soda
½ teaspoon baking powder
½ teaspoon salt

Over a large piece of waxed or parchment paper or a bowl, sift together the flour, baking soda, and baking powder. Add the salt and toss to blend well.

3 large, ripe bananas
¾ cup buttermilk
2 teaspoons pure vanilla extract

Place the bananas in a medium mixing bowl and use a fork to mash them. Add the buttermilk and vanilla and stir together until well blended.

With the mixer on low speed, add the dry ingredients alternately with the banana mixture to the butter mixture in 4 stages. Blend well after each addition and stop often to scrape down the bottom and sides of the bowl with a rubber spatula.

Transfer the cake batter to the cake pan. Smooth the top of the pan with a rubber spatula.

Bake the cake for 30 to 35 minutes, until golden and a cake tester inserted in the center comes out with no crumbs clinging to it.

Remove the cake pan from the oven and cool completely on a rack. Invert the pan to remove the cake, then peel the parchment paper off the back of the cake. Re-invert the cake onto a cardboard cake circle.

CREAM CHEESE ICING

12 ounces cream cheese, softened

Place the cream cheese in the bowl of an electric stand mixer or in a large mixing bowl. Use the flat beater attachment or a hand-held mixer and beat the cream cheese until it is fluffy, about 3 minutes.

¾ cup confectioners' sugar, sifted
2 tablespoons heavy whipping cream
2 teaspoons freshly squeezed lemon juice

Add the confectioners' sugar, cream, and lemon juice to the cream cheese and beat together well.

ASSEMBLY

Using a serrated knife, cut the cake into 3 layers horizontally (see page 34). Place one cake layer on a serving plate. Place strips of waxed paper around the bottom edges of the cake to protect the plate while assembling the cake. Use the flexible-blade spatula to

refrigerator, up to 4 days. To freeze the cake up to 3 months, wrap it snugly in several layers of plastic wrap and place in a freezer bag. Use a large piece of masking tape and an indelible marker to label and date the contents. If frozen, defrost the layers overnight in the refrigerator.

Adding Style

Add ½ cup toasted and finely chopped walnuts, almonds, or pecans to the cake. Add the nuts with the dry ingredients when mixing the cake batter.

Recovering from a Mishap

If one of the cake layers breaks during assembly, patch it together with some of the icing.

2 cups sweetened, shredded coconut	spread the layer evenly with ¼ cup of the icing, then sprinkle ¼ cup of the coconut evenly over the icing.
	Position the second cake layer evenly over the coconut and use the flexible-blade spatula to spread about ¼ cup of the icing over the layer and sprinkle with another ¼ cup coconut.
	Position the top layer of the cake over the coconut. Spread the remaining icing over the sides and top of the cake.
	Press the remaining shredded coconut into the sides of the cake and sprinkle lightly over the top.
	Let the cake chill for at least 2 hours before serving so it has time to set and will be easier to cut. Serve the cake at room temperature.

Banana Cream Pie

THIS PIE, chock full of bananas, is the perfect pie for banana lovers. Flaky pie dough that is prebaked holds a filling of whipped cream mixed with vanilla pastry cream. Bananas are nestled between two layers of the filling and whipped cream crowns the top of the pie. Because of the delicacy of the cream in the filling and on top, the pie needs to be served within a few hours of when its assembly, but the pie crust can be baked in advance. **Makes one 9-inch round pie, 12 to 14 servings**

Essential Gear
- Food processor
- Rolling pin
- 9-inch round pie pan
- Baking sheet
- Aluminum foil
- Pie weights
- Cooling rack
- Electric stand mixer with wire whip attachment, or large mixing bowl and hand-held mixer

Keeping
This pie needs to be served within 3 hours of assembling because the cream filling will start to weep after that.

Streamlining
The pie dough can be made in advance and kept in the refrigerator, tightly wrapped in a double layer of plastic

PIE DOUGH

1 cup all-purpose flour **1 tablespoon granulated sugar** **¼ teaspoon salt**	In the work bowl of a food processor fitted with the steel blade, combine the flour, sugar, and salt. Pulse briefly to blend.
4 ounces (8 tablespoons, 1 stick) unsalted butter, chilled	Cut the butter into small pieces and freeze for 20 minutes.
4 ounces cream cheese, chilled	Cut the cream cheese into small pieces and add to the dry ingredients. Pulse to cut the cream cheese into very tiny pieces. The texture should be sandy with very tiny lumps throughout.

Add the butter to the flour mixture. Pulse until the butter is cut into pea-sized pieces, 30 to 45 seconds.

2 to 3 tablespoons heavy whipping cream

Remove the top of the food processor and sprinkle on 2 tablespoons of the cream. Replace the top and pulse for 10 seconds. Squeeze a small amount of the dough in your hand. If it holds together, don't add any more cream. If the dough is still very crumbly, add another tablespoon of cream, pulse to blend, then check the dough again. It won't hold together unless you squeeze it, but that's the texture you want.

Shape the dough into a flat disk and wrap it tightly in a double layer of plastic wrap. Chill in the refrigerator until firm before using, about 2 hours. Chilling the dough relaxes the gluten in the flour so it won't be too elastic and will roll out easily. It also firms up the butter in the dough so it will need less flour when rolled out. If the dough is too firm it will splinter and break when rolled out. Let it stand at room temperature for 10 to 15 minutes before rolling to become more pliable.

On a smooth, flat surface, roll out the disk of pie dough between sheets of lightly floured waxed or parchment paper to a large circle about 12 inches in diameter. To tell if the dough will fit the pie pan, invert the pan over the dough. If there are 2 to 3 inches of dough that protrude beyond the sides of the pan, it will fit.

Carefully peel the paper off the top of the dough. Brush excess flour off the dough, then loosely roll the pastry dough around the rolling pin without the bottom piece of paper. Place the pie pan directly underneath the rolling pin and carefully unroll the pastry dough into the pan. Or loosely fold the dough in half. Carefully place it in half of the pie pan and gently unfold the dough. Gently lift up the sides and ease the pie dough into the bottom and sides of the pie pan. Trim off the excess pie dough at the top of the pan and crimp the sides (see page 40).

Transfer the pie pan to a baking sheet and chill in the freezer for 15 to 20 minutes. This helps prevent the pie dough from shrinking as it bakes and sets the butter in the dough to ensure flakiness.

Adjust an oven rack to the lower third and preheat the oven to 425°F.

Line the pie shell with aluminum foil that extends over the sides and weight with pie weights or a mixture of rice and beans. Bake the pie shell for 12 minutes. Remove the foil and weights and lightly pierce the bottom of the pie shell to release air. Continue to bake the pie shell until it is light golden brown, about 12 to 15 minutes more. Remove from the oven and cool completely on a rack.

wrap, up to 4 days. To freeze up to 3 months, wrap the dough snugly in several layers of plastic wrap and place it in a freezer bag. Use a large piece of masking tape and an indelible marker to label and date the contents. If frozen, defrost overnight in the refrigerator before using. The pie dough can also be fitted into the pie pan and frozen. Wrap as above and label.

The pastry cream can be made in advance and kept in the refrigerator in a tightly covered bowl or container for up to 4 days.

Troubleshooting

Don't overprocess the pie dough or it will be tough and not flaky.

4 large, ripe bananas **3 tablespoons freshly** **squeezed orange juice**	Peel the bananas and cut them into $^{1}/_{2}$-inch-thick slices. Place the slices in a shallow bowl and cover them with the orange juice. Cover the bowl with plastic wrap and let the bananas soak while preparing the cream filling. The orange juice keeps the bananas from turning brown.

2 cups heavy whipping
  cream
2 tablespoons granulated
  sugar
	Place the cream in the chilled bowl of an electric stand mixer or a large mixing bowl. Use the wire whip attachment or a hand-held mixer to whip the cream on medium speed until frothy. Add the sugar and whip on medium-high speed until the cream holds firm but not stiff peaks. Remove 1 cup of the whipped cream and set aside.

1 recipe Vanilla Pastry
  Cream (see Pluot Custard
  Tart, page 92)
	Whisk the pastry cream vigorously to break up any lumps. Fold the remaining whipped cream into the pastry cream and blend well.
	
	Spread half of the cream mixture in the cooled pie shell.

Remove the bananas from the orange juice and pat them dry on paper towels. Arrange the bananas over the filling in the pie shell, then cover the bananas with the remaining cream filling.

Spread the reserved whipped cream over the top of the filling, mounding it slightly in the center.

Chill the pie in the refrigerator up to 3 hours before serving.

Banana Loaf Cake with Walnuts and Dried Apricots

T HIS CAKE is not too sweet and has a wonderfully complex texture that comes from the bananas, walnuts, and dried apricots. I like to serve this for afternoon tea and also like to pack it into a lunch box. Try it toasted for breakfast, spread with cream cheese or a little butter and jam. **Makes one $8^{1}/_{2} \times 4^{1}/_{2} \times 2^{1}/_{2}$-inch loaf cake, 12 servings**

Essential Gear

- $8^{1}/_{2} \times 4^{1}/_{2} \times 2^{1}/_{2}$-inch loaf pan
- Aluminum foil
- Sifter
- Electric stand mixer with flat beater attachment, or large mixing bowl and hand-held mixer

CAKE

1 tablespoon unsalted butter, softened	Center rack in the oven and preheat it to 350°F. Line the loaf pan with aluminum foil that extends over the sides. Using a paper towel or your fingertips, generously butter the foil inside the pan.
½ cup granulated sugar 2 ounces (4 tablespoons, ¼ stick) unsalted butter, melted and cooled ¼ cup milk 1 extra-large egg, at room temperature 1 teaspoon pure vanilla extract ½ teaspoon salt	Combine the sugar, butter, milk, egg, vanilla, and salt in the bowl of an electric stand mixer or in a large mixing bowl. Use the flat beater attachment or hand-held mixer to blend the ingredients together.
1½ cups all-purpose flour 1 teaspoon baking powder 1 teaspoon baking soda ¼ teaspoon sea salt	Over a large piece of waxed or parchment paper or a bowl, sift together the flour, baking powder, and baking soda. Add the salt and toss to blend well. Add the dry ingredients to the butter mixture and blend briefly. The batter should not be lumpy.
1 large or 2 medium, ripe bananas, mashed (should measure 1 cup) ½ cup roughly chopped walnuts ½ cup roughly chopped dried apricots	Use a rubber spatula to fold the banana into the batter, then fold in the walnuts and dried apricots.
	Transfer the batter to the prepared loaf pan. The batter is very thick, so use a rubber spatula to spread it evenly into the pan. Bake for 45 to 50 minutes, until the cake is light golden on top and a cake tester inserted into the center comes out clean. Remove the pan from the oven and cool completely on a rack.

- Rubber spatula
- Cooling rack

Keeping

Store the cake, tightly wrapped in aluminum foil, at room temperature up to 4 days. To freeze up to 3 months, wrap the cake tightly in several layers of plastic wrap and aluminum foil. Use a large piece of masking tape and an indelible marker to label and date the contents. If frozen, defrost overnight in the refrigerator and bring to room temperature before serving.

Making a Change

Replace the walnuts with pecans, macadamia nuts, or whole, unblanched almonds.

Replace the dried apricots with dried peaches, pears, cranberries, or raisins.

Coconut Biscotti

THESE TWICE-BAKED cookies are full of shredded coconut and sliced almonds. I find them so yummy I have a hard time eating only one or two. Because they are so crunchy, they are perfect for dunking in coffee, tea, or milk. Like all biscotti, these keep a long time, but they usually are eaten very quickly. **Makes 2 dozen biscotti**

Center a rack in the oven and preheat it to 350°F. Line a baking sheet with parchment paper or a non-stick liner.

2 cups all-purpose flour
1¹/₃ cups sweetened, shredded coconut
1 cup sliced almonds
²/₃ cup granulated sugar
2 teaspoons baking powder
¹/₄ teaspoon salt

Combine the flour, coconut, almonds, sugar, baking powder, and salt in the bowl of an electric stand mixer or a large mixing bowl. Use the flat beater attachment or a hand-held mixer to blend together briefly on low speed.

2 extra-large eggs, at room temperature
4 ounces (8 tablespoons, 1 stick) unsalted butter, melted
1 teaspoon pure vanilla extract

Using a fork, lightly beat together the eggs, butter, and vanilla in a medium bowl. With the mixer speed on low, add to the dry ingredients and blend together thoroughly.

Divide the dough into 2 equal pieces. Dust your hands lightly with flour and shape each piece of dough into a loaf about 8 inches long, 2 to 3 inches wide, and ³/₄ inch high. Place both loaves on the baking sheet, leaving several inches of space between them.

Bake the biscotti for 22 to 24 minutes, until the loaves are light golden and set. Remove the baking sheet from the oven and cool on a rack for 10 minutes.

Using a serrated knife, slice each loaf on the diagonal into ¹/₂-inch-thick slices. Place these slices on their sides on the baking sheet. Bake for 15 to 20 minutes, until firm and golden colored.

Remove the pan from the oven and transfer the biscotti to racks to cool.

Essential Gear
- Baking sheet
- Electric stand mixer with flat beater attachment, or large mixing bowl and hand-held mixer
- Cooling rack
- Serrated knife

Keeping
Store the biscotti in an airtight container between layers of waxed paper at room temperature up to 1 week. To freeze up to 3 months, wrap the container tightly in several layers of plastic wrap and aluminum foil. Use a large piece of masking tape and an indelible marker to label and date the contents. If frozen, defrost overnight in the refrigerator and bring to room temperature before serving.

Making a Change
Replace the almonds with pecans, walnuts, or toasted and skinned hazelnuts.

Adding Style
Drizzle the biscotti with thin lines of bittersweet, semisweet, milk, or white chocolate after they are completely cool. Let the chocolate set for 15 minutes in the refrigerator before serving or storing.

Coconut Cream Pie with Chocolate Cookie Crust

A CRISP CHOCOLATE cookie crust holds a filling of whipped cream mixed with pastry cream and shredded coconut. The texture contrast between the filling and the crust enhances them both. Be sure to make the pastry cream at least a day before using so it has time to cool and chill. **Makes one 10-inch round pie, 12 to 14 servings**

CHOCOLATE COOKIE CRUST

7 ounces (about 30) chocolate wafer cookies
2 tablespoons granulated sugar

Place the wafers in the work bowl of a food processor fitted with the steel blade. Add the sugar and pulse until the wafers are finely ground, about 2 minutes. Or place the wafers in a sturdy plastic bag and seal it. Use a rolling pin to crush the cookies to a very fine crumb consistency.

3 ounces (6 tablespoons, ¾ stick) unsalted butter, melted and cooled

Transfer the crumbs to a medium bowl and add the butter. Use a rubber spatula to toss the mixture together and moisten all the crumbs.

Using your fingers, press the crumbs evenly into the bottom and partway up the sides of the pie pan. Chill the crust in the freezer for 15 minutes.

Adjust an oven rack to the lower third and preheat the oven to 350°F.

Place the pie pan on a baking sheet and bake the crust for 15 minutes, until set. Remove from the oven and cool completely on a rack.

COCONUT CREAM FILLING AND TOPPING

2 cups heavy whipping cream
2 tablespoons granulated sugar

Place the cream in the chilled bowl of an electric stand mixer or a large mixing bowl. Use the wire whip attachment or a hand-held mixer to whip the cream on medium speed until frothy. Add the sugar and whip on medium-high speed until the cream hold, firm but not stiff peaks. Remove 1 cup of the whipped cream and set aside.

1 recipe Vanilla Pastry Cream (see Pluot Custard Tart, page 92)
1½ cups sweetened, shredded or flaked coconut

Whisk the pastry cream to break up any lumps. Fold the remaining whipped cream into the pastry cream and blend well, then fold in the coconut.

Spread this mixture evenly in the cooled chocolate cookie shell.

Essential Gear

- Food processor
- Rolling pin
- Rubber spatula
- 10-inch round deep pie pan
- Baking sheet
- Cooling rack
- Electric stand mixer with wire whip attachment, or large mixing bowl and hand-held mixer

Streamlining

The chocolate cookie crust can be made in advance and kept at room temperature, tightly wrapped in aluminum foil up to 2 days.

Making a Change

Replace the chocolate wafer cookies with other wafer cookies for the crust.

Spread the reserved whipped cream over the top of the filling, mounding it slightly in the center.

½ cup toasted, sweetened, shredded or flaked coconut

Sprinkle the top of the pie with the toasted coconut.

Chill the pie in the refrigerator up to 3 hours before serving.

Coconut Macaroons

THESE ARE CLASSIC macaroons, crisp on the outside and chewy on the inside. To make them extra special, dip the bottoms in dark chocolate. **Makes 3½ dozen macaroons**

COCONUT MACAROONS

1½ cups granulated sugar
2 extra-large egg whites, at room temperature
1 tablespoon light corn syrup
1 teaspoon pure vanilla extract

Place the sugar, egg whites, corn syrup, and vanilla in a large bowl. Place the bowl in a pan of simmering water. Whisk the mixture together until it is smooth and warm to the touch.

Remove the bowl from the water and wipe the bottom and sides dry.

4 cups (10½ ounces) sweetened, shredded coconut
1 cup cake flour

In a large bowl, combine the coconut and flour and toss to blend well.

Stir this mixture into the egg white mixture until thoroughly blended.

Cover the bowl tightly with plastic wrap and chill for 1 hour.

Position the oven racks to the upper and lower thirds and preheat the oven to 325°F. Line three baking sheets with parchment paper or non-stick liners.

Using a spoon or a small ice cream scoop, shape 1-inch mounds of the macaroon mixture. Place them on the baking sheets, leaving 2 inches of space between them.

Essential Gear
- Large mixing bowl
- Whisk
- Microwave-proof bowl
- Three baking sheets
- Three parchment paper sheets or non-stick pan liners
- Three cooling racks
- Rubber spatula

Keeping
Store the macaroons in an airtight container between layers of waxed paper at room temperature up to 1 week. To freeze up to 3 months, wrap the container tightly in several layers of plastic wrap and aluminum foil. Use a large piece of masking tape and an indelible marker to label and date the contents. If frozen, defrost overnight in the refrigerator and bring to room temperature before serving.

Bake the macaroons for 8 minutes. Switch the baking sheets and bake another 7 to 10 minutes, until the macaroons are light golden and set. Remove the baking sheets from the oven and cool completely on racks.

CHOCOLATE GARNISH

8 ounces bittersweet, semisweet, or milk chocolate, finely chopped

Place 6 ounces of the chocolate in a microwave-proof bowl. Melt on low power for 30-second bursts, stirring with a rubber spatula after each burst. Or melt the chocolate in the top of a double boiler over warm water. Stir often with a rubber spatula.

When the chocolate is melted, stir in the remaining 2 ounces of chocolate in 2 to 3 batches. Make sure each batch is melted before adding the next. This cools down the melted chocolate and brings it to the right temperature for dipping.

Line two baking sheets with parchment or waxed paper. Hold a macaroon by the top and dip the bottom and about $1/2$ inch up the sides into the chocolate. Shake off any excess chocolate and place the macaroon on a lined baking sheet. When all the macaroons are dipped, chill them for 15 minutes to set the chocolate.

Double Fig Tart

FOR FIG LOVERS, this will be your favorite fig tart because it is filled with fig jam and topped with sliced figs. It's not possible to eat too many figs when they're so delicious! A delicate, sweet pastry crust holds the yummy filling. I ate a tart similar to this at Zuni Café in San Francisco when I took my mother to lunch there to celebrate her birthday. Since I'm a big fan of fresh figs, I wanted to recreate that tart at home. **Makes one $9^{1}/_{2}$-inch round tart, 12 to 14 servings**

PASTRY DOUGH

1½ cups all-purpose flour
½ cup confectioners' sugar
¼ teaspoon salt

In the work bowl of a food processor fitted with the steel blade, combine the flour, sugar, and salt. Pulse briefly to blend.

5 ounces (10 tablespoons, 1¼ sticks) unsalted butter, chilled

Cut the butter into small pieces and add to the flour mixture. Pulse until the butter is cut into very tiny pieces, about 30 seconds.

Essential Gear
- Food processor
- Rolling pin
- 9½-inch round, fluted-edge tart pan with removable bottom
- Aluminum foil
- Small saucepan
- Baking sheet
- Pie weights
- Cooling rack
- 2-quart mixing bowl

Keeping
Although the tart is best eaten the day it's made, it can last up to 3 days.

1 extra-large egg yolk, at
room temperature
2 teaspoons heavy whipping
cream
½ teaspoon pure vanilla
extract

In a small bowl, beat the egg yolk with the cream and vanilla. With the food processor running, pour this mixture through the feed tube. Process the dough until the mixture wraps itself around the blade, about 1 minute.

Turn the pastry dough onto a large piece of plastic wrap. Shape into a flat disk and wrap tightly in a double layer of plastic wrap. Chill in the refrigerator until firm before using, at least 2 hours.

Center a rack in the oven and preheat it to 375°F.

On a smooth, flat surface, roll out the pastry dough between sheets of lightly floured waxed or parchment paper to a large circle about 11 inches in diameter. To tell if the dough will fit the tart pan, hold the pan above the dough. If there are about 2 inches of dough that protrude beyond the sides of the pan, it will fit.

Carefully peel the paper off the top of the dough. Brush excess flour off the dough, then loosely roll the pastry dough around the rolling pin without the bottom piece of paper. Place the tart pan directly underneath the rolling pin and carefully unroll the pastry dough into the tart pan. Gently lift up the sides and ease the pastry dough into the bottom and sides of the tart pan. Trim off the excess pastry dough at the top of the pan. Transfer the tart pan to a baking sheet and chill for 15 minutes.

Line the pastry shell with a large piece of aluminum foil that fits well against the bottom and sides. Fill the pastry shell with pie weights or a mixture of rice and beans. Bake for 10 minutes, then remove the foil and weights. If the bottom of the pastry shell puffs up, gently pierce it in a few places with a fork or the point of a knife to release the air. Bake another 12 to 14 minutes, until light golden and set. Remove the pan from the oven and transfer the tart shell to a rack to cool completely

FIG FILLING

One 8-ounce jar (1 cup)
fig jam
2 tablespoons freshly
squeezed lemon juice
2 tablespoons granulated
sugar

Combine the fig jam, lemon juice, and sugar in a small saucepan. Bring to a boil over medium heat and cook, stirring often, until the mixture thickens slightly. Cool briefly and spread the mixture evenly in the bottom of the cooled tart shell

1¼ pounds ripe, fresh figs
(7 to 8 large), rinsed,
dried, and stemmed

Cut the figs lengthwise in ½-inch-thick slices. Arrange the slices overlapping each other to completely fill in the tart shell.

Store the tart, loosely covered with waxed paper and then tightly wrapped with aluminum foil, in the refrigerator.

Streamlining
The pastry dough can be made in advance and kept in the refrigerator, tightly wrapped in a double layer of plastic wrap, up to 4 days. To freeze up to 3 months, wrap the dough snugly in several layers of plastic wrap and place it in a freezer bag. Use a large piece of masking tape and an indelible marker to label and date the contents. If frozen, defrost overnight in the refrigerator before using.

Troubleshooting
Don't roll out the pastry dough before it is chilled. The dough will be too soft and it will require a lot of flour to roll out, which results in a tough dough.

Once the pastry dough is unrolled into the tart pan, don't push it down forcefully. This will stretch the dough, which will shrink as it bakes, making it flat instead of taking the shape of the tart pan.

Adding Style
Serve slices of the tart with vanilla or coconut ice cream or whipped cream.

1 tablespoon granulated sugar	Sprinkle the sugar evenly over the top of the figs.

Bake the tart for 10 to 15 minutes, until the figs are soft.

Remove the pan from the oven and cool on a rack. Carefully remove the side of the tart pan.

Serve the tart warm or at room temperature.

Fig and Almond Galette

A GALETTE is a free-form tart made without a tart pan. In this galette, almond pastry dough encloses frangipane, a creamy almond filling, and fresh figs. For an even tastier treat, serve this with vanilla ice cream. It's one of my favorite ways to use fresh figs. **Makes one 9-inch tart, 8 to 10 servings**

Essential Gear

- Food processor
- Fine grater or zester
- Sharp knife
- Baking sheet
- Parchment paper
- 1-inch natural-bristle pastry brush or a spoon
- Cooling rack

Keeping

Although the galette is best eaten the day it's made, it can last up to 2 days. Store the galette tightly covered with aluminum foil at room temperature.

Adding Style

Serve slices of the galette with vanilla ice cream.

PASTRY DOUGH

1 cup all-purpose flour ½ cup sliced or slivered almonds 2 teaspoons granulated sugar ¼ teaspoon salt	In the work bowl of a food processor fitted with the steel blade, combine the flour, almonds, sugar, and salt. Pulse until the almonds are very finely ground, about 1 minute.
4 ounces (8 tablespoons, 1 stick) unsalted butter, chilled	Cut the butter into small pieces and add. Pulse until the butter is cut into very tiny pieces, about 30 seconds. The texture should be sandy with very tiny lumps throughout.
2 teaspoons freshly squeezed lemon juice 2 to 3 tablespoons ice water Finely grated zest of 1 large lemon	In a small bowl, combine the lemon juice, 2 tablespoons of water, and the lemon zest.

With the food processor running, pour this mixture through the feed tube. Process until the dough wraps itself around the blade, 30 seconds to 1 minute. If the dough seems dry, add the remaining tablespoon of water and process until the dough comes together.

Turn the pastry dough onto a large piece of plastic wrap. Shape into a flat disk and wrap tightly in a double layer of plastic wrap. Chill in the refrigerator until firm before using, about 2 hours. Chilling the dough relaxes the gluten in the flour so it won't be too elastic and will roll out easily. It also firms up the butter in the dough so it will need less flour when rolled out. If the dough is too firm it will splinter and break when rolled out. Let it stand at room temperature for 10 to 15 minutes before rolling to become more pliable.

FIG FILLING

1 pound fresh figs (6 to 7 large), washed and dried	Using a sharp knife, cut the stem off the top of the figs and cut the figs in half lengthwise. Cut the fig halves in half again lengthwise, then cut each quarter into ¹/₂-inch-thick chunks.
2 tablespoons light brown sugar	Place the fig chunks in a bowl. Add the sugar and toss together to distribute evenly. Taste the fruit to see if it needs any more sugar.

ASSEMBLY

Center a rack in the oven and preheat it to 375°F.

On a smooth, flat surface, roll out the pastry dough between sheets of lightly floured waxed or parchment paper to a large circle 11 to 12 inches in diameter. Carefully peel the paper off the top of the dough. Brush excess flour off the dough, then loosely roll the pastry dough around the rolling pin without the bottom piece of paper. Place a baking sheet lined with parchment paper directly underneath the rolling pin and carefully unroll the pastry dough onto the baking sheet.

¹/₃ cup Frangipane Filling (see Apricot Frangipane Tart, page 54)	Spread the filling over the center of the pastry dough, leaving a 3-inch border all around.
	Mound the fig chunks in the center of the dough circle, leaving a 2¹/₂- to 3-inch border all around.
	Fold the border up so that it partially covers the figs. It will naturally form pleats as it is folded.
1 tablespoon heavy whipping cream **2 teaspoons granulated sugar**	Using a pastry brush, brush the dough border with cream, being careful that it doesn't run down the sides and under the galette. If it does, wipe it up because it can cause the bottom of the galette to burn. Gently lift up the folds of the dough and brush under those areas with cream, then replace the folds. Evenly sprinkle the sugar over the dough border.

Bake the galette for 40 to 45 minutes, until light golden. Remove the pan from the oven and transfer to a rack to cool. Cut the galette into pie-shaped wedges to serve.

Fresh Fig and Pistachio Nut Tart

FIGS AND PISTACHIO NUTS are a fabulous flavor combination. In this tart, almond pastry dough holds a creamy filling of ground pistachio nuts. Fig halves are fanned out over the top of the filling, which puffs up as it bakes and encloses them. The top of the warm tart is brushed with apricot glaze, making it glisten. **Makes one 9¹/₂-inch round tart, 8 to 12 servings**

PASTRY DOUGH

1 cup all-purpose flour
¹/₂ cup sliced or slivered almonds
2 teaspoons granulated sugar
¹/₄ teaspoon salt

In the work bowl of a food processor fitted with the steel blade, combine the flour, almonds, sugar, and salt. Pulse until the almonds are very finely ground, about 1 minute.

4 ounces (8 tablespoons, 1 stick) unsalted butter, chilled

Cut the butter into small pieces and add. Pulse until the butter is cut into very tiny pieces, about 30 seconds. The texture should be sandy with very tiny lumps throughout.

2 teaspoons freshly squeezed lemon juice
2 to 3 tablespoons ice water

In a small bowl, combine the lemon juice and 2 tablespoons of water. With the food processor running, pour this mixture through the feed tube. Process until the dough wraps itself around the blade, 30 seconds to 1 minute. If the dough seems dry, add the remaining tablespoon of water and process until the dough comes together.

Turn the pastry dough onto a large piece of plastic wrap. Shape into a flat disk and wrap tightly in a double layer of plastic wrap. Chill in the refrigerator until firm before using, about 2 hours. Chilling the dough relaxes the gluten in the flour so it won't be too elastic and will roll out easily. It also firms up the butter in the dough so it will need less flour when rolled out. If the dough is too firm it will splinter and break when rolled out. Let it stand at room temperature for 10 to 15 minutes before rolling to become more pliable.

Center a rack in the oven and preheat it to 375°F.

On a smooth, flat surface, roll out the pastry dough between sheets of lightly floured waxed or parchment paper to a large circle about 11 inches in diameter. To tell if the dough will fit the tart pan, hold the pan above the dough. If there are about 2 to 3 inches of dough that protrude beyond the sides of the pan, it will fit.

Essential Gear

- Food processor
- Rolling pin
- 9¹/₂-inch round, fluted-edge tart pan with removable bottom
- Baking sheet
- Cooling rack
- 2-cup saucepan
- Medium-size fine-mesh strainer
- Goose-feather pastry brush

Keeping

The tart can last up to 3 days in the refrigerator. Place a piece of waxed paper over the top of the tart, then tightly cover it with aluminum foil.

Streamlining

The pastry dough can be made in advance and kept in the refrigerator, tightly wrapped in a double layer of plastic wrap, up to 4 days. To freeze for up to 3 months, wrap the dough snugly in several layers of plastic wrap and place it in a freezer bag. Use a large piece of masking tape and an indelible marker to label and date the contents. If frozen, defrost overnight in the refrigerator before using. The dough can also be fitted into the pan and kept tightly covered in the refrigerator or frozen, wrapped and labeled as above.

Carefully peel the paper off the top of the dough. Brush excess flour off the dough, then loosely roll the pastry dough around the rolling pin without the bottom piece of paper. Place the tart pan directly underneath the rolling pin and carefully unroll the pastry dough onto it

Gently lift up the sides and ease the pastry dough into the bottom and sides of the tart pan, pushing it lightly into the fluted edges. Trim off the excess pastry dough at the top of the pan by running the rolling pin over the top. Or use your fingers to press against the top of the pan to remove the excess pastry dough.

Place the tart pan on a baking sheet and chill while preparing the filling.

PISTACHIO NUT FILLING

1 cup toasted, unsalted pistachio nuts
½ cup granulated sugar

In the work bowl of a food processor fitted with the steel blade, combine the pistachios and sugar. Pulse until the pistachios are very finely ground, about 1 minute.

1 extra-large egg, at room temperature
1 teaspoon pure vanilla extract

Add the egg and vanilla to the pistachio mixture and pulse several times to blend together well.

2½ ounces (5 tablespoons) unsalted butter, softened

Cut the butter into small pieces and add to the mixture. Pulse several times to blend.

2 tablespoons all-purpose flour

Add the flour and pulse until the mixture is smooth, about 15 seconds.

Transfer the mixture to the pastry shell and spread it out evenly with a rubber spatula.

ASSEMBLY

¾ to 1 pound fresh ripe figs (7 to 8 medium), washed and dried

Cut the stems off of the figs and cut them in half vertically. Place the fig halves around the outer edge of the tart, with the pointed ends facing out, leaving about 1 inch of space between them. Form another circle of figs in the center, filling the center of the tart.

Bake the tart for 40 to 45 minutes, until the filling is puffed and light golden.

Remove the tart from the oven and place on a cooling rack.

The pistachio nut filling can be made in advance and kept in a tightly covered plastic container in the refrigerator up to 4 days before using.

The apricot glaze can be made in advance and kept in a tightly covered plastic container in the refrigerator up to 1 month before using. Warm it in a small saucepan over medium heat or in a microwave oven on medium power before using.

Making a Change
Replace the almonds in the pastry dough with toasted, unsalted pistachio nuts.

Replace the pistachios in the filling with macadamia nuts, pecans, or toasted and skinned hazelnuts.

¼ cup apricot preserves

1 tablespoon amaretto, cognac, or water

Combine the apricot preserves and liquid in a small saucepan. Bring to a boil over medium heat. Remove the pan from the heat and strain the glaze into a small bowl, pushing through as much of the pulp as possible.

Use a goose-feather pastry brush to lightly brush the top of the tart with the glaze. Don't apply a thick glaze, which looks unappetizing. The purpose of the glaze is to keep the figs from drying out and to make the top of the tart glisten.

Remove the sides of the tart pan (see page 42) before serving. Serve the tart warm or at room temperature.

Fresh Fig Clafouti

A CLAFOUTI is a rustic fruit dessert from the Limousin region of France that is a cross between a tart and a custard dessert, baked in a deep pie dish. The fruit is covered with a batter that puffs up around it as the dessert bakes. Traditionally, a clafouti is made with cherries, but in this variation I use fresh figs. This is a very tasty and easy-to-prepare dessert that shows off fresh figs very well. **Makes one 10-inch clafouti, 8 to 10 servings**

Essential Gear

- 10-inch round deep pie dish
- Small sharp knife
- Large mixing bowl
- Whisk, rubber spatula, or wooden spoon
- Large fine-mesh strainer
- Cooling rack

Keeping

Although the clafouti is best eaten the day it's made, it can last up to 2 days. Store the clafouti tightly covered with plastic wrap in the refrigerator. Once the clafouti cools, it will fall slightly.

Adding Style

Serve slices of the clafouti with vanilla ice cream or whipped cream.

Center a rack in the oven and preheat it to 375°F.

1 tablespoon unsalted butter, softened

1 tablespoon granulated sugar

Use your fingertips or a paper towel to butter the bottom and sides of the pie dish. Sprinkle the inside of the pan with sugar. Tilt and shake the dish so the sugar sticks to the butter. Turn the dish over and shake out any excess sugar over the sink.

FRESH FIG FILLING

1 pound ripe fresh figs (6 to 7 large), rinsed and dried

Use a small sharp knife to remove the stems of the figs. Cut the figs in half vertically and arrange most of them in a circle around the perimeter of the pie dish, cut sides up and stem ends toward the outer edge of the pie dish. Arrange another smaller circle of figs in the center to fill in the pie dish.

1¼ cups milk	In a large bowl, combine the milk, cream, eggs, sugar, and vanilla. Stir together to blend.
1¼ cups heavy whipping cream	
3 extra-large eggs, at room temperature	
¼ cup granulated sugar	
1 teaspoon pure vanilla extract	

1 cup all-purpose flour, sifted	Add the flour, nutmeg, and salt and whisk together until smooth.
¼ teaspoon freshly grated nutmeg	
⅛ teaspoon salt	

	Pour the batter through a fine-mesh strainer to remove any lumps, spreading it evenly over the figs in the pie dish.

	Bake the clafouti for 45 to 50 minutes, until it is puffed and light golden. Remove the pan from the oven and transfer to a rack to cool.

GARNISH

2 tablespoons confectioners' sugar	Dust the top of the clafouti evenly with confectioners' sugar. Cut into pie-shaped wedges and serve warm or at room temperature.

Fresh Fig Pound Cake

FRESH FIGS make this pound cake very moist. It's wonderful on its own, but is also great with vanilla or coconut ice cream. It's also excellent toasted and spread with fig or blackberry jam for breakfast. **Makes one 8½ × 4½ × 2½-inch loaf cake, about 10 servings**

Essential Gear

- 8½ × 4½ × 2½-inch loaf pan
- Electric stand mixer with flat beater attachment, or large mixing bowl and hand-held mixer
- Rubber spatula
- Cooling rack
- Flexible-blade spatula

1 tablespoon unsalted butter, softened	Center a rack in the oven and preheat it to 325°F. Use your fingertips or a paper towel to butter the inside of the pan.
2 teaspoons all-purpose flour	Dust the inside of the pan with the flour. Shake and tilt the pan to coat it with flour. Turn the pan over the sink and tap out the excess flour.

½ pound fresh figs (3 to 4 large), rinsed and dried	Cut off the stems of the figs, then cut them in half vertically. Cut each half vertically in half again, then cut each quarter into small pieces. Place the fig pieces in a small bowl.	**Keeping** Store the cake, tightly covered with a double layer of plastic wrap, at room temperature up to 4 days. To freeze up to 3 months, wrap the cake tightly in several layers of plastic wrap and aluminum foil. Use a large piece of masking tape and an indelible marker to label and date the contents. If frozen, defrost overnight in the refrigerator and bring to room temperature before serving.
2 cups cake flour 1 teaspoon baking powder ¼ teaspoon salt	Over a large piece of waxed paper or parchment paper or a bowl, sift together the flour and baking powder. Add the salt and toss to blend well. Take 2 tablespoons of this mixture and toss with the fig pieces to coat them completely.	
8 ounces (16 tablespoons, 2 sticks) unsalted butter, softened	Place the butter in the bowl of an electric stand mixer or in a large mixing bowl. Use the flat beater attachment or a hand-held mixer to beat the butter on medium speed until it's fluffy, about 2 minutes.	
1 cup superfine sugar	Add the sugar, and cream together well. Stop occasionally and scrape down the sides and bottom of the bowl with a rubber spatula.	**Making a Change** Add ½ cup chopped toasted pecans, walnuts, macadamia nuts, or almonds after adding the figs.
4 extra-large eggs, at room temperature	Adjust the mixer speed to medium-low. One at a time, add the eggs to the butter mixture, mixing well after each addition. The eggs will sit on top of the butter mixture, so stop after each addition and scrape down the sides and bottom of the bowl with a rubber spatula to help mix evenly.	Add ½ cup toasted, sweetened coconut after adding the figs.
3 tablespoons milk 2 teaspoons pure vanilla extract	In a small bowl or measuring cup, combine the milk and vanilla. Add to the butter mixture and blend well.	**Adding Style** Serve slices of the cooled cake with vanilla or coconut ice cream.
	Turn the mixer speed to low and add the dry ingredients in 3 stages, mixing thoroughly after each addition. Add the fig pieces and mix to distribute evenly.	
	Pour the cake batter into the prepared pan. Bake for 1 hour and 10 to 15 minutes, until the cake is light golden and a cake tester inserted in the center comes out clean.	
	Remove the pan from the oven and cool on a rack for 20 minutes. Use a flexible-blade spatula or thin-bladed sharp knife to run around the outer edges to loosen the cake from the pan. Invert the pan over the cooling rack or a serving plate and gently pull the pan away from the cake.	

Fresh Fig Puff Pastry Tartlets

S LICED FRESH FIGS drizzled with honey are baked on top of puff pastry circles to form individual tartlets. These look so professional that when you serve them your guests will think you spent the whole day making them. But they are really quick to assemble, especially if you use store-bought puff pastry. **Makes eight 5^1/$_2$-inch round tartlets**

Essential Gear
- Rolling pin
- Chef's knife
- Two baking sheets
- Two parchment paper sheets
- 1-inch natural-bristle pastry brush or a spoon
- Two cooling racks
- Microplane grater or citrus zester

PUFF PASTRY DOUGH

1 pound Quick Puff Pastry (page 196) or store-bought puff pastry

If the puff pastry is frozen, defrost it in the refrigerator before rolling out. Divide the puff pastry into two equal pieces and roll each piece out between sheets of lightly floured waxed or parchment paper to a 9-inch square.

Use a ruler to cut each square into equal-sized quarters, making a total of eight 4^1/$_2$-inch squares.

On a smooth, flat work surface between sheets of lightly floured waxed or parchment paper, roll out each puff pastry piece to a circle about 5^1/$_2$ inches in diameter. Use a 5^1/$_2$-inch round plate or other shape to place gently on top of the puff pastry as a guide and trim off the excess puff pastry.

Use a 4^1/$_2$-inch round plate or other shape to place gently on top of the puff pastry as a guide and use a sharp knife to draw an inner circle in the puff pastry circle, but don't cut all the way through the puff pastry. Remove the guide and fold the outer pastry edges in toward the center to form a lip, pressing on them gently so they will stick.

Line two baking sheets with parchment paper sheets and place 4 puff pastry circles on each baking sheet, leaving at least 3 inches of space between them.

2 tablespoons heavy whipping cream
2 tablespoons granulated sugar
Finely grated zest of 1 lemon

Using a small pastry brush or a spoon, brush the center of each puff pastry circle lightly with the cream. Then sprinkle sugar and lemon zest over the cream in the center of each circle.

Place the baking sheets in the freezer for 20 minutes.

Keeping

Although the tartlets are best eaten the day they're made, they can last up to 2 days. Store the tartlets, loosely covered with waxed paper and then tightly wrapped with aluminum foil, in the refrigerator.

Streamlining

The puff pastry dough can be rolled out in advance and kept in the refrigerator, tightly wrapped in a double layer of plastic wrap, up to 3 days.

The figs can be sliced and kept in the refrigerator, tightly covered with plastic wrap, up to 1 day in advance of using.

Adjust the oven racks to the upper and lower thirds and preheat the oven to 450°F.

ASSEMBLY

8 large ripe figs (about 1¼ pounds), washed and dried

Cut off the stem and a ¼-inch slice from the end of each fig. Then slice each fig crosswise into ¼-inch-thick slices. Arrange a sliced fig on each puff pastry circle, overlapping the slices to fill in the center of each circle.

2 tablespoons honey

Drizzle a little honey over the fig slices.

Place the baking sheets in the oven and reduce the oven temperature to 425°F.

Bake for 10 minutes, then switch the baking sheets and bake another 6 to 8 minutes, until the pastry is golden.

Remove the baking sheets from the oven and cool on racks.

Serve the tartlets warm or at room temperature with vanilla ice cream or lightly sweetened whipped cream.

Fresh Fig Tart with Cornmeal Crust and Mascarpone Filling

A CRISP cornmeal crust holds a creamy filling of mascarpone topped with fresh figs. It's a wonderful combination of textures that is visually striking and exceptionally flavorful.
Makes one 9½-inch round tart, 12 to 14 servings

CORNMEAL PASTRY CRUST

1½ cups all-purpose flour
½ cup stone-ground fine yellow cornmeal
1 tablespoon granulated sugar
¼ teaspoon salt

In the work bowl of a food processor fitted with the steel blade, combine the flour, cornmeal, sugar, and salt. Pulse briefly to blend.

4 ounces (8 tablespoons, 1 stick) unsalted butter, chilled

Cut the butter into small pieces and add to the flour mixture. Pulse until the butter is cut into very tiny pieces, about 30 seconds. The texture should be sandy with very tiny lumps throughout.

Essential Gear
- Food processor
- 9½-inch round, fluted-edge tart pan with removable bottom
- Baking sheet
- Cooling rack
- Electric stand mixer with wire whip attachment, or large mixing bowl and hand-held mixer
- Small offset spatula or rubber spatula
- Small saucepan
- Medium fine-mesh strainer
- Goose-feather pastry brush

¼ cup cold water

With the food processor running, pour the water through the feed tube. Process the dough until the mixture wraps itself around the blade, about 1 minute.

Press the dough evenly into the bottom and up the sides of the tart pan. Trim off any excess pastry dough at the top by running a rolling pin over the top. Chill the pastry shell for 30 minutes in the refrigerator.

Center a rack in the oven and preheat it to 400°F.

Transfer the tart pan to a baking sheet. Bake the tart shell 25 to 30 minutes, until light golden. Remove the pan from the oven and transfer the tart pan to a rack to cool completely.

MASCARPONE FILLING

1 cup mascarpone (8 ounces), softened
⅓ cup heavy whipping cream

Place the mascarpone and cream in the bowl of an electric stand mixer or in a large mixing bowl. Use a wire whip attachment or a hand-held mixer to whip together on medium-low speed until smooth.

¼ cup granulated sugar
1 teaspoon freshly squeezed lemon juice
¼ teaspoon salt

Add the sugar, lemon juice, and salt to the mascarpone mixture and continue to whip together until completely blended, about 1 minute.

Transfer the filling to the cooled tart shell. Use a small offset spatula or rubber spatula to spread it out evenly in the shell.

ASSEMBLY

1 pound ripe, fresh figs (6 to 7 large), washed and dried

Cut off the stems and cut the figs in half lengthwise. Then cut each half in half again, lengthwise. Arrange the fig quarters over the top of the filling with the pointed ends facing the center. Completely cover the filling with figs.

¼ cup apricot preserves
1 tablespoon amaretto, cognac, or water

Combine the apricot preserves and liquid in a small saucepan. Bring to a boil over medium heat. Remove the pan from the heat and strain the glaze into a small bowl, pushing through as much of the pulp as possible.

Use a goose-feather pastry brush to lightly brush the top of the figs with the glaze. Don't apply a thick glaze, which looks unappetizing. The purpose of the glaze is to keep the fruit from drying out and to make it glisten.

Serve the tart immediately or chill about 1 hour before serving.

Keeping

Store the tart, loosely covered with waxed paper and then tightly wrapped with aluminum foil, in the refrigerator up to 3 days.

Streamlining

The pastry dough can be made in advance and kept tightly wrapped in a double layer of plastic wrap in the refrigerator up to 4 days. To freeze up to 3 months, wrap the dough snugly in several layers of plastic wrap and place it in a freezer bag. Use a large piece of masking tape and an indelible marker to label and date the contents. If frozen, defrost overnight in the refrigerator before using. If the dough is chilled, it is necessary to roll it out and ease it into the tart pan, rather than pressing it into the pan (see technique on page 39 or Raspberry-Blueberry Galette on page 199).

Grilled Pineapple Tart with Macadamia Nuts

A DELICATE cookie crust encloses luscious vanilla pastry cream that is topped with slices of grilled pineapple and decorated with finely chopped macadamia nuts. This is a quintessential summer dessert that makes you feel like you're in the tropics. It's refreshing and it tastes divine. The pastry dough and pastry cream filling can both be made in advance, so it's easy to assemble shortly before serving. **Makes one 9¹/₂-inch round tart, 12 to 14 servings**

PASTRY DOUGH

1¹/₄ cups all-purpose flour ¹/₂ cup confectioners' sugar ¹/₈ teaspoon salt	In the work bowl of a food processor fitted with the steel blade, combine the flour, sugar, and salt. Pulse briefly to blend.
4 ounces (8 tablespoons, 1 stick) unsalted butter, chilled	Cut the butter into small pieces and add to the flour mixture. Pulse until the butter is cut into very tiny pieces, about 30 seconds. The texture should be sandy with very tiny lumps throughout.
1 extra-large egg yolk, at room temperature ¹/₂ teaspoon pure vanilla extract	Use a fork to lightly beat the egg yolk with the vanilla in a small bowl. With the food processor running, pour the egg yolk and vanilla mixture through the feed tube. Process the dough until the mixture wraps itself around the blade, about 1 minute.

Turn the pastry dough onto a large piece of plastic wrap. Shape into a flat disk and wrap tightly in a double layer of plastic wrap. Chill in the refrigerator until firm before using, at least 2 hours.

Center a rack in the oven and preheat it to 375°F.

On a smooth, flat surface, roll out the pastry dough between sheets of lightly floured waxed or parchment paper to a large circle about 11 inches in diameter. To tell if the dough will fit the tart pan, hold the pan above the dough. If there are about 2 inches of dough that protrude beyond the sides of the pan, it will fit.

Carefully peel the paper off the top of the dough and brush off any excess flour. Loosely roll the pastry dough around the rolling pin without the bottom piece of paper. Place the tart pan directly underneath the rolling pin and carefully unroll the pastry dough into the tart pan. Gently lift up the sides and ease the pastry dough into the bottom and sides of the tart pan. Trim off the excess pastry dough

Essential Gear

- Food processor
- Rolling pin
- 9¹/₂-inch round, fluted-edge tart pan with removable bottom
- Aluminum foil
- Baking sheet
- Pie weights
- Cooling rack
- Whisk or rubber spatula
- 1-inch natural-bristle pastry brush or paper towel
- Grill or stove-top grill pan

Keeping

Store the tart, loosely covered with waxed paper and then tightly wrapped with aluminum foil, in the refrigerator up to 3 days.

Streamlining

The pastry dough can be made in advance and kept in the refrigerator up to 4 days, tightly wrapped in a double layer of plastic wrap. To freeze up to 3 months, place the wrapped dough in a freezer bag. Use a large piece of masking tape and an indelible marker to label and date the contents. If frozen, defrost in the refrigerator overnight before using. If the dough is very cold, let it stand at room temperature to become pliable.

The pastry shell can be baked up to 2 days in advance. Store it at room

at the top of the pan. Transfer the tart pan to a baking sheet and chill in the refrigerator for 15 minutes.

Line the pastry shell with a large piece of aluminum foil that fits well against the bottom and sides. Fill with pie weights or a mixture of rice and beans. Bake for 10 minutes, then remove the foil and weights. If the bottom of the pastry shell puffs up, gently pierce it in several places with a fork or a sharp knife to release the air. Bake another 12 to 14 minutes, until light golden and set. Remove the pan from the oven and transfer to a rack to cool completely.

temperature tightly covered with aluminum foil.

Troubleshooting
Don't roll out the pastry dough before it is chilled. The dough will be too soft and it will require a lot of flour to roll out, which results in a tough dough.

Rolling the delicate tart dough around the rolling pin and unrolling into the tart pan is an easy way to get the dough into the pan without stretching or tearing it.

Once the pastry dough is unrolled into the tart pan, don't push it down forcefully. This will stretch the dough, which will shrink as it bakes, making it flat instead of taking the shape of the tart pan.

GRILLED PINEAPPLE

1 large pineapple

Using a sharp chef's knife or serrated knife, cut off the top and bottom of the pineapple and trim off the outer skin. Cut the pineapple in half from top to bottom. Then cut each half in half from top to bottom and cut out the core from each pineapple quarter. Cut each quarter into $1/4$-inch-thick slices. Place the slices in a single layer on a baking sheet.

1 tablespoon canola oil
$1/2$ teaspoon freshly grated nutmeg
$1/2$ teaspoon ground cinnamon

Use a pastry brush to very lightly brush the top of each piece of pineapple with oil. Sprinkle the top of each piece with nutmeg and cinnamon.

Non-stick cooking spray

Lightly spray the grate of a preheated grill or a stove-top grill pan with non-stick cooking spray.

Grill the pineapple pieces on low to medium-low heat for 3 to 4 minutes on each side, until tender.

ASSEMBLY

1 recipe Vanilla Pastry Cream (see Pluot Custard Tart, page 92)

Stir the pastry cream vigorously to eliminate any lumps. Use a rubber spatula to evenly spread the pastry cream filling in the cooled tart shell.

Arrange the grilled pineapple on top of the pastry cream in concentric circles, filling in the tart shell.

2 tablespoons toasted, unsalted macadamia nuts
2 teaspoons sugar

In the work bowl of a food processor fitted with the steel blade, combine the nuts and sugar. Pulse until the nuts are finely ground. Or use a chef's knife to chop the nuts very finely.

Scatter the nuts over the top of the tart.

Serve the tart at room temperature.

Pineapple and Macadamia Nut Cake

THIS CAKE is similar in texture to a pound cake, but it's baked in a round cake pan instead of a loaf pan. It's full of fresh pineapple chunks and toasted macadamia nuts that complement each other and give the cake a delectable texture. **Makes one 9 × 2-inch round cake, 12 servings**

CAKE

1 tablespoon unsalted butter, softened

Center a rack in the oven and preheat it to 350°F. Use your fingertips or a paper towel to generously butter the inside of the pan.

2 teaspoons all-purpose flour

Dust the inside of the pan with the flour. Shake and tilt the pan to evenly distribute the flour, then turn the pan over and shake out the excess over the sink.

Cut a round of parchment paper to fit the bottom of the pan. Butter the parchment paper round and place in the pan, butter-side up.

6 ounces (12 tablespoons, 1½ sticks) unsalted butter, softened

Place the butter in the bowl of an electric stand mixer or in a large bowl. Use the flat beater attachment or a hand-held mixer to beat the butter on medium speed until it's fluffy, about 2 minutes.

¾ cup superfine sugar
⅓ cup firmly packed light brown sugar

Gradually add the superfine sugar and the brown sugar to the butter, and cream together well. Stop occasionally and scrape down the bottom and sides of the bowl with a rubber spatula.

4 extra-large eggs, at room temperature

One at a time, add the eggs to the butter mixture, stopping to scrape down the bottom and sides of the bowl after each addition. At first the mixture may look curdled as the eggs are added, but as you stop and scrape down the bowl, the mixture will smooth out.

1 medium, ripe pineapple or 3 ripe baby pineapples

Use a sharp knife to cut off the top and bottom of the pineapple. Then cut off all the outer skin. Cut the pineapple in half vertically and cut each half in half vertically again, to form quarters. If using a large pineapple, cut out the core of each quarter. If using baby pineapples, there's no need to cut out the core because it is edible. Cut each pineapple quarter into 1-inch pieces and place the pieces in a large bowl.

2 cups all-purpose flour
4 teaspoons baking powder
¼ teaspoon salt

Over a large piece of waxed or parchment paper or a bowl, sift together the flour and baking powder. Add the salt and toss to blend. Take 2 tablespoons of this mixture and toss with the cut pineapple to coat completely.

Essential Gear

- 9 × 2-inch round cake pan
- Scissors
- Parchment paper
- Electric stand mixer with flat beater attachment, or large mixing bowl and hand-held mixer
- Rubber spatula
- Cooling rack

Keeping

Store the cake tightly wrapped in aluminum foil at room temperature up to 4 days. To freeze up to 3 months, wrap the cake tightly in several layers of plastic wrap and aluminum foil. Use a large piece of masking tape and an indelible marker to label and date the contents. If frozen, defrost overnight in the refrigerator and bring to room temperature before serving.

Making a Change

Replace the macadamia nuts with walnuts, pecans, or finely chopped whole, unblanched almonds.

Add the dry ingredients to the butter mixture in 3 stages, blending well after each addition. Add the cut pineapple and stir in briefly.

½ cup finely chopped toasted, unsalted macadamia nuts	Add the macadamia nuts and stir to distribute evenly.

Transfer the batter to the prepared cake pan. The batter is very thick, so use a rubber spatula to spread it evenly into the pan.

Bake for 1 hour, until the cake is light golden on top and a cake tester inserted into the center comes out clean. If the cake is browning too much after 40 minutes, place a piece of aluminum foil on top to prevent it from becoming too dark.

Remove the pan from the oven and cool completely on a rack. Invert the pan to remove the cake, then peel the parchment paper off the back of the cake. Re-invert the layer onto a plate or a cardboard cake circle.

GARNISH

Confectioners' sugar	Lightly dust the top of the cake with confectioners' sugar. Cut into wedges and serve at room temperature.

Pineapple Tarte Tatin

THIS IS A VARIATION of the classic upside-down caramelized tart, typically made with apples. The name comes from two sisters in the Loire region of France who served the classic apple tart at their hotel in the late nineteenth and early twentieth centuries. Tarte Tatin is made using either puff pastry or pie dough. You can use either quick or store-bought puff pastry. **Makes one 10-inch round tarte, 10 to 12 servings**

PUFF PASTRY DOUGH

½ pound Quick Puff Pastry (page 196) or store-bought puff pastry	If the puff pastry is frozen, defrost it in the refrigerator before rolling out.

Adjust the oven rack to the lower third and preheat the oven to 400°F.

Essential Gear
- Rolling pin
- 1-quart heavy-bottomed saucepan
- 10-inch round pie pan
- 10-inch sauté pan or frying pan
- Heat-resistant spatula
- Cooling rack
- Pastry brush

Keeping
Although the tarte is best eaten the day it's made, it can last up to 2 days. Store

On a smooth, flat work surface, roll out the puff pastry between sheets of lightly floured waxed or parchment paper to a circle 12 inches in diameter. Chill the puff pastry while preparing the filling.

ASSEMBLY

½ cup granulated sugar
⅓ cup water
⅛ teaspoon cream of tartar

Combine the sugar, water, and cream of tartar in the saucepan and bring to a boil over medium-high heat, without stirring. Cook the mixture until it becomes a deep golden caramel, brushing down the sides of the pan two times with a pastry brush dipped in water to prevent stray crystals from coming out of the solution.

Immediately remove the saucepan from the heat and pour the caramel into the bottom of the pie pan. Swirl the pan to completely coat the bottom with the caramel.

1½ ounces (3 tablespoons) unsalted butter, cut into small pieces

Melt the butter in a large sauté pan over medium heat.

1 large pineapple, peeled and cored, cut into 1-inch cubes
⅓ cup granulated sugar
½ teaspoon ground allspice

Add the pineapple cubes to the butter and sprinkle them with the sugar and allspice. Use a heat-resistant spatula or wooden spoon to stir them gently to coat. Sauté the pineapple for 10 minutes, stirring occasionally, until lightly browned. Remove the pan from the heat and cool slightly.

Transfer the cooked pineapple mixture to the pie pan

Cover the top of the pineapple with the puff pastry circle, tucking it inside the edges of the pan so that the fruit is completely covered. Pierce the puff pastry in several places to release steam while it bakes.

Bake the tarte for 45 minutes, until the pastry is golden and puffed. Remove the tart from the oven and cool on a rack for 15 minutes.

Place a serving plate over the pie pan and carefully invert the tarte onto the plate. Gently lift the pan off of the tarte. If any pineapple pieces stick to the pan, use a spatula to carefully remove them and any remaining caramel sauce and arrange on top of the tarte.

Serve the tart warm or at room temperature with vanilla ice cream or lightly sweetened whipped cream.

the tarte, loosely covered with waxed paper and then tightly wrapped with aluminum foil, in the refrigerator.

Streamlining
The puff pastry dough can be rolled out in advance and kept in the refrigerator, tightly wrapped in a double layer of plastic wrap, up to 3 days.

Kiwi and Baby Pineapple Tartlets

THE FIRST TIME I saw baby pineapples, I grinned. They were so cute that I wanted to hug them! But just like larger pineapples, they are prickly on the outside and not very huggable. They're really just miniature versions of regular pineapples that come from South Africa. You can find them in many markets that carry unusual and unique produce. Don't worry if you can't find them though, because you can easily make this recipe with regular pineapple. The main point is to be sure that the pineapple is ripe before you cut into it. **Makes six 4½-inch round tartlets**

COCONUT PASTRY DOUGH

Center a rack in the oven and preheat it to 350°F.

¾ cup sweetened, shredded coconut	Place the coconut in a shallow cake or pie pan and toast for 12 to 15 minutes, until light golden. Every 5 minutes shake the pan to stir the coconut. Remove from the oven and cool.
1½ cups all-purpose flour **¼ cup granulated sugar** **⅛ teaspoon salt**	In the work bowl of a food processor fitted with the steel blade, combine the coconut, flour, sugar, and salt. Pulse briefly to blend.
6 ounces (12 tablespoons, 1½ sticks) unsalted butter, chilled	Cut the butter into small pieces and add to the flour mixture. Pulse until the butter is cut into very tiny pieces, about 30 seconds. The texture will be sandy with very tiny lumps throughout.
1 extra-large egg, at room temperature **1 tablespoon heavy whipping cream** **1 teaspoon pure vanilla extract**	In a small bowl, use a fork to lightly beat the egg with the cream and vanilla. With the food processor running, pour this mixture through the feed tube. Process the dough until the mixture wraps itself around the blade, about 1 minute.

Turn the pastry dough onto a large piece of plastic wrap. Shape into a flat disk and wrap tightly. Chill in the refrigerator until firm before using, at least 2 hours. Chilling the dough relaxes the gluten in the flour so it won't be too elastic and will roll out easily. It also firms up the butter in the dough so it will need less flour when rolled out. If the dough is too firm, it will splinter and break when rolled out. Let it stand at room temperature for 10 to 15 minutes before rolling to become more pliable.

Essential Gear

- Food processor
- Rolling pin
- Shallow cake pan
- Six 4½-inch round, fluted-edge tartlet pans with removable bottoms
- Baking sheet
- Pie weights
- Aluminum foil
- Chef's knife
- Small saucepan
- Medium fine-mesh strainer
- Two cooling racks
- Goose-feather pastry brush or a spoon

Keeping

Store the tartlets in a single layer on a baking sheet. Cover the top of the tartlets with a large piece of waxed paper to keep the surface from becoming marred. Tightly wrap the pan with plastic wrap and keep in the refrigerator up to 3 days

Streamlining

The pastry dough can be made in advance and kept in the refrigerator, tightly wrapped in a double layer of plastic wrap, up to 4 days before using. To freeze up to 4 months, wrap it in a double layer of plastic wrap and place it inside a freezer bag. Use a large piece of masking tape and an indelible marker to label and date the contents. If frozen, defrost in the refrigerator overnight before

Increase the oven temperature to 375°F.

On a smooth, flat surface, roll out the pastry dough between sheets of lightly floured waxed or parchment paper to a large rectangle about 16 × 12 inches. Carefully peel the paper off the top of the dough and brush off excess flour. Cut the dough in half horizontally, then into 3 equal sections vertically, making six 5 × 6-inch squares. Carefully peel the squares off the other piece of paper.

Gently place each square in a tartlet pan. Carefully lift up the sides of the pastry dough and ease the dough into the bottom and sides of each tart pan. Trim off the excess pastry dough at the top of the pan. Transfer the tartlet pans to a baking sheet and chill for at least 15 minutes to set.

Line each tartlet shell with a large piece of aluminum foil that fits well against the bottom and sides. Fill each pastry shell with pie weights or a mixture of rice and beans. Bake for 10 minutes, then remove the foil and weights. If the bottom of the tartlet shells puff up, gently pierce in a few places with a fork or the point of a knife to release the air. Bake another 12 to 14 minutes, until light golden and set. Remove the pan from the oven and transfer the tartlets to racks to cool completely.

ASSEMBLY

1 recipe Lemon Curd (page 140)

Vigorously stir the lemon curd to remove any lumps. Use a rubber spatula to spread the inside of each tartlet shell with lemon curd, filling it ¾ full. Use the rubber spatula to smooth the top of the lemon curd.

3 kiwifruit, peeled and stemmed

Cut each kiwi crosswise into ¼-inch-thick slices.

2 baby pineapples or 1 medium pineapple

Cut off the top and bottom of each pineapple, then cut off the outer skin of each. Cut each pineapple in half lengthwise, then cut into ¼-inch-thick slices. If using a regular pineapple, cut each half in half again lengthwise, then cut out the core of each quarter before slicing.

Arrange alternating slices of kiwi and pineapple on top of the lemon curd, covering it completely.

APRICOT GLAZE

¼ cup apricot preserves
1 tablespoon amaretto, cognac, or water

Combine the apricot preserves and liquid in a small saucepan. Bring to a boil over medium heat. Remove the pan from the heat and strain

using. If the dough is too cold to roll out, let it stand at room temperature to become pliable.

The tartlet shells can be baked and held at room temperature up to 2 days before filling. After they are completely cool, place them on a baking sheet between layers of waxed or parchment paper and tightly wrap the pan in aluminum foil.

The lemon curd filling can be made up to 1 month in advance and kept in the refrigerator in a tightly sealed plastic container.

Troubleshooting
Don't roll out the pastry dough before it is chilled. The dough will be too soft and it will require a lot of flour to roll out, which will make the dough tough.

Making a Change
Replace the toasted coconut in the pastry dough with finely ground, toasted, unsalted macadamia nuts.

the glaze into a small bowl, pushing through as much of the pulp as possible.

Use a goose-feather pastry brush to lightly brush the top of the tartlets with the glaze. Don't apply a thick glaze, which looks unappetizing. The purpose of the glaze is to keep the fruit from drying out and to make the top of the tart glisten.

Remove the sides of the tartlet pans (page 42) before serving. Refrigerate the tartlets until ready to serve.

Mango and Lime Tartlets

MANGOES AND LIME are a perfect complement to each other. In these tartlets, coconut pastry dough holds a lime curd filling that is topped with slices of fresh mango. An apricot glaze is brushed on top of the mango to protect it from the air and to make it glisten. These are the perfect dessert for a summer gathering. With one taste you'll be instantly transported to the tropics. **Makes eighteen 2¹/₂-inch round tartlets or six 4¹/₂-inch round tartlets**

COCONUT PASTRY DOUGH

Center a rack in the oven and preheat it to 350°F.

½ cup sweetened, shredded coconut	Place the coconut in a shallow pie or cake pan. Toast for 12 to 15 minutes, until light golden. Every 5 minutes shake the pan to stir the coconut. Remove the pan from the oven and cool.
1¼ cups all-purpose flour 3 tablespoons granulated sugar ⅛ teaspoon salt	In the work bowl of a food processor fitted with the steel blade, combine the coconut, flour, sugar, and salt. Pulse briefly to blend.
4 ounces (8 tablespoons, 1 stick) unsalted butter, chilled	Cut the butter into small pieces and add to the flour mixture. Pulse until the butter is cut into very tiny pieces, about 30 seconds. The texture will be sandy with very tiny lumps throughout.
1 extra-large egg yolk, at room temperature ½ teaspoon pure vanilla extract	In a small bowl, use a fork to lightly beat the egg yolk with the vanilla. With the food processor running, pour this mixture through the feed tube. Process the dough until the mixture wraps itself around the blade, about 1 minute.

Essential Gear

- Food processor
- Rolling pin
- 3¼-inch plain-edged cutter
- Thirty-six 2½-inch round, fluted-edge tartlet pans or six 4½-inch round, fluted-edge tartlet pans with removable bottom
- Baking sheet
- Aluminum foil
- Pie weights (for 4½-inch pans)
- Cooling rack
- Whisk or rubber spatula
- Double boiler
- Fine grater or citrus zester
- 2-cup saucepan
- Vegetable peeler
- Medium fine-mesh strainer
- Goose-feather pastry brush

Keeping

Although the tartlets are best eaten the day they are made, they can last up to 3 days. Store the tartlets on a baking sheet, loosely covered with waxed paper and then tightly

Turn the pastry dough onto a large piece of plastic wrap. Shape into a flat disk and wrap tightly. Chill in the refrigerator until firm before using, at least 2 hours. Chilling the dough relaxes the gluten in the flour so it won't be too elastic and will roll out easily. It also firms up the butter in the dough so it will need less flour when rolled out. If the dough is too firm it will splinter and break when rolled out. Let it stand at room temperature for 10 to 15 minutes before rolling to become more pliable.

Increase the oven temperature to 375°F.

On a smooth, flat surface, roll out the pastry dough between sheets of lightly floured waxed or parchment paper. Use the round cutter or a small bowl measuring $3^{1}/_{4}$ inches and cut out circles of the pastry dough. Carefully peel the circles off the other piece of paper. Gather together the dough scraps, reroll, and cut out any remaining circles.

For the $4^{1}/_{2}$-inch round tartlets, roll out the dough to a large rectangle about 16×12 inches. Carefully peel the paper off the top of the dough and brush off excess flour. Cut the dough in half horizontally, then vertically into 6 equal pieces. Carefully peel the squares off the other piece of paper.

Gently place each piece in a tartlet pan. Carefully lift up the sides of the pastry dough and ease the dough into the bottom and sides of each tart pan. Trim off the excess pastry dough at the top of the pan with your fingertips. Transfer the tartlet pans to a baking sheet and chill for at least 15 minutes to set.

If using the $2^{1}/_{2}$-inch pans, top each with another tartlet pan the same size to act as a weight while they bake. If using the $4^{1}/_{2}$-inch pans, line each pastry shell with a large piece of aluminum foil that fits well against the bottom and sides. Fill each pastry shell with tart weights or a mixture of rice and beans.

Bake for 8 minutes for the smaller pans and 10 minutes for the larger pans, then remove the top tartlet pan or the foil and weights. If the bottoms of the tartlet shells puff up, gently pierce in a few places with a fork or the point of a knife to release the air. Bake another 10 minutes for the smaller pans and 12 to 14 minutes for the larger pans, until light golden and set. Remove the baking pan from the oven and transfer the tartlets to racks to cool completely.

To remove the tartlet shells from their pans, gently tap each tartlet pan on a countertop. The tartlet shell should slip out of the pan eas-

wrapped with aluminum foil, in the refrigerator.

Streamlining

The pastry dough can be made in advance and kept in the refrigerator, tightly wrapped in a double layer of plastic wrap, up to 4 days. To freeze up to 3 months, wrap the dough snugly in several layers of plastic wrap and place it in a freezer bag. Use a large piece of masking tape and an indelible marker to label and date the contents. If frozen, defrost overnight in the refrigerator before using.

The tartlet shells can be baked and held at room temperature up to 2 days before filling. After they are completely cool, place them on a baking sheet between layers of waxed or parchment paper and tightly wrap the pan in aluminum foil.

The lime curd can be made in advance and kept in a tightly covered plastic container in the refrigerator up to 1 month before using.

The apricot glaze can be made in advance and kept in a tightly covered plastic container in the refrigerator up to 1 month before using. Warm it in a small saucepan over medium heat or in a microwave oven on medium power before using.

ily. If using the larger tartlet pans, set each pan on top of an upside-down bowl that is smaller than the pan and the sides will fall away. Gently lift the tartlet shell off of the bottom of the pan.

LIME CURD

4 large limes

Use a fine grater to remove the outer rind of the limes. Take care not to grate the inner white pith, which is very bitter. Or use a zester to remove the lime zest and chop it very finely with a chef's knife.

Squeeze the juice from the limes and strain it to remove any seeds.

6 extra-large egg yolks, at room temperature
½ cup granulated sugar

Place the egg yolks and sugar in the top pan of a double boiler over simmering water. Stir together to dissolve the sugar, about 3 minutes.

2 ounces (4 tablespoons, ½ stick) unsalted butter, melted

Add the lime zest, lime juice, and butter. Stir the mixture constantly with a heat-resistant spatula or wooden spoon until it thickens, about 12 minutes.

A good test to see if the mixture is at the right consistency is to dip the spatula or spoon into it. Lift the spatula or spoon from the mixture and hold it with the width of the spatula blade or spoon parallel to the top of the pan. With your finger, draw a parallel line across the middle of the spatula or spoon. If the mixture does not run over the line, it's thick enough. The mixture will thicken more as it cools and chills.

Remove the top pan of the double boiler and wipe the bottom and sides dry.

Transfer the lime curd to a bowl or plastic container. Cover tightly with plastic wrap or the container lid. Cool to room temperature, then place in the refrigerator until thoroughly chilled.

ASSEMBLY

Stir the lime curd vigorously with a whisk or rubber spatula to eliminate any lumps. Using a spoon or rubber spatula, spread the lime curd into the each tartlet shell, filling it ¾ full.

1 large, ripe mango

Use a vegetable peeler to remove the mango skin. Use a sharp knife to cut a large slice on each side of the large center pit of the mango. Cut each slice into ¼-inch-thick slices. Arrange slices of the mango on top of the lime curd. If the mango slices are too large, cut them in half crosswise. Fill the top of each tartlet with mango, overlapping the slices slightly.

¼ cup apricot preserves

**1 tablespoon amaretto,
cognac, or water**

Combine the apricot preserves and liquid in a small saucepan. Bring to a boil over medium heat. Remove the pan from the heat and strain the glaze into a small bowl, pushing through as much of the pulp as possible.

Use a goose-feather pastry brush to lightly brush the top of each tartlet with the glaze. Don't apply a thick glaze, which looks unappetizing. The purpose of the glaze is to keep the fruit from drying out and to make the top of each tartlet glisten.

Refrigerate the tartlets loosely covered with waxed paper, then loosely wrapped with aluminum foil for a few hours, until ready to serve.

Passion Fruit and Macadamia Nut Layer Cake

THIS CAKE is composed of alternating layers of rich, dense macadamia nut cake and passion fruit buttercream. Toasted, finely chopped macadamia nuts decorate the sides and top of the cake. It's an elegant cake with tropical flavors that's perfect for any summertime gathering. Passion fruit can be difficult to work with and it takes many of them to get the amount of juice needed, so I use passion fruit concentrate, available from Napa Valley Puree, listed in the sources (page 625). Although there are several steps involved in making this cake, most can be done in advance. Assemble the cake a few hours to a day before serving so the flavors and textures have time to blend together. **Makes one 9-inch round cake, 12 to 14 servings**

Essential Gear

- Two 9 × 2-inch round cake pans
- Scissors
- Parchment paper
- Two rubber spatulas
- Electric stand mixer with flat beater attachment, and wire whip attachment or large mixing bowl and hand-held mixer
- Two 9-inch cardboard cake circles
- Sifter
- Two cooling racks
- 2-quart heavy-bottomed saucepan
- Sugar or candy thermometer
- 1-inch natural-bristle pastry brush
- 10-inch flexible-blade icing spatula
- 12- or 14-inch pastry bag and large open star tip

MACADAMIA NUT CAKE

Center a rack in the oven and preheat it to 325°F.

1 tablespoon unsalted butter, softened

Using a paper towel or your fingertips, generously butter the inside of the cake pans, coating them thoroughly

1 tablespoon all-purpose flour

Dust the inside of each pan with some of the flour. Shake and tilt the pans to evenly distribute the flour, then turn the pans over and shake out the excess over the sink.

Cut a round of parchment paper to fit the bottom of each pan. Butter each parchment paper round and place in each pan, butter-side up.

12 ounces (24 tablespoons, 3 sticks) unsalted butter, softened	Place the butter in the bowl of an electric stand mixer or in a large mixing bowl. Use the flat beater attachment or hand-held mixer to beat the butter on medium speed until it's fluffy, about 2 minutes.
2¼ cups superfine sugar	Gradually add the sugar to the butter, and cream together well. Stop occasionally and scrape down the bottom and sides of the bowl with a rubber spatula.
6 extra-large eggs, at room temperature	One at a time, add the eggs, stopping to scrape down the bottom and sides of the bowl after each addition. At first the mixture may look curdled as the eggs are added, but as you stop and scrape down the bowl, the mixture will smooth out.
½ cup sour cream **2 teaspoons pure vanilla extract**	Add the sour cream and vanilla to the butter mixture and blend together well.
2¾ cups cake flour **1 teaspoon baking powder** **½ teaspoon baking soda** **½ teaspoon salt** **½ cup toasted, unsalted macadamia nuts**	Over a large piece of waxed or parchment paper or a bowl, sift together the flour, baking powder, and baking soda. Add the salt and toss to blend well. Combine ½ cup of this mixture with the macadamia nuts in the work bowl of a food processor. Pulse until the nuts are very finely ground, about 1 minute. Add the ground nuts to the rest of the dry ingredients and stir to blend completely.
	With the mixer on low speed, add the dry ingredients in 4 stages. Blend well after each addition and stop often to scrape down the bottom and sides of the bowl with a rubber spatula.
	Divide the batter evenly between the two cake pans. Smooth the top of each pan with a rubber spatula.
	Bake for 45 minutes, until the cakes are golden and a cake tester inserted in the center comes out with no crumbs clinging to it.
	Remove the cake pans from the oven and cool completely on racks. Invert the pans to remove the layers, then peel the parchment paper off the back of each layer. Re-invert the layers onto plates or cardboard cake circles.

SUGAR SYRUP

3 tablespoons granulated sugar **⅓ cup water**	Combine the sugar and water in a small saucepan. Bring to a boil over high heat to dissolve the sugar. Remove from the heat and cool.

Keeping

After the cake is chilled, store it loosely covered with aluminum foil in the refrigerator for up to 3 days. Place several toothpicks in the top outer edges of the cake to hold the foil away from it so it won't mar the buttercream.

Streamlining

Bake the cake layers up to 2 days before assembling and keep tightly covered with a double layer of plastic wrap at room temperature or in the refrigerator up to 4 days. To freeze the layers up to 3 months, wrap them snugly in several layers of plastic wrap and place them in freezer bags. Use a large piece of masking tape and an indelible marker to label and date the contents. If frozen, defrost the layers overnight in the refrigerator.

The buttercream can be prepared up to 3 days in advance and kept in an airtight plastic container in the refrigerator or up to 4 months in the freezer. If frozen, defrost overnight in the refrigerator. To reheat the buttercream, break it up into chunks and place in a mixing bowl. Place the bowl in a saucepan of warm water and let the buttercream begin to melt around the bottom. Wipe the bottom of the bowl dry and beat the buttercream with an electric mixer until it is fluffy and smooth.

PASSION FRUIT BUTTERCREAM

2 extra-large eggs, at room temperature
2 extra-large egg yolks, at room temperature
¼ cup granulated sugar

Place the eggs, egg yolks, and sugar in the bowl of an electric stand mixer or in a large mixing bowl. Use the wire whip attachment or a hand-held mixer and whip the eggs on medium speed until they are very pale colored and hold a slowly dissolving ribbon as the beater is lifted, about 5 minutes.

1¼ cups granulated sugar
½ cup water
¼ teaspoon cream of tartar

While the eggs are whipping, place the sugar, water, and cream of tartar in the saucepan. Bring the mixture to a boil, without stirring. Place a wet pastry brush at the point where the sugar syrup meets the sides of the pan and sweep it around completely. Do this two times.

Brushing down the sides of the pan while sugar is cooking prevents sugar crystals from coming out of the mixture, which causes crystallization. This is a condition that creates a crust around the side of the pan. Once crystallization occurs, the sugar syrup won't come up to temperature correctly and must be thrown away. Don't brush around the pan more than a few times. If you do, you're adding extra water to the sugar syrup, which takes more time to cook off and reach the desired temperature.

Cook over high heat until the mixture registers 242°F on a sugar thermometer (soft-ball stage). Immediately remove the thermometer and place it in a glass of warm water, then remove the pan from the heat so it won't continue to cook.

Adjust the mixer speed to low and pour the sugar syrup into the whipped eggs in a slow, steady stream. Aim the sugar syrup between the beater and the side of the bowl, so it doesn't get caught up in the beater or thrown against the sides of the bowl. Turn the mixer speed up to medium-high and whip until the bowl is cool to the touch, about 8 minutes.

Once the cooked sugar syrup is added to the whipped eggs, the mixture must whip until the bowl is completely cool to the touch before the butter is added, or the butter will melt. If this happens, the texture and consistency of the buttercream will be too soft and more butter will have to be added to bring it to the right point.

1 pound (2 cups, 4 sticks) unsalted butter, softened

Adjust the mixer speed to medium and add the butter, 2 tablespoons at a time. Continue to beat until the buttercream is thoroughly blended and fluffy.

½ cup passion fruit concentrate

Add the passion fruit concentrate to the buttercream and beat until it is thoroughly blended, about 2 minutes.

Making a Change
Replace the macadamia nuts with sliced almonds or finely chopped walnuts.

Replace the passion fruit preserves with apricot, peach, or mango preserves or orange marmalade.

Recovering from a Mishap
If one of the cake layers breaks during assembly, patch it together with some of the buttercream.

¼ cup passion fruit, apricot,
or peach preserves

Using a serrated knife, cut each cake layer in half horizontally (see page 34). With your fingertips, peel the skin off of the top of each cake layer. Place one cake layer on a serving plate. Place strips of waxed paper around the bottom edges of the cake to protect the plate while assembling the cake. Use the flexible-blade spatula to spread the layer evenly with the preserves.

Reserve ⅓ cup of the buttercream for the top decoration. Brush the layer generously with the sugar syrup. With a clean flexible-blade spatula, evenly spread some of the passion fruit buttercream over the cake layer.

Position the second cake layer evenly over the buttercream and brush with some of the sugar syrup. Use the flexible-blade spatula to spread some of the buttercream over the layer. Repeat with the remaining two cake layers and buttercream.

Spread the remaining buttercream over the sides and top of the cake.

1½ cups finely chopped
toasted, unsalted
macadamia nuts

Reserve ¼ cup of the nuts for the top decoration. Press the rest of them onto the sides of the cake just up to, but not over, the top edge.

Fit the pastry bag with the star tip and fill partway with the reserved buttercream. Visually divide the top of the cake into 12 pieces or use a small sharp knife to mark the outer top edge of the cake into serving pieces. Pipe a rosette at the center outer edge of each piece (see page 44). Sprinkle the reserved finely chopped macadamia nuts on top of each rosette.

Let the cake chill for at least 2 hours before serving so it has time to set and will be easier to cut, but serve it at room temperature.

Pavlova

THIS IS A CLASSIC meringue dessert created by an Australian pastry chef in 1926 to celebrate the visit of famed Russian prima ballerina Anna Pavlova. There is a bit of controversy surrounding the pavlova because both Australia and New Zealand claim to have created it. It doesn't matter which country invented this scrumptious dessert composed of a light, crisp meringue shell with a soft interior—but we're lucky someone did. It's filled with

Essential Gear
• Baking sheet
• Aluminum foil
• 9-inch cardboard cake circle or cake pan
• Electric stand mixer with wire whip attachment, or

whipped cream and topped with fruit such as kiwifruit, pineapple, raspberries, strawberries, blueberries, and bananas. This dessert can be made anytime during the year by varying the fruit. Once the dessert is assembled, the cream will begin to soften the meringue shell, so it's best to assemble no more than three hours before serving. **Makes one 9-inch round pastry, 12 to 14 servings**

MERINGUE SHELL

Center a rack in the oven and preheat it to 400°F. Line a baking sheet with aluminum foil. Using the cake circle or cake pan as a guide, trace a 9-inch circle onto the dull side of the foil with a pencil, then turn the foil over on the baking sheet.

4 extra-large egg whites, at room temperature
¼ teaspoon cream of tartar
1 cup superfine sugar
1 tablespoon plus 1 teaspoon cornstarch, sifted
½ teaspoon distilled white vinegar
½ teaspoon pure vanilla extract

Place the egg whites and cream of tartar in the grease-free bowl of an electric stand mixer. Use the wire whip attachment or a hand-held mixer to whip the egg whites on medium speed until frothy. Very slowly sprinkle on the sugar and continue beating the egg whites until they hold firm peaks, about 3 minutes. Turn the mixer speed to low and sprinkle on the cornstarch. Blend together well, then add the vinegar and vanilla and blend thoroughly.

Using a rubber spatula, spread the meringue mixture onto the foil on the baking sheet, using the circle as a guide. Mound the mixture around the edges so they are slightly thicker than the center, creating a shallow bowl. Place the baking sheet in the oven, lower the oven temperature to 250°F, and dry the meringue for 1½ hours.

Turn off the oven, prop open the oven door with a wooden spoon, and leave the meringue in the oven until it is cool.

Remove the baking sheet from the oven and carefully peel the foil off the back of the meringue shell. Place the meringue shell on a 9-inch cardboard cake circle or a serving plate.

CREAM FILLING

2 cups heavy whipping cream
3 tablespoons superfine sugar
2 teaspoons pure vanilla extract

Place the cream in the chilled bowl of an electric stand mixer. Using the wire whip attachment or a hand-held mixer and a chilled mixing bowl, whip the cream on medium speed until it thickens. Gradually sprinkle on the sugar, then beat in the vanilla and whip the cream until it holds soft peaks.

large mixing bowl and hand-held mixer
• Rubber spatula
• 12- or 14-inch pastry bag and large open star tip

Keeping
Although the pavlova is best eaten the same day it is assembled, it can keep for up to 2 days, loosely covered with waxed paper and then tightly wrapped with aluminum foil, in the refrigerator.

Streamlining
The meringue shell can be made up to 2 days in advance. Store it at room temperature tightly wrapped in aluminum foil to protect it from moisture, which will make it soft.

Making a Change
To make a Cocoa Pavlova, add ¼ cup unsweetened, sifted cocoa powder (natural or Dutch-processed) to the meringue with the cornstarch.

To make a Double Chocolate Pavlova, fold 5 ounces melted and cooled bittersweet or semisweet chocolate into the whipped cream before assembling the dessert.

Reserve ¼ of the cream for decoration and use a rubber spatula to spread the cream in the meringue shell, mounding it slightly in the center.

1 cup fresh raspberries, strawberries, or blackberries
1 ripe, medium banana, thinly sliced
2 to 3 kiwifruit, peeled and thinly sliced

Arrange the fruit in concentric circles over the cream. Fit the pastry bag with the star tip and fill with the reserved whipped cream. Pipe a border of shells around the outer edge of the fruit (see page 44).

Refrigerate the pavlova until ready to serve, no more than 3 hours.

Persimmon Coffee Cake

THIS IS AN easy-to-prepare cake that is great to serve for afternoon tea or warmed up for breakfast. It's full of fresh persimmon and finely ground walnuts. A little orange liqueur and freshly grated nutmeg also add their flavors to this tasty cake. You can use either type of persimmons for this cake; just be sure they are ripe so they are not too tart. **Makes one 9½-inch round cake, 12 servings**

CAKE

1 tablespoon unsalted butter, softened

Center an oven rack and preheat it to 350°F. Use your fingertips or a paper towel to generously butter the inside of the pan.

1 tablespoon all-purpose flour

Dust the inside of the pan with the flour. Shake and tilt the pan to evenly distribute the flour, then turn the pan over and shake out the excess over the sink.

Cut a round of parchment paper to fit the bottom of the pan. Butter the parchment paper round and place in the pan, butter-side up.

Or prepare the pan by spraying the inside with non-stick spray. Fit the parchment paper round to the bottom of the pan and spray it.

8 ounces (16 tablespoons, 2 sticks) unsalted butter, softened

Place the butter in the bowl of an electric stand mixer or in a large mixing bowl. Use the flat beater attachment or hand-held mixer to beat the butter on medium speed until it's fluffy, about 2 minutes.

Essential Gear
- 9½-inch round spring-form pan
- Electric stand mixer with flat beater attachment, or large mixing bowl and hand-held mixer
- Scissors
- Microplane grater or citrus zester
- Parchment paper
- Rubber spatula
- Food processor
- Cooling rack

Keeping
Store the cake tightly wrapped in aluminum foil at room temperature up to 4 days. To freeze up to 3 months, wrap the cake tightly in several layers of plastic wrap and aluminum foil. Use a large piece of masking tape and an indelible marker to label and

½ cup granulated sugar	Gradually add the granulated sugar and brown sugar to the butter, and cream together well. Stop occasionally and scrape down the bottom and sides of the bowl with a rubber spatula.
⅔ cup firmly packed light brown sugar	
3 extra-large eggs, at room temperature	One at a time, add the eggs, stopping to scrape down the bottom and sides of the bowl after each addition. At first the mixture may look curdled as the eggs are added, but as you stop and scrape down the bowl, the mixture will smooth out.
2 teaspoons pure vanilla extract	Add the vanilla and liqueur to the butter mixture and blend together well.
1 tablespoon orange liqueur	
1¾ cups all-purpose flour	Over a large piece of waxed or parchment paper or a bowl, sift together the flour and baking powder. Add the allspice, nutmeg, and salt and toss together to blend.
1 teaspoon baking powder	
½ teaspoon ground allspice	
½ teaspoon freshly grated nutmeg	
¼ teaspoon salt	
	Add the dry ingredients to the butter mixture in 3 stages, blending well after each addition.
½ cup walnuts	Place the walnuts in the work bowl of a food processor fitted with the steel blade. Add the sugar and pulse until the walnuts are very finely ground, about 1 minute. Add to the batter and stir together well.
1 tablespoon granulated sugar	
2 persimmons, peeled and cut into ½-inch pieces	Fold the persimmons and orange zest into the cake batter.
Finely grated zest of 1 medium orange	
	Transfer the batter to the prepared cake pan. The batter is very thick, so use a rubber spatula to spread it evenly into the pan.
	Bake for 1 hour, until the cake is light golden on top and a cake tester inserted into the center comes out clean.
	Remove the pan from the oven and cool completely on a rack. Release the sides of the springform pan and lift them off of the cake. Place a plate over the top of the cake and invert it. Peel off the parchment paper from the back of the cake and re-invert it onto a serving plate.

GARNISH

Confectioners' sugar	Lightly dust the top of the cake with confectioners' sugar. Cut the cake into wedges and serve at room temperature.

date the contents. If frozen, defrost overnight in the refrigerator and bring to room temperature before serving.

Making a Change

Replace the walnuts with almonds or pecans.

Persimmon Pudding

ALTHOUGH this is called a pudding, it's more of a cake. Persimmon puree is combined with sugar, eggs, buttermilk, flour, and spices to make a richly flavored dessert. It is perfect for afternoon tea topped with a dollop of whipped cream. **Makes one 9 × 13-inch cake, 20 servings**

CAKE

Non-stick baking spray	Center a rack in the oven and preheat it to 350°F. Spray the inside of the baking pan with non-stick spray.
5 to 7 large, ripe persimmons	Use a sharp knife to remove the papery leaves and the skin of the persimmons. Place the persimmons in a large bowl and use a fork to mash them. Or puree them in the work bowl of a food processor fitted with the steel blade. Pulse several times until the pulp is smooth, then transfer the pulp to the bowl.
2 cups granulated sugar	Add the sugar to the persimmon pulp and stir together until thoroughly blended.
2 extra-large eggs, at room temperature	Use a fork to lightly beat the eggs, then add them to the persimmon mixture and use a rubber spatula to blend them in well.
1 teaspoon baking soda **1 teaspoon pure vanilla extract** **1½ cups buttermilk**	Stir the baking soda and vanilla into the buttermilk. Add this mixture to the persimmon mixture and blend in thoroughly.
1½ cups all-purpose flour **1 teaspoon baking powder** **½ teaspoon ground cinnamon** **⅛ teaspoon ground ginger** **¼ teaspoon salt** **¼ teaspoon freshly grated nutmeg**	Over a large piece of waxed or parchment paper or a bowl, sift together the flour, baking powder, cinnamon, and ginger. Add the salt and nutmeg and toss together to blend.
	Add the dry ingredients to the persimmon mixture in 3 stages, stirring to blend completely after each addition.
¼ cup heavy whipping cream **2 ounces (4 tablespoons, ½ stick) unsalted butter, melted and cooled**	Add the cream and butter to the batter and stir to blend in thoroughly.

Transfer the batter to the prepared pan. Bake for 1 hour, until a cake tester inserted into the center comes out clean.

Remove the pan from the oven and cool completely on a rack.

Confectioners' sugar

Dust the top of the pudding lightly with confectioners' sugar.

Cut the pudding 5 rows across the width, then cut each row into 4 equal pieces to get 20 pieces.

GARNISH

²⁄₃ cup heavy whipping cream

Place the cream in the chilled bowl of an electric stand mixer or a medium mixing bowl. Using the wire whip attachment or a hand-held mixer, whip the cream on medium speed until it is frothy.

1 tablespoon confectioners' sugar, sifted
1 teaspoon pure vanilla extract

Add the confectioners' sugar and vanilla and continue to whip the cream on medium speed until it holds soft peaks.

Serve each piece of pudding with a large dollop of whipped cream on top.

Pomegranate Butter Cookies

THESE ARE GREAT refrigerator cookies because the dough needs to be made in advance of baking so it has time to set before it is cut. You can also keep the dough cylinders in the freezer and slice them just before baking. These have the unexpected burst of flavor that comes from juicy pomegranate seeds. Not only do they taste very good, but the bright red color of the seeds is striking against the soft tan color of the cookie dough. **Makes about 4 dozen cookies**

Essential Gear
- Electric stand mixer with flat beater attachment, or large mixing bowl and hand-held mixer
- Rubber spatula
- Chef's knife
- Waxed paper
- Two baking sheets
- Two parchment paper sheets or non-stick pan liners
- Two cooling racks

Keeping
Store the cookies in an airtight plastic container

8 ounces (16 tablespoons, 2 sticks) unsalted butter, softened

Place the butter in the bowl of an electric stand mixer or in a large mixing bowl. Use the flat beater attachment or hand-held mixer to beat the butter on medium speed until it's fluffy, about 2 minutes.

²⁄₃ cup firmly packed light brown sugar
¹⁄₄ teaspoon salt

Add the brown sugar and salt to the butter and cream together well. Stop occasionally and scrape down the sides and bottom of the bowl with a rubber spatula.

2 cups all-purpose flour	Add the flour in 2 stages to the butter mixture and blend thoroughly after each addition.
1 large pomegranate	To remove the seeds of the pomegranate, cut it in half across the width and score each half in half lengthwise. Soak the pomegranate in water for 5 minutes. Separate the pieces of the pomegranate and separate the seeds from the white membrane. Pat the seeds dry on paper towels and add to the dough mixture.
	Place two large sheets of waxed paper on a flat surface and divide the dough evenly onto them. Use the waxed paper to shape and roll the dough into cylinders about 8 inches long and 2 inches wide (see Refrigerator Cookies, page 37). Cover the cylinders tightly with the waxed paper, then wrap each roll in plastic wrap. Chill in the freezer for 45 minutes or in the refrigerator for at least 4 hours, until firm enough to slice.
	Adjust the oven racks to the upper and lower thirds and preheat the oven to 325°F. Line each baking sheet with parchment paper or with a non-stick pan liner.
	Place the cookie cylinders on a cutting board. Using a sharp knife, cut each cylinder into $1/2$-inch-thick slices. Cut straight down and roll the cylinder a quarter turn after every 6 slices so it will keep its round shape. If the dough becomes soft while you are working with it, rewrap it, chill for another 10 to 15 minutes, then continue slicing.
	Place the slices on the baking sheets, leaving at least 1 inch of space between them. Bake for 12 minutes. Switch the baking sheets and bake another 10 to 12 minutes, until set. Remove the baking sheets from the oven and leave the cookies on the sheets to cool on racks.

between layers of waxed paper at room temperature up to 1 week. A kitchen cupboard or pantry is the ideal storage place. To freeze up to 3 months, wrap the airtight container in several layers of plastic wrap and aluminum foil. Use a large piece of masking tape and an indelible marker to label and date the contents. If frozen, defrost overnight in the refrigerator and bring to room temperature before serving.

Streamlining
The dough cylinders can be made and kept in the refrigerator up to 3 days before baking. They can also be kept in the freezer up to 3 months. To refrigerate, wrap the cylinders tightly in several layers of plastic wrap. To freeze, wrap the same way and place each cylinder in a freezer bag. Use a large piece of masking tape and an indelible marker to label and date the contents. You can take them directly from the freezer and slice for baking, or defrost the cylinders overnight in the refrigerator.

Making a Change
Add $2/3$ cup toasted and finely chopped pecans, walnuts, or almonds to the dough after adding the pomegranate seeds.

Roasted Banana Tart with Coconut

OVEN-ROASTED BANANAS sit on top of vanilla pastry cream that is enclosed in a crisp pastry shell with finely chopped almonds scattered over the top. I like to make this tart in the fall and winter when other special fruit is not in season. The pastry dough and the vanilla pastry cream filling have to be made in advance, because they need time to chill. That makes it easy to assemble this tart a few hours before serving. **Makes one 9½-inch round tart, 12 to 14 servings**

PASTRY DOUGH

1¼ cups all-purpose flour
½ cup confectioners' sugar
⅛ teaspoon salt

In the work bowl of a food processor fitted with the steel blade, combine the flour, sugar, and salt. Pulse briefly to blend.

4 ounces (8 tablespoons, 1 stick) unsalted butter, chilled

Cut the butter into small pieces and add to the flour mixture. Pulse until the butter is cut into very tiny pieces, about 30 seconds. The texture should be sandy with very tiny lumps throughout.

1 extra-large egg yolk, at room temperature
½ teaspoon pure vanilla extract

In a small bowl, use a fork to lightly beat the egg yolk and vanilla. With the food processor running, pour the egg mixture through the feed tube. Process the dough until the mixture wraps itself around the blade, about 1 minute.

Turn the pastry dough onto a large piece of plastic wrap. Shape into a flat disk and wrap tightly in a double layer of plastic wrap. Chill in the refrigerator until firm before using, at least 2 hours. Chilling the dough relaxes the gluten in the flour so it won't be too elastic and will roll out easily. It also firms up the butter in the dough so it will need less flour when rolled out. If the dough is too firm, it will splinter and break when rolled out. Let it stand at room temperature for 10 to 15 minutes before rolling to become more pliable.

Center a rack in the oven and preheat it to 375°F.

On a smooth, flat surface, roll out the pastry dough between sheets of lightly floured waxed or parchment paper to a large circle about 11 inches in diameter. To tell if the dough will fit the tart pan, hold the pan above the dough. If there are about 2 to 3 inches of dough that protrude beyond the sides of the pan, it will fit.

Carefully peel the paper off the top of the dough and brush off any excess flour. Loosely roll the pastry dough around the rolling pin

Essential Gear

- Food processor
- Rolling pin
- 9½-inch round, fluted-edge tart pan with removable bottom
- Aluminum foil
- 4-quart baking dish
- Pie weights
- Small saucepan
- Whisk or rubber spatula
- Two baking sheets
- Parchment paper or non-stick liner
- Cooling rack

Keeping

Store the tart, loosely covered with waxed paper and then tightly wrapped with aluminum foil, in the refrigerator up to 3 days.

Streamlining

The pastry dough can be made in advance and kept in the refrigerator up to 4 days, tightly wrapped in a double layer of plastic wrap. To freeze up to 3 months, place the wrapped dough in a freezer bag. Use a large piece of masking tape and an indelible marker to label and date the contents. If frozen, defrost in the refrigerator overnight before using. If the dough is very cold, let it stand at room temperature to become pliable.

The pastry shell can be baked up to 2 days in

without the bottom piece of paper. Place the tart pan directly underneath the rolling pin and carefully unroll the pastry dough into the tart pan. Gently lift up the sides and ease the pastry dough into the bottom and sides of the tart pan.

Trim off the excess pastry dough at the top of the pan. Transfer the tart pan to a baking sheet and chill in the refrigerator for 15 minutes.

Line the pastry shell with a large piece of aluminum foil that fits well against the bottom and sides. Fill with pie weights or a mixture of rice and beans. Bake for 10 minutes, then remove the foil and weights. If the bottom of the pastry shell puffs up, gently pierce it in several places with a fork or a sharp knife to release the air. Bake another 12 to 14 minutes, until light golden and set. Remove the pan from the oven and transfer to a rack to cool completely. Leave the oven on.

ROASTED BANANAS

¼ cup granulated sugar
½ cup water

Place the sugar and water together in a small saucepan. Bring to a boil over high heat to dissolve the sugar. Remove from the heat and cool.

6 to 8 large ripe but firm bananas

Skin the bananas and cut in half lengthwise. Then cut each half in half across the width. Place the cut bananas in a 4-quart baking dish or on a baking sheet and pour the sugar syrup over them. Let the bananas soak in the sugar syrup for 15 minutes.

Remove the bananas from the sugar syrup and pat dry on paper towels.

Line a baking sheet with parchment paper or a non-stick liner. Place the banana slices on the lined baking sheet. Roast in the oven for 15 to 20 minutes, until soft and the sugar syrup is caramelized on the bananas.

Remove the baking sheet from the oven and cool slightly on a rack.

ASSEMBLY

1 recipe Vanilla Pastry Cream (see Pluot Custard Tart, page 92)

Vigorously stir the pastry cream to eliminate any lumps. Use a rubber spatula to evenly spread the vanilla pastry cream filling in the cooled tart shell. Arrange the roasted bananas on top of the pastry cream, filling in the tart shell.

2 tablespoons sweetened, flaked coconut

Scatter the coconut over the top of the tart.

Serve the tart at room temperature.

advance. Store it at room temperature, tightly covered with aluminum foil.

Troubleshooting
Don't roll out the pastry dough before it is chilled. The dough will be too soft and it will require a lot of flour to roll out, which results in a tough dough.

Rolling the delicate tart dough around the rolling pin and unrolling into the tart pan is an easy way to get the dough into the pan without stretching or tearing it.

Once the pastry dough is unrolled into the tart pan, don't push it down forcefully. This will stretch the dough, which will shrink as it bakes, making it flat instead of taking the shape of the tart pan.

Tropical Coconut Layer Cake

THIS CAKE will transport you to the tropics. It is made with alternating layers of coconut cake flavored with allspice and coconut buttercream, and toasted coconut decorates the sides and top of the cake. Cream of coconut flavors the buttercream. Cream of coconut is a smooth, thick liquid made from fresh coconut. It is sweet and is thicker than coconut milk. It is sold in cans and is available in many large liquor stores. Because cream of coconut tends to separate as it sits, be sure to stir it thoroughly before use. This is an elegant cake that can take center stage at any gathering. Several of the steps for this cake can be done in advance, which makes it easy to fit into a busy schedule. Assemble the cake a few hours to a day before serving so the flavors and textures have time to blend together. **Makes one 9-inch round cake, 10 to 12 servings**

COCONUT CAKE

Center a rack in the oven and preheat it to 350°F.

1 tablespoon unsalted butter, softened	Using a paper towel or your fingertips, generously butter the inside of the cake pan, coating it thoroughly.
2 teaspoons all-purpose flour	Dust the inside of the pan with the flour. Shake and tilt the pan to evenly distribute the flour, then turn the pans over and shake out the excess over the sink.
	Cut a round of parchment paper to fit the bottom of the pan. Butter the parchment paper round and place in the pan, butter-side up.
6 extra-large eggs, at room temperature **1 cup granulated sugar**	Place the eggs and sugar in the bowl of an electric stand mixer or in a large mixing bowl. Use the wire whip attachment or a hand-held mixer to whip the eggs and sugar on medium-high speed until they are very thick and pale colored and hold a slowly dissolving ribbon as the beater is lifted, about 5 minutes.
¾ cup all-purpose flour **2½ teaspoons ground allspice** **¼ cup sweetened, shredded coconut** **½ teaspoon freshly grated nutmeg** **⅛ teaspoon salt**	Over a large piece of waxed or parchment paper or a bowl, sift together the flour and allspice. Add the coconut, nutmeg, and salt and toss to blend together.

Essential Gear

- 9 × 2-inch round cake pan
- Scissors
- Parchment paper
- Two rubber spatulas
- Electric stand mixer with flat beater attachment and wire whip attachment, or large mixing bowl and hand-held mixer
- Cooling rack
- 2-quart heavy-bottomed saucepan
- Pastry brush
- Sugar or candy thermometer
- 10-inch flexible-blade icing spatula
- 12- or 14-inch pastry bag and large open star tip

Keeping

After the cake is chilled, store it loosely covered, tented with aluminum foil, in the refrigerator up to 3 days. Place several toothpicks in the top outer edge of the cake to hold the foil away from it so it won't mar the buttercream.

Streamlining

Bake the cake up to 2 days before assembling and keep it tightly covered with a double layer of plastic wrap at room temperature or in the refrigerator up to 4 days. To freeze the cake up to 3 months, wrap it snugly in several layers of plastic wrap and place in freezer bags.

Fold into the egg mixture in 3 stages, blending well after each addition.

1½ ounces (3 tablespoons) unsalted butter, melted and cooled	Place the butter in a small bowl. Take about 1 cup of the batter and blend it thoroughly with the butter. Then fold this mixture into the rest of the cake batter. This allows the butter to blend completely with the cake mixture.
1 teaspoon pure vanilla extract	Fold the vanilla into the batter and blend thoroughly.

Transfer the batter to the cake pan and smooth the top with a rubber spatula.

Bake the cake for 25 to 28 minutes, until golden and a cake tester inserted in the center comes out with no crumbs clinging to it.

Remove the cake pan from the oven and cool completely on a rack. Invert the pan to remove the cake, then peel the parchment paper off the back. Re-invert the cake onto a plate or a cardboard cake circle.

COCONUT BUTTERCREAM

2 extra-large eggs, at room temperature **2 extra-large egg yolks, at room temperature** **¼ cup granulated sugar**	Place the eggs, egg yolks, and sugar in the bowl of an electric stand mixer or in a large mixing bowl. Use the wire whip attachment or a hand-held mixer and whip the eggs on medium speed until they are very pale colored and hold a slowly dissolving ribbon as the beater is lifted, about 5 minutes.
1¼ cups granulated sugar **½ cup water** **¼ teaspoon cream of tartar**	While the eggs are whipping, place the sugar, water, and cream of tartar in the saucepan. Bring the mixture to a boil, without stirring. Place a wet pastry brush at the point where the sugar syrup meets the sides of the pan and sweep it around completely. Do this two times. This prevents the sugar from crystallizing by brushing any stray crystals back into the mixture. Cook over high heat until the mixture registers 242°F on a sugar thermometer (soft-ball stage).

Immediately remove the thermometer and place it in a glass of warm water, then remove the pan from the heat so it won't continue to cook.

Adjust the mixer speed to low and pour the sugar syrup into the whipped eggs in a slow, steady stream. Aim the sugar syrup between the beater and the side of the bowl, so it doesn't get caught up in the beater or thrown against the sides of the bowl. Turn the mixer speed up to medium-high and whip until the bowl is cool to the touch, about 8 minutes.

Use a large piece of masking tape and an indelible marker to label and date the contents. If frozen, defrost the cake overnight in the refrigerator.

The buttercream can be prepared up to 3 days in advance and kept in an airtight plastic container in the refrigerator or up to 4 months in the freezer. If frozen, defrost overnight in the refrigerator. To reheat the buttercream, break it up into chunks and place in a mixing bowl. Place the bowl in a saucepan of warm water and let the buttercream begin to melt around the bottom. Wipe the bottom of the bowl dry and beat the buttercream with an electric mixer until it is fluffy and smooth.

Recovering from a Mishap
If one of the cake layers breaks during assembly, patch it together with some of the buttercream.

Once the cooked sugar syrup is added to the whipped eggs, the mixture must whip until the bowl is completely cool to the touch before the butter is added, or the butter will melt. If this happens, the texture and consistency of the buttercream will be too soft and more butter will have to be added to bring it to the right point.

1 pound (2 cups, 4 sticks) unsalted butter, softened

Adjust the mixer speed to medium and add the butter, 2 tablespoons at a time. Continue to beat until the buttercream is thoroughly blended and fluffy.

**1/2 cup cream of coconut
1 teaspoon ground allspice
1/2 teaspoon freshly grated nutmeg**

Add the cream of coconut, allspice, and nutmeg to the buttercream and beat until it is thoroughly blended, about 2 minutes.

ASSEMBLY

1/4 cup passion fruit, apricot, or peach preserves

With your fingertips, peel the skin off of the top of the cake. Using a serrated knife, cut the cake into 3 equal pieces, horizontally (see page 34). Place the bottom cake layer on a serving plate. Place strips of waxed paper around the bottom edges of the cake to protect the plate while assembling the cake. Use the flexible-blade spatula to spread the layer evenly with the preserves.

Reserve 1/3 cup of the buttercream for the top decoration. With a clean flexible-blade spatula, evenly spread some of the buttercream over the cake layer.

Position the second cake layer evenly over the buttercream. Use the flexible-blade spatula to spread some of the buttercream over the layer. Repeat with the remaining cake layer and spread the remaining buttercream over the sides and top of the cake.

3/4 cup lightly toasted sweetened, shredded coconut

Press the toasted coconut into the sides of the cake and sprinkle lightly over the top.

Fit the pastry bag with the star tip and fill partway with the reserved buttercream. Pipe a border of alternating shells (see page 44) around the outside top edge of the cake, then pipe a rosette in the center of the cake.

Let the cake chill for at least 2 hours before serving so it has time to set and will be easier to cut, but serve it at room temperature.

6

DRIED FRUIT

SING DRIED FRUITS in baking is very popular. They are often used during the fall and winter months when many types of fresh fruit are not available. But for my taste, any time of the year is fine for using dried fruit in baking. As a matter of fact, dried fruit complements fresh fruit and goes exceptionally well with nuts.

One thing that I like to do when I am having several guests over is to make at least one of the desserts I'm serving with dried fruit. This way everyone is pleased. I have several favorites when it comes to dried fruit, so it's always hard to select what to bake. The recipes in this chapter are all equally my favorites and I believe they will become your favorites, too.

With dried fruit, there is no need to worry about seasons. They are available year-round in many markets and health food stores. If you don't find exactly what you are looking for in one store, look in another. There seems to be a proliferation of dried fruit in practically all supermarkets.

TIPS AND TECHNIQUES

Selecting dried fruit is fairly simple, but there are a few things you should watch for. If the fruit is packaged, check the date on the package to make sure it is not past the expiration date. Also, make sure that the package is sealed well. And, if it is a see through package, check to make sure the dried fruits are plump and have good color. I usually pick my dried fruit out of large bins in my local health food store. I like this because I know there is quick turnover and I know they're fresh. Also, I can get a close-up look and smell of what I'm buying. As I scoop them out of the bins, I look for them to be plump and moist and to have good color. What I don't want to see is a moldy or very dried-out look. Make sure there is no chemical or rancid scent. Some stores will allow you to taste dried fruit before you buy it. Note that the texture and taste of dried fruit does not change when it's used in baking.

There are two types of dried fruit: sulphured, which are treated with a sulphur dioxide solution, and unsulphured, which are left untreated. Sulphured dried fruits are lighter in color and moister than unsulphured. Either type of dried fruit is fine to use.

You can buy dried fruit well in advance of when you need it. Most dried fruit will keep fresh for up to a year in a tightly sealed container in a cool, dark place. But do check the dried fruit before using it to make sure that it's still good. Don't store it in the refrigerator or freezer, as this will cause it to become very hard and dried out.

Dried fruit requires little preparation. It is normally used in the same form as it's purchased. Sometimes it needs to be chopped into small- to medium-sized pieces, depending on the recipe. Or it may need to be soaked in liquid to soften it, such as orange juice or a liqueur. Again, this depends on the recipe you're making. When adding dried fruit to a dough or batter, it's a good idea to mix it with a few tablespoons of the flour from the recipe first. This keeps it from sinking to the bottom of the dough or batter while it's baking.

Currant-Molasses Tea Cake

T HIS LOAF CAKE has deep, rich flavor that comes from the molasses and brown sugar, and the currants give it an appealing texture. It makes a delicious addition to afternoon tea. Try it for breakfast spread with cream cheese. **Makes one 8½ × 4½ × 2½-inch loaf cake, 12 servings**

CAKE

Center a rack in the oven and preheat it to 375°F.

1 tablespoon unsalted butter, softened	Using a paper towel or your fingertips, generously butter the inside of the pan.
2 teaspoons all-purpose flour	Dust the inside of the pan with flour, then shake and tilt the pan to evenly coat the bottom and sides. Turn the pan over the sink and tap out the excess flour.
2 cups all-purpose flour 1¼ teaspoons baking powder ½ teaspoon baking soda ½ teaspoon salt 1 cup currants	Over a large piece of waxed or parchment paper or a bowl, sift together the flour, baking powder, and baking soda. Add the salt and toss together to blend well. Take 2 tablespoons of this mixture and toss with the currants in a bowl.
5 ounces (10 tablespoons, 1¼ sticks) unsalted butter, softened	Place the butter in the bowl of an electric stand mixer or in a large mixing bowl. Use the flat beater attachment or hand-held mixer to beat the butter until it is light and fluffy, about 2 minutes.
⅔ cup firmly packed light brown sugar	Add the sugar to the butter, and cream together until light and fluffy, about 2 minutes.
2 extra-large eggs, at room temperature 2 teaspoons pure vanilla extract	In a small bowl, lightly beat together the eggs and vanilla and add to the butter mixture. The eggs will sit on top of the butter mixture so stop after adding them and scrape down the sides and bottom of the bowl with a rubber spatula to help mix evenly. The mixture may look curdled but will smooth out when the dry ingredients are added.
¼ cup molasses	Add the dry ingredients alternately with the molasses to the butter mixture and blend briefly after each addition. Beat until smooth. Add the currants and blend well.

Essential Gear

- 8½ × 4½ × 2½-inch loaf pan
- Electric stand mixer with flat beater attachment, or large mixing bowl and hand-held mixer
- Rubber spatula
- Cooling rack

Keeping

Store the cake tightly wrapped in aluminum foil at room temperature up to 4 days. To freeze up to 3 months, wrap the cake tightly in several layers of plastic wrap and aluminum foil. Use a large piece of masking tape and an indelible marker to label and date the contents. If frozen, defrost overnight in the refrigerator and bring to room temperature before serving.

Making a Change

Replace the currants with raisins or chopped dried apricots, peaches, pears, or cranberries.

Adding Style

Add ⅔ cup finely chopped walnuts or pecans after adding the currants to the batter.

Transfer the batter to the prepared pan. The batter is very thick, so use a rubber spatula to spread it evenly into the pan.

Bake for 45 minutes, until the cake has risen and set and a cake tester inserted into the center comes out clean

Remove the pan from the oven and cool completely on a rack. Invert the pan to remove the cake. Cut the cake across the width into slices and serve at room temperature.

Date Spirals

DATES COOKED in sugar syrup are blended with walnuts and orange juice to make a delectable filling that is spread onto pastry dough and then rolled up tightly. After the roll is chilled, it is sliced across the width and baked, making cookies with a beautiful spiral pattern. These are some of my favorite cookies because they are not only yummy to eat, but they also look festive. These take a little work, but both the dough and the filling can be made in advance and put together right before baking. **Makes 3¹/₂ dozen cookies**

DATE FILLING

³/₄ cup coarsely chopped, pitted dates
¹/₂ cup water
¹/₃ cup granulated sugar

Combine the dates, water, and sugar in the saucepan. Bring to a boil and cook over medium heat, stirring occasionally, until the mixture thickens, about 10 minutes.

¹/₃ cup walnuts, coarsely chopped
1 tablespoon freshly squeezed orange or lemon juice

Remove the pan from the heat and stir in the walnuts and juice. Cool the mixture, then transfer it to the work bowl of a food processor fitted with the steel blade. Puree the mixture, then transfer to a bowl, cover tightly with plastic wrap, and let it stand at room temperature.

PASTRY DOUGH

2 cups all-purpose flour
¹/₄ teaspoon baking powder
¹/₈ teaspoon salt

Over a large piece of waxed or parchment paper or a bowl, sift together the flour and baking powder. Add the salt and toss to blend.

4 ounces (8 tablespoons, 1 stick) unsalted butter, softened

Place the butter in the bowl of an electric stand mixer or a large mixing bowl. Use the flat beater attachment or a hand-held mixer to beat

Essential Gear
• 2-quart heavy-bottomed saucepan
• Heat-resistant rubber spatula or wooden spoon
• Food processor
• Electric stand mixer with flat beater attachment, or large mixing bowl and hand-held mixer
• Rubber spatula
• Microplane grater or citrus zester
• Rolling pin
• Two baking sheets
• Two parchment paper sheets or non-stick liners
• Two cooling racks

Keeping
Store the cookies in an airtight plastic container between layers of waxed paper at room temperature up to 1 week. To freeze up to 3 months, wrap the container tightly in several layers of plastic wrap and aluminum foil. Use a large piece of masking tape and an indelible marker to label

| 1 cup firmly packed light
brown sugar |

| 1 extra-large egg, at room
temperature
1 teaspoon pure vanilla
extract
1 tablespoon finely grated
orange or lemon zest |

the butter until it is light and fluffy, about 2 minutes. Add the sugar and cream together well.

Use a fork to lightly beat the egg and vanilla in a small bowl. Add the zest, then add this mixture to the butter mixture and blend together. At first the mixture may look curdled as the egg is added, but as you stop and scrape down the bowl, the mixture will smooth out.

Add the flour mixture in 3 stages, stopping to scrape down the bottom and sides of the bowl after each addition.

Form the dough into a disk and wrap tightly in plastic wrap. Chill the dough for several hours or overnight.

ASSEMBLY

On a smooth, flat surface, roll out the dough between sheets of lightly floured waxed or parchment paper to a large rectangle, about $1/4$ inch thick and 10 × 15 inches. Carefully peel the paper off the top of the dough.

Evenly spread the date mixture over the rectangle. Starting at one long end, roll up the dough into a tight roll, peeling it off the bottom piece of paper as you go. Wrap the roll tightly in waxed paper and then in plastic wrap and chill for at least 1 hour, until firm enough to cut.

Adjust the oven racks to the upper and lower thirds and preheat the oven to 375°F.

Line two baking sheets with parchment paper or non-stick liners.

Slice the roll into cookies $1/4$ inch thick. Lay the cookies on the baking sheets, leaving 1 inch of space between them. Bake for 7 minutes, then switch the baking sheets and bake another 5 to 6 minutes, until set and golden.

Remove the baking sheets from the oven and cool the cookies on the baking sheets on racks.

and date the contents. If frozen, defrost overnight in the refrigerator. Bring to room temperature to serve.

Streamlining
The cookie dough can be made up to 3 days in advance and kept tightly wrapped in a double layer of plastic wrap in the refrigerator. To freeze up to 3 months, wrap the dough snugly in several layers of plastic wrap and place in a freezer bag. Use a large piece of masking tape and an indelible marker to label and date the contents. If frozen, defrost in the refrigerator. If the dough is very cold it will need to stand at room temperature until it is pliable enough to roll out.

Making a Change
Replace the dates with dried figs or dried apricots.

Dried Apricot and Date-Nut Squares

THESE SQUARES are very easy to make and they keep very well. They are great to pack into a lunch box or as a snack in the afternoon. Everyone, including children, will love them.

Makes sixteen 2-inch squares

Center a rack in the oven and preheat it to 350°F.

Non-stick baking spray	Spray the inside and bottom of the baking pan.
½ cup finely chopped dried apricots **½ cup finely chopped pitted dates** **2 tablespoons freshly squeezed orange juice**	Place the apricots and dates in a small mixing bowl and add the orange juice. Toss to blend together well.
2 extra-large eggs, at room temperature	Place the eggs in the bowl of an electric stand mixer or in a large mixing bowl. Using the wire whip attachment or a hand-held mixer, whip the eggs until they are frothy.
½ cup granulated sugar **¼ cup firmly packed light brown sugar**	Add the granulated sugar and brown sugar and continue to whip until the mixture is thick and pale yellow colored and holds a slowly dissolving ribbon as the beater is lifted, about 5 minutes.
¼ cup all-purpose flour **½ teaspoon baking powder**	Over a medium piece of waxed or parchment paper or a bowl, sift together the flour and baking powder. Fold the mixture into the egg mixture.
1 cup finely chopped walnuts	Fold in the apricots, dates, and orange juice, then fold in the walnuts.

Transfer the mixture to the prepared pan. Use the rubber spatula to smooth and even the top. Bake for 30 minutes, until the mixture is puffed and set and a cake tester inserted in the center comes out clean.

Remove the pan from the oven and cool on a rack.

Cut into 4 rows in each direction, forming sixteen 2-inch squares. Serve at room temperature.

Essential Gear
- 8-inch square baking pan
- Electric stand mixer with wire whip attachment, or large mixing bowl and hand-held mixer
- Rubber spatula
- Cooling rack

Keeping

Store the squares tightly wrapped with aluminum foil up to 3 days at room temperature. To freeze up to 4 months, tightly wrap the squares in several layers of plastic wrap and aluminum foil. Use a large piece of masking tape and an indelible marker to label and date the contents. If frozen, defrost overnight in the refrigerator and bring to room temperature before serving.

Making a Change

Replace the apricots and dates with dried figs, peaches, pears, or nectarines.

Replace the walnuts with pecans or almonds.

Adding Style

Lightly dust the top of the squares with confectioners' sugar.

Dried Apricot Loaf Cake

APRICOTS SOAKED in brandy are mixed into a batter rich with butter, brown sugar, eggs, and buttermilk, then baked to produce this delectable loaf cake. It's great for afternoon tea or to pack into a lunch box. Try it toasted for breakfast, spread with cream cheese or a little butter and jam. **Makes one 8$^{1}/_{2}$ × 4$^{1}/_{2}$ × 2$^{1}/_{2}$-inch loaf cake, 12 servings**

CAKE

Center a rack in the oven and preheat it to 325°F.

1 tablespoon unsalted butter, softened

Using a paper towel or your fingertips, generously coat the inside of the pan.

2 teaspoons all-purpose flour

Dust the inside of the pan with flour, then shake and tilt the pan to evenly coat the bottom and sides. Turn the pan over the sink and tap out the excess flour.

$^{1}/_{2}$ cup dried apricots, finely chopped
2 tablespoons brandy

Place the apricots in a small bowl and pour the brandy over them. Cover the bowl tightly with plastic wrap and let the apricots steep for at least 15 minutes.

6 ounces (12 tablespoons, 1$^{1}/_{2}$ sticks) unsalted butter, softened

Place the butter in the bowl of an electric stand mixer or in a large mixing bowl. Use the flat beater attachment or hand-held mixer to beat the butter until it is light and fluffy, about 2 minutes.

1 cup granulated sugar
$^{1}/_{2}$ cup firmly packed light brown sugar

Add the granulated sugar and the brown sugar to the butter, and cream together until light and fluffy, about 2 minutes.

2 extra-large eggs, at room temperature
1 extra-large egg yolk, at room temperature
1$^{1}/_{2}$ teaspoons pure vanilla extract

In a small bowl, lightly beat together the eggs, egg yolk, and vanilla and add to the butter mixture. The eggs will sit on top of the butter mixture, so scrape down the sides and bottom of the bowl with a rubber spatula after adding them to help mix evenly. The mixture may look curdled but will smooth out when the dry ingredients are added.

2 cups all-purpose flour
$^{1}/_{2}$ teaspoon baking powder
$^{1}/_{4}$ teaspoon baking soda
$^{1}/_{4}$ teaspoon salt

Over a large piece of waxed or parchment paper or a bowl, sift together the flour, baking powder, and baking soda. Add the salt and toss together.

Essential Gear:
- 8$^{1}/_{2}$ × 4$^{1}/_{2}$ × 2$^{1}/_{2}$-inch loaf pan
- Electric stand mixer with flat beater attachment, or large mixing bowl and hand-held mixer
- Rubber spatula
- Flexible-blade spatula
- Cooling rack

Keeping
Store the cake tightly wrapped in aluminum foil at room temperature up to 4 days. To freeze up to 3 months, wrap the cake tightly in several layers of plastic wrap and aluminum foil. Use a large piece of masking tape and an indelible marker to label and date the contents. If frozen, defrost overnight in the refrigerator and bring to room temperature before serving.

Making a Change
Replace the dried apricots with dried peaches, pears, cranberries, or raisins.

Adding Style
Add $^{2}/_{3}$ cup finely chopped walnuts or pecans after adding the dried apricots to the batter.

½ cup buttermilk

Add the dry ingredients to the butter mixture alternately with the buttermilk and blend well after each addition. Beat until smooth.

Add the dried apricots and brandy and blend well.

Transfer the batter to the prepared loaf pan. The batter is very thick, so use a rubber spatula to spread it evenly into the pan.

Bake for 1 hour and 5 minutes, until the cake is light golden on top and a cake tester inserted into the center comes out clean.

Remove the pan from the oven and cool completely on a rack. Use a flexible blade spatula or thin-blade sharp knife to run around the outer edges to loosen the cake from the pan. Invert the pan over the cooling rack or a serving plate and gently pull the pan away from the cake. Cut the cake across the width into slices and serve at room temperature.

Dried Berry Crisp with Apples

A LUSCIOUS COMBINATION of mixed dried berries and crisp apples are baked together with a crumbly topping of toasted oats, almonds, brown sugar, spices, and butter. This easy-to-prepare dessert is perfect for fall and winter. It can be eaten warm or at room temperature and is even better served with a scoop of vanilla ice cream or whipped cream. **Makes one 8-inch square crisp, 8 to 10 servings**

DRIED BERRY AND APPLE FILLING

2½ cups mixed dried berries (strawberries, cranberries, cherries, or blueberries)
1 cup freshly squeezed orange juice

Place the dried berries in a bowl and cover with the orange juice. Tightly cover the bowl with plastic wrap and let the berries soak for 30 minutes.

1¼ pounds Granny Smith or Gala apples (4 medium)

Using a vegetable peeler or a knife, peel the apples, then cut them into quarters and cut out the cores. Cut the apple quarters into 1-inch chunks. Place the apple chunks in a large bowl and add the dried berries and orange juice. The orange juice will keep the apples from turning brown.

Essential Gear
- 8-inch square baking pan
- Food processor
- Rubber spatula or wooden spoon
- Vegetable peeler
- Chef's knife
- Cooling rack
- Electric stand mixer with wire whip attachment, or large mixing bowl and hand-held mixer
- Microplane grater or citrus zester

Keeping
Although the crisp is best eaten the day it's made, it can last up to 2 days. Store the crisp tightly covered with aluminum foil in the refrigerator.

Finely grated zest of 1 large orange	Drain the dried fruit and apple mixture to remove most of the liquid. Add the orange zest and sugar and stir to mix thoroughly. Place the fruit mixture in the baking pan.
¼ cup granulated sugar	

TOPPING

Center a rack in the oven and preheat it to 350°F.

²/₃ cups rolled oats (not quick-cooking)	Place the rolled oats in a single layer in a cake or pie pan. Toast in the oven for 15 minutes, until light golden. Remove from the oven and cool slightly. Raise the oven heat to 400°F.
½ cup sliced or slivered almonds	In the work bowl of a food processor fitted with the steel blade, combine the oats, almonds, sugar, cinnamon, nutmeg, and salt. Pulse briefly to blend.
½ cup firmly packed light brown sugar	
¼ teaspoon cinnamon	
¼ teaspoon freshly ground nutmeg	
⅛ teaspoon salt	
2 ounces (4 tablespoons, ½ stick) unsalted butter, chilled	Cut the butter into small pieces and add to the dry ingredients. Pulse until the butter is cut into very small pieces, 30 seconds to 1 minute.

Evenly sprinkle the topping over the fruit in the baking pan.

Bake for 30 to 35 minutes, until the topping is light golden and crisp and the fruit is bubbling. Remove the pan from the oven and transfer to a rack to cool.

GARNISH

1 cup heavy whipping cream	Place the cream in the chilled bowl of an electric stand mixer or in a large mixing bowl. Use the wire whip attachment or a hand-held mixer to whip on medium speed until frothy.
2 tablespoons confectioners' sugar	Add the confectioners' sugar and continue whipping the cream until it holds soft peaks.

Cut squares of the crisp, scooping up the fruit. Serve each square with a large dollop of whipped cream.

Streamlining
The topping can be made in advance. Store it in a tightly covered plastic container in the refrigerator up to 4 days.

Adding Style
Serve squares of the crisp with vanilla ice cream.

Cranberry Nut Muffins

TART DRIED CRANBERRIES and walnuts are the prominent flavors in these muffins. These are great for breakfast, lunch, or as a snack. They taste good either at room temperature or warm, and they can be warmed up in a 350-degree oven for 10 minutes before serving. **Makes 12 muffins**

Center a rack in the oven and preheat it to 400°F. Line each cavity of the muffin pan with a paper muffin cup.

2 cups all-purpose flour
²/₃ cup firmly packed light brown sugar
1 tablespoon baking powder
¹/₂ teaspoon salt
¹/₄ teaspoon freshly grated nutmeg

In a large bowl, stir together the flour, sugar, baking powder, salt, and nutmeg. Use a rubber spatula or wooden spoon to stir together well.

1 cup heavy whipping cream
4 ounces (8 tablespoons, 1 stick) unsalted butter, melted
2 extra-large eggs, at room temperature
1¹/₂ teaspoons pure vanilla extract

Use a fork to whisk together the cream, butter, eggs, and vanilla in a bowl. Add this mixture to the dry ingredients and stir together just until combined. The batter doesn't have to be smooth. If the batter is overmixed, the muffins may crumble instead of rising as they bake.

³/₄ cup dried cranberries
³/₄ cup coarsely chopped walnuts

Add the cranberries and walnuts to the batter and stir briefly to distribute evenly.

Use a spoon to divide the batter evenly among the 12 muffin cups, filling them to the top.

Bake the muffins about 15 minutes, until they are light golden brown and a tester inserted in the center comes out clean. Remove the pan from the oven and cool on a rack. Serve warm or at room temperature.

To rewarm the muffins, place them in a 350°F oven for 8 to 10 minutes.

Essential Gear
- 12-cavity 3-inch muffin pan
- 3-inch pleated paper muffin cups
- Electric stand mixer with flat beater attachment, or large mixing bowl and hand-held mixer
- Rubber spatula
- Cooling rack

Keeping
Store the muffins in an airtight plastic container between layers of waxed paper at room temperature up to 3 days. To freeze up to 2 months, wrap the container tightly in several layers of plastic wrap and aluminum foil. Use a large piece of masking tape and an indelible marker to label and date the contents. If frozen, defrost overnight in the refrigerator and bring to room temperature before serving.

Making a Change
Replace the cranberries with dried cherries.

Replace the walnuts with toasted almonds, pecans, or hazelnuts.

Dried Cherry and Almond Scones

SCONES ARE classic English teatime treats that are not very sweet, which also makes them great for breakfast. These are made with oats, dried cherries, and almonds for a unique flavor and lots of texture. Scones are best served warm and can be reheated in a 350-degree oven for 10 to 15 minutes. **Makes ten 3-inch scones**

Center a rack in the oven and preheat it to 400°F. Line a baking sheet with parchment paper or a non-stick liner.

1½ cups all-purpose flour 1 cup rolled oats (not quick-cooking) ½ cup sliced or slivered almonds ¼ cup granulated sugar 1½ teaspoons baking powder ½ teaspoon baking soda ½ teaspoon freshly grated nutmeg ¼ teaspoon salt	In the work bowl of a food processor fitted with the steel blade, combine the flour, oats, almonds, sugar, baking powder, baking soda, nutmeg, and salt. Pulse a few times to blend.
4 ounces (8 tablespoons, 1 stick) unsalted butter, chilled	Cut the butter into small pieces and add to the mixture in the food processor. Pulse until the butter is cut into very tiny pieces, about 30 seconds. The texture should be sandy with very tiny lumps throughout.
½ cup dried cherries	Add the dried cherries and pulse a few times to mix.
⅔ cup buttermilk 1 extra-large egg, at room temperature	Using a fork, lightly beat the buttermilk and egg together in a liquid measuring cup. With the food processor running, pour this mixture through the feed tube and process until the dough wraps itself around the blade, about 30 seconds.

Dust a large piece of waxed or parchment paper with flour and turn the dough out onto it. Dust your hands with flour and shape the dough into a large rectangle, approximately 7 × 10 inches and ½ inch thick. Use the round cutter to cut out scones. Cut straight down through the dough without twisting the cutter. Twisting will seal the edges and keep them from rising well. Transfer the scones to the lined baking sheet, leaving at least 1 inch of space between them so they have room to expand as they bake.

Gather together any scraps, knead them briefly, and pat into a round. Use the cutter to cut out more scones and place them on the baking sheet.

Replace the almonds with walnuts, pecans, or macadamia nuts.

GARNISH

1 tablespoon heavy whipping cream
1 tablespoon granulated sugar

Brush the top of each scone with cream, taking care that it doesn't run down the sides and under the scones. If it does, wipe it up because it can cause the bottom of the scones to burn.

Lightly sprinkle the top of each scone with sugar.

Bake the scones for 18 to 20 minutes, until light golden.

Remove the baking sheet from the oven and cool completely on a rack.

To rewarm the scones, place them in a 350°F oven for 10 to 15 minutes.

Fig and Anise Cake

THE COMBINATION of flavors in this cake is sensational. The dried figs are highlighted and enhanced by the anise seed. This is a wonderful cake for afternoon tea or coffee and is equally good for dessert. Try serving it with rich vanilla ice cream. **Makes one 9-inch round cake, 12 to 14 servings**

Essential Gear
- 9 × 4-inch tube pan or Bundt pan
- Electric stand mixer with flat beater attachment, and wire whip attachment or large mixing bowl and hand-held mixer
- Rubber spatula
- Cooling rack
- Sugar dredger or fine-mesh strainer

Center a rack in the oven and preheat it to 325°F.

2 teaspoons unsalted butter, softened

Use your fingertips or a paper towel to butter the inside of the pan.

2 teaspoons all-purpose flour

Sprinkle the flour inside the pan and shake and tilt the pan to cover the bottom and sides. Turn the pan over the sink and shake out any excess flour.

Keeping
Store the cake tightly wrapped in plastic up to 4 days at room temperature. To freeze up to 4 months, tightly wrap the cake in several layers of plastic wrap and aluminum foil. Use a large piece of masking tape

8 ounces (16 tablespoons, 2 sticks) unsalted butter, softened

Place the butter in the bowl of an electric stand mixer or in a large mixing bowl. Use the flat beater attachment or a hand-held mixer to beat the butter on medium speed until it's light and fluffy, about 2 minutes.

1²/₃ cups granulated sugar

Add the sugar to the butter, and cream together well. Stop occasionally and scrape down the sides and bottom of the bowl with a rubber spatula.

5 extra-large eggs, at room temperature	One at a time, add the eggs to the butter mixture, stopping to scrape down the bottom and sides of the bowl after each addition. At first the mixture may look curdled as the eggs are added, but as you stop and scrape down the bowl, the mixture will smooth out.
1½ teaspoons anise extract	Add the anise extract and blend well.
2¼ cups cake flour **1 tablespoon baking powder** **3 tablespoons anise seeds** **¼ teaspoon salt**	Over a large piece of waxed or parchment paper or a bowl, sift together the cake flour and baking powder. Add the anise seeds and salt and toss together well.
3 tablespoons coarsely chopped dried figs	Place the figs in a small bowl and add 2 tablespoons of the flour mixture. Toss to coat the figs.

Alternately add the dry ingredients and the chopped figs to the butter mixture in 3 stages. Stop after each addition and scrape down the sides and bottom of the bowl. Blend the mixture thoroughly.

Transfer the mixture to the pan. Use the rubber spatula to smooth and even the top.

Bake for 55 minutes to 1 hour, until a cake tester inserted in the center of the cake comes out clean.

Remove the pan from the oven and cool on a rack for 15 minutes. Invert the pan onto the rack and leave it for a few minutes so the cake will drop out of the pan. Remove the pan and let the cake cool completely.

GARNISH

2 tablespoons confectioners' sugar, sifted	Dust the top of the cake with confectioners' sugar before serving.

and an indelible marker to label and date the contents. If frozen, defrost overnight in the refrigerator and bring to room temperature before serving.

Making a Change

Add 1½ cups coarsely chopped walnuts, pecans, or almonds to the dry ingredients.

Kolachys

THESE TRADITIONAL Eastern European cookies are made with a delicate, soft, cream cheese dough that encloses a filling of cooked and pureed prunes. The dough can be a little tricky to work with, but these are well worth the extra effort. Make the dough a day before you plan to assemble and bake these because it needs to chill in the refrigerator at least 12 hours. **Makes 2 dozen cookies**

Essential Gear
- Two baking sheets
- Two parchment paper sheets or non-stick liners
- Electric stand mixer with flat beater attachment, or

Line two baking sheet with parchment paper sheets or non-stick liners.

8 ounces (16 tablespoons, 2 sticks) unsalted butter, softened 8 ounces cream cheese, at room temperature	Place the butter and cream cheese in the bowl of an electric stand mixer or in a large mixing bowl. Use the flat beater attachment or a hand-held mixer to beat together until light and fluffy, about 2 minutes.
3 tablespoons granulated sugar	Add the sugar to the butter mixture and blend together thoroughly.
2 extra-large eggs, at room temperature	One at time, add the eggs to the butter mixture and blend together well. The eggs will sit on top of the mixture, so stop and scrape down the sides and bottom of the bowl with a rubber spatula to encourage even mixing.
2 cups all-purpose flour 1 teaspoon baking powder 1/4 teaspoon salt	Over a piece of waxed or parchment paper or a bowl, sift together the flour and baking powder. Add the salt and toss to blend. Add this mixture to the butter mixture in 2 stages, beating well after each addition.
	Divide the dough in two and shape each piece into a disk. Wrap the dough disks tightly in plastic and chill until firm, 12 hours to overnight.

PRUNE FILLING

1 cup pitted prunes 1/2 cup water 1/4 cup granulated sugar Grated zest of 1 large orange 1 tablespoon freshly squeezed orange or lemon juice	In a medium heavy-bottomed saucepan, combine the prunes, water, sugar, orange zest, and juice. Bring the mixture to a boil over medium-high heat. Reduce the heat to low and simmer the mixture for 15 minutes, until it thickens.
1 ounce (2 tablespoons) unsalted butter, softened	Transfer the prune mixture to the work bowl of a food processor fitted with the steel blade. Cut the butter into small pieces and add. Pulse the mixture several times until it is pureed, about 2 minutes.
	Adjust the oven racks to the upper and lower thirds and preheat the oven to 350°F.
	Work with one disk of dough and keep the other refrigerated. Roll out each disk of dough between sheets of lightly floured waxed or parchment paper to a large square about 12 inches wide. Cut the

large mixing bowl and hand-held mixer
• Medium heavy-bottomed saucepan
• Sifter
• Microplane grater or citrus zester
• Chef's knife
• Ruler
• Food processor
• Two cooling racks

Keeping
Store the Kolachys in a single layer in an airtight plastic container at room temperature up to 3 days. To freeze up to 4 months, wrap the container tightly in several layers of plastic wrap and aluminum foil. Use a large piece of masking tape and an indelible marker to label and date the contents. If frozen, defrost overnight in the refrigerator and bring to room temperature before serving.

Streamlining
The dough can be made up to 3 days in advance and kept tightly wrapped in a double layer of plastic wrap in the refrigerator. To freeze for up to 3 months, wrap the dough snugly in several layers of plastic wrap and place in a freezer bag. Use a large piece of masking tape and an indelible marker to label and date the contents. If frozen, defrost in the refrigerator. If the dough is very cold it will need to stand at room temperature

square into 3-inch squares, using a ruler as a guide, cutting 4 rows in each direction, to get 16 pieces.

Place the dough squares evenly on the lined baking sheets, leaving at least 1 inch of space between them.

Place a tablespoon of the prune filling in the center of each square.

Moisten the corners of the dough squares and bring opposite corners together so they overlap over the filling. Press gently so they stick together. Repeat with the remaining two opposite corners, forming small pillows.

Bake for 7 minutes. Switch the baking sheets and bake another 7 to 8 minutes, until light golden.

Remove the baking sheets from the oven and cool completely on racks.

GARNISH

½ cup confectioners' sugar, sifted

Dust the tops of the Kolachys with confectioners' sugar.

Mixed Dried Fruit Tart

THIS IS A SUMPTUOUS tart made with a variety of dried fruit. The tart dough is rich with ground almonds and butter and the filling is first soaked in orange juice, then cooked until soft and pureed. The top of the tart is decorated with the same type of dried fruit used in the filling. This is a gorgeous and luscious dessert that can easily be the centerpiece of your next party. **Makes one 11-inch round tart, 14 to 16 servings**

MARINATED MIXED DRIED FRUIT

3½ cups mixed dried fruit (peaches, pears, apricots, nectarines, currants, or raisins)
1 cup freshly squeezed orange juice

Place the dried fruit in a single layer in the baking pan. Pour the orange juice over the fruit. Tightly cover the baking pan with plastic wrap and let the fruit marinate for at least 12 hours or overnight at room temperature so it can soak in the juice. Occasionally stir the fruit to be sure it is soaking evenly.

Essential Gear
• 2-quart glass baking pan
• Food processor
• Rolling pin
• 11-inch round, fluted-edge tart pan with removable bottom
• Baking sheet
• Whisk or rubber spatula
• 2-quart heavy-bottomed saucepan
• Cooling rack

Keeping
Store the tart, loosely covered with waxed paper and

until it is pliable enough to roll out.

PASTRY DOUGH

1½ cups finely ground almonds or almond meal
1 cup all-purpose flour
½ cup granulated sugar
1½ teaspoons ground cinnamon
⅛ teaspoon salt

In the work bowl of a food processor fitted with the steel blade, combine the almonds, flour, sugar, cinnamon, and salt. Pulse briefly to blend.

9 ounces (18 tablespoons, 2¼ sticks) unsalted butter, chilled

Cut the butter into small pieces and add to the flour mixture. Pulse until the butter is cut into very tiny pieces, about 30 seconds. The texture will be sandy with very tiny lumps throughout.

1 extra-large egg yolk, at room temperature

In a small bowl, use a fork to lightly beat the egg yolk. With the food processor running, pour the egg yolk through the feed tube. Process the dough until the mixture wraps itself around the blade, about 1 minute.

Turn the pastry dough onto a large piece of plastic wrap. Shape into a flat disk and wrap tightly in a double layer of plastic wrap. Chill in the refrigerator until firm before using, about 2 hours. Chilling the dough relaxes the gluten in the flour so it won't be too elastic and will roll out easily. It also firms up the butter in the dough so it will need less flour when rolled out. If the dough is too firm it will splinter and break when rolled out. Let it stand at room temperature for 10 to 15 minutes before rolling to become more pliable.

On a smooth, flat surface, roll out the pastry dough between sheets of lightly floured waxed or parchment paper to a large circle about 13 inches in diameter. To tell if the dough will fit the tart pan, hold the pan above the dough. If there are about 2 inches of dough that protrude beyond the sides of the pan, it will fit.

Carefully peel the paper off the top of the dough. Brush excess flour off the dough, then loosely roll the pastry dough around the rolling pin without the bottom piece of paper. Place the tart pan directly underneath the rolling pin and carefully unroll the pastry dough into the tart pan. Gently lift up the sides and ease the pastry dough into the bottom and sides of the tart pan. Trim off the excess pastry dough at the top of the pan. Transfer the tart pan to a baking sheet and chill in the freezer for 15 minutes while preparing the filling.

then tightly wrapped with aluminum foil, at room temperature up to 4 days.

Streamlining
The pastry dough can be made in advance and kept in the refrigerator, tightly wrapped in a double layer of plastic wrap, up to 4 days. To freeze up to 3 months, wrap the dough snugly in several layers of plastic wrap and place it in a freezer bag. Use a large piece of masking tape and an indelible marker to label and date the contents. If frozen, defrost overnight in the refrigerator before using.

Troubleshooting
Don't roll out the pastry dough before it is chilled. The dough will be too soft and it will require a lot of flour to roll out, which results in a tough dough.

Once the pastry dough is unrolled into the tart pan, don't push it down forcefully. This will stretch the dough, which will shrink as it bakes, making it flat instead of taking the shape of the tart pan.

**2 tablespoons freshly
squeezed lemon juice**

**2 tablespoons granulated
sugar**

**1/2 teaspoon freshly grated
nutmeg**

Take approximately 1/3 of the marinated dried fruit and place it in a mixing bowl. Sprinkle the lemon juice, sugar, and nutmeg over the fruit and toss gently to evenly coat the fruit. Cover the bowl tightly with plastic wrap and set aside.

Center a rack in the oven and preheat it to 350°F.

MIXED DRIED FRUIT FILLING

Place the remaining marinated dried fruit in the saucepan. Add 1 cup of water and bring the mixture to a boil over medium heat. Reduce the heat to low and simmer the mixture, stirring frequently with a heatproof spatula or wooden spoon, until the liquid is absorbed and the fruit mixture is thick, 20 to 25 minutes.

1 cup sliced almonds

Transfer the filling to the work bowl of a food processor fitted with the steel blade. Add the almonds and process until the fruit mixture is pureed and the almonds are finely chopped, about 1 minute.

Remove the tart shell from the freezer and evenly spread the filling in it.

Arrange the dried fruit topping in circles over the filling.

Bake the tart for 40 minutes, until the tart shell is golden and the filling is set. Remove the pan from the oven and cool on a rack.

Carefully remove the side of the tart pan (see page 42). Serve slices of the tart at room temperature.

Raisin and Walnut Tart

THIS SUCCULENT TART is chock full of plump dark raisins and finely chopped walnuts nestled in a sweet pastry shell. It's a great tart to serve anytime, but seems to be especially good in the fall when the weather turns crisp. **Makes one 12 × 8-inch rectangular tart, 14 to 16 servings**

Essential Gear
- Food processor
- Rolling pin
- 12 × 8-inch fluted-edge tart pan with removable bottom

PASTRY DOUGH

2½ cups all-purpose flour

⅓ cup granulated sugar

½ teaspoon freshly grated
  nutmeg

⅛ teaspoon salt

In the work bowl of a food processor fitted with the steel blade, combine the flour, sugar, nutmeg, and salt. Pulse briefly to blend.

8 ounces (16 tablespoons,
  2 sticks) unsalted butter,
  chilled

Cut the butter into small pieces and add to the flour mixture. Pulse until the butter is cut into very tiny pieces, about 30 seconds. The texture will be sandy with very tiny lumps throughout.

1 extra-large egg, at room
  temperature

1 teaspoon pure vanilla
  extract

In a small bowl, use a fork to lightly beat the egg with the vanilla. With the food processor running, pour the egg mixture through the feed tube. Process the dough until the mixture wraps itself around the blade, about 1 minute.

Turn the pastry dough onto a large piece of plastic wrap. Shape into a flat disk and wrap tightly in a double layer of plastic wrap. Chill in the refrigerator until firm before using, at least 2 hours. Chilling the dough relaxes the gluten in the flour so it won't be too elastic and will roll out easily. It also firms up the butter in the dough so it will need less flour when rolled out. If the dough is too firm it will splinter and break when rolled out. Let it stand at room temperature for 10 to 15 minutes before rolling to become more pliable.

On a smooth, flat surface, roll out the pastry dough between sheets of lightly floured waxed or parchment paper to a large rectangle about 10 × 14 inches. To tell if the dough will fit the tart pan, hold the pan above the dough. If there are about 2 inches of dough that protrude beyond the sides of the pan, it will fit.

Carefully peel the paper off the top of the dough. Brush excess flour off the dough, then loosely roll the pastry dough around the rolling pin without the bottom piece of paper. Place the tart pan directly underneath the rolling pin and carefully unroll the pastry dough into the tart pan. Gently lift up the sides and ease the pastry dough into the bottom and sides of the tart pan. Trim off the excess pastry dough at the top of the pan. Transfer the tart pan to a baking sheet and chill in refrigerator while preparing the filling.

Center a rack in the oven and preheat it to 350°F.

- Baking sheet
- Whisk or rubber spatula
- Electric stand mixer with flat beater attachment, or large mixing bowl and hand-held mixer
- Cooling rack

Keeping
Store the tart, loosely covered with waxed paper and then tightly wrapped with aluminum foil, at room temperature up to 4 days.

Streamlining
The pastry dough can be made in advance and kept in the refrigerator, tightly wrapped in a double layer of plastic wrap, up to 4 days. To freeze up to 3 months, wrap the dough snugly in several layers of plastic wrap and place it in a freezer bag. Use a large piece of masking tape and an indelible marker to label and date the contents. If frozen, defrost overnight in the refrigerator before using.

Troubleshooting
Don't roll out the pastry dough before it is chilled. The dough will be too soft and it will require a lot of flour to roll out, which results in a tough dough.

Once the pastry dough is unrolled into the tart pan, don't push it down forcefully. This will stretch the dough, which will shrink as it bakes, making it flat instead of taking the shape of the tart pan.

RAISIN AND WALNUT FILLING

6 ounces (12 tablespoons, 1½ sticks) unsalted butter, softened

Place the butter in the bowl of an electric stand mixer or in a large mixing bowl. Use the flat beater attachment or hand-held mixer to beat the butter on medium speed until it's fluffy, about 2 minutes.

2 cups firmly packed light brown sugar

Add the sugar to the butter, and cream together well. Stop occasionally and scrape down the sides and bottom of the bowl with a rubber spatula.

3 extra-large eggs, at room temperature
1 teaspoon pure vanilla extract
¼ teaspoon freshly grated nutmeg

Using a fork, lightly beat the eggs, vanilla, and nutmeg together in a small bowl. Add the eggs to the butter mixture. The eggs will sit on top of the butter mixture, so stop after adding them and scrape down the sides and bottom of the bowl with a rubber spatula to help mix evenly. The mixture may look curdled but will smooth out as it is beaten.

3 cups plump dark raisins, such as Monukka or Thompson seedless

Add the raisins to the mixture and blend thoroughly.

Remove the tart shell from the refrigerator and evenly spread the filling in it.

1 cup walnuts, finely chopped

Evenly scatter the walnuts over the top of the filling.

Bake the tart for 45 to 50 minutes, until the tart shell is golden and the filling is set. Remove the pan from the oven and cool on a rack.

Carefully remove the sides of the tart pan (see page 42). Use a sharp knife to cut the tart into 2-inch squares.

Making a Change
Replace the raisins with finely chopped dried figs, apricots, peaches, pears, or nectarines.

Replace the walnuts with pecans or almonds.

Raisin Tartlets with Maple Syrup

THE SPECIAL FLAVOR of maple syrup makes these individual tartlets stand out. Be sure to use pure maple syrup, not imitation, for true maple flavor. The raisins in the filling become plump and chewy and the pastry dough is made with a combination of butter and cream cheese, making it easy to work with and very tasty. **Makes twenty 2½-inch tartlets**

PASTRY DOUGH

1 cup all-purpose flour
1 teaspoon granulated sugar
⅛ teaspoon salt

In the work bowl of a food processor fitted with the steel blade, combine the flour, sugar, and salt. Pulse briefly to blend.

Essential Gear
- Food processor
- Rolling pin
- 3-inch round, plain-edge cutter
- Twenty 2½-inch fluted-edge tartlet pans
- Baking sheet
- Cooling rack
- Electric stand mixer with flat beater attachment, or

4 ounces (8 tablespoons, 1 stick) unsalted butter, chilled 3 ounces cream cheese, chilled	Cut the butter and cream cheese into small pieces and add to the flour mixture. Pulse until they are cut into very tiny pieces, about 30 seconds. The texture will be sandy with very tiny lumps throughout. Continue to process until the mixture forms a ball, another 30 seconds.

Turn the pastry dough onto a large piece of plastic wrap. Shape into a flat disk and wrap tightly. Chill in the refrigerator until firm before using, at least 2 hours. Chilling the dough relaxes the gluten in the flour so it won't be too elastic and will roll out easily. It also firms up the butter in the dough so it will need less flour when rolled out. If the dough is too firm, it will splinter and break when rolled out. Let it stand at room temperature for 10 to 15 minutes before rolling to become more pliable.

Center a rack in the oven and preheat it to 375°F.

On a smooth, flat surface, roll out the pastry dough between sheets of lightly floured waxed or parchment paper to a large rectangle about 1/8 inch thick. Carefully peel the paper off the top of the dough. Use the round cutter to cut out circles of dough. Carefully peel the circles off the other piece of paper.

Gently place each circle in a tartlet pan and press the dough against the bottom and sides of each pan. Trim off the excess pastry dough at the top of the pan. Transfer the tartlet pans to a baking sheet and chill for at least 15 minutes to set while preparing the filling.

RAISIN AND MAPLE SYRUP FILLING

1 cup dark raisins 2 cups boiling water	Place the raisins in a small bowl and cover them with boiling water. Let them stand for 5 minutes. Drain the raisins and pat them dry, then transfer them to the work bowl of a food processor fitted with the steel blade. Pulse until they are roughly chopped, about 15 seconds.
1/2 cup firmly packed light brown sugar 1/3 cup pure maple syrup 1/4 cup freshly squeezed lemon juice 1 ounce (2 tablespoons) unsalted butter, melted 1 teaspoon pure vanilla extract 1/8 teaspoon ground cloves 1/8 teaspoon salt	Combine the sugar, maple syrup, lemon juice, butter, vanilla, cloves, and salt in the bowl of an electric stand mixer or a large mixing bowl. Use the flat beater attachment or a hand-held mixer to blend the ingredients together until they are smooth. Add the chopped raisins.

hand-held mixer with large mixing bowl

Keeping
Store the tartlets in a single layer on a baking sheet. Cover the top of the tartlets with a large piece of waxed paper to keep the surface from becoming marred. Tightly wrap the pan with aluminum foil and keep at room temperature up to 3 days.

Streamlining
The pastry dough can be made in advance and kept in the refrigerator, tightly wrapped in a double layer of plastic wrap, up to 4 days before using. To freeze up to 4 months, wrap it in a double layer of plastic wrap and place it inside a freezer bag. Use a large piece of masking tape and an indelible marker to label and date the contents. If frozen, defrost in the refrigerator overnight before using. If the dough is too cold to roll out, let it stand at room temperature to become pliable.

Troubleshooting
Don't roll out the pastry dough before it is chilled. The dough will be too soft and it will require a lot of flour to roll out, which will make the dough tough.

Making a Change
Replace the raisins with other chopped dried fruit such as apricots, figs, or dates.

Use a spoon to fill each tartlet shell ¾ full with the filling.

Bake the tartlets for 30 minutes, until the filling is puffed and set. Transfer the tartlets to racks to cool.

To remove the tartlets from the pans, gently tap them against a flat surface. They should easily slip out of the pans.

Replace the maple syrup with molasses.

Raisin-Walnut-Oatmeal Cookies

THESE ARE CLASSIC American cookies loaded with raisins and walnuts. They are best eaten warm from the oven or dunked in a cold glass of milk. Surprise someone you love by packing a few of these cookies into their lunch box. **Makes 3 dozen cookies**

Adjust the oven racks to the upper and lower thirds and preheat the oven to 350°F. Line 2 baking sheets with parchment paper or non-stick liners.

1½ cups rolled oats (not quick-cooking)
¾ cup all-purpose flour
1 teaspoon baking powder
1 teaspoon ground cinnamon
¼ teaspoon salt

In a large bowl, combine the oats, flour, baking powder, cinnamon, and salt. Toss gently to blend together.

4 ounces (8 tablespoons, 1 stick) unsalted butter, softened

Place the butter in the bowl of an electric stand mixer or in a large mixing bowl. Use the flat beater attachment or a hand-held mixer to beat the butter until light and fluffy, about 2 minutes.

¾ cup firmly packed light brown sugar

Add the sugar to the butter, and cream together well. Stop occasionally and scrape down the bottom and sides of the bowl with a rubber spatula.

1 extra-large egg at room temperature
1 teaspoon pure vanilla extract

Use a fork to lightly beat the egg with the vanilla in a small bowl. Add this mixture to the butter mixture. This will sit on top of the butter mixture, so stop after adding it and scrape down the sides and bottom of the bowl with a rubber spatula to help mix evenly. At first the mixture may look curdled as the eggs are added, but as you stop and scrape down the bowl, the mixture will smooth out.

Essential Gear
- Two baking sheets
- Two parchment paper sheets or non-stick liners
- Electric stand mixer with flat beater attachment, or large mixing bowl and hand-held mixer
- Rubber spatula
- 1½-inch-diameter ice cream scoop or spoon
- Two cooling racks

Keeping
Store the cookies between sheets of waxed paper in an airtight container at room temperature up to 1 week.

Making a Change
Replace the raisins with dried cherries, dried cranberries, chopped dried figs, or chopped dates.

Replace the walnuts with pecans or chopped almonds.

Add the dry ingredients in 3 stages, mixing well after each addition.

²/₃ **cup dark raisins**

²/₃ **cup coarsely chopped walnuts**

Add the raisins and walnuts to the dough and stir together to blend well.

Use the ice cream scoop or spoon to drop small mounds of the cookie dough onto the baking sheets. Leave at least 2 inches of space between the mounds so they have room to spread as they bake.

Bake the cookies for 5 minutes, then switch the baking sheets and bake another 6 to 7 minutes, until set and golden.

Remove the baking sheets from the oven and cool the cookies on the baking sheets on racks. Use a spatula to remove the cookies from the baking sheets.

CHAPTER

7

VEGETABLES

VEGETABLES MAY not be the first ingredients that come to mind when you think about baking. But I can tell you, some absolutely scrumptious things can be baked with vegetables as the main ingredient. Vegetables can impart a wonderfully sweet flavor and texture. Pumpkin pie and carrot cake are familiar to most of us, but there are other great vegetable ingredients that are used in baking. In this chapter, I have chosen some all-time favorites as well as some interesting surprises that I know you will really enjoy.

There's no problem finding carrots because they are always available. Cornmeal is also always available, either in boxes or in bulk. Fresh pumpkins are in season in late September and October and canned pumpkin puree can be found year-round. Fresh rhubarb is in season in late spring and summer, with the exception of rhubarb grown in greenhouses, which can be found in the fall and winter. The vegetables used as ingredients in this chapter are in supermarkets, produce stores, and at farmer's markets.

TIPS AND TECHNIQUES

Large carrots are commonly sold in bunches or packages. Baby carrots are packaged and peeled, so they can be used directly out of the package. Look for carrots that are uniformly shaped and have a smooth surface. The brighter the color of the carrots, the more likely they are to be sweet. If you buy carrots with the tops attached, they should be bright green and not wilted. Don't buy carrots that are soft, split, or overly dry. Baby carrots should be moist. Large carrots need to be peeled with a vegetable peeler. Whichever type of carrots you choose, they must be grated before use. This is done either by hand with a grater or using the grating or shredding disk of a food processor. Store carrots in a plastic bag in the refrigerator for several weeks.

If buying cornmeal in a box, make sure to check for the expiration date. When buying from a bin, check for even color, consistency in the grind, and no caking. Smell the cornmeal to be certain there is no chemical or rancid scent. Store cornmeal in a tightly sealed container in

291

a cool and dry place for up to a year. If I use cornmeal from a box, I transfer the remainder into another container.

I usually use canned pumpkin puree, not pumpkin pie filling. Make sure to check the expiration date on the can and use it before that date. Fresh pumpkin can be used, but it requires a good deal of effort. A ripe pumpkin will have uniform color and will give slightly on the bottom. You should even be able to smell the sweetness of the pumpkin when you bring it close to your nose. Watch out for bruises, scars, and large areas that are discolored. To prepare fresh pumpkin, cut it into quarters and scrape out the seeds and stringy fibers. Place the quarters on a baking sheet and bake in a 350°F oven for an hour, until the flesh is soft. Remove the baking sheet from the oven and scoop the flesh out of the quarters. Leftover canned pumpkin and freshly prepared pumpkin should be stored in an airtight container in the refrigerator no longer than five days.

Choose rhubarb that is brightly colored pink to deep red. Rhubarb should be firm without any bruises. Cut off the leaves of the rhubarb and pull off the strings if the stalks have them. Cut off both ends of the stalks and slice across the width. For the recipes in this book, rhubarb is baked, so there is no need to cook it separately. Store fresh rhubarb in a plastic bag in the refrigerator for three to four days.

Carrot Cake with Cream Cheese Frosting

THIS IS A CLASSIC carrot cake with cream cheese frosting that is full of raisins, walnuts, and spices. It's not at all boring or heavy like so many carrot cakes, but moist and very flavorful. I find it very easy to use the peeled baby carrots available in many supermarkets, so I don't have to spend time peeling them. The cake makes enough servings for a large group and is easy to transport. **Makes one 9 × 13-inch cake, 18 servings**

CARROT CAKE

Non-stick baking spray	Center a rack in the oven and preheat it to 350°F. Spray the inside of the baking pan with non-stick baking spray.
1¼ cups walnuts, coarsely chopped	Place the walnuts in a cake or pie pan and toast in the oven for 8 to 10 minutes, until a light golden color and there is a toasty aroma. Remove the pan from the oven and cool on a rack.
1 pound carrots, peeled	Coarsely grate the carrots in a food processor fitted with the grating disk or with a grater.
4 extra-large eggs, at room temperature **1½ cups granulated sugar** **1¼ cups canola or safflower oil** **⅔ cup firmly packed light brown sugar** **2 teaspoons pure vanilla extract** **Finely grated zest of 1 large orange**	In a large mixing bowl, whisk the eggs briefly to break them up. Add the granulated sugar, oil, brown sugar, vanilla, and orange zest.
2¼ cups all-purpose flour **1½ teaspoons baking powder** **1 teaspoon baking soda** **1 teaspoon ground cinnamon** **¼ teaspoon ground ginger** **½ teaspoon salt** **¼ teaspoon ground cloves** **¼ teaspoon freshly grated nutmeg**	Over a large piece of waxed or parchment paper or a bowl, sift together the flour, baking powder, baking soda, cinnamon, and ginger. Add the salt, cloves, and nutmeg and toss to blend well. Fold this mixture into the egg mixture in 3 stages, blending well after each addition.

Essential Gear

- 9 × 13-inch baking pan
- Food processor or grater
- Large mixing bowl
- Cake pan
- Microplane grater or citrus zester
- Rubber spatula
- Cooling rack
- Electric stand mixer with flat beater attachment, or large mixing bowl and hand-held mixer
- Offset spatula
- Sifter

Keeping

Store the frosted cake in an airtight container in the refrigerator up to 4 days. To freeze the cake without the frosting up to 4 months, wrap it tightly in several layers of plastic wrap and aluminum foil. Use a large piece of masking tape and an indelible marker to label and date the contents. If frozen, defrost overnight in the refrigerator and bring to room temperature before serving.

The frosting can be made up to 2 days in advance and kept in an airtight container in the refrigerator. Bring it to room temperature and rebeat before using.

Making a Change

Replace the walnuts with whole pecans.

1 cup dark raisins

Add the grated carrots, toasted walnuts, and raisins to the mixture and blend together thoroughly.

Pour the mixture into the prepared pan and use the rubber spatula to spread it evenly into the corners.

Bake the cake for 35 to 40 minutes, until a cake tester or toothpick inserted in the center comes out with no crumbs clinging to it.

Remove the pan from the oven and cool completely on a rack.

CREAM CHEESE FROSTING

12 ounces cream cheese, softened
4 ounces unsalted butter, softened

Place the cream cheese and butter in the bowl of an electric stand mixer or in a large mixing bowl. Use the flat beater attachment or a hand-held mixer to beat until light and fluffy, about 2 minutes.

3 tablespoons heavy whipping cream
2 teaspoons pure vanilla extract

Add the cream and vanilla to the cream cheese mixture and blend well. Stop and scrape down the sides and bottom of the bowl with a rubber spatula.

2½ cups confectioners' sugar, sifted

Add the sugar in 3 stages to the cream cheese mixture, blending well after each addition. The frosting should be easy to spread, but not too soft. If it is too soft, let it chill in the refrigerator for 15 minutes, then beat again.

Use a small offset spatula to spread the frosting evenly over the top of the cake. Let the frosting set in the refrigerator for 15 minutes, then cut the cake into 6 rows on the long side of the pan and into 3 rows on the short side of the pan to make 18 pieces.

Replace the nuts and raisins with 1½ cups lightly toasted shredded coconut.

Replace the cream cheese in the frosting with mascarpone.

Adding Style

Sprinkle the top of the frosting with finely chopped toasted walnuts, pecans, or shredded coconut, depending on which is used in the cake.

Cornmeal Muffins with Dried Cranberries

C ORNMEAL GIVES these muffins a delightfully crunchy texture. Dried cranberries also add tartness and texture. Try these warmed up and served with butter and jam for breakfast or afternoon tea. **Makes 12 muffins**

Center a rack in the oven and preheat it to 400°F. Line each cavity of the muffin pan with a paper muffin cup.

Essential Gear
- 12-cavity 3-inch muffin pan
- 3-inch pleated paper muffin cups
- Electric stand mixer with flat beater attachment, or large mixing bowl and hand-held mixer

1¹⁄₃ cups all-purpose flour	In a large mixing bowl, combine the flour, cornmeal, baking powder, and salt. Toss gently to blend together.	• Rubber spatula
²⁄₃ cup stone-ground fine yellow cornmeal		• Cooling rack

1¹⁄₃ cups all-purpose flour **²⁄₃ cup stone-ground fine yellow cornmeal** **1 tablespoon plus 1 teaspoon baking powder** **¹⁄₄ teaspoon salt**	In a large mixing bowl, combine the flour, cornmeal, baking powder, and salt. Toss gently to blend together.	• Rubber spatula • Cooling rack
¹⁄₂ cup dried cranberries	Add the dried cranberries to the flour mixture and toss together to coat them with the dry ingredients. This helps keep the cranberries suspended in the mixture as the muffins bake, so they don't sink to the bottom.	
1¹⁄₄ cups buttermilk **1 extra-large egg, at room temperature** **1¹⁄₂ ounces (3 tablespoons) unsalted butter, melted and cooled**	In a liquid measuring cup, combine the buttermilk, egg, and butter. Lightly beat the mixture with a fork to break up the egg. Pour this mixture into the dry ingredients and stir together just until the dry ingredients are moistened.	
	Use a spoon to divide the batter evenly among the 12 muffin cups, filling them to the top.	
	Bake the muffins 18 to 20 minutes, until they are set and a tester inserted in the center comes out clean. Remove the pan from the oven and cool on a rack. When the muffins are cool, gently pry them out of the pan. Serve warm or at room temperature. To rewarm the muffins, place them in a 325°F oven for 8 to 10 minutes.	

Keeping

Store the muffins in an airtight plastic container between layers of waxed paper at room temperature up to 3 days. To freeze up to 2 months, wrap the container tightly in several layers of plastic wrap and aluminum foil. Use a large piece of masking tape and an indelible marker to label and date the contents. If frozen, defrost overnight in the refrigerator and bring to room temperature before serving.

Making a Change

Replace the cranberries with dried cherries, raisins, chopped dates, chopped apricots, or chopped figs.

Pumpkin Cheesecake with Walnuts

THIS IS A RICH and very creamy cheesecake that is perfect for the fall and winter holiday season. I like to make this in place of pumpkin pie for Thanksgiving dinner. The crust is made with finely ground walnuts and provides an excellent textural contrast to the smoothness of the cheesecake. Make this cake at least a day before you plan to serve it because it needs several hours to cool and chill. **Makes one 9¹⁄₂-inch round cake, 12 to 14 servings**

Essential Gear

• 9¹⁄₂-inch round springform pan
• Heavy-duty aluminum foil
• Food processor or rolling pin
• Electric stand mixer with flat beater attachment and wire whip attachment, or

WALNUT CRUST

1 tablespoon unsalted butter, softened

Center a rack in the oven and preheat it to 350°F. Use a paper towel or your fingertips to generously butter the inside of the springform pan. Use a double layer of heavy-duty foil to wrap around the bottom of the pan. This prevents any water from the water bath from seeping into the pan.

One 8½-ounce package (about 22) small butter cookies, wafers, or shortbread
½ cup walnuts
2 tablespoons granulated sugar
1 teaspoon ground cinnamon

In the work bowl of a food processor fitted with the steel blade, combine the cookies, walnuts, sugar, and cinnamon. Pulse until the cookies and walnuts are finely ground, about 2 minutes.

Or place the butter cookies in a plastic bag and crush them with a rolling pin. Transfer the cookie crumbs to a bowl. Finely chop the walnuts and add to the cookie crumbs along with the sugar and cinnamon.

3 tablespoons unsalted butter, melted

Pour the butter through the feed tube of the food processor and pulse until the mixture holds together, about 30 seconds. Or add the butter to the bowl and toss to coat the ingredients.

Using your fingers, press the crust evenly into the bottom and most of the way up the sides of the springform pan. Chill the crust while preparing the filling.

PUMPKIN CHEESECAKE

1½ pounds cream cheese, softened

Place the cream cheese in the bowl of an electric stand mixer or in a large mixing bowl. Use the flat beater attachment or a hand-held mixer and beat the cream cheese until it is fluffy, about 2 minutes.

½ cup firmly packed light brown sugar
2 tablespoons all-purpose flour
¼ teaspoon salt

Add the sugar, flour, and salt and beat together until well blended, about 1 minute.

4 extra-large eggs, at room temperature
1 extra-large egg yolk, at room temperature

One at a time, add the eggs and egg yolk to the cream cheese mixture, beating well after each addition. Stop and scrape down the sides and bottom of the bowl with a rubber spatula. Mix until well blended and smooth, about 1 minute.

1¼ cups pumpkin puree (canned pumpkin)
½ cup heavy whipping cream
2 teaspoons pure vanilla extract

Add the pumpkin puree, cream, and vanilla and blend well..

hand-held mixer and large mixing bowl
• 12-inch round cake pan or large roasting pan
• Cooling rack
• Rubber spatula
• Thin-bladed knife
• 10- or 12-inch pastry bag with large open star tip

Keeping
Store the cheesecake tented with aluminum foil in the refrigerator up to 4 days. To freeze up to 2 months without the whipped cream garnish, wrap the cake tightly in several layers of plastic wrap and aluminum foil. Use a large piece of masking tape and an indelible marker to label and date the contents. If frozen, defrost overnight in the refrigerator and bring to room temperature before serving.

1½ teaspoons ground cinnamon	Combine the cinnamon, cloves, ginger, and nutmeg in a bowl and toss together to blend well. Add the walnuts and stir together. Add this mixture to the cheesecake mixture and blend thoroughly.
½ teaspoon ground cloves	
½ teaspoon ground ginger	
½ teaspoon freshly grated nutmeg	
1 cup coarsely chopped walnuts	

Transfer the cheesecake batter to the prepared pan. Smooth the top with a rubber spatula.

1 quart boiling water

Place the springform pan in the larger pan and set the pan on the oven rack. Carefully pour the boiling water into the bottom pan until it reaches halfway up the side of the springform pan. Baking the cake in a water bath cushions it from the heat and adds extra moisture to the oven, which keeps the top from cracking.

Bake the cake for 20 minutes. Reduce the oven temperature to 250°F, and continue to bake the cake for 1 hour and 30 minutes, until the top is no longer wet and the center moves slightly when the cake is shaken.

Remove the cheesecake pan from the oven and place on a rack to cool.

Remove the foil from the outside of the pan. When the cheesecake is completely cool, cover the top with waxed paper, then wrap tightly in aluminum foil. Refrigerate the cake for at least 6 hours before serving. To unmold the cheesecake, dip a thin-bladed knife in hot water and dry, then run it around the inner edge of the pan, release the clip on the rim of the pan, and gently lift it off the cake.

GARNISH

¼ cup heavy whipping cream

Place the cream in the chilled bowl of an electric stand mixer or in a mixing bowl. Use the wire whip attachment or a hand-held mixer to whip the cream on medium speed until it holds firm peaks.

Fit the pastry bag with the star tip and fill the bag partway with the whipped cream.

14 walnut halves

Mark the outside top edge of the cake into serving pieces. Pipe a rosette or star of cream in the center at the outside edge of each piece (see page 44). Or place a dollop of whipped cream in the same place. Top each rosette, star, or dollop of cream with a walnut half.

Pumpkin-Nut Muffins

THESE MUFFINS are full of pumpkin puree, a blend of spices, raisins, and walnuts. I love these warmed up for breakfast or afternoon tea served with butter, but they are equally good packed in a lunch box. It may look like there is too much batter right after they are mixed, but it's just the right amount. **Makes 12 muffins**

Center a rack in the oven and preheat it to 400°F. Line each cavity of the muffin pan with a paper muffin cup.

4 ounces (8 tablespoons, 1 stick) unsalted butter, softened

Cut the butter into pieces and melt it in a small saucepan over medium heat. Or melt the butter in a bowl in a microwave oven on low power. Cool the butter slightly, then pour it into a medium bowl.

¾ cup pumpkin puree (canned pumpkin)
¼ cup heavy whipping cream
2 extra-large eggs, at room temperature
3 tablespoons molasses
1 teaspoon pure vanilla extract

Add the pumpkin puree, cream, eggs, molasses, and vanilla. Whisk together until smooth and well blended.

2 cups all-purpose flour
¾ cup firmly packed light brown sugar
1½ teaspoons baking powder
½ teaspoon salt
½ teaspoon ground cinnamon
½ teaspoon ground ginger
¼ teaspoon baking soda
¼ teaspoon ground cloves
¼ teaspoon freshly grated nutmeg

In the bowl of an electric stand mixer or a large mixing bowl, combine the flour, sugar, baking powder, salt, cinnamon, ginger, baking soda, cloves, and nutmeg. Use the flat beater attachment or a hand-held mixer to blend briefly.

Add the pumpkin mixture and stir together quickly until combined.

1 cup raisins
1 cup coarsely chopped walnuts

Add the raisins and walnuts and stir to distribute evenly.

Use a spoon to divide the batter evenly among the 12 muffin cups, filling them to the top.

Essential Gear
- 12-cavity 3-inch muffin pan
- 3-inch pleated paper muffin cups
- Small saucepan
- Medium mixing bowl
- Electric stand mixer with flat beater attachment, or large mixing bowl and hand-held mixer
- Rubber spatula
- Cooling rack

Keeping
Store the muffins in an airtight plastic container between layers of waxed paper at room temperature up to 3 days. To freeze up to 2 months, wrap the container tightly in several layers of plastic wrap and aluminum foil. Use a large piece of masking tape and an indelible marker to label and date the contents. If frozen, defrost overnight in the refrigerator and bring to room temperature before serving.

Making a Change
Replace the raisins with dried chopped dates, chopped apricots, or chopped figs.

Replace the walnuts with toasted pecans, unblanched almonds, or hazelnuts.

Bake the muffins 20 to 25 minutes, until they are light golden brown and a tester inserted in the center comes out clean. Remove the pan from the oven and cool on a rack. When the muffins are cool, gently pry them out of the pan. Serve warm or at room temperature.

To rewarm the muffins, place them in a 325°F oven for 8 to 10 minutes.

Pumpkin Pie

PUMPKIN PIE is a classic that is a sure winner during the fall and winter holiday season. This pie has rich, deep flavor and a super creamy texture. It will have those who eat it asking for seconds! **Makes one 10-inch round pie, 12 to 14 servings**

PIE DOUGH

1 cup all-purpose flour
1 tablespoon granulated sugar
¼ teaspoon salt

In the work bowl of a food processor fitted with the steel blade, combine the flour, sugar, and salt. Pulse briefly to blend.

4 ounces (8 tablespoons, 1 stick) unsalted butter, chilled

Cut the butter into small pieces and freeze for 20 minutes.

4 ounces cream cheese, chilled

Cut the cream cheese into small pieces and add to the dry ingredients. Pulse to cut the cream cheese into very tiny pieces. The texture should be sandy with very tiny lumps throughout.

Add the butter to the flour mixture. Pulse until the butter is cut into pea-sized pieces, 30 to 45 seconds.

2 to 3 tablespoons heavy whipping cream

Remove the top of the food processor and sprinkle on 2 tablespoons of the cream. Replace the top and pulse for 10 seconds. Squeeze a small amount of the dough in your hand. If it holds together, don't add any more cream. If the dough is still very crumbly, add another tablespoon of cream, pulse to blend, then check the dough again. It won't hold together unless you squeeze it, but that's the texture you want.

Shape the dough into a disk and wrap it tightly in a double layer of plastic wrap. Chill in the refrigerator until firm before using, at least

Essential Gear
- Food processor
- Rolling pin
- 10-inch round deep pie pan
- Baking sheet
- Large mixing bowl
- Whisk or rubber spatula
- Cooling rack
- Electric stand mixer with wire whip attachment, or a hand-held mixer with large mixing bowl

Keeping
Store the pie, loosely covered with waxed paper and then tightly wrapped with aluminum foil, in the refrigerator up to 3 days.

Streamlining
The pie dough can be made in advance and kept in the refrigerator, tightly wrapped in a double layer of plastic wrap, up to 4 days. To freeze up to 3 months, wrap the dough snugly in several layers of plastic wrap and place it in a freezer bag. Use a large piece of masking tape and an indelible marker to label and date the

2 hours. Chilling the dough relaxes the gluten in the flour so it won't be too elastic and will roll out easily. It also firms up the butter in the dough so it will need less flour when rolled out. If the dough is too firm it will splinter and break when rolled out. Let it stand at room temperature for 10 to 15 minutes before rolling to become more pliable.

On a smooth, flat surface, roll out the pie dough between sheets of lightly floured waxed or parchment paper to a large circle about 12 inches in diameter. To tell if the dough will fit the pie pan, invert the pan over the dough. If there are 2 to 3 inches of dough that protrude beyond the sides of the pan, it will fit.

Carefully peel the paper off the top of the dough. Brush excess flour off the dough, then loosely roll the pastry dough around the rolling pin without the bottom piece of paper. Place the pie pan directly underneath the rolling pin and carefully unroll the pastry dough into the pan. Or loosely fold the dough in half. Carefully place it in half of the pie pan and gently unfold the dough. Gently lift up the sides and ease the pie dough into the bottom and sides of the pie pan. Trim off the excess pie dough at the top of the pan and crimp the sides (see page 40).

Transfer the pie pan to a baking sheet and chill in the freezer for 15 to 20 minutes. This helps prevent the pie dough from shrinking as it bakes and sets the butter in the dough to ensure flakiness.

Center an oven rack and preheat it to 425°F.

contents. If frozen, defrost overnight in the refrigerator before using. The pie dough can also be fitted into the pie pan and frozen. Wrap as above and label.

Troubleshooting

Don't overprocess the pie dough or it will be tough and not flaky.

Making a Change

Stir 1 tablespoon finely chopped crystallized ginger into the pumpkin filling after adding the cream.

Add 2/3 cup very finely chopped walnuts to the pie crust after adding the cream.

Replace the pumpkin puree with sweet potato puree.

Adding Style

Serve slices of the pie with vanilla ice cream.

PUMPKIN FILLING

3 extra-large eggs, at room temperature
2 cups pumpkin puree (canned pumpkin)

In a large bowl, use a whisk to lightly beat the eggs. Add the pumpkin puree and stir together until completely blended.

¾ cup firmly packed light brown sugar
¼ cup granulated sugar
½ teaspoon ground cinnamon
¼ teaspoon salt
¼ teaspoon ground ginger
¼ teaspoon ground cloves
¼ teaspoon freshly grated nutmeg

Add the brown sugar, granulated sugar, cinnamon, salt, ginger, cloves, and nutmeg and stir together well.

1½ cups heavy whipping cream ½ teaspoon pure vanilla extract	Add the cream and vanilla to the pumpkin mixture and stir to blend thoroughly.
	Pour the pumpkin filling into the chilled pie shell.
	Bake the pie for 10 minutes, then reduce the oven temperature to 350°F. Bake the pie another 50 to 60 minutes, until the filling is set and giggles very slightly when the pan is moved. Remove the pie from the oven and cool on a rack.
	GARNISH
½ cup heavy whipping cream 2 teaspoons confectioners' sugar, sifted	Place the cream in the chilled bowl of an electric stand mixer or in a large mixing bowl. Use the wire whip attachment or a hand-held mixer to whip the cream on medium speed until frothy. Add the confectioners' sugar and continue to whip the cream until it holds soft peaks.
	Serve slices of the pie with a scoop of whipped cream.

Pumpkin Roulade with Walnuts

T HIS CAKE is baked in a jelly-roll pan and rolled up tightly while warm. When cool, the cake is unrolled and spread with a filling of spiced whipped cream, then rerolled and decorated on the outside with more whipped cream and finely chopped walnuts. This is a very attractive cake that can easily be the star at any gathering. Try it for Thanksgiving dessert in place of pumpkin pie! **Makes one 15-inch cake, 12 to 14 servings**

Essential Gear
- Jelly-roll pan (12 × 17 inches)
- Two parchment paper sheets
- Electric stand mixer with wire whip attachment, or a hand-held mixer and a large mixing bowl
- Rubber spatula
- Sharp knife
- Sifter
- Ruler
- Rectangular serving plate
- Serrated knife
- Offset spatula
- Kitchen towel

PUMPKIN ROLLED CAKE

1 tablespoon unsalted butter, softened	Center a rack in the oven and preheat it to 375°F. Line a jelly-roll pan with a sheet of parchment paper. Use a paper towel or your fingertips to butter the parchment paper. Or spray the parchment paper with non-stick baking spray
4 extra-large eggs, at room temperature	Place the eggs in the bowl of an electric stand mixer or a large mixing bowl. Use the wire whip attachment or a hand-held mixer

	to whip the eggs on medium-high speed until they thicken, about 2 minutes.

• 14-inch pastry bag with large open star tip

1½ cups granulated sugar

Slowly sprinkle on the sugar and continue to whip on medium-high speed until the mixture is very thick and pale colored and holds a slowly dissolving ribbon as the beater is lifted, about 5 minutes.

Keeping

Store the filled and frosted cake tented with waxed paper and topped with aluminum foil in the refrigerator for 1 day. Store the unfilled and unfrosted cake tightly wrapped with plastic wrap in the refrigerator up to 4 days before filling. To freeze the cake without the filling and frosting up to 4 months, wrap it tightly in several layers of plastic wrap and aluminum foil. Use a large piece of masking tape and an indelible marker to label and date the contents. If frozen, defrost overnight in the refrigerator and bring to room temperature before serving.

¾ cup pumpkin puree (canned pumpkin)
1¼ teaspoons freshly squeezed lemon juice

Add the pumpkin puree and the lemon juice to the egg mixture and blend thoroughly.

1 cup all-purpose flour
2½ teaspoons ground cinnamon
1½ teaspoons baking powder
1½ teaspoons ground ginger
¾ teaspoon freshly grated nutmeg
½ teaspoon salt

Over a large piece of waxed or parchment paper or a bowl, sift together the flour, cinnamon, baking powder, and ginger. Add the nutmeg and salt and toss to blend well. Add to the egg mixture in 3 stages, blending well after each addition. Stop after each addition and scrape down the sides and bottom of the bowl with a rubber spatula.

1 cup finely chopped walnuts

Add the walnuts to the mixture and blend together thoroughly.

Pour the batter onto the prepared pan and use the rubber spatula or an offset spatula to spread it evenly into the corners.

Bake the cake for 15 to 18 minutes, until it is evenly colored and the tops springs back when touched lightly.

Remove the pan from the oven and use a sharp knife to loosen the sides and ends of the cake from the pan.

Making a Change

Replace the walnuts with pecans or almonds.

Place a sheet of parchment paper over the top of the cake and cover with a kitchen towel. Then invert the jelly-roll pan and lift it off the cake. Gently peel the parchment paper off of the back of the cake and discard.

Starting at one long end of the cake, immediately roll it up in the towel and parchment paper. Leave the cake seam-side down to cool completely.

WHIPPED CREAM FILLING AND FROSTING

2 cups heavy whipping cream

Place the cream in the chilled bowl of an electric stand mixer or in a large mixing bowl. Use the wire whip attachment or a hand-held mixer to whip the cream on medium speed until frothy.

1½ teaspoon pure vanilla extract	Add the vanilla to the cream and continue to whip.
2 tablespoons confectioners' sugar ½ teaspoon ground cinnamon ¼ teaspoon ground ginger ¼ teaspoon ground nutmeg	Over a small piece of waxed or parchment paper or a bowl, sift together the sugar, cinnamon, and ginger. Add the nutmeg and toss to blend well.
	Add this mixture to the whipped cream and continue to whip the cream until it holds soft peaks.
	Unroll the cooled cake and remove the towel. Use an offset spatula to spread ¼ of the whipped cream evenly over the inside of the cake, leaving a 1-inch border at the farthest long end of the cake. Roll up the cake, using the parchment paper as a guide.
	To make a tight cake roll, pull about one-third of the parchment paper over the top of the cake. Then place a ruler flat against the parchment that covers the top of the cake and push it against the roll while pulling the bottom part of the parchment paper toward you. This resistance motion of simultaneously pushing against the cake while pulling the parchment under the cake toward you compresses the roulade.
	Carefully place the roulade on a rectangular serving plate with the seam down and discard the parchment paper. Trim off the rough ends of the cake and discard.
	Fit the pastry bag with the star tip and fill partway with some of the remaining whipped cream. Pipe parallel rows of cream from one end of the roulade to the other, starting from the bottom and moving toward the top of the cake. Turn the plate around and repeat piping the cream on the other side of the roulade (see page 44).
⅓ cup toasted finely chopped walnuts	Sprinkle the top of the roulade with the walnuts.
	Use a serrated knife to cut the roulade crosswise for serving pieces.

Pumpkin Tartlets

A CREAMY pumpkin filling, enhanced with sour cream and classic pumpkin-pie spices, is baked in individual sweet pastry shells. Serve these in place of pumpkin pie for holiday meals or anytime you have a taste for a pumpkin dessert. **Makes eighteen 2½-inch round tartlets**

PASTRY DOUGH

1¼ cups all-purpose flour
3 tablespoons granulated sugar
⅛ teaspoon salt

In the work bowl of a food processor fitted with the steel blade, combine the flour, sugar, and salt. Pulse briefly to blend.

4 ounces (8 tablespoons, 1 stick) unsalted butter, chilled

Cut the butter into small pieces and add to the flour mixture. Pulse until the butter is cut into very tiny pieces, about 30 seconds. The texture will be sandy with very tiny lumps throughout.

1 extra-large egg yolk, at room temperature
½ teaspoon pure vanilla extract

In a small bowl, use a fork to lightly beat the egg yolk with the vanilla. With the food processor running, pour this mixture through the feed tube. Process the dough until the mixture wraps itself around the blade, about 1 minute.

Turn the pastry dough onto a large piece of plastic wrap. Shape into a flat disk and wrap tightly. Chill in the refrigerator until firm before using, at least 2 hours. Chilling the dough relaxes the gluten in the flour so it won't be too elastic and will roll out easily. It also firms up the butter in the dough so it will need less flour when rolled out. If the dough is too firm it will splinter and break when rolled out. Let it stand at room temperature for 10 to 15 minutes before rolling to become more pliable.

Center a rack in the oven and preheat it to 375°F.

On a smooth, flat surface, roll out the pastry dough between sheets of lightly floured waxed or parchment paper to a large rectangle about 16 × 12 inches. Carefully peel the paper off the top of the dough. Brush excess flour off the dough. Use the round cutter or a small bowl measuring 3¼ inches and cut out circles of the pastry dough. Carefully peel the circles off the other piece of paper. Gather together the dough scraps, reroll, and cut out any remaining circles. Carefully peel the circles off the other piece of paper.

Essential Gear
- Electric stand mixer with wire whip attachment, or a hand-held mixer with large mixing bowl
- Food processor
- Rolling pin
- 3¼-inch plain round cutter
- Baking sheet
- Thirty-six 2½-inch round, fluted-edge tartlet pans
- Cooling rack

Keeping
Store the tartlets ungarnished in a single layer on a baking sheet. Cover the top of the tartlets with a large piece of waxed paper to keep the surface from becoming marred. Tightly wrap the pan with plastic wrap and keep in the refrigerator up to 3 days.

Making a Change
Replace the pumpkin puree with sweet potato puree.

Streamlining
The pastry dough can be made in advance and kept in the refrigerator, tightly wrapped in a double layer of plastic wrap, up to 4 days before using. To freeze up to 4 months, wrap it in a double layer of plastic wrap and place it inside a freezer bag. Use a large piece of masking tape and an indelible marker to label and date the contents. If frozen, defrost in the refrigerator overnight before

Gently place each dough circle in a tartlet pan. Carefully lift up the sides of the pastry dough and ease the dough into the bottom and sides of each tartlet pan. Trim off the excess pastry dough at the top of the pan with your fingertips. Transfer the tartlet pans to a baking sheet and chill for at least 15 minutes to set.

Top each tartlet pan with another tartlet pan the same size to act as a weight while they bake.

Bake the tartlet shells for 5 minutes, then remove the top tartlet pan. If the bottom of the pastry shells puff up, gently pierce them in a few places with a fork or the point of a knife to release the air. Bake another 4 minutes, until very light colored and set. Remove the baking sheet from the oven and cool on a rack while making the filling.

using. If the dough is too cold to roll out, let it stand at room temperature to become pliable.

Troubleshooting
Don't roll out the pastry dough before it is chilled. The dough will be too soft and it will require a lot of flour to roll out, which will make the dough tough.

PUMPKIN FILLING

1 cup pumpkin puree (canned pumpkin) 1 extra-large egg, at room temperature 1 extra-large egg yolk, at room temperature	Place the pumpkin, egg, and egg yolk in the bowl of an electric stand mixer or a large mixing bowl. Use the flat beater attachment or a hand-held mixer to blend together until smooth, about 1 minute.
½ cup sour cream ¼ cup milk 1 tablespoon dark rum	Add the sour cream, milk, and rum to the pumpkin mixture and blend together until smooth.
½ cup granulated sugar ½ teaspoon ground ginger ½ teaspoon ground cinnamon ¼ teaspoon salt ¼ teaspoon ground cloves ¼ teaspoon freshly grated nutmeg	Add the sugar, ginger, cinnamon, salt, cloves, and nutmeg and stir to blend well.
½ cup finely chopped crystallized ginger	Stir in the crystallized ginger.

Spoon the filling into the tartlet shells until they are ¾ full. Bake for 10 minutes. Reduce the oven heat to 300°F and bake for 25 to 30 minutes, until the filling is set, but not dry or cracked.

Remove the baking pan from the oven and cool the tartlets on a rack.

To remove the tartlets from the pans, gently tap each tartlet pan on a countertop. The tartlets should slip out of their pans easily.

GARNISH

¼ cup heavy whipping cream

1 teaspoon granulated sugar

½ teaspoon pure vanilla extract

Place the cream in the chilled bowl of an electric stand mixer or a mixing bowl. Use the wire whip attachment or a hand-held mixer to whip the cream until it is frothy. Add the sugar and vanilla and continue to whip until the cream holds soft peaks.

Place a dollop of whipped cream in the center of each tartlet. Serve the tartlets at room temperature.

Rhubarb Custard Pie

MY GOOD FRIEND Bonnie Manion brought me fresh rhubarb from her garden and I decided to create this pie to use it. I used my favorite pie dough made with butter and cream cheese. The rhubarb is cut into 2-inch pieces and tossed with sugar, then arranged in the unbaked pie shell. A custard filling made with cream, eggs, sugar, and flavorings is poured over the rhubarb and it puffs up, enclosing the rhubarb as the pie bakes. A light dusting of confectioners' sugar is all this pie needs for garnish, but a scoop of vanilla ice cream is also a delicious accompaniment. Be sure to remove any leaves from the rhubarb stalks because they are not edible. **Makes one 10-inch round pie, 12 to 14 servings**

PIE DOUGH

1 cup all-purpose flour

1 tablespoon granulated sugar

¼ teaspoon salt

In the work bowl of a food processor fitted with the steel blade, combine the flour, sugar, and salt. Pulse briefly to blend.

4 ounces (8 tablespoons, ½ stick) unsalted butter, chilled

Cut the butter into small pieces and freeze for 20 minutes.

4 ounces cream cheese, chilled

Cut the cream cheese into small pieces and add to the dry ingredients. Pulse to cut the cream cheese into very tiny pieces. The texture should be sandy with very tiny lumps throughout.

Add the butter to the flour mixture. Pulse until the butter is cut into pea-sized pieces, 30 to 45 seconds.

Essential Gear

• Food processor
• Rolling pin
• 10-inch round deep pie pan
• Rolling pin
• Microplane grater or citrus zester
• Cooling rack

Keeping

Store the pie, loosely covered with waxed paper and then tightly wrapped with aluminum foil, at room temperature up to 3 days.

Streamlining

The pie dough can be made in advance and kept in the refrigerator, tightly wrapped in a double layer of plastic wrap, up to 4 days. To freeze up to 3 months, wrap the dough snugly in several layers of plastic wrap and place it in a freezer bag. Use a large piece of masking tape and an indelible

2 to 3 tablespoons heavy whipping cream

Remove the top of the food processor and sprinkle on the cream. Replace the top and pulse for 10 seconds. Squeeze a small amount of the dough in your hand. It should hold together. If the dough is still very crumbly, add another tablespoon of cream, pulse to blend, then check the dough again. It won't hold together unless you squeeze it, but that's the texture you want.

Shape the dough into a flat disk and wrap tightly in a double layer of plastic wrap. Chill in the refrigerator until firm before using, at least 2 hours. Chilling the dough relaxes the gluten in the flour so it won't be too elastic and will roll out easily. It also firms up the butter in the dough so it will need less flour when rolled out. If the dough is too firm it will splinter and break when rolled out. Let it stand at room temperature for 10 to 15 minutes before rolling to become more pliable.

On a smooth, flat surface, roll out the pie dough between sheets of lightly floured waxed or parchment paper to a large circle about 12 inches in diameter. To tell if the dough will fit the pie pan, invert the pan over the dough. If there are 2 to 3 inches of dough that protrude beyond the sides of the pan, it will fit.

Carefully peel the paper off the top of the dough. Brush excess flour off the dough, then loosely roll the pastry dough around the rolling pin without the bottom piece of paper. Place the pie pan directly underneath the rolling pin and carefully unroll the pastry dough into the pan. Or loosely fold the dough in half. Carefully place it in half of the pie pan and gently unfold the dough. Gently lift up the sides and ease the pie dough into the bottom and sides of the pie pan. Trim off the excess pie dough at the top of the pan and crimp the sides (see page 40).

Transfer the pie pan to a baking sheet and chill in the freezer for 15 to 20 minutes. This helps prevent the pie dough from shrinking as it bakes and sets the butter in the dough to ensure flakiness.

Adjust an oven rack to the lower third and preheat the oven to 425°F.

RHUBARB CUSTARD FILLING

1¼ pounds fresh rhubarb, cut into 2-inch pieces (about 4 cups)
¼ cup firmly packed light brown sugar

Place the rhubarb in a large bowl. Add the sugar and toss to coat the rhubarb. Remove the pie shell from the freezer and transfer the rhubarb to the pie shell, spreading it out evenly.

marker to label and date the contents. If frozen, defrost overnight in the refrigerator before using. The pie dough can also be fitted into the pie pan and frozen. Wrap as above and label.

Troubleshooting
Don't overprocess the pie dough or it will be tough and not flaky.

Adding Style
Add 2 tablespoons finely grated or minced lemon zest to the pie dough before adding the butter.

Serve slices of the pie with vanilla ice cream or whipped cream.

3/4 cup heavy whipping cream

2 extra-large eggs

3/4 cup firmly packed light brown sugar

2 tablespoons cornstarch, sifted

Finely grated zest of 1 large lemon

1/4 teaspoon freshly grated nutmeg

1/8 teaspoon salt

In a medium bowl, whisk together the cream and eggs to break up the eggs. Add the sugar, cornstarch, lemon zest, nutmeg, and salt and whisk together to blend well.

Pour this mixture over the rhubarb in the pie shell. Place the pie pan on a baking sheet.

Bake the pie for 30 minutes, then reduce the oven temperature to 350°F. Bake the pie another 20 to 30 minutes, until the filling is puffed and light golden.

Remove the pie from the oven and cool on a rack.

2 tablespoons confectioners' sugar

Lightly dust the top of the pie with confectioners' sugar. Serve warm or at room temperature.

Zalettini

I DISCOVERED these cookies in Venice, Italy, when I lived there and worked as an apprentice in a very fine pastry shop. These are traditional Venetian cookies made with cornmeal and raisins. The cornmeal gives them their crunchy texture and the raisins add sweetness. These are tasty on their own and are also excellent dunked in coffee or tea. **Makes about 28 cookies**

3/4 cup dark raisins

1/3 cup dark rum

Place the raisins in a small bowl and cover with the rum. Cover the bowl tightly with plastic wrap and let the raisins soak for at least 30 minutes.

Position the oven racks to the upper and lower thirds and preheat the oven to 375°F. Line two baking sheets with parchment paper or non-stick liners.

5 1/2 ounces (11 tablespoons) unsalted butter, softened

Place the butter in the bowl of an electric stand mixer or a large mixing bowl. Use the flat beater attachment or a hand-held mixer to

Essential Gear

- Two baking sheets
- Sifter
- Two parchment paper sheets or non-stick pan liners
- Electric stand mixer with flat beater attachment, or large mixing bowl and hand-held mixer
- Rubber spatula
- Two cooling racks

Keeping

Store the zalettini in an airtight container between layers of waxed paper at

½ cup granulated sugar	beat the butter until fluffy, about 2 minutes. Add the sugar, and cream together until light and fluffy, about 2 minutes.
2 extra-large eggs, at room temperature **½ teaspoon pure vanilla extract**	Using a fork, lightly beat together the eggs and vanilla in a small bowl. With the mixer speed on low, add the egg mixture to the butter mixture. The eggs will sit on top of the butter mixture, so stop after adding them and scrape down the sides and bottom of the bowl with a rubber spatula to help mix evenly. The mixture may look curdled as the eggs are added, but as you stop and scrape down the bowl, the mixture will smooth out.
1½ cups all-purpose flour **2 teaspoons baking powder** **1¼ cups fine yellow cornmeal** **½ teaspoon salt**	Over a large piece of waxed or parchment paper or a bowl, sift together the flour and baking powder. Add the cornmeal and salt and toss together lightly to blend.
	Add the dry ingredients to the butter mixture in 3 stages, blending well after each addition.
	Drain the raisins and pat dry. Add to the dough and blend briefly to distribute evenly.
	Pinch off 2 tablespoon-size pieces of the dough and roll in your hands into log shapes about 3 inches long, 1 inch wide, and ½ inch thick. Place the cookies on the lined baking sheets, leaving 2 inches of space between them so there is room for them to expand as they bake.
	Bake the cookies for 8 minutes. Switch the baking sheets and bake another 8 to 10 minutes, until they are light golden and set. Remove the baking sheets from the oven and cool on racks for 10 minutes. Remove the cookies from the baking sheets and cool completely on racks.

room temperature up to 1 week. To freeze up to 3 months, wrap the container tightly in several layers of plastic wrap and aluminum foil. Use a large piece of masking tape and an indelible marker to label and date the contents. If frozen, defrost overnight in the refrigerator and bring to room temperature before serving.

Making a Change
Replace the raisins with dried cherries or cranberries.

Adding Style
Add ½ cup finely chopped walnuts or pecans to the dough after adding the dry ingredients.

HAZELNUT SNOWFLAKE COOKIES, PAGE 336

MILK CHOCOLATE–CARAMEL PECAN TART, PAGE 422

DRIED CHERRY AND ALMOND SCONES, PAGE 279

DARK CHOCOLATE MADELEINES, PAGE 398

ALMOND BUTTER ROUNDS, PAGE 314, AND PECAN SHORTBREAD, PAGE 350

PASSION FRUIT AND MACADAMIA NUT LAYER CAKE, PAGE 254

ESPRESSO CHEESECAKE, PAGE 573

COCOA NIB AND WALNUT BISCOTTI, PAGE 485

PEANUT BUTTER AND CHOCOLATE TARTLETS, PAGE 345

MOCHA CREAM PUFFS, PAGE 583

LEMON TEA CAKE WITH PECANS, PAGE 158

COCONUT MACAROONS DIPPED IN DARK CHOCOLATE,
PAGE 231

DEVILISH CHOCOLATE LAYER CAKE
WITH CARAMEL-CHOCOLATE BUTTERCREAM,
PAGE 399

RAISIN AND WALNUT TART, PAGE 285

CHAMPAGNE GRAPE TARTLET, PAGE 211

PUMPKIN-NUT MUFFINS, PAGE 298

NECTARINE AND ALMOND GALETTE, PAGE 78

WHITE CHOCOLATE CUPCAKE WITH WHITE CHOCOLATE FROSTING, PAGE 452

RED, WHITE, AND BLUE BERRY PIZZA, PAGE 201

III.

NUTS AND

SEEDS

NUTS ARE ONE OF THE MOST TRADITIONAL INGREDIENTS in baking. Because I grew up eating baked goods with nuts, I enjoy eating just about anything with nuts. But if you only like certain types of nuts, that's not a problem because there are plenty to choose from. ✳ Almonds and walnuts are all-time favorites, but personally, I love hazelnuts. I developed my taste for hazelnuts when I worked in Europe many years ago, where I also discovered how well they go with so many other ingredients. Regardless of which nuts you prefer, they are all generally available year-round and are easy to find. ✳ Although they are not used as often as nuts, seeds are a popular ingredient in many baked goods too. They impart a wonderful taste as well as create a great texture. I am a big fan of poppy seeds. Seeds are easy to find year-round. ✳ You won't have any trouble selecting a recipe or two or more to make from this section. Just find the nut or seed that you like. If you're not familiar with a particular nut or seed, this is your chance to discover something new. Your satisfaction is guaranteed.

NUTS

ALMOST ALWAYS, if there's a choice between a dessert with nuts and one without, I'll go for the one with nuts. They have a wonderful flavor and there's that fabulous texture. And nuts are great as the decoration on desserts. Because I like all nuts, one of my problems is deciding which ones to use. But this is not really much of a problem because it is so easy to substitute one nut for another. This chapter contains a wide selection of recipes that will excite anyone who likes nuts.

In general, all nuts can be found throughout the year. But it has been my experience that hazelnuts and pecans are more plentiful in the fall and winter after their annual harvest. Nuts are available in packages in supermarkets and at some specialty produce markets. They are also sold in bins in natural and health food stores.

TIPS AND TECHNIQUES

Some nuts can be purchased in their shells; however, I recommend buying shelled nuts, which are normally fresh. When selecting nuts, inspect them closely to make sure they are clean and have good color and shape, and that there are no signs of mold. Also, if possible, smell the nuts to make sure there is no rancid or off scent. In addition, if you can taste the nuts before you buy them, you want to make sure they are crunchy. If nuts are soft, it is a sign that they have been stored improperly.

Nuts come in a variety of forms. They can always be purchased in their whole shape, but they often need to be used in another form, such as sliced or chopped. For example, almonds come sliced, slivered, and finely ground, known as almond meal or almond flour. Walnuts and pecans can commonly be found in halves and chopped, and hazelnuts and macadamia nuts are also sold chopped. Peanuts, pistachio nuts, and pine nuts are most commonly sold whole. And then there's another twist with almonds. They can be bought either blanched (skinned) or unblanched (natural). Also, I recommend buying peanuts, pistachio nuts, and macadamia nuts roasted, not raw. Many nuts are available salted, but I advise staying away from those for baking.

All nuts have a high content of natural oil, which is what gives them a lot of flavor. To prevent this natural oil from turning rancid, store nuts in an airtight container or tightly sealed plastic bag in the freezer, where they will last up to a year. Nuts that you will use soon after you buy them can be stored in a cool, dry place. Nuts can also be stored in the refrigerator, but will last half as long as those stored in the freezer because they may be exposed to moisture. Storing nuts in an airtight container or tightly sealed plastic bag will keep them from picking up the flavors of other foods around them.

Roasting enhances and deepens the flavor of nuts. Depending on your recipe, you may need to roast the following nuts: almonds, hazelnuts, pecans, pine nuts, and walnuts. To roast any nuts, place them in a single layer in a cake or baking pan and put them into a preheated 350°F oven; roast for 5 to 8 minutes, except hazelnuts, which should be roasted for 15 to 18 minutes. To remove most of their bitter outer skins, immediately place hazelnuts in a kitchen towel while warm, fold the towel around them, and rub them between your hands.

If you need whole blanched almonds and can't buy them that way, you can do this yourself. Plunge the nuts into a pot of boiling water for 1 minute. Use a skimmer or slotted spoon to remove them from the boiling water, and immediately put them into a bowl of cold water. Squeeze the almonds between your thumb and forefinger and they will pop out of their skins.

If your recipe calls for nuts to be finely ground, do this in a food processor fitted with the steel blade. To keep them from becoming nut butter when their oil is released during grinding, I add a tablespoon of sugar for each cup of nuts. Pulse them until they reach the desired texture. For hazelnuts and macadamia nuts, I add 2 tablespoons of sugar per cup of nuts because they have more natural oil than other nuts. To grind a small amount of nuts, use a mini food processor or a clean coffee grinder. Smaller batches of nuts can be chopped in the food processor, but this often results in an uneven texture. For just a few nuts, chop them with a sharp chef's knife on a cutting board, or use a mini food processor.

All nuts
have a high
content
of natural
oil . . .

Almond Butter Rounds

THESE ARE GREAT do-ahead refrigerator cookies because the dough is shaped into logs, which are chilled and then sliced when you're ready to bake the cookies. If you keep some of these cookie logs in the freezer, you'll always be prepared to make cookies when the mood strikes. **Makes 5 dozen cookies**

Essential Gear
- Electric stand mixer with flat beater attachment, or large mixing bowl and hand-held mixer
- Rubber spatula
- Two baking sheets
- Four parchment paper sheets or non-stick liners
- Two cooling racks

Keeping
Store the cookies in an airtight plastic container between layers of waxed paper at room temperature up to 4 days. To freeze up to 3 months, wrap the container tightly in several layers of plastic wrap and aluminum foil. Use a large piece of masking tape and an indelible marker to label and date the contents. If frozen, defrost overnight in the refrigerator and bring to room temperature before shaping.

To freeze the cookie dough logs up to 6 months, wrap them in several layers of plastic wrap and place in a freezer bag. Use masking tape and an indelible marker to label and date the dough logs. Let the logs stand at room temperature for about 20 minutes before slicing, because if they are too firm when cut, they may splinter.

4 ounces (8 tablespoons, 1 stick) unsalted butter, softened	Place the butter in the bowl of an electric stand mixer or in a large mixing bowl. Use the flat beater attachment or a hand-held mixer to beat the butter on medium speed until it's fluffy, about 2 minutes.
½ cup granulated sugar	Add the sugar, and cream together completely. Stop occasionally and scrape down the sides and bottom of the bowl with a rubber spatula.
1 cup finely ground almonds	Add the almonds to the butter mixture and blend together thoroughly. Stop and scrape down the sides and bottom of the bowl with a rubber spatula.
1 extra-large egg, at room temperature 2 teaspoons pure vanilla extract	Lightly beat the egg and vanilla together in a small bowl, then add to the butter mixture and beat together thoroughly.
2 cups all-purpose flour ¼ teaspoon salt	Mix the flour and salt together, then add in 3 stages to the butter mixture, blending well after each addition. Stop and scrape down the sides and bottom of the bowl between each addition to ensure even mixing.
	Divide the dough in half and place each part on a large piece of waxed paper. Use the waxed paper to shape and roll the dough into a log about 1½ inches wide and 8 to 10 inches long. Wrap the rolls tightly in the waxed paper and then in plastic wrap. Chill the logs 3 to 4 hours in the refrigerator or 1 to 2 hours in the freezer, until firm.
	Adjust the oven racks to the upper and lower thirds and preheat the oven to 350°F. Line the baking sheets with parchment paper sheets or non-stick liners.
	Unwrap one cookie log and place it on a cutting board. Use a sharp knife to cut the log into ½-inch-thick slices. Cut straight down and roll the cylinder a quarter turn after every 6 slices so it will keep its round shape. If the dough becomes soft while you're working with it, rewrap it, and chill for another 10 to 15 minutes, then continue

slicing. Place the slices on the baking sheets, leaving 1 inch of space between them.

Bake the cookies for 7 minutes, then switch the baking sheets. Bake another 6 to 7 minutes, until cookies are set and light golden. Remove the baking sheets from the oven and cool the cookies on the baking sheets on racks. Repeat as desired with any remaining cookie logs.

Making a Change
Replace the almonds with walnuts, hazelnuts, or pecans.

Financiers

FINANCIERS (pronounced fee-*nance*-cee-airs) are classic French cakes made with ground almonds and browned butter, which adds a nutty flavor. Financiers are made either as individual cakes or in a large size as the cake base for a more elaborate dessert. These individual cakes are very easy to make and are perfect for a casual gathering, for afternoon tea, or to pack in a lunch box. **Makes twelve 3-inch cakes**

Center a rack in the oven and preheat it to 350°F. Line the cavities of the muffin pan with paper muffin cups.

½ cup sliced almonds	Place the almonds in a cake or pie pan and toast in the oven for 5 minutes, until very light golden. Remove the pan from the oven and cool on a rack.
6 ounces (12 tablespoons, 1½ sticks) unsalted butter 1 tablespoon pure vanilla extract or vanilla paste	Cut the butter into small pieces and place in the saucepan with the vanilla. Cook over medium heat until the butter is foamy and light brown. Pour the mixture into a bowl and cool to lukewarm.
4 extra-large egg whites, at room temperature ½ teaspoon cream of tartar	Place the egg whites and cream of tartar in the bowl of an electric stand mixer or a large mixing bowl. Use the wire whip attachment or a hand-held mixer and whip on high speed until the egg whites hold soft peaks.
1⅓ cups confectioners' sugar, sifted	Slowly add the confectioners' sugar to the egg whites and continue whipping until they hold firm, glossy peaks.
1 cup all-purpose flour	Fold the flour into the egg whites in 3 stages, blending thoroughly.
¾ cup finely ground almonds	Fold the finely ground almonds into the flour mixture in 3 stages, blending thoroughly.

Essential Gear
- 12-cavity 3-inch muffin pan
- 3-inch pleated paper muffin cups
- Cake pan
- 1-quart saucepan
- Electric stand mixer with wire whip attachment, or large mixing bowl and hand-held mixer
- Rubber spatula
- Cooling rack

Keeping
Store the financiers in an airtight plastic container between layers of waxed paper at room temperature up to 3 days. To freeze up to 2 months, wrap the container tightly in several layers of plastic wrap and aluminum foil. Use a large piece of masking tape and an indelible marker to label and date the contents. If frozen, defrost overnight in the refrigerator and bring to room temperature before serving.

Making a Change
Replace the ground almonds with finely ground walnuts,

Fold the cooled browned butter mixture into the flour mixture in 3 stages, blending thoroughly.

Use a spoon to divide the batter evenly among the 12 muffin cups, filling each about ⅔ full.

½ cup sliced almonds, lightly toasted

Sprinkle the tops of the financiers with the sliced almonds.

Bake the financiers 12 to 15 minutes, until they are light golden brown and a tester inserted in the center comes out clean. Remove the pan from the oven and cool on a rack. Serve at room temperature.

pecans, or toasted hazelnuts. Replace the sliced almonds with finely chopped walnuts, pecans, or toasted, ground hazelnuts.

Linzertorte

L INZERTORTE is a classic Austrian pastry that comes from the town of Linz, not far from Vienna. Although this pastry is called a torte, which usually means a cake in German, it's really a tart with a lattice topping. Whatever the name, this is a scrumptious dessert made with buttery ground almond pastry dough that's filled with raspberry or apricot preserves. My husband always asks me to make a Linzertorte for his birthday cake. **Makes one 9½-inch round tart, 12 servings**

Essential Gear
- Food processor
- Rolling pin
- 9½-inch round, fluted-edge tart pan with removable bottom
- Long-blade offset spatula
- Baking sheet or jelly-roll pan
- Fluted-edge pastry cutting wheel
- Cooling rack

Keeping
Store the tart, tightly wrapped in aluminum foil, at room temperature up to 3 days.

PASTRY DOUGH

1½ cups finely ground almonds
1 cup all-purpose flour
½ cup granulated sugar
1½ teaspoons ground cinnamon
¼ teaspoon ground cloves

In the work bowl of a food processor fitted with the steel blade, combine the almonds, flour, sugar, cinnamon, and cloves. Pulse briefly to blend.

8 ounces (16 tablespoons, 2 sticks) unsalted butter, chilled

Cut the butter into small pieces and add to the flour mixture. Pulse until the butter is cut into very tiny pieces, about 30 seconds. The texture will be sandy with very tiny lumps throughout.

2 extra-large egg yolks, at room temperature

In a small bowl, beat the egg yolks lightly with a fork. With the food processor running, pour the egg yolks through the feed tube. Process the dough until the mixture wraps itself around the blade, about 1 minute.

Streamlining
The pastry dough can be made up to 3 days in advance. To freeze up to 3 months, place the wrapped pastry dough in a freezer bag. Use masking tape and an indelible marker to label

Turn the pastry dough onto a large piece of plastic wrap. Shape into a flat disk and wrap well. Chill in the refrigerator until firm before using, at least 2 hours. Chilling the dough relaxes the gluten in the flour so it won't be too elastic and will roll out easily. It also firms up the butter in the dough so it will need less flour when rolled out. If the dough is too firm, it will splinter and break when rolled out. Let it stand at room temperature for 10 to 15 minutes before rolling to become more pliable.

Center a rack in the oven and preheat it to 375°F.

Cut off ⅓ of the pastry dough and keep it chilled while working with the other portion. On a smooth, flat surface, roll out the pastry dough between sheets of lightly floured waxed or parchment paper to a large circle 11 to 12 inches in diameter. To tell if the dough will fit the tart pan, hold the pan above the dough. If there are 2 or 3 inches of dough that protrude beyond the sides of the pan, it will fit.

Carefully peel the paper off the top of the dough. Brush excess flour off the dough, then loosely roll the pastry dough around the rolling pin without the bottom piece of paper. Place the tart pan directly underneath the rolling pin and carefully unroll the pastry dough into the tart pan.

Gently lift up the sides and ease the pastry dough into the bottom and sides of the tart pan. Trim off any excess pastry dough at the top of the pan. Transfer the tart pan to a baking sheet.

FILLING

1¼ cups red raspberry preserves

Spread the preserves evenly in the tart shell.

On a smooth, flat surface, roll out the remaining pastry dough between sheets of lightly floured waxed or parchment paper to a large circle about 12 inches in diameter. Carefully peel the paper off the top of the dough. Use the pastry wheel to cut ½-inch-wide strips of the dough. Carefully peel the strips off the other piece of paper. Use a long-blade offset spatula to wedge underneath each strip of pastry dough and gently transfer it to the top of the linzertorte. Make a lattice by laying the strips in a woven pattern, first in one direction, then in the other direction, alternating as they are placed (see page 41).

Roll any remaining dough into a long rope about ¼ inch thick. Place this around the top outer edge where the ends of the lattice strips meet the edge of the tart. Use the tines of a fork to press the rope into the edges of the tart and make a pressed design. Chill the linzertorte for 15 minutes before baking.

and date the package. If frozen, defrost it in the refrigerator before using.

Troubleshooting
Once the pastry dough is unrolled into the tart pan, don't push it down forcefully. This will stretch the dough, which will shrink as it bakes.

Making a Change
Use apricot preserves in place of the raspberry preserves.

Use toasted hazelnuts in place of the almonds in the pastry dough.

Center an oven rack and preheat it to 375°F.

Bake for 30 minutes, until the pastry is set and the filling is bubbling. Remove the pan from the oven and transfer the tart pan to a rack to cool completely.

GARNISH

1 tablespoon confectioners' sugar

Remove the sides of the tart pan and lightly dust the top of the linzertorte with confectioners' sugar. Serve wedges of tart at room temperature.

Pithiviers

PITHIVIERS IS a classic round, flat cake made from two circles of puff pastry that enclose a filling of frangipane (almond) cream. The edges of the cake are scalloped and a sunburst or rosette pattern is etched on top. This cake is a specialty of the town of Pithiviers in the Orléans region in the Loire Valley of France. Puff pastry is renowned for its flaky layers that rise when baked. Making puff pastry can seem overwhelming, especially if you've never made it before. I encourage you to try my method for making puff pastry that is quick and easy and puffs up as well as the classic method. But don't let making your own puff pastry stand in the way of making this delicious dessert. You can use store-bought puff pastry. **Makes one 10-inch round cake, 12 to 14 servings**

PUFF PASTRY DOUGH

1½ pounds Quick Puff Pastry (see page 196) or store-bought puff pastry, thawed in the refrigerator

Divide the puff pastry into two equal pieces. Roll out one piece of the pastry dough between sheets of lightly floured waxed or parchment paper on a smooth, flat work surface to a large circle about 13 inches in diameter. Turn the dough to your right frequently as you roll it. This makes it easier to roll the dough and ensures that it rolls evenly. Several times, lift off the paper and lightly flour the dough, if needed. Turn the dough package over and lift off the other piece of paper. If the dough becomes too soft as you are working with it, transfer it to a jelly-roll pan and chill for 30 minutes in the refrigerator to firm the butter, then roll again.

Transfer the pastry circle to a parchment paper–lined baking sheet.

Essential Gear

- Rolling pin
- Baking sheet
- Parchment paper
- Food processor
- Rubber spatula
- 1-inch natural-bristle pastry brush
- Small knife
- Cooling rack

Keeping

Although the cake is best eaten the day it's made, it can last up to 2 days. Store it loosely covered with waxed paper, then tightly wrapped with aluminum foil at room temperature.

Streamlining

The puff pastry dough can be made in advance and kept in the refrigerator, tightly wrapped in a double layer of plastic wrap, up to 3 days. To freeze up to 3 months, wrap the dough

Roll out the second half of the dough to another large circle about 11 inches in diameter. Chill in the refrigerator while preparing the frangipane.

1 RECIPE FRANGIPANE FILLING

(see Apricot Frangipane Tart, page 54)

ASSEMBLY

Place the frangipane cream in the center of the 13-inch circle of puff pastry. Mound it slightly and leave a 2-inch border around the filling.

Use a damp pastry brush to brush around the edges of the circle.

Position the 11-inch circle over the filling, draping it over the center. Line up the edges of the puff pastry circles and press them together to seal, then crimp the outer edges (see page 40).

Use a small knife or toothpick to pierce a tiny hole in the top center of the pastry. Score the pastry, beginning at the top hole and working to the outside edges, in curved lines, forming a sunburst design. Do not cut all the way through the pastry.

EGG WASH

1 extra-large egg yolk, at room temperature
1 teaspoon water

Use a fork to lightly beat together the egg yolk and water in a small bowl.

Brush the entire top of the pastry dough with half of the egg wash. Be careful that the egg wash doesn't run down the sides and underneath the cake. If it does, wipe it up because it can cause the bottom of the cake to burn.

Chill the pastry in the refrigerator for 15 minutes.

Adjust an oven rack to the lower third and preheat the oven to 450°F.

Brush the Pithiviers with the remaining half of the egg wash and place the baking pan in the oven. Reduce the oven temperature to 400°F and bake for 15 minutes. Then reduce the oven temperature to 350°F and bake for 25 to 30 minutes longer, until puffed and golden brown.

Transfer the baking sheet to a rack to cool for 15 minutes. Cut the cake into wedges and serve warm.

snugly in several layers of plastic wrap and place it in a freezer bag. Use a large piece of masking tape and an indelible marker to label and date the contents. If frozen, defrost overnight in the refrigerator before using.

The frangipane filling can be made up to 4 days before using. Store it in a tightly covered container in the refrigerator.

Toasted Almond Scones

TOASTED ALMONDS give these scones a distinctive flavor and texture. Scones are classic English teatime treats that have become very popular in the U.S. They are not very sweet, which makes them great to serve for breakfast, afternoon tea, and snacks. These are best served warm and can be reheated in a 350°F oven for 10 to 15 minutes. **Makes twelve 3-inch scones**

Adjust the oven racks to the upper and lower thirds and preheat the oven to 350°F. Line the baking sheets with parchment paper or non-stick liners.

½ cup sliced almonds

Place the sliced almonds in a cake or pie pan and toast in the oven for 5 to 8 minutes, until light golden brown. Remove the pan from the oven and cool on a rack. Reserve 1 tablespoon of the almonds for the garnish. Raise the oven temperature to 425°F.

2½ cups all-purpose flour
3 tablespoons granulated sugar
1 tablespoon plus 1 teaspoon baking powder
¼ teaspoon salt

In the work bowl of a food processor fitted with the steel blade, combine the remaining almonds, flour, sugar, baking powder, and salt. Pulse a few times to blend and to chop the almonds.

4 ounces (8 tablespoons, 1 stick) unsalted butter, chilled

Cut the butter into small pieces and add to the flour mixture. Pulse until the butter is cut into very tiny pieces, about 30 seconds. The texture should be sandy with very tiny lumps throughout.

⅔ cup heavy whipping cream
2 extra-large eggs, at room temperature
Finely grated zest of 1 large lemon

Using a fork, lightly beat the cream and eggs together in a liquid measuring cup, then add the lemon zest. With the food processor running, pour this mixture through the feed tube and process until the dough wraps itself around the blade, about 30 seconds.

Turn the dough out onto a large piece of waxed or parchment paper dusted with flour. and divide it in two. Dust your hands with flour and shape each piece of dough into a circle about 1 inch thick and 6 inches in diameter. Using a chef's knife dipped in flour, cut each circle in half and each half into 3 equal triangles.

Transfer the scones to the lined baking sheets, leaving at least 1 inch of space between them so they have room to expand as they bake.

Essential Gear
- Two baking sheets
- Two parchment paper sheets or non-stick liners
- Cake pan
- Food processor
- Chef's knife
- 1-inch natural-bristle pastry brush
- Two cooling racks
- Microplane grater or citrus zester

Keeping
Store the scones in an airtight plastic container between layers of waxed paper at room temperature up to 4 days. To freeze up to 4 months, wrap the container tightly in several layers of plastic wrap and aluminum foil. Use a large piece of masking tape and an indelible marker to label and date the contents. If frozen, defrost overnight in the refrigerator and bring to room temperature before serving.

Streamlining
The unbaked scones can be frozen for up to 3 months, wrapped as above. It's not necessary to defrost the scones, but bake them 5 to 6 minutes longer.

Making a Change
Replace the toasted almonds with walnuts or pecans.

Repeat with the other half of the dough. Brush any excess flour off the scones.

GARNISH

1 tablespoon heavy whipping cream

Brush the top of each scone with cream, taking care that it doesn't run down the sides and under the scones. If it does, wipe it up because it can cause the bottom of the scones to burn.

2 tablespoons granulated sugar

Lightly sprinkle the top of each scone with sugar. Then sprinkle the remaining tablespoon of toasted almonds evenly over the tops of the scones.

Bake the scones for 8 minutes, then switch the baking sheets and bake another 5 to 7 minutes, until they are light golden.

Remove the baking sheets from the oven and cool completely on racks.

Baklava

BAKLAVA is a classic pastry that is found throughout the Middle East. Orange blossom water, found in many cookware shops, some liquor stores, and stores that sell Middle Eastern foods, adds its distinctively subtle floral flavor to the nutty filling enclosed between layers of flaky, crisp filo dough and to the sugar syrup poured over the pastry after it is baked. To keep the filo pastry crisp and prevent the baklava from becoming soggy, it's important to pour the hot syrup over the pastry when it is completely cool. Baklava is made in many variations, some using only one type of nut and others using a combination of nuts. I like to use a blend of almonds, pistachio nuts, and walnuts. Filo pastry dough is available frozen in packages in many supermarkets and specialty food shops. To prevent the sheets of filo dough from sticking together, thaw it overnight in the refrigerator, then let it stand at room temperature for an hour or two before using. Filo dough dries out very quickly when exposed to air. To prevent this from happening while you work with it, keep the dough covered with a damp paper towel or with a piece of plastic wrap covered with a damp towel. **Makes about 30 pieces**

Essential Gear

- Food processor
- Large mixing bowl
- Rubber spatula
- 13 × 9-inch baking pan
- 1-inch natural-bristle pastry brush
- Chef's knife
- Cooling rack
- 1-quart heavy-bottomed saucepan
- Small offset spatula

Keeping

Store the baklava, lightly covered with waxed paper and then tightly wrapped with aluminum foil, at room temperature up to 5 days.

Streamlining

The baklava can be assembled and kept tightly covered

BAKLAVA

Center a rack in oven and preheat it to 375°F.

1½ cups whole unblanched almonds 1½ cups walnuts 1 cup unsalted shelled pistachios, toasted	In the work bowl of a food processor fitted with the steel blade, combine the almonds, walnuts, and pistachios. Pulse until the nuts are coarsely chopped, about 1 minute. Transfer the nuts to a large bowl.
¼ cup granulated sugar 1 tablespoon orange blossom water 1 teaspoon ground cinnamon ⅛ teaspoon ground cloves	Add the sugar, orange blossom water, cinnamon, and cloves to the nuts and stir to combine thoroughly.
½ pound thawed frozen filo dough	Unroll the filo dough. If the sheets are larger than 13 × 9 inches, trim them to make that size. Cover the stack of filo dough sheets with a damp paper towel or a large piece of plastic wrap covered with a damp towel.
4 ounces (8 tablespoons, 1 stick) unsalted butter, melted	Use the pastry brush to brush the bottom of the baking pan with butter, then place one sheet of filo dough in the bottom of the baking pan. Brush lightly with butter. Don't use too much butter, though, or the pastry will become greasy and heavy. When you take a sheet of filo dough from the stack, be sure to cover the rest of the dough so it doesn't dry out and become stiff and crumbly.

Repeat with 7 more layers of filo dough.

Evenly spread the nut mixture over the layers of filo dough in the baking pan. Cover the nut filling with 8 more sheets of filo dough, brushing each lightly with butter.

If there is any filo dough left over, reroll and rewrap it tightly in plastic wrap. Refrigerate the filo dough, but use it within a few days. Don't freeze it again because this will cause it to become brittle and it will crack when it is defrosted again.

Cover the pan of baklava tightly with plastic wrap and chill in the freezer for 20 minutes. This makes it very easy to cut.

Use a sharp knife to score the pastry into criss-cross diagonal lines about 1½ inches wide, to create diamond shapes. Trim off any excess filo dough at the edges.

Or score the pastry into equal-sized large squares, then score each square in half diagonally to form triangles.

with a double layer of plastic wrap in the refrigerator up to 1 day before baking. To freeze up to 3 months, wrap the baking pan tightly in several layers of plastic wrap and aluminum foil. Use a large piece of masking tape and an indelible marker to label and date the contents. You can bake the frozen baklava, allowing about 5 extra minutes for it to bake.

Making a Change
Use all almonds or all walnuts in place of the mixed nuts.

Replace the cinnamon and cloves with 1¼ teaspoons ground cardamom.

Bake the baklava for 20 minutes. Reduce the oven temperature to 325°F and bake another 25 to 30 minutes, until light golden brown and crisp.

Remove the pan from the oven and cool completely on a rack.

Use a sharp knife to cut through the previously scored lines.

SUGAR SYRUP

1½ cups granulated sugar
¾ cup water

Place the sugar and water in the saucepan and bring to a boil over medium-high heat. Boil for 8 minutes, until the syrup begins to thicken.

2 teaspoons freshly squeezed lemon juice
2 tablespoons orange blossom water

Add the lemon juice and boil another 2 to 3 minutes. Remove from the heat and stir in the orange blossom water.

Immediately pour the hot sugar syrup evenly over the top of the cooled baklava. Let the baklava absorb the hot syrup for several minutes. Use a small offset spatula to remove the pieces from the baking pan and place on a serving tray. Serve warm or at room temperature.

Caramelized Walnut Tart

THIS IS A CLASSIC tart with both bottom and top pastry crusts, from the Engadine region of Switzerland, which I learned to make when I worked in Lausanne. The Engadine is a mountainous region and this tart is a staple that's included in the packs of many hikers because it stays moist for several days, holds its shape, and is full of energy. You don't have to be a hiker to enjoy it, though. I usually make this tart as one of the desserts for Thanksgiving dinner and it's always much appreciated. **Makes one 9½-inch round tart, 12 to 14 servings**

Essential Gear
- Food processor
- Rolling pin
- 9½-inch round, fluted-edge tart pan with removable bottom
- Baking sheet
- 3-quart heavy-bottomed saucepan
- Small saucepan
- 1-inch natural-bristle pastry brush
- Heat-resistant spatula or wooden spoon
- Small bowl
- Cooling rack

PASTRY DOUGH

2½ cups all-purpose flour
⅓ cup granulated sugar
⅛ teaspoon salt

In the work bowl of a food processor fitted with the steel blade, combine the flour, sugar, and salt. Pulse briefly to blend.

8 ounces (16 tablespoons, 2 sticks) unsalted butter, chilled	Cut the butter into small pieces and add. Pulse until the butter is cut into very tiny pieces, about 30 seconds. The texture should be sandy with very tiny lumps throughout.
1 extra-large egg, at room temperature **1 teaspoon pure vanilla extract**	In a small bowl, whisk the egg and vanilla together. With the food processor running, pour this mixture through the feed tube. Process until the dough wraps itself around the blade, 30 seconds to 1 minute.

Divide the pastry dough in half. Place each piece on a large piece of plastic wrap. Shape into flat disks and wrap tightly in a double layer of plastic wrap. Chill in the refrigerator until firm before using, about 2 hours. Chilling the dough relaxes the gluten in the flour so it won't be too elastic and will roll out easily. It also firms up the butter in the dough so it will need less flour when rolled out. If the dough is too firm it will splinter and break when rolled out. Let it stand at room temperature for 10 to 15 minutes before rolling to become more pliable.

Center a rack in the oven and preheat it to 425°F.

On a smooth, flat surface, roll out one piece of the pastry dough between sheets of lightly floured waxed or parchment paper to a large circle about 11 inches in diameter. Carefully peel the paper off the top of the dough. Brush excess flour off the dough, then loosely roll the pastry dough around the rolling pin without the bottom piece of paper. Place the tart pan directly underneath the rolling pin and carefully unroll the pastry dough onto it.

Gently lift up the sides and ease the pastry dough into the bottom and sides of the tart pan, pushing it lightly into the fluted edges. Trim off the excess pastry dough at the top of the pan by running the rolling pin over the top. Or use your fingers to press against the top of the pan to remove the excess pastry dough. Transfer the tart pan to a baking sheet and chill for at least 15 minutes to set.

CARAMELIZED WALNUT FILLING

1¼ cups granulated sugar **¼ cup water**	Place the sugar and water in the saucepan. Cook over high heat, without stirring, until the mixture begins to boil. Place a wet pastry brush at the point where the sugar syrup meets the sides of the pan and sweep it around completely. Do this two times. This prevents the sugar from crystallizing by brushing any stray crystals back into the mixture. Cook the mixture over high heat, without stirring, until it turns amber colored, about 10 minutes.

Keeping

The tart can last up to 5 days tightly wrapped with aluminum foil at room temperature.

Streamlining

The pastry dough can be made in advance and kept in the refrigerator, tightly wrapped in a double layer of plastic wrap, up to 4 days. To freeze up to 3 months, wrap the dough snugly in several layers of plastic wrap and place it in a freezer bag. Use a large piece of masking tape and an indelible marker to label and date the contents. If frozen, defrost overnight in the refrigerator before using. The tart dough can also be fitted into the tart pan and kept tightly covered in the refrigerator or frozen, wrapped and labeled as above.

Making a Change

Replace the walnuts with pecans or almonds.

Replace half of the walnuts with almonds, cashews, or pecans.

²/₃ **cup heavy whipping cream**	At the same time, heat the cream in a small saucepan until it begins to boil.
	Carefully pour the hot cream into the caramel mixture. Stir together using a long-handled wooden spoon or heat-resistant spatula. Be very careful because it will bubble and splatter. Stir for 1 to 2 minutes to dissolve any lumps.
1 tablespoon honey	Stir the honey into the caramel mixture.
2 cups walnuts, finely chopped	Add the walnuts to the caramel mixture and stir to coat them completely.
2 teaspoons unsalted butter, softened	Use your fingertips or a paper towel to coat the wooden spoon or spatula with butter to keep the mixture from sticking to it, then transfer the mixture quickly to the tart shell and spread it out evenly.
	On a smooth, flat surface, roll out the remaining piece of pastry dough between sheets of lightly floured waxed or parchment paper to a large circle about 9½ inches in diameter. Carefully peel the paper off the top of the dough.
	Brush the top edge of the bottom pastry shell lightly with water. Brush excess flour off the dough, then loosely roll the pastry dough around the rolling pin without the bottom piece of paper. Place the tart pan directly underneath the rolling pin and carefully unroll the top piece of pastry dough onto it. Press the pastry dough down at the edges so it will stick to the sides of the bottom dough and then remove any excess pastry dough. Use the tines of a fork to press around the outer edges of the dough to form a finished edge and help the bottom and top doughs stick together.
	Use a fork to pierce the top of the pastry dough in several places to create steam holes and make a design.
1 extra-large egg, at room temperature	Lightly beat the egg in a small bowl with a fork. Brush the top of the tart two times with the beaten egg.
	Place the tart pan on a baking sheet and bake for 25 minutes, until the pastry dough is golden. Remove the baking pan from the oven and cool the tart on a rack.
	Remove the sides of the tart pan (see page 42) before serving. Cut the tart into slices and serve at room temperature.

Greek Butter Cookies

T HESE RICH, buttery cookies are found in Greece as part of almost every celebration. Traditionally they are made with finely ground walnuts. Often, rosewater is sprinkled on the cookies while they are warm, adding its unique flavor. **Makes 6 dozen cookies**

Adjust the oven racks to the upper and lower thirds and preheat the oven to 350°F.

Line the baking sheets with parchment paper sheets or non-stick liners.

8 ounces (16 tablespoons, 2 sticks) unsalted butter softened	Place the butter in the bowl of an electric stand mixer or in a large mixing bowl. Use the flat beater attachment or a hand-held mixer to beat the butter on medium speed until it's fluffy, about 2 minutes.
½ cup confectioners' sugar, sifted	Add the confectioners' sugar and cream together well. Stop occasionally and scrape down the sides and bottom of the bowl with a rubber spatula.
1 extra-large egg yolk, at room temperature **1 tablespoon brandy or cognac** **2 teaspoons pure vanilla extract**	Add the egg yolk, brandy or cognac, and vanilla to the butter mixture. The egg yolk will sit on top of the butter mixture, so stop and scrape down the sides and bottom of the bowl with a rubber spatula to encourage even mixing. The mixture may look curdled as the egg yolk is added, but as you stop and scrape down the bowl, the mixture will smooth out.
2 cups all-purpose flour **1 teaspoon baking powder** **1¼ teaspoons ground cloves**	Over a large piece of waxed or parchment paper or a bowl, sift together the flour and baking powder. Add the cloves and toss to blend well. Add the flour to the butter mixture in 4 stages, mixing thoroughly after each addition. Stop occasionally and scrape down the sides and bottom of the bowl with a rubber spatula.
1 cup walnuts, finely ground	Add the walnuts to the dough mixture and stir to distribute evenly.
	Pinch off 2-tablespoon-size pieces of cookie dough and roll them into 1-inch balls. Place the balls on the lined baking sheets, leaving at least 1 inch of space between them so there is room for them to expand as they bake.
	Tightly cover one baking sheet with plastic wrap and chill while baking the other two baking sheets.

Essential Gear
- Three baking sheets
- Three parchment paper sheets or non-stick pan liners
- Food processor
- Electric stand mixer with flat beater attachment, or large mixing bowl and hand-held mixer
- Rubber spatula
- Sifter
- Two cooling racks

Keeping
Store the cookies coated in confectioners' sugar in an airtight container at room temperature up to 5 days. To freeze up to 3 months, wrap the container tightly in several layers of plastic wrap and aluminum foil. Use a large piece of masking tape and an indelible marker to label and date the contents. If frozen, defrost overnight in the refrigerator and bring to room temperature before serving.

Streamlining
The cookie dough can be made and kept tightly covered with a double layer of plastic wrap in the refrigerator up to 3 days before baking.

Making a Change
Replace the ground walnuts with finely ground maca-

Bake the cookies for 6 minutes. Switch the baking sheets and bake another 5 to 6 minutes, until the cookies are set and golden.

damia nuts, hazelnuts, or pecans.

3 to 4 tablespoons rosewater (optional)

Remove the baking sheets from the oven and place on cooling racks. Sprinkle the hot cookies with rosewater, if using. Let the cookies cool until they are warm.

3 to 4 cups confectioners' sugar, sifted

Place half of the confectioners' sugar on a baking sheet. Place the cookies on the confectioners' sugar and sift more confectioners' sugar on top of them. Let the cookies cool completely, then roll them in the confectioners' sugar.

Walnut Crescents

THESE TASTY COOKIES are very easy to make and even easier to eat. The dough needs to be made at least three hours in advance so it has time to chill, which makes it great to do ahead. Then the dough is shaped by hand into crescents. These are excellent for getting family and friends involved in shaping them, making it a fun project for everyone involved. **Makes 3½ dozen cookies**

Essential Gear

- Electric stand mixer with flat beater attachment, or large mixing bowl and hand-held mixer
- Rubber spatula
- Food processor
- Two to four baking sheets
- Four parchment paper sheets or non-stick liners
- Two cooling racks

Keeping

Store the cookies in an airtight plastic container between layers of waxed paper at room temperature up to 4 days. To freeze up to 3 months, wrap the container tightly in several layers of plastic wrap and aluminum foil. Use a large piece of masking tape and an indelible marker to label and date the contents. If frozen, defrost overnight in the refrigerator and bring to room temperature before serving.

6 ounces (12 tablespoons, 1½ sticks) unsalted butter, softened

Place the butter in the bowl of an electric stand mixer or in a large mixing bowl. Use the flat beater attachment or hand-held mixer to beat the butter on medium speed until it's fluffy, about 2 minutes.

⅓ cup light corn syrup
1 teaspoon pure vanilla extract

Add the corn syrup and vanilla to the butter, and cream together completely. Stop occasionally and scrape down the sides and bottom of the bowl with a rubber spatula.

1 cup walnuts
2 cups all-purpose flour

In the work bowl of a food processor fitted with the steel blade, combine the walnuts and 3 tablespoons of the flour. Pulse until the walnuts are finely ground.

¼ teaspoon freshly grated nutmeg
⅛ teaspoon salt

Transfer the mixture to a bowl and add the remaining flour, the nutmeg, and salt. Toss to blend.

Add the dry ingredients to the butter mixture in 4 stages, mixing well after each addition. Stop occasionally and scrape down the sides and bottom of the bowl with a rubber spatula.

Turn the dough out onto a large piece of plastic wrap. Shape the mixture into a disk, wrap tightly in plastic wrap, and chill at least 3 hours or overnight.

Adjust the oven racks to the upper and lower thirds and preheat the oven to 350°F.

Line the baking sheets with parchment paper or non-stick liners.

Take walnut-sized pieces of the dough and roll each into a ball, then shape each one into a rope about 3 inches long by rolling on a flat surface. Bend the rope into a crescent shape and place on a baking sheet. Leave 2 inches of space between the crescents. Repeat with the remaining dough.

Bake the cookies for 7 minutes, then switch the baking sheets. Bake another 6 to 8 minutes, until set and very pale golden. Remove the baking sheets from the oven and cool the cookies completely on the baking sheets on racks.

Confectioners' sugar

When the cookies are cool, dust them heavily with confectioners' sugar.

To freeze the cookie dough up to 6 months, wrap it in several layers of plastic wrap and place in a freezer bag. Use masking tape and an indelible marker to label and date the dough. Let the dough stand at room temperature for about 20 minutes before slicing, because if it is too firm when shaped, it may splinter.

Making a Change

Replace the walnuts with finely ground almonds, hazelnuts, or pecans.

Walnut-Oatmeal Crisps

THESE ARE CLASSIC refrigerator cookies. The dough is shaped into logs that are chilled, then sliced right before baking. You can keep the logs in the refrigerator for four days or freeze them up to six months. This makes it very easy to have freshly baked cookies when the kids come home from school or when an unexpected visitor drops by, because you can take the rolls from the freezer, warm them up briefly, slice, and bake. **Makes 4¹/₂ dozen cookies**

8 ounces (16 tablespoons, 2 sticks) unsalted butter, softened

Place the butter in the bowl of an electric stand mixer or in a large bowl. Use the flat beater attachment or hand-held mixer to beat the butter on medium speed until it's fluffy, about 2 minutes.

1 cup granulated sugar

Add the sugar to the butter, and cream together completely. Stop occasionally and scrape down the sides and bottom of the bowl with a rubber spatula.

2 teaspoons pure vanilla extract

Add the vanilla to the butter mixture and blend thoroughly.

Essential Gear

- Electric stand mixer with flat beater attachment, or large mixing bowl and hand-held mixer
- Rubber spatula
- Waxed paper
- Two baking sheets
- Four parchment paper sheets or non-stick liners
- Sharp knife
- Two cooling racks

Keeping

Store the cookies in an airtight plastic container between layers of waxed paper at room temperature up to 4 days. To freeze up to 3 months, wrap the con-

2 cups rolled oats (not quick-cooking) **1 cup all-purpose flour** **1 teaspoon baking soda**	In a large bowl, combine the oats, flour, and baking soda. Toss together to blend. Add the dry ingredients in 3 stages to the butter mixture, blending completely after each addition. Stop occasionally and scrape down the sides and bottom of the bowl with a rubber spatula to ensure even mixing.
1 cup finely chopped walnuts	Add the walnuts and stir to distribute evenly.

Divide the dough in half and place each part on a large piece of waxed paper. Use the waxed paper to shape and roll the dough into a log about 1½ inches wide and 8 to 10 inches long. Wrap the logs tightly in the waxed paper and then in plastic wrap. Chill the logs 3 to 4 hours in the refrigerator or 2 hours in the freezer, until firm

Adjust the oven racks to the upper and lower thirds and preheat the oven to 350°F. Line the baking sheets with parchment paper sheets or non-stick liners.

Unwrap one cookie log and place it on a cutting board. Use a sharp knife to slice the roll into ½-inch-thick slices. Cut straight down and roll the cylinder a quarter turn after every 6 slices so it will keep its round shape. If the dough becomes soft while you work with it, rewrap it, and chill for another 10 to 15 minutes, then continue slicing. Place the slices on the baking sheets, leaving 1 inch of space between them.

Bake the cookies for 7 minutes, then switch the baking sheets. Bake another 6 to 7 minutes, until set and light golden. Remove the baking sheets from the oven and cool the cookies completely on the baking sheets on racks. Repeat as desired with any remaining cookie logs.

tainer tightly in several layers of plastic wrap and aluminum foil. Use a large piece of masking tape and an indelible marker to label and date the contents. If frozen, defrost overnight in the refrigerator and bring to room temperature before serving.

To freeze the cookie dough logs up to 6 months, wrap them in several layers of plastic wrap and place in a freezer bag. Use masking tape and an indelible marker to label and date the dough logs. Let the logs stand at room temperature for about 20 minutes before slicing, because if they are too firm when cut, they may splinter.

Making a Change
Replace the walnuts with macadamia nuts, hazelnuts, or pecans.

Hazelnut Biscotti

ALTHOUGH BISCOTTI are of Italian origin, they are very popular in the United States. The name means "twice baked" and this double baking is what gives these cookies their renowned crispness and makes them ideal for dipping into a cup of coffee or hot chocolate. Biscotti keep very well but they usually don't last long enough for that to be much of a consideration, because they are eaten so quickly. **Makes about 3 dozen cookies**

Adjust the oven racks to the upper and lower thirds and preheat the oven to 350°F. Line the baking sheets with parchment paper sheets or non-stick liners.

Essential Gear
- Two baking sheets
- Two parchment paper sheets or non-stick liners
- Cake pan
- Kitchen towel
- Food processor
- Electric stand mixer with flat beater attachment, or large mixing bowl and hand-held mixer

1 cup unblanched hazelnuts	Place the hazelnuts in a single layer in a cake or pie pan. Toast in the oven for 15 to 18 minutes, until the skins split and the nuts turn light golden brown.
	Remove the pan from the oven and transfer the hazelnuts to a kitchen towel. Fold the towel around the nuts and then rub them to remove most of the skins.
	Place the hazelnuts in the work bowl of a food processor fitted with the steel blade. Pulse the nuts to chop them coarsely, about 1 minute.
2 cups all-purpose flour ½ cup granulated sugar ½ cup firmly packed light brown sugar 2 teaspoons baking powder ⅛ teaspoon salt	In the bowl of an electric stand mixer or a large mixing bowl, combine the flour, granulated sugar, brown sugar, baking powder, and salt. Use the flat beater attachment or a hand-held mixer to stir together briefly.
3 extra-large eggs, at room temperature 2 teaspoons pure vanilla extract 4 ounces (8 tablespoons, 1 stick) unsalted butter, melted	Using a fork, whisk the eggs with the vanilla in a small bowl. Add the egg and vanilla mixture and the butter to the dry ingredients. Mix on low speed until thoroughly combined. Stop occasionally and scrape down the sides and bottom of the mixing bowl with a rubber spatula.
	Add the chopped hazelnuts and stir to blend thoroughly.
	Divide the dough into 4 equal pieces. Dust your hands with flour to keep the dough from sticking and shape each piece into a log about 7 inches long, 3 inches wide, and ¾ inch high. Place 2 logs on each baking sheet, leaving at least 2 inches of space between them.
	Bake for 12 minutes, then switch the baking sheets and bake another 12 to 13 minutes, until set. Remove the baking sheets from the oven and rest for 10 minutes on cooling racks.
	Using a serrated knife, cut each log on the diagonal into ½-inch-thick slices. Place the slices back onto the baking sheet on their sides so the wide part of each slice faces up.
	Bake the biscotti again for 6 minutes, switch the baking sheets and bake another 6 to 7 minutes, until firm.
	Transfer the biscotti to racks to cool.

- Rubber spatula
- Serrated knife
- Two cooling racks

Keeping

Store the biscotti in an airtight container between sheets of waxed paper at room temperature up to 2 weeks. A kitchen cupboard or pantry is the ideal storage place.

To freeze up to 3 months, wrap the container tightly in several layers of plastic wrap and aluminum foil. Use a large piece of masking tape and an indelible marker to label and date the contents. If frozen, defrost overnight in the refrigerator and bring to room temperature before serving.

Making a Change

Replace the hazelnuts with almonds, walnuts, or pistachios.

Adding Style

Drizzle the biscotti with thin lines of bittersweet, semisweet, milk, or white chocolate after they are completely cool. Let the chocolate set for 15 minutes in the refrigerator before serving or storing.

Dip one end or one lengthwise side of the biscotti into tempered bittersweet, semisweet, milk, or white chocolate after they are completely cool (see page 43). Let the chocolate set for 15 minutes in the refrigerator before serving or storing.

Hazelnut Cheesecake

THIS IS A CLASSIC dense and creamy cheesecake with the addition of toasted, skinned, and chopped hazelnuts that give the cake both flavor and texture. The crust is made from store-bought butter cookies combined with toasted hazelnuts, sugar, butter, and a touch of cinnamon. This is a great cake to make for a gathering because it is very rich and yields several servings. The cake needs to be made at least a day in advance so it has time to cool and chill. **Makes one 9½-inch round cake, 12 to 14 servings**

Center a rack in the oven and preheat it to 350°F.

1 tablespoon unsalted butter, softened

Use your fingertips or a paper towel to generously butter the inside of the springform pan. Use a double layer of heavy-duty foil to wrap around the bottom of the pan. This prevents any water from the water bath from seeping into the pan

1½ cups unblanched hazelnuts

Place the hazelnuts in a cake or pie pan and toast in the oven for 15 to 18 minutes, until the skins begin to split and the nuts turn golden brown.

Remove the pan from the oven and transfer the hazelnuts to a kitchen towel. Fold the towel around the nuts and then rub them to remove most of the skins.

CHEESECAKE CRUST

8½ ounces (1 package) butter biscuit cookies, wafers, or shortbread
2 tablespoons granulated sugar
½ teaspoon ground cinnamon
2½ ounces (5 tablespoons) unsalted butter, melted

In the work bowl of a food processor fitted with the steel blade, combine ½ cup of the skinned hazelnuts, the cookies, sugar, and cinnamon. Pulse until the cookies and hazelnuts are finely ground, about 1 minute. With the food processor on, pour the butter through the feed tube. Process the mixture until it begins to clump together.

Or place the cookies in a plastic bag and crush them with a rolling pin, then transfer the crumbs to a mixing bowl. Very finely chop the hazelnuts and add to the crumbs. Add the sugar and cinnamon and toss to blend thoroughly. Pour the butter onto the mixture and stir until the mixture begins to hold together.

Transfer the crust to the prepared springform pan and use your fingertips to press it into the bottom and partway up the sides of the pan. Chill the crust while preparing the cheesecake batter.

Essential Gear
- 9½-inch round spring-form pan
- Heavy-duty aluminum foil
- Cake pan
- Kitchen towel
- Food processor or rolling pin
- Electric stand mixer with flat beater attachment, or hand-held mixer and 3 quart mixing bowl
- Rubber spatula
- 12-inch round cake pan or large roasting pan
- Cooling rack

Keeping
Store the cheesecake tightly covered with aluminum foil in the refrigerator up to 4 days. To freeze up to 2 months, wrap the cake tightly in several layers of plastic wrap and aluminum foil. Use a large piece of masking tape and an indelible marker to label and date the contents. If frozen, defrost overnight in the refrigerator and bring to room temperature before serving.

Adding Style
Serve slices of the cheese-cake with raspberry sauce (see Meyer Lemon Soufflés, page 143) and a few fresh raspberries.

CHEESECAKE BATTER

2 pounds cream cheese, softened
1⅓ cups granulated sugar
¼ teaspoon salt

Place the cream cheese in the bowl of an electric stand mixer or a large mixing bowl. Use the flat beater attachment or a hand-held mixer to beat the cream cheese until it is fluffy, about 2 minutes. Add the sugar and salt and beat until well blended. Stop occasionally and scrape down the sides and bottom of the bowl with a rubber spatula.

4 extra-large eggs, at room temperature

One at a time, add the eggs to the cream cheese mixture. The eggs will sit on top of the cream cheese, so stop frequently and scrape down the bottom and sides of the bowl with a rubber spatula to help mix evenly.

1 cup sour cream
½ cup heavy whipping cream
1 tablespoon pure vanilla extract

Add the sour cream, cream, and vanilla and blend thoroughly.

In the work bowl of a food processor fitted with the steel blade, finely chop the remaining 1 cup of hazelnuts. Add to the cheesecake batter and blend well.

Pour the cheesecake batter into the crust in the springform pan. Use a rubber spatula to smooth and even the top.

1 quart boiling water

Place the springform pan in the larger pan and set the pan on the oven rack. Carefully pour the boiling water into the bottom pan until it reaches halfway up the side of the springform pan. Baking the cake in a water bath cushions it from the heat and adds extra moisture to the oven, which keeps the top from cracking.

Bake the cake for 1 hour and 15 minutes, until set and very pale golden, and the top jiggles only slightly when the cake is moved. Turn off the oven and hold the door ajar with a wooden spoon. Let the cake stand in the oven for 1 hour.

Remove the cheesecake pan from the oven, lift it from the water, and remove the foil from the pan. Place the cheesecake on a rack to cool to room temperature. Cover the top of the cheesecake with waxed paper and wrap tightly in aluminum foil. Refrigerate the cake for at least 6 hours before serving. To unmold the cheesecake, dip a thin-bladed knife in hot water and dry it, then run it around the inner edge of the pan, release the clip on the rim of the pan, and gently lift it off the cake.

Hazelnut Dacquoise with Mocha Buttercream

DACQUOISE (pronounced da *kwahz*) is a classic French cake made with layers of thin, crisp hazelnut meringue filled and decorated with rich mocha buttercream. The cake is garnished on top with confectioners' sugar, and finely ground, toasted hazelnuts are pressed into the sides. This is an elegant cake and takes a bit of work, but is well worth it. The meringue layers are delicate and can break easily, so take extra care with them. They can be made several days before you assemble the cake. **Makes one 9-inch round cake, 12 to 14 servings**

HAZELNUT MERINGUE CIRCLES

1½ cups unblanched hazelnuts

Center an oven rack and preheat it to 350°F. Place the hazelnuts in a single layer in a cake or pie pan and toast for 15 to 18 minutes, until the skins split and the nuts turn light golden brown.

Remove the pan from the oven and transfer the hazelnuts to a kitchen towel. Fold the towel around the hazelnuts and rub them together to remove most of the skins.

Reduce the oven temperature to 200°F. Adjust the racks to the upper and lower thirds of the oven.

2 tablespoons granulated sugar

Place the hazelnuts in the work bowl of a food processor fitted with the steel blade. Add the sugar and pulse until the nuts are very finely ground.

2 tablespoons cornstarch

Place 1 cup of the ground hazelnuts in a small bowl. Add the cornstarch and stir together to blend thoroughly.

Line the baking sheets with aluminum foil. Use the cake circle or cake pan as a guide and trace a 9-inch circle onto the dull side of each piece of foil with a pencil, then turn the foil over onto the baking sheets.

5 extra-large egg whites, at room temperature
½ teaspoon cream of tartar

Place the egg whites in the grease-free bowl of an electric stand mixer or a large bowl. Use the wire whip attachment or a hand-held mixer to whip the egg whites on medium speed until frothy. Add the cream of tartar and whip on medium-high speed until the egg whites hold soft peaks.

¾ cup superfine sugar

With the mixer running, gradually sprinkle on the sugar and continue to whip until the egg whites hold glossy and firm, but not stiff, peaks.

Essential Gear
- Cake pan
- Kitchen towel
- Food processor
- 9-inch round cardboard cake circle or cake pan
- Three baking sheets
- Aluminum foil
- Electric stand mixer with wire whip attachment, or hand-held mixer and large mixing bowl
- 14-inch pastry bag with ½-inch plain round tip
- 8- or 10-inch flexible-blade spatula
- 2-quart heavy-bottomed saucepan
- 1-inch natural-bristle pastry brush
- Sugar or candy thermometer
- Rubber spatula
- Small sharp knife
- 10-inch pastry bag with large open star tip

Keeping
Store the dacquoise tented with aluminum foil in the refrigerator up to 3 days. Place several toothpicks in the top outer edges of the dacquoise to hold the foil away from it so it won't mar the buttercream.

Streamlining
The meringue circles can be made up to 2 weeks in advance and stored at room temperature wrapped in aluminum foil. They are subject

Fold the ground hazelnuts into the egg whites in 3 stages, blending thoroughly.

Fit the 14-inch pastry bag with the plain tip. Fill the pastry bag partway with the hazelnut meringue mixture. Hold the pastry bag straight and about 1 inch above the center of one of the circles. Pipe out concentric circles of the meringue mixture into the traced circles, filling in each circle completely.

Or, instead of using a pastry bag, divide the meringue mixture evenly into 3. Place a mound of the meringue in the center of each traced circle. Use an offset spatula to evenly spread the mixture to the edges of each circle, keeping the meringue at least ¼ inch thick.

Place the baking sheets in the oven and dry the meringues for 2 hours. Turn off the oven and leave the meringues in the oven with the door closed until it is completely cool.

Very carefully peel the aluminum foil off the back of each meringue circle.

MOCHA BUTTERCREAM

2 extra-large eggs, at room temperature
2 extra-large egg yolks, at room temperature
¼ cup granulated sugar

Place the eggs, egg yolks, and sugar in the bowl of an electric stand mixer or in a large mixing bowl. Use the wire whip attachment or a hand-held mixer and whip the eggs on medium speed until they are very pale colored and hold a slowly dissolving ribbon as the beater is lifted, about 5 minutes.

1¼ cups granulated sugar
½ cup water
¼ teaspoon cream of tartar

While the eggs are whipping, place the sugar, water, and cream of tartar in the saucepan. Bring the mixture to a boil, without stirring. Place a wet pastry brush at the point where the sugar syrup meets the sides of the pan and sweep it around completely. Do this two times. This prevents the sugar from crystallizing by brushing any stray crystals back into the mixture. Cook over high heat until the mixture registers 242°F on a sugar thermometer (soft-ball stage). Immediately remove the sugar thermometer and place it in a glass of warm water, then remove the pan from the heat so it won't continue to cook.

Adjust the mixer speed to low and pour the sugar syrup into the whipped eggs in a slow, steady stream. Aim the sugar syrup between the beater and the side of the bowl, so it doesn't get caught up in the beater or thrown against the sides of the bowl. Turn the mixer speed up to medium-high and whip until the bowl is cool to the touch, about 8 minutes. Once the cooked sugar syrup is added to the whipped eggs, the mixture must whip until the bowl is completely cool to the touch before the butter is added or the butter will melt.

to humidity and may soften if it is too humid or damp. If this happens, they can be redried. Place them on a baking sheet lined with aluminum foil in the oven at 200°F for 1 hour.

Recovering from a Mishap
If one of the meringue circles cracks or breaks, place it on top of a layer of buttercream and patch it back together with buttercream on top. Use the cracked or broken layer as the center meringue layer of the cake.

Making a Change
Replace the hazelnuts with almonds, pecans, walnuts, or macadamia nuts.

Leave the espresso out of the buttercream.

Flavor the buttercream with milk chocolate or white chocolate, with ½ cup fresh raspberry puree, or with 3 tablespoons Grand Marnier, Frangelico, or Chambord.

Adding Style
Serve slices of the dacquoise with raspberry sauce (page 143) and a few fresh raspberries.

Troubleshooting
Don't dry the meringue at a temperature higher than 200°F. This will cause the sugar to seep out of the meringue and make it sticky.

If this happens, the texture and consistency of the buttercream will be too soft and more butter will have to be added to bring it to the right point.

1 pound (2 cups, 4 sticks) unsalted butter, softened	Adjust the mixer speed to medium and add the butter, 2 tablespoons at a time. Continue to beat until the buttercream is thoroughly blended and fluffy.
1 tablespoon instant espresso powder **1 tablespoon water**	In a small bowl, stir together the espresso powder and water until the mixture is thoroughly blended and forms a thick paste. Add this mixture to the buttercream and blend well.
4 ounces bittersweet chocolate, very finely chopped	Place the chocolate in a microwave-proof bowl and melt on low power for 30-second bursts (see page 374). Stir with a rubber spatula after each burst. When the chocolate is completely melted, stir it for a couple of minutes to cool. Then add it to the buttercream and blend well.

ASSEMBLY

Place 1 hazelnut meringue disk on a 9-inch cardboard cake circle or serving plate. Use a small sharp knife to carefully trim the edges to make them even, if necessary. Place waxed paper strips around the bottom edges of the cake to protect the plate while assembling the cake.

Use a flexible-blade spatula to spread $\frac{1}{3}$ of the buttercream evenly over the meringue layer.

Carefully trim the edges of a second meringue layer and position it evenly over the buttercream, lining up the edges with the bottom meringue disk. Spread another $\frac{1}{3}$ of the buttercream evenly over the second meringue layer.

Carefully trim the edges of the third meringue layer and position it over the buttercream with the bottom of the layer facing up. This provides a flat surface for the top of the dacquoise.

Reserve $\frac{1}{3}$ cup of the buttercream and use the rest to cover the sides of the cake evenly.

Confectioners' sugar	Heavily dust the top of the cake with confectioners' sugar. Place the remaining ground hazelnuts on a sheet of waxed or parchment paper. Press the ground hazelnuts into the sides of the cake just up to, but not over, the top edges. The waxed paper will catch the hazelnuts that don't stick to the sides of the cake.

Fit the 10-inch pastry bag with the star tip. Fill the bag with the reserved buttercream. Pipe a border of shells around the top outer edge of the cake and pipe a large rosette in the center (see page 44). If there are any remaining ground hazelnuts, sprinkle them over the center rosette.

Let the dacquoise chill for at least 2 hours before serving so it has time to set and will be easier to cut. To cut the dacquoise into serving pieces, dip a knife in hot water and dry it between slices. Serve the cake at room temperature.

Hazelnut Snowflake Cookies

THE COOKIE CUTTER used to shape these cookies makes them look like snowflakes. These can be single cookies or they can be made into sandwich cookies by putting them together with apricot jam. Either way, I predict that they will become some of your favorite cookies! **Makes about 3 dozen sandwich cookies or 6 dozen single cookies**

Essential Gear
- Electric stand mixer with flat beater attachment, or large mixing bowl and hand-held mixer
- Rubber spatula
- Two baking sheets
- Two parchment paper sheets or non-stick pan liners
- Rolling pin
- 2½-inch fluted-edge snowflake cookie cutter or other cutter
- Two cooling racks

Keeping
Store the cookies in an airtight plastic container between layers of waxed paper at room temperature up to 1 week for single cookies or 3 days for sandwich cookies. A kitchen cupboard or pantry is an ideal storage place. To freeze unassembled cookies up to 3 months, wrap the airtight container

COOKIES

4 ounces (8 tablespoons, 1 stick) unsalted butter, softened	Place the butter in the bowl of an electric stand mixer or in a large mixing bowl. Use the flat beater attachment or a hand-held mixer to beat the butter on medium speed until it's fluffy, about 2 minutes.
⅓ cup granulated sugar	Add the sugar to the butter and cream together well. Stop occasionally and scrape down the sides and bottom of the bowl with a rubber spatula.
½ cup toasted, skinned, and finely ground hazelnuts	Add the hazelnuts to the butter mixture and mix well.
2 extra-large egg yolks, at room temperature ½ teaspoon pure vanilla extract.	Using a fork, lightly beat the egg yolks and vanilla in a small bowl. Add to the butter mixture and blend well. Stop and scrape down the sides and bottom of the bowl with a rubber spatula.
1½ cups all-purpose flour	Add the flour to the butter mixture in 2 stages, blending well after each addition.

Turn the dough out of the bowl onto a large piece of plastic wrap and shape into a disk. Cover the dough tightly in a double layer of plastic wrap and chill in the refrigerator at least 2 hours.

Adjust the oven racks to the upper and lower thirds and preheat the oven to 375°F.

Line two baking sheets with parchment paper or non-stick pan liners.

If the dough is too firm, let it stand at room temperature for 10 to 15 minutes to become more pliable before rolling it out.

Roll out the dough on a smooth, flat surface between sheets of lightly floured waxed or parchment paper to a thickness of 1/4 inch. Turn the dough a quarter turn often while rolling it out to make it easier to roll it evenly.

Remove the top piece of paper. Dip the cookie cutter into flour and shake off the excess. Use the cutter to cut out cookies. Transfer the cut cookies to the baking sheets, leaving at least 1 inch of space between them.

Gather the dough scraps back together and roll them out again, then cut out more cookies.

Bake the cookies for 5 minutes, then switch the baking sheets. Bake another 5 to 7 minutes, until light golden.

Remove the baking sheets from the oven and cool the cookies completely on the baking sheets on racks.

ASSEMBLY AND GARNISH

1/3 cup apricot preserves

To make sandwich cookies, use a spoon or a parchment paper pastry cone (see page 25) to place a small amount of apricot preserves on the flat side of one cookie. Top the apricot preserves with the flat side of another cookie, lining up the edges of the snowflakes. Dust the top of the cookies lightly with confectioners' sugar.

Confectioners' sugar

For single cookies, dust them lightly with confectioners' sugar.

in several layers of plastic wrap and aluminum foil. Use a large piece of masking tape and an indelible marker to label and date the contents. If frozen, defrost overnight in the refrigerator and bring to room temperature before serving.

Streamlining
The dough can be made and kept in the refrigerator up to 3 days before baking. It can also be kept in the freezer up to 3 months. To refrigerate, wrap the dough tightly in several layers of plastic wrap. To freeze, wrap the same way and place the dough in a freezer bag. Use a large piece of masking tape and an indelible marker to label and date the contents. Defrost the dough overnight in the refrigerator.

Making a Change
Replace the ground hazelnuts with almonds, walnuts, or pecans.

Replace the apricot preserves with orange marmalade or raspberry or strawberry preserves.

Macadamia Nut Blondies

BLONDIES ARE a light version of brownies that are made without dark or milk chocolate. Macadamia nuts and chopped white chocolate are mixed with light brown sugar and other typical brownie ingredients to create these treats. **Makes nine 2¹⁄₂-inch squares or sixteen 2-inch squares**

Essential Gear
- 8-inch square baking pan
- Aluminum foil
- Electric stand mixer with flat beater attachment, or large mixing bowl and hand-held mixer
- Sifter
- Rubber spatula
- Cooling rack

1 tablespoon unsalted butter, softened	Center a rack in the oven and preheat it to 350°F. Line the baking pan with aluminum foil, letting it hang about 2 inches over the sides. Using a paper towel or your fingertips, generously butter the inside of the foil or spray the foil with non-stick baking spray.
4 ounces (8 tablespoons, 1 stick) unsalted butter, softened	Place the butter in the bowl of an electric stand mixer or in a large mixing bowl. Use the flat beater attachment or a hand-held mixer to beat the butter until it is fluffy, about 2 minutes.
1 cup firmly packed light brown sugar	Add the sugar to the butter and cream together well.
2 extra-large eggs, at room temperature 2 teaspoons pure vanilla extract	Use a fork to lightly beat the eggs and vanilla together in a small bowl. Add to the butter mixture and blend well.
1 cup all-purpose flour ¹⁄₄ teaspoon baking powder ¹⁄₄ teaspoon salt	Over a large piece of waxed or parchment paper or a bowl, sift together the flour, baking powder, and salt. In 3 stages, add the dry ingredients to the butter mixture, blending well after each addition. Scrape down the sides and bottom of the bowl with the rubber spatula.
²⁄₃ cup coarsely chopped toasted, unsalted macadamia nuts 3 ounces white chocolate, coarsely chopped	Add the nuts and white chocolate to the batter and stir to distribute evenly.

Pour the batter into the prepared pan and use the rubber spatula to spread it evenly into the corners.

Bake the blondies for 28 to 30 minutes, until a cake tester or toothpick inserted in the center comes out with no crumbs clinging to it. Remove the pan from the oven and cool completely on a rack.

Lift the brownies from the pan with the aluminum foil. Carefully peel the foil away from the sides of the blondies. Cut into 3 or 4 equal-sized rows in each direction.

Keeping
Store the blondies in an airtight container between layers of waxed paper at room temperature up to 4 days. To freeze up to 4 months, wrap the container tightly in several layers of plastic wrap and aluminum foil. Use a large piece of masking tape and an indelible marker to label and date the contents. If frozen, defrost overnight in the refrigerator and bring to room temperature before serving.

Making a Change
Replace the macadamia nuts with walnuts, whole blanched almonds, or toasted hazelnuts.

Adding Style
Serve the cooled blondies with a dollop of lightly sweetened whipped cream.

Serve the cooled blondies with a scoop of caramel ice cream.

Macadamia Nut, White Chocolate, and Mango Tart

A BUTTERY macadamia nut crust encloses a light and airy white chocolate filling. Fresh mango slices, lightly glazed with apricot preserves, adorn the top. As a garnish, chopped macadamia nuts are sprinkled over the top. This tart is visually stunning and tastes divine. When your guests eat it they will think they've been magically transported to the tropics. **Makes one 11-inch round tart, 14 to 16 servings**

MACADAMIA NUT PASTRY DOUGH

1½ cups all-purpose flour
1 cup toasted, salted
  macadamia nuts
⅓ cup granulated sugar
¼ teaspoon salt

In the work bowl of a food processor fitted with the steel blade, combine the flour, macadamia nuts, sugar, and salt. Pulse until the nuts are finely ground, about 1 minute.

5 ounces (10 tablespoons,
  1¼ sticks) unsalted butter,
  chilled

Cut the butter into small pieces and add to the flour. Pulse until the butter is cut into very tiny pieces, about 30 seconds. The texture should be sandy with very tiny lumps throughout.

1 extra-large egg yolk,
  at room temperature
½ teaspoon pure vanilla
  extract

In a small bowl, lightly beat together the egg yolk and vanilla. With the food processor running, pour this mixture through the feed tube. Process until the dough wraps itself around the blade, 30 seconds to 1 minute.

Turn the pastry dough onto a large piece of plastic wrap. Shape into a flat disk and wrap tightly in a double layer of plastic wrap. Chill in the refrigerator until firm before using, at least 2 hours. Chilling the dough relaxes the gluten in the flour so it won't be too elastic and will roll out easily. It also firms up the butter in the dough so it will need less flour when rolled out. If the dough is too firm it will splinter and break when rolled out. If the pastry dough is too cold and firm, let it stand at room temperature for 10 to 15 minutes before rolling to become more pliable.

On a smooth, flat surface, roll out the pastry dough between sheets of lightly floured waxed or parchment paper to a large circle about 13 inches in diameter. Carefully peel the paper off the top of the dough. Brush excess flour off the dough, then loosely roll the pastry dough around the rolling pin without the bottom piece of paper. Place the tart pan directly underneath the rolling pin and carefully unroll the pastry dough onto it

Essential Gear
- Food processor
- Rolling pin
- 11-inch round, fluted-edge tart pan with removable bottom
- Baking sheet
- Pie weights
- Cooling rack
- Electric stand mixer with flat beater attachment, or a medium mixing bowl and hand-held mixer
- Pie weights
- Aluminum foil
- Vegetable peeler
- Sharp knife
- Small saucepan
- Medium fine-mesh strainer
- Goose-feather pastry brush

Keeping
The tart can last up to 2 days at room temperature or 4 days in the refrigerator. Place a piece of waxed paper over the top of the tart, then tightly cover it with aluminum foil. It is best served at room temperature.

Streamlining
The pastry dough can be made in advance and kept in the refrigerator, tightly wrapped in a double layer of plastic wrap, up to 4 days. To freeze up to 3 months, wrap the dough snugly in several layers of plastic wrap and place it in a freezer bag. Use a large piece of mask-

Gently lift up the sides and ease the pastry dough into the bottom and sides of the tart pan, pushing it lightly into the fluted edges. Trim off the excess pastry dough at the top of the pan by running the rolling pin over the top. Or use your fingers to press against the top of the pan to remove the excess pastry dough.

Place the tart pan on a baking sheet. Chill for at least 1 hour in the refrigerator.

Center a rack in the oven and preheat it to 375°F. Line the pastry shell with a large piece of aluminum foil that fits well against the bottom and sides. Fill with pie weights or a mixture of rice and beans.

Bake for 12 minutes. Remove the foil and weights. If the bottom of the pastry shell puffs up, gently pierce it in several places with a fork to release the air. Bake the pastry shell another 12 to 15 minutes, until light golden and set. Remove the pan from the oven and transfer to a rack to cool completely.

WHITE CHOCOLATE GANACHE FILLING

1 pound white chocolate, finely chopped

Place the white chocolate in a large bowl.

¾ cup heavy whipping cream
1 teaspoon pure vanilla extract

Place the cream in a small saucepan and bring to a boil over medium heat. Pour the cream over the chocolate and let it stand for 1 minute. Stir the mixture together using a heat-resistant spatula, whisk, or immersion blender until very smooth. Stir in the vanilla. Cover the bowl tightly with plastic wrap and let the mixture cool to room temperature. Chill for 1 hour, until it is firm, but still pliable.

Place the white chocolate ganache in the bowl of an electric stand mixer or a large mixing bowl. Use the flat beater attachment or a hand-held mixer and beat on medium speed until the mixture is fluffy, 30 seconds to 1 minute.

If the chocolate is beaten too long it will become stiff and may curdle. To repair this, place the mixing bowl in a large pan of warm water and let the mixture begin to melt. Return it to the mixer and add ¼ cup heavy whipping cream. Beat lightly until the mixture is restored.

Transfer the filling to the cooled tart shell and spread it out evenly in the shell.

3 large, ripe mangoes

Use a vegetable peeler to remove the mango skin. Use a sharp knife to cut a large slice from each side of the large center pit of the mango,

ing tape and an indelible marker to label and date the contents. If frozen, defrost overnight in the refrigerator before using.

The white chocolate ganache filling can be made in advance and kept in the refrigerator in a tightly covered container for up to 1 week. Bring it to room temperature before whipping or it will break and separate.

Making a Change
Replace the macadamia nuts with whole blanched almonds or pecans.

Replace the mangoes with papayas, peaches, apricots, kiwifruit, persimmons, or pineapple.

then cut each slice into ½-inch-thick slices. Overlap the slices on top of the filling in a large circle, filling in the center.

APRICOT GLAZE

¼ cup apricot preserves
1 tablespoon orange liqueur
  or water

Combine the apricot preserves and the liquid in a small saucepan. Bring to a boil over medium heat. Strain the mixture, pushing through as much of the pulp as possible.

Using the pastry brush, lightly brush the glaze on top of the mango slices. Don't apply a thick glaze, which looks unappetizing. The purpose of the glaze is to keep the mango slices from drying out and to make the top of the tart glisten.

¼ cup toasted, coarsely
  chopped macadamia nuts

Sprinkle the chopped macadamia nuts over the center of the tart and the mango slices.

Remove the sides of the tart pan by placing it on top of an upside-down bowl that is smaller than the pan. The sides should fall away. Cut the tart into slices to serve.

Double Peanut Butter Cookies

I F YOU'RE A peanut lover, these cookies are for you. These classic cookies are loaded with peanut butter and peanuts. I prefer to use natural-style or freshly ground peanut butter because I like the texture. I also recommend using chunky peanut butter instead of smooth. **Makes 5½ dozen cookies**

Adjust the oven racks to the upper and lower thirds and preheat the oven to 350°F. Line the baking sheets with parchment paper sheets or non-stick liners.

2¼ cups all-purpose flour
1 teaspoon baking soda
¼ teaspoon salt

Over a large piece of waxed or parchment paper or a bowl, sift together the flour and baking soda. Add the salt and toss to blend well.

6 ounces (12 tablespoons,
  1½ sticks) unsalted butter,
  softened

Place the butter in the bowl of an electric stand mixer or in a large mixing bowl. Use the flat beater attachment or a hand-held mixer to beat the butter on medium speed until it's fluffy, about 2 minutes.

1 cup chunky peanut butter,
  at room temperature

Add the peanut butter to the butter and blend together well.

Essential Gear
- Three baking sheets
- Three parchment paper sheets or non-stick liners
- Sifter
- Electric stand mixer with flat beater attachment, or large mixing bowl and hand-held mixer
- Rubber spatula
- Spoon or small ice cream scoop
- Fork
- Two cooling racks

Keeping
Store the cookies in an airtight plastic container between layers of waxed paper at room temperature

1 cup firmly packed light brown sugar 1 cup granulated sugar	Add the brown sugar and granulated sugar to the peanut butter mixture and cream together completely. Stop occasionally and scrape down the sides and bottom of the bowl with a rubber spatula.
2 extra-large eggs, at room temperature 1 teaspoon pure vanilla extract	Using a fork, lightly beat the egg and vanilla together in a small bowl. Add to the peanut butter mixture and blend thoroughly. The egg will sit on top of the mixture, so be sure to scrape down the sides and bottom of the bowl to help mix evenly. The mixture may look curdled as the eggs are added, but as you stop and scrape down the bowl, the mixture will smooth out.
	Add the dry ingredients in 4 stages, blending completely after each addition. Stop occasionally and scrape down the sides and bottom of the bowl with a rubber spatula to ensure even mixing.
½ cup toasted, lightly salted peanuts	Add the peanuts to the cookie mixture and blend well.
	Use a large spoon or a small ice cream scoop to scoop out mounds about 1½ inches in diameter. Place the mounds on the lined baking sheets, leaving 2 inches of space between them so they have room to expand as they bake. Dampen the back of a fork and press each mound of dough slightly to flatten it. Then press the fork across the first set of marks to form a cross-hatch pattern.
½ cup toasted, salted peanuts	Press two or three peanuts into the top of each cookie. Tightly cover one baking sheet with plastic wrap and chill while baking the other two baking sheets. Bake the cookies for 7 minutes. Switch the baking sheets and bake another 7 to 8 minutes, until the cookies are set and light golden. Remove the baking sheets from the oven and cool the cookies completely on the baking sheets. Carefully remove the cookies from the parchment paper or non-stick liners.

up to 5 days. To freeze up to 3 months, wrap the container tightly in several layers of plastic wrap and aluminum foil. Use a large piece of masking tape and an indelible marker to label and date the contents. If frozen, defrost overnight in the refrigerator and bring to room temperature before serving.

Making a Change
Replace the peanut butter with cashew or almond butter and replace the peanuts with cashews or almonds.

Peanut Butter and Banana Layer Cake with Mascarpone Filling and Frosting

PEANUT BUTTER and banana lovers will think they are in heaven when they eat a slice of this incredible cake. Three layers of rich, dense peanut butter and banana cake are alternated with mascarpone filling and sliced bananas. The entire cake is covered with mascarpone frosting, and chopped toasted peanuts decorate the sides. Since the cake is very rich, it can be cut into thin slices, making it great to serve at any large gathering. Most of the steps involved in making this cake can be done in advance, so it's easy to assemble a few hours to a day before serving. **Makes one 9-inch round cake, 14 to 16 servings**

PEANUT BUTTER AND BANANA CAKE

Center a rack in the oven and preheat it to 325°F.

1 tablespoon unsalted butter, softened	Using a paper towel or your fingertips, generously butter the inside of the cake pan, coating it thoroughly
2 teaspoons all-purpose flour	Dust the inside of the pan with the flour. Shake and tilt the pan to evenly distribute the flour, then turn the pan over and shake out the excess over the sink.
	Cut a round of parchment paper to fit the bottom of the pan. Butter the parchment paper round and place in the pan, butter-side up.
4 ounces (8 tablespoons, 1 stick) unsalted butter, softened	Place the butter in the bowl of an electric stand mixer or in a large mixing bowl. Use the flat beater attachment or hand-held mixer to beat the butter on medium speed until it's fluffy, about 2 minutes.
⅓ cup natural-style (old-fashioned) chunky peanut butter	Add the peanut butter to the butter and beat together until smooth, about 1 minute.
1 cup firmly packed light brown sugar	Gradually add the sugar to the peanut butter mixture and cream together well. Stop occasionally and scrape down the bottom and sides of the bowl with a rubber spatula.
3 extra-large egg yolks, at room temperature	One at a time, add the egg yolks to the peanut butter mixture, stopping to scrape down the bottom and sides of the bowl after each addition. At first the mixture may look curdled as the eggs are added, but as you stop and scrape down the bowl, the mixture will smooth out.

Essential Gear

- 9 × 2-inch round cake pan
- Scissors
- Parchment paper
- Electric stand mixer with flat beater attachment and wire whip attachment, or large mixing bowl and hand-held mixer
- Two rubber spatulas
- Sifter
- Cooling rack
- 9-inch cardboard cake circle
- Serrated knife
- 10-inch flexible-blade icing spatula

Keeping

Store the cake loosely covered with aluminum foil in the refrigerator up to 3 days. Place several toothpicks in the top outer edges of the cake to hold the foil away from it so it won't mar the icing.

Streamlining

Bake the cake up to 2 days before assembling and keep tightly covered with a double layer of plastic wrap, at room temperature or in the refrigerator, up to 3 days. To freeze the cake up to 3 months, wrap it snugly in several layers of plastic wrap and place in a freezer bag. Use a large piece of masking tape and an indelible marker to label and date the contents.

| | | If frozen, defrost the cake overnight in the refrigerator. |

| 1 large, ripe banana
1½ teaspoons pure vanilla extract | Use a fork to mash the banana in a bowl. Add the vanilla and then add to the peanut butter mixture and beat until smooth. |

Recovering from a Mishap
If one of the cake layers breaks during assembly, patch it together with some of the icing.

| 1½ cups all-purpose flour
1 teaspoon baking powder
1 teaspoon baking soda
¼ teaspoon salt | Over a large piece of waxed or parchment paper or a bowl, sift together the flour, baking powder, and baking soda. Add the salt and toss to blend well. |

| ⅓ cup buttermilk | With the mixer on low speed, add the dry ingredients alternately with the buttermilk in 3 stages. Blend well after each addition and stop often to scrape down the bottom and sides of the bowl with a rubber spatula. |

| 3 extra-large egg whites
⅛ teaspoon cream of tartar | Place the egg whites in the grease-free bowl of an electric stand mixer or a large mixing bowl. Use the wire whip attachment or a hand-held mixer to whip the whites until they are frothy. Add the cream of tartar and continue to whip the whites on medium-high speed until they hold firm, but not stiff, glossy peaks.

Fold the whites into the cake batter in 4 stages. |

Transfer the cake batter to the cake pan. Smooth the top of the pan with a rubber spatula.

Bake the cake for 40 to 45 minutes, until golden and a cake tester inserted in the center comes out with no crumbs clinging to it.

Remove the cake pan from the oven and cool completely on a rack. Place a 9-inch round cardboard cake circle over the top of the pan and invert the pan to remove the cake, then peel the parchment paper off the back of the cake.

MASCARPONE FILLING AND FROSTING

| 1½ pounds mascarpone, softened | Place the mascarpone in the bowl of an electric stand mixer or in a large mixing bowl. Use the flat beater attachment or a hand-held mixer and beat the mascarpone until it is fluffy, about 3 minutes. |

| ¾ cup confectioners' sugar, sifted
½ cup heavy whipping cream
1 tablespoon pure vanilla extract | Add the sugar, cream, and vanilla to the mascarpone and beat together until the mixture holds soft peaks, about 1 minute. |

**2 medium, ripe bananas,
thinly sliced**

Using a serrated knife, cut the cake horizontally into 3 layers (see page 34). Place one cake layer on a serving plate. Place strips of waxed paper around the bottom edges of the cake to protect the plate while assembling the cake. Use the flexible-blade spatula to spread the layer evenly with ¼ cup of the icing. Cover the top of the icing with concentric circles of banana slices, then spread another ¼ cup of the icing evenly over the sliced bananas.

Position the second cake layer evenly over the icing and use the flexible-blade spatula to spread about ¼ cup of the icing over the layer. Arrange another layer of thinly sliced bananas over the icing and spread with another ¼ cup icing.

Position the top layer of the cake over the icing. Spread the remaining icing over the sides and top of the cake.

**1 cup toasted peanuts, finely
chopped**

Press the finely chopped peanuts into the sides of the cake just up to, but not over, the top edge.

Let the cake chill for at least 2 hours before serving so it has time to set and will be easier to cut. Serve the cake at room temperature.

Peanut Butter and Chocolate Tartlets

I F YOU LIKE the combination of peanut butter and chocolate, these tartlets are for you! A crispy cocoa pastry crust holds a delectable filling of peanut butter, cream cheese, and whipping cream, topped off with a creamy layer of chocolate ganache. There is a blend of several textures—crispy, crunchy, creamy, and velvety—in these tartlets, making them a divine eating experience. **Makes eighteen 2¹/₂-inch round tartlets**

Essential Gear
- Food processor
- Rolling pin
- ³/₄-inch round plain-edge cutter
- Thirty-six 2¹/₂-inch fluted-edge tartlet pans
- Baking sheet
- Aluminum foil
- Cooling rack
- Electric stand mixer with flat beater and wire whip attachments, or large mixing bowl and hand-held mixer
- 3¹/₄-inch plain-edged cutter
- Pie weights

COCOA PASTRY DOUGH

1¹/₄ cups all-purpose flour
¹/₂ cup superfine sugar
**¹/₄ cup cocoa powder (natural
or Dutch-processed)**
¹/₈ teaspoon salt

In the work bowl of a food processor fitted with the steel blade, combine the flour, sugar, cocoa, and salt. Pulse briefly to blend.

**4 ounces (8 tablespoons,
1 stick) unsalted butter,
chilled**

Cut the butter into small pieces and add to the flour mixture. Pulse until the butter is cut into very tiny pieces, about 30 seconds. The texture should be sandy with tiny lumps throughout.

**1 extra-large egg yolk,
  at room temperature
1 teaspoon pure vanilla
  extract**

Use a fork to beat the egg yolk with the vanilla in a small bowl. With the food processor running, pour the egg and vanilla mixture through the feed tube. Process the dough until the mixture wraps itself around the blade, about 1 minute.

Turn the pastry dough onto a large piece of plastic wrap. Shape into a flat disk and wrap tightly in two layers of plastic wrap. Chill in the refrigerator until firm before using, at least 2 hours. Chilling the dough relaxes the gluten in the flour so it won't be too elastic and will roll out easily. It also firms up the butter in the dough so it will need less flour when rolled out. If the dough is too firm it will splinter and break when rolled out. Let it stand at room temperature for 10 to 15 minutes before rolling to become more pliable.

Center a rack in the oven and preheat it to 375°F.

On a smooth, flat surface, roll out the pastry dough between sheets of lightly floured waxed or parchment paper to a large round, about ¼ inch thick. Carefully peel the paper off the top of the dough and brush off any excess flour. Use the round cutter or a small bowl measuring 3¼ inches and cut out circles of the pastry dough. Carefully peel the circles off the other piece of paper. Gather together the dough scraps, reroll, and cut out any remaining circles.

To fit a circle of pastry dough into a tartlet pan, gently lift up the sides and ease the pastry dough into the bottom and sides of the tart pan, pushing it lightly into the fluted edges. Trim off the excess pastry dough at the top of the pan with your fingertips. Transfer the tartlet pan to a baking sheet and chill in the freezer for 30 minutes.

If you have enough tartlet pans, top each pan with another to act as a weight or line each pastry shell with a piece of aluminum foil that fits well against the bottom and sides. Fill the pastry shells with pie weights. Bake for 10 minutes, then remove the top tartlet pan or the foil and weights. If the bottom of the pastry shells puff up, gently pierce them in a few places with a fork to release the air. Bake another 10 to 12 minutes, until set. Remove the baking pan from the oven and transfer to a rack to cool completely.

PEANUT BUTTER FILLING

**½ cup natural-style
  (old-fashioned) chunky
  peanut butter, at room
  temperature
4 ounces cream cheese,
  softened**

Place the peanut butter and cream cheese in the bowl of an electric stand mixer or a large mixing bowl. Use the flat beater attachment or a hand-held mixer to beat together until fluffy, about 2 minutes.

- Two rubber spatulas
- 12- or 14-inch pastry bag and ¾-inch plain round pastry tip
- Small saucepan

Keeping

Store the tartlets on a baking sheet in the refrigerator up to 3 days. Cover the tops with a large piece of waxed paper to protect them from becoming marred and tightly cover the tartlets with aluminum foil.

Streamlining

The pastry dough can be made in advance and kept in the refrigerator, tightly wrapped in a double layer of plastic wrap, up to 4 days before using. To freeze up to 4 months, wrap it in a double layer of plastic wrap and place it inside a freezer bag. Use a large piece of masking tape and an indelible marker to label and date the contents. If frozen, defrost in the refrigerator overnight before using. If the dough is too cold to roll out, let it stand at room temperature to become pliable.

The tartlet shells can be baked and held at room temperature up to 2 days before filling. Cover the top of the cooled tartlet shells with a large piece of waxed or parchment paper and tightly wrap the pan in aluminum foil.

⅓ cup firmly packed light brown sugar	Add the sugar to the peanut butter mixture, and cream together well.
½ cup heavy whipping cream 1 teaspoon pure vanilla extract	Place the cream in the chilled bowl of an electric stand mixer or a medium mixing bowl. Using the wire whip attachment or a hand-held mixer, whip the cream on medium speed until it is frothy. Add the vanilla and continue to whip the cream on medium speed until it holds soft peaks. Fold the whipped cream into the peanut butter mixture in 3 stages, blending thoroughly.
	Fit the pastry bag with the plain round tip and fill partway with the peanut butter filling. Pipe the filling into each tartlet shell up to the top edge. Dampen the back of a spoon and smooth down any points on the top of the filling. Chill the tartlets in the freezer for 30 minutes, until the filling is set.

CHOCOLATE GANACHE TOPPING

4 ounces semisweet or bittersweet chocolate, finely chopped	Place the chocolate in a large bowl.
⅓ cup heavy whipping cream	Place the cream in a small saucepan and bring to a boil over medium heat. Pour the cream over the chopped chocolate. Let it stand for 30 seconds to 1 minute, then stir together with a rubber spatula, whisk, or immersion blender until very smooth.
½ teaspoon pure vanilla extract	Add the vanilla to the ganache and stir to blend well. Using a spoon, cover the top of each tartlet with the ganache.

GARNISH (OPTIONAL)

1 tablespoon roasted peanuts	Place a roasted peanut in the center of each tartlet. Let the tartlets set at room temperature before serving.

Troubleshooting

Once the pastry dough is placed in the tartlet pans, don't push it down forcefully. This will stretch the dough, which will shrink as it bakes, making it flat instead of taking the shape of the tartlet pans.

Pecan Pie

P ECAN PIE is a much-loved classic that takes center stage during the fall and winter holiday season. Its rich, deep flavor and texture that is creamy, crunchy, and gooey always leaves you wanting just a little bit more. This is sure to please everyone who eats it. **Makes one 10-inch round pie, 12 to 14 servings**

PIE DOUGH

1 cup all-purpose flour
1 tablespoon granulated
    sugar
¼ teaspoon salt

In the work bowl of a food processor fitted with the steel blade, combine the flour, sugar, and salt. Pulse briefly to blend.

4 ounces (8 tablespoons,
    1 stick) unsalted butter,
    chilled

Cut the butter into small pieces and freeze for 20 minutes.

4 ounces cream cheese,
    chilled

Cut the cream cheese into small pieces and add to the dry ingredients. Pulse to cut the cream cheese into very tiny pieces. The texture should be sandy with very tiny lumps throughout.

Add the butter to the flour mixture. Pulse until the butter is cut into pea-sized pieces, 30 to 45 seconds.

2 to 3 tablespoons heavy
    whipping cream

Remove the top of the food processor and sprinkle on 2 tablespoons of the cream. Replace the top and pulse for 10 seconds. Squeeze a small amount of the dough in your hand. If it holds together, don't add any more cream. If the dough is still very crumbly, add another tablespoon of cream, pulse to blend, then check the dough again. It won't hold together unless you squeeze it, but that's the texture you want.

Shape the dough into a disk and wrap it tightly in a double layer of plastic wrap. Chill in the refrigerator until firm before using, about 2 hours. Chilling the dough relaxes the gluten in the flour so it won't be too elastic and will roll out easily. It also firms up the butter in the dough so it will need less flour when rolled out. If the dough is too firm it will splinter and break when rolled out. Let it stand at room temperature for 10 to 15 minutes before rolling to become more pliable.

On a smooth, flat surface, roll out the pie dough between sheets of lightly floured waxed or parchment paper to a large circle about

Essential Gear
- Food processor
- Rolling pin
- 10-inch round deep
  pie pan
- Baking sheet
- Large mixing bowl
- Whisk
- Cake pan
- Rubber spatula
- Cooling rack

Keeping
Store the pie, loosely covered with waxed paper and then tightly wrapped with aluminum foil, at room temperature up to 3 days.

Streamlining
The pie dough can be made in advance and kept in the refrigerator, tightly wrapped in a double layer of plastic wrap, up to 4 days. To freeze up to 3 months, wrap the dough snugly in several layers of plastic wrap and place it in a freezer bag. Use a large piece of masking tape and an indelible marker to label and date the contents. If frozen, defrost overnight in the refrigerator before using. The pie dough can also be fitted into the pie pan and frozen. Wrap as above and label.

Troubleshooting
Don't overprocess the pie dough or it will be tough and not flaky.

12 inches in diameter. To tell if the dough will fit the pie pan, invert the pan over the dough. If there are 2 to 3 inches of dough that protrude beyond the sides of the pan, it will fit.

Carefully peel the paper off the top of the dough. Brush excess flour off the dough, then loosely roll the pastry dough around the rolling pin without the bottom piece of paper. Place the pie pan directly underneath the rolling pin and carefully unroll the pastry dough into the pan. Or loosely fold the dough in half. Carefully place it in half of the pie pan and gently unfold the dough. Gently lift up the sides and ease the pie dough into the bottom and sides of the pie pan. Trim off the excess pie dough at the top of the pan and crimp the sides (see page 40).

Transfer the pie pan to a baking sheet and chill in the freezer for 15 to 20 minutes. This helps prevent the pie dough from shrinking as it bakes and sets the butter in the dough to ensure flakiness.

Center an oven rack and preheat it to 375°F.

PECAN FILLING

1⅓ cups pecan halves or coarsely chopped pecans	Place the pecans in a single layer in a cake or pie pan and toast in the oven for 5 minutes. Remove the pan from the oven and cool. Raise the oven temperature to 425°F.
3 extra-large eggs, at room temperature **¾ cup dark corn syrup** **1 tablespoon molasses**	Use a whisk to lightly beat the eggs in a large mixing bowl. Add the corn syrup and molasses and stir together until completely blended.
⅔ cup firmly packed light brown sugar **2 ounces (4 tablespoons, ½ stick) unsalted butter, melted** **1 teaspoon pure vanilla extract** **⅛ teaspoon salt**	Add the sugar, butter, vanilla, and salt and stir together well.
	Add the toasted pecans to the filling mixture and stir to distribute them evenly.
	Transfer the pecan filling to the pie shell and use a rubber spatula to spread it out evenly.

Don't the cut the pie while it is too warm or it won't hold together.

Making a Change
Replace ½ cup of flour in the pie dough with finely chopped pecans. Pulse with the remaining flour in the recipe until the pecans are very finely ground.

To make Chocolate Pecan Pie, add 6 ounces melted bittersweet or semisweet chocolate to the filling before adding the pecans.

Adding Style
Serve slices of the pie with vanilla ice cream or whipped cream.

Bake the pie for 10 minutes, then reduce the oven temperature to 350°F. Bake the pie another 35 to 40 minutes, until the filling is set and no longer jiggles when the pan is moved.

Remove the pie from the oven and cool at least 30 minutes on a rack. Serve warm or at room temperature.

Pecan Shortbread

CLASSIC SHORTBREAD is made with only a few ingredients: butter, flour, sugar, and salt. This is a variation with the addition of brown sugar, vanilla extract, pecans, and a bit of freshly grated nutmeg. The result is deep flavor with a delicate and slightly crunchy texture. **Makes 32 pieces**

5 ounces (10 tablespoons, 1¼ sticks) unsalted butter, softened	Place the butter in the bowl of an electric stand mixer or in a large mixing bowl. Using the flat beater attachment or a hand-held mixer, beat the butter on medium speed until light and fluffy, about 2 minutes.
½ cup granulated sugar **2 tablespoons light brown sugar**	Add the granulated sugar and brown sugar and beat together until thoroughly blended, about 2 minutes. Stop occasionally and scrape down the bottom and sides of the bowl with a rubber spatula.
1 cup pecans, coarsely chopped **2 teaspoons pure vanilla extract**	Add the pecans and vanilla to the butter mixture and blend thoroughly. Stop and scrape down the bottom and sides of the bowl with a rubber spatula.
1½ cups all-purpose flour **¼ teaspoon salt** **⅛ teaspoon freshly grated nutmeg**	Over a large piece of waxed or parchment paper or a bowl, sift the flour. Add the salt and nutmeg and toss to blend together. Add this mixture to the butter mixture in 3 stages, blending well after each addition.

Transfer the shortbread dough to the baking pan. Use your fingertips to press the dough evenly into the pan and the corners. Use a ruler and a sharp knife to score the shortbread into 1 × 2-inch rectangles. Use a fork to pierce each shortbread rectangle in 2 places on the diagonal. Cover the baking pan tightly with plastic wrap and chill in the refrigerator for at least 2 hours.

Adjust the oven racks to the upper and lower thirds and preheat the oven to 300°F. Line the baking sheets with parchment paper.

Essential Gear

- Electric stand mixer with flat beater attachment, or large mixing bowl and hand-held mixer
- Rubber spatula
- Sifter
- 8-inch square baking pan
- Ruler
- Sharp knife
- Two baking sheets
- Two parchment paper sheets
- Two cooling racks

Keeping

Store the shortbread in an airtight plastic container between layers of waxed paper at room temperature up to 1 week.

Streamlining

The shortbread dough can be made up to 3 days in advance and kept tightly wrapped in a double layer of plastic wrap in the refrigerator. To freeze up to 3 months, wrap the dough snugly in several layers of plastic wrap and place in a freezer bag. Use a large piece of masking tape and an indelible marker to label and

Use a sharp knife and cut through the scored pieces of shortbread. Transfer the shortbread rectangles to the baking sheets, leaving at least 1 inch of space between them.

Bake for 12 minutes, then switch the baking sheets and bake another 12 to 15 minutes, until the shortbreads are set and very lightly colored. Remove the baking sheets from the oven and cool the shortbread completely on the baking sheets on racks.

date the contents. If frozen, defrost in the refrigerator.

Making a Change
Replace the pecans with walnuts, almonds, or macadamia nuts.

Pecan Tassies

THESE ARE small pecan pies made in 2½-inch round tartlet pans. The name "tassie" comes from two different sources. In the southern United States, *tassie* means tiny pies. In Scotland, *tassie* means a small cup, which describes how these tiny pies look. These are very easy to eat out of hand, which makes them perfect for a buffet gathering. **Makes twenty-four 2½-inch round tartlets**

PASTRY DOUGH

4 ounces (8 tablespoons, 1 stick) unsalted butter, softened
3 ounces cream cheese, softened

Place the butter and cream cheese in the bowl of an electric stand mixer or a large mixing bowl. Use the flat beater attachment or a hand-held mixer to beat together until fluffy, about 2 minutes.

1 cup all-purpose flour

Add the flour to the butter mixture and beat on medium speed until the dough comes together in a ball.

Turn the pastry dough onto a large piece of plastic wrap. Shape into a flat disk and wrap tightly. Chill in the refrigerator until firm before using, at least 2 hours. Chilling the dough relaxes the gluten in the flour so it won't be too elastic and will roll out easily. It also firms up the butter in the dough so it will need less flour when rolled out. If the dough is too firm, it will splinter and break when rolled out. Let it stand at room temperature for 10 to 15 minutes before rolling to become more pliable.

Center a rack in the oven and preheat it to 350°F.

On a smooth, flat surface, roll out the pastry dough between sheets of lightly floured waxed or parchment paper to a thickness of about

Essential Gear
- Electric stand mixer with flat beater attachment, or large mixing bowl and hand-held mixer
- Rolling pin
- 3¼-inch round plain-edge cutter
- Forty-eight 2½-inch round, fluted-edge tartlet pans
- Baking sheet
- Cake pan
- Liquid measuring cup
- Whisk
- Cooling rack

Keeping
Store the tartlets in a single layer on a baking pan. Cover the top of the tartlets with a large piece of waxed paper and then tightly wrap the pan with aluminum foil and keep at room temperature up to 3 days

Streamlining
The pastry dough can be made in advance and kept in the refrigerator, tightly wrapped in a double layer of plastic wrap, up to 4 days

¼ inch. Carefully peel the paper off the top of the dough. Brush excess flour off the dough. Use the round cutter or a small bowl measuring 3¼ inches to cut the dough into circles. Carefully peel the circles off the other piece of paper. Gather together the dough scraps, reroll, and cut out any remaining circles.

Gently place each circle in a tartlet pan. Carefully lift up the sides and ease the pastry dough into the bottom and sides of each pan, pushing it lightly into the fluted edges. Trim off the excess pastry dough at the top of the pan with your fingertips. Transfer the tartlet pans to a baking sheet and chill while preparing the filling. Gather together the dough scraps, re-roll, and cut out any remaining circles.

PECAN FILLING

1 cup pecans

Place the pecans in a single layer in a cake or pie pan and toast in the oven for 5 minutes. Remove the pan and cool on a rack. Roughly chop the pecans.

Divide the chopped pecans among the tartlet pans.

1 extra-large egg, at room temperature
3 tablespoons dark corn syrup
1 ounce (2 tablespoons) unsalted butter, melted
2 teaspoons pure vanilla extract

In a medium bowl, whisk together the egg, corn syrup, butter, and vanilla.

¾ cup firmly packed light brown sugar
¼ teaspoon salt

Add the sugar and salt and whisk together until the mixture is very smooth.

Pour the filling into a liquid measuring cup and distribute the filling evenly among the tartlet pans.

Bake the tartlets for 25 to 30 minutes, until the filling is set and the tartlet dough is light golden brown.

Remove the baking pan from the oven and cool the tartlets completely on a rack.

To remove the tartlets from the pans, tap each pan lightly on a flat surface. The tartlets should slip out easily. If they are stuck to the pan, use the point of a sharp knife to help release them from the pans.

before using. To freeze up to 4 months, wrap it in a double layer of plastic wrap and place it inside a freezer bag. Use a large piece of masking tape and an indelible marker to label and date the contents. If frozen, defrost in the refrigerator overnight before using. If the dough is too cold to roll out, let it stand at room temperature to become pliable.

Troubleshooting
Don't roll out the pastry dough before it is chilled. The dough will be too soft and it will require a lot of flour to roll out, which will make the dough tough.

Making a Change
Replace the pecans with walnuts or almonds.

Adding Style
Serve each tartlet with a scoop of whipped cream or vanilla ice cream.

Pine Nut Butter Cake

Y OU DON'T NEED an electric mixer to make this cake because it is mixed by hand in a large bowl. Pine nuts are scattered over the top before the cake is baked, adding their own special nutty flavor. The cake is delicious for afternoon tea, packed in a lunch box, or as dessert with a scoop of vanilla or caramel ice cream. **Makes one 9-inch round cake, 12 servings**

CAKE

1 tablespoon unsalted butter, softened	Center a rack in the oven and preheat it to 350°F. Use your fingertips or a paper towel to generously butter the inside of the cake pan.
2 teaspoons all-purpose flour	Dust the inside of the pan with the flour. Shake and tilt the pan to evenly distribute the flour, then turn the pan over and shake out the excess over the sink.
	Cut a round of parchment paper to fit the bottom of the pan. Butter the parchment paper round and place in the pan, butter-side up.
6 ounces (12 tablespoons, ³/₄ stick) unsalted butter, melted	Place the butter in a large bowl.
1 cup granulated sugar **²/₃ cup firmly packed light brown sugar**	Add the granulated sugar and brown sugar and stir together with a rubber spatula until thoroughly blended.
2 extra-large eggs, at room temperature **2 teaspoons pure vanilla extract**	One at a time, add the eggs to the butter mixture. The eggs will sit on top of the butter mixture, so stop and scrape down the sides and bottom of the bowl with a rubber spatula to help mix evenly. The mixture may look curdled as the eggs are added, but as you scrape down the bowl, the mixture will smooth out. Then add the vanilla and stir to blend.
1¹/₂ cups all-purpose flour **¹/₂ teaspoon salt**	Over a large piece of waxed or parchment paper or a bowl, sift together the flour and salt, then add to the butter mixture in 3 stages, blending well after each addition.
	Transfer the batter to the prepared cake pan. The batter is very thick, so use a rubber spatula to spread it evenly into the pan.
3 tablespoons pine nuts	Sprinkle the pine nuts evenly over the top of the cake.

Essential Gear
- 9 × 2-inch round cake pan
- Scissors
- Parchment paper
- Large mixing bowl
- Rubber spatula
- Sifter
- Cooling rack

Keeping

Store the cake, tightly wrapped in aluminum foil, at room temperature up to 4 days. To freeze up to 3 months, wrap the cake tightly in several layers of plastic wrap and aluminum foil. Use a large piece of masking tape and an indelible marker to label and date the contents. If frozen, defrost overnight in the refrigerator and bring to room temperature before serving.

Making a Change

Replace the pine nuts with finely chopped macadamia nuts.

Bake the cake for 35 to 40 minutes, until a cake tester inserted into the center comes out clean

Remove the pan from the oven and cool completely on a rack. Invert the pan to remove the cake, then peel the parchment paper off the back of the cake. Re-invert the cake onto a plate or a cardboard cake circle.

Cut into wedges and serve at room temperature.

Pine Nut Sablé Cookies

SABLÉ IS a French word that means "sandy." It's often used to describe cookie or tart doughs that are delicate and crumbly. In this case, it is the sugar sprinkled on top of the cookies before they are baked that gives them a sandy texture and the dough itself can be a bit crumbly. Pine nuts add their special texture and flavor to these cookies. Use any shape cookie cutter you like. **Makes about thirty 2¹/₂-inch or fifty 1¹/₂-inch cookies**

Essential Gear

• Electric stand mixer with flat beater attachment, or large mixing bowl and hand-held mixer
• Rubber spatula
• Sifter
• Waxed or parchment paper
• Three baking sheets
• Three parchment paper sheets or non-stick pan liners
• Rolling pin
• 2¹/₂-inch or 1¹/₂-inch round plain-edged cookie cutter
• Three cooling racks

Keeping

Store the cookies in an airtight plastic container between layers of waxed paper at room temperature up to 1 week. A kitchen cupboard or pantry is an ideal storage place. To freeze up to 3 months, wrap the airtight container in several layers of plastic wrap and aluminum foil. Use a large piece of masking tape and an indelible marker to label and date the contents. If

4 ounces (8 tablespoons, 1 stick) unsalted butter, softened	Place the butter in the bowl of an electric stand mixer or in a large mixing bowl. Use the flat beater attachment or hand-held mixer to beat the butter on medium speed until it's fluffy, about 2 minutes.
²/₃ cup confectioners' sugar, sifted	Add the sugar to the butter, and cream together well. Stop occasionally and scrape down the sides and bottom of the bowl with a rubber spatula.
1 extra-large egg yolk, at room temperature 1 teaspoon pure vanilla extract	Using a fork, lightly beat the egg yolk and vanilla in a small bowl. Add to the butter mixture and blend well. Stop and scrape down the sides and bottom of the bowl with a rubber spatula. The egg will sit on top of the butter mixture, so stop and scrape down the sides and bottom of the bowl with a rubber spatula to help mix evenly. The mixture may look curdled as the egg is added, but as you scrape down the bowl, the mixture will smooth out.
1¹/₄ cups all-purpose flour ¹/₄ teaspoon baking powder 1 cup pine nuts ¹/₈ teaspoon salt	Over a large piece of waxed or parchment paper or a bowl, sift together the flour and baking powder. Add the pine nuts and salt. Toss to blend well and to coat the nuts with flour.
1 or 2 teaspoons water (optional)	In 2 stages, add this mixture to the dough, blending well after each addition. The dough should be smooth and pliable. If it seems stiff and crumbly, add 1 to 2 teaspoons water and blend thoroughly.

Turn the dough out onto a large piece of plastic wrap and shape into a disk. Cover the dough tightly in a double layer of plastic wrap and chill in the refrigerator until firm enough to roll, about 30 minutes. Chilling the dough relaxes the gluten in the flour so it won't be too elastic and will roll out easily. It also firms up the butter in the dough so it will need less flour when rolled out. If the dough is too firm, it will splinter and break when rolled out. If the dough is too cold and firm, let it stand at room temperature for 10 to 15 minutes before rolling to become more pliable.

Adjust the oven racks to the upper and lower thirds and preheat the oven to 325°F.

Line the baking sheets with parchment paper or non-stick pan liners.

On a smooth, flat surface, roll out the dough between sheets of lightly floured waxed or parchment paper to a thickness of ¼ inch. Turn the dough often while rolling it out to make it easier to roll evenly.

Remove the top piece of paper. Dip the cookie cutter into flour and shake off the excess. Use the cutter to cut out cookies, dipping in flour as needed to keep it from sticking. Transfer the cut cookies to the baking pan, leaving at least 1 inch of space between them.

Gather the dough scraps back together, roll them out, and cut out more cookies.

Bake the cookies for 10 minutes. Switch the baking sheets and bake another 8 to 9 minutes, until light golden.

Remove the baking pans from the oven and cool the cookies completely on the baking sheets on racks.

frozen, defrost overnight in the refrigerator and bring to room temperature before serving.

Streamlining
The dough can be made and kept in the refrigerator up to 3 days before baking. It can also be kept in the freezer up to 3 months. To refrigerate, wrap the dough tightly in several layers of plastic wrap. To freeze, wrap the same way and place the dough in a freezer bag. Use a large piece of masking tape and an indelible marker to label and date the contents. Defrost the dough overnight in the refrigerator.

Making a Change
Replace the pine nuts with finely chopped toasted hazelnuts or toasted sliced almonds.

Pine Nut Tart

IN THIS RECTANGULAR tart, rich, sweet pastry dough encloses a soft, chewy pine nut filling. After this tart is cooled, a light dusting of confectioners' sugar is the only garnish needed. **Makes one 12 × 8-inch tart, 15 servings**

PASTRY DOUGH

Place the butter in the bowl of an electric stand mixer or in a large mixing bowl. Use the flat beater attachment or a hand-held mixer to beat the butter until soft and fluffy, about 2 minutes.

8 ounces (16 tablespoons, 2 sticks) unsalted butter, softened

Essential Gear
- Electric stand mixer with flat beater attachment, or large mixing bowl and hand-held mixer
- Rolling pin
- Sifter
- 12 × 8-inch fluted-edge tart pan with removable bottom

1 cup granulated sugar	Add the sugar, and cream together well. Stop occasionally and scrape down the sides and bottom of the bowl with a rubber spatula.
1 extra-large egg, at room temperature **1 teaspoon pure vanilla extract**	In a small bowl, whisk the egg and vanilla together. Add this mixture to the butter mixture. The egg will sit on top of the butter mixture, so stop and scrap down the sides and bottom of the bowl with a rubber spatula to encourage even mixing. The mixture may look curdled as the eggs are added, but as you scrape down the bowl, the mixture will smooth out.
2½ cups all-purpose flour **1 teaspoon baking powder** **½ teaspoon salt**	Over a large piece of waxed or parchment paper or a bowl, sift together the flour and baking powder. Add the salt and toss to blend together well. In 3 stages, add the flour mixture to the butter mixture, blending well after each addition. Stop occasionally and scrape down the sides and bottom of the bowl with a rubber spatula.

Transfer the dough to a large piece of plastic wrap. Shape into a flat disk and wrap tightly in a double layer of plastic wrap. Chill in the refrigerator until firm before using, about 2 hours. Chilling the dough relaxes the gluten in the flour so it won't be too elastic and will roll out easily. It also firms up the butter in the dough so it will need less flour when rolled out. If the dough is too firm it will splinter and break when rolled out. Let it stand at room temperature for 10 to 15 minutes before rolling to become more pliable.

Center a rack in the oven and preheat it to 375°F.

On a smooth, flat surface, roll out the pastry dough between sheets of lightly floured waxed or parchment paper to a large rectangle about 14 × 10 inches. Carefully peel the paper off the top of the dough. Brush excess flour off the dough, then loosely roll the pastry dough around the rolling pin without the bottom piece of paper. Place the tart pan directly underneath the rolling pin and carefully unroll the pastry dough onto it.

Gently lift up the sides and ease the pastry dough into the bottom and sides of the tart pan, pushing it lightly into the fluted edges. Trim off any excess pastry dough at the top of the pan by running the rolling pin over the top. Or use your fingers to press against the top of the pan to remove the excess pastry dough.

Place the tart pan on a baking sheet and chill in the freezer for 15 to 20 minutes while preparing the filling. This helps prevent the dough from shrinking as it bakes.

- Baking sheet
- Large mixing bowl
- Rubber spatula or wooden spoon
- Cooling rack

Keeping
The tart can last up to 5 days tightly wrapped in aluminum foil at room temperature.

Streamlining
The pastry dough can be made in advance and kept in the refrigerator, tightly wrapped in a double layer of plastic wrap, up to 4 days. To freeze up to 3 months, wrap the dough snugly in several layers of plastic wrap and place in a freezer bag. Use a large piece of masking tape and an indelible marker to label and date the contents. If frozen, defrost overnight in the refrigerator before using.

Making a Change
Replace the pine nuts with walnuts, pecans, or whole unblanched almonds.

1 cup firmly packed light brown sugar	Place the sugar in a large bowl. Add the butter and blend together until smooth.
3 tablespoons unsalted butter, melted and cooled	
1 extra-large egg, at room temperature	Add the egg, egg yolk, vanilla, and salt to the sugar mixture and blend together thoroughly.
1 extra-large egg yolk, at room temperature	
1½ teaspoons pure vanilla extract	
½ teaspoon salt	
2⅓ cups pine nuts	Add the pine nuts and stir to blend them in completely.
	Transfer the mixture to the tart shell and spread it out evenly with a rubber spatula.
	Bake the tart for 25 to 30 minutes, until the filling is set and golden. Remove the baking pan from the oven and cool the tart on a rack.
Confectioners' sugar	Remove the sides of the tart pan (see page 42) before serving. Lightly dust the top of the tart with confectioners' sugar. Cut the tart into 3 equal rows across the 8-inch side, then cut 5 equal rows across the 12-inch side.

Pistachio and Dried Cherry Biscotti

PISTACHIO NUTS AND DRIED CHERRIES add flavor, texture, and color to these twice-baked cookies. The green of the pistachio nuts and the red of the dried cherries make these look very festive, but they're too tasty to save just for holiday time. These are crisp and crunchy, the perfect texture for dunking into a cup of coffee or a glass of milk. **Makes about 2 dozen cookies**

Adjust the oven racks to the upper and lower thirds and preheat the oven to 350°F. Line the baking sheets with parchment paper sheets or non-stick liners.

Essential Gear
- Two baking sheets
- Two parchment paper sheets or nonstick liners
- Electric stand mixer with flat beater attachment, or large mixing bowl and hand-held mixer
- Small bowl
- Serrated knife
- Two cooling racks

2 cups all-purpose flour 1 cup granulated sugar 2 teaspoons baking powder ¼ teaspoon salt	In the bowl of an electric stand mixer or a large bowl, combine the flour, sugar, baking powder, and salt. Use the flat beater attachment or a hand-held mixer to stir together briefly.

2 extra-large eggs, at room
   temperature
1 teaspoon pure vanilla
   extract
4 ounces (8 tablespoons,
   1 stick) unsalted butter,
   melted
	Using a fork, lightly whisk the eggs with the vanilla in a small bowl. Add the egg and vanilla mixture and the butter to the dry ingredients. Mix on low speed until thoroughly combined. Stop occasionally and scrape down the sides and bottom of the mixing bowl with a rubber spatula.

1 cup shelled, toasted pistachios . 1 cup dried cherries	Add the pistachios and cherries and stir to blend thoroughly.

Divide the dough into 2 equal pieces. Dust your hands with flour to keep the dough from sticking and shape each piece into a log about 10 inches long, 4 inches wide, and ¾ inch high. Place each log on a baking sheet.

Bake for 13 minutes, then switch the baking sheets. Bake another 12 minutes, until set. Remove the baking sheets from the oven and let the dough logs rest on the baking sheets for 10 minutes on racks.

Using a serrated knife, cut the logs on the diagonal into ¾-inch-thick slices. Place the slices back on the baking sheet on their sides so the wide part of each faces up.

Bake the biscotti again for 7 minutes. Then switch the baking sheets and bake until firm, 8 to 12 minutes.

Transfer the biscotti to racks to cool.

Keeping

Store the biscotti in an airtight container between sheets of waxed paper at room temperature up to 2 weeks. A kitchen cupboard or pantry is the ideal storage place.

To freeze up to 3 months, wrap the container tightly in several layers of plastic wrap and aluminum foil. Use a large piece of masking tape and an indelible marker to label and date the contents. If frozen, defrost overnight in the refrigerator and bring to room temperature before serving.

Making a Change

Replace the pistachios with almonds, walnuts, or hazelnuts.

Replace the cherries with dried cranberries, raisins, or finely chopped apricots.

9

SEEDS

IT'S NOT VERY often that someone asks for something baked with seeds. And seeds are frequently only thought of as a garnish. However, when seeds are baked into the batter or dough, you get their great flavor and their slightly chewy texture, which I love. I am sure you will enjoy these recipes made with poppy seeds, sesame seeds, and sunflower seeds.

There is never a problem finding seeds, because they are available year-round. In supermarkets, they are usually found in the spice section, and in health food stores, they are available in bulk.

TIPS AND TECHNIQUES

If buying seeds that are in sealed containers, check for the expiration date and that the top seal is not broken. When buying them from open bins, watch for any foreign material that may be mixed with the seeds and that the seeds are uniform in shape and color. Also, smell the seeds to make sure they don't have a rancid odor, because seeds have a high content of natural oil that can go rancid quickly.

Whether they are raw or toasted, store seeds in an airtight container or a tightly sealed plastic bag in the refrigerator for about three months. As a reminder, be sure to smell them before using to make sure they haven't gone bad.

Seeds are available raw, toasted, and toasted and salted. Generally it's better to use either raw or toasted seeds, but not salted. If raw seeds are the only ones you can find, you can toast them yourself in a preheated 350°F oven in a shallow pan for 5 to 8 minutes.

Poppy Seed and Lemon Pound Cake

POPPY SEEDS are complemented perfectly by the tartness of lemon in this rich and moist pound cake. This cake is delicious on its own or served for afternoon coffee or tea, and becomes divine when served with a dollop of whipped cream, fresh raspberry sauce, or a scoop of your favorite ice cream. Another great way to serve this cake is lightly toasted and spread with a bit of butter for breakfast. **Makes one 8½ × 4½ × 2½-inch loaf cake, 12 servings**

CAKE

1 tablespoon unsalted butter, softened	Center a rack in the oven and preheat it to 350°F. Using a paper towel or your fingertips, generously butter the inside the loaf pan.
2 teaspoons all-purpose flour	Dust the inside of the pan with the flour. Shake and tilt the pan to distribute the flour evenly, then turn the pan over the sink and tap out the excess. Or spray the inside of the pan with non-stick baking spray.
8 ounces (16 tablespoons, 2 sticks) unsalted butter, softened	Place the butter in the bowl of an electric stand mixer or in a large mixing bowl. Use the flat beater attachment or hand-held mixer to beat the butter on medium speed until it's fluffy, about 2 minutes.
1½ cups superfine sugar	Add the sugar to the butter, and cream together well. Stop occasionally and scrape down the bottom and sides of the bowl with a rubber spatula.
4 extra-large eggs, at room temperature	One at a time, add the eggs, stopping to scrape down the bottom and sides of the bowl after each addition. At first the mixture may look curdled as the eggs are added, but as you stop and scrape down the bowl, the mixture will smooth out.
3 tablespoons milk 1 tablespoon pure vanilla extract Finely grated zest of 1 large lemon 2 teaspoons freshly squeezed lemon juice	Combine the milk and vanilla and add to the butter mixture with the lemon zest and lemon juice. Mix together until well blended.
2¼ cups cake flour 1 teaspoon baking powder ¼ teaspoon salt	Over a large piece of waxed or parchment paper or a bowl, sift together the flour and baking powder. Add the salt and toss to blend well.

Essential Gear
- 8½ × 4½ × 2½-inch loaf pan
- Electric stand mixer with flat beater attachment, or large mixing bowl and hand-held mixer
- Rubber spatula
- Sifter
- Microplane grater or zester
- Cooling rack

Keeping

Store the cake, tightly wrapped in aluminum foil, at room temperature up to 4 days. To freeze up to 3 months, wrap the cake tightly in several layers of plastic wrap and aluminum foil. Use a large piece of masking tape and an indelible marker to label and date the contents. If frozen, defrost overnight in the refrigerator and bring to room temperature before serving.

Adding Style

Serve each slice of cake with a dollop of whipped cream.

Serve each slice of cake with a spoonful of raspberry sauce (see Meyer Lemon Soufflés, page 143).

Serve each slice of cake with a scoop of ice cream.

Add the dry ingredients to the butter mixture in 3 stages, blending well after each. Stop after each addition and scrape down the sides and bottom of the bowl to ensure even mixing.

¼ cup poppy seeds	Add the poppy seeds to the batter and blend well.

Transfer the batter to the prepared loaf pan. The batter is very thick, so use a rubber spatula to spread it evenly into the pan.

Bake for 1 hour and 12 minutes, until the cake is light golden on top and a cake tester inserted into the center comes out with only a few crumbs clinging to it.

Remove the pan from the oven and cool completely on a rack.

Invert the pan to remove the cake, then turn the cake top-side up. Slice the cake into serving pieces, about ³/₄ inch thick.

Poppy Seed Cake

I T'S BEST to wait a few hours after baking to eat this yummy cake loaded with poppy seeds, because as it rests, its intriguing flavor develops. I like to bake it in a tube pan with deeply grooved sections. The only decoration this cake needs is a light dusting of confectioners' sugar before serving. To make it extra special, serve it with a scoop of rich vanilla ice cream. **Makes one 9-inch round cake, 12 to 14 servings**

Center a rack in the oven and preheat it to 350°F.

1 tablespoon unsalted butter, melted **2 teaspoons all-purpose flour**	Use a pastry brush or a paper towel to butter the inside of the pan, taking care to get into all the grooves. Sprinkle the flour inside the pan, then shake and tilt the pan to cover the bottom and sides. Turn the pan upside down over the sink and shake out any excess flour. Or spray the inside of the pan with non-stick baking spray.
1 cup poppy seeds **½ cup honey** **¼ cup water**	Combine the poppy seeds, honey, and water in the saucepan over low heat. Cook, stirring frequently with a heat-resistant spatula or wooden spoon, until the poppy seeds absorb the liquid, about 5 minutes. Remove the pan from the heat and transfer the poppy seed mixture to a bowl to cool.

Essential Gear

- 9 × 4-inch grooved tube pan
- 1-inch natural-bristle pastry brush
- 1-quart heavy-bottomed saucepan
- Heat-resistant spatula or wooden spoon
- Electric stand mixer with flat beater and wire whip attachment, or large mixing bowl and hand-held mixer
- Rubber spatula
- Sifter
- Cooling rack
- Thin-bladed knife

Keeping

Store the cake, tightly wrapped in plastic wrap,

8 ounces (16 tablespoons, 2 sticks) unsalted butter, softened	Place the butter in the bowl of an electric stand mixer or in a large mixing bowl. Use the flat beater attachment or hand-held mixer to beat the butter on medium speed until it's fluffy, about 2 minutes.
1½ cups granulated sugar	Add the sugar, and cream together well. Stop occasionally and scrape down the sides and bottom of the bowl with a rubber spatula.
4 extra-large egg yolks, at room temperature	One at a time, add the egg yolks to the butter mixture, stopping to scrape down the bottom and sides of the bowl after each addition. At first the mixture may look curdled as the egg yolks are added, but as you stop and scrape down the bowl, the mixture will smooth out.
½ cup sour cream ¼ cup buttermilk 1 teaspoon pure vanilla extract	In a small bowl, combine the sour cream, buttermilk, and vanilla. Add to the butter mixture and blend well.
2¼ cups all-purpose flour 1 teaspoon baking soda ¼ teaspoon salt	Over a large piece of waxed or parchment paper or a bowl, sift together the flour and baking soda. Add the salt and toss to blend. Add the dry ingredients to the butter mixture in 3 stages. Stop after each addition and scrape down the sides and bottom of the bowl. Blend the mixture thoroughly.
4 extra-large egg whites, at room temperature ¼ teaspoon cream of tartar	Place the egg whites in the grease-free bowl of an electric stand mixer. Use the wire whip attachment or a hand-held mixer to whip the egg whites on medium speed until frothy. Add the cream of tartar and whip on medium-high speed until the egg whites hold firm and glossy, but not stiff, peaks. In 3 stages, fold the whipped egg whites into the batter.
	Transfer the mixture to the pan. Use a rubber spatula to smooth and even the top. Bake for 1 hour and 5 minutes, until a cake tester inserted in the center of the cake comes out clean. Remove the pan from the oven and cool on a rack for 15 minutes. Invert the pan onto the rack and leave it for a few minutes so the cake will drop out of the pan. Remove the pan and let the cake cool completely.

GARNISH

2 tablespoons confectioners' sugar, sifted	Dust the top of the cake with confectioners' sugar before serving.

up to 4 days at room temperature. To freeze up to 4 months, tightly wrap the cake in several layers of plastic wrap and aluminum foil. Use a large piece of masking tape and an indelible marker to label and date the contents. If frozen, defrost overnight in the refrigerator and bring to room temperature before serving.

Adding Style

Serve slices of the cake with a dollop of whipped cream or a scoop of vanilla ice cream.

Sesame Seed Biscotti

T OASTED SESAME SEEDS are an unusual, but delicious, addition to these classic twice-baked cookies. Biscotti's crispness makes them the perfect accompaniment to coffee or tea. **Makes about 2 dozen cookies**

Center a rack in the oven and preheat it to 350°F. Line a baking sheet with parchment paper or a non-stick liner.

½ cup plus 2 tablespoons raw, unhulled sesame seeds	Place the sesame seeds in a shallow baking pan and toast in the oven for 5 minutes. Shake the pan and toast another 3 to 4 minutes, until light golden. Remove the pan from the oven and cool on a rack.
2 cups all-purpose flour **⅔ cup firmly packed light brown sugar** **½ cup granulated sugar** **1 teaspoon baking powder** **¼ teaspoon salt**	In the bowl of an electric stand mixer or a large mixing bowl, combine the flour, brown sugar, granulated sugar, baking powder, and salt. Use the flat beater attachment or a hand-held mixer to stir together briefly.
2 extra-large eggs, at room temperature **2 extra-large egg yolks, at room temperature** **1 teaspoon pure vanilla extract**	Using a fork, whisk the eggs and egg yolks with the vanilla in a small bowl. Add the egg and vanilla mixture to the dry ingredients. Mix on low speed until thoroughly combined. Stop occasionally and scrape down the sides and bottom of the mixing bowl with a rubber spatula.
	Add the toasted sesame seeds to the mixture and stir to blend thoroughly.

Divide the dough into 2 equal pieces. Dust your hands with flour to keep the dough from sticking and shape each piece into a log about 10 inches long, 2 to 3 inches wide, and ¾ inch high. Place the logs on the baking sheet, leaving at least 2 inches of space between them.

Bake for 25 minutes, until lightly browned and set. Remove the baking sheet from the oven and let the dough logs rest on the baking sheet for 10 minutes on a rack. Lower the oven temperature to 325°F.

Using a serrated knife, cut the logs on the diagonal into ¾-inch-thick slices. Place the slices back on the baking sheet on their sides so the wide part of each faces up.

Bake the biscotti for 12 to 15 minutes, until very firm. Transfer the biscotti to racks to cool.

Essential Gear
- Baking sheet
- Parchment paper sheet or non-stick liner
- Electric stand mixer with flat beater attachment, or large mixing bowl and hand-held mixer
- Rubber spatula
- Two cooling racks
- Serrated knife

Keeping
Store the biscotti in an airtight container between sheets of waxed paper at room temperature up to 2 weeks. A kitchen cupboard or pantry is the ideal storage place. To freeze up to 3 months, wrap the container tightly in several layers of plastic wrap and aluminum foil. Use a large piece of masking tape and an indelible marker to label and date the contents. If frozen, defrost overnight in the refrigerator and bring to room temperature before serving.

Sesame Seed Wafers

THE DOUGH for these cookies is shaped into cylinders that are rolled in sesame seeds and chilled before they are baked. The sesame seeds on the outside add extra texture and flavor to these chewy, yummy cookies. The dough needs to be made ahead so it has at least an hour to chill before it is shaped, and it needs to chill again before it is cut and baked. Keep the dough cylinders in the freezer, tightly wrapped in several layers of plastic wrap and inside a freezer bag, and you'll always be ready to bake cookies when the mood strikes you. Sesame seeds can be found in bulk bins at natural- and health food stores and in the spice section of supermarkets. I bake these cookies on baking sheets lined with aluminum foil brushed with butter or non-stick liners, not parchment paper, because they tend to stick to the parchment. **Makes about 6 dozen cookies**

Center a rack in the oven and preheat it to 350°F.

2 cups raw, unhulled sesame seeds	Spread the sesame seeds out in a single layer in a jelly-roll pan. Toast them for 5 minutes. Shake the pan and toast another 3 to 4 minutes, until light golden. Remove the pan from the oven and cool on a rack.
½ cup pecans	Place the pecans in a shallow baking pan and toast in the oven for 8 minutes. Remove the pan from the oven and cool on a rack, then chop the pecans finely with a chef's knife on a cutting board or in a food processor fitted with the steel blade.
3 ounces (6 tablespoons, ¾ stick) unsalted butter, softened	Place the butter in the bowl of an electric stand mixer or in a large mixing bowl. Use the flat beater attachment or a hand-held mixer to beat the butter on medium speed until it's fluffy, about 2 minutes.
¾ cup firmly packed light brown sugar	Add the sugar to the butter, and cream together well. Stop occasionally and scrape down the sides and bottom of the bowl with a rubber spatula.
1 extra-large egg, at room temperature **1 teaspoon pure vanilla extract**	Use a fork to blend the egg and vanilla together in a small bowl. Add this mixture to the butter mixture and blend thoroughly.
1 cup all-purpose flour **½ teaspoon baking powder** **⅛ teaspoon salt**	Over a large piece of waxed or parchment paper or a bowl, sift together the flour and baking powder. Add 1 cup of the sesame seeds and the salt and toss to blend together well.

Essential Gear

- Electric stand mixer with flat beater attachment, or large mixing bowl and hand-held mixer
- Jelly-roll pan
- Shallow baking pan
- Chef's knife
- Sifter
- Rubber spatula
- Waxed paper
- Three baking sheets
- Three aluminum foil sheets or non-stick liners
- 1-inch natural-bristle pastry brush or a paper towel
- Three cooling racks

Keeping

Store the cookies in an airtight plastic container at room temperature up to 1 week. A kitchen cupboard or pantry is an ideal storage place. To freeze up to 3 months, wrap the airtight container in several layers of plastic wrap and aluminum foil. Use a large piece of masking tape and an indelible marker to label and date the contents. If frozen, defrost overnight in the refrigerator and bring to room temperature before serving.

Streamlining

The dough cylinders can be made and kept in the refrigerator up to 3 days before baking. They can also be kept in the freezer up to

Add this mixture in 3 stages to the butter mixture. Stop after each addition and scrape down the sides and bottom of the bowl with a rubber spatula. Add the chopped toasted pecans and mix thoroughly.

Cover the bowl tightly with plastic wrap and chill the dough in the refrigerator until it is firm enough to shape into cylinders, at least 1 hour.

Place two large sheets of waxed paper on a flat surface. Sprinkle each piece of waxed paper with ½ cup of the remaining toasted sesame seeds. Divide the dough evenly between the two pieces of waxed paper. Use the waxed paper to shape and roll the dough into cylinders 8 to 10 inches long and about 2 inches wide (see Refrigerator Cookies, page 37). Roll the cylinders in the sesame seeds to make sure they stick. Cover the cylinders tightly with the waxed paper and wrap each roll in plastic wrap. Chill in the refrigerator until firm enough to slice, about 1 hour.

Adjust the oven racks to the upper and lower thirds and preheat the oven to 400°F. Line each baking sheet with a sheet of aluminum foil.

1 ounce (2 tablespoons) unsalted butter, melted

Use a pastry brush or paper towel to brush the top of the foil with melted butter. This keeps the cookies from sticking to the foil as they cool, after baking.

Place a dough cylinder on a cutting board. Using a sharp knife, cut each cylinder into ¼-inch-thick slices. Cut straight down and rotate the cylinder a quarter turn after every 6 slices so it will keep its round shape. If the dough becomes soft while you are working with it, rewrap it, chill for another 10 to 15 minutes, then continue slicing. Repeat with the remaining cylinder of dough, if desired.

Place the slices on the baking sheets, leaving at least 1 inch of space between them.

Bake for 5 minutes. Switch the baking sheets and bake another 5 to 6 minutes, until set. Remove the baking sheets from the oven and cool the cookies completely on the baking sheets on racks.

3 months. To refrigerate, wrap the cylinders tightly in several layers of plastic wrap. To freeze, wrap the same way and place each cylinder in a freezer bag. Use a large piece of masking tape and an indelible marker to label and date the contents. You can take them directly from the freezer and slice for baking, or defrost the cylinders overnight in the refrigerator.

Sunflower Seed Muffins

T HESE INDIVIDUAL cakes are not overly sweet and are delicious any time of day—for breakfast, at afternoon tea, as a snack, or for dessert. They are great on their own, but are especially tasty warmed up and served with butter, jam, or honey. **Makes 2 dozen muffins**

Center a rack in the oven and preheat it to 325°F. Line each cavity of the muffin pans with a paper muffin cup.

8 ounces (16 tablespoons, 2 sticks) unsalted butter, softened	Place the butter in the bowl of an electric stand mixer or in a large mixing bowl. Use the flat beater attachment or hand-held mixer to beat the butter on medium speed until it's fluffy, about 2 minutes.
1 cup granulated sugar **1²/₃ cups firmly packed light brown sugar**	Add the granulated sugar and brown sugar to the butter, and cream together well. Stop occasionally and scrape down the sides and bottom of the bowl with a rubber spatula.
5 extra-large eggs, at room temperature	One at a time, add the eggs to the butter mixture, stopping to scrape down the bottom and sides of the bowl after each addition. At first the mixture may look curdled as the eggs are added, but as you stop and scrape down the bowl, the mixture will smooth out.
2³/₄ cups cake flour **¹/₂ teaspoon baking soda** **¹/₄ teaspoon salt** **¹/₄ teaspoon freshly grated nutmeg**	Over a large piece of waxed or parchment paper or a bowl, sift together the flour and baking powder. Add the salt and nutmeg and toss to blend well.
¹/₂ cup buttermilk	Add the dry ingredients to the butter mixture alternately with the buttermilk in 3 stages, stopping to scrape down the sides and bottom of the bowl with a rubber spatula after each addition.
1 cup toasted, unsalted sunflower seeds	Add the sunflower seeds to the batter and blend thoroughly.
	Use a spoon to divide the batter evenly among the 24 muffin cups, filling them to just below the top. These rise very high, so it's best not to fill the muffin cups all the way to the top
¹/₃ cup toasted, unsalted sunflower seeds	Sprinkle the top of each muffin evenly with the sunflower seeds.

Essential Gear

- Two 12-cavity 3-inch muffin pans
- Twenty-four 3-inch pleated paper muffin cups
- Electric stand mixer and flat beater attachment, or hand-held mixer and large mixing bowl
- Rubber spatula or wooden spoon
- Sifter
- Two cooling racks

Keeping

Store the muffins in an airtight plastic container between layers of waxed paper at room temperature up to 3 days. To freeze up to 2 months, wrap the container tightly in several layers of plastic wrap and aluminum foil. Use a large piece of masking tape and an indelible marker to label and date the contents. If frozen, defrost overnight in the refrigerator and bring to room temperature before serving.

Bake the muffins about 25 minutes, until they have risen and set and a tester inserted in the center comes out clean. Remove the pans from the oven and cool on racks. When the muffins are cool, gently remove them from the pan. Serve warm or at room temperature.

To rewarm the muffins, place them in a 325°F oven for 8 to 10 minutes.

IV.

CHOCOLATE

C HOCOLATE IS VERY NEAR AND DEAR to me. It was my love for chocolate that inspired me to become a pastry chef and confectioner. Working with chocolate continues to fascinate and excite me. And I love to eat it, too, and share it with my family, friends, and students. ✳ Chocolate is used in a wide variety of ways and comes in many different forms. The three basic types of chocolate are dark, milk, and white. Also, there is cocoa powder, which is produced by extracting most of the cocoa butter when chocolate is made. And then there are specialty chocolates such as chocolate chips, cocoa nibs, and gianduia. ✳ Some bakers have shied away from chocolate, believing that it's difficult to use. Nothing is further from the truth. Using chocolate in baking is very easy to do with very little that is required in the way of special equipment and tools. You can be very creative with chocolate, but that's not necessary to make a fabulous chocolate dessert. ✳ The great news about dark chocolate and cocoa powder is that they are very good for you. They have no cholesterol and are high in antioxidants and flavonols. Also, chocolate has a combination of "feel-good" compounds that release endorphins. ✳ In this section I have provided a good deal of background information on chocolate. This will help you gain even more appreciation for chocolate and greatly assist you in working with it. I am sure you will enjoy this and all of my favorite chocolate recipes.

10

ABOUT

CHOCOLATE

ALTHOUGH CHOCOLATE'S ORIGINS are shrouded in the mists of time, there are archaeological findings that point to its genesis in the Amazon basin of South America close to 1,000 years ago. The ancient Maya and other Meso-American indigenous peoples used cacao as early as 600 A.D. in ritualistic ceremonies. The cacao bean was so highly prized that it was even used as currency by the Maya. Chocolate is definitely very special, and I agree with the Swedish naturalist, Linnaeus, who first called chocolate "Food of the Gods." It's my favorite flavor.

CACAO BEANS

Ironically, chocolate *does* grow on trees. But it can't be picked from the tree and eaten directly. It has to go through several processes to become edible. Cacao, the name given to the bean

before it is processed into chocolate or cocoa, is a tropical crop grown within twenty degrees of the equator. Ghana and the Ivory Coast are the world's biggest producers of cacao, but far from the only ones. Cacao is grown in many other countries, including Indonesia, Venezuela, Brazil, Trinidad, Cuba, Madagascar, Papua New Guinea, Malaysia, Ecuador, Mexico, Honduras, Peru, and the United States on the big island of Hawaii.

There are three main varieties of cacao beans: *criollo, forastero,* and *trinitario.* Criollo is the first type of cacao that was grown and still is the most sought-after because it is the most flavorful. In fact, it is known as "the flavor bean." Criollo is also the trickiest type of cacao to grow and, because of this, it is produced in the smallest quantity. Forastero has a rougher flavor that can be bitter. It is known as "the bulk bean" because it is the most widely grown type of cacao in the world. Trinitario is a cross between criollo and forastero cacao that was developed in Trinidad. Trinitario takes the best of both of these varieties of cacao beans, because it has some of the flavor qualities of criollo and the heartiness of forastero. Also, depending on the specifics of the growing region, these varieties can take on their own unique flavor characteristics.

Most chocolates are a blend of two or more varieties of cacao beans. Each manufacturer has its own formulas for particular blends that are closely guarded because it is what makes their chocolate unique. Also, like fine wine, chocolate is now available in single-origin varieties. This is chocolate made from one variety of cacao grown in a particular region or sub-region, which produces a distinct flavor profile as a result of the unique growing conditions of the soil and the climate of that area. The same situation occurs with regions where wine grapes are grown, known as *terroir* in French. The labels on single-origin chocolate bars state the name of the region or sub-region where the cacao is grown. I like to use both blended and single-origin chocolates. My favorite brand of blended chocolate is Scharffen Berger and my favorite brands of single-origin chocolates are E. Guittard and Valrhona. But there are many other high-quality blended and single-origin chocolates.

MAKING CHOCOLATE
A cacao pod is about the size of a football. When the pods are ripe, they are cut from the trees and split open. Inside the pods is a milky white membrane that holds between twenty and forty almond-shaped beans. The membrane and beans are removed from the pod and placed in the sun to dry and ferment for a period ranging from a few days to as long as a week. The amount of time the beans are left to dry and ferment is determined by the variety of bean and

the grower. This step is critical and is one of the factors that determine the flavor quality of the chocolate made from the cacao beans. Unfermented cacao beans never develop good chocolate flavor. At this point, only the tiniest hint of chocolate flavor develops. If you were to eat one of the beans, you would find it extremely bitter. After the beans are dried, they are shipped to chocolate factories.

When the beans arrive at the factories, they are roasted at a temperature between 250°F and 350°F for about an hour. The exact temperature and time depend on the bean and the manufacturer. While the beans are roasting, the outer shells crack. These are blown away during the next process, called winnowing. The inner nib or kernel is left, and this goes on to become chocolate. The nibs are ground between heavy rollers. The heat and friction from this process melts the cocoa butter in the nibs and produces a thick, viscous liquid called chocolate liquor, which is the foundation for chocolate. When most of the cocoa butter is extracted from chocolate liquor, the end product is a dry cake called press cake, which goes on to become cocoa powder (see Cocoa chapter, page 462).

To make dark and milk chocolate, the chocolate liquor is mixed with varying amounts of sugar and cocoa butter. White chocolate is made from cocoa butter mixed with sugar (see Dark Chocolate, page 377; Milk Chocolate, page 414; and White Chocolate chapters, page 437). A small amount of lecithin and vanilla are added to all of these. Then these mixtures are stirred constantly for several hours, a process called conching, named after the original shell-shaped machine. This removes any residual grittiness and produces the velvety-smooth texture we expect when eating fine-quality chocolate. How long chocolate is conched is one of the factors that determines final quality. High-end chocolates are conched for a long period of time, some for as long as seventy-two hours. After conching, the chocolate is tempered and molded into its ultimate form, which is usually bars.

Couverture is chocolate that has a higher percentage of cocoa butter than baking or eating chocolate does. Most professional chefs use couverture. It is the perfect chocolate to use for dipping truffles and candies and for molding because it makes a thin coating and it's also great to use for baking. Most high-quality chocolates are couverture, so it's not difficult to find. Couverture chocolate must be tempered to stabilize the cocoa butter before it is used for dipping or molding. Tempering gives chocolate a glossy sheen and allows it to set up quickly (Techniques chapter, page 25). All chocolate comes from the factory tempered, but once it is melted it must be tempered again if used for dipping or molding. Tempering is done primarily for cosmetic reasons, so the finished chocolate looks good and pops out of molds easily, but tempering is not necessary for baking.

Chocolate bars come as small as one ounce and as large as eleven pounds. Pistoles, buttons, ribbons, and calets are small wafers, disks, pieces, or ovals of chocolate that some chocolate manufacturers are producing in addition to bars. Mostly these are available to professionals, but some of the sources in this book offer these forms (see page 625). What I like most about these forms of chocolate is that they are convenient, because it's not necessary to spend time chopping them up to melt. An exception here is chocolate chips, which are readily available in supermarkets for the home baker.

CHOCOLATE TASTING

I have found that the best way to taste chocolate is in its plain state. This allows the true flavor of the chocolate to come through. In general, the flavor of chocolate does not change when used in baked goods. However, the flavor of chocolate can be influenced by other ingredients, and sometimes the flavor that is the hallmark of a particular chocolate may get lost among all the other ingredients. A factor that does play a role in tasting chocolate is our individual palate chemistry. Also, our personal experiences with flavor and food memories come into play

I recommend looking for the following characteristics when tasting chocolate, no matter which chocolate you are using.

Appearance

The surface should be smooth, unblemished, and glossy with consistent color. Look out for chocolate or sugar bloom (see Storing Chocolate, below), which are indications of poor handling and storage. Watch out for cracks and an overall dull look. These can also indicate that the chocolate has passed its prime.

Aroma

Hold a small piece of chocolate up to your nose with one hand. Cup your other hand around your nose to block off other aromas. Take several small bunny-like sniffs of the chocolate. This helps bring the aroma into your nose and to your palate. Chocolate should smell good. It should entice you to want to take a bite. If you detect off odors, this is an indication that the chocolate may not taste good. If there are other ingredients in the chocolate, they shouldn't overpower the chocolate aroma. Depending on the type of chocolate and the cacao beans used, it will have aromas of berries, flowers, fruit, spice, citrus, smoke, grass, tobacco, or roasted nuts.

Snap

When you break a piece of chocolate it should have a clean, sharp snap. If it crumbles or

Experience how it feels as it melts.

splinters, this indicates that the chocolate is of poor quality and has been handled improperly. Also, chocolate that is too cold when it is broken will splinter.

Mouthfeel

Chocolate melts at a few degrees less than body temperature, which is why it melts rapidly in the mouth. Good-quality chocolate will melt evenly, with a velvety smooth texture, and will not have lumps or feel gritty, greasy, or waxy.

Close your eyes and place a small piece of chocolate in your mouth. Press it against the upper part of your mouth with your tongue. Experience how it feels as it melts.

Flavor

This is the most important part. Chocolate should be pleasing with a well-balanced, harmonious flavor. Many of the same words used to describe wine are used to describe the flavor of chocolate, such as rich, deep, full-bodied, delicate, mellow, sweet, spicy, fruity, berry, caramel, toasted nuts, bitter, tart, harsh, and burned.

Aftertaste

The chocolate flavor should linger in the mouth for a minute or longer and diminish slowly, leaving you satisfied.

See each chocolate chapter (Dark, Milk, and White) for tasting tables with several brands of that type of chocolate.

SELECTING AND WORKING WITH CHOCOLATE

There isn't one chocolate that's best for everything. Use the brand and flavor of chocolate that appeals to you the most, but also follow what the recipes call for as a guide. Unsweetened chocolate is used for cakes, brownies, and cookies that are on the sweet side. It's also used to add extra flavor depth in combination with bittersweet and semisweet chocolate. Bittersweet chocolate provides assertive, deep chocolate flavor in baked goods. Single-origin and varietal chocolates are shown to their best advantage in uncomplicated baked goods where their complex flavor can come through. Semisweet chocolate is the right choice for presenting the pure flavor of the chocolate. It's the perfect chocolate to use for all kinds of desserts and baked goods. Milk chocolate is much sweeter than the darker chocolates and blends very well with lots of other flavors. Dark milk chocolate has more flavor depth than milk chocolate and can hold its own in baked goods. White chocolate has the most delicate chocolate flavor and it's the sweetest of all the types of chocolate. It works very well with fruit and berries. I like to use white chocolate when I want subtle chocolate flavor.

Most chocolate recipes call for melted chocolate, though many recipes only require finely chopped chocolate. In order to melt chocolate, it must be chopped or cut into fine pieces so it will melt quickly and evenly. Chop chocolate with a large chef's knife on a cutting board or use a tool called a "chocolate chipper," which looks like a large, wide fork, to chop chocolate into pieces.

There are two ways to melt chocolate: in the top of a double boiler and in a microwave oven. Both of these methods work well, but do require that you pay attention to the chocolate so it doesn't burn. Chocolate is delicate and temperamental. If it's treated properly, though, it behaves beautifully.

To melt chocolate in the top of a double boiler, here are a few tips to keep in mind:

- **The water level in the bottom pot should be only about 1 inch deep and it shouldn't touch the bottom of the**

Chocolate
is like a
sponge
that easily
picks
up other
flavors.

top pan or bowl. The water should be hot and close to simmering, but not boiling. If the water boils, immediately remove the pan from the heat and stir the chocolate to release extra heat.

- The top pan or bowl should fit very snugly over the bottom pan, so no steam can escape and mix with the chocolate.
- Don't crowd the chocolate in the top pan or bowl. There should be enough room for the chocolate to be stirred while it melts. If there's too much chocolate in the pan or bowl, it will take too long to melt and some of it may burn.
- All utensils used with chocolate must be completely dry. A stray drop or two of water will cause chocolate to "seize up" and become like a fist. Once this happens, there's no way to bring the chocolate back to its smooth, velvety state.
- Never put a cover on the top pan or bowl. This will cause moisture to condense onto the chocolate and it will seize.
- Chocolate melts slowly. Don't increase the heat to try to melt it quickly. Chocolate that becomes too hot will seize up and become like mud.
- Stir chocolate frequently as it's melting, to encourage it to melt evenly.
- Use only a rubber or heat-resistant spatula to stir chocolate. Wooden utensils are porous and hold onto other flavors, which shouldn't be mixed with the chocolate.
- When the chocolate is halfway melted, turn off the heat and leave it to finish melting. There is plenty of

residual heat in the water and bottom pan. This prevents the chocolate from overheating. Dark chocolate shouldn't be heated over 120°F. Milk chocolate and white chocolate are more delicate than dark chocolate because of the milk solids they contain. They shouldn't be heated over 115°F. If they are overheated, the milk solids will coagulate. I have had numerous phone calls from students who are melting milk or white chocolate. They tell me about how the chocolate just won't melt smoothly so they turn up the heat to get it to melt. What they're actually doing is causing the milk solids to coagulate from too much heat and to form lumps. It's impossible to reverse this condition once it's started. Chocolate that's overheated and burned, like burned anything, doesn't taste good. If chocolate burns, throw it away and start over with fresh chocolate.

- When the chocolate is completely melted, remove the top pan or bowl of the double boiler and place it on a dry kitchen towel. Use the towel to completely dry the bottom and sides of the pan or bowl. This prevents any stray drop of water mixing with the chocolate when the pan or bowl is turned over to remove the melted chocolate.

Follow these tips to melt chocolate in a microwave oven:

- Place the finely chopped chocolate in a microwave-safe bowl.
- Melt the chocolate on low power for 15- to 30-second bursts.

- Stir the chocolate after each burst so you can tell if it's melting evenly. Since microwaves melt food from the inside out, it's hard to tell if the chocolate is melting unless it's stirred.
- Don't crowd the chocolate in the bowl. There should be enough room for the chocolate to be stirred. Crowding the chocolate will cause it to take too long to melt, and some of it may burn.
- Use only a rubber or heat-resistant spatula to stir chocolate. Wooden utensils are porous and hold onto other flavors, which shouldn't be mixed with the chocolate.
- Don't cover the bowl. This will build up too much heat and can cause moisture to condense onto the chocolate, which will cause it to seize.

One of the most important factors to be aware of when working with chocolate is moisture. One or two drops of moisture will cause a batch of chocolate to seize up like a ball of mud. This is because the dry cocoa and sugar particles in chocolate are attracted to the moisture. There are two ways to prevent this from happening. The first is to keep all utensils that come into contact with chocolate completely dry. The second is that, when adding liquid to chocolate, there needs to be enough liquid so it will blend with the chocolate and keep the mixture smooth. The general formula is to use one tablespoon of liquid for each two ounces of chocolate. Many recipes call for chocolate to be finely chopped, then to heat cream to a boil, pour it over the chocolate, and stir the two together.

A technique I use for adding chocolate to some of my recipes is to grind it in a food processor. When a recipe calls for finely ground chocolate, I chop the chocolate into small pieces and place them in the work bowl of a food processor fitted with the steel blade. I never grind the chocolate by itself, which would overheat the chocolate and possibly melt it. I always add some of the dry ingredients (flour, sugar, confectioners' sugar) from the recipe to the chocolate. Then I pulse the mixture until the chocolate is very finely ground. This usually takes a couple of minutes. Check the mixture as you go very carefully (watch out for the sharp blade) by feeling it to see how fine the grind is.

STORING CHOCOLATE

Chocolate is like a sponge that easily picks up other flavors. Store chocolate in a cool (ideally about 65°F), dry place away from other food, wrapped in foil or its original packaging. Wrapping chocolate in plastic wrap is tricky because the plastic holds moisture and may cause problems if moisture mixes with the chocolate. Chocolate should not be stored in the refrigerator for the same reason. Moisture may accumulate and mix with the chocolate when it is melted. It is possible to freeze chocolate, if it is extremely well wrapped. If it's frozen, defrost it completely in its wrapping in the refrigerator and bring it to room temperature before using. This shouldn't be necessary, however, because dark chocolate can last for years if stored properly at cool room temperature. Milk chocolate and white chocolate contain milk products, which makes their shelf-life much shorter, usually eight to ten months. It's important to buy chocolate from a source with good turnover so you can be sure the chocolate is fresh. Also, buy the amount that you know you will use within a specific period of time, so it won't be necessary to store it for very long.

Chocolate bloom and sugar bloom are two conditions that occur if chocolate is not stored properly. With chocolate bloom, when the chocolate becomes too warm, the cocoa butter begins to melt, comes out of the emulsion, and drifts to the surface. This is visible as gray or white streaks. Sugar bloom is the result of chocolate being exposed to moisture, which leaches the sugar out of the mixture and brings it to the surface. Gritty dots or streaks on the surface of the chocolate are the symptoms of sugar bloom. Neither of these conditions is fatal. Once the chocolate is chopped up and melted, it is fine to use for baking.

11

DARK

CHOCOLATE

WHEN IT COMES to chocolate, the darker the better for me, but that's not to say that I don't like milk chocolate and white chocolate, too. However, dark chocolate is my first choice.

Dark chocolate is made from chocolate liquor and has lecithin added to it, which acts as an emulsifier, along with vanilla and sugar in most cases. Bitter or unsweetened chocolate is pure chocolate liquor with no sugar. A popular trend in the chocolate industry is dark chocolate with high cocoa percentages. The easy way to figure the percentage of cocoa components is to start with 100 percent. If the label of the chocolate bar states it contains 60 percent cocoa components, then the rest of the mixture is approximately 39 percent sugar, and 1 percent lecithin and vanilla. It's not unusual to find dark chocolates with 60 percent, 62 percent, 70 per-

cent, and 72 percent cocoa components. Some manufacturers are pushing the limit and making dark chocolate with as high as 85 percent cocoa. For dark-chocolate lovers, this is all good news. Many high-quality chocolate brands, such as Scharffen Berger, Valrhona, E. Guittard, and El Rey label their chocolates by percentage of cocoa components.

Extra-bittersweet chocolate has less sugar than bittersweet, which has less sugar than semisweet. At this time, there are no exact standards for labeling dark chocolate as extra-bittersweet, bittersweet, or semisweet. But the FDA requires dark chocolates to contain at least 35 percent cocoa components. By reading the label and seeing the percentage of cocoa components, it becomes easy to decipher exactly what the dark chocolate is composed of. For extra-bittersweet, bittersweet, and semisweet, the percentage of cocoa components normally ranges between 72 and 50 percent. The higher the percentage of cocoa components (56 percent, 60 percent, 62 percent, 70 percent, etc.), the less sugar it contains. With less sugar the chocolate flavor is deeper and more intense.

Dark chocolate is available year-round in supermarkets, cookware shops, gourmet food shops, and natural and health food stores, and through many online and catalog sources. If you are looking for a particular chocolate that you like, just search for it by name on the Web and you will most likely find the manufacturer's Web site, where you will be able to buy it.

TIPS AND TECHNIQUES

Dark chocolates that are close in cocoa percentages are interchangeable in recipes, except for unsweetened chocolate. The recipes in this chapter call for bittersweet chocolate, but if all you have on hand is extra-bittersweet or semi-sweet there should be no problem because these chocolates are easily interchangeable. However, don't substitute a dark chocolate with a very high percentage of cocoa components, such as 85 percent, because it will unbalance the recipe. The recipes in this chapter call for plain dark chocolate. Don't use dark chocolates that are mixed with other flavors, such as spices, or have other ingredients, like nuts.

Note that milk chocolate and white chocolate are not interchangeable with dark chocolate in recipes. Both of these chocolates contain milk products and have much less, or no, chocolate liquor and, therefore, less body than dark chocolate.

For more tips and techniques see Chocolate Tasting, Selecting and Working with Chocolate, and Storing Chocolate in About Chocolate (page 370). The following tables describe the tasting characteristics for twelve brands of dark chocolates that are readily available.

DARK CHOCOLATE TASTING TABLE 1

Brand and Cocoa Components Percentage	Callebaut 56.9%	E. Guittard 61%	El Rey 70%	Ghirardelli Premium Semisweet approx. 51%	Ghirardelli Premium Bittersweet approx. 56%	Lindt Excellence 70%
Appearance	Even Smooth	Even Smooth	Even Smooth	Even Smooth	Even Smooth	Shiny Even
Aroma	Full Deep	Mild	Complex	Earthy	Coffee	Earthy
Snap	Clean Crisp	Sharp Clean	Clean Crisp	Sharp Clean	Sharp Clean	Clean Crisp
Texture/ Mouthfeel	Smooth Light	Waxy	Firm Not much melt	Thick Not much melt	Thick Not much melt	Smooth
Flavor	Sweet Mellow	Mild	Smoky Tobacco	Bland One-dimensional	Bland One-dimensional	Coffee Tobacco
Aftertaste	Moderate	None	Long	Short	Short	Moderate

DARK CHOCOLATE TASTING TABLE 2

Brand and Cocoa Components Percentage	Scharffen Berger 62%	Scharffen Berger 70%	Schokinag 71%	Trader Joe's 70%	Valrhona Manjari 64%	Valrhona Araguani 72%
Appearance	Even Smooth Shiny	Even Smooth Shiny	Even Smooth	Even Smooth	Even Smooth	Even Smooth
Aroma	Complex Fruity Rich	Complex Fruity	Powdery Smokey	Complex Full	Fragrant Flowery	Complex Fruity
Snap	Crisp Clean	Crisp Clean	Crisp Clean	Sharp Clean	Sharp Clean	Sharp Clean
Texture/ Mouthfeel	Velvety Smooth	Smooth Melts easily	Dense	Smooth	Creamy	Creamy
Flavor	Complex Rich Layers	Astringent Complex Fruity	Toasted grain Coffee Earthy	Light Mellow	Astringent Fruity Winey	Cinnamon Fruity
Aftertaste	Long	Long	Long	Short	Moderate	Long

Baked Chocolate Tart

A DELICATE cookie crust encloses a rich, creamy, dark chocolate filling in this tart. It is excellent served either warm or at room temperature. To make this delectable tart even better, serve slices with whipped cream or raspberry sauce. **Makes one 9¹/₂-inch round tart, 12 to 14 servings**

PASTRY DOUGH

1¹/₄ cups all-purpose flour
¹/₂ cup confectioners' sugar
¹/₈ teaspoon salt

In the work bowl of a food processor fitted with the steel blade, combine the flour, sugar, and salt. Pulse briefly to blend.

4 ounces (8 tablespoons, 1 stick) unsalted butter, chilled

Cut the butter into small pieces and add to the flour mixture. Pulse until the butter is cut into very tiny pieces, about 30 seconds. The texture should be sandy with very tiny lumps throughout.

1 extra-large egg yolk, at room temperature
¹/₂ teaspoon pure vanilla extract

Using a fork, lightly beat the egg yolk with the vanilla in a small bowl. With the food processor running, pour the egg yolk and vanilla mixture through the feed tube. Process the dough until the mixture wraps itself around the blade, about 1 minute.

Turn the pastry dough onto a large piece of plastic wrap. Shape into a flat disk and wrap tightly in a double layer of plastic wrap. Chill in the refrigerator until firm before using, at least 2 hours. Chilling the dough relaxes the gluten in the flour so it won't be too elastic and will roll out easily. It also firms up the butter in the dough so it will need less flour when rolled out. If the dough is too firm it will splinter and break when rolled out. Let it stand at room temperature for 10 to 15 minutes before rolling to become more pliable.

Center a rack in the oven and preheat it to 375°F.

On a smooth, flat surface, roll out the pastry dough between sheets of lightly floured waxed or parchment paper to a large circle about 11 inches in diameter. To tell if the dough will fit the tart pan, hold the pan above the dough. If there are about 2 inches of dough that protrude beyond the sides of the pan, it will fit.

Carefully peel the paper off the top of the dough and brush off any excess flour. Loosely roll the pastry dough around the rolling pin without the bottom piece of paper. Place the tart pan directly underneath the rolling pin and carefully unroll the pastry dough into the

Essential Gear

- Food processor
- Rolling pin
- 9¹/₂-inch round, fluted-edge tart pan with removable bottom
- Aluminum foil
- Pie weights
- Baking sheet
- Double boiler
- Whisk or rubber spatula
- Cooling rack

Keeping

Store the tart, loosely covered with waxed paper and then tightly wrapped with aluminum foil, in the refrigerator up to 3 days.

Streamlining

The pastry dough can be made in advance and kept in the refrigerator up to 4 days, tightly wrapped in a double layer of plastic wrap. To freeze up to 3 months, place the wrapped dough in a freezer bag. If frozen, defrost in the refrigerator overnight before using. If the dough is very cold, let it stand at room temperature to become pliable.

Troubleshooting

Don't roll out the pastry dough before it is chilled. The dough will be too soft and it will require a lot of flour to roll out, which results in a tough dough.

tart pan. The tart dough is delicate and needs to be handled gently. Rolling it around the rolling pin and unrolling into the tart pan is an easy way to get the dough into the pan.

Gently lift up the sides and ease the pastry dough into the bottom and sides of the tart pan. Trim off the excess pastry dough at the top of the pan. Transfer the tart pan to a baking sheet and chill in the freezer for 15 minutes.

Line the pastry shell with a large piece of aluminum foil that fits well against the bottom and sides. Fill with pie weights or a mixture of rice and beans. Bake for 10 minutes, then remove the foil and weights. If the bottom of the pastry shell puffs up, gently pierce it in several places with a fork or a sharp knife to release the air. Bake another 12 to 14 minutes, until light golden and set. Remove the pan from the oven and transfer to a rack while preparing the filling.

Lower the oven heat to 350°F.

Once the pastry dough is unrolled into the tart pan, don't push it down forcefully. This will stretch the dough, which will shrink as it bakes, making it flat instead of taking the shape of the tart pan.

Adding Style
Serve each slice of the cooled tart with a dollop of lightly sweetened whipped cream or in a small pool of raspberry sauce (see Meyer Lemon Soufflés, page 143).

FILLING

---

6 ounces bittersweet chocolate, finely chopped
1½ cups heavy whipping cream

Place the chopped chocolate and cream in the top of a double boiler over hot water (see page 373). Stir often with a rubber spatula to help melt evenly. Remove the top of the double boiler and wipe the bottom and sides very dry.

Or place the chocolate and cream in a microwave-safe bowl and melt on low power for 30-second bursts, stirring after each burst.

¼ cup granulated sugar
1 extra-large egg, at room temperature

Use a whisk or rubber spatula to stir the sugar and egg together in a large bowl. Pour the melted chocolate mixture into the egg mixture and stir together until very smooth.

Pour the filling into the tart shell. Bake for 30 to 35 minutes, until the tart looks set and a cake tester inserted 2 inches in from the outside edge comes out clean.

Remove the pan from the oven and cool on a rack.

Remove the sides of the tart pan (see page 42) before serving. Serve the tart at room temperature

Bittersweet Chocolate Pots de Crème

P OTS DE CRÈME (pronounced poh du *krem*) is the French style of baked chocolate custard. This sophisticated dessert is full of deep chocolate flavor. Because it's baked in a water bath that provides cushioning and a humid environment in the oven, the custard won't have any cracks on top and retains a silky smooth texture. Traditionally pots de crème are baked in individual custard cups that have a lid on top, but you can use any custard cups or small, ovenproof glass bowls. **Makes eight ¹/₂-cup servings**

Center a rack in the oven and preheat it to 325°F. Place the custard cups in the baking dish or roasting pan.

6 ounces bittersweet chocolate, finely chopped	Place the chopped chocolate in the large bowl.
2 cups heavy whipping cream	Place the cream in the saucepan and bring to a boil over medium heat. Pour the cream over the chocolate and let it stand for 1 minute. Stir the mixture together using a heat-resistant spatula, whisk, or immersion blender until very smooth.
2 teaspoons pure vanilla extract	Add the vanilla to the chocolate mixture and blend well.
6 extra-large egg yolks, at room temperature **2 tablespoons superfine sugar** **¹/₈ teaspoon salt**	Place the egg yolks, sugar, and salt in a medium bowl. Whisk or stir together until smooth and the sugar is dissolved, about 1 minute.
	Add the chocolate mixture and whisk or stir together until smooth and thoroughly combined.
	Strain the mixture into the liquid measuring cup. Pour the mixture into the custard cups, dividing it evenly among them. Tightly cover the tops of the cups with aluminum foil.
1 quart boiling water	Place the baking dish on the oven rack. Carefully pour boiling water into the baking dish until it reaches halfway up the sides of the cups.
	Bake the custards for 25 minutes, until they look set on the edges but jiggle slightly in the center.

Essential Gear

- Eight ¹/₂-cup custard cups or shallow ovenproof bowls
- 3-quart baking dish or roasting pan
- Large bowl
- 1-quart heavy-bottomed saucepan
- Medium bowl
- Whisk or heat-resistant spatula
- Aluminum foil
- Large fine-mesh strainer
- 4-cup liquid measuring cup
- Cooling rack
- Electric stand mixer with wire whip attachment, or medium mixing bowl and hand-held mixer
- 10- or 12-inch pastry bag and large open star tip

Keeping

Store the baked custards, without the whipped cream decoration, tightly covered with a double layer of plastic wrap in the refrigerator up to 3 days. Decorate before serving.

Making a Change

To make Chocolate Espresso Pots de Crème, add 1 tablespoon plus 1 teaspoon instant espresso powder to the cream before it comes to a boil. Whisk together until very smooth, then pour over the chopped chocolate.

Remove the baking dish from the oven, then remove the cups or bowls from the water bath and place them on a rack to cool completely. Remove the aluminum foil and cover the cups or bowls tightly with plastic wrap. Chill in the refrigerator for at least 2 hours before serving, which helps them to set.

GARNISH

½ cup heavy whipping cream

Place the cream in the chilled bowl of an electric stand mixer or a medium mixing bowl. Using the wire whip attachment or a hand-held mixer, whip the cream on medium speed until it is frothy.

2 teaspoons confectioners' sugar, sifted
½ teaspoon pure vanilla extract

Add the sugar and vanilla and continue to whip the cream on medium speed until it holds firm peaks.

Fit the pastry bag with the star tube and fill partway with the whipped cream. Holding the pastry bag straight up and down about 1 inch above the top of the custard, pipe a star or rosette in the center of each custard (see page 44).

2 tablespoons finely shaved bittersweet chocolate

Scatter the chocolate on top of each custard. Serve the custards chilled.

Bittersweet Chocolate Soufflés

THIS IS A CLASSIC airy soufflé that rises high in the oven. It's a very impressive dessert and always elicits "oohs" and "aahs" when I bring it to the table. A soufflé has to be eaten as soon as it comes out of the oven or it begins to collapse. If it does collapse, the taste is the same, but the dramatic impact is lost. Unlike other soufflés, chocolate soufflé base can be made a day in advance and kept tightly covered in the refrigerator until it's ready to be baked, because the chocolate mixture is thick enough to retain the air bubbles in the whipped egg whites. This is a great time saver and makes it easy to serve a chocolate soufflé for your next dinner party. **Makes eight 1-cup servings**

Essential Gear
- Eight 1-cup soufflé ramekins or straight-sided custard cups or ovenproof bowls
- Double boiler
- Medium bowl
- Electric stand mixer with wire whip attachment, or large mixing bowl and hand-held mixer
- Rubber spatula
- Baking sheet

Streamlining
Prepare the soufflé batter and place it in the ramekins.

1 tablespoon unsalted butter, softened
1 tablespoon granulated sugar

Center a rack in the oven and preheat it to 375°F. Use a paper towel or your fingertips to butter the inside of the ramekins, cups, or bowls. Sprinkle the inside of each with sugar. Tilt the ramekins so the sugar sticks to the butter. Set aside while preparing the soufflé batter.

8 ounces bittersweet chocolate, finely chopped **3 ounces (6 tablespoons, ¾ stick) unsalted butter, cut into small pieces**	Place the chopped chocolate and butter together in the top of a double boiler over hot water (see page 373). Stir often with a rubber spatula to help melt evenly. Or place the chocolate and butter in a microwave-safe bowl and melt on low power for 30-second bursts. Stir with a rubber spatula after each burst. Remove the top pan of the double boiler, if using, and wipe the bottom and sides very dry.
1½ teaspoons pure vanilla extract **¼ teaspoon salt**	Add the vanilla and salt to the chocolate mixture and stir until well blended. Let the mixture cool, stirring occasionally with a rubber spatula to prevent a skin from forming on top.
4 extra-large eggs, at room temperature	Separate the eggs and place the egg yolks in a medium bowl. While stirring the yolks, pour about 1 cup of the chocolate mixture into them to temper them and bring them up to the temperature of the chocolate. Stir together well. Transfer this mixture back to the chocolate mixture and blend together thoroughly.
2 extra-large egg whites, at room temperature	Place the egg whites from the separated eggs plus 2 more egg whites in the grease-free bowl of an electric stand mixer or in a large grease-free mixing bowl. Using the wire whip attachment or a hand-held mixer, whip the egg whites on medium-high speed until they are frothy.
¼ teaspoon cream of tartar **½ cup superfine sugar**	Add the cream of tartar and continue to whip. When soft peaks form, gradually sprinkle on the sugar and continue to whip until the egg whites hold glossy and firm, but not stiff, peaks. Fold the whipped egg whites into the chocolate mixture in 4 stages.
	Divide the mixture evenly among the ramekins. Place the ramekins on a baking sheet and bake for 14 to 16 minutes, until the soufflés are puffed over the top, look set, and the center wiggles a little. You can also test for doneness with a cake tester inserted into the center of a soufflé. It should come out moist, but not runny.
2 tablespoons confectioners' sugar	Remove the baking sheet from the oven, sprinkle the top of each soufflé with confectioners' sugar, and serve immediately.

Tightly cover the ramekins with plastic wrap and refrigerate up to 1 day before baking.

Making a Change
Add 1 cup finely ground toasted almonds or hazelnuts to the soufflé batter before turning it into the ramekins to bake.

To make milk chocolate soufflés, replace the bittersweet chocolate with 12 ounces of milk chocolate and reduce the sugar to ¼ cup.

Adding Style
Serve each soufflé with a dollop of lightly sweetened whipped cream, vanilla or caramel ice cream, or a spoonful of hot fudge sauce, or Raspberry Sauce (see Meyer Lemon Soufflés, page 143).

Chocolate Chip Cookies

THESE ARE CLASSIC cookies that most of us ate while growing up. There are many versions of chocolate chip cookies—crisp, chewy, thin, or puffed. I prefer cookies that are chewy and puffy. Traditionally, these cookies call for milk chocolate chips, but you can use dark chocolate, milk chocolate, or white chocolate chips and any type of nuts you prefer. **Makes 5 dozen cookies**

Adjust the oven racks to the upper and lower thirds and preheat the oven to 350°F. Line the baking sheets with parchment paper or non-stick liners.

1 cup pecans

Place the pecans in a cake or pie pan and toast in the oven for 7 to 8 minutes, until golden. Remove the pan from the oven and cool on a rack.

Place the pecans in the work bowl of a food processor fitted with the steel blade and pulse until they are coarsely chopped. Or chop them on a cutting board using a chef's knife.

¾ cup all-purpose flour
¾ cup cake flour
½ teaspoon baking soda
¼ teaspoon salt

Over a large piece of waxed or parchment paper or a bowl, sift together the all-purpose flour, cake flour, and baking soda. Add the salt and toss to blend well.

4 ounces (8 tablespoons, 1 stick) unsalted butter, softened

Place the butter in the bowl of an electric stand mixer or in a large mixing bowl. Use the flat beater attachment or hand-held mixer to beat the butter on medium speed until it's fluffy, about 2 minutes.

½ cup firmly packed light brown sugar
½ cup granulated sugar

Add the brown sugar and granulated sugar to the butter, and cream together completely. Stop occasionally and scrape down the sides and bottom of the bowl with a rubber spatula.

1 extra-large egg, at room temperature
1 extra large egg yolk, at room temperature
2 teaspoons pure vanilla extract

Using a fork, lightly beat the egg, egg yolk, and vanilla together in a small bowl. Add to the butter mixture and blend thoroughly. The eggs will sit on top of the butter mixture, so be sure to scrape down the sides and bottom of the bowl to help mix evenly. The mixture may look curdled as the eggs are added, but as you stop and scrape down the bowl, the mixture will smooth out.

Add the dry ingredients in 4 stages, blending completely after each addition. Stop occasionally and scrape down the sides and bottom of the bowl with a rubber spatula to ensure even mixing.

Essential Gear
- Three baking sheets
- Three parchment paper sheets or non-stick liners
- Cake pan
- Food processor or chef's knife
- Sifter
- Electric stand mixer with flat beater attachment, or large mixing bowl and hand-held mixer
- Rubber spatula
- Spoon or small ice cream scoop
- Two cooling racks

Keeping
Store the cookies in an airtight plastic container between layers of waxed paper at room temperature up to 5 days. To freeze up to 3 months, wrap the container tightly in several layers of plastic wrap and aluminum foil. Use a large piece of masking tape and an indelible marker to label and date the contents. If frozen, defrost overnight in the refrigerator and bring to room temperature before serving.

Making a Change
Replace the pecans with walnuts or whole unblanched almonds or cocoa nibs.

Replace the semisweet chocolate chips with special dark or 60 percent cocoa chocolate chips, milk

1½ cups semisweet chocolate chips	Add the chocolate chips and the chopped pecans and stir to distribute evenly.

Cover the bowl tightly with plastic wrap and chill the cookie dough for at least 30 minutes.

Use a large spoon or a small ice cream scoop to scoop out mounds of dough about 1 inch in diameter. Place the mounds on the lined baking sheets, leaving 2 inches of space between them so they have room to expand as they bake.

Tightly cover one baking sheet with plastic wrap and chill while baking the other two. Bake the cookies for 5 minutes. Switch the baking sheets and bake another 5 to 6 minutes, until the cookies are set and light golden.

Remove the baking sheets from the oven and cool the cookies completely on the baking sheets on racks. Carefully remove the cookies from the sheets.

Chocolate Linzertorte

LINZERTORTE is an Austrian specialty that comes from the town of Linz. Although it's called a torte, which usually means a cake, it's really a tart with a lattice topping. Whatever the name, though, it's a delicious dessert made with a buttery, ground almond pastry dough that's filled with apricot or raspberry preserves. I always bake a Linzertorte for my husband's birthday cake. It's hard to improve on a classic, but this chocolate version is spectacular and all my tasters agreed. **Makes one 9½-inch round tart, 12 servings**

PASTRY DOUGH

1⅔ cups unblanched sliced almonds **½ cup granulated sugar**	In the work bowl of a food processor fitted with the steel blade, combine the almonds and 2 tablespoons of the sugar. Pulse until the almonds are finely ground, about 2 minutes.
5 ounces bittersweet chocolate, chopped into small pieces	Add the chocolate to the almonds and pulse until it is finely ground, about 2 minutes.

chocolate, or white chocolate chips.

Essential Gear
- Food processor
- Rolling pin
- 9½-inch round, fluted-edge tart pan with removable bottom
- Baking sheet
- Fluted-edge pastry cutting wheel
- Long-handled offset spatula
- Cooling rack

To Keep
Store the tart tightly wrapped in aluminum foil at room temperature up to 3 days.

Streamlining
The pastry dough can be made up to 3 days in

1 cup all-purpose flour 1½ teaspoons ground cinnamon ¼ teaspoon ground cloves	Add the flour, cinnamon, cloves, and the remaining sugar and pulse briefly to blend.
6 ounces (12 tablespoons, 1½ sticks) unsalted butter, chilled	Cut the butter into small pieces and add to the flour mixture. Pulse until the butter is cut into very tiny pieces, about 30 seconds. The texture will be sandy with very tiny lumps throughout.
2 extra-large egg yolks, at room temperature	In a small bowl, beat the egg yolks lightly with a fork. With the food processor running, pour the egg yolks through the feed tube. Process the dough until the mixture wraps itself around the blade, about 1 minute. Turn the pastry dough onto a large piece of plastic wrap. Shape into a flat disk and wrap well. Chill in the refrigerator until firm before using, at least 2 hours. Chilling the dough relaxes the gluten in the flour so it won't be too elastic and will roll out easily. It also firms up the butter in the dough so it will need less flour when rolled out. If the dough is too firm, it will splinter and break when rolled out. Let it stand at room temperature for 10 to 15 minutes before rolling to become more pliable.

Center a rack in the oven and preheat it to 375°F.

Cut off ⅓ of the pastry dough and keep it chilled while working with the other portion. On a smooth, flat surface, roll out the pastry dough between sheets of lightly floured waxed or parchment paper to a large circle 11 to 12 inches in diameter. To tell if the dough will fit the tart pan, hold the pan above the dough. If there are 2 or 3 inches of dough that protrude beyond the sides of the pan, it will fit.

Carefully peel the paper off the top of the dough. Brush excess flour off the dough, then loosely roll the pastry dough around the rolling pin without the bottom piece of paper. Place the tart pan directly underneath the rolling pin and carefully unroll the pastry dough into the tart pan. Gently lift up the sides and ease the pastry dough into the bottom and sides of the tart pan. Trim off any excess pastry dough at the top of the pan. Transfer the tart pan to a baking sheet and chill in the freezer for 15 minutes.

FILLING

1¼ cups apricot preserves	Spread the apricot preserves evenly in the tart shell.

advance. It can also be frozen up to 3 months. To freeze, place the wrapped pastry dough in a freezer bag. Use masking tape and an indelible marker to label and date the package. If frozen, defrost it in the refrigerator before using.

Troubleshooting
Once the pastry dough is unrolled into the tart pan, don't push it down forcefully. This will stretch the dough, which will shrink as it bakes.

Making a Change
Use red raspberry preserves in place of the apricot preserves.

Use toasted hazelnuts in place of the almonds in the pastry dough.

On a smooth, flat surface, roll out the remaining pastry dough between sheets of lightly floured waxed or parchment paper to a large circle about 12 inches in diameter. Carefully peel the paper off the top of the dough. Use the pastry wheel to cut ½-inch-wide strips of the dough. Carefully peel the strips off the other piece of paper. Use a long-handled offset spatula to wedge underneath each strip of pastry dough and gently transfer it to the top of the Linzertorte. Make a lattice by laying the strips in a woven pattern (see page 41).

Roll any remaining dough into a long rope about ¼ inch thick. Place this around the top outer edge where the ends of the lattice strips meet the edge of the tart. Use the tines of a fork to press the rope into the edges of the tart and make a pressed design. Chill the Linzertorte for 15 minutes before baking.

Center a rack in the oven and preheat it to 375°F.

Bake for 30 minutes, until the pastry is set and the filling is bubbling. Remove the pan from the oven and transfer the tart pan to a rack to cool completely.

GARNISH

1 tablespoon confectioners' sugar

Remove the sides of the tart pan (see page 42) and lightly dust the top of the Linzertorte with confectioners' sugar. Serve wedges of the tart at room temperature.

Chocolate Meringue Cake with Whipped Ganache Filling and Frosting

Essential Gear
- Aluminum foil
- Two baking sheets
- 9-inch round cardboard cake circle or cake pan
- Food processor
- Electric stand mixer with wire whip attachment and flat beater attachment, or large mixing bowl and hand-held mixer
- Small saucepan

DELICATE AND CRUNCHY chocolate meringue layers are filled like a layer cake and frosted with whipped ganache to make this extraordinary cake. Although this looks like a regular layer cake, it's much lighter because of the airy meringue layers. I made this for a good friend's birthday party and everyone wanted second helpings. Now it's one of my most requested recipes at dinner parties. Since this cake is rich, cut thin slices so there will be plenty to go around. The meringue layers can be made up to a month in advance. Assemble the cake several hours to a day ahead of when you plan to serve it because it's easier to cut when the ganache has time to soften the meringue layers a bit. **Makes one 9-inch round cake, 12 to 14 servings**

CHOCOLATE MERINGUE LAYERS

Adjust the oven racks to the upper and lower thirds and preheat the oven to 200°F.

Cut sheets of aluminum foil to fit the baking sheets. Use a cake circle or cake pan as a guide and trace two 9-inch circles onto the dull side of each piece of foil with a pencil, then turn the foil over onto the baking sheets.

6 ounces bittersweet chocolate, cut into small pieces
1/3 cup superfine sugar
1 tablespoon unsweetened cocoa powder (natural or Dutch-processed)

In the work bowl of a food processor fitted with the steel blade, combine the chocolate, sugar, and cocoa. Pulse until the chocolate is finely ground, about 2 minutes.

6 extra-large egg whites, at room temperature
1/4 teaspoon cream of tartar

Place the egg whites in the grease-free bowl of an electric stand mixer or in a large grease-free mixing bowl. Using the wire whip attachment or a hand-held mixer, whip the egg whites on medium speed until they are frothy. Add the cream of tartar and whip on medium-high speed until the egg whites hold soft peaks.

2/3 cup superfine sugar

Slowly sprinkle on the sugar and continue to whip the egg whites until they hold glossy and firm, but not stiff, peaks.

Fold the ground chocolate mixture into the egg whites in 4 stages.

Fit the 14-inch pastry bag with the round tip and fill halfway with the meringue mixture. Hold the pastry bag straight up and down, 1 inch above the baking sheet. Start at the center of each circle and pipe close-fitting concentric circles of the meringue mixture, filling each traced circle completely. Or divide the meringue mixture evenly between the four circles and spread it out with a small offset spatula to fill each circle. If you do this, don't spread it so that it's too thin. The meringue should be about 1/4 inch thick.

Dry the meringues in the oven for 2 hours. Turn off the oven and hold the door ajar with a wooden spoon. Leave the meringues in the oven until it is completely cool. Remove the pans from the oven and very gently peel the aluminum foil off of the backs of the meringues.

GANACHE FILLING AND FROSTING

1 pound bittersweet chocolate, finely chopped

Place the chocolate in a large bowl.

- Rubber spatula
- 12- or 14-inch pastry bag with 1/2-inch plain round pastry tip
- 10-inch flexible-blade metal spatula
- Whisk or heat-resistant spatula
- Small sharp knife

Keeping

Store the cake, loosely covered with waxed paper. Place several toothpicks in the top outer edges of the cake to hold the waxed paper away from it so it won't mar the icing. Wrap the cake with aluminum foil and it will keep in the refrigerator up to 4 days.

Streamlining

The meringue layers can be made up to 1 month in advance. Tightly wrap them individually in aluminum foil and store them in a cool, dry place. If they become sticky from humidity, place them on aluminum foil–lined baking sheets in a 200°F oven and dry them again for about 1 hour. Let them cool completely before using.

The ganache for the filling can be made up to 3 weeks in advance and kept in an airtight plastic container away from strong-flavored foods in the refrigerator. Bring it to room temperature before using.

1½ cups heavy whipping cream

Place the cream in a saucepan and bring to a boil over medium heat. Pour the cream over the chocolate and let it stand for 1 minute. Stir the mixture together using a heat-resistant spatula, whisk, or immersion blender until very smooth.

Pour the ganache into a cool bowl, cover tightly with plastic wrap, and cool to room temperature. Chill in the refrigerator until the mixture is thick but pliable, about 1 hour. The ganache should be able to hold the indentation of your finger and not be too soft. If it is too firm, let it stand at room temperature until it reaches the right consistency.

8 ounces (16 tablespoons, 2 sticks) unsalted butter, softened

Place the butter in the bowl of an electric stand mixer or in a large bowl. Using the flat beater attachment or a hand-held mixer, beat the butter on medium speed until it's very fluffy, about 2 minutes.

Add the ganache in 3 or 4 stages while the butter is beating. Stop occasionally and scrape down the bottom and sides of the bowl with a rubber spatula. The ganache will become lighter in color while it is beaten. Don't beat the ganache more than 1 or 2 minutes or it will curdle and separate.

ASSEMBLY

To assemble the cake, place one of the meringue layers on a cardboard cake circle or on a serving place. Use a small sharp knife to carefully trim the edges to make them even, if necessary. Cover the edges of the plate with wide strips of waxed paper to protect it. Using a flexible-blade spatula, spread about ¼ of the whipped ganache evenly over the meringue layer. Position a second meringue layer over the ganache and spread this layer evenly with more whipped ganache. Continue to assemble the cake with the remaining two layers of meringue.

Spread the top of the cake and fill in the sides with whipped ganache. Run the spatula under hot water and dry it, then use it to smooth and even the top of the cake.

1 cup toasted, finely chopped pecans

Press the pecans into the sides of the cake up to, but not over, the top edge. Some of the nuts will not stick to the cake. If there are any holes where there are no nuts, try again to press them into the sides.

Let the cake chill for at least 2 hours before serving so it has time to set and will be easier to cut. To cut the cake into serving pieces, dip a knife in hot water and dry it between each slice. Serve the cake at room temperature.

Troubleshooting

Don't dry the meringue at a temperature higher than 200°F. This will cause the sugar to seep out of the meringues and make them sticky.

Recovering from a Mishap

If a meringue layer breaks, piece it together carefully on top of the ganache. Use more ganache to hold it together.

Making a Change

Add 1 cup finely ground, toasted hazelnuts, walnuts, or almonds to the ground chocolate mixture and fold this into the meringue. Finish the sides of the cake with the same nuts as those used in the meringue.

Adding Style

Make individual 4-inch round or heart-shaped meringue cakes by tracing and piping out 4-inch circles or hearts on the lined pans.

Chocolate Shortbread Rounds

CLASSIC SHORTBREAD is buttery, delicate, slightly crunchy, and always delicious. Rounds or disks are one of the traditional shortbread shapes. This chocolate shortbread is a variation of the original, but equally delectable. In this recipe I use finely ground chocolate, which adds both flavor and texture. This recipe also uses rice flour, found occasionally in traditional shortbread recipes. It adds a bit of crispness to the texture of the cookies. You can find rice flour in bulk bins in health and natural-food stores. Since there are so few ingredients in shortbread, you always want to use the best quality you can find. **Makes 3½ dozen cookies**

Essential Gear
- Electric stand mixer with flat beater attachment, or large mixing bowl and hand-held mixer
- Rubber spatula
- Food processor
- Rolling pin
- Two baking sheets
- Two parchment paper sheets or non-stick liners
- 2-inch round cutter with plain or fluted edges
- Two cooling racks

Keeping
Store the shortbread rounds in an airtight plastic container between layers of waxed paper at room temperature up to 1 week.

Streamlining
The shortbread dough can be made up to 3 days in advance and kept tightly wrapped in a double layer of plastic wrap in the refrigerator. To freeze up to 3 months, wrap the dough snugly in several layers of plastic wrap and place in a freezer bag. Use a large piece of masking tape and an indelible marker to label and date the contents. If frozen, defrost in the refrigerator. If the dough is very cold, it will need to stand at room temperature until it is pliable enough to roll out.

Adding Style
Drizzle the cooled shortbread rounds with thin lines

---

8 ounces (16 tablespoons, 2 sticks) unsalted butter, softened

Place the butter in the bowl of an electric stand mixer or in a large mixing bowl. Using the flat beater attachment or a hand-held mixer, beat the butter on medium speed until light and fluffy, about 2 minutes.

½ cup superfine sugar

Add the sugar and beat together until thoroughly blended, about 2 minutes. Stop occasionally and scrape down the bottom and sides of the bowl with a rubber spatula.

1⅔ cups all-purpose flour
⅓ cup rice flour
4 ounces bittersweet chocolate, coarsely chopped
¼ teaspoon salt

In the work bowl of a food processor fitted with the steel blade, combine the flour, rice flour, chocolate, and salt. Pulse until the chocolate is very finely ground, about 2 minutes. Add to the butter mixture in 4 stages, blending well after each addition.

Turn the dough out onto a large piece of plastic wrap and form into a flat disk. Cover the dough tightly, wrap again in plastic wrap, and chill until firm enough to roll, about 30 minutes.

Line the baking sheets with parchment paper or non-stick liners.

On a smooth, flat work surface, roll out the dough between sheets of lightly floured waxed or parchment paper to a thickness of about ¼ inch. Carefully peel the paper off the top of the dough. Brush excess flour off the dough, then use the cutter to cut out shortbread rounds. Dip the cutter into flour and shake off the excess. Cut straight down through the dough without twisting and pull the cutter straight up. Twisting changes the shape of the edges and seals them, making the rounds bake unevenly.

Transfer the rounds to the baking sheets, leaving at least 1 inch of space between them. Chill the rounds for 15 minutes before baking.

Gather together the scraps of dough, roll them, and cut out rounds. Proceed as above.

Adjust the oven racks to the upper and lower thirds and preheat the oven to 325°F.

Bake the shortbread rounds for 10 minutes, then switch the baking sheets and bake another 6 to 8 minutes, until the rounds are set. Remove the baking sheets from the oven and cool the cookies completely on the baking sheets on racks.

of bittersweet, semisweet, milk, or white chocolate (see page 43). Let the chocolate set firmly for 15 minutes in the refrigerator before storing.

Dip the cooled shortbread rounds in tempered bittersweet chocolate (see page 43). Let the chocolate set firmly for 15 minutes in the refrigerator before storing.

Chocolate Soufflé Cake

DON'T BE ALARMED when this flourless chocolate cake falls slightly as it cools after baking. That's exactly what it's supposed to do. This cake not only tastes divine, it has two distinct textures depending on how it's stored. When served at room temperature shortly after baking, the cake has a creamy texture. It becomes dense and fudgy when stored in the refrigerator. Either way it's one of my all-time favorites. **Makes one 9½-inch round cake, 12 to 14 servings**

Center a rack in the oven and preheat it to 350°F.

1 tablespoon unsalted butter, softened

Use a paper towel or your fingertips to butter the inside of the spring-form pan.

2 teaspoons all-purpose flour

Dust the inside of the pan with the flour. Shake and tilt the pan to evenly distribute the flour, then turn the pan over and shake out the excess over the sink.

Cut a round of parchment paper to fit the bottom of the pan. Butter the parchment paper round and place in the pan, butter-side up.

6 ounces (12 tablespoons, 1½ sticks) unsalted butter
½ cup heavy whipping cream

Place the butter and cream together in the saucepan over medium heat. Stir often with a heatproof spatula or wooden spoon until the mixture is close to a simmer.

1 pound bittersweet chocolate, finely chopped

Take the pan off of the heat and add the chocolate. Stir until the chocolate is completely melted and the mixture is smooth.

Essential Gear
- 9½-inch round spring-form pan
- Parchment paper
- Small heavy-bottomed saucepan
- Heatproof spatula or wooden spoon
- Electric stand mixer with wire whip attachment, or large mixing bowl and hand-held mixer
- Rubber spatula
- Cooling rack
- Sugar dredger or fine-mesh strainer

Keeping
Store the cake tightly wrapped with aluminum foil at room temperature for 2 days or in the refrigerator up to 4 days.

Making a Change
Add 1 cup finely ground toasted almonds or hazelnuts to the cake mixture before turning into the pan to bake.

2 teaspoons pure vanilla extract ¼ teaspoon salt	Add the vanilla and salt and stir until well blended. Let the mixture cool, stirring frequently with a rubber spatula to prevent a skin from forming on top.
6 extra-large egg yolks, at room temperature ⅓ cup granulated sugar	Place the egg yolks and sugar in the bowl of an electric stand mixer or in a large bowl. Using the wire whip attachment or a hand-held mixer, whip the egg yolks and sugar until they are very thick and pale colored and hold a slowly dissolving ribbon as the beater is lifted, about 5 minutes.
	Pour the melted chocolate mixture into the whipped egg yolks and blend together thoroughly on low speed.
6 extra-large egg whites, at room temperature ⅓ cup granulated sugar	Place the egg whites in the grease-free bowl of an electric stand mixer or in a large grease-free bowl. Using the wire whip attachment or a hand-held mixer, whip the egg whites on medium-high speed until they are frothy. Gradually sprinkle on the sugar and continue to whip until the egg whites hold glossy and firm, but not stiff, peaks.
	Fold the whipped egg whites into the chocolate mixture in 4 stages.
	Pour the cake mixture into the prepared springform pan.
	Bake the cake for 35 to 40 minutes, until a cake tester or toothpick inserted in the center comes out slightly moist. The top of the cake may be slightly cracked. This adds to the rustic look of the cake and doesn't affect the flavor.
	Remove the cake from the oven and cool on a rack. Release the hinge on the side of the springform pan and carefully lift the side away from the cake.

GARNISH

2 tablespoons confectioners' sugar	Place the sugar in a sugar dredger or a fine-mesh strainer and dust the top of the cake.
	Run a knife under hot water and wipe it dry to cut the cake into thin slices.

Adding Style

Serve each slice of cake with a dollop of lightly sweetened whipped cream, a scoop of vanilla or caramel ice cream, or in a pool of raspberry sauce (see Meyer Lemon Soufflés, page 143), and scatter fresh raspberries around the plate.

Dark Chocolate Crème Brûlée

C RÈME BRÛLÉE (pronounced krem brew *lay*) is the French name for "burnt cream," which is cold baked custard with a crisp, brittle topping of caramelized sugar. The topping is a wonderful textural contrast to the silky smooth custard underneath. I love this dark chocolate version of crème brûlée because of its rich deep flavor. Crème brûlée is baked in a water bath to help retain its creamy texture. You can use custard cups, ramekins, or small oven-proof bowls to bake this delectable custard. The custard needs to chill for a few hours before serving, so make it a day ahead or early on the day you plan to serve it. **Makes eight ¹/₂-cup servings**

Center a rack in the oven and preheat it to 300°F. Place the custard cups in the baking dish or roasting pan.

3 cups heavy whipping cream

¹/₃ cup superfine sugar

Place the cream and sugar together in the saucepan and bring to a boil over medium heat, stirring occasionally to blend evenly.

8 ounces bittersweet chocolate, finely chopped

Take the saucepan off the heat and add the chocolate. Let it stand for 1 minute, then stir together using a heat-resistant spatula, whisk, or immersion blender until very smooth.

1 teaspoon pure vanilla extract

Add the vanilla and stir in completely.

6 extra-large egg yolks, at room temperature

Place the egg yolks in a medium bowl. Slowly pour in the chocolate mixture, whisking or stirring constantly until well blended.

Strain the mixture into a large liquid measuring cup.

Pour the mixture into the custard cups or bowls, dividing it evenly among them.

1 quart boiling water

Place the baking dish or roasting pan on the oven rack. Carefully pour boiling water into the baking dish or roasting pan until it reaches halfway up the sides of the cups or bowls. Tightly cover the top of the pan with aluminum foil.

Bake the custards for 1 hour until a tester inserted in the center comes out slightly moist and the centers jiggle slightly when the pan is moved.

Essential Gear

- Eight ¹/₂-cup custard cups or shallow ovenproof bowls
- 3-quart baking dish or roasting pan
- Aluminum foil
- Large liquid measuring cup (2- or 4-cup capacity)
- 2-quart heavy-bottomed saucepan
- Medium bowl
- Whisk or heat-resistant spatula
- Large fine-mesh strainer
- Cooling rack
- Propane kitchen torch (optional)

Keeping

Store the baked custards, without the caramelized sugar topping, tightly covered with a double layer of plastic wrap in the refrigerator up to 3 days. Caramelize the top of the custard before serving.

Remove the baking dish from the oven, then remove the cups or bowls from the water bath and place them on a rack to cool completely. Remove the aluminum foil and cover the cups or bowls tightly with plastic wrap, and chill in the refrigerator at least 4 hours before serving, which helps them to set.

¹⁄₂ cup superfine sugar

Sprinkle the top of each custard evenly with a teaspoon or two of sugar.

To caramelize the top of the custards, use a propane kitchen torch. Hold the torch a few inches above the custard and move it around the top. The sugar will become bubbly and golden brown. Or place the custards on a baking sheet or roasting pan and place them under the broiler for 2 to 3 minutes. Watch carefully, because the sugar can burn quickly.

Serve the custards immediately or hold at room temperature for up to 1 hour.

Dark Chocolate Cupcakes

ALTHOUGH THESE MAY remind you of the cupcakes you ate as a child at birthday parties, they are far different. An elegant dark chocolate cake dressed up with ganache frosting makes these individual cakes a stand-out whenever they are served. Cupcakes are fun because they're easy to eat and everyone enjoys having their own little cake. **Makes 2 dozen cupcakes**

Adjust the oven racks to the upper and lower thirds and preheat the oven to 350°F. Line each cavity of the muffin pan with a paper muffin cup.

CUPCAKES

9 ounces bittersweet chocolate, finely chopped

9 ounces (18 tablespoons, 1¹⁄₄ sticks) unsalted butter, cut into small pieces

Place the chocolate and the butter together in the top of a double boiler over low heat. Stir often with a rubber spatula to help melt evenly. Remove the top pan of the double boiler and wipe the bottom and sides very dry. Let the mixture cool, stirring occasionally with a rubber spatula to prevent a skin from forming on top.

Or place the chocolate and butter in a microwave-safe bowl and melt on low power for 30-second bursts. Stir with a rubber spatula after each burst.

Essential Gear

- Two 12-cavity 3-inch muffin pans
- 3-inch pleated paper muffin cups
- Double boiler
- Rubber spatula
- Electric stand mixer with wire whip attachment and the flat beater attachment, or large mixing bowl and hand-held mixer
- Siter
- 2-cup liquid measuring cup
- Two cooling racks
- Large bowl
- Small saucepan

Keeping

Store the cupcakes in a single layer in an airtight plastic

6 extra-large eggs, at room temperature	Place the eggs in the bowl of an electric stand mixer or in a large bowl. Using the wire whip attachment or a hand-held mixer, whip the eggs on medium speed until they are frothy.
1 cup superfine sugar **½ cup firmly packed light brown sugar**	Add the superfine sugar and brown sugar and whip together until the mixture is very thick and pale colored and holds a slowly dissolving ribbon as the beater is lifted, about 5 minutes.
2 teaspoons pure vanilla extract	Add the vanilla and stir to blend thoroughly.
	Add the chocolate mixture to the egg mixture and blend completely on low speed. Stop and scrape down the sides and bottom of the bowl with the rubber spatula.
¾ cup all-purpose flour **¼ teaspoon salt**	Over a medium piece of waxed or parchment paper or a bowl, sift the flour. Add the salt and toss to blend together.
	In 2 stages, add the flour mixture to the chocolate mixture, blending well after each addition. Stop and scrape down the sides and bottom of the bowl with the rubber spatula. This is now the cupcake batter.
1½ cups walnuts, finely chopped	Add the walnuts to the batter and stir to distribute them evenly.
	Pour half of the batter into the liquid measuring cup. Divide the batter evenly among the cavities of one muffin pan, filling them ¾ full. Repeat with the remaining batter and muffin pan.
	Bake the cupcakes for 9 minutes, then switch the pans and bake another 9 minutes, until a cake tester or toothpick inserted in the center comes out slightly moist.
	Remove the pans from the oven and cool on a rack for 15 minutes.
	Lift the cupcakes from the pan and cool completely on racks.

GANACHE FROSTING

10 ounces bittersweet chocolate, finely chopped	Place the chocolate in a large bowl.
¾ cup heavy whipping cream	In a small saucepan, warm the cream over medium heat until it boils. Pour the cream over the chopped chocolate. Let it stand for 1 minute, then stir together well using a rubber spatula, whisk, or immersion blender until very smooth.

container at room temperature up to 4 days. To freeze up to 4 months, wrap the container tightly in several layers of plastic wrap and aluminum foil. Use a large piece of masking tape and an indelible marker to label and date the contents. If frozen, defrost overnight in the refrigerator and bring to room temperature before serving.

Making a Change
Replace the walnuts with 1½ cups toasted and finely ground hazelnuts or unblanched almonds.

Adding Style
Sprinkle the top of the frosted cupcakes with ground toasted hazelnuts or ground toasted almonds if using hazelnuts or almonds inside.

Press toasted whole, unblanched almonds on the top of the frosted cupcakes in a random design if using almonds inside.

Drizzle the top of the frosted cupcakes with melted white chocolate or melted semisweet chocolate in close lines or in concentric circles (see page 43).

| 1 teaspoon pure vanilla extract | Add the vanilla and mix in completely. |
| | |

Cover the ganache mixture tightly with plastic wrap and cool to room temperature. Chill in the refrigerator until the mixture is firm but pliable, about 1 hour. A good test is to press a finger into the mixture. If it takes the indentation of your finger easily, it's at the right point. If the ganache is too soft, it will feel runny, and if it is too firm, it will be hard to press your finger in it. If the ganache is too firm, let it stand at room temperature until it is soft enough to use.

| 3 ounces (6 tablespoons, ¾ stick) unsalted butter, softened | Place the butter in the bowl of an electric stand mixer or in a large bowl. Using the flat beater attachment or a hand-held mixer, beat the butter on medium speed until it is fluffy, about 2 minutes. Add the ganache in 2 or 3 stages and beat until the mixture holds soft peaks, 1 to 2 minutes. As the ganache beats it becomes lighter in color. Don't beat the ganache too long or it may separate and curdle. |

| ¼ cup lightly toasted, finely chopped walnuts | Use a small offset spatula, a rubber spatula, or a spoon to spread the top of each cupcake with ganache frosting. Sprinkle the top of each cupcake with finely chopped walnuts. |

Dark Chocolate Madeleines

MADELEINES are cake-like cookies that take their characteristic ribbed shell shape from the pans in which they are baked. These are a different twist on traditional madeleines, which are light in color, because they are made with dark chocolate. Make plenty of these because they tend to disappear quickly. **Makes 2 dozen cakes**

Essential Gear

- 1-inch natural-bristle pastry brush or paper towel
- Two 12-cavity, 3-inch madeleine pans
- Double boiler
- Electric stand mixer with wire whip attachment, or large mixing bowl and hand-held mixer
- Rubber spatula
- Sifter
- 2-cup liquid measuring cup
- Two baking sheets
- Two cooling racks

Keeping

Store the madeleines in an airtight plastic container between layers of waxed

| 1 tablespoon unsalted butter, melted and slightly cooled | Adjust the oven racks to the upper and lower thirds and preheat the oven to 350°F. Using a pastry brush or a paper towel, coat the inside of each cavity of both madeleine pans with butter. |

| 3 ounces bittersweet chocolate, finely chopped
3 ounces (6 tablespoons, ¾ stick) unsalted butter, cut into small pieces | Place the chocolate and butter together in the top of a double boiler over low heat. Stir often with a rubber spatula to help melt evenly. Remove the top pan of the double boiler and wipe the bottom and sides very dry. Stir the mixture with a rubber spatula occasionally to prevent a skin from forming on top. |

Or place the chocolate and butter in a microwave-safe bowl and melt on low power for 30-second bursts. Stir with a rubber spatula after each burst.

1 teaspoon pure vanilla extract	Add the vanilla and blend well.
2 extra-large eggs, at room temperature	Place the eggs in the bowl of an electric stand mixer or in a large bowl. Using the wire whip attachment or a hand-held mixer, whip the eggs on medium speed until they are frothy, about 1 minute.
⅓ cup superfine sugar	Add the sugar and whip together until the mixture is very thick and pale colored and holds a slowly dissolving ribbon as the beater is lifted, about 5 minutes.
½ cup all-purpose flour **¼ teaspoon salt**	Over a medium piece of waxed or parchment paper or a bowl, sift the flour. Add the salt and toss to blend well.
	With the mixer speed on low, add the flour mixture to the egg mixture in 3 stages, blending well after each addition. Stop and scrape down the sides and bottom of the bowl. The mixture should be smooth.
	Pour the chocolate mixture into the batter and blend in thoroughly.
	Transfer the batter to the liquid measuring cup. Pour the batter slowly into each cavity of the madeleine molds, filling them ¾ full. Place each madeleine pan on a baking sheet.
	Bake the madeleines for 7 minutes. Switch the baking sheets and bake for another 6 to 7 minutes, until the tops spring back lightly when touched.
	Remove the pans from the oven. Holding the madeleine pans upside down over cooling racks, gently shake them to release the madeleines. Cool the madeleines completely on the racks.

paper at room temperature up to 3 days.

Adding Style

Drizzle the cooled madeleines with thin lines of bittersweet, semisweet, milk, or white chocolate (see page 43).

Half-dip the cooled madeleines in tempered bittersweet or semisweet chocolate (see page 43).

Make madeleine sandwich cookies by spreading a thin layer of raspberry or apricot jam on the flat side of one cooled madeleine and topping it with the flat side of another cooled cookie.

Make madeleine ganache sandwich cookies by spreading the flat side of one cooled madeleine with ganache (see page 393: use half of recipe) and topping it with the flat side of another cooled cookie.

Devilish Chocolate Layer Cake with Caramel-Chocolate Buttercream

THIS CAKE is about as close to sinful as you can get when it comes to eating pure chocolate. Rich, dark chocolate cake layers are alternated with sensuous, creamy caramel-chocolate buttercream in this extraordinary cake. It's elegant and luscious enough for any special occasion. Although there are several steps to making this cake, many can be done in advance, making it easy to assemble on the day it's served. **Makes one 9-inch round cake, 12 to 14 servings**

Essential Gear

- Two 9 × 2-inch round cake pans
- Scissors
- Parchment paper
- Double boiler
- Two rubber spatulas
- Sifter

CAKE

Center a rack in the oven and preheat it to 350°F.

1 tablespoon unsalted butter, softened	Using a paper towel or your fingertips, generously butter the inside of the cake pans.
1 tablespoon all-purpose flour	Dust the inside of each pan with some of the flour. Shake and tilt the pans to cover the inside completely, then turn the pans over and shake out the excess over the sink. Cut a round of parchment paper to fit the bottom of each pan. Butter each parchment paper round and place one in each pan, butter-side up.
6 ounces unsweetened chocolate, finely chopped	Place the chocolate in the top of a double boiler over low heat. Stir often with a rubber spatula to help melt evenly. Or melt the chocolate in a microwave oven on low power for 30-second bursts. Stir with a rubber spatula after each burst to help melt evenly.
1¾ .cups cake flour **1 teaspoon baking soda** **½ teaspoon salt**	Over a large piece of waxed or parchment paper or a bowl, sift together the flour and baking soda. Add the salt and toss to blend well.
4 ounces (8 tablespoons, 1 stick) unsalted butter, softened	Place the butter in the bowl of an electric stand mixer or in a large bowl. Use the flat beater attachment or a hand-held mixer to beat the butter on medium speed until it's light and fluffy, about 2 minutes.
1 cup superfine sugar **⅔ cups firmly packed light brown sugar**	Add the superfine sugar and the brown sugar to the butter, and cream together well on medium speed. Stop occasionally and scrape down the sides and bottom of the mixing bowl with a rubber spatula.
2 extra-large eggs, at room temperature **1 tablespoon pure vanilla extract**	Using a fork, lightly beat the eggs with the vanilla in a small bowl. Add to the butter mixture. Mix together, stopping a few times to scrape down the sides and bottom of the bowl. At first the mixture may look curdled as the eggs are added, but as you stop and scrape down the bowl, the mixture will smooth out.
1 cup sour cream	Alternately add the dry ingredients and sour cream in 4 or 5 stages, mixing well after each addition. Start with the dry ingredients and end with the sour cream. Stop after each addition and scrape down the bottom and sides of the bowl with a rubber spatula. This helps mix the ingredients together uniformly.
	Add the melted chocolate to the batter and blend together thoroughly.

- Electric stand mixer with flat beater attachment and wire whip attachment, or large mixing bowl and hand-held mixer
- Two cooling racks
- Two 9-inch cardboard cake circles
- Small saucepan
- 2-quart heavy-bottomed saucepan
- 1-inch natural-bristle pastry brush
- Wooden spoon or heat-resistant spatula
- Sugar or candy thermometer
- Serrated knife
- 10-inch flexible-blade icing spatula
- 10- or 12-inch pastry bag and large open star tip

Keeping .

Store the cake loosely covered with aluminum foil in the refrigerator up to 4 days. Place several tooth-picks in the top outer edges of the cake to hold the foil away from it so it won't mar the buttercream. To freeze up to 3 months, place the cake in a cake box and wrap with several layers of plastic wrap and aluminum foil. Or place the cake on a lined baking sheet in the freezer and let it freeze (about 3 hours). Loosely wrap the cake in layers of plastic wrap and aluminum foil. If frozen, defrost overnight in the refrigerator. Bring the cake to room temperature at least 30 minutes before serving.

Divide the batter evenly between the two cake pans. Smooth the top of each pan with a rubber spatula.

Bake the layers for 30 to 35 minutes, until a cake tester inserted in the center comes out with no crumbs clinging to it.

Remove the cake pans from the oven and cool completely on racks. Invert the pans to remove the layers, then peel the parchment paper off the back of each layer. Re-invert the layers onto plates or cardboard cake circles.

CARAMEL SAUCE

¾ cup heavy whipping cream	Place the cream in the small saucepan and warm over medium heat until bubbles form at the edges.
1 cup granulated sugar ¼ cup water 1 tablespoon light corn syrup	While the cream is heating, combine the sugar, water, and corn syrup in the 2-quart saucepan. Cook over high heat, without stirring, until the mixture begins to boil. Place a wet pastry brush at the point where the sugar syrup meets the sides of the pan and sweep it around completely. Do this two times. This prevents the sugar from crystallizing by brushing any stray crystals back into the mixture. Cook the mixture over high heat without stirring until it turns amber colored, about 10 minutes.
	Remove the saucepan from the heat and stir in the hot cream using a long-handled spoon or heat-resistant spatula. Be very careful because it will bubble and splatter. Return the saucepan with the caramel mixture to medium heat and stir to dissolve any lumps.
2 ounces (4 tablespoons, ½ stick) unsalted butter, softened	Add the butter to the caramel mixture and stir until it is melted.
1½ teaspoons pure vanilla extract	Remove the saucepan from the heat and stir in the vanilla. Transfer the caramel sauce to another container and cover tightly. Let the caramel sauce cool, then chill in the refrigerator until it is thick, about 2 hours.

BUTTERCREAM

2 extra-large eggs, at room temperature 2 extra-large egg yolks, at room temperature	Place the eggs, egg yolks, and sugar in the bowl of an electric stand mixer or in a large bowl. Use the wire whip attachment or a hand-held mixer and whip the eggs on medium speed until they are very

Streamlining

Bake the cake layers up to 2 days before assembling. After the layers are completely cool, cover them tightly with plastic wrap and hold at room temperature. The layers can be frozen for up to 3 months. To freeze, wrap them snugly in several layers of plastic wrap and place them in freezer bags. Use a large piece of masking tape and an indelible marker to label and date the contents. If frozen, defrost the layers overnight in the refrigerator.

The caramel sauce can be prepared up to 1 week in advance and kept in a tightly covered plastic container in the refrigerator. If it is too firm, soften it on low power in a microwave oven for 20-second bursts.

The buttercream can be prepared up to 3 days in advance and kept in an airtight plastic container in the refrigerator or up to 4 months in the freezer. If frozen, defrost overnight in the refrigerator. To rebeat the buttercream, break it up into chunks and place in a mixing bowl. Place the bowl in a saucepan of warm water and let the buttercream begin to melt around the bottom. Wipe the bottom of the bowl dry and beat the buttercream with an electric mixer until it is fluffy and smooth.

¼ cup granulated sugar	pale colored and hold a slowly dissolving ribbon as the beater is lifted, about 5 minutes.
1¼ cups granulated sugar ½ cup water ¼ teaspoon cream of tartar	While the eggs are whipping, place the sugar, water, and cream of tartar in the clean heavy-bottomed saucepan. Bring the mixture to a boil, without stirring. Place a wet pastry brush at the point where the sugar syrup meets the sides of the pan and sweep it around completely. Do this two times. Don't brush around the pan more than a few times. If you do, you're adding extra water to the sugar syrup, which takes more time to cook off and reach the desired temperature. Cook over high heat until the mixture registers 242°F on a sugar thermometer (soft-ball stage). Immediately remove the thermometer and place it in a glass of warm water, then remove the pan from the heat so it won't continue to cook. Adjust the mixer speed to low and pour the sugar syrup into the whipped eggs in a slow, steady stream. Aim the sugar syrup between the beater and the side of the bowl, so it doesn't get caught up in the beater or thrown against the sides of the bowl. Turn the mixer speed up to medium-high and whip until the bowl is cool to the touch, about 8 minutes. Once the cooked sugar syrup is added to the whipped eggs, the mixture must whip until the bowl is completely cool to the touch before the butter is added, or the butter will melt. If this happens, the texture and consistency of the buttercream will be too soft and more butter needs to be added to bring it to the right point.
1 pound (2 cups, 4 sticks) unsalted butter, softened	Adjust the mixer speed to medium and add the butter, 2 tablespoons at a time. Continue to beat until the buttercream is thoroughly blended and fluffy.
	Add the cooled caramel sauce and stir until it is thoroughly blended.
6 ounces bittersweet chocolate, very finely chopped	Place the chocolate in a microwave-safe bowl and melt on low power for 30-second bursts. Stir with a rubber spatula after each burst. When the chocolate is completely melted, stir it to cool for a couple of minutes. Then add it to the buttercream and blend well.

ASSEMBLY

1½ cups walnuts	Use a chef's knife or food processor to finely chop the walnuts.
	With your fingertips, gently peel the skin off the top of each cake layer. Using a serrated knife, cut each cake layer in half horizontally (see

Making a Change
Replace the walnuts with finely ground toasted hazelnuts or almonds.

Replace the buttercream with lightly sweetened whipped cream or vanilla buttercream. To make vanilla buttercream, leave out the melted chocolate and flavor the buttercream with 2 tablespoons pure vanilla extract.

Recovering from a Mishap
Don't worry if one of the cake layers breaks during assembly. You can patch it together with some of the buttercream and no one will know the difference.

¹⁄₃ cup apricot preserves

page 34). Place the bottom of one cake layer on a serving plate. Place strips of waxed paper around the bottom edges of the cake to protect the plate while assembling the cake. Use the flexible-blade spatula to spread the layer evenly with the apricot preserves (see page 35).

Set aside ¹⁄₃ cup of the buttercream for final decoration. With a clean flexible-blade spatula, evenly spread some of the remaining buttercream over the cake layer.

Position the second cake layer evenly over the buttercream. Spread buttercream over the layer. Repeat with the remaining two cake layers and more buttercream. Then spread the remaining buttercream over the sides and top of the cake.

Press the chopped walnuts onto the sides of the cake up to, but not over, the top edge (see page 35).

12 walnut halves

Fit the pastry bag with the star tip and fill with the reserved buttercream. Visually divide the top of the cake into 12 pieces or use a small sharp knife to mark the outer top edge of the cake into serving pieces. Pipe a rosette at the center outer edge of each piece (see page 44). Center a walnut on top of each rosette.

Let the cake chill for at least 2 hours before serving so it has time to set and will be easier to cut. Serve the cake at room temperature.

Ganache Lemon Tartlets

A CREAMY CHOCOLATE ganache with the tangy flavor of lemon is a refreshing surprise as the filling for these individual tartlets. The soft, velvety filling is nestled in a delicate, crisp, sweet pastry shell, making an exciting textural contrast. **Makes six 4¹⁄₂-inch tartlets**

Essential Gear

- Food processor
- Rolling pin
- Six 4¹⁄₂-inch round, fluted-edge tartlet pans with removable bottoms
- Baking sheet
- Pie weights
- Two cooling racks
- Double boiler
- 1-inch natural-bristle pastry brush or a spoon
- Microplane grater or citrus zester
- 10- or 12-inch pastry bag and large open star tip

PASTRY DOUGH

2 cups all-purpose flour
²⁄₃ cup confectioners' sugar
¹⁄₄ teaspoon salt

In the work bowl of a food processor fitted with the steel blade, combine the flour, sugar, and salt. Pulse briefly to blend.

6 ounces (12 tablespoons, 1¹⁄₂ sticks) unsalted butter, chilled

Cut the butter into small pieces and add to the flour mixture. Pulse until the butter is cut into very tiny pieces, about 30 seconds. The texture will be sandy with very tiny lumps throughout.

1 extra-large egg yolk,
at room temperature
1 tablespoon heavy whipping
cream
1 teaspoon pure vanilla
extract

In a small bowl, use a fork to lightly beat the egg yolk with the cream and vanilla. With the food processor running, pour this mixture through the feed tube. Process the dough until the mixture wraps itself around the blade, about 1 minute.

Turn the pastry dough onto a large piece of plastic wrap. Shape into a flat disk and wrap tightly. Chill in the refrigerator until firm before using, at least 2 hours. Chilling the dough relaxes the gluten in the flour so it won't be too elastic and will roll out easily. It also firms up the butter in the dough so it will need less flour when rolled out. If the dough is too firm it will splinter and break when rolled out. Let it stand at room temperature for 10 to 15 minutes before rolling to become more pliable.

Center a rack in the oven and preheat it to 375°F.

On a smooth, flat surface, roll out the pastry dough between sheets of lightly floured waxed or parchment paper to a large rectangle about 16 × 12 inches. Carefully peel the paper off the top of the dough. Brush excess flour off the dough. Cut the dough in half horizontally, then into 3 equal sections vertically, making six 6 × 5-inch squares. Carefully peel the squares off the other piece of paper.

Gently place each square in a tart pan. Carefully lift up the sides of the pastry dough and ease the dough into the bottom and sides of each tart pan. Trim off the excess pastry dough at the top of the pan. Transfer the tart pans to a baking sheet and chill for at least 15 minutes to set.

Line each pastry shell with a large piece of aluminum foil that fits well against the bottom and sides. Fill each pastry shell with pie weights or a mixture of rice and beans. Bake for 10 minutes, then remove the foil and weights. If the bottom of a pastry shell puffs up, gently pierce it in a few places with a fork or the point of a knife to release the air. Bake another 12 to 14 minutes, until light golden and set. Remove the pan from the oven and transfer the tartlets to racks to cool completely.

ASSEMBLY

2 ounces bittersweet
chocolate, finely chopped

Place the chocolate in the top of a double boiler over hot water. Stir often with a rubber spatula to help melt evenly. Remove the top of the double boiler and wipe the bottom and sides very dry.

Keeping
Store the tartlets, without the whipped cream garnish, in a single layer on a baking sheet. Cover the top of the tartlets with a large piece of waxed paper to keep the surface from becoming marred. Tightly wrap the pan with plastic wrap and keep in the refrigerator up to 3 days. Bring the tartlets to room temperature and garnish before serving.

Streamlining
The pastry dough can be made in advance and kept in the refrigerator, tightly wrapped in a double layer of plastic wrap, up to 4 days before using. To freeze up to 4 months, wrap it in a double layer of plastic wrap and place it inside a freezer bag. Use a large piece of masking tape and an indelible marker to label and date the contents. If frozen, defrost in the refrigerator overnight before using. If the dough is too cold to roll out, let it stand at room temperature to become pliable.

The tartlet shells can be baked and held at room temperature up to 2 days before filling. After they are completely cool, place them on a baking sheet between layers of waxed or parchment paper and tightly wrap the pan in aluminum foil.

Or place the chocolate in a microwave-safe bowl and melt on low power for 30-second bursts. Stir with a rubber spatula after each burst.

Using the pastry brush or the back of a spoon, paint the inside of each tartlet shell with the melted chocolate. Place the tartlet shells on a cool baking sheet while preparing the filling.

LEMON GANACHE FILLING

12 ounces bittersweet chocolate, finely chopped

Place the chopped chocolate in a large bowl.

1 cup heavy whipping cream

Place the cream in a small saucepan and bring to a boil over medium heat. Pour the cream over the chocolate. Let it stand for 1 minute, then stir together with a rubber spatula, whisk, or immersion blender until very smooth.

4 large lemons

Grate or zest the rind of the lemons into the chocolate mixture. Be careful to use only the lemon zest and not to take any of the bitter white pith underneath the zest. Stir the mixture to blend well.

Divide the lemon ganache evenly among the six tartlet shells. Gently shake each tartlet shell from side to side to smooth the filling and release any air bubbles that will make holes in the chocolate once it is set. Chill the tartlets until the filling is no longer liquid, about 1 hour.

GARNISH

⅓ cup heavy whipping cream

Place the cream in the chilled bowl of an electric stand mixer or in a large bowl. Using the wire whip attachment or a hand-held mixer, whip on medium speed until frothy.

1 tablespoon confectioners' sugar, sifted

Add the sugar and continue whipping the cream until it holds soft peaks.

Fit the pastry bag with the star tip. Fill the pastry bag partway with the whipped cream. Holding the pastry bag straight up and down, about 1 inch above the surface, pipe a large rosette in the center of each tartlet (see page 44). Sprinkle the top of each rosette with the

Finely grated zest of 1 large lemon

grated lemon zest.

Serve the tartlets at room temperature.

Troubleshooting

Don't roll out the pastry dough before it is chilled. The dough will be too soft and it will require a lot of flour to roll out, which will make the dough tough.

Making a Change

Use fresh oranges or limes in place of the lemons.

Adding Style

Pipe a row of whipped cream shells (see page 44) around the outside edge of each tartlet, then sprinkle the center with grated lemon zest.

Individual Molten Chocolate Cakes

THE LUSCIOUS liquid chocolate center of these delicate cakes oozes out when a fork breaks them open. This dessert is total heaven for chocolate lovers. Not only is it easy to make, but it can be assembled in advance and kept covered in the refrigerator for several hours, so all you have to do is bake it right before serving. This is my husband's favorite chocolate cake. **Makes six 6-ounce servings**

1 tablespoon unsalted butter, melted

1 tablespoon plus 1 teaspoon superfine sugar

Use the pastry brush or a paper towel to butter the inside of the custard cups or bowls completely. Sprinkle the inside of each cup or bowl with sugar and rotate the cup or bowl so it is completely covered with sugar, then shake out any excess. Place the cups or bowls on the baking sheet.

3 ounces bittersweet chocolate, finely chopped

Place the chocolate in a medium bowl.

¼ cup heavy whipping cream

1 teaspoon pure vanilla extract

Place the cream in a saucepan and bring to a boil over medium heat. Pour the cream over the chocolate and let it stand for 1 minute. Stir the mixture together using a heat-resistant spatula, whisk, or immersion blender until very smooth. Add the vanilla and stir to blend completely.

Line the cake pan or other shallow container with plastic wrap. Pour the ganache mixture into the pan, cover with plastic wrap, cool to room temperature, and chill in the freezer until firm, about 1 hour.

Use the round cutter to cut out 12 ganache disks. Stack 2 disks and press them so they stick together, making 6 disks. Keep the disks covered with plastic wrap to keep them from drying out and keep them chilled while preparing the cakes.

6 ounces bittersweet chocolate, finely chopped

6 ounces (12 tablespoons, 1½ sticks) unsalted butter, cut into small pieces

Place the chocolate and butter in the top of a double boiler and melt over low heat. Stir frequently with a rubber spatula to help melt evenly. Remove the top pan of the double boiler and wipe the bottom and sides very dry.

Or place the chocolate and butter in a microwave-safe bowl and melt on low power for 30-second bursts. Stir with a rubber spatula after each burst to be sure it's melting evenly.

3 extra-large eggs, at room temperature

Separate the eggs and add the yolks to the chocolate mixture one at a time, stirring well after each addition.

Essential Gear

- Six 6-ounce custard cups or ovenproof glass bowls
- 1-inch natural-bristle pastry brush or paper towel
- Baking sheet
- Small saucepan
- Heat-resistant spatula or whisk
- 6-inch round cake pan or other shallow pan
- 1-inch round, plain-edge cutter
- Double boiler
- Electric stand mixer with wire whip attachment, or large mixing bowl and hand-held mixer
- Rubber spatula
- Sifter
- Sharp knife

Streamlining

The cakes can be assembled and held tightly covered with plastic wrap in the refrigerator up to 3 days before baking. Take them directly from the refrigerator, remove the plastic wrap, and bake.

Adding Style

Serve each cake with a dollop of lightly sweetened whipped cream, or a scoop of vanilla or caramel ice cream.

Serve each cake in a pool of raspberry sauce (see Meyer Lemon Soufflés, page 143) and scatter fresh raspberries around the plate.

⅛ teaspoon cream of tartar	Place the egg whites in the grease-free bowl of an electric stand mixer or in a large grease-free bowl. Using the wire whip attachment or a hand-held mixer, whip the egg whites on medium high speed until they are frothy. Add the cream of tartar and continue to whip until the egg whites hold soft peaks. Gradually sprinkle on the sugar and whip until the egg whites hold glossy and firm, but not stiff, peaks.
⅓ cup superfine sugar	
	Fold the whipped egg whites into the chocolate mixture in 4 stages.
¼ cup cake flour, sifted	Sprinkle the cake flour over the chocolate mixture and fold in completely.
	Center a rack in the oven and preheat it to 350°F.
	Fill each custard cup or bowl ½ full of batter, then place the ganache disks in the center of each cup, and fill with the remaining batter.
	Bake the cakes for 15 to 18 minutes, until a toothpick inserted near the top outer edge comes out moist.
	Remove the pan from the oven and immediately run a sharp knife around the edges of each cup or bowl. Turn the cakes upside down onto individual serving plates and carefully remove the cups or bowls.
2 tablespoons confectioners' sugar	Dust the top of each cake with confectioners' sugar. Serve immediately.

Marbleized Chocolate Tart

THIS LOOKS LIKE a work of art, but the fun part is that it's edible. A velvety dark chocolate ganache filling is nestled in a buttery, cocoa cookie-crust shell. Milk chocolate and white chocolate are swirled into the filling, making the tart look like a beautiful piece of Venetian endpaper. **Makes one 11-inch round tart, 16 to 20 servings**

COCOA PASTRY DOUGH

1¼ cups all-purpose flour	In the work bowl of a food processor fitted with the steel blade, combine the flour, sugar, cocoa, and salt. Pulse briefly to blend.
½ cup superfine sugar	
¼ cup cocoa powder (natural or Dutch-processed)	
⅛ teaspoon salt	

Essential Gear
- Food processor
- Rolling pin
- One 11-inch round, fluted-edge tart pan with removable bottom
- Baking sheet
- Aluminum foil
- Pie weights
- Cooling rack
- Small saucepan
- Two microwave-safe bowls
- Two rubber spatulas
- Two small parchment paper pastry cones

4 ounces (8 tablespoons, 1 stick) unsalted butter, chilled	Cut the butter into small pieces and add to the flour mixture. Pulse until the butter is cut into very tiny pieces, about 30 seconds. The texture should be sandy with tiny lumps throughout.
1 extra-large egg yolk, at room temperature 1 teaspoon pure vanilla extract	Use a fork to beat the egg yolk with the vanilla in a small bowl. With the food processor running, pour the egg and vanilla mixture through the feed tube. Process the dough until the mixture wraps itself around the blade, about 1 minute.

Turn the pastry dough onto a large piece of plastic wrap. Shape into a flat disk and wrap tightly in two layers of plastic wrap. Chill in the refrigerator until firm before using, at least 2 hours. Chilling the dough relaxes the gluten in the flour so it won't be too elastic and will roll out easily. It also firms up the butter in the dough so it will need less flour when rolled out. If the dough is too firm it will splinter and break when rolled out. Let it stand at room temperature for 10 to 15 minutes before rolling to become more pliable.

Center a rack in the oven and preheat it to 375°F.

On a smooth, flat surface, roll out the pastry dough between sheets of lightly floured waxed or parchment paper to a large circle about 13 inches in diameter. To tell if the dough will fit the tart pan, hold the pan above the dough. If there are 2 or 3 inches of dough that protrude beyond the sides of the pan, it will fit.

Carefully peel the paper off the top of the dough and brush off any excess flour. Loosely roll the pastry dough around the rolling pin without the bottom piece of paper. Place the tart pan directly underneath the rolling pin and carefully unroll the pastry dough into the tart pan.

Gently lift up the sides and ease the pastry dough into the bottom and sides of the tart pan, pushing it lightly into the fluted edges.

The crust is delicate so it's very important to handle it gently. Rolling it around the rolling pin and unrolling into the tart pan is an easy way to get the dough into the pan without tearing it.

Trim off the excess pastry dough at the top of the pan. Transfer the tart pan to a baking sheet and chill in the freezer for 30 minutes. This helps prevent the dough from shrinking as it bakes.

Line the pastry shell with a large piece of aluminum foil that fits well against the bottom and sides. Fill the pastry shell with pie weights or a mixture of rice and beans. Bake for 10 minutes, then remove the foil and weights. If the bottom of the pastry shell puffs up, gently

- Scissors
- Toothpick or sharp knife

Keeping
Store the tart in the refrigerator up to 4 days. Cover the top with a large piece of waxed paper to protect it from becoming marred and tightly cover the tart with aluminum foil.

Streamlining
The pastry dough can be made in advance and kept in the refrigerator, tightly wrapped in a double layer of plastic wrap, up to 4 days before using. To freeze up to 4 months, wrap it in a double layer of plastic wrap and place it inside a freezer bag. Use a large piece of masking tape and an indelible marker to label and date the contents. If frozen, defrost in the refrigerator overnight before using. If the dough is too cold to roll out, let it stand at room temperature to become pliable.

The tart shell can be baked and held at room temperature up to 2 days before filling. Cover the top of the cooled tart shell with a large piece of waxed or parchment paper and tightly wrap the pan in aluminum foil.

Troubleshooting
Once the pastry dough is unrolled into the tart pan, don't push it down forcefully. This will stretch the dough, which will shrink as it bakes,

pierce it in a few places with a fork to release the air. Bake another 12 to 14 minutes, until set. Remove the pan from the oven and transfer the tart pan to a rack to cool completely.

making it flat instead of taking the shape of the tart pan.

DARK CHOCOLATE GANACHE FILLING

1 pound bittersweet chocolate, finely chopped

Place the chopped chocolate in a large bowl.

1 cup heavy whipping cream

Place the cream in the saucepan and bring to a boil over medium heat. Pour the cream over the chopped chocolate. Let it stand for 1 minute, then stir together with a rubber spatula, whisk, or immersion blender until very smooth.

1 teaspoon pure vanilla extract

Add the vanilla and stir to blend well.

Pour the ganache into the cooled tart shell. Use a rubber spatula to smooth and even the filling. Gently shake the pan from side to side to release any air bubbles that would make holes in the filling when it is set.

CHOCOLATE SWIRL GARNISH

½ ounce milk chocolate, finely chopped
½ ounce white chocolate, finely chopped

Place the milk chocolate and white chocolate in separate microwave-safe bowls and melt on low power for 30-second bursts. Stir each with a separate rubber spatula in between each burst.

Make two small parchment paper pastry cones (see page 25) and stand each in a glass for support. Pour the milk chocolate into one pastry cone and the white chocolate into the other pastry cone. Fold down the top and sides of each pastry cone tightly and snip off a small opening at the pointed end.

Holding a pastry cone straight up and down about 1 inch above the tart, separately drizzle swirls of each chocolate over the top of the ganache filling. Use a toothpick or the point of a sharp knife to drag through the drizzled chocolate a few times to create a marbleized look. But don't mix all the chocolates together and lose the effect. It's important to work quickly with the milk chocolate and white chocolate swirls so the ganache filling doesn't begin to set up.

Chill the tart until the filling is firm, about 2 hours. Let the tart stand at room temperature for 45 minutes before serving.

Use a knife that has been dipped in hot water and dried to cut the tart into serving slices.

Rolled Chocolate Cake with Spiked Cream Filling

THIS CAKE reminds me of one of my favorite childhood desserts, ice cream cake roll. It had vanilla ice cream rolled up inside of a thin chocolate cake, and when it was cut across the grain a spiral of chocolate and vanilla was revealed. In this version, a dark chocolate cake is baked in a jelly-roll pan and rolled up while warm so it will hold the rolled shape. The filling is a tantalizing blend of whipped cream, mascarpone, and orange liqueur. A simple decoration of whipped cream and orange zest finishes this scrumptious cake. **Makes one 15-inch cake, 12 to 15 servings**

ROLLED CHOCOLATE CAKE

1 tablespoon unsalted butter, melted	Center a rack in the oven and preheat it to 450°F. Line the jelly-roll pan with a sheet of parchment paper. Use the pastry brush or a paper towel to coat the parchment paper with butter.
¼ cup unsweetened Dutch-processed cocoa powder 2 tablespoons all-purpose flour ⅛ teaspoon salt	Over a medium piece of waxed or parchment paper or a bowl, sift together the cocoa powder, flour, and salt. Set aside briefly.
5 extra-large egg whites, at room temperature ¼ teaspoon cream of tartar 2 tablespoons superfine sugar	Place the egg whites in the grease-free bowl of an electric stand mixer or in a large grease-free bowl. Using the wire whip attachment or a hand-held mixer, whip the egg whites on medium-high speed until they are frothy. Add the cream of tartar and whip until the egg whites hold soft peaks. Sprinkle on the sugar and continue to whip the egg whites on medium-high speed until they hold glossy and firm, but not stiff, peaks.
5 extra-large egg yolks at room temperature ½ cup superfine sugar	Place the egg yolks in the bowl of an electric stand mixer or in a large bowl. Using the wire whip attachment or a hand-held mixer, whip the egg yolks with the sugar on medium-high speed until they are very thick and pale colored and hold a slowly dissolving ribbon as the beater is lifted, about 5 minutes.
	In 4 stages, alternately fold the whipped egg whites and dry ingredients into the whipped egg yolks, starting with the egg whites.
	Turn the batter out onto the lined jelly-roll pan. Use a long-blade offset spatula or rubber spatula to spread the mixture smoothly and evenly over the parchment paper and into the corners of the pan.

Essential Gear

- Jelly-roll pan (12 × 17 inches)
- Two parchment paper sheets
- 1-inch natural-bristle pastry brush or paper towel
- Electric stand mixer with wire whip attachment, or large mixing bowl and hand-held mixer
- Rubber spatula
- Long-blade offset spatula or rubber spatula
- Cocoa dredger or small fine-mesh sifter
- Ruler
- Small sharp knife
- Kitchen towel
- 12- or 14-inch pastry bag and large open star tip
- Serrated knife

Keeping

Store the cake lightly tented with waxed paper and aluminum foil in the refrigerator up to 4 days.

Streamlining

The cake can be baked up to 3 days before filling. When the cake is completely cool, wrap it tightly in a double layer of plastic wrap and store in the refrigerator.

Recovering from a Mishap

If the cake breaks or cracks while it is being rolled,

Bake the cake for 8 to 10 minutes, until the cake looks set and springs back when touched lightly on top.

1 tablespoon unsweetened Dutch-processed cocoa powder

Remove the pan from the oven and transfer it to a cooling rack. Lightly dust the top of the cake with cocoa powder in a dredger or fine-mesh sifter.

Use a small sharp knife to cut around the outer edges of the cake to release it from the pan. Place a sheet of parchment paper over the top of the cake and cover with a kitchen towel. Then invert the jelly-roll pan and lift it off the cake. Gently peel the parchment paper off the back of the cake and discard.

Starting at one long end, roll up the cake inside the towel and parchment paper and leave it seam-side down to cool to room temperature.

FILLING

1½ cups heavy whipping cream
3 tablespoons superfine sugar
1 tablespoon orange liqueur
1 teaspoon pure vanilla extract

Place the cream in the chilled bowl of an electric stand mixer or in a chilled large bowl. Using the wire whip attachment or a hand-held mixer, whip the cream on medium speed until it is frothy. Add the sugar, orange liqueur, and vanilla and continue to whip the cream on medium speed until it holds soft peaks. Reserve ⅓ of the whipped cream for the garnish.

½ cup mascarpone, at room temperature

Adjust the mixer speed to low and add the mascarpone to the whipped cream. Blend well.

Unroll the cake and remove the towel. Use the offset spatula or a rubber spatula to evenly spread the filling over the cake, leaving a 1-inch border at the farthest long end of the cake. Use the parchment paper to help roll up the filled cake.

To make a tight cake roll, pull about one-third of the parchment paper over the top of the cake. Then place a ruler flat against the parchment that covers the top of the cake and push it against the roll while pulling the bottom part of the parchment paper toward you. This resistance motion of simultaneously pushing against the cake while pulling the parchment under the cake toward you compresses the roulade.

Using the offset spatula, transfer the cake to a serving plate or a jelly-roll pan covered with waxed paper with the seam side down. Trim off the rough ends of the cake and discard.

position the cracked part of the cake on the bottom of the roll or patch with whipped cream.

Making a Change
Replace the orange liqueur with the same amount of vanilla extract.

Fold 1 cup toasted and finely ground hazelnuts or pecans into the batter before spreading it on the pan. Replace the orange liqueur with Frangelico or dark rum and sprinkle ground toasted hazelnuts or pecans over the top of the cake roll instead of orange zest.

Fill the cake with whipped Dark Chocolate Ganache (page 409) or Mocha Buttercream (see Mocha Bûche de Noël, page 580) instead of the cream filling.

Finely grated zest of 1 large orange

Fit the pastry bag with the star tip and fill partway with the reserved whipped cream. Pipe a design of swirls over the top of the rolled cake in a swag design (alternating S's) or pipe a design of rosettes over the top (see page 44). Randomly scatter the orange zest over the whipped cream.

2 tablespoons unsweetened Dutch-processed cocoa powder

Cut the cake crosswise into 1-inch slices. Place each slice on its side on a plate and dust lightly with cocoa powder. Serve immediately.

The World's Best Brownies

D EEP, DARK CHOCOLATE flavor bursts in your mouth with every bite of these brownies. And they have a great fudgy, creamy texture. Because these are so intensely flavored, a small square is all you need to satisfy any chocolate craving, but it is okay to indulge a little and have more than one. **Makes twenty-five 1½-inch brownies**

1 tablespoon unsalted butter, softened

Center a rack in the oven and preheat it to 350°F. Line the baking pan with aluminum foil, letting it hang about 2 inches over the sides. Use a paper towel or your fingertips to generously butter the inside of the foil.

5 ounces unsweetened chocolate, finely chopped
2 ounces bittersweet chocolate, finely chopped
6 ounces (12 tablespoons, 1½ sticks) unsalted butter, cut into small pieces

Place the unsweetened chocolate, bittersweet chocolate, and the butter together in the top of a double boiler over low heat. Stir often with a rubber spatula to help melt evenly. Remove the top pan of the double boiler and wipe the bottom and sides very dry. Let the mixture cool while mixing the rest of the brownie batter, stirring with a rubber spatula occasionally to prevent a skin from forming on top.

Or place the chocolates and butter in a microwave-safe bowl and melt on low power for 30-second bursts. Stir with a rubber spatula after each burst to make sure it's melting.

2 extra-large eggs, at room temperature
1 extra-large egg yolk, at room temperature

Place the eggs and egg yolk in the bowl of an electric stand mixer or in a large bowl. Using the wire whip attachment or a hand-held mixer, whip the eggs until they are frothy.

Essential Gear

- 8-inch square baking pan
- Aluminum foil
- Double boiler
- Electric stand mixer with wire whip attachment, or large mixing bowl and hand-held mixer
- Rubber spatula
- Cooling rack

Keeping

Store the brownies between layers of waxed paper in an airtight plastic container at room temperature up to 4 days. To freeze up to 4 months, wrap the container tightly in several layers of plastic wrap and aluminum foil. Use a large piece of masking tape and an indelible marker to label and date the contents. If frozen, defrost overnight in the refrigerator and bring to room temperature before serving.

¾ cup superfine sugar ¾ cup firmly packed light brown sugar	Add the superfine sugar and brown sugar to the eggs and whip together until the mixture is very thick and pale colored and holds a slowly dissolving ribbon as the beater is lifted, about 5 minutes.	**Making a Change** Add 1 cup roughly chopped walnuts, hazelnuts, or unblanched almonds to the batter before turning into the pan to bake and mix them in thoroughly.
1 teaspoon pure vanilla extract	Add the vanilla and stir to blend well.	

Add the melted chocolate mixture to the egg mixture and blend completely on low speed. Stop and scrape down the sides and bottom of the bowl with the rubber spatula. The mixture will look smooth and will be dark chocolate colored.

¾ cup all-purpose flour 3 tablespoons unsweetened natural cocoa powder ¼ teaspoon salt	Over a large piece of waxed or parchment paper or a bowl, sift the flour and cocoa powder together. Add the salt and stir to combine.	**Adding Style** Serve the cooled brownies with a dollop of lightly sweetened whipped cream or a scoop of caramel ice cream.
	In 3 stages, add the dry ingredients to the batter, blending well after each addition. Stop and scrape down the sides and bottom of the bowl with the rubber spatula, to make sure the mixture is mixing evenly.	Drizzle the top of the cooled brownies with melted white chocolate semisweet chocolate in close lines (see page 43).

Pour the batter into the prepared pan and use the rubber spatula to spread it evenly.

Bake the brownies for 35 minutes, until a cake tester or toothpick inserted in the center comes out slightly moist.

Remove the pan from the oven and cool completely on a rack.

Lift the brownies from the pan with the aluminum foil. Carefully peel the foil away from the sides of the brownies. Cut into 5 equal-sized rows in each direction.

Use a 1½-inch round or heart-shaped plain-edge cutter to cut the cooled brownies. Top the center of each brownie with a whipped cream star or rosette (see page 44) and garnish with a walnut half, a whole unblanched almond, or a whole toasted and skinned hazelnut, depending on the nuts used in the brownie.

MILK

CHOCOLATE

LIKE MANY AMERICANS, I grew up eating milk chocolate. I have fond memories of my dad bringing home milk chocolate bars as a special treat for my brothers and me. He would always bring a little extra for me. I used to try to hold some back for later, but I usually ate it all within a day. I'll have to admit, it's pretty hard to pace yourself when eating milk chocolate. It's just too darn good.

Like dark chocolate, milk chocolate is made from chocolate liquor and sugar, along with lecithin and vanilla. What's different is that milk solids or powder is also added. This is the reason why milk chocolate is a lighter brown color than dark chocolate. The percentage of cocoa components in milk chocolate is far less than with dark chocolates. The FDA requires as little as 10 percent cocoa components for milk chocolate. Like the new categories of dark chocolate,

there is a new category of milk chocolate called "dark milk chocolate," which contains between 23 and 45 percent cocoa components. This makes it less sweet and provides a richer chocolate flavor.

Milk chocolate is always available in supermarkets, cookware shops, gourmet food shops, natural and health food stores, and through many online and catalog sources. If you are looking for a particular milk chocolate that you like, just search for it by name on the Web and you will most likely find the manufacturer's Web site, where you will be able to buy it.

TIPS AND TECHNIQUES

Milk chocolate is not interchangeable with dark chocolate or white chocolate in recipes, because milk chocolate has less body than dark chocolate and more body than white chocolate. However, because there is only a small variance in the percentage of cocoa components between milk chocolate and dark milk chocolate, it is fine to use either in the recipes. Also, for the recipes in this chapter, don't use milk chocolates that are infused with other flavors, such as spices, or mixed with other ingredients, like nuts.

For more tips and techniques, see Chocolate Tasting, Selecting and Working with Chocolate, and Storing Chocolate in About Chocolate (page 370). The following table describes the tasting characteristics for ten brands of milk chocolate that are readily available.

MILK CHOCOLATE TASTING TABLE

Brand and Cocoa Components Percentage	Cocoa Barry 34%	E. Guittard Soleil d'Or 38%	El Rey Caoba 41%	Felchlin Maracaibo Criolait 38%	Ghirardelli	Lindt Excellence	Scharffen Berger 41%	Trader Joe's	Valrhona Jivara 38%	Valrhona Lacté 41%
Appearance	Even Smooth	Even Smooth Glossy	Even Smooth	Even Smooth	Even Smooth	Even Smooth	Even Smooth	Even Smooth	Even Smooth	Even Smooth
Aroma	Light Sweet	Light Milky	Rich Deep Chocolate milk	Light	Light	Rich Deep Caramel Cream	Rich Deep Full-bodied	Light Creamy	Sharp Floral	Sweet Milk
Snap	Clean	Sharp Clean	Crisp Clean	Crisp Clean	Clean	Crisp Clean	Sharp Clean	Clean	Sharp Clean	Sharp Clean
Texture/ Mouthfeel	Firm	Firm Not much melt	Moderately firm	Firm Not much melt	Smooth Moderately firm	Very smooth Creamy Good melt	Very smooth Creamy Good melt	Smooth Creamy Good melt	Smooth Moderately firm	Smooth Good melt
Flavor	Bland Slightly sweet	Very light caramel	Caramel Heavy roast	Bland Hint of fruit	Bland Sweet	Caramel Toasty	Coffee Toasty	Caramel Malt	Heavy Sweet Cream	Very sweet Floral
Aftertaste	Short	Short	Moderate	Short	Short	Moderate	Long	Moderate	Moderate	Moderate

Dark Milk Chocolate Ganache and Hazelnut Tart

A SILKY, dark milk chocolate ganache mixed with finely ground, toasted hazelnuts gives this tart a sophisticated flavor. The tart shell is baked and cooled, then the ganache is poured in and left to set up at room temperature. It's easy to prepare the tart shell in advance and assemble the dessert a few hours before serving. **Makes one 9½-inch round tart, 12 to 14 servings**

PASTRY DOUGH

1½ cups all-purpose flour
⅓ cup granulated sugar
¼ teaspoon salt

In the work bowl of a food processor fitted with the steel blade, combine the flour, sugar, and salt. Pulse briefly to blend.

3 ounces (6 tablespoons, ¾ stick) unsalted butter, chilled

Cut the butter into small pieces and add to the flour mixture. Pulse until the butter is cut into very tiny pieces, about 30 seconds. The texture should be sandy with very tiny lumps throughout.

1 extra-large egg, at room temperature
½ teaspoon pure vanilla extract

Use a fork to lightly beat the egg with the vanilla in a small bowl. With the food processor running, pour this mixture through the feed tube. Process the dough until the mixture wraps itself around the blade, about 1 minute.

Turn the pastry dough onto a large piece of plastic wrap. Shape into a flat disk and wrap tightly in two layers of plastic wrap. Chill in the refrigerator until firm before using, at least 2 hours. Chilling the dough relaxes the gluten in the flour so it won't be too elastic and will roll out easily. It also firms up the butter in the dough so it will need less flour when rolled out. If the dough is too firm, it will splinter and break when rolled out. Let it stand at room temperature for 10 to 15 minutes before rolling to become more pliable.

Center a rack in the oven and preheat it to 350°F.

On a smooth, flat surface, roll out the pastry dough between sheets of lightly floured waxed or parchment paper to a large circle about 11 inches in diameter. To tell if the dough will fit the tart pan, hold the pan above the dough. If there are about 2 inches of dough that protrude beyond the sides of the pan, it will fit.

Carefully peel the paper off the top of the dough. Brush excess flour off the dough. Loosely roll the pastry dough around the rolling pin

Essential Gear

- Food processor
- Rolling pin
- 9½-inch round, fluted-edge tart pan with removable bottom
- Baking sheet
- Aluminum foil
- Pie weights
- Cooling rack
- Whisk
- Small saucepan
- Medium fine-mesh strainer
- Heat-resistant spatula or whisk

Keeping

Store the tart, loosely covered with waxed paper and then tightly wrapped with aluminum foil, at room temperature for 2 days or in the refrigerator up to 4 days.

Streamlining

The pastry dough can be made in advance and kept in the refrigerator, tightly wrapped in a double layer of plastic wrap, up to 4 days. To freeze up to 3 months, wrap the dough tightly in several layers of plastic wrap and place them in a freezer bag. Use a large piece of masking tape and an indelible marker to label and date the contents. If frozen, defrost overnight in the refrigerator before using.

without the bottom piece of paper. Place the tart pan directly underneath the rolling pin and carefully unroll the pastry dough into the tart pan.

Gently lift up the sides and ease the pastry dough into the bottom and sides of the tart pan. Trim off the excess pastry dough at the top of the pan. Transfer the tart pan to a baking sheet and chill in the freezer for 15 minutes.

Line the pastry shell with a large piece of aluminum foil that fits well against the bottom and sides. Fill with pie weights or a mixture of rice and beans. Bake for 10 minutes, then remove the foil and weights. If the bottom of the pastry shell puffs up, gently pierce it in several places with a fork to release the air. Bake for another 12 to 15 minutes, until light golden and set. Remove the pan from the oven and transfer to a rack to cool completely.

GANACHE FILLING

9 ounces dark milk chocolate, finely chopped

Place the chocolate in a large bowl.

½ cup heavy whipping cream
½ vanilla bean

Place the cream in the saucepan and bring to a boil over medium heat. Turn off the heat. Split the vanilla bean down the center and add to the cream. Cover the pan and let steep together for 10 minutes. Remove the cover and bring the cream to a boil again over medium heat. Strain the cream over the chocolate and let it stand for 1 minute. Stir the mixture together using a heat-resistant spatula, a whisk, or an immersion blender until very smooth.

¾ cup toasted and finely ground hazelnuts

Reserve 1 tablespoon of the hazelnuts for the top of the tart. Add the remaining hazelnuts to the ganache mixture and stir to blend together well.

Transfer the filling to the tart shell and use a rubber spatula to spread it out evenly.

Sprinkle the top of the tart with the reserved tablespoon of hazelnuts.

Let the tart set up at room temperature or chill in the refrigerator for 30 minutes. Use a knife dipped in hot water and dried to cut the tart into serving slices. Serve the tart at room temperature.

Troubleshooting

Don't roll out the pastry dough before it is chilled. The dough will be too soft and it will require a lot of flour to roll out, which results in a tough dough.

Once the pastry dough is unrolled into the tart pan, don't push it down forcefully. This will stretch the dough, which will shrink as it bakes, making it flat instead of taking the shape of the tart pan.

Making a Change

Replace the hazelnuts with pecans or walnuts.

Adding Style

Add ⅓ cup toasted and finely ground hazelnuts to the pastry crust and reduce the sugar to ¼ cup.

Scatter the top of the tart with 2 tablespoons finely shaved dark milk chocolate.

Malted Milk Chocolate Cheesecake

O NE OF MY very favorite treats when I was growing up was malted milk balls. I couldn't seem to get enough of them. I vividly remember biting through the crunchy exterior of milk chocolate to find the malt ball inside. Yum! I still love the flavor of malt and believe it goes especially well with milk chocolate. This cheesecake is inspired by those malted milk balls I loved as a child. It's dense and creamy, with a crunchy cookie crust and a deep malt flavor. As with other cheesecakes, this one has to be made in advance of serving because it needs hours to cool and chill. But it also freezes beautifully, so you can make it well in advance of when you plan to serve it. **Makes one 9¹/₂-inch round cake, 12 to 14 servings**

Center a rack in the oven and preheat it to 300°F.

1 tablespoon unsalted butter, softened

Using a paper towel or your fingertips, generously butter the inside of the springform pan. Use a double layer of heavy-duty foil to wrap tightly around the bottom of the pan. This prevents any water from the water bath from seeping into the pan.

COOKIE CRUST

One 10-ounce package butter biscuits, wafers, or shortbread cookies
¹/₃ cup walnuts
2 tablespoons granulated sugar

In the work bowl of a food processor fitted with the steel blade, combine the cookies, walnuts, and sugar and pulse until the cookies are finely ground, about 2 minutes. Or place the cookies in a sturdy plastic bag and seal it. Use a rolling pin to crush the cookies to a very fine crumb consistency. Finely chop the walnuts and add them with the sugar to the cookies, seal the bag, and shake to blend together evenly.

4 ounces (8 tablespoons, 1 stick) unsalted butter, melted and cooled

Transfer the cookie crumb mixture to a medium bowl and add the butter. Use a rubber spatula or a spoon to toss the mixture together to moisten all of the cookie crumbs.

Transfer the crust to the prepared springform pan and use your fingertips to press it into the bottom and partway up the sides of the pan. Chill the crust while preparing the cheesecake batter.

CHEESECAKE

14 ounces milk chocolate, finely chopped

Place the milk chocolate in the top of a double boiler over low heat. Stir often with a rubber spatula to help melt evenly. Remove the top pan of the double boiler and wipe the bottom and sides very dry.

Or place the milk chocolate in a microwave-safe bowl and melt on low power for 30-second bursts. Stir with a rubber spatula after each burst.

Essential Gear
- 9¹/₂-inch round spring-form pan
- Heavy-duty aluminum foil
- Food processor or rolling pin
- Double boiler
- Small saucepan
- Whisk
- Electric stand mixer with flat beater attachment, or large mixing bowl and hand-held mixer
- Two rubber spatulas
- Fine-mesh strainer
- 12-inch round cake pan or large roasting pan
- Cooling rack

Keeping
Store the cheesecake, covered with waxed paper and tightly wrapped with aluminum foil, in the refrigerator up to 4 days. To freeze up to 2 months, wrap the cake pan tightly in several layers of plastic wrap and aluminum foil. Use a large piece of masking tape and an indelible marker to label and date the contents. If frozen, defrost overnight in the refrigerator and bring to room temperature at least 30 minutes before serving.

Making a Change
Add 1¹/₂ cups finely chopped walnuts to the batter before turning it into the pan.

½ cup heavy whipping cream ½ cup malted milk powder	Place the cream in a small saucepan and bring to a boil over medium heat. Turn off the heat, add the malted milk powder, and whisk to distribute evenly. Cover the pan and let the mixture steep for 10 minutes, then strain the cream.
2 pounds cream cheese, softened	Place the cream cheese in the bowl of an electric stand mixer or in a large bowl. Use the flat beater attachment or a hand-held mixer to beat the cream cheese on medium speed until it's fluffy, about 2 minutes.
1 cup granulated sugar	Add the sugar and cream together very well. Stop occasionally and scrape down the sides and bottom of the bowl with a rubber spatula.
4 extra-large eggs, at room temperature	One at a time, add the eggs to the cream cheese mixture, beating well after each addition. At first the eggs will sit on top of the cream cheese mixture, but stop often to scrape down the sides and bottom of the mixing bowl with a rubber spatula. This will help the mixture to blend. The mixture may also look curdled as the eggs are added, but as you stop and scrape down the bowl, the mixture will smooth out.
1 cup sour cream 2 teaspoons pure vanilla extract	Add the sour cream and vanilla to the cream cheese mixture and stir together to combine.
	Add the strained cream to the batter and blend thoroughly, then add the melted milk chocolate and mix together.
	Transfer the batter into the crust in the springform pan. Use a rubber spatula to smooth and even the top.
1 quart boiling water	Place the springform pan in the larger cake pan or roasting pan and set the pan on the oven rack. Carefully pour the boiling water into the bottom pan until it reaches halfway up the side of the springform pan. Baking the cake in a water bath cushions it from the heat and adds extra moisture to the oven, which keeps the top of the cake from cracking.
	Bake the cake for 1 hour and 45 minutes, until the top is set, but jiggles slightly. Remove the pan from the oven and transfer the cheesecake to a rack.
	Remove the foil and let the cheesecake cool completely. Cover the top of the cheesecake with waxed paper and wrap the pan tightly with aluminum foil. Refrigerate the cake for at least 6 hours before serving. To unmold the cheesecake, dip a thin-bladed knife in hot water and dry, then run it around the inner edge of the pan. Release the clip on the rim of the pan and gently lift it off the cake.

Adding Style

Drizzle the top of the cooled and chilled cheesecake with fine lines or designs of milk chocolate (see page 43).

Serve each slice of cheesecake with a dollop of lightly sweetened whipped cream and scatter about 1 teaspoon of shaved milk chocolate over the cream.

Milk Chocolate Brownies

BROWNIES are typically made with dark chocolate, so these are a little unusual. But I have no doubt that you'll like them once you taste them. These are good unadorned, but a garnish of piped chocolate lines on top gives them a striking visual element. Try using a round or heart-shaped cutter to create different shapes. **Makes sixteen 2-inch brownies**

Essential Gear
- 8-inch square baking pan
- Aluminum foil
- Double boiler
- Whisk
- Rubber spatula
- Sifter
- Cooling rack
- Parchment paper pastry cone

1 tablespoon unsalted butter, softened

Center a rack in the oven and preheat it to 350°F. Line the baking pan with aluminum foil, letting it hang about 2 inches over the sides. Use a paper towel or your fingertips to generously butter the inside of the foil.

3½ ounces milk chocolate, finely chopped

3½ ounces (7 tablespoons) unsalted butter, cut into small pieces

Place the chocolate and the butter together in the top of a double boiler over low heat. Stir often with a rubber spatula to help melt evenly. Remove the top pan of the double boiler and wipe the bottom and sides very dry. Stir the chocolate mixture with a rubber spatula occasionally to prevent a skin from forming on top.

Or place the chocolate and butter in a microwave-safe bowl and melt on low power for 30-second bursts. Stir with a rubber spatula after each burst.

½ cup granulated sugar

Add the sugar to the chocolate mixture and whisk together.

2 extra-large eggs, at room temperature

1 teaspoon pure vanilla extract

Use a fork to lightly beat the eggs and vanilla together in a small bowl. Add to the chocolate mixture and stir together well.

1 cup all-purpose flour

1 teaspoon baking powder

Over a medium piece of waxed or parchment paper or a small bowl, sift together the flour and baking powder. In 3 stages, add the dry ingredients to the chocolate mixture, blending well after each addition. Scrape down the sides and bottom of the bowl with the rubber spatula.

½ cup walnuts, coarsely chopped

Add the walnuts to the batter and stir to distribute evenly.

Pour the batter into the prepared pan and use the rubber spatula to spread it evenly into the corners.

Bake the brownies for 30 minutes, until a cake tester or toothpick inserted in the center comes out with no crumbs clinging to it.

Keeping

Store the brownies in an airtight container between layers of waxed paper at room temperature up to 4 days. To freeze up to 4 months, wrap the container tightly in several layers of plastic wrap and aluminum foil. Use a large piece of masking tape and an indelible marker to label and date the contents. If frozen, defrost overnight in the refrigerator and bring to room temperature before serving.

Making a Change

Replace the walnuts with toasted unblanched almonds or hazelnuts.

Adding Style

Serve the cooled brownies with a dollop of lightly sweetened whipped cream or a scoop of caramel ice cream.

Remove the pan from the oven and cool completely on a rack.

GARNISH

1 ounce milk chocolate, finely chopped

Place the chocolate in the top of a double boiler over low heat. Stir often with a rubber spatula to help melt evenly. Remove the top pan of the double boiler and wipe the bottom and sides very dry.

Or place the chocolate in a microwave-safe bowl and melt on low power for 30-second bursts. Stir with a rubber spatula after each burst.

Stand a parchment paper pastry cone (see page 25) in a tall glass. Pour the melted chocolate into the cone. Fold each side of the pastry cone into the center and fold the top down to make a tight package. Cut off a very small amount of the pastry cone at the pointed end.

Hold the pastry cone about 1 inch above and straight up and down over the brownies. Start at one corner and pipe thin lines close together diagonally across the top of the brownies to the opposite corner. Repeat from the other corners, creating a cross-hatch pattern across the top. Let the chocolate set for 15 minutes at room temperature.

Lift the brownies from the pan with the aluminum foil. Carefully peel the foil away from the sides of the brownies. Cut into 4 equal-sized rows in each direction.

Replace the top milk chocolate garnish with white chocolate or dark chocolate.

Use a 1½-inch round or heart-shaped plain-edge cutter to cut the brownies. Top each brownie with a star or rosette of whipped cream (see page 44). Garnish with a half walnut, a whole unblanched almond, or a whole toasted and skinned hazelnut, depending on the nuts used in the brownies.

Milk Chocolate–Caramel Pecan Tart

SIMILAR TO the flavors in a popular candy bar, this rich tart is far better and definitely more elegant than that. A glossy, smooth layer of milk chocolate tops a caramel-pecan filling that is enclosed in a sweet pastry shell. A thin slice of this rich tart is all it takes to satisfy those sweet cravings. **Makes one 9½-inch round tart, 12 to 14 servings**

PASTRY DOUGH

1¼ cups all-purpose flour
½ cup confectioners' sugar
¼ teaspoon salt

In the work bowl of a food processor fitted with the steel blade, combine the flour, sugar, and salt. Pulse briefly to blend.

Essential Gear
- Food processor
- Rolling pin
- 9½-inch round, fluted-edge tart pan with removable bottom
- Baking sheet
- Aluminum foil
- Pie weights
- Cooling rack
- Small saucepan
- 2-quart heavy-bottomed saucepan
- 1-inch natural-bristle pastry brush

4 ounces (8 tablespoons, 1 stick) unsalted butter, chilled	Cut the butter into small pieces and add to the flour mixture. Pulse until the butter is cut into very tiny pieces, about 30 seconds. The texture should be sandy with very tiny lumps throughout.
1 extra-large egg yolk, at room temperature **½ teaspoon pure vanilla extract**	Use a fork to lightly beat the egg yolk with the vanilla in a small bowl. With the food processor running, pour this mixture through the feed tube. Process the dough until the mixture wraps itself around the blade, about 1 minute.

Turn the pastry dough onto a large piece of plastic wrap. Shape into a flat disk and wrap tightly in a double layer of plastic wrap. Chill in the refrigerator until firm before using, at least 2 hours. Chilling the dough relaxes the gluten in the flour so it won't be too elastic and will roll out easily. It also firms up the butter in the dough so it will need less flour when rolled out. If the dough is too firm, it will splinter and break when rolled out. Let it stand at room temperature for 10 to 15 minutes before rolling to become more pliable.

Center a rack in the oven and preheat it to 375°F.

On a smooth, flat surface, roll out the pastry dough between sheets of lightly floured waxed or parchment paper to a large circle about 11 inches in diameter. To tell if the dough will fit the tart pan, hold the pan above the dough. If there are about 2 inches of dough that protrude beyond the sides of the pan, it will fit.

Carefully peel the paper off the top of the dough. Brush excess flour off the dough, then loosely roll the pastry dough around the rolling pin without the bottom piece of paper. Place the tart pan directly underneath the rolling pin and carefully unroll the pastry dough into the tart pan. Gently lift up the sides and ease the pastry dough into the bottom and sides of the tart pan. Trim off the excess pastry dough at the top of the pan.

The tart dough is delicate and needs to be handled gently. Rolling it around the rolling pin and unrolling into the tart pan is an easy way to get the dough into the pan.

Transfer the tart pan to a baking sheet and chill in the refrigerator for 15 minutes. This helps prevent the dough from shrinking as it bakes.

Line the pastry shell with a large piece of aluminum foil that fits well against the bottom and sides. Fill with pie weights or a mixture of rice and beans. Bake for 10 minutes, then remove the foil and weights and bake another 8 minutes, until very light golden and set. If the

- Heat-resistant spatula
- Small metal offset spatula

Keeping

Store the tart, loosely covered with waxed paper. Place several toothpicks around the top outer edge to hold up the waxed paper so it won't mar the surface. Tightly wrap with aluminum foil and hold at room temperature up to 3 days.

Streamlining

The pastry dough can be made in advance and kept in the refrigerator, tightly wrapped in a double layer of plastic wrap, up to 4 days. To freeze up to 3 months, wrap the dough snugly in several layers of plastic wrap and place it in a freezer bag. Use a large piece of masking tape and an indelible marker to label and date the contents. If frozen, defrost overnight in the refrigerator before using.

Troubleshooting

Don't roll out the pastry dough before it is chilled. The dough will be too soft and it will require a lot of flour to roll out, which results in a tough dough.

Once the pastry dough is unrolled into the tart pan, don't push it down forcefully. This will stretch the dough, which will shrink as it bakes, making it flat instead of taking the shape of the tart pan.

bottom of the pastry shell puffs up, gently pierce it with a fork or sharp knife in a few places to release the air. Remove the pan from the oven and transfer to a rack while preparing the filling.

Making a Change
Replace the pecans with walnuts.

CARAMEL-PECAN FILLING

¾ cup heavy whipping cream	Place the cream in a small saucepan and warm over medium heat until bubbles form at the edges.
1 cup granulated sugar ¼ cup water 1 tablespoon light corn syrup	While the cream is heating, combine the sugar, water, and corn syrup in the heavy-bottomed saucepan. Cook over high heat, without stirring, until the mixture begins to boil. Place a wet pastry brush at the point where the sugar syrup meets the sides of the pan and sweep it around completely. Do this two times. This prevents the sugar from crystallizing by brushing any stray crystals back into the mixture. Continue to cook the mixture, without stirring, until it turns amber colored, about 10 minutes.
	Remove the saucepan from the heat and carefully stir in the hot cream using a long-handled spoon or heat-resistant spatula. Be very careful because it will bubble and splatter. Return the saucepan to the heat and stir for 1 to 2 minutes to dissolve any lumps.
4 ounces (8 tablespoons, 1 stick) unsalted butter, softened	Add the butter to the caramel mixture and stir until it is completely melted.
1½ teaspoons pure vanilla extract	Remove the saucepan from the heat and stir in the vanilla.
2 cups pecans, coarsely chopped	Add the pecans to the caramel mixture and quickly stir to coat them completely before the caramel begins to set up.
2 teaspoons unsalted butter, softened	Use your fingertips or a paper towel to coat the wooden spoon or spatula with butter to keep the mixture from sticking to it. Working quickly, transfer the filling to the partially baked pastry shell and spread it out evenly. Bake the tart for 15 to 18 minutes, until the filling is bubbling and the tart shell is golden. Remove from the oven and cool completely on a rack.

MILK CHOCOLATE GANACHE TOPPING

5 ounces milk chocolate, finely chopped	Place the chocolate in a large bowl.

⅓ **cup heavy cream**	Place the cream in a saucepan and bring to a boil over medium heat. Pour the cream over the chocolate and let it stand for 1 minute. Stir the mixture together using a heat-resistant spatula, whisk, or immersion blender until very smooth. Let the ganache cool until it begins to thicken, stirring it frequently so a skin doesn't form on top, about 20 minutes. Pour the topping over the tart and use an offset spatula to spread it out to the edges.

GARNISH

20 pecan halves	While the topping is still fluid, place the pecan halves close together around the outer edges of the tart, facing the center. Let the topping set up at room temperature or chill in the refrigerator for 15 minutes.

Remove the sides of the tart pan (see page 42) before serving. Use a sharp knife dipped in hot water and dried to cut the tart into serving slices. Serve at room temperature.

Milk Chocolate Chunk and Peanut Butter Brownies

THE COMBINATION of milk chocolate, peanut butter, and brown sugar make these delectable brownies very hard to resist. Although these are not the usual dark color of brownies, the chocolate flavor definitely comes through. I like to use dark milk chocolate to increase the depth of chocolate flavor, but these work very well with regular milk chocolate. **Makes sixteen 2-inch square brownies**

Essential Gear

- 8-inch square baking pan
- Aluminum foil
- Electric stand mixer with flat beater attachment, or large mixing bowl with hand-held mixer
- Rubber spatula
- Sifter
- Cooling rack

Keeping

Store the brownies in an airtight plastic container between layers of waxed paper at room temperature up to 4 days. To freeze up to 4 months, wrap the container tightly in several layers of plastic wrap and

1 tablespoon unsalted butter, softened	Center a rack in the oven and preheat it to 350°F. Line the baking pan with aluminum foil, letting it hang about 2 inches over the sides. Use a paper towel or your fingertips to generously butter the inside of the foil.
3 ounces (6 tablespoons, ¾ stick) unsalted butter, softened	Place the butter in the bowl of an electric stand mixer or in a large bowl. Use the flat beater attachment or a hand-held mixer to beat the butter on medium speed until it's fluffy, about 2 minutes.
½ cup natural-style (old-fashioned) chunky peanut butter	Add the peanut butter, and cream together well. Stop occasionally and scrape down the sides and bottom of the pan with a rubber spatula.

1¼ cups firmly packed light brown sugar	Add the sugar to the peanut butter mixture and cream together well.	aluminum foil. Use a large piece of masking tape and an indelible marker to label and date the contents. If frozen, defrost overnight in the refrigerator and bring to room temperature before serving.
2 extra-large eggs, at room temperature	One at a time, add the eggs to the peanut butter mixture and beat well after each addition. At first the eggs will sit on top of the mixture, but once you scrape down the sides and bottom of the bowl with a rubber spatula, the mixture will smooth out.	
2 teaspoons pure vanilla extract	Add the vanilla and blend completely.	**Adding Style** Drizzle the top of the cooled brownies with melted milk chocolate or bittersweet chocolate in close lines (see page 43). Let the chocolate set for 15 minutes before cutting the brownies.
¾ cup all-purpose flour **1 teaspoon baking powder** **¼ teaspoon salt**	Over a medium piece of waxed or parchment paper or a bowl, sift together the flour and baking powder. Add the salt and toss to mix. Add the flour mixture to the peanut butter mixture in 2 stages and stir together thoroughly. Stop occasionally and scrape down the sides and bottom of the bowl with a rubber spatula.	
5 ounces milk chocolate (or dark milk chocolate), chopped into small chunks	Add the chocolate chunks to the batter and stir to distribute evenly.	Use a 1½-inch round or heart-shaped plain edge cutter to cut the cooled brownies. Top the center of each brownie with a star or rosette of whipped cream (see page 44). Sprinkle the whipped cream with finely chopped salted peanuts.
	Pour the batter into the prepared pan and use a rubber spatula to spread it evenly into the corners. Bake the brownies for 35 to 38 minutes, until a cake tester or toothpick inserted in the center comes out slightly moist. Remove the pan from the oven and cool completely on a rack. Lift the brownies from the pan with the aluminum foil. Carefully peel the foil away from the sides of the brownies. Cut into 4 equal-sized rows in each direction.	

Milk Chocolate Chunk–Peanut Butter Cookies

MILK CHOCOLATE and peanut butter are an excellent flavor combination that is showcased in these cookies. I prefer to use natural-style or freshly ground peanut butter for the maximum flavor. Kids of all ages love these cookies, so don't be surprised when they disappear quickly. **Makes 4½ dozen cookies**

Adjust the oven racks to the upper and lower thirds and preheat the oven to 350°F. Line the baking sheets with parchment paper or non-stick liners.

Essential Gear
- Four baking sheets
- Four parchment paper sheets or non-stick liners
- Electric stand mixer with flat beater attachment, or large mixing bowl and hand-held mixer
- Rubber spatula

6 ounces (12 tablespoons, 1½ sticks) unsalted butter, softened	Place the butter in the bowl of an electric stand mixer or in a large bowl. Use the flat beater attachment or a hand-held mixer to beat the butter on medium speed until it's fluffy, about 2 minutes.
1 cup unsalted natural-style (old-fashioned) chunky peanut butter, at room temperature	Add the peanut butter to the butter and mix together well. Stop and scrape down the sides and bottom of the bowl with a rubber spatula.
1 cup firmly packed light brown sugar **¾ cup granulated sugar**	Add the brown sugar and granulated sugar to the peanut butter mixture and cream together well. Stop occasionally and scrape down the sides and bottom of the bowl with a rubber spatula.
2 extra-large eggs, at room temperature **1 teaspoon pure vanilla extract**	Use a fork to lightly beat the egg and vanilla together in a small bowl. Add to the peanut butter mixture and blend thoroughly. At first the eggs will sit on top of the mixture, but stop often to scrape down the sides and bottom of the mixing bowl with a rubber spatula to help mix evenly. The mixture may also look curdled, but will smooth out when the dry ingredients are added.
2 cups all-purpose flour **1 teaspoon baking soda** **½ teaspoon salt**	Over a large piece of waxed or parchment paper or a bowl, sift together the flour and baking soda. Add the salt and toss to blend well.
	Add the dry ingredients in 4 stages, blending well after each addition. Stop occasionally and scrape down the sides and bottom of the bowl with a rubber spatula.
6 ounces milk chocolate, cut into small chunks	Add the chocolate chunks and stir to distribute evenly.

Use a large spoon or a small ice cream scoop to scoop out mounds about 2 inches in diameter. Place the mounds on the baking sheets, leaving 2 inches of space between them so they will have room to spread as they bake. Dip a fork in water and shake off any excess. Press the top of each mound with the fork to flatten them into disks.

Cover two of the baking sheets with plastic wrap and refrigerate.

Bake two sheets of the cookies for 5 minutes. Switch the baking sheets and bake another 5 to 6 minutes, until the cookies are set and light golden.

Remove the baking sheets from the oven and cool the cookies completely on the baking sheets on racks.

- Spoon or small ice cream scoop
- Two cooling racks

Keeping

Store the cookies in an airtight container between layers of waxed paper at room temperature up to 5 days. To freeze up to 3 months, wrap the container tightly in several layers of plastic wrap and aluminum foil. Use a large piece of masking tape and an indelible marker to label and date the contents. If frozen, defrost overnight in the refrigerator and bring to room temperature before serving.

Adding Style

Drizzle the tops of the cooled cookies with thin lines of milk, dark, or white chocolate (see page 43). Let the chocolate set for 15 minutes before storing.

Half dip the cookies into tempered milk or dark chocolate (see page 43). Let the chocolate set for 15 minutes before storing.

Make sandwich cookies by spreading a thin layer of Milk Chocolate Ganache (page 424) on the flat side of one cookie and topping it with the flat side of another cookie.

Make peanut butter–milk chocolate sandwich cookies by spreading a thin layer of peanut butter on the flat side of one cookie and topping it with the flat side of another cookie.

Milk Chocolate Layer Cake with Milk Chocolate Frosting

LAYERS OF LIGHT, airy milk chocolate cake are alternated with creamy milk chocolate frosting to make an old-fashioned layer cake. Although there are several steps involved in making this cake, it's easy to do some of them in advance. This is a perfect cake to adorn with candles for a birthday or any special celebration. But don't wait for a special occasion to savor this treat; make it the next time you bake a cake. **Makes one 9-inch round cake, 12 to 14 servings**

CAKE

Center a rack in the oven and preheat it to 350°F.

1 tablespoon unsalted butter, softened	Use a paper towel or your fingertips to butter the inside of the cake pans.
1 tablespoon all-purpose flour	Dust the inside of each pan with some of the flour. Shake and tilt the pans to cover the inside completely, then turn the pans over and shake out the excess over the sink.
	Cut a round of parchment paper to fit the bottom of each pan. Butter each parchment paper round and place in each pan, butter-side up.
5 ounces milk chocolate, finely chopped	Place the chocolate in the top of a double boiler over low heat. Stir often with a rubber spatula to help melt evenly.
	Or place the chocolate in a microwave-safe bowl and melt on low power for 30-second bursts. Stir with a rubber spatula after each burst.
2⅓ cups cake flour **1 teaspoon baking soda** **¼ teaspoon baking powder** **1 teaspoon salt**	Over a large piece of waxed or parchment paper or a bowl, sift together the flour, baking soda, and baking powder. Add the salt and toss to mix.
5 ounces (10 tablespoons, 1¼ sticks) unsalted butter, softened	Place the butter in the bowl of an electric stand mixer or in a large bowl. Use the flat beater attachment or a hand-held mixer to beat the butter on medium speed until it's light and fluffy, about 2 minutes.
1¼ cups granulated sugar **¼ cup firmly packed light brown sugar**	Add the granulated sugar and brown sugar to the butter and cream together well on medium speed. Stop occasionally and scrape down the sides and bottom of the mixing bowl with a rubber spatula.

Essential Gear

- Two 9 × 2-inch round cake pans
- Scissors
- Parchment paper
- Double boiler
- Two rubber spatulas
- Sifter
- Electric stand mixer with flat beater attachment and wire whip attachment, or large mixing bowl and hand-held mixer
- Two cooling racks
- Small saucepan
- Serrated knife
- 1-inch natural-bristle pastry brush
- 10-inch flexible-blade icing spatula

Keeping

Store the cake loosely tented with waxed paper and covered with aluminum foil in the refrigerator up to 4 days. Place several toothpicks in the top outer edges of the cake to hold the waxed paper away from it so it won't mar the frosting. To freeze up to 3 months, place the cake in a cake box and wrap with several layers of plastic wrap and aluminum foil. Or place the cake on a lined baking sheet in the freezer and let it freeze (about 3 hours). Loosely wrap the cake in layers of plastic wrap and aluminum foil. If frozen, defrost overnight in the refrigerator. Bring the

4 extra-large eggs, at room temperature	One at a time, add the eggs to the butter mixture, blending well after each addition. At first the eggs will sit on top of the mixture, but stop often to scrape down the sides and bottom of the mixing bowl with a rubber spatula. This will help smooth it out. The mixture may also look curdled as the eggs are added, but as you stop and scrape down the bowl, the mixture will smooth out..
2 teaspoons pure vanilla extract	Add the vanilla to the butter mixture and mix in thoroughly.
	Remove the top pan of the double boiler and wipe the bottom and sides of the pan very dry. Stir the milk chocolate for 30 seconds to 1 minute to cool, then add the to the butter mixture and blend thoroughly.
⅔ cup buttermilk	Add the dry ingredients to the butter mixture in 3 stages, alternating with the buttermilk. Blend well after each addition and stop often to scrape down the sides and bottom of the bowl with a rubber spatula. This helps mix the ingredients together uniformly.
	Divide the batter evenly between the two cake pans. Smooth the top of each pan with a rubber spatula.

Bake the layers for 30 to 35 minutes, until a cake tester inserted in the center comes out with no crumbs clinging to it.

Remove the cake pans from the oven and cool completely on racks. Invert the pans to remove the layers and peel the parchment paper off the back of each layer. Re-invert the layers onto plates or cardboard cake circles. |

SUGAR SYRUP

¼ cup granulated sugar **½ cup water**	Combine the sugar and water in a small saucepan. Bring to a boil over medium-high heat to dissolve the sugar. Remove from the heat and cool to room temperature.

MILK CHOCOLATE FROSTING

1 pound milk chocolate, finely chopped	Place the chocolate in the top of a double boiler over low heat. Stir often with a rubber spatula to help melt evenly.

Or melt the chocolate in a microwave-safe bowl on low power for 30-second bursts. Stir with a rubber spatula after each burst. |

cake to room temperature at least 30 minutes before serving.

Streamlining
Bake the cake layers up to 2 days before assembling and keep tightly covered with plastic wrap at room temperature. To freeze the layers up to 3 months, wrap them snugly in several layers of plastic wrap and place them in freezer bags. Use a large piece of masking tape and an indelible marker to label and date the contents. If frozen, defrost the layers overnight in the refrigerator.

The sugar syrup can be prepared up to 2 weeks in advance and stored in a tightly covered plastic container in the refrigerator.

Recovering from a Mishap
If one of the cake layers breaks during assembly, patch it together with some of the frosting.

Making a Change
Stir 1 cup finely chopped toasted pecans, walnuts, hazelnuts, or almonds into the cake batter before baking.

If using nuts in the cake batter, garnish the sides of the cake by pressing the same type of finely chopped nuts into the sides up to the top edge (see page 35).

12 ounces (24 tablespoons, 3 sticks) unsalted butter, softened	Place the butter in the bowl of an electric stand mixer or in a large bowl. Use the flat beater attachment or hand-held mixer to beat the butter on medium speed until it's fluffy, about 2 minutes.
1 tablespoon light corn syrup 2 teaspoons pure vanilla extract	Add the corn syrup and the vanilla to the butter and blend together well on medium speed.
	Remove the top pan of the double boiler and wipe the bottom and sides of the pan very dry. Add the melted chocolate to the butter mixture and combine thoroughly.
4 cups confectioner's sugar, sifted	Add the sugar in 4 stages to the chocolate mixture. Stop after each addition and scrape down the sides and bottom of the bowl with a rubber spatula. Mix together thoroughly.
1 to 2 tablespoons water	If the frosting seems too firm, blend in 1 or 2 tablespoons of water, as needed. The consistency should be soft enough to spread, but not so soft that it won't hold its shape.

Replace the apricot preserves with mango or passion fruit preserves or orange marmalade.

Adding Style

Press finely shaved milk chocolate into the top and sides of the cake (see page 35).

ASSEMBLY

With your fingertips, gently peel the skin off the top of each cake layer. Using a serrated knife, cut each cake layer in half horizontally (see page 34). Take your time and go slowly when cutting the cake layers in half so you don't turn the knife at an angle and make uneven cuts.

1/3 cup apricot preserves

Place the bottom of one cake layer on a serving plate. Use a pastry brush to brush the layer with sugar syrup. Place strips of waxed paper around the bottom edges of the cake to protect the plate while assembling the cake. Use a flexible-blade spatula to spread the layer evenly with the apricot preserves.

With a clean flexible-blade spatula, evenly spread some of the frosting over the cake layer.

Position the second cake layer evenly over the frosting. Brush the layer with the sugar syrup, then spread frosting over the layer. Repeat with the remaining two cake layers, sugar syrup, and more frosting. Spread the remaining frosting over the sides and top of the cake. Use the spatula to make swirls in the frosting on the sides and top of the cake by twisting your wrist lightly from side to side.

Let the cake chill for at least 2 hours before serving so it has time to set and will be easier to cut. Serve the cake at room temperature.

Milk Chocolate Roulade

FINELY GROUND milk chocolate flavors this light, airy cake that is baked in a jelly-roll pan and rolled up while warm so it will hold the rolled shape. After the cake is cool, it's filled and decorated with sweetened and flavored whipped cream. This is a great cake for a party because it looks spectacular, tastes divine, and makes several servings. **Makes one 15-inch cake, 12 to 15 servings**

CAKE

1 tablespoon unsalted butter, melted

Center a rack in the oven and preheat it to 400°F. Line the jelly-roll pan with a sheet of parchment paper. Use a pastry brush or paper towel to coat the parchment paper with butter.

3 ounces milk chocolate, coarsely chopped
1 tablespoon granulated sugar

In the work bowl of a food processor fitted with the steel blade, combine the chocolate and sugar. Pulse until the chocolate is very finely ground, about 2 minutes.

3 extra-large eggs, at room temperature
½ cup granulated sugar

Place the eggs and sugar in the bowl of an electric stand mixer or in a large mixing bowl. Use the wire whip attachment or a hand-held mixer and whip on medium speed until the mixture is very pale colored and holds a slowly dissolving ribbon as the beater is lifted, about 5 minutes.

1 cup all-purpose flour
1 tablespoon unsweetened cocoa powder (natural or Dutch-processed)
⅛ teaspoon salt

Over a large piece of waxed or parchment paper or a bowl, sift together the flour and cocoa powder. Add the salt and toss to mix well.

Transfer this mixture to a large bowl and add the ground milk chocolate. Stir together to blend thoroughly.

In 3 stages, fold the dry ingredients into the whipped egg mixture, blending well after each addition.

Turn the batter out onto the lined jelly-roll pan. Use an offset spatula or rubber spatula to spread the mixture smoothly and evenly over the parchment paper and into the corners of the pan.

Bake the cake for 8 to 10 minutes, until the cake looks set and springs back when lightly touched on top.

Remove the pan from the oven and transfer to a rack.

Essential Gear

- Jelly-roll pan (12 × 17 inches)
- Two parchment paper sheets
- 1-inch natural-bristle pastry brush or paper towel
- Food processor
- Electric stand mixer with wire whip attachment, or large mixing bowl and hand-held mixer
- Sifter
- Medium saucepan
- Rubber spatula
- Long-blade offset spatula
- Kitchen towel
- Ruler
- 12- or 14-inch pastry bag and large open star tip
- Serrated knife

Keeping

Store the cake lightly tented with waxed paper and aluminum foil in the refrigerator up to 2 days. Place several toothpicks in the top edges of the cake to hold the waxed paper away from it so it won't mar the icing.

Streamlining

The cake can be baked up to 3 days before filling. Wrap it tightly in a double layer of plastic wrap and store in the refrigerator.

Recovering from a Mishap

If the cake breaks or cracks while it is being rolled, posi-

After the cake is baked and while it is still hot, use a small, sharp knife to loosen the edges from the sides of the pan. Place a sheet of parchment paper over the top of the cake and cover with a kitchen towel. Then invert the jelly-roll pan and lift it off the cake. Gently peel the parchment paper off of the back of the cake and discard.

Starting at one long end, roll up the cake inside the towel and parchment paper and leave it seam-side down to cool to room temperature.

FILLING AND DECORATION

2 cups heavy whipping cream

2 tablespoons superfine sugar

1 teaspoon pure vanilla extract

Place the cream in the chilled bowl of an electric stand mixer or in a large bowl. Using the wire whip attachment or a hand-held mixer, whip the cream on medium speed until it is frothy. Add the sugar and vanilla and continue to whip the cream on medium speed until it holds soft peaks.

Unroll the cake and remove the towel. Use the offset spatula to evenly spread half of the whipped cream over the cake, leaving a 1-inch border at the farthest long end of the cake. Use the parchment paper to help roll up the cake.

To make a tight cake roll, pull about one-third of the parchment paper over the top of the cake. Then place a ruler flat against the parchment that covers the top of the cake and push it against the roll while pulling the bottom part of the parchment paper toward you. This resistance motion of simultaneously pushing against the cake while pulling the parchment under the cake toward you compresses the roulade.

Using the offset spatula, transfer the cake to a serving plate or a baking sheet covered with waxed or parchment paper, with the seam side down. Trim off the rough ends of the cake and discard.

Fit the pastry bag with the star tip and fill partway with the remaining whipped cream. Starting on the bottom side of the cake and working towards the top, pipe a row of whipped cream across the cake from one end to the other (see page 44). Repeat this, piping rows of whipped cream close together to cover the entire cake. Turn the plate or pan around after completing one side of the cake to make it easier for you to work.

1 ounce milk chocolate, finely chopped or shaved

Sprinkle the top of the cake with the milk chocolate.

Cut the cake crosswise into 1-inch slices. Place each slice on its side on a plate and serve immediately.

tion the cracked part of the cake on the bottom of the roll or patch with whipped cream.

Making a Change

Fold 1 cup toasted and finely ground hazelnuts or pecans into the batter before spreading it on the pan and sprinkle ground toasted hazelnuts or pecans over the top of the cake along with the milk chocolate.

Fill and decorate the cake with Milk Chocolate Buttercream instead of the whipped cream filling. To make Milk Chocolate Buttercream, follow the recipe for buttercream in Fresh Peach Buttercream Layer Cake (page 70), and replace the peach puree with 5 ounces melted milk chocolate.

Profiteroles with Milk Chocolate Filling and Sauce

PROFITEROLES are small cream puffs, one to two inches in diameter. They are traditionally filled with whipped ice cream and topped with dark chocolate sauce, but this recipe calls for whipped milk chocolate ganache for the filling. The typical serving of profiteroles is either three or five, depending on their size, stacked into a pyramid and drizzled with chocolate sauce. The same pastry dough is used to make cream puffs, which are simply a larger version of profiteroles and are typically filled with pastry cream. Profiteroles and cream puffs are made from choux pastry (pâte à choux, pronounced "pot ah *shoe*"), also known as cream puff pastry, which is one of the basics of French pastry. **Makes 84 profiteroles or 36 cream puffs**

CREAM PUFF PASTRY DOUGH

Adjust the oven racks to the upper and lower thirds and preheat the oven to 425°F. Line the baking sheets with aluminum foil or non-stick pan liners.

²/₃ cup water	Place the water, butter, milk, sugar, and salt in the saucepan. Bring to a boil over medium-high heat.
4 ounces (8 tablespoons, 1 stick) unsalted butter, cut into small pieces	
¹/₃ cup milk	
1 tablespoon granulated sugar	
¹/₄ teaspoon salt	
1 cup all-purpose flour, sifted	Remove the saucepan from the heat and add the flour all at once. Stir vigorously with a long-handled wooden spoon or heat-resistant spatula until the dough pulls away from the sides of the pan and forms a ball around the spoon. Return the saucepan to medium heat and cook for 3 minutes, stirring continuously, until the dough is smooth. This helps to develop the gluten in the flour, the protein that gives flour its elasticity. The result is that the puffs rise very well as they bake.

Transfer the dough to the bowl of an electric stand mixer or a large bowl. Use the flat beater attachment or a hand-held mixer to beat the dough on medium speed for about 3 minutes to release the heat and steam.

Or transfer the dough to the work bowl of a food processor fitted with the steel blade. Leave the feed tube open to release steam and process the mixture for 30 seconds to 1 minute.

Essential Gear

- Two baking sheets
- Aluminum foil or non-stick pan liners
- Medium heavy-bottomed saucepan
- Sifter
- Wooden spoon or heat-resistant spatula
- Electric stand mixer with flat beater attachment, or hand-held mixer and large mixing bowl or food processor
- Rubber spatula
- 14-inch pastry bag and ½-inch plain round pastry tip
- 1-inch natural-bristle pastry brush
- Small sharp knife
- Two cooling racks
- Small saucepan
- Serrated knife
- Microwave-safe bowl

Keeping

Store the puffs in a single layer on a cool baking sheet, tightly wrapped with aluminum foil, at room temperature for 1 day. To freeze up to 2 months, store the puffs in a single layer in freezer bags. Use a large piece of masking tape and an indelible marker to label and date the contents. Place them in a single layer on a baking sheet and warm them in a 300°F oven for 10 minutes before filling.

4 extra-large eggs, at room temperature

Using a fork, lightly beat each egg in a small bowl, and add to the dough, 1 at a time. Mix completely after each addition, then stop and scrape down the sides and bottom of the bowl with a rubber spatula. Mix or process the dough until it is smooth and glossy, 30 seconds to 1 minute.

Fit the pastry bag with the round tip and fill partway with the dough. Holding the pastry bag straight up and down and 1 inch above a baking sheet, pipe out mounds about $^3/_4$ to 1 inch in diameter and $^1/_2$ inch high, leaving at least 1 inch of space between puffs so there will be room for them to expand as they bake. This is the size for profiteroles.

To make cream puffs, pipe mounds about 2 to 2$^1/_4$ inches in diameter and $^3/_4$ inch high, with 2 inches of space between mounds.

Spacing the puffs evenly on the baking sheet helps them bake evenly. If the puffs are crowded on the baking sheet, they may collapse because air won't be able to circulate around them.

Make sure the puffs on each baking sheet are the same size so they will bake thoroughly. Different sizes require different baking times.

Dip a spoon or fork in water and shake off the excess. Lightly smooth the top of each mound with the back of the spoon or fork to even the tops.

EGG WASH

1 extra-large egg
1 teaspoon milk

Using a fork, lightly beat the egg and milk together in a small bowl. Lightly brush the top of each mound with the egg wash. Be careful that the egg wash doesn't run down the sides and get underneath the puffs. If this happens, wipe it up because it will cause the puffs to stick to the foil or pan liner.

Bake the puffs for 10 minutes. Reduce the oven temperature to 375°F. Switch the baking sheets and bake another 10 to 15 minutes for small puffs or 15 to 20 minutes for large puffs. The puffs should be deep golden brown. The initial heat of the oven creates steam inside of the puffs, which causes them to rise. If the oven heat is too low, the puffs won't rise properly.

Remove the baking sheets from the oven and put them on racks. Use a small sharp knife to cut a small horizontal slit in the side of each puff, about halfway from the top, to release steam.

Streamlining

The puffs can be baked in advance and kept in the freezer up to 2 months before using. They can also be filled and frozen for the same length of time. If filled and frozen, defrost briefly in the refrigerator before serving so they won't be too firm to eat.

Making a Change

Use dark milk chocolate for both the filling and the sauce, which gives a richer, deeper chocolate flavor.

Replace the filling with whipped milk chocolate ice cream or caramel ice cream.

Replace the milk chocolate sauce with Caramel Sauce (see Rum-Raisin Pound Cake, page 614).

Return the baking sheets to the oven, turn off the heat, and prop the door open with a wooden spoon. Leave the puffs in the oven for 30 to 45 minutes to dry completely. Test a puff to make sure it is dry inside by slitting it open. If the puffs are not dry, leave them in the oven another 10 to 15 minutes. When the puffs are dry, cool them completely on racks. If the puffs are not properly dried out inside before they are removed from the oven, they will collapse as they cool.

FILLING

10 ounces milk chocolate, finely chopped

Place the chocolate in a large bowl.

2/3 cup heavy whipping cream

Place the cream in the small saucepan and bring to a boil over medium heat. Pour the cream over the chocolate and let it stand for 1 minute. Stir the mixture together using a heat-resistant spatula, whisk, or immersion blender until very smooth.

Divide the mixture into 2 equal portions. Cover each portion and let cool to room temperature. Reserve one portion of the ganache for the sauce and refrigerate the other portion until it is firm but pliable. A good test is to press a finger into the mixture. If it takes the indentation of your finger easily, it's at the right point. If the mixture is too soft, it will feel runny, and if it is too firm, it will be hard to press your finger in it. If the mixture is too firm, let it stand at room temperature until it is ready to use.

Place the ganache in the bowl of an electric stand mixer or in a large bowl. Using the flat beater attachment or a hand-held mixer, beat the ganache on medium speed until it holds soft peaks, 1 to 2 minutes. The ganache will become lighter in color as it beats. Be careful not to beat the ganache too long or it will curdle and separate.

Fit a clean pastry bag with a clean round tip and fill partway with the whipped ganache.

Use a serrated knife to cut each profiterole in half horizontally. Pipe a mound of whipped ganache into the cavity of each puff until it mounds slightly over the top. Cover each profiterole with its top.

MILK CHOCOLATE SAUCE

Place the ganache set aside for the sauce in a microwave-safe bowl and heat on low power for 30 second bursts until it is liquid. Stir the ganache in after each burst to make sure it is melting evenly.

Or heat the ganache in the top of a double boiler over hot water. Stir often to ensure even melting. Remove the top pan of the double boiler and wipe the bottom and sides very dry.

ASSEMBLY

Place 3 to 5 profiteroles in a bowl, stacked in a pyramid shape. Drizzle the tops with warm milk chocolate sauce and serve immediately.

13

WHITE

CHOCOLATE

THE MOST FREQUENTLY asked question about white chocolate: "Is white chocolate really chocolate?" It most certainly *is* chocolate if it contains cocoa butter. Actually, this is a good question because there are many confections that call themselves white chocolate, but do not contain cocoa butter. Instead of cocoa butter they are made from other fats and oils. These are usually referred to as confectionery coating and are often used in place of real white chocolate. The imitations taste nothing like chocolate, but taste exactly like the fat or oil used to make them, and in most cases this is not appealing.

Technically, white chocolate is made from cocoa butter, sugar, lecithin, and vanilla. Because it doesn't contain any chocolate liquor, it was only in 2005 that the FDA allowed it to be labeled as chocolate. I am very fond of white

chocolate, but my husband absolutely loves it. While working in Switzerland, he learned to love white chocolate and hasn't turned back. I think it's the extra sweetness that he likes the most. Once you've eaten good-quality white chocolate, there's no substitute.

White chocolate is available year-round in supermarkets, cookware shops, gourmet food shops, natural and health food stores, and through many online and catalog sources. If you are looking for a particular brand of white chocolate that you like, just search for it by name on the Web and you will most likely find the manufacturer's Web site, where you will be able to buy it.

TIPS AND TECHNIQUES

White chocolate is not interchangeable with milk chocolate or dark chocolate in recipes because white chocolate has less body than either. I strongly urge you to taste white chocolate in plain bar form before using it in your recipes to make certain you like it, because the flavor won't change when you bake with it. There can be a good deal of variance in taste between brands of white chocolate. And, of course, make sure you are buying real white chocolate, not the imitation.

For more tips and techniques, see Chocolate Tasting, Selecting and Working with Chocolate, and Storing Chocolate in About Chocolate (page 370). The following tasting table describes the tasting characteristics for seven brands of white chocolate that are easy to find.

WHITE CHOCOLATE TASTING TABLE

Brand and Cocoa Components Percentage	Callebaut	Cocoa Barry	Ghirardelli	Lindt Swiss Classic	Perugina	Sarotti	Valrhona Ivoire
Appearance	Even Smooth Pale ivory	Even Smooth Pale ivory	Even Smooth Light yellow	Even Smooth Pale ivory	Even Smooth Pale ivory	Even Smooth Light yellow	Even Smooth Pale ivory
Aroma	Clean Floral Cocoa butter	Clean Cocoa butter	Heavy Medicinal	Clean Vanilla	Clean Light chocolate	Heavy Chocolate	Sweet Cream Light Clean
Snap	Clean Crisp	Clean Crisp	Clean	Clean Firm	Clean Sharp	Sharp	Clean Crisp
Texture/ Mouthfeel	Creamy Smooth	Creamy Smooth	Firm Moderate melt	Firm Moderate melt	Firm Not much melt	Firm Not much melt	Creamy Smooth
Flavor	Light Creamy Floral	Light Creamy	Milky Sour	Light Cocoa butter	Sweet Chocolate	Fruity Citrus·	Milky Toasty Lightly sweet
Aftertaste	Moderate	Moderate	Short	Moderate	Short	Short	Moderate

White Chocolate and Lemon Chiffon Cake

CHIFFON CAKE is a light, airy cake that adapts extremely well to a variety of flavors. In this version, white chocolate and lemon blend together beautifully. Both flavors complement and balance each other. This is one of my favorite cakes. **Makes one 10-inch round cake, 14 to 16 servings**

Center a rack in the oven and preheat it to 325°F.

4 ounces white chocolate, cut into small pieces **½ cup superfine sugar**	In the work bowl of a food processor fitted with the steel blade, combine the chocolate and sugar. Pulse until the chocolate is very finely ground, about 2 minutes.
2¼ cups cake flour **1 tablespoon baking powder**	In the bowl of an electric stand mixer or in a large bowl, sift together the flour and baking powder.
½ cup superfine sugar **½ teaspoon salt**	Add the sugar and salt and stir together well.
	Add the ground white chocolate to the dry ingredients and mix together.
⅔ cup water **½ cup canola or safflower oil** **1 teaspoon lemon extract**	In the measuring cup, mix together the water, oil, and lemon extract.
Finely grated zest of 4 large lemons **4 extra-large egg yolks, at room temperature**	Make a well in the center of the dry ingredients by pushing them toward the sides of the bowl. Add the lemon zest, the egg yolks, and the liquid mixture. Use the flat beater attachment or a hand-held mixer to blend together until smooth.
4 extra-large egg whites, at room temperature **½ teaspoon cream of tartar**	Place the egg whites in the grease-free bowl of an electric stand mixer or a large grease-free bowl. Using the wire whip attachment or a hand-held mixer, whip together on medium-high speed until the egg whites are frothy. Add the cream of tartar and whip until the egg whites hold soft peaks.
½ cup superfine sugar	Gradually sprinkle on the sugar and continue to whip the egg whites on medium-high speed until they hold glossy and firm, but not stiff, peaks.
	Using a rubber spatula, fold the egg whites into the egg yolk mixture in 4 stages, until thoroughly combined.

Essential Gear

- Food processor
- Microplane grater or citrus zester
- Electric stand mixer with flat beater attachment and wire whip attachment, or large mixing bowl and hand-held mixer
- 2-cup liquid measuring cup
- Rubber spatula
- 10-inch round tube pan
- Cooling rack
- Thin-bladed knife

Keeping

Store the cake tightly covered with a double layer of plastic wrap at room temperature up to 4 days. To freeze up to 3 months, wrap the cake tightly in several layers of plastic wrap and aluminum foil. Use a large piece of masking tape and an indelible marker to label and date the contents. If frozen, defrost overnight in the refrigerator and bring to room temperature before serving.

Making a Change

Add 1 cup unsweetened lightly toasted coconut to the cake batter before turning it into the pan to bake.

Add 1 cup toasted and finely chopped pecans, walnuts, or almonds to the batter before turning it into the pan to bake.

Pour the cake batter into the tube pan and smooth the top with the spatula.

Bake for 55 to 60 minutes, until the cake is light golden and springs back when lightly touched, and a cake tester inserted near the center comes out clean.

Remove the pan from the oven and invert it over a cooling rack. Leave the cake to cool completely. Don't set the pan on a cooling rack on its base. This will cause the cake to collapse.

Don't shake the cake out of the pan before it is cool. Once it is cool, use a thin-bladed knife or flexible-blade spatula to run around the outer edges and around the tube to loosen the cake from the pan. Push the bottom of the pan up, away from the sides. Gently run the knife or spatula between the bottom of the cake and the bottom of the pan. Invert the cake onto a serving plate.

Serve the cake at room temperature.

Add 1 cup finely ground, toasted hazelnuts to the batter before turning it into the pan to bake.

Adding Style
Serve slices of the cooled cake with lightly sweetened whipped cream and fresh strawberries, raspberry sauce (see Meyer Lemon Soufflés, page 143), or Blueberry Compote (page 147).

White Chocolate and Lemon Tart

A CREAMY FILLING of white chocolate blended with lemon curd is enclosed in a crisp cookie crust and topped with fresh berries in this tart. The colors and textures blend together very well and greatly enhance each other. This is a perfect springtime dessert. **Makes one 9^1/$_2$-inch round tart, 12 to 14 servings**

Essential Gear
- Food processor
- Rolling pin
- 9^1/$_2$-inch round, fluted-edge tart pan with removable bottom
- Baking sheet
- Aluminum foil
- Pie weights
- Cooling rack
- Double boiler
- Whisk
- Rubber spatula
- Small saucepan
- Medium fine-mesh strainer
- Goose-feather pastry brush

Keeping
Store the tart, loosely covered with waxed paper and then tightly wrapped

PASTRY DOUGH

1^1/$_4$ **cups all-purpose flour**
^{1}/$_2$ **cup confectioners' sugar**
^{1}/$_8$ **teaspoon salt**

In the work bowl of a food processor fitted with the steel blade, combine the flour, sugar, and salt. Pulse briefly to blend.

4 **ounces (8 tablespoons, 1 stick) unsalted butter, chilled**

Cut the butter into small pieces and add to the flour mixture. Pulse until the butter is cut into very tiny pieces, about 30 seconds. The texture should be sandy with very tiny lumps throughout.

1 **extra-large egg yolk, at room temperature**
^{1}/$_2$ **teaspoon pure vanilla extract**

Use a fork to lightly beat the egg yolk with the vanilla in a small bowl. With the food processor running, pour this mixture through the feed tube. Process the dough until the mixture wraps itself around the blade, about 1 minute.

Turn the pastry dough onto a large piece of plastic wrap. Shape into a flat disk and wrap tightly in a double layer of plastic wrap. Chill in the refrigerator until firm before using, at least 2 hours. Chilling the dough relaxes the gluten in the flour so it won't be too elastic and will roll out easily. It also firms up the butter in the dough so it will need less flour when rolled out. If the dough is too firm, it will splinter and break when rolled out. Let it stand at room temperature for 10 to 15 minutes before rolling to become more pliable.

Center a rack in the oven and preheat it to 375°F.

On a smooth, flat surface, roll out the pastry dough between sheets of lightly floured waxed or parchment paper to a large circle about 11 inches in diameter. To tell if the dough will fit the tart pan, hold the pan above the dough. If there are about 2 inches of dough that protrude beyond the sides of the pan, it will fit.

Carefully peel the paper off the top of the dough. Brush off the excess flour, then loosely roll the pastry dough around the rolling pin without the bottom piece of paper.

The tart dough is delicate and needs to be handled gently. Rolling it around the rolling pin and unrolling into the tart pan is an easy way to get the dough into the pan.

Place the tart pan directly underneath the rolling pin and carefully unroll the pastry dough into the tart pan. Gently lift up the sides and ease the pastry dough into the bottom and sides of the tart pan. Trim off the excess pastry dough at the top of the pan. Transfer the tart pan to a baking sheet and chill in the freezer for 15 minutes. This helps prevent the dough from shrinking as it bakes.

Line the pastry shell with a large piece of aluminum foil that fits well against the bottom and sides. Fill with pie weights or a mixture of rice and beans. Bake for 10 minutes. If the bottom of the pastry shell puffs up, gently pierce it in several places with a fork to release the air. Remove the foil and weights and bake another 12 to 14 minutes, until light golden and set. Remove the pan from the oven and transfer to a rack to cool completely.

FILLING

1 recipe Lemon Curd (see Double Lemon Layer Cake, page 140), chilled

Place the lemon curd in a large bowl and whisk until it's smooth and creamy, about 1 minute.

Streamlining

The pastry dough can be made in advance and kept in the refrigerator, tightly wrapped in a double layer of plastic wrap, up to 4 days. To freeze up to 3 months, wrap the dough snugly in several layers of plastic wrap and place it in a freezer bag. Use a large piece of masking tape and an indelible marker to label and date the contents. If frozen, defrost overnight in the refrigerator before using.

with aluminum foil, in the refrigerator up to 3 days.

Troubleshooting

Don't roll out the pastry dough before it is chilled. The dough will be too soft and it will require a lot of flour to roll out, which results in a tough dough.

Once the pastry dough is unrolled into the tart pan, don't push it down forcefully. This will stretch the dough, which will shrink as it bakes, making it flat instead of taking the shape of the tart pan.

Making a Change

Instead of topping the tart with fresh berries, scatter shaved white chocolate over the filling.

Adding Style

Serve each slice of tart in a small pool of Raspberry

12 ounces white chocolate, finely chopped	Place the chopped chocolate in the top of a double boiler over low heat. Stir often with a rubber spatula to help melt evenly. Remove the top pan of the double boiler and wipe the bottom and sides very dry.	Sauce (see Meyer Lemon Soufflés, page 143).

Or place the chocolate in a microwave-safe bowl and melt on low power for 30-second bursts. Stir with a rubber spatula after each burst.

Pour the melted white chocolate into the lemon curd and whisk or stir the two together until smooth.

Transfer the filling to the tart shell and spread it out evenly, using a rubber spatula.

4 cups fresh strawberries, rinsed and patted dry on paper towels, or 2 cups fresh blueberries, black-berries, or raspberries	If using strawberries, place one whole strawberry in the center of the tart. Cut the remaining strawberries in half vertically and arrange them around the center berry to completely cover the tart filling.

If using other berries, arrange them in concentric circles to cover the tart filling.

⅓ cup apricot preserves **2 tablespoons amaretto or water**	Combine the apricot preserves and liquid in a small saucepan. Bring to a boil over medium heat. Remove the pan from the heat and strain the glaze into a small bowl, pushing through as much of the pulp as possible.

Use the goose-feather pastry brush to lightly glaze the tops of the berries. Don't apply a thick glaze, which looks unappetizing. The purpose of the glaze is to keep the fruit from drying out and to make it glisten.

Serve the tart at room temperature.

White Chocolate Biscotti

BISCOTTI are purposely made to be very crunchy because they are double baked, which dries them out. This makes them the perfect cookies for dunking in coffee, tea, or milk and helps them keep a long time, although they get eaten so quickly, how long they last is usually not an issue. Enjoy! **Makes 3 dozen cookies**

Adjust the oven racks to the upper and lower thirds and preheat the oven to 350°F. Line the baking sheets with parchment paper or non-stick liners.

Essential Gear
- Two baking sheets
- 2 parchment paper sheets or non-stick pan liners
- Electric stand mixer with flat beater attachment, or large mixing bowl and hand-held mixer
- Rubber spatula

3 cups all-purpose flour

1¾ cups granulated sugar

1 teaspoon baking powder

¼ teaspoon salt

Combine the flour, sugar, baking powder, and salt in the bowl of an electric stand mixer or a large bowl. Use the flat beater attachment or a hand-held mixer to blend together briefly on low speed.

3 extra-large eggs, at room temperature

3 extra-large egg yolks, at room temperature

2 teaspoons pure vanilla extract

Using a fork, lightly beat together the eggs, egg yolks, and vanilla in a medium bowl. With the mixer speed on low, add the egg mixture to the dry ingredients and blend together thoroughly.

1 cup unblanched whole almonds, roughly chopped

4 ounces white chocolate, cut into small chunks

Add the almonds and white chocolate to the dough and mix until the dough holds together, about 30 seconds.

Divide the dough into 4 equal pieces. Dust your hands lightly with flour and shape each piece of dough into a loaf about 8 inches long, 3 inches wide, and 1 inch high. Place 2 loaves on each baking sheet, leaving at least 2 inches of space between them.

Bake the biscotti for 12 minutes. Switch the baking sheets and bake another 10 to 12 minutes, until the loaves are light golden and set. Remove the baking pans from the oven and cool on racks for 10 minutes.

Using a serrated knife, slice each loaf on the diagonal into ½-inch-thick slices. Place these slices on their sides on the baking sheets, with the wide part facing up.

Bake the biscotti again for 5 minutes, switch the baking sheets, and bake another 5 to 7 minutes, until firm.

Remove the baking sheets from the oven and transfer the biscotti to racks to cool.

- Two cooling racks
- Serrated knife

Keeping

Store the biscotti in an airtight container between layers of waxed paper at room temperature up to 2 weeks. To freeze up to 3 months, wrap the container tightly in several layers of plastic wrap and aluminum foil. Use a large piece of masking tape and an indelible marker to label and date the contents. If frozen, defrost overnight in the refrigerator and bring to room temperature before serving.

Making a Change

Replace the almonds with toasted pecans, walnuts, or skinned hazelnuts.

Adding Style

Drizzle the cooled biscotti with thin lines of bittersweet, semisweet, milk, or white chocolate (see page 43). Let the chocolate set for 15 minutes in the refrigerator before serving or storing.

White Chocolate Cheesecake

THIS IS THE QUINTESSENTIAL cheesecake. It's dense and creamy, with a crunchy cookie crust that's a great contrast to the cake. Try serving it with raspberry sauce and fresh raspberries. One of the things I like most about cheesecake is that it has to be made in advance of serving because it needs hours to cool and

Essential Gear

- 9½-inch round springform pan
- Heavy-duty aluminum foil

chill. It also freezes beautifully, so it's easy to have on hand for when you receive an invitation to a party. **Makes one 9¹/₂-inch round cake, 12 to 14 servings**

Center a rack in the oven and preheat it to 300°F.

1 tablespoon unsalted butter, softened	Using a paper towel or your fingertips, butter the inside of the spring-form pan. Use a double layer of heavy-duty foil to wrap around the bottom of the pan. This prevents any water from the water bath from seeping into the pan.

COOKIE CRUST

7 ounces (about 18) butter biscuit cookies, wafers, or shortbread **2 tablespoons granulated sugar**	In the work bowl of a food processor fitted with the steel blade, combine the cookies and sugar and pulse until the cookies are finely ground, about 2 minutes. Or place the cookies and sugar in a sturdy plastic bag and seal it. Use a rolling pin to crush the cookies to a very fine crumb consistency.
3 ounces (6 tablespoons, ³/₄ stick) unsalted butter, melted and cooled	Transfer the crumbs to a medium bowl and add the butter. Use a rubber spatula to toss the mixture together and moisten all the crumbs.
	Transfer the crust to the prepared springform pan, Using your fingers, press the crumb mixture evenly into the bottom and partway up the sides of the pan. Chill the crust while preparing the cheesecake batter.

CHEESECAKE

1 pound white chocolate, finely chopped	Place the chopped chocolate in the top of a double boiler over low heat. Stir often with a rubber spatula to help it melt evenly. Remove the top pan of the double boiler and wipe the bottom and sides very dry.
	Or place the chopped chocolate in a microwave-safe bowl and melt on low power for 30-second bursts. Stir with a rubber spatula after each burst.
2 pounds cream cheese, softened	Place the cream cheese in the bowl of an electric stand mixer or in a large bowl. Use the flat beater attachment or hand-held mixer to beat the cream cheese on medium speed until it's fluffy, about 2 minutes.
¹/₃ cup firmly packed light brown sugar	Add the sugar to the cream cheese and mix thoroughly.

- Food processor or rolling pin
- Double boiler
- Rubber spatula
- Electric stand mixer with flat beater attachment, or hand-held mixer and large mixing bowl
- 12-inch round cake pan or large roasting pan
- Cooling rack
- Thin-bladed knife

Keeping
Store the cheesecake tightly covered with aluminum foil in the refrigerator up to 4 days. To freeze up to 2 months, wrap the cake tightly in several layers of plastic wrap and aluminum foil. Use a large piece of masking tape and an indelible marker to label and date the contents. If frozen, defrost overnight in the refrigerator and bring to room temperature before serving.

Making a Change
Add 1½ cups toasted and finely ground hazelnuts to the batter before turning it into the pan.

Replace the butter wafers in the crust with gingersnaps and add 1 teaspoon ground ginger. Add 1 cup finely diced crystallized ginger to the cheesecake batter before turning it into the pan.

4 extra-large eggs, at room temperature	One at a time, add the eggs to the cream cheese, beating well after each addition. The eggs will sit on top of the cream cheese, so stop frequently and scrape down the bottom and sides of the bowl with a rubber spatula to help mix evenly. The mixture may look curdled as the eggs are added, but as you stop and scrape down the bowl, the mixture will smooth out.
2 teaspoons pure vanilla extract	Add the vanilla to the cream cheese mixture and blend well.
	Add the melted chocolate to the mixture and blend thoroughly.
	Pour the batter into the crust in the springform pan. Use a rubber spatula to smooth and even the top.
1 quart boiling water	Place the springform pan in the larger pan and set the pan on the oven rack. Carefully pour the boiling water into the bottom pan until it reaches halfway up the side of the springform pan. Baking the cake in a water bath cushions it from the heat and adds extra moisture to the oven, which keeps the top from cracking.

Bake the cake for 1½ hours, until the top is light golden and jiggles only slightly when the cake is moved. Remove the pan from the oven, remove the foil, and cool the cheesecake on a rack to room temperature.

Cover the top of the cheesecake with waxed paper and wrap the pan tightly in aluminum foil. Refrigerate the cake for at least 6 hours before serving. To unmold the cheesecake, dip a thin-bladed knife in hot water and dry, then run it around the inner edge of the pan; release the clip on the rim of the pan and gently lift it off the cake.

White Chocolate Chunk and Walnut Muffins

THESE MUFFINS are chock full of white chocolate chunks and walnuts, which are a natural flavor pair. They are great with afternoon tea, as a snack, and in a loved one's lunch box.

Makes 12 muffins

Center a rack in the oven and preheat the oven to 400°F. Line each cavity of the muffin pan with a paper muffin cup.

Essential Gear

- 12-cavity 3-inch muffin pan
- 3-inch pleated paper muffin cups
- Electric stand mixer with flat beater attachment, or large mixing bowl and hand-held mixer
- Spoon
- Cooling rack

2 cups all-purpose flour

²/₃ cup firmly packed light
brown sugar

2 teaspoons baking powder

¼ teaspoon salt

Combine the flour, sugar, baking powder, and salt in the bowl of an electric stand mixer or a large bowl. Use the flat beater attachment or a hand-held mixer to mix together briefly on low speed.

1 cup whole milk

4 ounces (8 tablespoons,
1 stick) unsalted butter,
melted and cooled

1 extra-large egg, at room
temperature

2 teaspoons pure vanilla
extract

In a separate bowl, combine the milk, butter, egg, and vanilla. Stir together and add to the dry ingredients with the mixer speed on low. Mix together thoroughly.

10 ounces white chocolate,
cut into small chunks

1 cup walnuts, roughly
chopped

Add the white chocolate and walnuts to the batter and mix together completely.

Use a spoon to divide the batter evenly among the 12 muffin cups, filling them to the top.

Bake the muffins about 20 minutes, until they are light golden brown and a tester inserted in the center comes out clean. Remove the pan from the oven and cool on a rack. Serve warm or at room temperature.

To rewarm the muffins, place them in a 350°F oven for 8 to 10 minutes.

Keeping

Store the muffins in an airtight plastic container between layers of waxed paper at room temperature up to 3 days. To freeze up to 2 months, wrap the container tightly in several layers of plastic wrap and aluminum foil. Use a large piece of masking tape and an indelible marker to label and date the contents. If frozen, defrost overnight in the refrigerator and bring to room temperature before serving.

Making a Change

Replace the walnuts with lightly toasted macadamia nuts, almonds, pecans, or hazelnuts.

Adding Style

Drizzle the tops of the cooled muffins with thin lines of white, milk, or dark chocolate (see page 43). Let the chocolate set for 15 minutes in the refrigerator before serving or storing.

White Chocolate Chunk–Oatmeal Cookies

T HESE CHEWY COOKIES will become favorites around your house. They are filled with chunks of white chocolate, macadamia nuts, and raisins that make each bite a little bit of flavor heaven. **Makes 5 dozen cookies**

Adjust the oven racks to the upper and lower thirds and preheat the oven to 375°F. Line the baking sheets with parchment paper or non-stick liners.

Essential Gear

• Four baking sheets
• Four parchment paper
sheets or non-stick liners
• Electric stand mixer with
flat beater attachment, or
large mixing bowl and
hand-held mixer

1²/₃ cups all-purpose flour	Over a large piece of waxed or parchment paper or a bowl, combine the flour, oats, baking soda, baking powder, and salt. Stir or toss to blend together thoroughly.	• Rubber spatula
1¹/₂ cups rolled oats (not quick cooking)		• Spoon or small ice cream scoop
³/₄ teaspoon baking soda		• Two cooling racks
¹/₂ teaspoon baking powder		
¹/₄ teaspoon salt		

1²/₃ cups all-purpose flour
1¹/₂ cups rolled oats
  (not quick cooking)
³/₄ teaspoon baking soda
¹/₂ teaspoon baking powder
¹/₄ teaspoon salt

Over a large piece of waxed or parchment paper or a bowl, combine the flour, oats, baking soda, baking powder, and salt. Stir or toss to blend together thoroughly.

• Rubber spatula
• Spoon or small ice cream scoop
• Two cooling racks

Keeping

Store the cookies in an airtight plastic container between layers of waxed paper at room temperature up to 5 days. To freeze up to 3 months, wrap the container tightly in several layers of plastic wrap and aluminum foil. Use a large piece of masking tape and an indelible marker to label and date the contents. If frozen, defrost overnight in the refrigerator and bring to room temperature before serving.

---

8 ounces (16 tablespoons, 2 sticks) unsalted butter, softened

Place the butter in the bowl of an electric stand mixer or in a large bowl. Use the flat beater attachment or a hand-held mixer to beat the butter on medium speed until it's fluffy, about 2 minutes.

---

³/₄ cup firmly packed light brown sugar
¹/₃ cup granulated sugar

Add the brown sugar and granulated sugar to the butter and cream together completely. Stop occasionally and scrape down the sides and bottom of the bowl with a rubber spatula.

Making a Change

Replace the macadamia nuts with walnuts, hazelnuts, or pecans.

---

1 extra-large egg, at room temperature
2 teaspoons pure vanilla extract

Using a fork, lightly beat the egg and vanilla together in a small bowl. Add to the butter mixture and blend thoroughly. The egg will sit on top of the butter mixture, so be sure to scrape down the sides and bottom of the bowl to help mix evenly. The mixture may look curdled as the eggs are added, but as you stop and scrape down the bowl, the mixture will smooth out.

Replace the macadamia nuts with cocoa nibs.

Add the dry ingredients in 4 stages, blending completely after each addition. Stop occasionally and scrape down the sides and bottom of the bowl with a rubber spatula to ensure even mixing.

Replace the raisins with dried cherries, cranberries, apricots, peaches, pears, or dates.

---

10 ounces white chocolate, cut into small chunks
¹/₂ cup toasted macadamia nuts, coarsely chopped
1 cup large raisins

Add the white chocolate chunks, macadamia nuts, and raisins and stir to distribute evenly.

Use a large spoon or a small ice cream scoop to scoop out mounds about 2 inches in diameter. Place the mounds on the baking sheets, leaving 2 inches of space between them so they have room to expand as they bake.

Tightly cover two baking sheets with plastic wrap and chill while baking the other two. Bake the cookies for 5 minutes. Switch the baking sheets and bake another 5 to 6 minutes, until the cookies are set and light golden.

Remove the baking sheets from the oven and cool the cookies completely on the baking sheets on racks. Carefully remove the cookies from the parchment paper or nonstick liners Repeat with the remaining two baking sheets.

White Chocolate Chunk Scones
with Almonds and Dried Apricots

SCONES ARE CLASSIC English teatime treats that are served after the sandwiches and before the sweet course. These tender, delicate scones are loaded with goodies. White chocolate chunks and dried apricots provide sweetness and almonds add texture. These are perfect for afternoon tea, but you don't have to wait until then to treat yourself. I like to eat these for breakfast. **Makes twenty-four 3-inch scones**

Essential Gear
- Two baking sheets
- Two parchment paper sheets or non-stick liners
- Food processor
- 1- or 2-inch natural-bristle pastry brush
- Chef's knife
- Two cooling racks

Adjust the oven racks to the upper and lower thirds and preheat the oven to 400°F. Line the baking sheets with parchment paper or non-stick liners.

2½ cups all-purpose flour ¼ cup granulated sugar 1 tablespoon baking powder ¼ teaspoon salt	In the work bowl of a food processor fitted with the steel blade, combine the flour, sugar, baking powder, and salt and pulse a few times to mix.
3 ounces (6 tablespoons, ¾ stick) unsalted butter, chilled	Cut the butter into small pieces and add to the flour mixture. Pulse until the butter is cut into very tiny pieces, about 30 seconds. The texture should be sandy with very tiny lumps throughout.
5 ounces white chocolate, chopped into small chunks ½ cup roughly chopped dried apricots ½ cup toasted whole unblanched almonds, roughly chopped	Add the white chocolate, dried apricots, and almonds and pulse a few times to mix.
2 extra-large eggs, at room temperature ⅔ cup heavy whipping cream	Using a fork, lightly beat the eggs and cream together in a small bowl. With the food processor running, pour this mixture through the feed tube and process until the dough wraps itself around the blade, about 30 seconds.

Dust a large piece of waxed or parchment paper with flour and turn the dough out onto it. Divide the dough into 3 equal pieces and pat and shape each piece into a circle about 6 inches in diameter and ¾ inch high.

Using a sharp chef's knife dipped in flour, cut each circle into quarters, then cut each quarter in half, forming 8 triangular-shaped

Keeping
Store the scones in an airtight plastic container between layers of waxed paper at room temperature up to 4 days. To freeze up to 4 months, wrap the container tightly in several layers of plastic wrap and aluminum foil. Use a large piece of masking tape and an indelible marker to label and date the contents. If frozen, defrost overnight in the refrigerator and bring to room temperature before serving.

Streamlining
The unbaked scones can be frozen for up to 3 months, wrapped as above. It's not necessary to defrost the scones, but bake them 5 to 6 minutes longer.

Making a Change
Replace the apricots with dried cherries, cranberries, raisins, or dates.

scones. Separate the scones and place them on the baking sheets, leaving at least 1 inch of space between them so they have room to expand as they bake.

EGG WASH AND GARNISH

1 extra-large egg yolk
1 tablespoon heavy cream

Using a fork, lightly beat the egg yolk and cream together in a small bowl. Brush the top of each scone with egg wash, being careful that it doesn't run down the sides and under the scones. If it does, wipe it up because it can cause the bottom of the scones to burn.

2 tablespoons granulated
sugar

Lightly sprinkle the top of each scone with sugar.

Bake the scones for 7 minutes. Switch the baking sheets and bake another 6 to 7 minutes, until the scones are light golden.

Remove the baking sheets from the oven and cool completely on racks.

Replace the almonds with walnuts or macadamia nuts.

Adding Style
Use a 2-inch round plain-edge cutter to cut the scones into circles instead of cutting them into triangles. If there are scraps after cutting the scones, gather them together, knead slightly, then cut out more scones.

White Chocolate–Citrus Ganache Napoleons

WHITE CHOCOLATE GANACHE flavored with fresh lemons and oranges and topped with fresh berries is alternated with layers of sugar-encrusted filo dough squares. This takes a bit of time to prepare, but the "oohs" and "aahs" that come when you serve it are well worth the effort. Also, the component parts can be prepared in advance and assembled a few hours before serving. **Makes 6 servings**

WHITE CHOCOLATE CITRUS GANACHE

1½ pounds white chocolate,
finely chopped

Place the white chocolate in a large bowl.

¾ cup heavy whipping cream
Finely grated zest of 2 large
lemons and 1 large orange

Place the cream in a saucepan and bring to a boil over medium heat. Turn off the heat. Add the citrus zests, cover the pan, and let them steep for 10 minutes. Remove the cover and bring the cream to a boil again over medium heat. Strain the cream over the white chocolate and let it stand for 1 minute. Stir the mixture together using a heat-resistant spatula, whisk, or immersion blender until very smooth.

Tightly cover the ganache with plastic wrap and chill until thick, but not stiff, about 1 hour.

Essential Gear
- Large bowl
- Small saucepan
- Micorplane grater or citrus zester
- Heat-resistant spatula or whisk
- Four baking sheets
- Four parchment paper sheets or non-stick liners
- Kitchen towel
- Electric stand mixer with flat beater attachment, or large mixing bowl and hand-held mixer
- Serrated knife
- 1-inch natural bristle pastry brush
- Two cooling racks
- Medium fine-mesh strainer

FILO DOUGH SQUARES

Adjust the oven racks to the upper and lower thirds and preheat the oven to 350°F. Line the baking sheets with parchment paper or non-stick liners.

Twelve 9 × 14-inch sheets thawed frozen filo pastry dough (¼ pound)

Place the filo dough on a smooth, flat surface and cover with plastic wrap and a damp kitchen towel to keep it from drying out.

3 ounces (6 tablespoons, ¾ stick) unsalted butter, melted
¼ cup granulated sugar

Take 1 sheet of filo dough and lay it flat on the work surface. Lightly brush it all over with butter, then sprinkle with about ½ teaspoon sugar. Top with a second sheet of filo dough, brush with butter, and sprinkle with about ½ teaspoon sugar. Repeat with two more filo dough sheets.

Using a serrated knife, cut the stack of filo dough in half widthwise, then cut across the length to make six 4½-inch squares. Use a wide, flat spatula to transfer the filo squares to a baking sheet. Repeat twice more to form 12 more filo squares.

Keep two baking sheets of filo dough squares tightly covered with plastic wrap so they don't dry out, and bake the other two sheets for 5 minutes. Switch the baking sheets and bake another 3 minutes, until light golden. Remove the baking sheets from the oven and use a wide, flat spatula to transfer the filo squares to racks to cool completely. Remove the plastic wrap from the remaining two baking sheets of filo dough squares and bake as above.

ASSEMBLY

Take the white chocolate ganache from the refrigerator. If it is very firm, soften it in a microwave oven on low power for 5-second bursts. The consistency should be like thick pudding; you should be able to stick your finger into it easily but it will hold the indentation. Take care not to soften it so much that it becomes liquid. Or let the ganache stand at room temperature until it reaches the right consistency.

Place the ganache in the bowl of an electric stand mixer or a large bowl. Use the flat beater attachment or a hand-held mixer to beat the ganache on medium speed until it holds soft peaks, 1 to 2 minutes. Don't beat the ganache too much or it will become grainy and may separate.

4 cups fresh strawberries, washed, dried, and hulled

Thinly slice the strawberries vertically.

• Small offset spatula or flexible-blade spatula

Keeping
Store the napoleons on baking sheets, loosely covered with waxed paper and then wrapped with aluminum foil, in the refrigerator up to 2 days.

Streamlining
The filo dough squares can be baked in advance and kept tightly covered with aluminum foil at room temperature up to 3 days.

Place 6 of the filo squares onto a lined baking sheet. Using a small offset spatula or flexible-blade spatula, evenly spread each square with about 1 tablespoon of the whipped ganache. Arrange cut strawberries over the ganache and spread another tablespoon of ganache over the berries.

2 cups fresh blueberries, blackberries, or raspberries

Place another filo dough square over the filling so that the corners are not lined up with the bottom square but are off-center. Evenly spread each square with about 1 tablespoon of the whipped ganache. Top the ganache on the second square with blueberries, blackberries, or raspberries and spread with about 1 tablespoon of the ganache.

Place the top filo dough square over the filling with the corners off-center and spread about 1 tablespoon of filling on top of each square. Top each square with the remaining berries.

Serve the napoleons at room temperature.

White Chocolate Cupcakes with White Chocolate Frosting

THESE INDIVIDUAL LITTLE cakes are elegant enough for any celebration or gathering. A light, moist, white chocolate cake is baked into individual cupcakes and topped with a creamy white chocolate and cream cheese frosting. Cupcakes are fun to serve because everyone gets his own little cake and they are just the right serving size. **Makes 12 cupcakes**

Essential Gear

- 12-cavity 3-inch muffin pan
- 3-inch pleated paper muffin cups
- Small saucepan
- Electric stand mixer with flat beater attachment and wirw whip attachment, or large mixing bowl and hand-held mixer
- Heat-resistant spatula or whisk
- Rubber spatula
- Sifter
- Cooling rack
- Double boiler
- 6-inch flexible-blade spatula

Center a rack in the oven and preheat it to 350°F. Line each cavity of the muffin pan with a paper muffin cup.

2 ounces white chocolate, finely chopped

Place the chopped chocolate in a small bowl.

¼ cup heavy whipping cream

Place the cream in a small saucepan and bring to boil over medium heat. Pour the cream over the chocolate and let it stand for 1 minute. Stir the mixture together using a heat-resistant spatula, whisk, or immersion blender until very smooth.

2½ ounces (5 tablespoons) unsalted butter, softened

Place the butter in the bowl of an electric stand mixer or in a bowl. Use the flat beater attachment or a hand-held mixer to beat the butter on medium speed until it's fluffy, about 2 minutes.

Keeping

Store the cupcakes in a single layer in an airtight

½ cup superfine sugar ¼ cup firmly packed light brown sugar	Add the superfine sugar and brown sugar, and cream together well. Stop occasionally and scrape down the sides and bottom of the bowl with a rubber spatula.
1 extra-large egg yolk, at room temperature 1 teaspoon pure vanilla extract	Use a fork to lightly beat together the egg yolk and vanilla in a small bowl. Add to the butter mixture and blend together well. The egg mixture will sit on top of the butter mixture, so scrape down the sides and bottom of the bowl with a rubber spatula to help mix evenly. The mixture will look curdled as the eggs are added, but as you stop and scrape down the bowl, the mixture will smooth out.
1 cup all-purpose flour ¾ teaspoon baking soda ¼ teaspoon salt	Over a medium piece of waxed or parchment paper or a bowl, sift together the flour and baking soda. Add the salt and toss to mix.
¼ cup buttermilk	Add the dry ingredients to the butter mixture alternately with the buttermilk in 3 stages. Mix completely after each addition. Stop occasionally and scrape down the sides and bottom of the bowl with a rubber spatula.
	Add the melted white chocolate to the batter and blend together thoroughly.
2 extra-large egg whites, at room temperature ¼ teaspoon cream of tartar	Place the egg whites in the grease-free bowl of an electric stand mixer or in a grease-free medium bowl. Use the wire whip attachment or a hand-held mixer to whip the egg whites on medium speed until frothy. Add the cream of tartar and whip on medium-high speed until the egg whites hold glossy and firm, but not stiff, peaks
	Fold the whipped egg whites into the batter in 4 stages, blending thoroughly.
	Use a spoon to divide the batter evenly among the 12 muffin cups, filling them about ¾ full.
	Bake the cupcakes 20 to 25 minutes, until they are light golden brown and a tester inserted in the center comes out clean. Remove the pan from the oven and cool completely on a rack. Lift the cupcakes from the muffin pan.

WHITE CHOCOLATE–CREAM CHEESE FROSTING

8 ounces white chocolate, finely chopped	Place the chopped chocolate in the top of a double boiler over low heat. Stir often with a rubber spatula to help melt evenly. Remove the top pan of the double boiler and wipe the bottom and sides very dry.

container in the refrigerator up to 3 days. To freeze up to 2 months, wrap the container tightly in several layers of plastic wrap and aluminum foil. Use a large piece of masking tape and an indelible marker to label and date the contents. If frozen, defrost overnight in the refrigerator and bring to room temperature before serving.

Making a Change
Add 1 cup roughly chopped walnuts, almonds, pecans, hazelnuts, or lightly toasted macadamia nuts to the batter before baking.

Adding Style
Sprinkle the tops of the frosted cupcakes with shavings of dark chocolate.

Sprinkle the tops of the frosted cupcakes with the same type of finely chopped nuts used in the batter.

Sprinkle the tops of the frosted cupcakes with sweetened shaved or flaked coconut.

	Or place the chocolate in a microwave-safe bowl and melt on low power for 30-second bursts. Stir with a rubber spatula after each burst.
8 ounces cream cheese, softened	Place the cream cheese in the bowl of an electric stand mixer or in a large bowl. Use the flat beater attachment or hand-held mixer to beat the cream cheese on medium speed until it's fluffy, about 2 minutes.
1 teaspoon pure vanilla extract	Add the vanilla to the cream cheese and mix together thoroughly.
1½ cups confectioners' sugar, sifted	Add the sugar to the cream cheese in 3 stages. Stop occasionally and scrape down the sides and bottom of the bowl with a rubber spatula. Beat together until thoroughly blended.
	Add the melted white chocolate and blend together completely.
	Use a flexible-blade spatula to spread the top of each cupcake with an equal amount of the frosting in a small mound. Make swirls in the frosting with the spatula or the back of a spoon.
	Chill the cupcakes for about 1 hour loosely covered with waxed paper, then tented with aluminum foil. Serve at room temperature.

White Chocolate Layer Cake with White Chocolate Buttercream

THIS CAKE is rich and satisfying. It's an elegant cake, with four layers of white chocolate cake alternated with white chocolate buttercream filling. There are several steps involved in making this cake, but many can be done in advance, making it easy to assemble when you're ready. It's a good idea to assemble the cake a few hours before you plan to serve it so the cake and buttercream flavors have time to blend together. **Makes one 9-inch round cake, 12 to 14 servings**

Essential Gear
- Two 9 × 2-inch round cake pans
- Scissors
- Parchment paper
- Double boiler
- Two rubber spatulas
- Sifter
- Electric stand mixer with flat beater attachment and wire whip attachment, or large mixing bowl and hand-held mixer
- Small saucepan
- Two cooling racks

CAKE

Center a rack in the oven and preheat it to 350°F.

1 tablespoon unsalted butter, softened	With your fingertips or a paper towel, butter the inside of the cake pans, coating them thoroughly.

1 tablespoon all-purpose flour	Dust the inside of each pan with some of the flour. Shake and tilt the pans to evenly distribute the flour, then turn the pans over and shake out the excess into the sink.
	Cut a round of parchment paper to fit the bottom of each pan. Butter each parchment paper round and place in each pan, butter-side up.
8 ounces white chocolate, finely chopped	Place the chopped chocolate in the top of a double boiler over low heat. Stir often with a rubber spatula to help melt evenly.
	Or melt the chocolate in a microwave-safe bowl on low power for 30-second bursts. Stir with a rubber spatula after each burst.
2¼ cups all-purpose flour 2½ teaspoons baking powder ¼ teaspoon salt	Over a large piece of waxed or parchment paper or a bowl, sift together the flour and baking powder. Add the salt and toss to mix.
6 ounces (12 tablespoons, 1½ sticks) unsalted butter, softened	Place the butter in the bowl of an electric stand mixer or in a large bowl. Use the flat beater attachment or a hand-held mixer to beat the butter on medium speed until it's light and fluffy, about 2 minutes.
1½ cups granulated sugar	Add the sugar, and cream together well on medium speed. Stop occasionally and scrape down the sides and bottom of the bowl with a rubber spatula.
4 extra-large eggs, at room temperature	Add the eggs one at a time to the butter mixture, blending well after each addition. Stop often to scrape down the sides and bottom of the bowl with a rubber spatula. The eggs will sit on top of the mixture, so it's important to scrape down the sides of the bowl to help mix evenly. The mixture may look curdled as the eggs are added, but as you stop and scrape down the bowl, the mixture will smooth out.
1 teaspoon pure vanilla extract	Add the vanilla and blend in thoroughly.
1¼ cups milk	Add the dry ingredients in 3 stages, alternating with the milk. Mix thoroughly after each addition and stop often to scrape down the sides and bottom of the mixing bowl with a rubber spatula.
	Remove the top pan of the double boiler and wipe the bottom and sides of the pan very dry. Stir the melted white chocolate to cool it slightly, add to the batter, and combine thoroughly.
1 cup toasted and finely chopped pecans	Add the pecans to the batter and stir to distribute evenly.

- 2-quart heavy-bottomed saucepan
- 1- or 2-inch natural-bristle pastry brush
- Sugar or candy thermometer
- Rubber spatula
- Serrated knife
- 10-inch flexible-blade icing spatula

Keeping
Store the cake loosely covered with aluminum foil in the refrigerator up to 4 days. Place several toothpicks in the top outer edges of the cake to hold the foil away from it so it won't mar the buttercream. To freeze up to 3 months, place the cake in a cake box and wrap with several layers of plastic wrap and aluminum foil. Or place the cake on a lined baking sheet in the freezer and let it freeze (about 3 hours). Loosely wrap the cake in layers of plastic wrap and aluminum foil. If frozen, defrost overnight in the refrigerator. Bring the cake to room temperature at least 30 minutes before serving.

Streamlining
Bake the cake layers up to 2 days before assembling the cake and keep tightly covered with a double layer of plastic wrap at room temperature. To freeze the layers up to 3 months, wrap them snugly in several layers of

Divide the batter between the two cake pans. Smooth the top of each pan with a rubber spatula.

Bake the layers for 40 minutes, until a cake tester inserted in the center comes out with no crumbs clinging to it.

Remove the cake pans from the oven and cool completely on racks. Invert the pans to remove the layers, then peel the parchment paper off the back of each layer. Re-invert the layers onto plates or cardboard cake circles.

SUGAR SYRUP

¼ cup granulated sugar
½ cup water

Combine the sugar and water in the small saucepan. Bring to a boil over medium-high heat, without stirring, to dissolve the sugar. Remove from the heat and cool to room temperature.

WHITE CHOCOLATE BUTTERCREAM

5 ounces white chocolate, finely chopped

Place the chopped chocolate in the top of a double boiler over low heat. Stir often with a rubber spatula to help melt evenly.

Or melt the chocolate in a microwave-safe bowl on low power for 30-second bursts. Stir with a rubber spatula after each burst.

2 extra-large eggs, at room temperature
2 extra-large egg yolks, at room temperature
¼ cup granulated sugar

Place the eggs, egg yolks, and sugar in the bowl of an electric stand mixer or in a large bowl. Use the wire whip attachment or a hand-held mixer to whip the egg mixture on medium speed until it is very pale colored and holds a slowly dissolving ribbon as the beater is lifted, about 5 minutes.

1¼ cups granulated sugar
½ cup water
¼ teaspoon cream of tartar

While the eggs are whipping, place the sugar, water, and cream of tartar in the heavy-bottomed saucepan. Bring the mixture to a boil, without stirring. Place a wet pastry brush at the point where the sugar syrup meets the sides of the pan and sweep it around completely. Do this two times. Brushing down the sides of the pan while sugar is cooking prevents sugar crystals from coming out of the mixture, which causes crystallization. This is a condition that creates a crust around the side of the pan. Once crystallization occurs, the sugar syrup won't come up to temperature correctly and needs to be thrown away. Don't brush around the pan more than a few times. If you do, you're adding extra water to the sugar syrup, which takes more time to cook off and reach the desired temperature. Cook the mixture over high heat until it registers 242°F on a sugar thermometer. Immediately remove the thermometer and place it in a glass of warm water, then remove the pan from the heat so it won't continue to cook.

plastic wrap and place them in freezer bags. Use a large piece of masking tape and an indelible marker to label and date the contents. If frozen, defrost the layers overnight in the refrigerator.

The buttercream can be prepared up to 3 days in advance and kept in an airtight plastic container in the refrigerator or up to 4 months in the freezer. If frozen, defrost overnight in the refrigerator. To reheat the buttercream, break it up into chunks and place in a mixing bowl. Place the bowl in a saucepan of warm water and let the buttercream begin to melt around the bottom. Wipe the bottom of the bowl dry and beat the buttercream with an electric mixer until it is fluffy and smooth.

Recovering from a Mishap
If one of the cake layers breaks during assembly, patch it together with some of the buttercream.

Making a Change
Replace the pecans with toasted finely chopped walnuts, hazelnuts, or almonds.

Replace the apricot preserves with mango or passion fruit preserves or orange marmalade.

Adjust the mixer speed to low and pour the sugar syrup into the whipped eggs in a slow, steady stream. Aim the sugar syrup between the beater and the side of the bowl, so it doesn't get caught up in the beater or thrown against the sides of the bowl. Adjust the mixer speed to medium-high and whip until the bowl is cool, about 8 minutes. Once the cooked sugar syrup is added to the whipped eggs, the mixture must whip until the bowl is completely cool to the touch before the butter is added, or the butter will melt. If this happens the texture and consistency of the buttercream will be too soft, and more butter needs to be added to bring it to the right point.

1 pound (2 cups, 4 sticks) unsalted butter, softened

Adjust the mixer speed to medium and add the butter, 2 tablespoons at a time. Continue to beat until the buttercream is thoroughly mixed and fluffy.

Add the melted white chocolate to the buttercream and mix in thoroughly.

ASSEMBLY

⅓ cup apricot preserves

With your fingertips, gently peel the skin off the top of each cake layer. Using a serrated knife, cut each cake layer in half horizontally (see page 34). Place the bottom of one cake layer on a serving plate. Use a pastry brush to brush the layer with sugar syrup. Use the flexible-blade spatula to spread the layer evenly with the apricot preserves. Place waxed paper strips around the bottom edge of the layer to protect the plate while you assemble the cake.

Reserve ⅓ of the buttercream to frost the top and sides of the cake. With a clean flexible-blade spatula, evenly spread about ⅓ of the remaining buttercream over the cake layer.

Position the second cake layer evenly over the buttercream. Brush the layer with the sugar syrup, then spread another ⅓ of the remaining buttercream over the layer. Repeat with the remaining two cake layers, sugar syrup, and more buttercream. Then spread the reserved ⅓ of the buttercream over the sides and top of the cake.

1 cup pecans, toasted and finely chopped

Press the chopped pecans onto the sides of the cake and scatter about 1 tablespoon of the pecans over the top.

Let the cake chill for at least 2 hours before serving so it has time to set and will be easier to cut. Serve the cake at room temperature.

White Chocolate Madeleines

MADELEINES are classic shell-shaped little cakes that take their form from the pan in which they are baked. These are a scrumptious white chocolate variation of the original madeleines. They are moist and delicate and I think perfect for afternoon tea or coffee. **Makes 2 dozen cakes**

1 tablespoon unsalted butter, melted and slightly cooled

Adjust the oven racks to the upper and lower thirds and preheat the oven to 350°F. Using the pastry brush or a paper towel, coat the inside of each cavity of both madeleine pans with melted butter.

2 ounces white chocolate, finely chopped
3 ounces (6 tablespoons, ¾ stick) unsalted butter, cut into small pieces

Place the white chocolate and butter together in the top of a double boiler over low heat. Stir often with a rubber spatula to help melt evenly. Remove the top pan of the double boiler and wipe the bottom and sides very dry. Stir the chocolate mixture with a rubber spatula occasionally to prevent a skin from forming on top.

Or place the chocolate and butter in a microwave-safe bowl and melt on low power for 30-second bursts. Stir with a rubber spatula after each burst.

2 extra-large eggs, at room temperature

Place the eggs in the bowl of an electric stand mixer or in a large bowl. Using the wire whip attachment or a hand-held mixer, whip the eggs on medium speed until they are frothy, about 1 minute.

⅓ cup superfine sugar

Add the sugar and whip together on medium-high speed until the mixture is very thick and pale colored and holds a slowly dissolving ribbon as the beater is lifted, about 5 minutes.

½ cup all-purpose flour
¼ teaspoon salt

Over a medium piece of waxed or parchment paper or a bowl, sift the flour. Add the salt and toss to mix.

With the mixer speed on low, add the flour mixture to the egg mixture in 3 stages, blending well after each addition. Stop and scrape down the sides and bottom of the bowl with a rubber spatula a few times while mixing.

Pour the white chocolate mixture into the batter and blend in thoroughly.

Transfer the batter to the liquid measuring cup. Pour the batter slowly into each cavity of the madeleine molds, filling them ¾ full. Place each madeleine pan on a baking sheet.

Essential Gear
- 1-inch natural-bristle pastry brush or paper towel
- Two 12-cavity, 3-inch madeleine pans
- Double boiler
- Electric stand mixer with wire whip attachment, or large mixing bowl and hand-held mixer
- Rubber spatula
- Sifter
- 2-cup liquid measuring cup
- Two baking sheets
- Two cooling racks

Keeping
Store the madeleines in an airtight container between layers of waxed paper at room temperature up to 3 days. To freeze up to 3 months, wrap the container tightly in several layers of plastic wrap and aluminum foil. Use a large piece of masking tape and an indelible marker to label and date the contents. If frozen, defrost overnight in the refrigerator and bring to room temperature before serving.

Making a Change
Add ½ cup toasted and finely chopped pecans, walnuts, or hazelnuts to the batter before turning into the pans to bake.

Adding Style
Drizzle the cooled madeleines with thin lines of bittersweet, semisweet,

Bake the madeleines for 6 minutes. Switch the baking sheets and bake for another 6 to 8 minutes, until the tops spring back lightly when touched.

Remove the pans from the oven. Holding the madeleine pans upside down over cooling racks, gently shake them to release the madeleines. Cool completely on the racks.

milk, or white chocolate (see page 43) or dip the madeleines in tempered bittersweet or semisweet chocolate (see page 43). Let the chocolate set in the refrigerator for 15 minutes before serving or storing.

White Chocolate Shortbread Triangles

FINELY GROUND white chocolate adds both texture and flavor, and light brown sugar boosts the flavor in this version of shortbread. It's a delectable variation on a classic. These are cut into triangles or wedges, as they are often called, which are one of the classic shortbread shapes. **Makes 16 triangles**

Essential Gear
- 9-inch round pie pan
- Food processor
- Electric stand mixer with flat beater attachment, or large mixing bowl and hand-held mixer
- Rubber spatula
- Small sharp knife
- Fork
- Cooling rack

Keeping
Store the shortbread in an airtight container between layers of waxed paper at room temperature up to 1 week. To freeze up to 2 months, wrap the container tightly in several layers of plastic wrap and aluminum foil. Use a large piece of masking tape and an indelible marker to label and date the contents. If frozen, defrost overnight in the refrigerator and bring to room temperature before serving.

Making a Change
Add 1/2 cup toasted and finely chopped pecans, walnuts, or hazelnuts to the dough before turning into the pans to bake.

1 tablespoon unsalted butter, softened	Use your fingertips or a paper towel to generously butter the inside of the pie pan.
5 ounces white chocolate, broken into small pieces **1 cup all-purpose flour** **1/4 teaspoon salt**	In the work bowl of a food processor fitted with the steel blade, combine the chocolate, flour, and salt. Pulse until the chocolate is very finely ground, about 2 minutes.
4 ounces (8 tablespoons, 1 stick) unsalted butter, softened	Place the butter in the bowl of an electric stand mixer or in a large bowl. Use the flat beater attachment or a hand-held mixer to beat the butter on medium speed until it's fluffy, about 2 minutes.
1/4 cup firmly packed light brown sugar	Add the sugar, and cream together. Stop occasionally and scrape down the sides and bottom of the bowl with a rubber spatula.
	With the mixer speed on low, add the flour and chocolate mixture to the butter mixture in 3 stages, mixing completely after each addition. Stop and scrape down the sides and bottom of the bowl with a rubber spatula.
	Transfer the mixture to the pie pan and use your fingertips to pat and press the dough evenly into the pan. Dust your fingertips with flour if the dough sticks to them.
	Use a small sharp knife to score the dough into quarters, then score each quarter into 4 equal pieces (they naturally form triangles

when cut this way). Use a fork to pierce each piece on the diagonal 2 times.

Cover the pan tightly with plastic wrap and chill for at least 1 hour.

Center a rack in the oven and preheat it to 350°F.

Bake the shortbread for 30 to 35 minutes, until light golden brown.

Remove the pan from the oven and cool on a rack for 5 minutes. Use a sharp knife to cut through the scored lines. Cool the shortbread completely. Use a small offset spatula to remove the shortbread triangles from the pie pan.

Adding Style

Drizzle the cooled shortbread triangles with thin lines of bittersweet, semisweet, milk, or white chocolate (see page 43) or dip them on the diagonal in tempered bittersweet or semisweet cocolate (see page 43). Let the chocolate set for 15 minutes in the refrigerator before serving or storing.

White Chocolate Tube Cake with Toasted Pecans

TOASTED PECANS and white chocolate balance each other very well in this yummy cake baked in a tube-shaped pan. Raspberry sauce is an excellent accompaniment. **Makes one 10-inch round cake, 14 to 16 servings**

Essential Gear

- 10-inch round tube pan
- Cake pan
- Chef's knife
- Sifter
- Food processor
- Electric stand mixer with flat beater attachment, or large mixing bowl and hand-held mixer
- Rubber spatula
- Cooling rack
- Flexible-blade spatula

1 tablespoon unsalted butter, softened	Center a rack in the oven and preheat it to 325°F. Use your fingertips or a paper towel to generously butter the inside of the cake pan.
1 tablespoon all-purpose flour	Dust the inside of the pan with the flour. Shake and tilt the pan to cover the inside completely, then turn the pan over and shake out the excess over the sink.
1 cup pecans	Place the pecans in a shallow cake or pie pan and toast in the oven until light golden, about 12 minutes. Every 4 minutes, shake the pan so the pecans toast evenly. Remove from the oven and cool completely, then chop finely with a chef's knife on a cutting board.
3 cups all-purpose flour **1 teaspoon baking powder** **¼ teaspoon salt**	Over a large piece of waxed or parchment paper or a bowl, sift together the flour and baking powder. Add the salt and toss to mix.
5 ounces white chocolate, cut into small pieces	In the work bowl of a food processor fitted with the steel blade, combine the chocolate and 1 cup of the flour mixture. Pulse until the chocolate is very finely ground, about 2 minutes. Add to the remaining dry ingredients and mix together.

Keeping

Store the cake tightly covered with a double layer of plastic wrap at room temperature up to 4 days. To freeze up to 3 months, wrap the cake tightly in several layers of plastic wrap and aluminum foil. Use a large piece of masking tape and an indelible marker to label

8 ounces (16 tablespoons, 2 sticks) unsalted butter, softened	Place the butter in the bowl of an electric stand mixer or in a large bowl. Use the flat beater attachment or hand-held mixer to beat the butter on medium speed until it's fluffy, about 2 minutes.
1¼ cups granulated sugar **1 cup firmly packed light brown sugar**	Add the granulated sugar and brown sugar to the butter, and cream together. Stop occasionally and scrape down the sides and bottom of the bowl with a rubber spatula.
4 extra-large eggs, at room temperature	Adjust the mixer speed to medium-low. One at a time, add the eggs to the butter mixture, mixing well after each addition. The eggs will sit on top of the butter mixture, so stop after adding each one and scrape down the sides and bottom of the bowl with a rubber spatula to help mix evenly. The mixture may look curdled as the eggs are added, but as you scrape down the bowl, the mixture will smooth out.
	Turn the mixer speed to low and add the dry ingredients in 3 stages, mixing completely after each addition. Stop occasionally and scrape down the sides and bottom of the bowl with a rubber spatula. Add the pecans and blend thoroughly.
	Pour the cake batter into the prepared pan. Use a rubber spatula to smooth the top. Bake for 1½ hours, until the cake is light golden and a cake tester inserted 2 inches from the outer edge comes out clean.
	Remove the pan from the oven and turn it upside down over a cooling rack. Leave the cake to cool completely. Use a flexible-blade spatula or thin-bladed knife to run around the outer and inner edges to loosen the cake from the pan. Invert the pan over a serving plate and gently pull the pan away from the cake. To release the bottom of the tube pan, run the spatula under the cake. Push the bottom up and the sides should fall away from the cake.
	Serve the cake at room temperature.

and date the contents. If frozen, defrost overnight in the refrigerator and bring to room temperature before serving.

Making a Change

Replace the pecans with walnuts or finely ground, toasted hazelnuts.

Replace the pecans with finely chopped dried fruit such as cherries, figs, pineapple, dates, papaya, or mango.

Adding Style

Serve slices of the cooled cake with Raspberry Sauce (see Meyer Lemon Soufflés page 143) and fresh raspberries or Blueberry Compote (page 147).

COCOA

COCOA IS OFTEN thought of as what you sprinkle on top of something else. And it is great to dust a little cocoa on top of a cup of cappuccino or to decorate the top of a cake. It provides a great flavor accent, but so much more can be done with cocoa. When it is used as a main ingredient to bake with, it offers an absolutely delectable flavor. Most bakers of chocolate desserts commonly use dark, milk, and white chocolate, but I encourage you to explore everything that cocoa has to offer. I am positive these recipes will become part of your chocolate baking repertoire.

Cocoa is available year-round in supermarkets, gourmet food shops, and natural and health food stores, and through catalog and on-line sources.

WHAT IS COCOA?

Cocoa is a product of the cacao bean. It is produced during the process of making chocolate. After the cacao beans are roasted, winnowed, and ground to a thick paste known as chocolate liquor (see About Chocolate, page 370), the mass is put through a hydraulic press that extracts the liquid, which is cocoa butter. The result is a dry cake called press cake or cocoa cake, which is then pulverized through a machine to produce a very fine powder.

Cocoa retains between 10 and 25 percent fat from cocoa butter. Low-fat cocoa contains between 10 and 18 percent fat, while high-fat cocoa contains between 20 and 25 percent fat. Low-fat cocoa powder is used to make cocoa drinks that often have a large amount of added sugar and other flavorings. Most cocoa used for baking is considered to be high-fat cocoa. Also, unsweetened cocoa is the only type used for baking.

There are two types of cocoa: natural, also called regular, and Dutch-processed, also called Dutched or European-style. The difference between these two is that an alkali is added to make Dutch-processed cocoa. Coenraad Van Houten, a Dutch chemist, discovered this process in the early nineteenth century, when he developed a screw press that extracted cocoa butter from chocolate. He found that when he added an alkali to the cocoa after removing the cocoa butter, it softened the flavor of the cocoa by eliminating some of the natural fruit flavors and it deepened the color. The addition of an alkali injects the cocoa with its own distinctive flavor. However, one of the reasons for adding an alkali to Dutch-processed cocoa is that natural cocoa has a deep bitterness, primarily due to the use of inferior-quality cocoa beans to make it. Scharffen Berger Chocolate Maker, a relatively young American company, is a pioneer in producing high-quality natural cocoa because they use the same quality cacao beans to produce cocoa as they do to produce their high-quality chocolates. Their cocoa retains the natural fruitiness of the cocoa beans without the inherent bitterness associated with it.

Keep in mind that the alkali added to produce Dutch-processed cocoa acts to balance out some of the acidity of natural cocoa and tends to make Dutched cocoa more neutral on the flavor scale. There is a difference between that and the harshness associated with astringency and tartness. Astringency is the dry sensation that you can feel on the sides of the mouth, while tartness is experienced more on the tongue. It's the balance of sweet and tart that gives natural cocoa powder its unique flavor.

TIPS AND TECHNIQUES

Because natural cocoa has an acidic quality that tends to give it a strong bitter edge, it is often recommended for baking, especially in American-style desserts such as brownies and cakes, rather than for decorations. There is a long-standing tradition of baking with Dutch-processed cocoa in Europe, and in the U.S., it is often the choice for decorating baked goods and desserts because it has a softer, less acidic flavor.

Generally, containers of cocoa are labeled Dutch-processed.. They may also state that it is cocoa processed with an alkali. If there is no identification, the cocoa is most likely natural.

I have found one brand of cocoa made by Seattle Chocolates that is a blend of both types, and it is stated so on the label. There is also one brand of cocoa, Pernigotti, that has a slight amount of vanilla blended in with it. This is one of my personal favorite cocoas. Most supermarkets carry several brands of cocoa, including Ghirardelli and Hershey's. Droste is an excellent Dutch-processed cocoa.

It is important to keep in mind that because natural cocoa is on the acidic side, baking soda is the leavener of choice with it because baking soda is alkaline and acts as a neutralizer for the acid. When using Dutch-processed cocoa, baking powder is the best leavener to use, although you can use small amounts of baking soda. Using too much baking soda with Dutch-processed cocoa is where the problem comes in because it produces a soapy taste, and who wants their baked goods to taste like soap? Combining acid ingredients such as yogurt and buttermilk with Dutch-processed cocoa also produces a sweeter flavor and gives many baked goods their delicious underlying flavors.

The recipes in this chapter call for a specific type of cocoa and the leavening that works best with that type. It's not a good idea to substitute one type of cocoa for another randomly. If you do want to change the type of cocoa called for in a recipe, then you also need to change the leavening to suit whichever type of cocoa is used. Keep in mind that baking soda is about four times stronger in its leavening ability than baking powder. If you change the type of leavening, you will need to make adjustments in the quantity.

Leaveners for cocoa powder
- Natural cocoa
  - Quality: acidic
  - Leavener: baking soda
- Dutch-processed cocoa
  - Quality: alkaline
  - Leavener: baking powder

Cocoa is a product of the cacao bean.

It's not a good idea to substitute one type of cocoa for another randomly.

- Other ingredients used to balance alkalinity of Dutch-processed cocoa:
  - Yogurt
  - Buttermilk
  - Sour cream
  - Chocolate
  - Honey

It may sound unusual, but cocoa powder can produce a deeper chocolate flavor than chocolate. That's because cocoa powder has a more highly concentrated amount of cocoa particles than chocolate. The way to produce the most intense chocolate flavor is to mix cocoa powder with boiling water before mixing it with the other ingredients. When cocoa is used dry in baking, the best way to use it is to sift it with the flour and other dry ingredients called for in the recipe.

Cocoa can be stored for an unlimited period of time in a covered container in a cool, dark, dry place.

TASTING COCOA

To judge the differences between natural and Dutch-processed cocoas for yourself, I recommend that you set up a cocoa tasting using a few different brands of cocoa. Then you will know for sure which cocoa(s) you prefer. It's also a good idea to try different brands of cocoa when baking the same cake or dessert to see and taste the differences.

It's unusual to eat cocoa by itself, but it is a good way to taste the differences in types and brands. Sprinkle about a teaspoon of different types and brands of cocoa onto a plate or a piece of parchment or waxed paper. These are the characteristics to look for in choosing cocoa.

Color

The color should be consistent. Be aware of the differences in color with different types and brands of cocoa powder. Words used to describe the color of cocoa powder are even, light, medium, dark, tan, red, and brown.

Texture

The texture of cocoa powder might be rather obvious. It should be a fine powder similar to the texture of flour, without lumps or graininess.

Aroma

Place a little of the cocoa powder on a spoon and bring it close to your nose. Lightly breathe in the aroma (not the powder). Words used to describe the aroma of cocoa powder are strong, mild, floral, faintly fruity, vanilla, and of course, chocolate.

Flavor

Place a little of the cocoa powder on the tip of your tongue and allow it to dissolve and be processed by your sense of taste. Words used to describe the flavor of cocoa powder include intense, mild, tart, acidic, fruity, vanilla, and chocolaty.

The following table describes the tasting characteristics for ten brands of cocoa that are readily available.

COCOA TASTING TABLE

Brand and Type	Bensdorp (D)	Cluziel (D)	Cocoa Barry Extra Brute (D)	Droste (D)	Hershey's (N)	Pernigotti (D)	Scharffen Berger (N)	Schokinag (D)	Valrhona (D)	Van Houten (D)
Color	Dark brown Warm	Reddish brown Warm	Red-brown Mink Warm Dark	Taupey grey Looks like natural, not Dutch-processed	Very light tan	Dark brown	Light tan	Dark brown Earthy	Dark red brown	Light reddish tan Ochre
Aroma	Earthy Loamy soil	Floral Strong Coffee	Not much	Bland Not much	None	Vanilla	Fruity Chocolaty	Not much	Floral Orchid	Not much
Texture/ Mouthfeel	Soft Velvety	Soft Velvety Smooth	Soft Almost gritty	Almost chalky	Dry Tart Astringent Pucker	Soft	Soft Smooth	Smooth	Smooth Rich Velvety	Gritty
Flavor	Mild chocolate Slight soapy aftertaste (alkali)	Fruity Not bitter	Not much Soapy Dusty	Chocolaty	Bitter Dry Tart	Vanilla Rich Chocolaty	Balanced More acidic but not dramatic difference Slightly bitter	Very roasted Nutty	Flowery Soapy (alkali) at the end	Bland Soapy aftertaste

N = Natural • D = Dutch-processed

Cocoa Angel Food Cake

THIS IS A CLASSIC angel food cake with a definitive chocolate flavor that comes from the cocoa powder. It's light and airy and very satisfying. If you have frozen egg whites, making this cake is a perfect opportunity to use them, but be sure to defrost them and bring them to room temperature. Fresh fruit, fruit sauce, caramel sauce, or ice cream is a great accompaniment for this cake. **Makes one 10-inch round cake, serves 12 to 14**

Center a rack in the oven and preheat it to 325°F.

¾ cup cake flour
¼ cup unsweetened cocoa powder (natural or Dutch-processed)
⅛ teaspoon salt
1½ cups superfine sugar, divided

Over a large piece of waxed paper or parchment paper or a bowl, sift together the flour, cocoa powder, and salt. Add ¾ cup of the sugar and stir together well.

12 extra-large egg whites, at room temperature

Place the egg whites in the grease-free bowl of an electric stand mixer or in a large grease-free bowl. Use the wire whip attachment or a hand-held mixer and whip the egg whites on medium speed until they are frothy.

1 teaspoon cream of tartar

Add the cream of tartar. Adjust the mixer speed to medium-high and slowly sprinkle on the remaining ¾ cup sugar, a few tablespoons at a time, until the egg whites hold glossy and firm, but not stiff, peaks, about 5 minutes.

1 tablespoon pure vanilla extract

Add the vanilla and blend in well.

Using a rubber spatula, fold the dry ingredients into the egg whites in 3 to 4 stages.

Transfer the mixture to the tube pan. Use the rubber spatula to smooth and even the top, then tap the pan gently on the countertop a few times. This releases air bubbles so there won't be any holes in the cake when it's baked. This cake is baked in an ungreased pan because greasing the pan would keep the batter from rising and gripping the sides of the pan as the cake bakes.

Bake for 40 minutes, until a cake tester inserted in the center of the cake comes out clean.

Essential Gear
- Sifter
- Electric stand mixer with wire whip attachment, or large mixing bowl and hand-held mixer
- Rubber spatula
- 10 × 4-inch tube pan with removable bottom
- Cooling rack

Keeping
Store the cake tightly wrapped in plastic up to 3 days at room temperature. To freeze up to 4 months, tightly wrap the cake in several layers of plastic wrap and aluminum foil. Use a large piece of masking tape and an indelible marker to label and date the contents. If frozen, defrost overnight in the refrigerator and bring to room temperature before serving.

Making a Change
Add 2 teaspoons five-spice powder or cinnamon to the dry ingredients.

Add 1½ cups coarsely chopped nuts; sweetened, shredded coconut; or finely chopped dried apricots, raisins, or figs to the dry ingredients.

Adding Style
Serve slices of the cooled cake with mixed fresh berries, Raspberry Sauce

Remove the cake from the oven and invert it over a cooling rack onto its feet or over a funnel or a thin-necked bottle. Don't set the pan on a cooling rack on its base. This will cause the cake to collapse onto itself. Let the cake hang to cool completely.

Don't shake the cake out of the pan before it is cool. It should slide out of the pan on its own, because it shrinks as it cools. If the cake doesn't come out of the pan on its own, use a thin-bladed knife to run around the outer edge of the center tube to help release the cake from the pan.

Serve the cake at room temperature.

(see Chocolate Lover's Pound Cake, below), caramel sauce (see Rum-Raisin Pound Cake, page 614), or ice cream.

Chocolate Lover's Pound Cake

COCOA POWDER, bittersweet chocolate, and bittersweet chocolate chips are all used to create deep chocolate flavor in this cake. The technique of combining the cocoa powder with boiling water brings out the most intense chocolate flavor. To enhance the chocolate experience, serve each slice of cake with a spoonful of raspberry sauce. This is a great cake to serve to your chocolate-loving guests. I like it with tea or coffee in the afternoon. **Makes one 8½ × 4½ × 2½-inch loaf cake, 12 servings**

Center a rack in the oven and preheat it to 325°F.

2 teaspoons unsalted butter, melted	Use a pastry brush or a paper towel to coat the inside of the loaf pan with the butter.
2 teaspoons all-purpose flour	Sprinkle the inside of the pan with the flour. Shake and tilt the pan to coat it with the flour, then turn it upside down over the sink and shake out the excess.
½ cup unsweetened Dutch-processed cocoa powder, sifted 5 tablespoons boiling water	Place the cocoa powder in small bowl. Add the boiling water. Use a heatproof spatula or a spoon to stir together until it forms a smooth cocoa paste.
2 teaspoons pure vanilla extract	Add the vanilla and stir together well.
8 ounces (16 tablespoons, 2 sticks) unsalted butter, softened	Place the butter in the bowl of an electric stand mixer or a large bowl. Use the flat beater attachment or a hand-held mixer to beat the butter on medium speed until fluffy, about 2 minutes.

Essential Gear

- 1-inch natural-bristle pastry brush or a paper towel
- 8½ × 4½ × 2½-inch loaf pan
- Sifter
- 2 heatproof rubber spatulas
- Electric stand mixer with flat beater attachment and wire whip attachment, or hand-held mixer and large mixing bowl
- Rubber spatula
- Cooling rack
- Food processor
- Medium mixing bowl
- Fine-mesh strainer
- Double boiler or 1-quart bowl (glass or ceramic)

Keeping

Store the cake tightly wrapped in aluminum foil at room temperature up to 4 days. To freeze up to 4 months, wrap the cake tightly in several layers of plastic wrap and aluminum

1 ²/₃ cups superfine sugar	Reduce the mixer speed to low and add the sugar gradually to the butter. Turn the mixer to medium speed and beat the mixture until creamy, about 1 minute. Stop and scrape down the bottom and sides of the bowl with the rubber spatula. This helps the mixture to blend evenly.
4 extra-large eggs, at room temperature	One at a time, add the eggs to the butter mixture, beating well after each addition. Stop frequently and scrape down the bottom and sides of the bowl with the rubber spatula. At first the mixture may look curdled as the eggs are added, but as you stop and scrape down the bowl, the mixture will smooth out.
	Add the cocoa paste to the butter mixture and mix together to a smooth texture.
1 ²/₃ cups cake flour **1 teaspoon baking powder** **¼ teaspoon salt**	Over a large piece of waxed or parchment paper or a bowl, sift together the cake flour and baking powder. Add the salt and toss to mix.
	Add the dry ingredients to the butter mixture in 3 stages, beating well after each addition. Stop frequently and scrape down the bottom and sides of the bowl with the rubber spatula.
4 ounces bittersweet chocolate, finely chopped	Melt the chocolate in the top of a double boiler over low heat or in a microwave-safe bowl on low power for 30-second bursts. Stir with a heatproof rubber spatula after each burst to ensure even melting.
	Remove the top pan of the double boiler and wipe the bottom and sides very dry. Stir the chocolate for 1 minute to cool and prevent a skin from forming on top.
	Add the melted chocolate to the batter and blend together well.
1 cup (6 ounces) bittersweet chocolate chips	Add the chocolate chips to the batter and stir to distribute evenly.
	Transfer the batter to the prepared pan. Use the rubber spatula to smooth and even the top.
	Bake the cake for 1 hour and 10 minutes, until a cake tester inserted in the center comes out with no crumbs clinging to it.
	Remove the pan from the oven and cool on a rack for 20 minutes. Invert the pan and turn the cake out. Re-invert the cake, so the top is facing up. Leave the cake to cool completely on the rack.

foil. Use a large piece of making tape and an indelible marker to label and date the contents. If frozen, defrost overnight in the refrigerator, and bring to room temperature before serving.

Making a Change
Replace the bittersweet chocolate chips with white chocolate chips or roughly chopped bittersweet chocolate.

Replace the chocolate chips with 1½ cups roughly chopped nuts or dried apricots.

Adding Style
Serve slices of the cooled cake with Caramel Sauce (see Rum-Raisin Pound Cake, page 614), or ice cream.

2 cups fresh or fresh-frozen raspberries, defrosted	Place the raspberries in the work bowl of a food processor fitted with the steel blade or in a blender. Pulse until the berries are pureed into liquid, about 1 minute.
	Strain the raspberry puree into a medium bowl. Push through the strainer as much of the liquid as possible, without the seeds.
3 tablespoons superfine sugar **2 tablespoons framboise, Chambord, kirsch, or Grand-Marnier** **2 teaspoons freshly squeezed lemon juice**	Add the sugar, liquor, and lemon juice to the raspberry puree and blend together thoroughly.
	Slice the cake and place each slice on a plate, and drizzle with a large spoonful of the raspberry sauce. Or pass the sauce separately.

Chocolate Macaroons

THESE ARE NOT the typical American-style macaroons, but elegant French-style macaroons like those found in the best French pastry shops. Two cocoa cookies that are round and smooth enclose a velvety dark chocolate ganache filling. The cookies are small, usually no more than two or three bites each, and are perfect to serve for afternoon tea or anytime you're in the mood for something elegant and very satisfying. **Makes about 3 dozen sandwich cookies**

COOKIES

Adjust the oven racks to the upper and lower thirds and preheat the oven to 350°F. Line the jelly-roll pans with aluminum foil with the shiny side up.

4 extra-large egg whites, at room temperature	Place the egg whites in the grease-free bowl of an electric stand mixer or in a large grease-free bowl. Using the wire whip attachment or a hand-held mixer, beat the egg whites on medium speed until they are frothy. This takes about 1 minute.

Essential Gear

- Two jelly-roll pans
- Aluminum foil
- Electric stand mixer with wire whip attachment and flat beater attachment, or large mixing bowl and hand-held mixer
- Two rubber spatulas
- Sifter
- Two 12- or 14-inch pastry bags with two 1/2-inch plain round pastry tips
- Two cooling racks
- Whisk, heat-resistant spatula, or immersion blender

Keeping

Store the cookies in a single layer, between sheets of waxed paper and tightly

¼ teaspoon cream of tartar	Add the cream of tartar to stabilize the egg white foam and continue to whip on medium speed.
1½ cups confectioners' sugar, sifted	Slowly add the sugar and continue to whip the egg whites until they hold firm, but not stiff, peaks.
1⅓ cups finely ground almonds ¼ cup unsweetened cocoa powder (natural or Dutch-processed), sifted ⅛ teaspoon salt	In a medium mixing bowl, combine the almonds, cocoa powder, and salt. Use a rubber spatula or large spoon and toss to mix together well.
	Fold this mixture into the whipped egg whites in 3 stages. Blend well after each addition. Be sure each batch is mixed in before adding the next or it becomes too difficult to get a smooth mixture.
1 teaspoon pure vanilla extract	Add the vanilla and mix together well.
	Fit a pastry bag with a plain round tip. Fill the pastry bag partway with the macaroon mixture. Holding the pastry bag vertically, 1 inch above the jelly-roll pan, pipe out mounds 1 inch in diameter. Leave at least 2 inches between mounds because they will spread as they bake. As you pipe out the macaroons, concentrate on keeping the size uniform and small. They spread slightly as they bake, which makes them bigger. Also, it looks more attractive to have macaroons of the same size when they are assembled.
	Bake the macaroons for 8 minutes. Switch the jelly-roll pans and bake another 7 minutes, until set. Remove the jelly-roll pans from the oven and immediately lift up a corner of the aluminum foil on each pan.
½ cup water	Pour ¼ cup of water under the foil on each pan. This creates steam, which makes it easy to remove the macaroons from the foil. Be careful to pour the water under the foil and not on top. Place each pan on a cooling rack and let the macaroons cool completely. Carefully remove the macaroons from the foil.

DARK CHOCOLATE GANACHE FILLING

4 ounces bittersweet chocolate, very finely chopped	Place the finely chopped chocolate in a medium bowl.
½ cup heavy whipping cream	In a small saucepan over medium heat, bring the cream to a boil. Immediately pour the cream over the chocolate. Let it stand for

covered with plastic wrap in the refrigerator up to 2 days. The texture will soften slightly, but this doesn't affect their flavor.

Streamlining
The macaroons can be baked up to 2 days in advance of assembling them. Cool them completely, then store them between layers of waxed paper on a jelly-roll pan or cookie sheet tightly covered with aluminum foil in a cool, dry place.

The ganache filling can be made up to 3 weeks in advance. Store it in an air-tight plastic container tightly covered with plastic wrap or a freezer bag in the refrigerator, away from any strong-flavored foods. Bring the ganache to room temperature before using. It should be pliable enough to hold the indentation of your finger, but not so soft that it runs.

Making a Change
Fill the macaroons with whipped vanilla, caramel, or gianduia ice cream.

Fill the macaroons with whipped milk chocolate ganache. To make the ganache, use 5 ounces milk chocolate and ⅓ cup heavy whipping cream. Follow the directions in the recipe for the Dark Chocolate Ganache Filling.

1 minute, then blend together with a heat-resistant spatula, whisk, or an immersion blender until very smooth.

Cover the bowl tightly with plastic wrap to prevent a skin from forming on top and let the mixture cool to room temperature. Chill in the refrigerator until thick, but not firm, about 1 hour.

Place the ganache filling in the bowl of an electric stand mixer or in a medium bowl. Use the flat beater attachment or a hand-held mixer and beat the ganache until it holds soft peaks, about 1 minute.

Fit a clean pastry bag with a clean round tip. Fill the pastry bag partway with the whipped ganache. Pipe a small mound of ganache on the flat side of 1 macaroon and top it with the flat side of a similar-sized macaroon. Gently press the cookies together to spread the ganache filling out to the edges

Serve the cookies immediately or chill in the refrigerator, covered tightly with plastic wrap, until 30 minutes before serving.

Adding Style

Dust the top of the assembled macaroons lightly with a mixture of 2 teaspoons confectioners' sugar and 2 teaspoons unsweetened cocoa powder sifted together.

Cocoa Biscotti

Biscotti is the Italian word for "little dry cookies" and it also means "twice baked." The double baking is what gives these cookies their characteristic crunchiness, which makes them perfect for dipping into a cup of coffee or hot chocolate. These keep for up to two weeks, but that's usually not a big consideration because they are so popular and disappear rapidly. **Makes about 2½ dozen cookies**

Center a rack in the oven and preheat it to 350°F. Line a baking sheet with parchment paper or a non-stick liner.

1½ cups all purpose flour
½ cup unsweetened natural cocoa powder
2 teaspoons baking soda
⅛ teaspoon salt

Over a large piece of waxed or parchment paper or a bowl, sift together the flour, cocoa, and baking soda. Add the salt and toss to mix. Transfer the mixture to the bowl of an electric stand mixer or a large bowl.

½ cup granulated sugar
⅓ cup firmly packed light brown sugar

Add the granulated sugar and brown sugar and stir to blend together well.

Essential Gear

- Baking sheet
- Parchment paper sheet or non-stick liner
- Sifter
- Electric stand mixer with flat beater attachment, or large mixing bowl and hand-held mixer
- Cooling rack
- Serrated knife

Keeping

Store the biscotti in an air-tight container between sheets of waxed paper at room temperature up to 2 weeks. A kitchen cupboard or pantry is the ideal storage place. To freeze up to 3 months, wrap the container

3 extra-large eggs, at room temperature

2 teaspoons pure vanilla extract

Using a fork, whisk the eggs with the vanilla extract in a small bowl. Add the egg and vanilla mixture to the dry ingredients. Mix on low speed until thoroughly combined. Stop occasionally and scrape down the sides and bottom of the bowl with a rubber spatula.

2 ounces bittersweet chocolate, cut into small pieces

1½ cups sliced almonds

Add the chocolate and almonds to the dough mixture and blend thoroughly on low speed. The dough should be smooth and pliable at this point.

Divide the dough into 2 equal pieces. Dust your hands with flour to keep the dough from sticking and shape each piece into a log about 10 inches long, 2 inches wide, and ¾ inch high. Place the logs on the baking sheet, leaving at least 2 inches space between them.

Bake until set, about 20 minutes. Remove the baking sheet from the oven and let the dough logs rest for 10 minutes on a rack

Using a serrated knife, cut the logs on the diagonal into ¾-inch-thick slices. Place the slices back on the baking sheet on their sides so the wide part of each slice faces up.

Bake the biscotti again until firm, 15 to 20 minutes.

Transfer the biscotti to racks to cool.

tightly in several layers of plastic wrap and aluminum foil. Use a large piece of masking tape and an indelible marker to label and date the contents. If frozen, defrost overnight in the refrigerator and bring to room temperature before serving.

Making a Change

Replace the almonds with walnuts or pistachios, or replace half of the almonds with dried cherries or cranberries.

Replace the natural cocoa powder with Dutch-processed cocoa powder and substitute ½ teaspoon baking powder for the baking soda.

Adding Style

Drizzle the biscotti with thin lines of bittersweet, semisweet, milk, or white chocolate after they are completely cool (see page 43). Let the chocolate set for 15 minutes in the refrigerator before serving or storing.

Cocoa Chiffon Cake

C HIFFON CAKE is an American classic that is a cross between a butter cake and an angel food cake. Oil replaces the butter used in a butter cake to give this cake its characteristic soft texture and extra moistness. Although this looks like an angel food cake, it's a bit richer and less sweet. Chiffon cake was developed in the 1920s and became very well known in the 1940s when its creator sold the recipe to General Mills. The technique of mixing cocoa powder with boiling water brings out the most concentrated chocolate flavor. **Makes one 10-inch round cake, serves 12 to 14**

Essential Gear
- Sifter
- Electric stand mixer with wire whip attachment, or large mixing bowl and hand-held mixer
- 10 × 4-inch tube pan with removable bottom
- Rubber spatula
- Cooling rack
- Thin-bladed knife

Center a rack in the oven and preheat it to 325°F.

¼ **cup unsweetened Dutch-processed cocoa powder** ¾ **cup boiling water** 1½ **teaspoons pure vanilla extract**	Place the cocoa powder in a small bowl and pour the boiling water over it. Stir together until the mixture forms a smooth cocoa paste. Let the mixture cool, stirring often to prevent a skin from forming on top, then blend in the vanilla.
1¾ **cups cake flour** 1 **tablespoon baking powder** 1¼ **cups granulated sugar** ¼ **teaspoon salt**	Over a large piece of waxed or parchment paper or a bowl, sift together the flour and baking powder. Add the sugar and salt and toss to mix.
½ **cup unflavored vegetable oil, such as canola or safflower** 6 **extra-large eggs yolks, at room temperature**	Make a well in the center of the mixture by pushing the dry ingredients toward the sides of the bowl. Add the oil, egg yolks, and the cocoa paste to the well. Using a rubber spatula, stir together until thoroughly combined.
6 **extra-large egg whites, at room temperature** ½ **teaspoon cream of tartar** ½ **cup granulated sugar**	Place the egg whites in the grease-free bowl of an electric stand mixer or a large grease-free bowl. Using the wire whip attachment or a hand-held mixer, whip the egg whites on medium speed until they are frothy. Add the cream of tartar. Slowly sprinkle on the sugar and continue whipping until the egg whites hold glossy and firm, but not stiff, peaks, about 5 minutes.

Fold the egg whites into the chocolate mixture in 3 to 4 stages, blending well after each addition.

Transfer the mixture to the tube pan. Use the rubber spatula to smooth and even the top. This cake is baked in an ungreased pan because greasing the pan would keep the batter from rising and gripping the sides of the pan as the cake bakes.

Bake for 1 hour, until a cake tester inserted in the center of the cake comes out clean.

Remove the pan from the oven and invert it over a cooling rack onto its feet or over a funnel or a thin-necked bottle. Let the cake hang to cool completely. Don't set the pan on a cooling rack on its base. This will cause the cake to collapse onto itself.

Don't shake the cake out of the pan before it is cool. Once it is cool, use a thin-bladed knife or flexible-blade spatula to run around the outer edge and the inside tube to help release the cake from the pan. Push the bottom of the pan up, away from the sides. Gently run the

- Sugar dredger or fine-mesh strainer

Keeping

Store the cake tightly wrapped in plastic up to 3 days at room temperature. To freeze up to 4 months, tightly wrap the cake in several layers of plastic wrap and aluminum foil. Use a large piece of masking tape and an indelible marker to label and date the contents. If frozen, defrost overnight in the refrigerator and bring to room temperature before serving.

Making a Change

Add 2 teaspoons five-spice powder or ground cinnamon to the dry ingredients.

Add 1½ cups coarsely chopped nuts; sweetened, shredded coconut; or finely chopped dried apricots, peaches, raisins, or figs to the dry ingredients.

Adding Style

Serve slices of the cooled cake with mixed berries, Raspberry Sauce (see Chocolate Lover's Pound Cake, page 467), Caramel Sauce (see Rum-Raisin Pound Cake, page 614), or ice cream.

knife or spatula between the bottom of the cake and the bottom of the pan. Invert the cake onto a serving plate.

GARNISH

2 tablespoons confectioners' sugar

2 tablespoons cocoa powder (natural or Dutch-processed)

Combine the sugar and cocoa powder in a small bowl and toss to combine. Using a sugar dredger or a fine-mesh strainer, dust the top of the cake with this mixture. Serve the cake at room temperature.

Diamond-Studded Cocoa Spice Coins

T HESE COOKIES look like they are studded with diamonds because of the crystal sugar on their surface, which also adds extra texture that is a sweet surprise. These are quintessential refrigerator cookies because the dough needs to be made ahead so it has plenty of time to set before cutting and baking. Keep the dough cylinders in the freezer, tightly wrapped in several layers of plastic wrap and inside a freezer bag. Having the dough cylinders on hand in the freezer makes it easy to slice and bake the cookies when the mood strikes. These have deep chocolate flavor that is enhanced by the spices blended into the cookie dough. **Makes about 3 dozen cookies**

Essential Gear
- Food processor
- Chef's knife
- Rubber spatula
- Waxed paper
- Two baking sheets
- Two parchment paper sheets or non-stick liners
- 1-inch natural-bristle pastry brush or a spoon
- Two cooling racks

2¼ cups all-purpose flour

1 cup granulated sugar

⅓ cup unsweetened Dutch-processed cocoa powder

1¼ teaspoons ground cinnamon

¾ teaspoon ground ginger

½ teaspoon freshly grated nutmeg

½ teaspoon baking powder

⅛ teaspoon salt

In the work bowl of a food processor fitted with the steel blade, combine the flour, sugar, cocoa powder, cinnamon, ginger, nutmeg, baking powder, and salt. Pulse briefly to blend the ingredients together, about 30 seconds.

Keeping

Store the cookies in an airtight plastic container between layers of waxed paper at room temperature up to 1 week. A kitchen cupboard or the pantry is the ideal storage place. To freeze up to 3 months, wrap the airtight container in several layers of plastic wrap and aluminum foil. Use a large piece of masking tape and an indelible marker to label and date the contents. If frozen, defrost overnight in the refrigerator and bring to room temperature before serving.

8 ounces (16 tablespoons, 2 sticks) unsalted butter, chilled

Cut the butter into small pieces and add to the flour mixture. Pulse until the butter is cut into very tiny pieces, about 1 minute. The mixture should feel sandy with tiny lumps throughout.

1 extra-large egg, at room temperature

2 teaspoons pure vanilla extract

Using a fork, lightly beat the egg and vanilla together in a small bowl. With the food processor running, pour the egg mixture through the feed tube. Pulse until blended, about 30 seconds.

4 ounces bittersweet chocolate, finely chopped	Add the chocolate and pulse to blend thoroughly, 30 seconds to 1 minute. The mixture will be smooth with very tiny chocolate pieces embedded within and will feel like soft pie or tart dough.
	Place two large sheets of waxed paper on a flat surface and divide the dough evenly onto them. Use the waxed paper to shape and roll the dough into cylinders about 8 inches long and 2 inches wide (see Refrigerator Cookies, page 37). Cover the cylinders tightly with the waxed paper, then wrap each roll in plastic wrap. Chill in the freezer for 45 minutes or in the refrigerator for at least 4 hours, until firm enough to slice.
	Adjust the oven racks to the upper and lower thirds and preheat the oven to 350°F. Line the baking sheets with parchment paper or non-stick liners.
1 extra-large egg yolk **¼ cup crystal sugar**	Using a fork, lightly beat the egg yolk in a small bowl. Divide the crystal sugar evenly between two sheets of waxed or parchment paper. Unwrap each dough cylinder. Using a pastry brush or a spoon, coat the outside of each dough cylinder with egg yolk, then roll in the crystal sugar, coating each completely.
	Place a dough cylinder on a cutting board. Using a sharp knife, cut each cylinder into ½-inch-thick slices. Cut straight down and roll the cylinder a quarter turn after every 6 slices so it will keep its round shape. If the dough becomes soft while you work with it, rewrap it, and chill for another 10 to 15 minutes, then continue slicing.
	Place the slices on the baking sheets, leaving at least 1 inch of space between them. Bake for 5 minutes. Switch the baking sheets and bake another 5 to 6 minutes, until set. Remove the baking sheets from the oven and cool the cookies completely on the baking sheets on racks

Streamlining

The dough cylinders can be made and kept in the refrigerator up to 3 days before baking. They can also be kept in the freezer up to 3 months. To refrigerate, wrap the cylinders tightly in several layers of plastic wrap. To freeze, wrap the same way and place each cylinder in a freezer bag. You can take them directly from the freezer and slice for baking, or defrost the cylinders overnight in the refrigerator.

Making a Change

To add a different flavor to the cinnamon blend, add ¼ teaspoon finely ground cloves. Replace the blend of spices with 2 teaspoons of a single spice, such as cinnamon, ginger, nutmeg, cardamom, five-spice powder, or allspice.

To replace the Dutch-processed cocoa powder with natural cocoa powder, use the same amount and substitute ¼ teaspoon baking soda for the ½ teaspoon baking powder.

Devil's Food Cake

T HIS IS A CLASSIC American cake of rich, deep, dark chocolate layers alternated with mocha buttercream. This cake takes a bit of work, but is more than worth it. The name comes from the dark brown color that occurs when the baking soda neutralizes the acid of the natural cocoa powder and because it is completely opposite from the pure whiteness of angel food cake. The

Essential Gear
- Two 9 × 2-inch round cake pans
- Scissors
- Parchment paper
- Medium fine-mesh strainer

technique of combining cocoa powder and boiling water brings out the deepest chocolate flavor. **Makes one 9-inch round cake, 12 to 14 servings**

CAKE

Center a rack in the oven and preheat it to 350°F.

1 tablespoon unsalted butter, softened	Using a paper towel or your fingertips, butter the inside of the cake pans.
1 tablespoon all-purpose flour	Dust the inside of each pan with some of the flour, then turn the pans over and shake out the excess.
	Cut a round of parchment paper to fit the bottom of each pan and place on the bottom. Butter each parchment paper round and place in each pan, butter-side up.
2 cups cake flour **1 teaspoon baking soda** **1/8 teaspoon salt**	Over a large piece of waxed or parchment paper or a bowl, sift together the flour and baking soda. Add the salt and toss to blend well.
1/2 cup unsweetened natural cocoa powder **1/2 cup boiling water**	Place the cocoa powder in a medium bowl and pour the boiling water over it. Use a heatproof spatula or a large spoon to blend together until it forms a smooth cocoa paste.
4 ounces (8 tablespoons, 1 stick) unsalted butter, softened	Place the butter in the bowl of an electric stand mixer or in a large bowl. Use the flat beater attachment or a hand-held mixer to beat the butter on medium speed until it's light and fluffy, about 2 minutes.
1 2/3 cups firmly packed light brown sugar **1/2 cup granulated sugar**	Add the brown sugar and granulated sugar, and cream together well on medium speed. Stop occasionally and scrape down the sides and bottom of the bowl with a rubber spatula.
2 extra-large eggs, at room temperature	Use a fork to lightly beat the eggs together in a small bowl, then add to the butter mixture. Blend well, stopping to scrape down the sides and bottom of the mixing bowl. At first the mixture may look curdled, but as you scrape down the bowl, it will smooth out.
1 cup buttermilk	Alternately add the dry ingredients and buttermilk in 4 or 5 stages, mixing well after each addition. Also scrape down the sides and bottom of the mixing bowl with a rubber spatula to encourage even mixing.
	Divide the batter evenly between the two cake pans. Smooth the top of each pan with a rubber spatula.

- Sifter or large fine-mesh strainer
- Heat-resistant spatula or wooden spoon
- 2 rubber spatulas
- Electric stand mixer with flat beater attachment and wire whip attachment, or large mixing bowl and hand-held mixer
- Two cooling racks
- 2-quart heavy-bottomed saucepan
- 1-inch natural-bristle pastry brush
- Sugar or candy thermometer
- Microwave-safe bowl
- Pie pan
- Chef's knife
- Serrated knife
- 10-inch flexible-blade icing spatula
- 10- or 12-inch pastry bag and large open star tip

Keeping
Store the cake loosely covered with aluminum foil in the refrigerator up to 4 days. Place several toothpicks in the top outer edges of the cake to hold the foil away from it so it won't mar the buttercream. To freeze up to 3 months, place the cake in a cake box and wrap with several layers of plastic wrap and aluminum foil. Or place the cake on a lined baking sheet in the freezer and let it freeze (about 3 hours). Loosely wrap the cake in layers of plastic wrap and aluminum foil. If frozen, defrost overnight in the

Bake the layers for 30 to 35 minutes, until a cake tester inserted in the center comes out with no crumbs clinging to it.

Remove the cake pans from the oven and cool completely on racks. Invert the pans to remove the layers, then peel the parchment paper off the back of each layer. Re-invert the layers onto plates or cardboard cake circles. Leave the oven on.

MOCHA BUTTERCREAM

2 extra-large eggs, at room temperature
2 extra-large egg yolks, at room temperature
¼ cup granulated sugar

Place the eggs, egg yolks, and sugar in the bowl of an electric stand mixer or in a large bowl. Use the wire whip attachment or a hand-held mixer to whip the eggs on medium speed until they are thick, very pale colored, and hold a slowly dissolving ribbon as the beater is lifted, about 5 minutes.

1¼ cups granulated sugar
½ cup water
¼ teaspoon cream of tartar

While the eggs are whipping, place the sugar, water, and cream of tartar in the heavy-bottomed saucepan. Bring the mixture to a boil over medium-high heat, without stirring. Place a wet pastry brush at the point where the sugar syrup meets the sides of the pan and sweep it around completely. Do this two times. This prevents the sugar from crystallizing by brushing any stray crystals back into the mixture. Brushing down the sides of the pan while sugar is cooking prevents sugar crystals from coming out of the mixture, which causes crystallization. This is a condition that creates a crust around the side of the pan. Once crystallization occurs, the sugar syrup won't come up to temperature correctly and needs to be thrown away. Don't brush around the pan more than a few times. If you do, you're adding extra water to the sugar syrup, which takes more time to cook off and reach the desired temperature. Cook over high heat until the mixture registers 242°F on a sugar thermometer (soft-ball stage).

Immediately remove the thermometer and place it in a glass of warm water, then remove the pan from the heat so it won't continue to cook.

Adjust the mixer speed to low and pour the sugar syrup into the whipped eggs in a slow, steady stream. Aim for the space between the side of the bowl and the wire whip or beaters, so the mixture doesn't wind up on the sides of the bowl. Adjust the mixer speed to medium-high and whip until the bowl is cool to the touch, about 8 minutes. Once the cooked sugar syrup is added to the whipped eggs, the mixture must whip until the bowl is completely cool to the touch before the butter is added, or the butter will melt. If this happens, the texture and consistency of the buttercream will be too soft and more butter needs to be added to bring it to the right point.

refrigerator. Bring the cake to room temperature at least 30 minutes before serving.

Streamlining
Bake the layers up to 2 days before assembling the cake. After the layers are completely cool, cover them tightly with plastic wrap and hold at room temperature. The layers can be frozen up to 3 months. To freeze, wrap them snugly in several layers of plastic wrap and place them in freezer bags. Use a large piece of masking tape and an indelible marker to label and date the contents. If frozen, defrost the layers overnight in the refrigerator.

The buttercream can be prepared up to 3 days in advance and kept in an airtight plastic container in the refrigerator or up to 4 months in the freezer. Label and date the buttercream. If frozen, defrost overnight in the refrigerator. To reheat the buttercream, break it up into chunks and place in a mixing bowl. Place the bowl in a saucepan of warm water and let the buttercream begin to melt around the bottom. Wipe the bottom of the bowl dry and beat the buttercream with an electric mixer until it is fluffy and smooth.

Making a Change
Replace the almonds with finely ground, toasted hazelnuts or walnuts.

1 pound (2 cups, 4 sticks) unsalted butter, softened	Adjust the mixer speed to medium and add the butter, 2 tablespoons at a time. Continue to beat until the buttercream is thoroughly blended and fluffy.
6 ounces bittersweet chocolate, very finely chopped	Place the chocolate in a microwave-safe bowl and melt on low power for 30-second bursts. Stir with a rubber spatula after each burst. When the chocolate is completely melted, add it to the buttercream. Blend well.
2 teaspoons instant espresso powder **1 tablespoon water**	In a small bowl, stir together the espresso powder and water until the mixture is thoroughly blended and forms a thick paste. Add to the buttercream and stir together thoroughly.

ASSEMBLY

1 cup sliced almonds Place the almonds in a pie or cake pan and toast in the oven until light golden, about 5 minutes.

Remove the pan from the oven and cool on a rack.

Use a chef's knife to finely chop the almonds.

Using your fingertips, peel the skin off the top of each cake layer. Using a serrated knife, cut each cake layer in half horizontally (see page 34). Place the bottom of one cake layer on a serving plate. Place several wide strips of waxed paper under the cake layer to protect the plate while assembling the cake. Set aside ⅓ cup of the buttercream for final decoration. Use the flexible-blade spatula to evenly spread some of the remaining buttercream over the cake layer to the edges (see page 35).

Position the second cake layer evenly over the buttercream. Spread buttercream over the layer to the edges. Repeat with the remaining two cake layers and more buttercream. Then spread the remaining buttercream over the sides and top of the cake.

Press the chopped toasted almonds onto the sides of the cake just up to, but not over, the top edge (see page 35).

Fit the pastry bag with the star tip and fill partway with the reserved buttercream. Pipe a row of shells around the top outer edge of the cake (see page 44).

Let the cake chill for at least 2 hours before serving so it has time to set and will be easier to cut. To cut the cake into serving pieces, dip a knife in hot water and dry after each slice. Serve the cake at room temperature.

Replace the mocha buttercream with vanilla buttercream or lightly sweetened whipped cream.

Recovering from a Mishap
Don't worry if one of the cake layers breaks during assembly. You can patch it together with some of the icing and no one will know the difference.

Panforte di Siena

ANFORTE is a classic Italian confection that's a cross between a cake and a candy. It's very dense and rich, loaded with nuts, dried fruit, and spices. The origins of panforte are cloudy, but the first references to it are found in the very early Middle Ages. Many sources state that originally, panforte was made by the tenants and servants of the monks of Siena as a tithe. Apothecaries and herbalists who were the purveyors of spices for both culinary and medicinal purposes kept the tradition and the recipe intact. Panforte has come to be a traditional Italian Christmas confection, but can be enjoyed anytime. It keeps very well because of the high proportion of dried fruit, nuts, and spices, and the honey, which keeps it moist. This good keeping quality may be one reason the Crusaders took it with them on their voyages to conquer foreign lands. Its rich, spicy taste is a great reason to make and serve it to your family and friends. And don't forget to pack some into your lunch bag. **Makes one 9^1/$_2$-inch round cake, 12 servings**

Essential Gear
- Cake or pie pan
- Kitchen towel
- Food processor
- Rice paper (see page 124 for information)
- 9½-inch round spring-form pan
- Microplane grater or citrus grater
- 1-quart heavy-bottomed saucepan
- Sugar or candy thermometer
- 1-inch natural-bristle pastry brush
- Heat-resistant spatula or wooden spoon
- Cooling rack
- Small flexible-blade spatula or kitchen knife
- Sugar dredger or fine-mesh strainer

Keeping
Store the panforte in an airtight plastic container between layers of waxed paper at room temperature up to 1 month. To freeze up to 4 months, wrap the container in several layers of plastic wrap and aluminum foil. Use a large piece of masking tape and an indelible marker to label and date the contents. If frozen, defrost overnight in the refrigerator and bring to room temperature before serving.

Center a rack in the oven and preheat it to 350°F.

1 cup hazelnuts

Place the hazelnuts in a cake or pie pan and toast in the oven for 15 to 18 minutes, until the skins split and the nuts turn light golden brown. Remove the pan from the oven and transfer the hazelnuts to a large kitchen towel. Fold the towel up around the nuts and leave them for 10 minutes. Rub the nuts between your hands to remove most of the skins.

1 cup unblanched whole almonds

Place the almonds in the cake or pie pan and toast in the oven for 5 to 8 minutes, shaking the pan every 2 to 3 minutes. Remove the pan from the oven and cool on a rack.

When the nuts are cool, combine the hazelnuts and almonds in the work bowl of a food processor fitted with the steel blade. Pulse to chop the nuts coarsely, about 30 seconds.

Reduce the oven temperature to 300°F.

Use a pencil to trace the bottom of a 9½-inch springform pan onto a piece of rice paper. Cut the rice paper slightly inside the pencil lines to make a pan liner.

1 tablespoon unsalted butter, softened

Use a paper towel or your fingertips to butter the bottom and halfway up the sides of the springform pan. Place the rice paper round in the bottom of the pan and butter it.

1½ cups finely chopped
   candied orange peel
   (page 171)
½ cup finely chopped
   candied lemon peel or
   citron (page 171)
½ cup all-purpose flour
3 tablespoons unsweetened
   cocoa powder (natural or
   Dutch-processed)
Zest of 1 small lemon,
   finely grated or minced
1 teaspoon ground
   cinnamon
¼ teaspoon ground cloves
¼ teaspoon freshly ground
   nutmeg
Large pinch of freshly
   ground white pepper

In a large bowl, combine the orange peel, lemon peel, flour, cocoa powder, lemon zest, and spices. Use a rubber spatula or large spoon and toss to blend.

Streamlining
Toast the hazelnuts and almonds before making the panforte. They will keep in an airtight plastic container in the freezer up to 1 year.

Add the chopped nuts and stir together to blend thoroughly.

¾ cup granulated sugar
¾ cup honey
1 ounce (2 tablespoons,
   ¼ stick) unsalted butter,
   cut into small pieces

In the saucepan, combine the sugar, honey, and butter. Over medium heat, bring the mixture to a boil. Place a damp pastry brush at the point where the sugar syrup meets the sides of the pan and sweep it completely around the pan. Do this two times. Brushing down the sides of the pan while sugar is cooking prevents sugar crystals from coming out of the mixture, which causes crystallization. This is a condition that creates a crust around the side of the pan. Once crystallization occurs, the sugar syrup won't come up to temperature correctly and needs to be thrown away. Don't brush around the pan more than a few times. If you do, you're adding extra water to the sugar syrup that will make the syrup take longer to reach its finished temperature.

Cook the mixture until it registers 246°F on a sugar thermometer (firm-ball stage), about 12 minutes. Watch the sugar syrup closely as it gets close to the right temperature because it can very quickly become too hot.

Immediately remove the sugar thermometer and pour the hot sugar syrup into the flour mixture. Using a heat-resistant spatula or wooden spoon, work quickly and stir the sugar syrup into the mixture until thoroughly blended.

Turn the mixture out into the prepared springform pan. With damp hands, press the top of the cake out to the edges of the pan and smooth out the top.

Bake the cake for 30 minutes. It will not look set, but will firm up as it cools. Remove the pan from the oven and cool completely on a rack.

Run a thin-bladed, small, flexible-blade spatula or knife between the edges of the pan and the cake to loosen the cake from the sides of the pan. Release the sides of the springform pan and lift them off of the cake.

¼ cup confectioners' sugar

Use a sugar dredger or fine-mesh sifter to heavily dust the top of the cake with the sugar. Use a sharp knife to cut the panforte into very thin slices.

Ultimate Cocoa Brownies

T HESE ARE the most intensely chocolate brownies I've ever eaten. They are fudgy, dense, and very rich—just what I want in a brownie. Because they are made with cocoa powder instead of chocolate, the flavor is extremely concentrated and very satisfying, which is why I nicknamed them "killer" brownies. **Makes twenty-five 1½-inch brownies**

Essential Gear
- 8-inch square baking pan
- Aluminum foil
- Small saucepan
- Rubber spatula
- Whisk
- Cooling rack

Keeping

Store the brownies in an airtight plastic container between layers of waxed paper at room temperature up to 4 days. A kitchen cupboard or the pantry is the ideal storage place. To freeze up to 4 months, wrap the airtight container in several layers of plastic wrap and aluminum foil. Use a large piece of masking tape and an indelible marker to label and date the contents. If frozen, defrost overnight in the refrigerator and bring to room temperature before serving.

Center a rack in the oven and preheat to 325°F. Line the baking pan with aluminum foil, letting it hang about 2 inches over the sides.

8 ounces (16 tablespoons, 2 sticks) unsalted butter, cut into small pieces

Melt the butter in a small saucepan over low heat or in a microwave-safe bowl on low powder for 30-second bursts.

¾ cup all-purpose flour
1 cup unsweetened natural cocoa powder
¼ teaspoon salt

Sift together the flour and cocoa powder into a large bowl. Add the salt and toss to mix.

1 cup granulated sugar
⅔ cup firmly packed light brown sugar

Add the granulated sugar and brown sugar and stir to mix well.

Add the melted butter and stir until very well combined.

1 tablespoon instant espresso powder
1 tablespoon water

In a small bowl, stir together the espresso powder and water until the mixture is thoroughly blended and forms a thick paste.

2 extra-large eggs, at room temperature 1 teaspoon pure vanilla extract	Using a fork, lightly beat the eggs together in a small bowl. Add the vanilla and espresso paste and whisk together well. Add this mixture to the butter mixture and stir together until shiny and well blended.
1 cup walnuts, coarsely chopped	Stir the walnuts into the batter. Spread the batter evenly into the lined baking pan. Use a rubber spatula to spread it evenly.
	Bake the brownies for 27 minutes, until a cake tester or toothpick inserted in the center comes out slightly moist. Remove the pan from the oven and cool completely on a rack.
	Lift the brownies from the pan with the aluminum foil. Carefully peel the foil away from the sides of the brownies. Cut into 5 equal-sized rows in each direction.

Making a Change

Replace the walnuts with chopped whole, unblanched almonds, pecans, or macadamia nuts.

Adding Style

Serve the cooled brownies with a dollop of lightly sweetened whipped cream or ice cream.

Use a 1½-inch round or heart-shaped plain-edge cutter to cut the brownies after they are cooled. Top each with a star or rosette of whipped cream (see page 44) and place a candy coffee bean or a walnut half, whole unblanched almond, pecan half, or macadamia half on top of the cream, depending on the nuts used in the brownie.

SPECIALTY

CHOCOLATE

TWO GREAT SPECIALTY chocolates that are used in baking are cocoa nibs and gianduia (pronounced john-*do*-ya). Cocoa nibs are a relatively new form of chocolate available for baking. The nibs are the hulled, unsweetened kernels of the cacao bean that are roasted and broken into small pieces. These pieces would normally be ground to make chocolate liquor. Nibs are crunchy and add lots of texture to recipes that call for them. Since nibs are unsweetened, they are bitter but also full of chocolate flavor. I love to watch the expression on people's faces when they eat something made with cocoa nibs. It's one of those curious, "I really like this" expressions. It's fun, also, to explain to people just what cocoa nibs are.

Gianduia is a commercially blended mixture of chocolate and hazelnuts that has a vel-

vety smooth, soft texture and a unique flavor. Occasionally, almonds are used in place of hazelnuts in the mixture. Gianduia is made in dark chocolate, milk chocolate, and white chocolate versions. Gianduia and I go back a long way. I've used it since the beginning of my journey with chocolate and absolutely love everything made with gianduia. Europeans commonly use gianduia in pastries and confections, but it is not used very much in the U.S. If you haven't tried gianduia, I highly recommend that you do.

Cocoa nibs and gianduia can be found year-round in specialty food and cookware shops and through online and catalog sources. There are only a few chocolate manufacturers that produce cocoa nibs. If you cannot find these where you normally shop and don't want to mail order them, ask the store manager to order them for you. I'm sure he or she would be happy to do this.

TIPS AND TECHNIQUES

Cocoa nibs are added directly to a dough or batter, as called for in a specific recipe. Store cocoa nibs in their original container in a cool, dry place for an unlimited period of time.

Gianduia comes in bars or in pieces of large bars that have been cut. Gianduia is used in the same way as other chocolate. For more tips and techniques, see Working with Chocolate and Storing Chocolate in About Chocolate (page 370).

Cocoa Nib and Walnut Biscotti

COCOA NIBS add a new flavor dimension and unusual texture to these classic twice-baked cookies. **Makes about 3 dozen cookies**

Center a rack in the oven and preheat it to 350°F. Line the baking sheets with parchment paper sheets or non-stick liners.

1 cup walnuts

Place the walnuts in a single layer in a cake or pie pan. Toast in the oven for 7 to 8 minutes, until the nuts turn light golden brown.

Remove the pan from the oven and transfer to a rack to cool.

Place the walnuts in the work bowl of a food processor fitted with the steel blade. Pulse the nuts to chop them coarsely.

2 cups all-purpose flour
1/2 cup granulated sugar
1/2 cup firmly packed light brown sugar
2 teaspoons baking powder
1/8 teaspoon salt

In the bowl of an electric stand mixer or a large bowl, combine the flour, granulated sugar, brown sugar, baking powder, and salt. Use the flat beater attachment or a hand-held mixer to stir together briefly.

3 extra-large eggs, at room temperature
2 teaspoons pure vanilla extract
4 ounces (8 tablespoons, 1 stick) unsalted butter, melted

Using a fork, whisk the eggs with the vanilla in a small bowl. Add the egg and vanilla mixture and the butter to the dry ingredients. Mix on low speed until thoroughly combined. Stop occasionally and scrape down the sides and bottom of the mixing bowl with a rubber spatula.

1 cup cocoa nibs

Add the cocoa nibs and the walnuts and stir to blend thoroughly.

Divide the dough into 4 equal pieces. Dust your hands with flour to keep the dough from sticking and shape each piece into a log about 7 inches long, 3 inches wide, and 3/4 inch high. Place 2 logs on each baking sheet, leaving at least 2 inches space between them.

Bake for 12 minutes. Switch the baking sheets and bake until set, about 13 minutes. Remove the baking sheets from the oven and rest for 10 minutes on racks.

Place a dough log on a cutting board. Using a serrated knife, cut the log on the diagonal into 1/2 - to 3/4-inch-thick slices. Place the slices

Essential Gear
- Two baking sheets
- Two parchment paper sheets or non-stick liners
- Cake pan
- Food processor
- Electric stand mixer with flat beater attachment, or large mixing bowl and hand-held mixer
- Two cooling racks
- Serrated knife

Keeping
Store the biscotti in an airtight container between sheets of waxed paper at room temperature up to 2 weeks. A kitchen cupboard or the pantry is the ideal storage place. To freeze up to 3 months, wrap the container tightly in several layers of plastic wrap and aluminum foil. Use a large piece of masking tape and an indelible marker to label and date the contents. If frozen, defrost overnight in the refrigerator and bring to room temperature before serving.

Making a Change
Replace the walnuts with almonds.

Adding Style
Drizzle the biscotti with thin lines of bittersweet or semisweet chocolate after they are completely cool (see page 43). Let the chocolate set for 15 minutes in the

back on the baking sheet on their sides so the wide part of each slice faces up. Repeat with the remaining logs.

Bake the biscotti again for 7 minutes. Switch the pans and bake 6 to 8 minutes, until firm.

Transfer the biscotti to racks to cool.

refrigerator before serving or storing.

Dip one end or one lengthwise side of the biscotti into tempered bittersweet or semisweet chocolate after they are completely cool (see page 43). Let the chocolate set for 15 minutes in the refrigerator before serving or storing.

Cocoa Nib Butter Cookies

COCOA NIBS and toasted walnuts give these classic butter cookies extra-special flavor and crunchy texture. These are quintessential do-ahead refrigerator cookies because the dough is shaped into logs, which need to be chilled, then the logs are sliced when you're ready to bake the cookies. When you're in the mood, make up a couple of batches of these cookie logs and keep them in the freezer. That way you can make cookies in a snap. **Makes 6½ dozen cookies**

Center a rack in the oven and preheat it to 350°F.

1 cup walnuts

Place the walnuts in a single layer in a shallow baking pan and toast in the oven for 7 to 8 minutes, until the nuts turn light golden brown.

Remove the pan from the oven and cool completely on a rack. Use a chef's knife to chop the walnuts finely. Or chop the walnuts in the work bowl of a food processor fitted with the steel blade.

Adjust the oven racks to the upper and lower thirds and raise the oven heat to 375°F.

6 ounces (12 tablespoons, 1½ sticks) unsalted butter, softened

Place the butter in the bowl of an electric stand mixer or in a large bowl. Use the flat beater attachment or a hand-held mixer to beat the butter on medium speed until it's fluffy, about 2 minutes.

½ cup granulated sugar
⅔ cup firmly packed light brown sugar

Add the granulated sugar and light brown sugar to the butter, and cream together completely. Stop occasionally and scrape down the sides and bottom of the bowl with a rubber spatula.

1 extra-large egg, at room temperature
1 teaspoon pure vanilla extract

Lightly beat the egg and vanilla together in a small bowl, then add to the butter mixture and blend together well.

Essential Gear
- Shallow baking pan
- Chef's knife
- Electric stand mixer with flat beater attachment, or large mixing bowl and hand-held mixer
- Rubber spatula
- Sifter
- 2 baking sheets
- Four parchment paper sheets or non-stick liners
- Two cooling racks

Keeping
Store the cookies in an airtight plastic container between layers of waxed paper at room temperature up to 4 days. To freeze up to 3 months, wrap the container tightly in several layers of plastic wrap and aluminum foil. Use a large piece of masking tape and an indelible marker to label and date the contents. If frozen, defrost overnight in the refrigerator and bring to room temperature before serving.

2 cups all-purpose flour
2 teaspoons baking powder
¼ teaspoon salt

Over a large piece of waxed or parchment paper or a bowl, sift together the flour and baking powder. Add the salt and toss to blend.

Add the dry ingredients in 3 stages to the butter mixture, blending well after each addition. Stop and scrape down the sides and bottom of the bowl after each addition to ensure even mixing.

⅔ cup cocoa nibs

Combine the cocoa nibs and walnuts in a bowl. Stir to blend well. Add this mixture in 2 stages to the dough and blend thoroughly.

Cover the bowl tightly with plastic wrap and chill for 1 hour, until firm enough to roll into logs.

Divide the dough in two and place each half on a large piece of waxed paper. Use the waxed paper to shape and roll the dough into logs about 1¼ inches wide and 12 to 13 inches long. Wrap the rolls tightly in the waxed paper and then in plastic wrap. Chill the logs 3 to 4 hours in the refrigerator or 1 hour in the freezer, until firm enough to slice.

Line the baking sheets with parchment paper sheets or non-stick liners.

Unwrap the cookie logs and place them on a cutting board. Use a sharp knife to slice each roll into ½-inch-thick slices. Cut straight down and roll the cylinder a quarter turn after every 6 slices so it will keep its round shape. If the dough becomes soft while you work with it, rewrap it and chill for another 10 to 15 minutes, then continue slicing. Place the slices on the baking sheets, leaving 1 inch of space between them.

Bake the cookies for 5 minutes, then switch the baking sheets. Bake another 5 to 7 minutes, until set and light golden. Remove the baking sheets from the oven and cool the cookies completely on the baking sheets on racks.

Repeat with any remaining cookie logs.

To freeze the cookie dough logs up to 6 months, wrap them in several layers of plastic wrap and place in a freezer bag. Use masking tape and an indelible marker to label and date the dough logs. Let the logs stand at room temperature for about 20 minutes before slicing, because if they are too firm when cut, they may splinter.

Making a Change
Replace the walnuts with hazelnuts, almonds, or pecans.

Gianduia Brownies

GIANDUIA is a blended chocolate made with hazelnuts. Even though gianduia contains nuts, its texture is silky smooth and it looks and behaves like chocolate. Gianduia chocolate can be found in some specialty food shops and through online and catalog sources (see page 625). The scrumptious flavor of gianduia

Essential Gear
• 8-inch square baking pan
• Aluminum foil
• Rubber spatula
• Double boiler

permeates these brownies. Toasted hazelnuts add more depth to the flavor and a crunchy texture. These are hard to resist, so bake them when you know friends and family will be around to help you eat them. **Makes twenty-five 1½-inch brownies**

1 tablespoon unsalted butter, softened	Center a rack in the oven and preheat it to 350°F. Line the baking pan with aluminum foil, letting it hang about 2 inches over the sides. Use a paper towel or your fingertips to butter the inside of the foil.
10 ounces gianduia chocolate, finely chopped **4 ounces (8 tablespoons, 1 stick) unsalted butter, cut into small pieces**	Place the gianduia chocolate and the butter together in the top of a double boiler over low heat. Stir often with a rubber spatula to help melt evenly. Remove the top pan of the double boiler and wipe the bottom and sides very dry. Let the mixture cool, stirring occasionally with a rubber spatula to prevent a skin from forming on top. Or place the gianduia chocolate and butter in a microwave-safe bowl and melt on low power for 30-second bursts. Stir with a rubber spatula after each burst.
½ cup granulated sugar	Add the sugar to the chocolate mixture and mix well.
2 extra-large eggs, at room temperature **1 teaspoon pure vanilla extract**	Using a fork, lightly beat the eggs together in a small bowl. Add the vanilla and stir together. Add the egg mixture to the chocolate mixture and mix together.
1½ cups toasted and partially skinned hazelnuts (see page 479) **1 tablespoon all-purpose flour**	In the work bowl of a food processor fitted with the steel blade, combine the hazelnuts and flour. Pulse until the hazelnuts are finely chopped, about 30 seconds. Stir the hazelnuts into the chocolate mixture and blend well.
½ cup all-purpose flour **½ teaspoon baking powder** **¼ teaspoon salt**	Over a medium piece of waxed or parchment paper or a bowl, sift together the flour and baking powder. Add the salt and toss to blend together. Add the dry ingredients to the chocolate mixture and stir together thoroughly.
	Pour the batter into the prepared pan and use a rubber spatula to spread it evenly into the corners.

- Food processor
- Sifter
- Cooling rack

Keeping

Store the brownies in an airtight plastic container between layers of waxed paper at room temperature up to 4 days. To freeze up to 4 months, wrap the container tightly in several layers of plastic wrap and aluminum foil. Use a large piece of masking tape and an indelible marker to label and date the contents. If frozen, defrost overnight in the refrigerator and bring to room temperature before serving.

Adding Style

Serve the cooled brownies with a dollop of lightly sweetened whipped cream.

Drizzle the top of the cooled brownies with melted bittersweet chocolate in close lines (see page 43). Let the chocolate set for 15 minutes before storing.

Use a 1½-inch round or heart-shaped plain-edge cutter to cut the cooled brownies. Top the center of each brownie with a star or rosette of whipped cream (see page 44). Center a whole toasted and skinned hazelnut on the whipped cream.

Bake the brownies for 35 to 40 minutes, until a cake tester or tooth-pick inserted in the center comes out slightly moist.

Remove the pan from the oven and cool completely on a rack.

Lift the brownies from the pan with the aluminum foil. Carefully peel the foil away from the sides of the brownies. Cut into 5 equal-sized rows in each direction.

Gianduia Crostata

CROSTATA is the Italian word for "tart" and gianduia is a much-loved flavor combination of chocolate and hazelnuts often found in Northern Italy. This yummy tart is chock full of hazelnuts and chocolate baked into a flaky pastry crust. It's perfect to serve for any gathering. **Makes one 11-inch round tart, 14 to 16 servings**

PASTRY DOUGH

1¾ cups all-purpose flour
⅓ cup granulated sugar
Finely grated zest of 1 orange
½ teaspoon baking powder
¼ teaspoon freshly grated nutmeg
⅛ teaspoon salt

In the work bowl of a food processor fitted with the steel blade, combine the flour, sugar, orange zest, baking powder, nutmeg, and salt. Pulse briefly to blend.

5 ounces (10 tablespoons, 1¼ sticks) unsalted butter, chilled

Cut the butter into small pieces and add to the flour mixture. Pulse until the butter is cut into very tiny pieces, about 30 seconds. The texture should be sandy with very tiny lumps throughout.

1 extra-large egg, at room temperature
1½ teaspoons pure vanilla extract

In a small bowl, combine the egg and vanilla extract. With the food processor running, pour this mixture through the feed tube. Process until the dough wraps itself around the blade, 30 seconds to 1 minute.

Turn the pastry dough onto a large piece of plastic wrap. Shape into a flat disk and wrap tightly in a double layer of plastic wrap. Chill in the refrigerator until firm before using, about 2 hours. Chilling the dough relaxes the gluten in the flour so it won't be too elastic and will roll out easily. It also firms up the butter in the dough so it will need less flour when rolled out. If the dough is too firm it will splin-ter and break when rolled out. If the pastry dough is too cold and

Essential Gear

- Food processor
- Microplane grater or citrus zester
- Rolling pin
- 11-inch round, fluted-edge tart pan with removable bottom
- Jelly-roll pan
- Kitchen towel
- Electric stand mixer with flat beater attachment, or a medium mixing bowl and hand-held mixer
- Rubber spatula
- Cooling rack

Keeping

The tart can last up to 4 days at room temperature. Place a piece of waxed paper over the top of the tart, then tightly cover it with aluminum foil.

Streamlining

The pastry dough can be made in advance and kept in the refrigerator, tightly wrapped in a double layer of plastic wrap, up to 4 days. To freeze up to 3 months, wrap

firm, let it stand at room temperature for 10 to 15 minutes before rolling to become more pliable.

On a smooth, flat surface, roll out the pastry dough between sheets of lightly floured waxed or parchment paper to a large circle about 13 inches in diameter. To tell if the dough will fit the tart pan, hold the pan above the dough. If there are about 2 inches of dough that protrude beyond the sides of the pan, it will fit.

Carefully peel the paper off the top of the dough. Brush excess flour off the dough, then loosely roll the pastry dough around the rolling pin without the bottom piece of paper. Place the tart pan directly underneath the rolling pin and carefully unroll the pastry dough onto it.

Gently lift up the sides and ease the pastry dough into the bottom and sides of the tart pan, pushing it lightly into the fluted edges. Trim off the excess pastry dough at the top of the pan by running the rolling pin over the top. Or use your fingers to press against the top of the pan to remove the excess pastry dough.

Place the tart pan on a baking sheet. Use a fork to pierce the bottom of the pastry shell Chill for at least 30 minutes. This helps prevent the dough from shrinking as it bakes.

Center a rack in the oven and preheat it to 350°F.

HAZELNUT AND CHOCOLATE (GIANDUIA) FILLING

1³/₄ cups hazelnuts	Place the hazelnuts in a single layer in a jelly-roll pan and toast for 15 to 18 minutes, until the skins split and the nuts turn light golden brown.
	Remove the pan from the oven and transfer the hazelnuts to a kitchen towel. Fold the towel around the hazelnuts and rub them together to remove most of the skins.
2 tablespoons granulated sugar	In the work bowl of a food processor fitted with the steel blade, combine the hazelnuts and sugar. Pulse until the hazelnuts are finely ground. The sugar absorbs the oil that is released when the nuts are ground and keeps them from becoming a paste.
3 ounces (6 tablespoons, ³/₄ stick) unsalted butter, softened	Place the butter in the bowl of an electric stand mixer or in a large bowl. Use the flat beater attachment or hand-held mixer to beat the butter on medium speed until it's fluffy, about 2 minutes.
¹/₃ cup granulated sugar	Add the sugar, and cream together thoroughly. Stop occasionally and scrape down the sides and bottom of the bowl with a rubber spatula.

the dough snugly in several layers of plastic wrap and place it in a freezer bag. Use a large piece of masking tape and an indelible marker to label and date the contents. If frozen, defrost overnight in the refrigerator before using.

The filling can be made in advance and kept in the refrigerator in a tightly covered container up to 3 days.

Adding Style
Garnish each slice of tart with a dollop of whipped cream.

2 extra-large eggs, at room temperature **Finely grated zest of 1 orange**	Use a fork to lightly beat the eggs and orange zest together in a small bowl. Adjust the mixer speed to medium-low. Add the lightly beaten eggs to the butter mixture, mixing well. The eggs will sit on top of the butter mixture, so stop after adding each one and scrape down the sides and bottom of the bowl with a rubber spatula to help mix evenly. The mixture may look curdled as the eggs are added, but as you scrape down the bowl, the mixture will smooth out.
1 tablespoon all-purpose flour **2 ounces milk chocolate, finely chopped** **2 ounces bittersweet chocolate, finely chopped**	Add the flour, milk chocolate, and bittersweet chocolate to the butter mixture and blend thoroughly.
1 tablespoon pure vanilla extract	Add the vanilla and the ground hazelnuts and blend thoroughly.
	Transfer the filling to the chilled pastry shell. Use a rubber spatula to spread the mixture out evenly.
	Bake the tart for 25 to 30 minutes, until the filling is puffed, set, and a cake tester inserted in the center comes out clean.
	Remove the pan from the oven and cool on a rack.
	Cut the tart into serving slices and serve at room temperature.

Gianduia Mousse Cake

DARK CHOCOLATE, milk chocolate, and toasted hazelnuts combine to create the incomparable flavor of gianduia. When served at room temperature on the day it's baked, this cake has a creamy, soft texture that is similar to mousse. After it's refrigerated, the consistency of the cake firms up and is denser, but not hard. Whichever texture you prefer, the rich, full-bodied flavor of this cake is always very satisfying. **Makes one 9¹/₂-inch round cake, 12 to 14 servings**

Essential Gear

- 9¹/₂-inch round spring-form pan
- Heavy-duty aluminum foil
- Jelly-roll pan
- Kitchen towel
- Food processor
- Double boiler
- Electric stand mixer with wire whip attachment, or large mixing bowl and hand-held mixer

1 tablespoon unsalted butter, softened	Center a rack in the oven and preheat it to 350°F. Use a paper towel or your fingertips to butter the inside of the springform pan. Wrap a double layer of heavy-duty foil around the bottom of the pan. This prevents any water from seeping into the cake.

2¼ cups hazelnuts	Place the hazelnuts in a single layer on a jelly-roll pan and toast for 15 to 18 minutes, until the skins split and the nuts turn light golden brown.	• Heat-resistant spatula or wooden spoon
		• Rubber spatula
	Remove the pan from the oven and transfer the hazelnuts to a kitchen towel. Fold the towel around the hazelnuts and rub them together to remove most of the skins.	• 12-inch round cake pan or roasting pan
		• Cooling rack

Keeping

Store the cake tightly wrapped with aluminum foil at room temperature up to 2 days or in the refrigerator up to 4 days.

½ cup unflavored vegetable oil, such as canola or safflower

In the work bowl of a food processor fitted with the steel blade, combine the hazelnuts and oil. Pulse until the nuts are finely ground and become a paste, about 2 minutes.

9 ounces bittersweet chocolate, finely chopped
7 ounces milk chocolate, finely chopped

Place the bittersweet chocolate and milk chocolate in the top of a double boiler over low heat. Stir often with a rubber spatula to help melt evenly. Remove the top pan of the double boiler and wipe the bottom and sides very dry. Or place the chocolates in a microwave-safe bowl and melt on low power for 30-second bursts. Stir with a rubber spatula after each burst.

Add the hazelnut paste to the melted chocolate and stir together until thoroughly blended.

Adding Style

Serve each slice of cake with a scoop of vanilla or caramel ice cream.

Serve each slice of cake in a pool of Raspberry Sauce (see Meyer Lemon Soufflés, page 143) and scatter fresh raspberries around the plate.

6 extra-large eggs, at room temperature
½ cup superfine sugar

Place the eggs in the bowl of an electric stand mixer or in a large bowl. Using the wire whip attachment or a hand-held mixer, whip the eggs on medium-high speed until they are frothy. Gradually sprinkle on the sugar and continue to whip until the eggs are very thick and pale colored and hold a slowly dissolving ribbon as the beater is lifted, about 5 minutes.

Add the chocolate-hazelnut mixture to the whipped eggs and blend together thoroughly.

1 cup heavy whipping cream

Place the cream in the chilled bowl of an electric stand mixer or a medium bowl. Using the wire whip attachment or a hand-held mixer, whip the cream on medium speed until it holds soft peaks.

Fold the whipped cream into the chocolate mixture in 3 stages, blending thoroughly.

1 quart boiling water

Pour the mixture into the prepared springform pan. Place the springform pan in the larger pan. Pour hot water into the bottom pan until it reaches halfway up the sides of the springform pan.

Bake the cake for 1 hour. Turn off the oven and let the cake stand in the oven for another 15 minutes with the door closed.

Remove the cake from the oven. Unwrap the foil and cool the cake on a rack. Release the hinge on the side of the springform pan and carefully lift the side away from the cake.

GARNISH

1 cup heavy whipping cream
1 tablespoon confectioners' sugar, sifted
½ teaspoon pure vanilla extract

Place the cream in the chilled bowl of an electric stand mixer or a medium bowl. Using the wire whip attachment or a hand-held mixer, whip the cream on medium speed until frothy. Add the sugar and vanilla and continue to whip the cream until it holds soft peaks.

Serve slices of the cake with a large dollop of whipped cream.

V.

DAIRY

PRODUCTS

AIRY PRODUCTS PLAY a vital role in baking. Some of my most requested baked desserts are dairy based, especially those that use cream. It may be from our childhood, but the combination of dairy products with the sweetness of many desserts is very comforting. ✳ There are many more dairy products to use in baking than one would imagine. Buttermilk, cream, and sour cream are widely used. But there are wonderful cheeses, such as cream cheese, ricotta cheese, and even goat cheese. A cheese that I really love to use is mascarpone. It imparts a tangy flavor and has a smooth texture. And it's easy to find any of these. ✳ There are many recipes you will want to try in this section. My family and friends, as do I, enjoy eating baked goods made with buttermilk, so you might want to start there. One thing I do recommend—make enough to go around because everyone will want seconds.

16

MILK AND CREAM

BAKING USING milk or cream as a primary ingredient may not seem so exciting. But it definitely can be, especially when more than just regular milk and regular cream are used. In this chapter, I use buttermilk, heavy whipping cream, crème fraîche, milk, and sour cream. Buttermilk has a long tradition of use in baked goods. It offers a mildly sour taste that is very pleasing. Heavy whipping cream provides a mildly sweet taste, while milk gives a more subtle sweetness. Crème fraîche imparts a hint of tartness, while sour cream gives a more distinct sour taste. And all of these help to make baked goods moist and tender. All of the recipes in this chapter are good to bake any time of the year, but I generally like to make them during cooler seasons.

Buttermilk, heavy whipping cream, milk, and sour cream are available any time of the year in supermarkets. Crème fraîche is generally found at specialty food shops, or you can make it yourself (see below).

TIPS AND TECHNIQUES

Buttermilk, heavy whipping cream, and milk come in cartons with pour spouts. Buttermilk is normally found in quarts; heavy whipping cream in pints; and milk in all sizes. I prefer to use whole milk. Make sure to check the expiration dates on these when you buy them because some stores will leave them on the shelf past their expiration date. Crème fraîche and sour cream come in small round containers, which also have expiration dates on them that need to be checked. Crème fraîche is generally available in a 1-cup size, while sour cream comes in both 1- and 2-cup sizes.

All of these products should be stored in the refrigerator, preferably not in the door because it is has more temperature variation from being opened. Although the expiration date on the carton is the date by which these products should be sold, I generally don't buy or use any of these past their expiration dates.

For the recipes in this chapter, buttermilk, crème fraîche, and sour cream are used directly out of the refrigerator. Heavy whipping cream and milk are also used directly out of the refrigerator, but occasionally they are heated in a double boiler, sometimes with other ingredients, depending on the specific recipe.

If you want to make your own crème fraîche, combine 1 cup of heavy whipping cream with 1 tablespoon of buttermilk, or equal parts of heavy whipping cream and sour cream, in a mixing bowl and blend together thoroughly. Cover the bowl and let the mixture stand in a warm (about 70°F), draft-free place for 12 hours, or overnight, to thicken. Stir the crème, cover tightly again, and refrigerate for at least 4 hours before using. The crème will keep for up to 1 week in a tightly sealed container in the refrigerator.

Buttermilk and Raisin Pie

A CREAMY buttermilk custard full of plump raisins is baked in a classic cream cheese pie dough shell for this delectable pie. This is an easy pie to make, and you can make it all year-round. **Makes one 9-inch round pie, 12 to 14 servings**

Essential Gear
- Food processor
- Rolling pin
- 9-inch round pie pan
- Baking sheet
- Cooling rack

PIE DOUGH

1 cup all-purpose flour

1 tablespoon granulated sugar

¼ teaspoon salt

In the work bowl of a food processor fitted with the steel blade, combine the flour, sugar, and salt. Pulse briefly to blend.

Keeping

Cover the top of the pie with waxed paper, then wrap it tightly with plastic wrap and keep in the refrigerator up to 3 days.

4 ounces (8 tablespoons, 1 stick) unsalted butter, chilled

Cut the butter into small pieces and freeze for 20 minutes.

4 ounces cream cheese, chilled

Cut the cream cheese into small pieces and add to the dry ingredients. Pulse to cut the cream cheese into very tiny pieces. The texture should be sandy with very tiny lumps throughout.

Add the butter to the flour mixture. Pulse until the butter is cut into pea-sized pieces, 30 to 45 seconds.

Streamlining

The pie dough can be made in advance and kept in the refrigerator, tightly wrapped in a double layer of plastic wrap, up to 4 days. To freeze up to 3 months, wrap the dough snugly in several layers of plastic wrap and place it in a freezer bag. Use a large piece of masking tape and an indelible marker to label and date the contents. If frozen, defrost overnight in the refrigerator before using. The pie dough can also be fitted into the pie pan and frozen. Wrap as above and label.

2 to 3 tablespoons heavy whipping cream

Remove the top of the food processor and sprinkle on 2 tablespoons of the cream. Replace the top and pulse for 10 seconds. Squeeze a small amount of the dough in your hand. If it holds together, don't add any more cream. If the dough is still very crumbly, add another tablespoon of cream, pulse to blend, then check the dough again. It won't hold together unless you squeeze it, but that's the texture you want.

Shape the dough into a flat disk and wrap it tightly in a double layer of plastic wrap. Chill in the refrigerator until firm before using, at least 1 hour. Chilling the dough relaxes the gluten in the flour so it won't be too elastic and will roll out easily. It also firms up the butter in the dough so it will need less flour when rolled out. If the dough is too firm it will splinter and break when rolled out. Let it stand at room temperature for 10 to 15 minutes before rolling to become more pliable.

On a smooth, flat surface, roll out the disk of pie dough between sheets of lightly floured waxed or parchment paper to a large circle about 12 inches in diameter. To tell if the dough will fit the pie pan,

Troubleshooting

Don't overprocess the pie dough or it will be tough and not flaky.

invert the pan over the dough. If there are 2 to 3 inches of dough that protrude beyond the sides of the pan, it will fit.

Carefully peel the paper off the top of the dough. Brush excess flour off the dough, then loosely roll the pastry dough around the rolling pin without the bottom piece of paper. Place the pie pan directly underneath the rolling pin and carefully unroll the pastry dough into the pan. Or loosely fold the dough in half. Carefully place it in half of the pie pan and gently unfold the dough. Gently lift up the sides and ease the pie dough into the bottom and sides of the pie pan. Trim off the excess pie dough at the top of the pan and crimp the sides (see page 40).

Transfer the pie pan to a baking sheet and chill in the freezer for 15 to 20 minutes. This helps prevent the pie dough from shrinking as it bakes and sets the butter in the dough to ensure flakiness.

Adjust an oven rack to the lower third and preheat the oven to 375°F.

BUTTERMILK AND RAISIN FILLING

1 extra-large egg, at room temperature
1 cup buttermilk
1 tablespoon apple cider vinegar

Place the egg in a large bowl and beat it lightly with a fork. Add the buttermilk and vinegar and stir together to blend.

¾ cup granulated sugar
2 tablespoons all-purpose flour
¼ teaspoon freshly grated nutmeg
¼ teaspoon salt

Stir together the sugar, flour, nutmeg, and salt in a small bowl, then add to the egg and buttermilk mixture and stir together until well combined.

2 cups raisins

Add the raisins to the filling and stir to blend.

Transfer the filling to the chilled pie shell. Bake for 40 minutes, until the filling is set, jiggles very slightly when the pan is moved, and is very lightly colored.

Remove the pan from the oven and cool completely on a rack. Chill the pie before serving.

Buttermilk Biscuits

BUTTERMILK PROVIDES the characteristic tangy flavor in these very easy-to-bake biscuits. To make flaky biscuits, mix the batter just until the dry ingredients are moistened. Although this makes a slightly sticky dough, the steam that is created in the oven makes the biscuits rise and gives them their airy texture. **Makes fourteen 2-inch round biscuits**

Essential Gear
- Baking sheet
- Parchment paper sheet or non-stick liner
- Food processor
- 2-inch round, plain-edge cutter
- Cooling rack

Center a rack in the oven and preheat it to 450°F. Line a baking sheet with parchment paper or a non-stick liner.

Keeping

Store the biscuits in an airtight plastic container between layers of waxed paper at room temperature up to 2 days. To freeze up to 2 months, wrap the container tightly in several layers of plastic wrap and aluminum foil. Use a large piece of masking tape and an indelible marker to label and date the contents. If frozen, defrost overnight in the refrigerator and bring to room temperature before serving.

2 cups all-purpose flour 2 teaspoons baking powder 1/2 teaspoon baking soda 1/2 teaspoon salt	In the work bowl of a food processor fitted with the steel blade combine the flour, baking powder, baking soda, and salt. Pulse briefly to blend.
4 ounces (8 tablespoons, 1 stick) unsalted butter, cold	Cut the butter into small pieces and add to the dry ingredients. Pulse until the butter is cut into very tiny pieces. The texture should be sandy with very tiny lumps throughout.
2/3 cup cold buttermilk	With the food processor on, pour the buttermilk through the feed tube. Process just until the dry ingredients are moistened and begin to clump together.

Transfer the mixture to a floured flat work surface and knead briefly to form a rough ball. Pat the ball into a 1-inch-thick round. Use the round cutter to cut out biscuits. Plunge the cutter straight down into the dough and lift straight up without twisting. Twisting seals the edges of the dough and keeps the biscuits from rising. Place the biscuits on the lined baking sheet with at least 1 inch of space between them.

To cut square biscuits, use a sharp knife to cut off 1/4 inch from all the edges. Then cut the dough into equal-sized squares. Cut straight down and lift the knife straight up to avoid sealing the edges.

Bake the biscuits 10 to 12 minutes, until they are risen and light golden. Remove the pan from the oven and cool on a rack.

The biscuits are best served warm and can be reheated in a 350°F oven for 10 to 12 minutes.

Buttermilk Scones

T HESE SCONES are great not only for afternoon tea, but also for breakfast. This recipe uses chopped dried figs, but you can substitute raisins or other dried fruit if you like. Scones are best served warm and can be reheated in a 350°F oven for 10 to 15 minutes. **Makes eight 3-inch scones**

Center a rack in the oven and preheat it to 400°F. Line a baking sheet with parchment paper or a non-stick liner.

1¾ cups all-purpose flour
¼ cup granulated sugar
2 teaspoons baking powder
¼ teaspoon baking soda
¼ teaspoon salt

In the work bowl of a food processor fitted with the steel blade, combine the flour, sugar, baking powder, baking soda, and salt. Pulse a few times to blend.

1½ ounces (3 tablespoons) unsalted butter, chilled

Cut the butter into small pieces and add to the flour mixture. Pulse until the butter is cut into very tiny pieces, about 30 seconds. The texture should be sandy with very tiny lumps throughout.

1 cup finely chopped dried figs

Add the dried figs and pulse a few times to mix.

½ cup buttermilk
1 extra-large egg, at room temperature
2 teaspoons pure vanilla extract

Using a fork, lightly beat the buttermilk, egg, and vanilla together in a liquid measuring cup. With the food processor running, pour this mixture through the feed tube and process until the dough wraps itself around the blade, about 30 seconds.

Dust a large piece of waxed or parchment paper with flour and turn the dough out onto it. Dust your hands with flour and shape the dough into an 8-inch round, about ½ inch thick. Use a sharp knife to cut the circle into quarters, then cut each quarter in half, forming 8 triangular scones.

Transfer the scones to the lined baking sheet, leaving at least 1 inch of space between them so they have room to expand as they bake. Brush any excess flour off the scones.

GARNISH

1 tablespoon heavy cream

Brush the top of each scone with cream, taking care that it doesn't run down the sides and under the scones. If it does, wipe it up because it can cause the bottom of the scones to burn.

Keeping

Store the scones in an airtight plastic container between layers of waxed paper at room temperature up to 4 days. To freeze up to 4 months, wrap the container tightly in several layers of plastic wrap and aluminum foil. Use a large piece of masking tape and an indelible marker to label and date the contents. If frozen, defrost overnight in the refrigerator and bring to room temperature before serving.

Making a Change

Replace the dried figs with raisins, dried apricots, cherries, cranberries, or dates.

Adding Style

Add ⅔ cup roughly chopped almonds, walnuts, or pecans when adding the dried figs.

2 tablespoons granulated sugar	Lightly sprinkle the top of each scone with sugar.
	Bake the scones for 15 to 18 minutes, until they are light golden.
	Remove the baking sheet from the oven and cool completely on a rack.

Buttermilk Spice Layer Cake

THREE LAYERS of tangy buttermilk and spice cake alternate with cream cheese icing sprinkled with chopped walnuts to make up this delectable cake. Chopped walnuts decorate the sides of the cake, with walnut halves on top. This yummy dessert is just right to serve for practically any event. Some of the steps involved in making this cake can be done in advance, so it's easy to assemble a few hours or a day before serving. **Makes one 9-inch round cake, 12 to 14 servings**

BUTTERMILK SPICE CAKE

Center a rack in the oven and preheat it to 350°F.

1 tablespoon unsalted butter, softened	Using a paper towel or your fingertips, generously butter the inside of the cake pan, coating it thoroughly
2 teaspoons all-purpose flour	Dust the inside of the pan with the flour. Shake and tilt the pan to evenly distribute the flour, then turn the pan over and shake out the excess over the sink.
	Cut a round of parchment paper to fit the bottom of the pan. Butter the parchment paper round and place in the pan, butter-side up.
6 ounces (12 tablespoons, 1½ sticks) unsalted butter, softened	Place the butter in the bowl of an electric stand mixer or in a large bowl. Use the flat beater attachment or a hand-held mixer to beat the butter on medium speed until it's fluffy, about 2 minutes.
1²/₃ cups granulated sugar	Gradually add the sugar to the butter, and cream together well. Stop occasionally and scrape down the bottom and sides of the bowl with a rubber spatula.
3 extra-large eggs, at room temperature	One at a time, add the eggs to the butter mixture, stopping to scrape down the bottom and sides of the bowl after each addition. At first

Essential Gear

- One 9 × 2-inch round cake pan
- Scissors
- Parchment paper
- Two rubber spatulas
- Electric stand mixer with flat beater attachment and wire whip attachment, or large mixing bowl and hand-held mixer
- Sifter
- Cooling rack
- Cardboard cake circle
- Serrated knife
- 10-inch flexible-blade icing spatula

Keeping

Store the cake loosely covered with aluminum foil in the refrigerator up to 3 days. Place several toothpicks in the top outer edges of the cake to hold the foil away from it so it won't mar the icing.

Streamlining

Bake the cake up to 2 days before assembling and keep tightly covered with a double layer of plastic wrap

the mixture may look curdled as the eggs are added, but as you stop and scrape down the bowl, the mixture will smooth out.

2½ cups cake flour

1½ teaspoons baking powder

½ teaspoon baking soda

1 teaspoon ground cinnamon

½ teaspoon salt

½ teaspoon freshly grated nutmeg

¼ teaspoon ground cloves

¼ teaspoon ground ginger

Over a large piece of waxed or parchment paper or a bowl, sift together the flour, baking powder, and baking soda. Add the cinnamon, salt, nutmeg, cloves, and ginger and toss to blend thoroughly.

2 teaspoons pure vanilla extract

¾ cup buttermilk

Stir the vanilla into the buttermilk. With the mixer on low speed, add the dry ingredients to the butter mixture alternately with the buttermilk mixture in 4 stages. Blend well after each addition and stop often to scrape down the bottom and sides of the bowl with a rubber spatula.

Transfer the cake batter to the cake pan. Smooth the top of the pan with a rubber spatula.

Bake the cake for 40 to 45 minutes, until golden and a cake tester inserted in the center comes out with no crumbs clinging to it.

Remove the cake pan from the oven and cool completely on a rack. Invert the pan to remove the cake, then peel the parchment paper off the back of the cake. Re-invert the cake onto a cardboard cake circle.

CREAM CHEESE ICING

1 pound cream cheese, softened

Place the cream cheese in the bowl of an electric stand mixer or in a large bowl. Use the flat beater attachment or a hand-held mixer and beat the cream cheese until it is fluffy, about 3 minutes.

1 cup confectioners' sugar, sifted

¼ cup heavy whipping cream

Add the confectioners' sugar and cream and beat together well.

ASSEMBLY

2 cups roughly chopped walnuts

Using a serrated knife, cut the cake into 3 layers horizontally (see page 34). Place the bottom cake layer on a serving plate. Place strips of waxed paper around the bottom edges of the cake to protect the

at room temperature or in the refrigerator for up to 4 days. To freeze the cake up to 3 months, wrap it snugly in several layers of plastic wrap and place in a freezer bag. Use a large piece of masking tape and an indelible marker to label and date the contents. If frozen, defrost the layers overnight in the refrigerator.

Making a Change

Replace the walnuts with pecans.

Adding Style

Add ½ cup finely chopped walnuts to the cake. Add the nuts with the dry ingredients when mixing the cake batter.

Recovering from a Mishap

If one of the cake layers breaks during assembly, patch it together with some of the icing.

plate while assembling the cake. Use the flexible-blade spatula to spread the layer evenly with ¼ cup of the icing, then sprinkle ¼ cup of the chopped walnuts evenly over the icing.

Position the second cake layer evenly over the walnuts. Spread about ¼ cup of the icing over the layer, then sprinkle with another ¼ cup walnuts.

Position the top layer of the cake over the walnuts. Spread the remaining icing over the sides and top of the cake. Press the remaining chopped walnuts into the sides of the cake.

12 walnut halves

Visually divide the cake into 12 serving pieces. Place a walnut half in the center of each serving piece near the top outer edge.

Let the cake chill for at least 2 hours before serving so it has time to set and will be easier to cut. Serve the cake at room temperature.

Crème Brûlée

CRÈME BRÛLÉE (pronounced krem brew *lay*) is the French name for "burnt cream," which is cold baked custard with a crisp, brittle topping of caramelized sugar. The topping is a wonderful textural contrast to the silky smooth custard underneath and is what gives this classic dessert its well-deserved reputation. Crème brûlée is baked in a water bath to help retain its creamy texture. You can use custard cups, ramekins, or small ovenproof bowls to bake this delectable custard. **Makes eight ½-cup servings**

Essential Gear
- Eight ½-cup custard cups or shallow ovenproof bowls
- 3-quart baking dish or roasting pan
- Double boiler
- Heat-resistant rubber spatula
- Medium bowl
- Whisk or rubber spatula
- Large fine-mesh strainer
- Aluminum foil
- Propane kitchen torch (optional)

Keeping
Store the baked custard, without the caramelized sugar topping, tightly covered with a double layer of plastic wrap in the refrigerator up to 3 days. Caramelize the top of the custard before serving.

Place the custard cups in the baking dish or roasting pan.

2 cups heavy whipping cream
½ cup superfine sugar
1 vanilla bean, split lengthwise

Place the cream, sugar, and vanilla bean together in the top of a double boiler over hot water. Stir often with a heat-resistant rubber spatula or a wooden spoon until the mixture is hot, about 15 minutes.

Take the top of the double boiler off and wipe the outside of the pan dry. Remove the vanilla bean and reserve it.

6 extra-large egg yolks, at room temperature

Whisk the egg yolks into the cream mixture and blend thoroughly. Strain the custard into a bowl or other container. Add the reserved vanilla bean, cover the bowl tightly with plastic wrap, and refrigerate at least 4 hours.

Center an oven rack and preheat it to 350°F. Whisk the chilled custard mixture and remove the vanilla bean. Pour the mixture into the custard cups or bowls, dividing it evenly among them.

1 quart boiling water

Place the baking dish or roasting pan on the oven rack. Carefully pour boiling water into the baking dish until it reaches halfway up the sides of the cups or bowls. Tightly cover the top of the pan with aluminum foil.

Bake the custard for 40 minutes. Remove the foil and gently tap or shake the custard cups. The custards should be fairly firm but the centers will jiggle slightly when the pan is moved.

If the custards are too soft, cover with the foil and bake another 5 to 10 minutes, until set.

Remove the baking dish from the oven. Remove the foil, and let the custard stand in the water bath for 30 minutes to cool. Cover each custard with plastic wrap and chill in the refrigerator for at least 4 hours before serving, which helps them to set.

¹⁄₂ cup superfine sugar

Sprinkle the top of each custard evenly with a teaspoon or two of superfine sugar.

To caramelize the top of the custards, use a propane kitchen torch. Hold the torch a few inches above the custard and move it around the top. The sugar will become bubbly and golden brown. Or place the custards on a baking sheet or roasting pan and place them under the broiler for 2 to 3 minutes. Watch carefully, because the sugar can burn quickly.

Serve the custards immediately or hold at room temperature for up to 1 hour.

Crème Caramel

THIS IS A CLASSIC egg custard that is baked in a caramel-lined mold. Because the custard has a delicate texture, it is baked in a water bath that cushions it from the heat. The custard is turned out of the mold after it is baked and chilled, and the caramel forms a topping and sauce. **Makes eight ¹⁄₂-cup servings**

Essential Gear
- 1-quart heavy-bottomed saucepan
- Wooden spoon or heat-resistant spatula

Center a rack in the oven and preheat it to 350°F.

CARAMEL

½ cup granulated sugar
¼ cup water

Combine the sugar and water in the 1-quart saucepan over medium-high heat. Bring the mixture to a boil and stir to dissolve the sugar. Cook the mixture, without stirring, until it turns a rich golden brown, about 8 minutes.

2 tablespoons water

Remove the pan from the heat and stir in the water. Be careful because the water may bubble and foam up. Return the pan to the heat and stir with a wooden spoon or a heat-resistant spatula to dissolve any lumps.

Divide the caramel evenly between the custard cups. Tilt and rotate each cup so the caramel completely covers the bottoms. Place the custard cups in the baking dish or roasting pan.

CUSTARD

2½ cups milk
1 vanilla bean or 1 teaspoon vanilla paste

Place the milk in the 2-quart saucepan. Split the vanilla bean lengthwise and scrape out the seeds. Add the seeds and vanilla bean to the milk. If using the vanilla paste instead of the vanilla bean, add the paste to the milk. Warm the milk over medium heat to the point when tiny bubbles become visible at the edges. Remove the pan from the heat, cover it, and let the milk infuse.

3 extra-large eggs, at room temperature
3 extra-large egg yolks, at room temperature

Place the eggs and egg yolks in the bowl of an electric stand mixer or in a large bowl. Use the wire whip attachment or a hand-held mixer to whisk together until they are frothy.

½ cup granulated sugar

With the mixer on medium speed, slowly sprinkle on the sugar.

In a steady stream, pour in the warm milk and mix thoroughly.

Strain the custard into the measuring cup and remove the vanilla bean. Pour the custard into the cups, dividing it evenly among them.

1 quart boiling water

Place the roasting pan on the oven rack. Carefully pour boiling water into the baking dish until it reaches halfway up the sides of the cups or bowls.

Reduce the oven temperature to 325°F.

- Eight ½-cup custard cups or shallow ovenproof bowls
- 3-quart baking dish or roasting pan
- 2-quart heavy-bottomed saucepan
- Electric stand mixer with wire whip attachment, or a large mixing bowl and hand-held mixer
- Large fine-mesh strainer
- Large liquid measuring cup (2- or 4-cup capacity)
- Cooling rack
- Thin-bladed knife

Keeping
Store the baked custard in the custard cups, tightly covered with a double layer of plastic wrap, in the refrigerator up to 3 days.

Adding Style
Decorate the top of each custard with a sprig of fresh mint and a few raspberries or strawberries after turning them out of the cups.

Bake the custard for 40 minutes, until a toothpick or cake tester inserted in the center comes comes out slightly moist and the centers jiggle slightly when the pan is moved.

Remove the roasting pan from the oven and transfer the custard cups to a rack to cool completely.

To unmold the custards, run a thin-bladed knife around the edges of the custard cups. Place a serving plate over the top of a custard cup and invert the custard onto the plate. Repeat with each custard cup.

Serve the custards immediately or refrigerate until ready to serve.

Crème Fraîche Chocolate Cake

CRÈME FRAÎCHE is a thick, tangy cream with a nutty, slightly sour flavor and a velvety smooth texture. It's very easy to make your own crème fraîche by combining cream with buttermilk or sour cream and letting the ingredients stand at room temperature for about twelve hours until the mixture is thick (see page 497). Crème fraîche adds its characteristic tangy flavor to this yummy chocolate cake that is sure to please any chocolate lover. **Makes one 9½-inch round cake, 12 to 14 servings**

CAKE

1 tablespoon unsalted butter, softened	Center a rack in the oven and preheat it to 350°F. Using a paper towel or your fingertips, generously butter the inside of the springform pan. Or spray the inside of the pan with non-stick baking spray.
4 ounces (8 tablespoons, 1 stick) unsalted butter, softened	Place the butter in the bowl of an electric stand mixer or in a large bowl. Use the flat beater attachment or a hand-held mixer to beat the butter on medium speed until it's fluffy, about 2 minutes.
½ cup granulated sugar	Add the sugar to the butter and cream together thoroughly. Stop occasionally and scrape down the bottom and sides of the bowl with a rubber spatula.
2 extra-large eggs, at room temperature	Add the eggs one at a time, stopping to scrape down the bottom and sides of the bowl after each addition. At first the mixture may look curdled as the eggs are added, but as you stop and scrape down the bowl, the mixture will smooth out.

Essential Gear

- 9½-inch round springform pan
- Electric stand mixer with flat beater attachment and wire whip attachment, or large mixing bowl and hand-held mixer
- Rubber spatula
- Sifter
- Cooling rack

Keeping

Store the cake tightly wrapped in aluminum foil at room temperature up to 4 days. To freeze up to 3 months, wrap the cake tightly in several layers of plastic wrap and aluminum foil. Use a large piece of masking tape and an indelible marker to label and date the contents. If frozen, defrost overnight in the refrigerator and bring to room temperature before serving.

1 cup cake flour	Over a large piece of waxed or parchment paper or a bowl, sift to-
½ cup unsweetened cocoa powder (natural or Dutch-processed)	gether the flour, cocoa powder, and baking soda. Add the salt and toss together to blend well.
¼ teaspoon baking soda	
¼ teaspoon salt	

⅔ cup crème fraîche (see page 497)	Add the dry ingredients to the butter mixture in 3 stages, alternating with the crème fraîche. Blend well after each addition. Stir in the vanilla.
1 teaspoon pure vanilla extract or vanilla paste	

4 extra-large egg whites, at room temperature	Place the egg whites in the grease-free bowl of an electric stand mixer or large grease-free bowl. Use the wire whip attachment or a hand-held mixer to whip the egg whites on medium speed until frothy. Add the cream of tartar and whip on medium-high speed until the egg whites hold soft peaks. Gradually sprinkle on the sugar and whip the egg whites until they hold firm and glossy, but not stiff, peaks.
¼ teaspoon cream of tartar	
½ cup granulated sugar	

Fold the whipped egg whites into the cake batter in 3 additions, blending thoroughly.

Transfer the cake batter to the pan. Bake for 35 minutes, until a cake tester inserted in the center comes out clean. Remove the pan from the oven and cool on a rack.

Release the sides of the springform pan and lift off of the cake.

GARNISH

¼ cup confectioners' sugar	Dust the top of the cake with confectioners' sugar.
⅓ cup crème fraîche	Serve each slice of cake with a dollop of crème fraîche.

Irish Soda Bread

THIS CLASSIC quick bread made with buttermilk and leavened with baking soda is loved throughout Ireland and has been made in some form for centuries. Traditionally, soda bread has caraway seeds, but can be made without them. I like to add raisins to soda bread and sometimes include walnuts. This is great served warm with butter and jam. **Makes one 8-inch round loaf**

Essential Gear
- Baking sheet
- Parchment paper sheet or non-stick liner
- Food processor
- Chef's knife
- Cooling rack

Center a rack in the oven and preheat it to 425°F. Line the baking sheet with parchment paper or a non-stick liner.

3 cups all-purpose flour **2 tablespoons granulated sugar** **2 tablespoons caraway seeds (optional)** **1 teaspoon baking soda** **½ teaspoon salt**	In the work bowl of a food processor fitted with the steel blade, combine the flour, sugar, caraway seeds (if using), baking soda, and salt. Pulse a few times to blend.
1 cup raisins	Add the raisins to the flour mixture and pulse a few times to mix.
1¼ cups buttermilk	With the food processor running, pour the buttermilk through the feed tube and process until the dough forms itself into a ball, about 30 seconds.

Dust a large piece of waxed or parchment paper with flour and turn the dough out onto it. Knead the dough briefly and form it into an 8-inch round, about ½ inch thick. Use a sharp knife to cut a shallow X in the top of the round.

Transfer the soda bread to the lined baking sheet.

Bake for 35 minutes, until golden and set. If a cake tester is inserted in the center, it will come out clean..

Remove the baking sheet from the oven and cool completely on a rack.

Keeping

Store the soda bread tightly wrapped in aluminum foil at room temperature up to 4 days. To freeze up to 4 months, wrap tightly in several layers of plastic wrap and aluminum foil. Use a large piece of masking tape and an indelible marker to label and date the contents. If frozen, defrost overnight in the refrigerator and bring to room temperature before serving.

Adding Style

Add ½ cup roughly chopped almonds, walnuts, or pecans when adding the raisins.

Sour Cream Coffee Cake

T HIS IS THE TYPE of cake you dream about when you think of a classic coffee cake. It's rich with the flavor of sour cream and has a crunchy filling and topping made with brown sugar, cinnamon, and chopped walnuts. It is excellent served warm for breakfast, afternoon tea, or just about anytime. This cake holds a lot of warm, yummy memories for me because my grandmother used to bake it often when I was young. **Makes one 9½-inch round cake, 12 to 14 servings**

Essential Gear

- 9½-inch round spring-form pan
- Electric stand mixer with flat beater attachment, or large mixing bowl and hand-held mixer
- Rubber spatula
- Sifter
- Cooling rack

CAKE

1 tablespoon unsalted butter, softened	Center a rack in the oven and preheat it to 350°F. Using a paper towel or your fingertips, generously butter the inside of the pan.

6 ounces (12 tablespoons, 1½ sticks) unsalted butter, softened	Place the butter in the bowl of an electric stand mixer or in a large bowl. Use the flat beater attachment or a hand-held mixer to beat the butter on medium speed until it's fluffy, about 2 minutes.
1½ cups granulated sugar	Add the sugar to the butter, and cream together well. Stop occasionally and scrape down the bottom and sides of the bowl with a rubber spatula.
3 extra-large eggs, at room temperature	Add the eggs one at a time, stopping to scrape down the bottom and sides of the bowl after each addition. At first the mixture may look curdled as the eggs are added, but as you stop and scrape down the bowl, the mixture will smooth out.
1 cup sour cream **2 teaspoons pure vanilla extract**	Add the sour cream and vanilla to the butter mixture and blend together thoroughly
3 cups all-purpose flour **1 tablespoon baking powder** **½ teaspoon salt**	Over a large piece of waxed or parchment paper or a bowl, sift together the flour and baking powder. Add the salt and toss together to blend. Add the dry ingredients to the butter mixture in 3 stages, blending thoroughly after each.

TOPPING

½ cup walnuts, finely chopped **¼ cup granulated sugar** **¼ cup firmly packed light brown sugar** **½ teaspoon ground cinnamon**	Combine the walnuts, sugar, brown sugar, and cinnamon in a small bowl and toss together to blend thoroughly.

ASSEMBLY

Transfer half of the batter to the prepared pan. The batter is very thick, so use a rubber spatula to spread it evenly into the pan.

Sprinkle half of the topping over the batter in the pan.

Transfer the remaining batter to the pan and spread it out evenly over the topping. Sprinkle the remaining topping over the batter.

Keeping

Store the cake tightly wrapped in aluminum foil at room temperature up to 4 days. To freeze up to 3 months, wrap the cake tightly in several layers of plastic wrap and aluminum foil. Use a large piece of masking tape and an indelible marker to label and date the contents. If frozen, defrost overnight in the refrigerator and bring to room temperature before serving.

Making a Change

Replace the walnuts with pecans, whole unblanched almonds, or macadamia nuts.

Bake the cake for 40 to 45 minutes, until a cake tester inserted into the center comes out with a few moist crumbs clinging to it.

Remove the pan from the oven and cool on a rack. Remove the sides of the springform pan (page 36) and lift off of the cake.

Slice the cake into serving pieces.

Sour Cream–White Chocolate Cheesecake

A COMBINATION of sour cream, cream cheese, and white chocolate makes a rich, dense, and very creamy cheesecake. This cheesecake is baked directly in the pan, with no crust. After the cheesecake is baked, a sour cream mixture is spread over the top and it's returned to the oven for a few minutes to set the topping. Although very tasty on its own, this cheesecake is even better when served with raspberry sauce. Cheesecake is the perfect do-ahead dessert because it needs hours to cool and chill. **Makes one 9¹/₂-inch round cake, 12 to 14 servings**

Center a rack in the oven and preheat it to 400°F. Use a double layer of heavy-duty foil to wrap around the bottom of the pan. This prevents any water from the water bath from seeping into the pan.

12 ounces white chocolate, finely chopped

Place the chopped chocolate in the top of a double boiler over low heat. Stir often with a rubber spatula to help melt evenly. Remove the top pan of the double boiler and wipe the bottom and sides very dry.

Or place the chopped chocolate in a microwave-safe bowl and melt on low power for 30-second bursts. Stir with a rubber spatula after each burst.

1¹/₂ pounds cream cheese, softened
¹/₂ cup granulated sugar
¹/₄ teaspoon salt

In the work bowl of a food processor fitted with the steel blade, combine the cream cheese, sugar, and salt. Process for about 1 minute, then scrape down the sides of the work bowl with a rubber spatula.

4 extra-large eggs, at room temperature
1¹/₂ cups sour cream
1 tablespoon pure vanilla extract

Lightly beat the eggs in a small bowl and add to the cream cheese mixture. Add the melted white chocolate, the sour cream, and vanilla. Process until the mixture is thoroughly blended and smooth, about 1 minute.

Essential Gear

- 9¹/₂-inch round spring-form pan
- Heavy-duty aluminum foil
- Double boiler
- Two rubber spatulas
- Food processor or rolling pin
- Electric stand mixer with flat beater attachment, or hand-held mixer and large mixing bowl
- 12-inch round cake pan or large roasting pan
- Cooling rack
- Thin-bladed knife

Keeping

Store the cheesecake tightly covered with aluminum foil in the refrigerator up to 4 days. To freeze up to 2 months, wrap the cake tightly in several layers of plastic wrap and aluminum foil. Use a large piece of masking tape and an indelible marker to label and date the contents. If frozen, defrost overnight in the refrigerator and bring to room temperature before serving.

Transfer the mixture to the springform pan. Smooth the top with a rubber spatula.

1 quart boiling water

Place the springform pan in the larger pan and set the pan on the oven rack. Carefully pour the boiling water into the bottom pan until it reaches halfway up the side of the springform pan. Baking the cake in a water bath cushions it from the heat and adds extra moisture to the oven, which keeps the top from cracking.

Bake the cake for 1 hour, until very pale golden on top and the center jiggles only slightly when moved. Remove the cheesecake pan from the oven and place on a rack to cool for 10 to 15 minutes. The top of the cake will sink slightly as the cake cools.

SOUR CREAM TOPPING

2 cups sour cream
2 tablespoons granulated sugar
2 teaspoons pure vanilla extract

In a small bowl, combine the sour cream, sugar, and vanilla. Stir together until completely blended and smooth. Spread this mixture evenly over the top of the cheesecake. Return the cheesecake to the oven for 5 minutes to set the topping.

Remove the pan from the oven and place it on a cooling rack. Run a sharp thin-bladed knife around the edge of the cheesecake so it won't stick to the pan as it cools. Let the cheesecake cool to room temperature.

Cover the top of the cheesecake with waxed paper and wrap the pan tightly with aluminum foil. Refrigerate the cake for at least 6 hours before serving. To unmold the cheesecake, dip a thin-bladed knife in hot water and dry, then run it around the inner edge of the pan; release the clip on the rim of the pan and gently lift it off the cake.

Chill the cheesecake until ready to serve.

Adding Style
Serve slices of the cheesecake with Raspberry Sauce (see page 143) and a few fresh raspberries.

CHAPTER
17

CHEESES

ANY PEOPLE have experienced cheese in baking through cheesecake. However, there are other baked goods that can be made using cheese as a main ingredient. Cheese can be baked into dough, used as a filling, and baked into the body of a cake, as with cheesecake. In general, cheese creates a delicate and moist texture. And, depending on the type of cheese that is used, a very distinct flavor can be achieved. This is especially true when using cheeses such as mascarpone and chèvre (soft) goat cheese. Also, in my judgment, there is a huge difference between store-bought, restaurant-ordered, and homemade cheese desserts. Personally, anything baked with cheese is near the top of my favorites list.

All of the cheeses used in this chapter are always available. Cream cheese is easy to find in most supermarkets. Ricotta cheese is commonly sold in a small plastic tub in most supermarkets, but it's possible to find a higher quality ricotta in a specialty deli or cheese shop. Mascarpone also comes in small, round, plastic tubs and chèvre goat cheese comes in round logs and disks, tightly sealed in plastic. Neither of these cheeses is usually found in supermarkets. You will have to rely on a deli or specialty cheese shop to find mascarpone and chèvre goat cheese.

TIPS AND TECHNIQUES

When buying any of these cheeses, it's essential to check the expiration date. Do not buy low-fat, fat-free, or whipped cream cheese for these recipes, because they don't have the same body and texture as full-fat cream cheese. Make sure to always buy the full-fat or whole-milk variety of ricotta cheese for the same reason. Always buy plain chèvre goat cheese, not the flavored variety, for sweet pastry recipes.

Store all of these cheeses in the refrigerator, preferably not on the door. Also, when opened, store them away from other strongly flavored foods, as they will easily pick up other flavors.

Bring cream cheese, mascarpone, and chèvre goat cheese to room temperature before using. Ricotta cheese can be used straight out of the refrigerator; however, it needs to be drained of excess water before use. To do this, line a mesh strainer with a double thickness of paper towels and transfer the ricotta cheese to the paper towels. Place the strainer over a bowl and let the ricotta drain for thirty minutes. Replace the damp paper towels with dry ones and again let the ricotta drain for thirty minutes. The ricotta can be drained as long as overnight. To do this, tightly cover it with plastic wrap and place the strainer and bowl in the refrigerator.

Chèvre Goat Cheese Cake

YOU MAY NOT THINK that goat cheese would be used in a dessert, but chèvre goat cheese gives this cake a delicate, creamy texture and mildly tangy flavor. You can either bake this cake with no crust or add a crust made from finely chopped walnuts for extra texture and flavor. This cake needs to be made at least a day before you plan to serve it because it needs several hours to cool and chill. Although the cake is excellent on its own, try serving it with raspberry sauce or caramel sauce. **Makes one 9-inch round cake, 12 to 14 servings**

Center a rack in the oven and preheat it to 325°F.

2 tablespoons granulated sugar	Spray the inside of the springform pan with non-stick baking spray. Sprinkle the inside of the pan with sugar, then tilt and rotate the pan to distribute the sugar evenly over the bottom and sides. Turn the pan upside down over the sink and shake out any excess sugar. Use a double layer of heavy-duty foil to wrap around the bottom of the pan. This prevents any water from the water bath from seeping into the pan.
6 extra-large egg yolks, at room temperature 1 cup superfine sugar	Place the egg yolks and sugar in the bowl of an electric stand mixer or a large bowl. Use the wire whip attachment or a hand-held mixer to beat on medium-high speed until the mixture is very thick and pale colored and holds a slowly dissolving ribbon as the beater is lifted, about 5 minutes.
1½ pounds chèvre goat cheese, softened	With the mixer running on medium speed, add the goat cheese a few tablespoons at a time to the egg yolk mixture. Beat until the mixture is smooth.
3 tablespoons all-purpose flour 2 tablespoons orange liqueur Finely grated zest of 1 large orange 1 tablespoon freshly squeezed orange juice	Add the flour, orange liqueur, orange zest, and orange juice to the egg mixture and blend until smooth.
6 extra-large egg whites, at room temperature ¼ teaspoon cream of tartar ½ cup superfine sugar	Place the egg whites in the grease-free bowl of an electric stand mixer or a large grease-free bowl. Use the wire whip attachment or a hand-held mixer to whip the egg whites on medium speed until frothy. Add the cream of tartar and continue to whip on medium-high speed. Sprinkle on the sugar and continue to whip until the egg whites hold soft peaks.

Essential Gear

- 9-inch round spring-form pan
- Heavy-duty aluminum foil
- Electric stand mixer with wire whip attachment, or hand-held mixer and large mixing bowl
- Microplane grater or citrus zester
- Rubber spatula
- 12-inch round cake pan or large roasting pan
- Cooling rack
- Thin-bladed knife

Keeping

Store the cheesecake tightly covered with aluminum foil in the refrigerator up to 4 days. To freeze up to 2 months, wrap the cake tightly in several layers of plastic wrap and aluminum foil. Use a large piece of masking tape and an indelible marker to label and date the contents. If frozen, defrost overnight in the refrigerator and bring to room temperature before serving.

Adding Style

Serve slices of the cheesecake with Raspberry Sauce (see Meyer Lemon Soufflés, page 143) and a few fresh raspberries, or caramel sauce (see Rum-Raisin Pound Cake, page 614).

Making a Change

Make a walnut and cookie crust for the cheesecake

In 3 stages, fold the whipped egg whites into the cheesecake mixture, blending thoroughly after each edition.

Transfer the batter to the prepared springform pan. Smooth the top with a rubber spatula.

(see Malted Milk Chocolate Cheesecake, page 419).

1 quart boiling water

Place the springform pan in the larger pan and set the pan on the oven rack. Carefully pour the boiling water into the bottom pan until it reaches halfway up the side of the springform pan. Baking the cake in a water bath cushions it from the heat and adds extra moisture to the oven, which keeps the top from cracking.

Loosely cover the top of the cake with aluminum foil and bake the cake for 45 minutes. Remove the foil and bake another 10 to 15 minutes, until the center of the cake doesn't jiggle when the cake pan is lightly shaken. Remove the cheesecake pan from the oven, remove the foil from the outside of the pan, and place on a rack to cool.

Cover the top of the cake with waxed paper and wrap the pan tightly with aluminum foil. Chill the cake for at least 4 hours before serving. To unmold the cake, dip a thin-bladed knife in hot water and dry, then run it around the inner edge of the pan; release the clip on the rim of the pan and gently lift it off the cake.

Mascarpone Cheesecake with Almond and Butter Cookie Crust

THIS CREAMY mascarpone cheesecake has a unique and special flavor that comes from the cheese. The cheesecake sits in a crunchy almond and butter cookie crust that's a great contrast to the cake. Although this cheesecake is excellent on its own, try serving it with raspberry sauce and fresh raspberries. Like other cheesecakes, this one must be made in advance of serving because it needs hours to cool and chill. **Makes one 9½-inch round cake, 12 to 14 servings**

Essential Gear

- 9½-inch round springform pan
- Heavy-duty aluminum foil
- Food processor or rolling pin
- Rubber spatula
- Electric stand mixer with flat beater attachment, or hand-held mixer and large mixing bowl
- 12-inch round cake pan or large roasting pan
- Cooling rack
- Thin-bladed knife

Center a rack in the oven and preheat it to 350°F.

1 tablespoon unsalted butter, softened

Using a paper towel or your fingertips, butter the inside of the springform pan. Use a double layer of heavy-duty foil to wrap around the bottom of the pan. This prevents any water from seeping into the pan.

ALMOND AND BUTTER COOKIE CRUST

1 cup whole, unblanched almonds

3½ ounces (about 9) butter cookies, wafers, or shortbread

2 tablespoons light brown sugar

In the work bowl of a food processor fitted with the steel blade, combine the almonds, cookies, and sugar. Pulse until the mixture is finely ground, about 2 minutes. Or place the almonds, cookies, and sugar in a sturdy plastic bag and seal it. Use a rolling pin to crush the mixture to a very fine crumb consistency.

2 ounces (4 tablespoons, ½ stick) unsalted butter, melted and cooled

Transfer the crumb mixture to a medium bowl and add the butter. Use a rubber spatula to toss the mixture together and moisten all the crumbs.

Using your fingers, press the crumbs evenly into the bottom and partway up the sides of the springform pan. Chill the crust while preparing the filling.

CHEESECAKE

12 ounces mascarpone, at room temperature

6 ounces cream cheese, softened

Place the mascarpone and the cream cheese in the bowl of an electric stand mixer or in a large bowl. Use the flat beater attachment or hand-held mixer to beat the cheeses on medium speed until they are fluffy, about 2 minutes.

1 cup granulated sugar

2 tablespoons light brown sugar

¼ teaspoon salt

Add the granulated sugar, brown sugar, and salt to the cheese and mix thoroughly.

3 extra-large eggs, at room temperature

One at a time, add the eggs to the cheese mixture, beating well after each addition. The eggs will sit on top of the mixture, so stop frequently and scrape down the bottom and sides of the bowl with a rubber spatula to help mix evenly. The mixture may look curdled as the eggs are added, but as you scrape down the bowl, the mixture will smooth out.

2 tablespoons freshly squeezed lemon juice

2 teaspoons pure vanilla extract or vanilla paste

Add the lemon juice and vanilla to the cheese mixture and blend well.

2 cups sour cream

Add the sour cream to the cheese mixture and blend thoroughly.

Turn the batter into the crust in the springform pan. Use a rubber spatula to smooth and even the top.

Keeping

Store the cheesecake tightly covered with aluminum foil in the refrigerator up to 4 days. To freeze up to 2 months, wrap the cake tightly in several layers of plastic wrap and aluminum foil. Use a large piece of masking tape and an indelible marker to label and date the contents. If frozen, defrost overnight in the refrigerator and bring to room temperature before serving.

Adding Style

Serve slices of the cheesecake with Raspberry Sauce (see Meyer Lemon Soufflés, page 143) and a few fresh raspberries.

1 quart boiling water	Place the springform pan in the larger pan and set the pan on the oven rack. Carefully pour the boiling water into the bottom pan until it reaches halfway up the side of the springform pan. Baking the cake in a water bath cushions it from the heat and adds extra moisture to the oven, which keeps the top from cracking.
	Bake the cake for 1 hour and 15 minutes, until the top is light golden and jiggles only slightly when the pan is moved. Turn off the oven and leave the cheesecake in the oven with the door closed until it is cool, about 1 hour. Remove the cheesecake pan from the oven, remove the foil from the outside of the pan, and place on a rack to cool.
	Cover the top of the cheesecake with waxed paper and wrap the pan tightly in aluminum foil. Refrigerate the cake for at least 6 hours before serving. To unmold the cake, dip a thin-bladed knife in hot water and dry, then run it around the inner edge of the pan; release the clip on the rim of the pan and gently lift it off the cake.

Mascarpone Layer Cake with Fresh Berries

A BLEND of mascarpone, sour cream, and brown sugar makes the layers in this cake rich, dense, and full of flavor. The cake layers are brushed with sugar syrup and filled with a creamy blend of mascarpone and whipped cream, which is topped with thinly sliced fresh strawberries. The whole cake is iced with the same mixture as the filling and decorated with toasted sliced almonds and fresh strawberries. This gorgeous cake is the perfect way to announce that spring has arrived. **Makes one 9-inch round cake, 12 to 14 servings**

Essential Gear
- 9 × 2-inch round cake pan
- Scissors
- Parchment paper
- 2 rubber spatulas
- Electric stand mixer with flat beater attachment and wire whip attachment, or large mixing bowl and hand-held mixer
- Sifter
- Cooling rack
- Small saucepan
- Serrated knife
- 2-inch natural-bristle pastry brush
- 10-inch flexible-blade icing spatula
- 12- or 14-inch pastry bag and large open star tip

Keeping
Store the cake, loosely tented with aluminum foil, in

CAKE

Center a rack in the oven and preheat it to 325°F.

1 tablespoon unsalted butter, softened	Using a paper towel or your fingertips, generously butter the inside of the cake pan, coating it thoroughly
2 teaspoons all-purpose flour	Dust the inside of the pan with the flour. Shake and tilt the pan to evenly distribute the flour, then turn the pan over and shake out the excess over the sink.
	Cut a round of parchment paper to fit the bottom of the pan. Butter the parchment paper round and place in the pan, butter-side up.

6 ounces (12 tablespoons, 1½ sticks) unsalted butter, softened	Place the butter in the bowl of an electric stand mixer or in a large bowl. Use the flat beater attachment or hand-held mixer to beat the butter on medium speed until it's fluffy, about 2 minutes.
1 cup plus 2 tablespoons superfine sugar	Gradually add the sugar to the butter and cream together well. Stop occasionally and scrape down the bottom and sides of the bowl with a rubber spatula.
3 extra-large eggs, at room temperature	One at a time, add the eggs to the butter mixture, stopping to scrape down the bottom and sides of the bowl after each addition. At first the mixture may look curdled as the eggs are added, but as you stop and scrape down the bowl, the mixture will smooth out.
¼ cup sour cream **1 teaspoon pure vanilla extract or vanilla paste**	Add the sour cream and vanilla to the butter mixture and blend together well.
1½ cups cake flour **½ teaspoon baking powder** **¼ teaspoon baking soda** **¼ teaspoon salt**	Over a large piece of waxed or parchment paper or a bowl, sift together the flour, baking powder, and baking soda. Add the salt and toss to blend thoroughly.
	With the mixer on low speed, add the dry ingredients in 4 stages. Blend thoroughly after each addition and stop often to scrape down the bottom and sides of the bowl with a rubber spatula.
	Transfer the batter to the cake pan and smooth the top with a rubber spatula.
	Bake the cake for 45 minutes, until the top is golden and a cake tester inserted in the center comes out with no crumbs clinging to it.
	Remove the cake pan from the oven and cool completely on a rack. Invert the pan to remove the cake, then peel the parchment paper off the back of the cake. Re-invert the cake onto a plate or a cardboard cake circle.

SUGAR SYRUP

¼ cup granulated sugar **½ cup water**	Combine the sugar and water in a small saucepan. Bring to a boil over medium-high heat, without stirring, to dissolve the sugar. Remove from the heat and cool to room temperature.

MASCARPONE FILLING AND ICING

2¼ cups heavy whipping cream	Place the cream in the chilled bowl of an electric stand mixer or a large bowl. Using the wire whip attachment or a hand-held mixer, whip the cream on medium speed until it is frothy.

the refrigerator up to 2 days. Place several toothpicks in the top outer edges of the cake to hold the foil away from it so it won't mar the icing.

Streamlining

Bake the cake up to 2 days before assembling and keep it tightly covered with a double layer of plastic wrap at room temperature. To freeze the unfilled cake up to 3 months, wrap it snugly in several layers of plastic wrap and place in a freezer bag. Use a large piece of masking tape and an indelible marker to label and date the contents. If frozen, defrost the layers overnight in the refrigerator.

Making a Change

Replace the sliced almonds with toasted, finely chopped walnuts or hazelnuts.

Replace the strawberries with raspberries, blueberries, blackberries, or thinly sliced peaches, apricots, or nectarines.

Recovering from a Mishap

If one of the cake layers breaks during assembly, patch it together with some of the filling.

⅓ cup firmly packed light brown sugar	Gradually add the sugar and continue to whip the cream on medium speed until it holds soft peaks.
1 pound mascarpone, at room temperature	Place the mascarpone in the clean bowl of an electric stand mixer or a medium bowl. Use the flat beater attachment or a hand-held mixer to beat gently on low speed for about 30 seconds. Take care not to beat too much or the mascarpone will become grainy.
2 to 3 tablespoons heavy whipping cream or buttermilk	Stir ⅓ of the whipped cream into the mascarpone, then fold in the remaining whipped cream in 2 or 3 stages. If the filling is too thick to spread, stir in 2 or 3 tablespoons of whipping cream or buttermilk.

ASSEMBLY

With your fingertips, gently peel the skin off the top of the cake. Using a serrated knife, cut the cake into 3 equal layers horizontally (see page 34). Place the bottom layer on a serving plate or a cardboard cake circle. Place strips of waxed paper around the bottom edges of the cake to protect the plate while assembling the cake. Use a pastry brush to brush the layer with the cooled sugar syrup.

4 cups strawberries, washed, dried, hulled, and sliced very thinly	With a flexible-blade spatula, evenly spread about 3 tablespoons of the filling over the cake layer. Cover the filling with a layer of the thinly sliced strawberries. Spread another thin layer of the filling over the strawberries.

Position the second cake layer evenly over the filling and brush with the sugar syrup. Spread about 3 tablespoons of the filling over the layer. Cover the filling with another layer of thinly sliced strawberries, then spread with a thin layer of filling.

Position the top layer over the filling and gently press down. Brush the layer with sugar syrup. Reserve about ⅔ cup of the filling for the final decoration and spread the remaining filling and icing over the sides and top of the cake. |
| 1½ cups sliced almonds, lightly toasted | Press the toasted sliced almonds onto the sides of the cake just up to, but not over, the top edge. |

Fit the pastry bag with the star tip and fill with the reserved icing. Pipe a border of shells around the top outer edge of the cake and pipe a large rosette in the center (see page 44). Arrange 2 halves of a large strawberry around the rosette, with their points facing in opposite directions.

Serve immediately, cutting the cake into wedges, or refrigerate for up to 4 hours, covered with waxed paper.

Ricotta Cheesecake with Chocolate Wafer Cookie Crust

RICOTTA CHEESECAKE is an Italian classic. Usually the cheesecake filling is enclosed in a cookie crust or pastry dough crust. This chocolate wafer cookie crust is a bit unusual, but I chose it to hold the creamy cheesecake filling because it makes an interesting textural and flavor contrast. I like to add chopped candied orange peel to this cheesecake to make it in the classic way, but the orange peel can be left out and the cake will still be very tasty. This is an elegant dessert to serve with afternoon coffee or tea or after a light dinner. The cake needs to be made at least a day before you plan to serve it, so there is enough time for it to cool and chill. **Makes one 9$^1/_2$-inch round cake, 12 to 14 servings**

Essential Gear

- Large fine-mesh strainer
- 9$^1/_2$-inch round spring-form pan
- Food processor or rolling pin
- Microplane grater or citrus zester
- Rubber spatula
- Baking sheet
- Cooling rack
- Thin-bladed knife

2 pounds ricotta cheese

Line the strainer with a double thickness of paper towels and transfer the ricotta cheese to the paper towels. Place the strainer over a bowl and let the ricotta drain for 30 minutes. Replace the damp paper towels with dry ones and again let the ricotta drain for 30 minutes. The ricotta can be drained as long as overnight. To do this, tightly cover it with plastic wrap and place the strainer and bowl in the refrigerator. Draining the excess water off the ricotta makes a creamier cheesecake filling.

Center a rack in the oven and preheat it to 325°F.

1 tablespoon unsalted butter, softened

Use your fingertips or a paper towel to butter the inside of the springform pan.

Keeping

Store the cheesecake covered with waxed paper and tightly wrapped with aluminum foil in the refrigerator up to 4 days. To freeze up to 2 months, wrap the cake pan tightly in several layers of plastic wrap and aluminum foil. Use a large piece of masking tape and an indelible marker to label and date the contents. If frozen, defrost overnight in the refrigerator and bring to room temperature at least 30 minutes before serving.

CHOCOLATE WAFER COOKIE CRUST

One 9-ounce package chocolate wafer cookies
2 tablespoons granulated sugar

In the work bowl of a food processor fitted with the steel blade, combine the cookies and sugar. Pulse until the cookies are finely ground, about 2 minutes. Or place the cookies in a sturdy plastic bag and seal it. Use a rolling pin to crush the cookies to a very fine crumb consistency. Add the sugar to the cookies, seal the bag, and shake to blend together evenly.

4 ounces (8 tablespoons, 1 stick) unsalted butter, melted and cooled

Transfer the cookie crumbs to a medium bowl and add the butter. Use a rubber spatula or a spoon to toss the mixture together to moisten all of the cookie crumbs.

Press the crumbs evenly into the bottom and about halfway up the sides of the springform pan. Refrigerate the pan while preparing the filling.

Making a Change

Replace the orange zest and candied orange peel with lemon zest and candied lemon peel.

Replace the whipping cream with light rum.

Add 3 tablespoons lightly toasted pine nuts to the

RICOTTA CHEESECAKE

Place the drained ricotta cheese in the work bowl of a food processor fitted with the steel blade. Process until the ricotta is smooth and creamy, about 1 minute.

²/₃ cup granulated sugar

Add the sugar to the ricotta and process until thoroughly blended and smooth.

4 extra-large eggs, at room temperature
¼ cup heavy whipping cream
Finely grated zest of 1 large orange
1½ teaspoons pure vanilla extract or vanilla paste
1 tablespoon all-purpose flour
¼ teaspoon ground cinnamon
⅛ teaspoon salt

Add the eggs, cream, orange zest, vanilla, flour, cinnamon, and salt to the ricotta mixture and process until fully blended, about 1 minute.

⅓ cup finely chopped candied orange peel (page 171, optional)

Remove the work bowl and remove the steel blade. Stir the chopped candied orange peel, if using, into the ricotta mixture evenly.

Transfer the batter into the springform pan. Use a rubber spatula to smooth and even the top.

Place the springform pan on a baking sheet. Bake the cake for 1 hour and 15 minutes, until the top is light golden and set, but jiggles slightly. Remove the pan from the oven and transfer the cheesecake to a rack to cool completely. Cover the top of the cheesecake with waxed paper and wrap the pan tightly in aluminum foil. Refrigerate the cake for at least 6 hours before serving. To unmold the cake, dip a thin-bladed knife in hot water and dry, then run it around the inner edge of the pan; release the clip on the rim of the pan and gently lift it off the cake.

batter before turning it into the pan.

Add 2 ounces coarsely chopped milk chocolate or dark chocolate to the batter before turning it into the pan.

Adding Style

Drizzle the top of the cooled and chilled cheesecake with fine lines or designs of dark chocolate (see page 43). Let the chocolate set for 15 minutes in the refrigerator before serving or storing.

Serve each slice of cheesecake with Raspberry Sauce (see Meyer Lemon Soufflés, page 143).

Pinwheel Cookies

THESE FESTIVE COOKIES are made with delicate cream cheese pastry dough. Bright spots of jam peek out from the center when the cookies are assembled. The dough is soft and can be a little trouble to work with, but these are well worth the extra effort. **Makes 2 dozen cookies**

Line the baking sheets with parchment paper or non-stick liners.

6 ounces (12 tablespoons, 1½ sticks) unsalted butter, softened **8 ounces cream cheese, at room temperature**	Place the butter and cream cheese in the bowl of an electric stand mixer or in a large bowl. Use the flat beater attachment or a hand-held mixer to beat together until light and fluffy, about 2 minutes.
1 extra-large egg yolk, at room temperature	Add the egg yolk to the butter mixture and blend together well. The egg yolk will sit on top of the mixture, so stop and scrape down the sides and bottom of the bowl with a rubber spatula to encourage even mixing. The mixture may look curdled as the eggs are added, but as you scrape down the bowl, the mixture will smooth out.
1½ cups all-purpose flour **1 tablespoon baking powder**	Over a large piece of waxed or parchment paper or a bowl, sift together the flour and baking powder. Add to the butter mixture in 2 stages, beating well after each addition.
	Divide the dough in two and shape each piece into a disk. Wrap the dough disks tightly in plastic and chill until firm, at least 2 hours.
	Adjust the oven racks to the upper and lower thirds and preheat the oven to 375°F.

Work with one disk of dough and keep the other refrigerated. Roll out each disk of dough between sheets of lightly floured waxed or parchment paper to a large rectangle about 9 × 18 inches. Carefully peel the paper off the top of the dough. Cut the rectangle into 3-inch squares, using a ruler as a guide. Carefully peel the squares off the other piece of paper.

Place the dough squares evenly on the lined baking sheets, leaving at least 1 inch of space between them.

Cut the corners of each square almost to the center, leaving them attached at the center. Fold half of every corner to the center and press down firmly so they will stick. This forms a pinwheel.

Essential Gear

- Two baking sheets
- Two parchment paper sheets or non-stick liners
- Electric stand mixer with flat beater attachment, or large mixing bowl and hand-held mixer
- Rubber spatula
- Sifter
- Rolling pin
- Ruler
- Small sharp knife
- Two cooling racks

Keeping

Store the cookies in a single layer in an airtight plastic container at room temperature up to 3 days. To freeze up to 4 months, wrap the container tightly in several layers of plastic wrap and aluminum foil. Use a large piece of masking tape and an indelible marker to label and date the contents. If frozen, defrost overnight in the refrigerator and bring to room temperature before serving.

1½ cups strawberry, apricot, or raspberry jam	Place a teaspoon of jam in the center of each pinwheel over the sealed tips.
	Bake the pinwheels for 7 minutes. Switch the baking sheets and bake the pinwheels for another 7 to 8 minutes, until light golden.
	Remove the baking sheets from the oven and cool the cookies completely on the baking sheets on racks.

GARNISH

½ cup confectioners' sugar	Dust the tops of the pinwheels with confectioners' sugar

VI.

SPICES

AND HERBS

THE USE OF SPICES AND HERBS gives a special personality to baked goods. Their flavors are tantalizing and they have a way of transporting you. It's always fun to watch someone's expression when they bite into a baked dessert made with spices or herbs. You know they're thinking, "What is that?" ✱ Everyone knows the more common spices, such as vanilla and cinnamon. But there are many others that are equally good. Nutmeg, anise, and cardamom are great to use in baked desserts, as is my personal favorite, ginger. ✱ Like spices, herbs are perfect to bake with. Lavender and rosemary are two of my favorite herbs, although you may not often think of them in sweet goods. Additional favorites are lemon verbena, chocolate mint, and cinnamon basil. It is okay to experiment with other herbs that you like but make sure you taste-test before serving them. Just about any spice can be found in large supermarkets and other food shops, but for some herbs you may have to find a specialty source or grow them yourself. ✱ Some of the recipes in this section will be completely new to your family and friends. But I can assure you, once they experience desserts baked with spices and herbs, they are going to want more.

18

SPICES

F YOU'RE LOOKING to spice up your life, you are in the right place—the recipes in this chapter use a variety of spices as the primary ingredient. I love baked goods made with spices because there are so many unique flavors that it's always exciting. There's also something adventurous about baking with spices. The smells are rich and unusual and transport you to an exotic place. And the flavors that come through are both tantalizing and, I think, stimulating. This chapter contains recipes using spices such as allspice, anise, cardamom, cinnamon, cloves, ginger, nutmeg, and vanilla. Some of the recipes call for five-spice powder as an option. Five-spice powder is a seasoning used primarily in Chinese cooking and is made from a combination of spices such as star anise, cloves, cinnamon, fennel, and pepper. All these recipes will definitely excite your taste buds.

It's easy to find spices any time of the year in your local supermarket, health food store, or specialty shop.

TIPS AND TECHNIQUES

As a general rule, it's best to buy spices whole and grind or grate them yourself using a clean coffee grinder or a specialty grater. The reason for buying whole spices is that if you buy them ground, they will not be as flavorful because they begin to lose flavor quickly as soon as they're ground. But it is an option to buy already ground spices, since it may be difficult to find some whole spices. Whether the spice is bought whole or ground, usually in a tightly sealed glass jar, check for an expiration date. Occasionally spices are sold in bulk bins, in which case you want to smell the spice to make sure that it has good aroma, and look closely for even color and consistency. Also, watch that there are no foreign materials mixed with the spices, like stems.

Store cardamom pods in a tightly sealed glass jar in the refrigerator for up to 1 year. Store ground cardamom under the same conditions, no longer than 3 months. Store both whole and ground spices in tightly sealed glass jars in a cool, dry place. Use whole spices within 2 years and ground spices within 6 months.

For grinding allspice berries, cardamom, and cloves, use a clean coffee grinder and grind them to a fine powder. Anise seeds and dried ground ginger and cinnamon are used in the form in which they are purchased. However, fresh ginger must be peeled and chopped using a chef's knife, according to the directions in the recipe. Fresh peeled ginger is now available in jars, which is a good option if you would rather skip the step of peeling it yourself. Nutmeg can be purchased and used ground, but I always buy whole nutmegs and use a specialty grater to obtain fine shavings. You have three options with vanilla, depending on the recipe. Vanilla extract is used directly from its bottle and vanilla paste is used straight out of the jar. Vanilla paste contains tiny black flecks that are vanilla bean seeds, which give a bit more texture than vanilla extract. But it's fine to substitute vanilla paste for vanilla extract in any recipe. I do this often. Using a whole vanilla bean, which I like to do, requires more effort. To do this, use a sharp knife to slit the vanilla bean down the center. With the back of the knife, scrape out the vanilla seeds and add to the liquid in a saucepan, as called for in the recipe, along with the vanilla bean. Bring the mixture to a boil over medium-high heat. Cover the pan, turn off the heat, and let the vanilla infuse into the liquid for 10 to 30 minutes. Use a pair of tongs or a fork to lift the vanilla bean out of the mixture after infusing. After you have used a vanilla bean for making a sauce or custard, rinse it off thoroughly and let it dry completely on a paper towel. Add the vanilla bean to a canister of vanilla sugar (see page 552).

Allspice Layer Cake with Classic Genoise

THE BASE for this layer cake is a classic genoise, which is one of the most versatile cakes in the baker's repertoire. It is a light, airy cake that is the foundation for many classic French layered cakes and desserts. On its own, genoise is drier than most other cakes, so the layers are always brushed with sugar syrup. Genoise really takes on character when it is assembled with buttercream or other fillings and frostings. Buttercream flavored with allspice and a combination of other spices is used to create this delicious and elegant cake that is worthy of center stage at any celebration. Some of the preparation steps can be done in advance. Be sure to assemble the cake a few hours before serving so it has time to set. **Makes one 9-inch round cake, 10 to 12 servings**

GENOISE

Center a rack in the oven and preheat it to 350°F.

1 tablespoon unsalted butter, softened

Using a paper towel or your fingertips, generously butter the inside of the cake pan, coating it thoroughly.

2 teaspoons all-purpose flour

Dust the inside of the pan with some of the flour. Shake and tilt the pan to evenly distribute the flour, then turn the pan over and shake out the excess over the sink.

Cut a round of parchment paper to fit the bottom of the pan. Butter the parchment paper round and place in the pan, butter-side up.

6 extra-large eggs, at room temperature
½ cup granulated sugar

Place the eggs and sugar in the bowl of an electric stand mixer or in a large bowl. Place the bowl over a large saucepan of simmering water. Use a whisk and stir together constantly until the mixture registers 110°F on an instant-read thermometer. This process helps the sugar dissolve so it will incorporate thoroughly with the eggs.

Remove the bowl from the water and wipe the bottom dry. Use the wire whip attachment or a hand held mixer to whip the eggs and sugar on medium-high speed until they are very thick and pale colored and hold a slowly dissolving ribbon as the beater is lifted, about 5 minutes.

1 cup cake flour
1 tablespoon granulated sugar
⅛ teaspoon salt

Over a large piece of waxed or parchment paper or a bowl, sift together the flour and sugar. Add the salt and toss to blend.

Essential Gear

- 9 × 2-inch round cake pan
- Scissors
- Parchment paper
- Electric stand mixer with flat beater attachment and wire whip attachment, or large mixing bowl and hand-held mixer
- Sifter
- Two rubber spatulas
- Cooling rack
- Small heavy-bottomed saucepan
- Instant-read thermometer
- Large heavy-bottomed saucepan
- 1-inch natural-bristle pastry brush
- Sugar or candy thermometer
- Coffee grinder
- Serrated knife
- 10-inch flexible-blade icing spatula
- 10- or 12-inch pastry bag and large open star tip

Keeping

Store the cake loosely covered with waxed paper and then tightly wrapped with aluminum foil in the refrigerator up to 4 days. Place several toothpicks in the top outer edges of the cake to hold the waxed paper away from it so it won't mar the buttercream.

Fold this mixture into the beaten eggs in 3 stages. Fold gently, taking care not to deflate the egg mixture. The air beaten into the eggs is what makes this cake rise as it bakes.

1 ounce (2 tablespoons, ¼ stick) unsalted butter, melted	Place the butter in a small bowl. Take about 1 cup of the batter and blend it thoroughly with the butter. Then fold this mixture into the rest of the cake batter. This allows the butter to blend completely with the cake mixture.
½ teaspoon pure vanilla extract or vanilla paste	Fold the vanilla into the batter and blend thoroughly.

Transfer the batter to the cake pan and smooth the top with a rubber spatula.

Bake the cake for 30 to 35 minutes, until it is golden and springs back when lightly touched on top.

Remove the cake pan from the oven and cool completely on a rack. Invert the pan to remove the cake, then peel the parchment paper off the back. Re-invert the cake onto a plate or a cardboard cake circle.

SUGAR SYRUP

¼ cup sugar **½ cup water**	Combine the sugar and water in the small saucepan and bring to a boil over medium heat to dissolve the sugar. Remove the saucepan from the heat and let the sugar syrup cool.

ALLSPICE BUTTERCREAM

2 extra-large eggs, at room temperature **2 extra-large egg yolks, at room temperature** **¼ cup granulated sugar**	Place the eggs, egg yolks, and sugar in the clean bowl of an electric stand mixer or in a large bowl. Use a clean wire whip attachment or a hand-held mixer and whip on medium speed until the mixture is very pale colored and holds a slowly dissolving ribbon as the beater is lifted, about 5 minutes.
1¼ cups granulated sugar **½ cup water** **¼ teaspoon cream of tartar**	While the eggs are whipping, place the sugar, water, and cream of tartar in the clean, large saucepan. Bring the mixture to a boil, without stirring. Place a wet pastry brush at the point where the sugar syrup meets the sides of the pan and sweep it around completely. Do this two times. This prevents the sugar from crystallizing by brushing any stray crystals back into the mixture. Cook over high heat until the mixture registers 242°F on a sugar thermometer (soft-ball stage).

Immediately remove the thermometer and place it in a glass of warm water, then remove the pan from the heat so it won't continue to cook.

Streamlining

Bake the genoise up to 2 days before assembling and keep it tightly covered with a double layer of plastic wrap at room temperature or in the refrigerator up to 4 days. To freeze the cake up to 3 months, wrap it snugly in several layers of plastic wrap and place in freezer bags. Use a large piece of masking tape and an indelible marker to label and date the contents. If frozen, defrost the cake overnight in the refrigerator.

The sugar syrup can be prepared up to 2 weeks in advance and kept in an airtight plastic container in the refrigerator.

The buttercream can be prepared up to 3 days in advance and kept in an airtight plastic container in the refrigerator or up to 4 months in the freezer. If frozen, defrost overnight in the refrigerator. To reheat the buttercream, break it up into chunks and place in a mixing bowl. Place the bowl in a saucepan of warm water and let the buttercream begin to melt around the bottom. Wipe the bottom of the bowl dry and beat the buttercream with an electric mixer until it is fluffy and smooth.

Recovering from a Mishap

If one of the genoise layers breaks during assembly, patch it together with some of the buttercream.

Adjust the mixer speed to low and pour the sugar syrup into the whipped eggs in a slow, steady stream. Aim the sugar syrup between the beater and the side of the bowl, so it doesn't get caught up in the beater or thrown against the sides of the bowl. Turn the mixer speed up to medium-high and whip until the bowl is cool to the touch, about 8 minutes, before adding the butter. Once the cooked sugar syrup is added to the whipped eggs, the mixture must whip until the bowl is completely cool to the touch before the butter is added, or the butter will melt. If this happens, the texture and consistency of the buttercream will be too soft and more butter needs to be added to bring it to the right point.

1 pound (2 cups, 4 sticks) unsalted butter, softened	Adjust the mixer speed to medium and add the butter, 2 tablespoons at a time. Continue to beat until the buttercream is thoroughly blended and fluffy.
16 allspice berries or 1¼ teaspoons ground allspice **¼ teaspoon ground ginger** **¼ teaspoon ground cloves** **¼ teaspoon freshly grated nutmeg**	Grind the allspice berries, if using, in a clean coffee grinder until they are a fine powder. Transfer the ground allspice to a small bowl. Add the ginger, cloves, and nutmeg and stir together to blend thoroughly. Add this mixture to the buttercream and beat until it is thoroughly blended, about 2 minutes.

ASSEMBLY

With your fingertips, carefully peel the skin off of the top of the cake. Using a serrated knife, cut the genoise horizontally into 3 equal layers (see page 34). Place the bottom layer on a serving plate. Place strips of waxed paper around the bottom edges of the cake to protect the plate while assembling the cake.

⅓ cup apricot preserves

Brush the layer with sugar syrup. Use the flexible-blade spatula to spread the layer evenly with the apricot preserves.

Reserve ¼ cup of the buttercream for the top decoration. With a clean flexible-blade spatula, evenly spread some of the buttercream over the apricot preserves.

Position the second cake layer evenly over the buttercream and brush with sugar syrup. Spread some of the buttercream over the layer. Repeat with the top cake layer and spread the remaining buttercream over the sides and top of the cake.

¾ cup toasted and finely ground hazelnuts

Press the ground hazelnuts into the sides of the cake just up to, but not over, the top edge.

Making a Change

Replace the cake flour in the genoise with ½ cup all-purpose flour and ½ cup cornstarch sifted together.

To make a spiced genoise, sift together a mixture of 1 teaspoon ground cinnamon, 1 teaspoon ground coriander, 1 teaspoon ground ginger, ¼ teaspoon ground cardamom, and ¼ teaspoon ground cloves. Add this spice mixture to the flour before adding to the cake batter.

Fit the pastry bag with the star tip and fill partway with the reserved buttercream. Pipe a reverse shell border (see page 44) around the outer top edge of the cake.

7 to 8 whole toasted and skinned hazelnuts

Place the whole hazelnuts, pointed ends up, equally spaced around the reverse shell border.

Let the cake chill for at least 2 hours before serving so it has time to set and will be easier to cut. Serve the cake at room temperature.

Anise and Almond Biscotti

ANISE HAS a pronounced licorice flavor and it is a classic flavor combination with almond for biscotti. The name of these cookies means "twice baked" and this double baking is what gives biscotti their renowned crispness. It also makes them perfect for dipping into a cup of coffee or hot chocolate. These biscotti keep very well, making them great do-ahead cookies. **Makes about 3 dozen cookies**

Adjust the oven racks to the upper and lower thirds and preheat the oven to 350°F. Line the baking sheets with parchment paper sheets or non-stick liners.

2³/₄ cups all-purpose flour
1³/₄ cups granulated sugar
1 tablespoon plus 1 teaspoon anise seed
1 teaspoon baking powder
¹/₄ teaspoon salt

In the bowl of an electric stand mixer or a large bowl, combine the flour, sugar, anise seed, baking powder, and salt. Use the flat beater attachment or a hand-held mixer to stir together briefly.

3 extra-large eggs, at room temperature
3 extra-large egg yolks, at room temperature
2 teaspoons pure vanilla extract or vanilla paste

Using a fork, whisk the eggs and egg yolks with the vanilla in a small bowl. Add the egg and vanilla mixture to the dry ingredients. Mix on low speed until thoroughly combined. Stop occasionally and scrape down the sides and bottom of the mixing bowl with a rubber spatula.

1²/₃ cups unblanched whole almonds

Add the almonds to the mixture and stir to blend thoroughly.

Divide the dough into 4 equal pieces. Dust your hands with flour to keep the dough from sticking and shape each piece into a log about

Essential Gear

- Electric stand mixer with flat beater attachment, or large mixing bowl and hand-held mixer
- Rubber spatula
- Two baking sheets
- Two parchment paper sheets or non-stick liners
- Two cooling racks
- Serrated knife

Keeping

Store the biscotti in an airtight container between sheets of waxed paper at room temperature up to 2 weeks. A kitchen cupboard or the pantry is the ideal storage place.

To freeze up to 3 months, wrap the container tightly in several layers of plastic wrap and aluminum foil. Use a large piece of masking tape and an indelible marker to label and date the contents. If frozen, defrost overnight in the refrigerator and bring to room temperature before serving.

8 inches long, 3 inches wide, and 1 inch high. Place 2 logs on each baking sheet, leaving at least 2 inches between them.

Bake for 10 to 15 minutes. Switch the baking sheets and bake another 8 to 10 minutes, until the logs are lightly browned and set. Remove the baking sheets from the oven to rest for 10 minutes on a rack. Lower the oven temperature to 325°F.

Using a serrated knife, cut the logs on the diagonal into ½-inch-thick slices. Place the slices back on the baking sheet on their sides so the wide part of each slice faces up.

Bake the biscotti for 10 minutes, then switch the baking sheets and bake another 10 to 12 minutes, until very firm.

Transfer the biscotti to racks to cool.

Making a Change
Replace the almonds with walnut halves or coarsely chopped walnuts.

Leave out the anise seed if you don't like the flavor of licorice.

Cardamom and Pear Crisp

CARDAMOM LENDS its distinct lemony flavor to this crisp. I use Bosc pears because they are my favorite eating pears, but many other varieties also work well. One of the best ways to serve this crisp is warm, accompanied by whipped cream or vanilla ice cream. **Makes one 8-inch square crisp, 8 to 10 servings**

Essential Gear
- Vegetable peeler or sharp knife
- Chef's knife
- Small sharp knife
- 8-inch square baking pan
- Food processor
- Cooling rack
- Electric stand mixer with wire whip attachment, or large mixing bowl and hand-held mixer

PEAR FILLING

2 pounds ripe pears (5 to 6 medium)

Use a vegetable peeler or a knife to peel the pears. Use a chef's knife to cut the pears into quarters, then use a small sharp knife to remove the core and seeds. Slice the pears into ½-inch-thick slices and place them in the baking pan.

1 tablespoon light brown sugar
1 teaspoon ground cardamom
Finely grated zest of 1 large lemon

Sprinkle the sugar, cardamom, and lemon zest over the pears and toss to blend together.

Keeping
Although the crisp is best eaten the day it's made, it can last up to 2 days. Store the crisp tightly covered with aluminum foil in the refrigerator.

TOPPING

Center a rack in the oven and preheat it to 400°F.

Streamlining
The topping can be made in advance. Store it in a tightly

1 cup walnuts	In the work bowl of a food processor fitted with the steel blade, combine the walnuts, flour, sugar, cardamom, and salt. Pulse until the walnuts are finely chopped, 30 seconds to 1 minute.
2/3 cup all-purpose flour	
1/2 cup firmly packed light brown sugar	
2 teaspoons ground cardamom	
1/8 teaspoon salt	

covered plastic container in the refrigerator up to 4 days.

Adding Style
Serve squares of the crisp with vanilla ice cream.

2 ounces (4 tablespoons, 1/2 stick) unsalted butter, chilled	Cut the butter into small pieces and add to the dry ingredients. Pulse until the butter is cut into very small pieces, about 30 seconds.

Evenly sprinkle the topping over the fruit in the baking pan.

Bake the crisp for 25 to 30 minutes, until the topping is light golden. Remove the pan from the oven and transfer to a rack to cool.

GARNISH

1 cup heavy whipping cream	Place the cream in the chilled bowl of an electric stand mixer or in a large bowl. Use the wire whip attachment or a hand-held mixer to whip on medium speed until frothy.
2 tablespoons confectioners' sugar	Add the sugar and continue whipping the cream until it holds soft peaks.

Cut squares of the crisp, scooping up the fruit. Serve each square with a large dollop of whipped cream.

Gingerbread

THIS IS MY FAVORITE gingerbread. Its soft and cake-like texture is rich and aromatic with the spicy flavors of ginger, cinnamon, cloves, and nutmeg. Although good on its own, I like it best served with a dollop of whipped cream or a scoop of vanilla ice cream. **Makes sixteen 2-inch squares**

Essential Gear
- 8-inch square baking pan
- Aluminum foil
- Sifter
- Electric stand mixer with flat beater attachment, or large mixing bowl and hand-held mixer
- Rubber spatula
- Cooling rack
- Microplane grater

1 tablespoon unsalted butter, softened	Center a rack in the oven and preheat it to 350°F. Line the baking pan with aluminum foil, letting it hang about 2 inches over the sides. Use a paper towel or your fingertips to butter the inside of the foil.

2½ cups all-purpose flour	Over a large piece of waxed or parchment paper or a bowl, sift together the flour, ginger, baking soda, cinnamon, and cloves. Add the nutmeg and salt and toss to blend.
1 tablespoon ground ginger	
2 teaspoons baking soda	
1 teaspoon ground cinnamon	
½ teaspoon ground cloves	
¼ teaspoon freshly grated nutmeg	
¼ teaspoon salt	
4 ounces (8 tablespoons, 1 stick) unsalted butter, softened	Place the butter in the bowl of an electric stand mixer or a large bowl. Use the flat beater attachment or a hand-held mixer to beat the butter until light and fluffy, about 2 minutes.
¼ cup firmly packed light brown sugar	Add the brown sugar and granulated sugar and cream together until smooth. Stop and scrape down the sides and bottom of the bowl with a rubber spatula.
¼ cup granulated sugar	
2 extra-large eggs, at room temperature	Use a fork to lightly beat the eggs in a small bowl. Add the eggs and molasses to the butter mixture. The eggs will sit on top of the butter mixture, so stop after adding each one and scrape down the sides and bottom of the bowl with a rubber spatula to help mix evenly. The mixture may look curdled as the eggs are added, but as you scrape down the bowl, the mixture will smooth out.
1 cup molasses	
1 cup boiling water	Add the water to the mixture and beat to blend thoroughly.
	Adjust the mixer speed to low and add the dry ingredients in 4 stages, blending thoroughly after each edition. Stop often and scrape down the sides and bottom of the bowl with a rubber spatula.
	Pour the batter into the prepared pan and use a rubber spatula to spread it evenly.
	Bake for 45 minutes, until a tester inserted in the center comes out clean.
	Remove the pan from the oven and cool completely on a rack.
	Lift the gingerbread from the pan with the aluminum foil. Carefully peel the foil away from the sides. Cut into 4 equal-sized rows in each direction. Serve the gingerbread at room temperature.

Keeping

Store the gingerbread tightly wrapped in aluminum foil at room temperature up to 4 days. To freeze up to 4 months, wrap the container tightly in several layers of plastic wrap and aluminum foil. Use a large piece of masking tape and an indelible marker to label and date the contents. If frozen, defrost overnight in the refrigerator and bring to room temperature before serving.

Making a Change

Add 1 cup finely chopped crystallized ginger to the flour mixture before adding it to the batter.

Adding Style

Serve squares of gingerbread with a dollop of lightly sweetened whipped cream, a scoop of vanilla ice cream, or Lemon Curd (see Double Lemon Layer Cake, page 143).

Pain d'Epices

PAIN D'EPICES is a classic French spice and honey cake that is closely related to gingerbread. This cake developed during medieval times, when it was influenced by contact with bakers from Germany. Anise is the main spice in this cake, but cinnamon and cloves add their special flavors as well. Rye flour, which can be found in many natural and health food stores, as well as some supermarkets, is also characteristic of this traditional cake. Pain d'Epices is best served warm, spread with butter, for afternoon tea or breakfast. **Makes one $8^{1}/_{2} \times 4^{1}/_{2} \times 2^{1}/_{2}$-inch loaf cake, 18 to 20 servings**

Center a rack in the oven and preheat it to 350°F.

1 tablespoon unsalted butter, softened

Using a paper towel or your fingertips, generously butter the inside of the pan.

2 teaspoons all-purpose flour

Dust the inside of the pan with the flour, then shake and tilt the pan to evenly coat the bottom and sides. Turn the pan over the sink and tap out the excess flour.

Cut a rectangle of parchment paper to fit the bottom of the pan. Butter the parchment and place in the pan, butter-side up.

3/4 cup honey
1/2 cup water
1/2 cup superfine sugar

In the saucepan, combine the honey, water, and sugar over low heat. Stir with a heat-resistant spatula or wooden spoon until the sugar dissolves. Increase the heat to medium and bring the mixture to a boil. Remove the pan from the heat and transfer the mixture to the bowl of an electric stand mixer or a large bowl.

2 teaspoons anise seeds
2 tablespoons dark rum
2 teaspoons ground cinnamon
1/2 teaspoon ground cloves
1/4 teaspoon salt

Place the anise seeds in a plastic bag or between 2 sheets of waxed or parchment paper. Roll a rolling pin over them several times to crush the seeds. Add the crushed seeds, the rum, cinnamon, cloves, and salt to the honey mixture. Use the flat beater attachment or a hand-held mixer to blend together thoroughly.

1 1/2 cups rye flour
1 cup all-purpose flour
1 teaspoon baking soda
1/2 teaspoon baking powder

Over a large piece of waxed or parchment paper or a bowl, sift together the rye flour, all-purpose flour, baking soda, and baking powder. Add to the honey mixture in 4 or 5 stages, blending well after each addition. Stop after each addition and scrape down the sides and bottom of the bowl with a rubber spatula. The batter will be sticky.

⅔ cup finely ground almonds **½ cup finely chopped candied orange peel (page 171)**	Stir in the almonds and peel and blend thoroughly.
	Transfer the batter to the prepared pan. The batter is very thick, so use a rubber spatula to spread it evenly into the pan.
	Bake for 35 to 40 minutes, until the cake has risen to the top of the pan and a cake tester inserted into the center comes out clean. Remove the pan from the oven and cool on a rack for 15 minutes. Turn the cake out of the pan, peel the parchment paper off of the bottom, and re-invert the cake onto the cooling rack. Let it cool completely. Slice the cake crosswise into serving pieces.

Spiced Sugar Coins

EXTRA TEXTURE and flavor is added to these yummy cookies by rolling the dough cylinders in sugar before they are baked. These are classic refrigerator cookies because the dough needs to be made ahead so it has plenty of time to chill before it is cut and baked. You can keep the dough cylinders in the freezer, tightly wrapped in several layers of plastic wrap and inside a freezer bag, so you can be ready to bake cookies when unexpected guests drop by. **Makes about 5 dozen cookies**

6 ounces (12 tablespoons, 1½ sticks) unsalted butter, softened	Place the butter in the bowl of an electric stand mixer or in a large bowl. Use the flat beater attachment or a hand-held mixer to beat the butter on medium speed until it's fluffy, about 2 minutes.
½ cup granulated sugar	Add the sugar, and cream together well. Stop occasionally and scrape down the sides and bottom of the bowl with a rubber spatula.
1 teaspoon pure vanilla extract or vanilla paste	Add the vanilla to the butter mixture and blend thoroughly.
1¾ cups all-purpose flour **1 teaspoon ground cinnamon** **½ teaspoon ground ginger** **¼ teaspoon ground cloves** **¼ teaspoon freshly grated nutmeg** **⅛ teaspoon salt**	Over a large piece of waxed or parchment paper or a bowl, sift together the flour, cinnamon, ginger, and cloves. Add the nutmeg and salt and toss to blend.

Essential Gear

- Electric stand mixer with flat beater attachment, or large mixing bowl and hand-held mixer
- Rubber spatula
- Waxed paper
- Sifter
- Two baking sheets
- Two parchment paper sheets or non-stick liners
- Microplane grater
- 1-inch natural-bristle pastry brush or a spoon
- Chef's knife
- Two cooling racks

Keeping

Store the cookies in an airtight plastic container between layers of waxed paper at room temperature up to 1 week. A kitchen cupboard or the pantry is the ideal storage place. To freeze up to 3 months, wrap the

Add this mixture in 3 stages to the butter mixture. Stop after each addition and scrape down the sides and bottom of the bowl with a rubber spatula. Mix thoroughly.

Place two large sheets of waxed paper on a flat surface and divide the dough evenly onto them. Use the waxed paper to shape and roll the dough into cylinders about 10 inches long and 1 inch wide (see Refrigerator Cookies, page 37). Cover the cylinders tightly with the waxed paper and wrap each roll in plastic wrap. Chill in the freezer for 45 minutes or in the refrigerator for at least 2 hours, until firm enough to slice.

Adjust the oven racks to the upper and lower thirds and preheat the oven to 400°F. Line each baking sheet with parchment paper or a non-stick baking liner.

1 extra-large egg yolk
⅓ cup granulated sugar

Using a fork, lightly beat the egg yolk in a small bowl. Divide the sugar evenly between sheets of waxed or parchment paper. Unwrap each dough cylinder. Using a pastry brush or a spoon, coat the outside of each cylinder with egg yolk, then roll in the sugar, coating each completely.

Place a cylinder on a cutting board. Using a sharp knife, cut each cylinder into ¼-inch-thick slices. Cut straight down and roll the cylinder a quarter turn after every 6 slices so it will keep its round shape. If the dough becomes soft while you work with it, rewrap it and chill for another 10 to 15 minutes, then continue slicing.

Place the slices on the baking sheets, leaving at least 1 inch of space between them. Bake for 5 minutes. Switch the baking sheets and bake another 5 to 6 minutes, until set. Remove the baking sheets from the oven and cool the cookies completely on the baking sheets on racks.

airtight container in several layers of plastic wrap and aluminum foil. Use a large piece of masking tape and an indelible marker to label and date the contents. If frozen, defrost overnight in the refrigerator and bring to room temperature before serving.

Streamlining
The dough cylinders can be made and kept in the refrigerator up to 3 days before baking, tightly wrapped in several layers of plastic wrap. To freeze up to 3 months, wrap the same way and place each cylinder in a freezer bag. Use a large piece of masking tape and an indelible marker to label and date the contents. You can take them directly from the freezer and slice for baking, or defrost the cylinders overnight in the refrigerator.

Making a Change
Use 2 teaspoons of another single spice, such as cardamom, five-spice powder, cinnamon, ginger, nutmeg, or allspice, in place of the blend of cinnamon, ginger, and nutmeg.

Spiced Bread Pudding

BREAD PUDDING is true comfort food and is the perfect dessert when it's cold outside. A blend of ground cloves and nutmeg gives this dessert its rich, warm flavor. Bread pudding is usually made from leftover bread, but there's no reason you can't use good-quality, fresh white bread or a baguette. **Makes 6 to 8 servings**

Center a rack in the oven and preheat it to 400°F.

Essential Gear
- 3-quart roasting pan or baking dish
- Baking sheet
- 2-quart baking dish
- Whisk
- Large mixing bowl
- Rubber spatula

¾ (about 8 ounces) fresh or day-old baguette or ½ loaf (8 ounces) fresh or day-old good-quality white bread	Cut the crusts off the bread and cut the bread into 1-inch cubes. If using fresh bread, place the cubes in a shallow layer in the 3-quart baking pan and dry in the oven for 15 minutes.
1 tablespoon unsalted butter, softened 1 tablespoon granulated sugar	Use a paper towel or your fingertips to butter the inside of the 2-quart baking dish. Sprinkle the inside of the baking dish with the sugar.
⅔ cup raisins	Transfer the dry bread cubes to the prepared baking dish. Sprinkle the raisins evenly over the bread.
2 cups milk 1 cup heavy whipping cream 5 extra-large eggs, at room temperature ½ cup granulated sugar ½ cup firmly packed light brown sugar 2 teaspoons pure vanilla extract 2 teaspoons ground cloves ¼ teaspoon freshly grated nutmeg ¼ teaspoon salt	In a large bowl, combine the milk, cream, eggs, granulated sugar, light brown sugar, vanilla, cloves, nutmeg, and salt. Whisk together to blend thoroughly. Pour this mixture over the bread and raisins. Cover the pan tightly with plastic wrap and place in the refrigerator for 30 minutes. This gives the bread time to soak up the liquid.
	Adjust the oven heat to 350°F.
1 quart boiling water	Remove the plastic from the baking dish. Place the bread pudding in a larger baking pan. Place the baking pan on the oven rack and pour boiling water halfway up the sides of the dish. Bake for 35 to 45 minutes, until the pudding is puffed and a cake tester or toothpick inserted in the center comes out clean. Remove the baking pan from the oven. Remove the bread pudding from the water bath and cool on a rack.

GARNISH

1 cup heavy whipping cream 2 tablespoons confectioners' sugar, sifted 1 teaspoon pure vanilla extract or vanilla paste	Place the cream in the chilled bowl of an electric stand mixer or in a chilled bowl. Use the wire whip attachment or a hand-held mixer to whip the cream until it is frothy. Add the sugar and vanilla and continue to whip the cream until it holds soft peaks. Serve scoops of the warm bread pudding topped with a large spoonful of whipped cream.

- Cooling rack
- Electric stand mixer with wire whip attachment, or large mixing bowl and hand-held mixer

Keeping
Store the bread pudding tightly covered with plastic wrap in the refrigerator up to 3 days.

Making a Change
Sprinkle 1 cup finely chopped walnuts over the top of the bread pudding before baking it in the oven.

Spiced Maple Layer Cake

T HE FIRST THING I said when I made this cake was, "It tastes like pancakes." And my niece, who ate a piece, said the same thing. That's because of the flavor of the maple syrup used in both the cake and the buttercream filling and frosting. Maple syrup comes in grades. Grade A is lighter in color and flavor than Grade B, but both work very well in this cake. You might think this cake would be very sweet because of the maple syrup, but it's not. It has a rich, satisfying flavor and a light texture. Ginger, nutmeg, and cloves also add flavor dimension to this scrumptious cake. There are a few steps involved in making this cake, but they can be done in advance. Assemble the cake a few hours to a day before serving so the flavors and textures have time to blend together. **Makes one 9-inch round cake, 14 to 16 servings**

SPICED MAPLE CAKE

Center a rack in the oven and preheat it to 350°F.

1 tablespoon unsalted butter, softened	Using a paper towel or your fingertips, generously butter the inside of the cake pans, coating them thoroughly
1 tablespoon all-purpose flour	Dust the inside of each pan with some of the flour. Shake and tilt the pans to evenly distribute the flour, then turn the pans over and shake out the excess over the sink.
	Cut a round of parchment paper to fit the bottom of each pan. Butter each parchment paper round and place in each pan, butter-side up.
4 ounces (8 tablespoons, 1 stick) unsalted butter, softened	Place the butter in the bowl of an electric stand mixer or in a large bowl. Use the flat beater attachment or hand-held mixer to beat the butter on medium speed until it's fluffy, about 2 minutes.
2 cups pure maple syrup	Gradually add the maple syrup to the butter, and cream together well. Stop occasionally and scrape down the bottom and sides of the bowl with a rubber spatula.
3 extra-large eggs, at room temperature	One at a time, add the eggs to the butter mixture, stopping to scrape down the bottom and sides of the bowl after each addition. At first the mixture may look curdled as the eggs are added, but as you scrape down the bowl, the mixture will smooth out.

Essential Gear

- Two 9 × 2-inch round cake pans
- Scissors
- Parchment paper
- Two rubber spatulas
- Electric stand mixer with flat beater attachment and wire whip attachment, or large mixing bowl and hand-held mixer
- Sifter
- Liquid measuring cup
- Two cooling racks
- Large heavy-bottomed saucepan
- 1-inch natural-bristle pastry brush
- Sugar or candy thermometer
- Serrated knife
- 10-inch flexible-blade icing spatula
- 10- or 12-inch pastry bag and large open star tip
- Microplane grater

Keeping

Store the cake loosely covered with waxed paper and tented with aluminum foil in the refrigerator up to 3 days. Place several toothpicks in the top outer edges of the cake to hold the waxed paper away from it so it won't mar the buttercream.

Streamlining

Bake the cake layers up to 2 days before assembling the cake and keep tightly covered with a double layer

2¾ cups all-purpose flour 1 tablespoon baking powder 1 teaspoon ground ginger ⅛ teaspoon ground cloves ¼ teaspoon salt ¼ teaspoon freshly grated nutmeg	Over a large piece of waxed or parchment paper or a bowl, sift together the flour, baking powder, ginger, and cloves. Add the salt and nutmeg and toss to blend.
	Add the dry ingredients to the butter mixture in 3 stages, blending well after each addition. Stop often to scrape down the bottom and sides of the bowl with a rubber spatula.
1 cup milk 1½ teaspoons pure vanilla extract or vanilla paste	Combine the milk and vanilla in a liquid measuring cup. Add to the batter in 3 stages, blending thoroughly after each addition.

¾ cup walnuts, finely
  chopped
½ cup crystallized ginger,
  finely chopped
	Add the walnuts and crystallized ginger to the batter in 2 stages, blending thoroughly.

	Divide the batter evenly between the two cake pans. Smooth the top of each pan with a rubber spatula. Bake the layers for 40 minutes, until the cakes are golden and a cake tester inserted in the center comes out with no crumbs clinging to it. Remove the cake pans from the oven and cool completely on racks. Invert the pans to remove the layers, then peel the parchment paper off the back of each layer. Re-invert the layers onto plates or cardboard cake circles.

MAPLE SYRUP BUTTERCREAM

2 extra-large eggs, at room
  temperature
2 extra-large egg yolks, at
  room temperature
	Place the eggs and egg yolks in the bowl of an electric stand mixer or in a large bowl. Use the wire whip attachment or a hand-held mixer and whip the eggs on medium speed until they are very pale colored and hold a slowly dissolving ribbon as the beater is lifted, about 5 minutes.

2 cups pure maple syrup	While the eggs are whipping, place the maple syrup in the saucepan. Bring the syrup to a boil over medium heat, without stirring. Place a wet pastry brush at the point where the maple syrup meets the sides of the pan and sweep it around completely. Do this two times. This prevents the maple syrup from crystallizing by brushing any stray crystals back into the mixture. Cook over medium-high heat until the mixture registers 242°F on a sugar thermometer (soft-ball stage).

of plastic wrap at room temperature or in the refrigerator up to 4 days. To freeze the layers up to 3 months, wrap them snugly in several layers of plastic wrap and place them in freezer bags. Use a large piece of masking tape and an indelible marker to label and date the contents. If frozen, defrost the layers overnight in the refrigerator.

The buttercream can be prepared up to 3 days in advance and kept in an airtight plastic container in the refrigerator or up to 4 months in the freezer. If frozen, defrost overnight in the refrigerator. To reheat the buttercream, break it up into chunks and place in a mixing bowl. Place the bowl in a saucepan of warm water and let the buttercream begin to melt around the bottom. Wipe the bottom of the bowl dry and beat the buttercream with an electric mixer until it is fluffy and smooth.

Making a Change
Replace the finely chopped walnuts with pecans or almonds.

Recovering from a Mishap
If one of the cake layers breaks during assembly, patch it together with some of the buttercream.

Immediately remove the thermometer and place it in a glass of warm water, then remove the pan from the heat so it won't continue to cook.

Adjust the mixer speed to low and pour the maple syrup into the whipped eggs in a slow, steady stream. Aim between the beater and the side of the bowl, so it doesn't get caught up in the beater or thrown against the sides of the bowl. Turn the mixer speed up to medium-high and whip until the bowl is cool to the touch, about 8 minutes. Once the cooked maple syrup is added to the whipped eggs, the mixture must whip until the bowl is completely cool to the touch before the butter is added, or the butter will melt. If this happens, the texture and consistency of the buttercream will be too soft and more butter needs to be added to bring it to the right point.

1 pound (2 cups, 4 sticks) unsalted butter, softened

Adjust the mixer speed to medium and add the butter, 2 tablespoons at a time. Continue to beat until the buttercream is thoroughly blended and fluffy.

ASSEMBLY

With your fingertips, peel the skin off of the top of each cake layer. Using a serrated knife, cut each cake layer in half horizontally (see page 34). Place the bottom of one cake layer on a serving plate. Place strips of waxed paper around the bottom edges of the cake to protect the plate while assembling the cake.

Reserve 1/4 cup of the buttercream for the top decoration. With the flexible-blade spatula, evenly spread some of the buttercream over the cake layer.

Position the second cake layer evenly over the buttercream. Spread some of the buttercream over the layer. Repeat with the remaining two cake layers and buttercream.

Spread the remaining buttercream over the sides and top of the cake.

1¼ cups walnuts, finely chopped

Press the walnuts onto the sides of the cake just up to, but not over, the top edge.

16 walnut halves

Fit the pastry bag with the star tip and fill with the reserved buttercream. Visually divide the top of the cake into 16 pieces or use a small sharp knife to mark the outer top edge of the cake into serving pieces. Pipe a star at the center outer edge of each piece (see page 44). Top each star with a walnut half set at an angle.

Let the cake chill for at least 2 hours before serving so it has time to set and will be easier to cut, but serve at room temperature.

Spiced Sablé Cookies with Hazelnuts

I MADE sandy-textured cookies like these almost daily when I worked at the Stanford Court Hotel in San Francisco. These are great do-ahead refrigerator cookies because the dough needs to chill before it is cut and baked. I like to serve these with afternoon coffee and tea or as an assortment of small cookies after dinner. Although these cookies are delicious on their own, to dress them up, dip them halfway or on the diagonal into dark chocolate. **Makes 6 to 7 dozen cookies**

Essential Gear
- 2-quart baking pan
- Three baking sheets
- Three parchment paper sheets or non-stick liners
- Electric stand mixer with flat beater attachment, or large mixing bowl and hand-held mixer
- Rubber spatula
- Ruler
- Two cooling racks
- Microplane grater

Keeping
Store the cookies in an airtight plastic container between layers of waxed paper at room temperature up to 4 days. To freeze up to 3 months, wrap the container tightly in several layers of plastic wrap and aluminum foil. Use a large piece of masking tape and an indelible marker to label and date the contents. If frozen, defrost overnight in the refrigerator and bring to room temperature before serving.

To freeze the cookie dough up to 6 months, wrap the pan tightly in several layers of plastic wrap and place in a freezer bag. Use masking tape and an indelible marker to label and date the dough. Let the dough stand at room temperature for about 20 minutes before slicing, because if it is too firm when cut, it may splinter.

8 ounces (16 tablespoons, 2 sticks) unsalted butter, softened	Place the butter in the bowl of an electric stand mixer or in a large bowl. Use the flat beater attachment or a hand-held mixer to beat the butter on medium speed until it's fluffy, about 2 minutes.
1¼ cups confectioners' sugar, sifted	Add the sugar to the butter and cream together completely. Stop occasionally while mixing and scrape down the sides and bottom of the bowl with a rubber spatula.
1 extra-large egg white, at room temperature **1 teaspoon pure vanilla extract**	In a small bowl, blend together the egg white and vanilla, then add to the butter mixture. Mix on medium speed, then stop to scrape down the sides and bottom of the bowl with a rubber spatula. Continue to mix until well blended.
2¼ cups all-purpose flour **½ teaspoon ground cinnamon** **¼ teaspoon ground cloves** **½ teaspoon freshly grated nutmeg** **¼ teaspoon salt**	Over a large piece of waxed or parchment paper or a bowl, sift together the flour, cinnamon, and cloves. Add the nutmeg and salt and toss together to blend.
	Add the dry ingredients in 3 stages to the butter mixture, blending thoroughly after each addition. Stop and scrape down the sides and bottom of the bowl after each addition to ensure even mixing.
1 cup toasted, skinned, and coarsely chopped hazelnuts	Add the hazelnuts and blend in thoroughly.
1 tablespoon granulated sugar	Sprinkle the sugar over the bottom of the baking pan. Transfer the cookie dough to the pan. Dip your fingertips in flour to keep them from sticking to the dough and press the dough evenly into the pan, making sure to fill in the corners. Cover the pan tightly with plastic wrap and chill at least 2 hours or overnight, until firm.

Adjust the oven racks to the upper and lower thirds and preheat the oven to 350°F. Line the baking sheets with parchment paper or non-stick liners.

Making a Change
Replace the hazelnuts with almonds or pecans.

Use a sharp knife and a ruler to cut the dough across the width of the pan into strips 1½ inches wide. Then cut each strip into ½-inch-thick slices.

Arrange the cookies on the baking sheets. leaving at least 1 inch of space between them. Cover 1 baking sheet with plastic wrap and chill in the refrigerator while baking the other two sheets.

Bake the cookies for 9 minutes, then switch the baking sheets. Bake another 9 to 10 minutes, until set and light golden. Remove the baking sheets from the oven and cool on racks. Repeat with the remaining baking sheet.

Spicy Apple and Dried Cherry Pie

THIS PIE has a great balance of sweet and tart, as well as crunchy texture from the apples and dried cherries. It also has a good measure of spice. I love to make this when the weather turns crisp and cool in the fall. Serve each slice of pie with a dollop of freshly whipped cream or vanilla ice cream. **Makes one 10-inch round pie, 12 to 14 servings**

Essential Gear
- Food processor
- Rolling pin
- 10-inch round deep pie pan
- Baking sheet
- Microplane grater or citrus grater
- 1-inch natural-bristle pastry brush
- Vegetable peeler or sharp knife
- Small sharp knife
- Rubber spatula
- Cooling rack

Keeping
Store the pie, loosely covered with waxed paper and then tightly wrapped with aluminum foil, in the refrigerator up to 3 days.

Streamlining
The pie dough can be made in advance and kept in the

PIE DOUGH

2 cups all-purpose flour
2 tablespoons granulated sugar
½ teaspoon salt

In the work bowl of a food processor fitted with the steel blade, combine the flour, sugar, and salt. Pulse briefly to blend.

8 ounces (16 tablespoons, 2 sticks) unsalted butter, chilled

Cut the butter into small pieces and freeze for 20 minutes.

8 ounces cream cheese, chilled

Cut the cream cheese into small pieces and add to the dry ingredients. Pulse to cut the cream cheese into very tiny pieces. The texture should be sandy with very tiny lumps throughout.

Add the butter to the flour mixture. Pulse until the butter is cut into pea-sized pieces, 30 to 45 seconds.

3 to 4 tablespoons heavy whipping cream

Remove the top of the food processor and sprinkle on 3 tablespoons of the cream. Replace the top and pulse for 10 seconds. Squeeze a small amount of the dough in your hand. If it holds together, don't add any more cream. If the dough is still very crumbly, add another tablespoon of cream, pulse to blend, then check the dough again. It won't hold together unless you squeeze it, but that's the texture you want.

Divide the dough in two equal pieces and shape each piece into a flat disk. Wrap the disks tightly in a double layer of plastic wrap. Chill in the refrigerator until firm before using, about 2 hours. Chilling the dough relaxes the gluten in the flour so it won't be too elastic and will roll out easily. It also firms up the butter in the dough so it will need less flour when rolled out. If the dough is too firm it will splinter and break when rolled out. Let it stand at room temperature for 10 to 15 minutes before rolling to become more pliable.

On a smooth, flat surface, roll out one of the disks of pie dough between sheets of lightly floured waxed or parchment paper to a large circle about 12 inches in diameter. To tell if the dough will fit the pie pan, invert the pan over the dough. If there are 2 to 3 inches of dough that protrude beyond the sides of the pan, it will fit.

Carefully peel the paper off the top of the dough. Brush excess flour off the dough, then loosely roll the pastry dough around the rolling pin without the bottom piece of paper. Place the pie pan directly underneath the rolling pin and carefully unroll the pastry dough into the pan. Or loosely fold the dough in half. Carefully place it in half of the pie pan and gently unfold the dough. Gently lift up the sides and ease the pie dough into the bottom and sides of the pie pan.

Transfer the pie pan to a baking sheet and chill in the freezer for 15 to 20 minutes. This helps prevent the pie dough from shrinking as it bakes and sets the butter in the dough to ensure flakiness.

APPLE, DRIED CHERRY, AND SPICE FILLING

1/2 cup dried tart cherries
Finely grated zest of 1 large orange
Juice of 1 large orange

Place the dried cherries in a small bowl. Add the orange zest and juice. Cover the bowl tightly with plastic wrap and let the mixture stand for at least 30 minutes.

2 1/2 pounds Granny Smith or other tart apples (7 to 8 medium)

Use a vegetable peeler to peel the apples. Cut each apple in half, then cut each half in half again. Use a small sharp knife to remove the core of each quarter, then cut them into 1/2-inch-thick slices. Place the apple slices in a large bowl.

refrigerator tightly wrapped in a double layer of plastic wrap up to 4 days. To freeze up to 3 months, wrap the dough snugly in several layers of plastic wrap and place it in a freezer bag. Use a large piece of masking tape and an indelible marker to label and date the contents. If frozen, defrost overnight in the refrigerator before using. The pie dough can also be fitted into the pie pan and kept tightly covered in the refrigerator or frozen, wrapped and labeled as above.

The assembled unbaked pie can be frozen up to 3 months. To freeze the pie, cover it snugly in several layers of plastic wrap and place it in a freezer bag. Use a large piece of masking tape and an indelible marker to label and date the contents. Do not defrost the pie to bake, but extend the baking time by 5 to 10 minutes.

Troubleshooting
Don't overprocess the pie dough or it will be tough and not flaky.

Adding Style
Serve slices of the pie with vanilla ice cream or whipped cream.

½ cup firmly packed light
   brown sugar
2 tablespoons all-purpose
   flour
1¼ teaspoons ground
   cinnamon
½ teaspoon freshly grated
   nutmeg
½ teaspoon ground allspice
⅛ teaspoon ground cloves
¼ teaspoon salt

Sprinkle the sugar, flour, cinnamon, nutmeg, allspice, cloves, and salt over the apples. Add the cherries with the orange zest and any remaining juice and use a rubber spatula to gently toss and stir the apples to evenly distribute the ingredients and coat the apples completely.

---

1 tablespoon unsalted
   butter

Transfer the filling to the pie shell. Dot the top of the filling with the butter.

Adjust an oven rack to the lower third and preheat the oven to 375°F.

1 extra-large egg yolk,
   at room temperature
1 tablespoon heavy whipping
   cream

Use a fork to lightly beat the egg yolk and cream together in a small bowl. Use a pastry brush to brush the edges of the bottom pastry shell to help the bottom and top crusts stick together.

Roll out the remaining disk of pie dough on a smooth, flat surface between sheets of lightly floured waxed or parchment paper to a large circle about 12 inches in diameter. Peel off the top piece of paper. Brush excess flour off the dough, then loosely roll the pastry dough around the rolling pin without the bottom piece of paper. Place the pie pan directly underneath the rolling pin and carefully unroll the pastry dough onto the filling. Or loosely fold the dough in half. Carefully place it on half of the filling and gently unfold the dough. Trim off the edges of both the top and the bottom pie shell evenly, leaving a ¾-inch overhang.

1 tablespoon granulated
   sugar

Fold the edges of the top crust over the bottom crust and press them to seal together. Crimp or flute the edges (see page 40). Brush the top of the pie with the egg mixture and sprinkle sugar over the top of the dough. Use a small, sharp knife to cut several slits in the top of the pie to allow steam to escape as it bakes.

Bake the pie for 10 minutes, then lower the oven temperature to 350°F. Bake for another 40 to 45 minutes, until the crust is light golden and the filling is thickly bubbling inside.

Remove the pie from the oven and cool on a rack. Serve warm or at room temperature.

Triple Ginger Cake

YOU CAN'T MISS the ginger in this cake, but it's not overpowering. Fresh ginger, crystallized ginger, and powdered ginger all add their unique flavor to this cake that has a wonderful moist texture contributed in part by fresh, ripe pears. A good friend came to visit in January, which is the month she chooses to abstain from sugar and alcohol. However, she ate a thin slice of this cake because, as she said, "Ginger is good for you!" But you won't need that justification to eat this scrumptious cake. **Makes one 9 × 2-inch round cake, 12 servings**

CAKE

1 tablespoon unsalted butter, softened	Center a rack in the oven and preheat it to 350°F. Use your fingertips or a paper towel to butter the inside of the pan.
1 tablespoon all-purpose flour	Dust the inside of the pan with the flour. Shake and tilt the pan to evenly distribute the flour, then turn the pan over and shake out the excess over the sink.
	Cut a round of parchment paper to fit the bottom of the pan. Butter the parchment paper round and place in the pan, butter-side up.
4 ounces (8 tablespoons, 1 stick) unsalted butter, softened	Place the butter in the bowl of an electric stand mixer or in a large bowl. Use the flat beater attachment or hand-held mixer to beat the butter on medium speed until it's fluffy, about 2 minutes.
½ cup granulated sugar **1 cup firmly packed light brown sugar**	Add the granulated sugar and the light brown sugar to the butter and cream together well. Stop occasionally and scrape down the bottom and sides of the bowl with a rubber spatula.
2 extra-large eggs, at room temperature	One at a time, add the eggs, stopping to scrape down the bottom and sides of the bowl after each addition. The mixture may look curdled as the eggs are added, but as you scrape down the bowl, the mixture will smooth out.
1 pound very ripe pears (2 large)	Use a vegetable peeler or a knife to peel the pears. Cut them in half lengthwise and use a melon baller or ice cream scoop to remove the stem, core, and seeds. Dice the pears very finely or mash with a fork against the side of a bowl. Add the pears to the butter mixture and blend together. At this point the mixture may look curdled, but it will smooth out as the dry ingredients are added.

Essential Gear

- 9-inch round spring-form pan
- Scissors
- Parchment paper
- Electric stand mixer with flat beater attachment and wire whip attachment, or large mixing bowl and hand-held mixer
- Vegetable peeler or sharp knife
- Melon baller or small ice cream scoop
- Rubber spatula
- Sifter
- Cooling rack

Keeping

Store the cake tightly wrapped in aluminum foil at room temperature up to 4 days. To freeze up to 3 months, wrap the cake tightly in several layers of plastic wrap and aluminum foil. Use a large piece of masking tape and an indelible marker to label and date the contents. If frozen, defrost overnight in the refrigerator and bring to room temperature before serving.

Making a Change

Replace the pears with peeled, cored apples that have been cooked briefly in a heavy-bottomed saucepan over medium heat until they are the consistency of applesauce, or use 2 cups applesauce.

⅓ cup peeled and finely diced fresh ginger 2 teaspoons pure vanilla extract or vanilla paste ¾ teaspoon ground ginger ½ teaspoon freshly grated nutmeg	Add the fresh ginger, vanilla, ground ginger, and nutmeg to the butter mixture and blend together thoroughly.
2 cups cake flour 1 teaspoon baking soda ½ teaspoon salt	Over a large piece of waxed or parchment paper or a bowl, sift together the flour and baking soda. Add the salt and toss together to blend.
½ cup buttermilk	Add the dry ingredients to the butter mixture in 3 stages, alternately with the buttermilk, blending thoroughly after each addition. Stop occasionally to scrape down the bottom and sides of the bowl to ensure even mixing.
¾ cup finely chopped crystallized ginger	Add the crystallized ginger to the batter and stir to distribute evenly.
	Transfer the batter to the prepared springform pan. Use a rubber spatula to spread it evenly into the pan.
	Bake for 45 to 50 minutes, until a cake tester inserted into the center comes out clean.
	Remove the pan from the oven and cool completely on a rack. Release the clip on the side of the springform pan and gently lift it off of the cake.

GARNISH

1 cup heavy whipping cream	Place the cream in the chilled bowl of an electric stand mixer or in a large mixing bowl. Use the wire whip attachment or a hand-held mixer to whip the cream on medium speed until it is frothy.
2 tablespoons confectioners' sugar, sifted ¼ teaspoon ground ginger	Add the sugar and the ground ginger and continue to whip the cream until it holds soft peaks.
2 tablespoons finely chopped crystallized ginger	Serve each slice of cake with a large dollop of whipped cream on top. Sprinkle a little crystallized ginger over the center of the whipped cream.

Gingersnaps

CRYSTALLIZED GINGER gives these cookies both extra added sweet-hot flavor and texture. The cookies are rolled in sugar before baking, making them crackly on top. I love to eat these when it's cold outside because they warm me up. These keep well, but usually get eaten very quickly. **Makes about 5 dozen cookies**

2¼ cups all-purpose flour
2 teaspoons ground ginger
1 teaspoon baking soda
1 teaspoon ground cinnamon
½ teaspoon ground cloves
¼ teaspoon salt
¼ cup finely chopped
  crystallized ginger

Over a large piece of waxed or parchment paper or a bowl, sift together the flour, ginger, baking soda, cinnamon, and cloves. Add the salt and stir to blend. Add the crystallized ginger and toss to blend well. Set this mixture aside briefly.

6 ounces (12 tablespoons,
  1½ sticks) unsalted butter,
  softened
½ cup granulated sugar
⅓ cup firmly packed light
  brown sugar

Place the butter in the bowl of an electric stand mixer or a large mixing bowl. Use the flat beater attachment or a hand-held mixer to beat the butter until it is light and fluffy, about 2 minutes. Add the granulated sugar and brown sugar and cream together until light and fluffy, about 2 minutes.

1 extra-large egg, at room
  temperature
⅓ cup molasses

Add the egg and molasses to the butter mixture and blend together thoroughly. The egg and molasses will sit on top of the butter mixture, so after adding them stop and scrape down the sides and bottom of the bowl with a rubber spatula to help mix evenly. The mixture may look curdled but will smooth out when the dry ingredients are added.

Add the dry ingredients to the butter mixture in 3 stages, blending well after each addition. Tightly cover the bowl with plastic wrap and chill in the refrigerator at least 30 minutes.

Adjust the oven racks to the upper and lower thirds and preheat the oven to 350°F. Line two baking sheets with parchment paper sheets or non-stick liners.

½ cup granulated sugar

Dampen your hands with water. Pinch off 2 tablespoon-sized pieces of the dough and roll them in your hands into balls, then roll in the sugar. Place the balls on the baking sheets, leaving 2 inches of space between them so there is room for them to expand as they bake.

Essential Gear
- Sifter
- Electric stand mixer with flat beater attachment, or large mixing bowl and hand-held mixer
- Rubber spatula
- Two baking sheets
- Two parchment paper sheets or non-stick pan liners
- Two cooling racks
- Metal spatula

Keeping
Store the gingersnaps in an airtight container between layers of waxed paper at room temperature up to 1 week. To freeze up to 3 months, wrap the container tightly in several layers of plastic wrap and aluminum foil. Use a large piece of masking tape and an indelible marker to label and date the contents. If frozen, defrost overnight in the refrigerator and bring to room temperature before serving.

Bake the cookies for 6 minutes. Switch the baking sheets and bake another 6 to 7 minutes, until the cookies are set and the tops are cracked.

Remove the baking pans from the oven and cool on racks for 5 minutes. Use a metal spatula to transfer the cookies to racks to cool completely.

Double Ginger Shortbread

CRYSTALLIZED GINGER and ground ginger add their sweet-hot, piquant flavor to classic buttery shortbread. These are especially good when the weather is cold because ginger warms you up. **Makes 5 dozen 1 × 2-inch cookies**

1 pound (2 cups, 4 sticks) unsalted butter, softened

Place the butter in the bowl of an electric stand mixer or in a large mixing bowl. Using the flat beater attachment or a hand-held mixer, beat the butter on medium speed until light and fluffy, about 2 minutes.

1 cup superfine sugar

Add the sugar and beat together until thoroughly blended, about 2 minutes. Stop occasionally and scrape down the bottom and sides of the bowl with a rubber spatula.

4 cups all-purpose flour
2¼ teaspoons ground ginger
½ teaspoon salt
¼ teaspoon freshly grated nutmeg
⅔ cup finely chopped crystallized ginger

In a medium mixing bowl, combine the flour, ground ginger, salt, and nutmeg. Toss to blend together. Add this mixture to the butter mixture in 4 stages, blending well after each addition. Add the crystallized ginger and stir to blend evenly.

2 tablespoons all-purpose flour

Sprinkle the inside of the baking pan evenly with the flour, then transfer the shortbread dough to the pan. Use your fingertips and a rolling pin to press and roll the dough evenly into the pan and the corners. Use a ruler and a sharp knife to score the shortbread into 1 × 2-inch rectangles. Use a fork to pierce each shortbread rectangle in 2 places on the diagonal. Cover the baking pan tightly with plastic wrap and chill in the refrigerator at least 2 hours.

Adjust the oven racks to the upper and lower thirds and preheat the oven to 300°F. Line 2 baking sheets with parchment paper or non-stick pan liners.

Use a sharp knife to cut through the scored pieces of shortbread. Transfer the shortbread rectangles to the baking sheets, leaving at

Essential Gear

- Electric stand mixer with flat beater attachment, or large mixing bowl and hand-held mixer
- Rubber spatula
- 9 × 13-inch baking pan
- Ruler
- Sharp knife
- Fork
- Rolling pin
- Two baking sheets
- Two parchment paper sheets or non-stick pan liners
- Two cooling racks

Keeping

Store the shortbread in an airtight plastic container between layers of waxed paper at room temperature up to 1 week.

Streamlining

The shortbread dough can be made up to 3 days in advance and kept tightly wrapped in a double layer of plastic wrap in the refrigerator. To freeze up to 3 months, wrap the dough snugly in several layers of plastic wrap and place in a freezer bag. Use a large piece of masking tape and an

least 1 inch of space between them. Chill the shortbread for 15 minutes before baking.

Bake the shortbread for 15 minutes, then switch the baking sheets and bake another 15 to 18 minutes, until they are set and very lightly colored. Remove the baking sheets from the oven and cool the shortbread completely on the baking sheets on racks.

Triple Ginger Cheesecake

GINGER, GINGER, and more ginger give this cheesecake its distinctive sweet, warm flavor. Gingersnaps are the basis of the crust that holds the creamy filling accented with both fresh ginger and crystallized ginger. Layering the flavor in this way brings out its best qualities. As with all cheesecakes, this one needs to be made at least a day in advance of serving so there is enough time for it to cool and chill. **Makes one 9½-inch round cake, 12 to 14 servings**

Center a rack in the oven and preheat it to 325°F.

1 tablespoon unsalted butter, softened

Using a paper towel or your fingertips, butter the inside of the springform pan. Use a double layer of heavy-duty foil to wrap around the bottom of the pan. This prevents any water from the water bath from seeping into the pan.

GINGERSNAP COOKIE CRUST

9 ounces (about 34) gingersnaps
2 tablespoons granulated sugar
1 teaspoon finely ground ginger

In the work bowl of a food processor fitted with the steel blade, combine the gingersnaps, sugar, and ground ginger. Pulse until the mixture is finely ground, about 2 minutes. Or place the gingersnaps, sugar, and ginger in a sturdy plastic bag and seal it. Use a rolling pin to crush the mixture to a very fine crumb consistency.

3 ounces (6 tablespoons, ¾ stick) unsalted butter, melted and cooled

Transfer the crumbs to a medium bowl and add the butter. Use a rubber spatula to toss the mixture together and moisten all the crumbs.

Using your fingers, press the crumbs evenly into the bottom and partway up the sides of the springform pan.

Chill the crust while preparing the cheesecake batter.

indelible marker to label and date the contents. If frozen, defrost in the refrigerator.

Adding Style

Dip one end of each shortbread rectangle on the diagonal into tempered bittersweet or semisweet chocolate (see page 43).

Essential Gear

- 9½-inch round springform pan
- Heavy-duty aluminum foil
- Food processor or rolling pin
- Electric stand mixer with flat beater attachment or hand-held mixer and large mixing bowl
- Microplane grater or citrus zester
- 12-inch round cake pan or large roasting pan
- Cooling rack
- 10- or 12-inch pastry bag with large open star tip

Keeping

Store the undecorated cheesecake tightly covered with aluminum foil in the refrigerator up to 4 days. To freeze up to 2 months, wrap the cake tightly in several layers of plastic wrap and aluminum foil. Use a large piece of masking tape and an indelible marker to label and date the contents. If frozen, defrost overnight in the refrigerator and bring to room temperature before serving.

CHEESECAKE

2 pounds cream cheese, softened	Place the cream cheese in the bowl of an electric stand mixer or in a large mixing bowl. Use the flat beater attachment or hand-held mixer to beat the cream cheese on medium speed until it's fluffy, about 2 minutes.
1¼ cups granulated sugar	Add the sugar and mix thoroughly. Stop occasionally and scrape down the sides and bottom of the bowl with a rubber spatula.
4 extra-large eggs, at room temperature	One at a time, add the eggs to the cream cheese mixture, beating well after each addition. The eggs will sit on top of the cream cheese, so stop frequently and scrape down the bottom and sides of the bowl with a rubber spatula to help mix evenly.
1 cup sour cream **½ cup heavy whipping cream**	Add the sour cream and cream to the cream cheese mixture and blend thoroughly.
2 tablespoons finely grated fresh gingerroot **Finely grated zest of 2 large lemons** **1 tablespoon freshly squeezed lemon juice**	Add the gingerroot, lemon zest, and lemon juice to the cream cheese mixture and blend well.
1 cup finely chopped crystallized ginger	Add the crystallized ginger and stir to blend thoroughly.
	Turn the cheesecake batter into the crust in the springform pan. Use a rubber spatula to smooth and even the top.
1 quart boiling water	Place the springform pan in the larger pan and set the pan on the oven rack. Carefully pour the boiling water into the bottom pan until it reaches halfway up the side of the springform pan. Baking the cake in a water bath cushions it from the heat and adds extra moisture to the oven, which keeps the top from cracking.
	Bake the cake for 1 hour and 25 minutes, until the top is light golden and jiggles only slightly when moved. Turn off the oven and leave the cheesecake in the oven, with the door closed, until it is cool, about 1 hour.
	Remove the pan from the oven and remove it from the water. Place it on a cooling rack. Let the cheesecake cool to room temperature. Remove the foil from the outside of the pan. Cover the top of the cheesecake with waxed paper and wrap tightly in aluminum foil. Refrigerate the cake for at least 6 hours before serving. To unmold

the cheesecake, dip a thin-bladed knife in hot water and dry, then run it around the inner edge of the pan; release the clip on the rim of the pan and gently lift it off the cake.

GARNISH

⅓ cup heavy whipping
cream
1 tablespoon confectioners'
sugar, sifted

Place the cream in the chilled bowl of an electric stand mixer or a medium mixing bowl. Using the wire whip attachment or a hand-held mixer, whip the cream on medium speed until it is frothy. Add the confectioners' sugar and continue to whip the cream on medium speed until it holds firm peaks.

12 pieces crystallized ginger

Fit the pastry bag with the star tip. Visually divide the top of the cake into 12 pieces. At the outer edge of each piece, center a whipped cream rosette (see page 44). Place a piece of crystallized ginger on top of each whipped cream rosette.

Chill the cheesecake until ready to serve

Triple Vanilla Soufflé

THIS CLASSIC airy soufflé is always very impressive when it's served. Soufflés are delicate and must be eaten as soon as they come out of the oven before they collapse. The soufflé mixture can be partially made several hours in advance and kept in the refrigerator until it's ready to be finished and baked. Using three forms of vanilla—vanilla sugar, vanilla beans, and pure vanilla extract—builds layers that give this soufflé its rich depth of flavor. **Makes one 5-cup soufflé, 8 servings**

VANILLA SUGAR

3 (or more) fresh, moist
vanilla beans

Use a small sharp knife to slit the vanilla beans down the center, taking care not to cut them all the way through. Carefully open up the sides of the beans so the tiny vanilla seeds are exposed.

2 to 5 pounds granulated or
superfine sugar

Place about ⅓ of the sugar in a canister or other container. Add 1 of the vanilla beans. Repeat layering the sugar and vanilla beans, ending with sugar.

Let the sugar stand for a few days, shaking it occasionally to evenly distribute the vanilla flavor.

As you use sugar from the canister, add more so that it will remain full.

Essential Gear
- 5-cup soufflé dish
- 2-quart heavy-bottomed
  saucepan
- Whisk or heat-resistant
  spatula
- Electric stand mixer with
  wire whip attachment, or
  large mixing bowl and
  hand-held mixer
- Rubber spatula

Keeping
Store vanilla sugar in a tightly sealed canister or other container in a cool, dry place, such as the pantry.

Streamlining
Prepare the soufflé batter through adding the vanilla extract. Transfer the batter

After you have used a vanilla bean for making a sauce or custard, rinse it off thoroughly and let it dry completely on a paper towel. Add the vanilla bean to the canister of vanilla sugar. By adding both sugar and vanilla beans, you will always have a good supply of vanilla sugar on hand.

SOUFFLÉ

1 tablespoon unsalted butter, softened 1 tablespoon vanilla sugar	Use a paper towel or your fingertips to butter the inside of the soufflé dish, then sprinkle the inside with vanilla sugar. Tilt the dish so the sugar sticks to the butter. Set aside while preparing the soufflé batter.
⅓ cup milk 2 vanilla beans	Place the milk in the saucepan. Use a sharp knife to slit each vanilla bean down the center. With the back of the knife, scrape out the vanilla seeds and add to the milk with the vanilla beans. Bring the milk to a boil over medium-high heat. Cover the pan, turn off the heat, and let the vanilla infuse into the milk for 10 minutes.
	Adjust an oven rack to the lower third and preheat the oven to 400°F.
	Use a fork or a pair of tongs to remove the vanilla beans from the milk. Reheat the milk over medium heat.
3 tablespoons all-purpose flour	Add the flour to the milk and whisk or stir together until there are no lumps remaining, about 1 minute.
⅓ cup vanilla sugar	Add the sugar and whisk or stir together constantly until the mixture comes to a boil and thickens, about 2 minutes. Remove the pan from the heat.
4 extra-large egg yolks, at room temperature	One at a time, whisk or stir the egg yolks into the milk mixture, blending thoroughly.
1 tablespoon unsalted butter, softened	Add the butter and stir until it is melted and thoroughly blended into the mixture.
1 teaspoon pure vanilla extract	Stir in the vanilla.
5 extra-large egg whites, at room temperature ½ teaspoon cream of tartar 2 tablespoons granulated sugar	Place the egg whites in the grease-free bowl of an electric stand mixer or in a large grease-free bowl. Using the wire whip attachment or a hand-held mixer, whip the egg whites on medium-high speed until they are frothy. Add the cream of tartar and continue to whip. When soft peaks form, gradually sprinkle on the sugar and continue to whip until the egg whites hold glossy and firm, but not stiff, peaks.
	Fold ¼ of the whipped egg whites into the egg yolk mixture. Gently fold the yolk mixture into the whipped egg whites, blending thor-

to a bowl, cover tightly with plastic wrap, and refrigerate up to 8 hours. When ready to bake, whip the egg whites, fold them into the soufflé batter, transfer to the soufflé dish, and bake.

Making a Change
Fold 1 cup finely ground toasted almonds or hazelnuts into the soufflé batter before turning into the soufflé dish to bake.

Adding Style
Serve the soufflé with a scoop of vanilla or caramel ice cream.

Serve the soufflé with Raspberry Sauce (see Meyer Lemon Soufflés, page 143).

oughly. Be careful not to mix vigorously and deflate the air beaten into the egg whites, which is what makes the soufflé rise as it bakes.

Transfer the soufflé mixture to the prepared soufflé dish. Use the rubber spatula to run around the rim of the dish and slightly mound the soufflé mixture. Bake for 30 minutes, until the soufflé is puffed over the top of the dish, and looks set, and the center wiggles a little. You can also test for doneness with a cake tester inserted into the center of the soufflé. It should come out moist, but not runny.

1 tablespoon confectioners' sugar

Remove the soufflé dish from the oven, sprinkle the top with sugar, and serve immediately.

Vanilla and Macadamia Nut Tart

V ANILLA IS USED in three forms—beans, extract, and powder— to contribute its rich, full-bodied flavor to this yummy tart. The filling is soft and chewy but also crunchy with the texture of macadamia nuts. **Makes one 11-inch round tart, 14 to 16 servings**

VANILLA PASTRY DOUGH

1³/₄ cup all-purpose flour
¼ cup granulated vanilla sugar (see page 552)
½ teaspoon vanilla powder

In the work bowl of a food processor fitted with the steel blade, combine the flour, sugar, and vanilla powder. Pulse briefly to blend.

2 ounces (4 tablespoons, ½ stick) unsalted butter, chilled

Cut the butter into small pieces and add. Pulse until the butter is cut into very tiny pieces, about 30 seconds. The texture should be sandy with very tiny lumps throughout.

1 extra-large egg yolk, at room temperature
1 tablespoon heavy whipping cream
1 teaspoon pure vanilla extract

In a small bowl, combine the egg yolk, cream, and vanilla. With the food processor running, pour this mixture through the feed tube. Process until the dough wraps itself around the blade, 30 seconds to 1 minute.

Turn the pastry dough onto a large piece of plastic wrap. Shape into a flat disk and wrap tightly in a double layer of plastic wrap. Chill in the refrigerator until firm before using, about 2 hours. Chilling the dough relaxes the gluten in the flour so it won't be too elastic and will roll out easily. It also firms up the butter in the dough so it will

Essential Gear

- Food processor
- Rolling pin
- 11-inch round, fluted-edge tart pan with removable bottom
- Baking sheet
- Aluminum foil
- Pie weights
- Cooling rack
- Whisk
- Small saucepan
- Sharp knife
- Rubber spatula
- Electric stand mixer with wire whip attachment, or a medium bowl and hand-held mixer

Keeping

The tart can last up to 4 days at room temperature. Place a piece of waxed paper over the top of the tart, then tightly cover it with aluminum foil.

Streamlining

The pastry dough can be made in advance and kept

need less flour when rolled out. If the dough is too firm it will splinter and break when rolled out. Let it stand at room temperature for 10 to 15 minutes before rolling to become more pliable.

Center a rack in the oven and preheat it to 350°F.

On a smooth, flat surface, roll out the pastry dough between sheets of lightly floured waxed or parchment paper to a large circle about 13 inches in diameter. To tell if the dough will fit the tart pan, hold the pan above the dough. If there are 2 or 3 inches of dough that protrude beyond the sides of the pan, it will fit.

Carefully peel the paper off the top of the dough. Brush excess flour off the dough, then loosely roll the pastry dough around the rolling pin without the bottom piece of paper. Place the tart pan directly underneath the rolling pin and carefully unroll the pastry dough onto it.

Gently lift up the sides and ease the pastry dough into the bottom and sides of the tart pan, pushing it lightly into the fluted edges. Trim off the excess pastry dough at the top of the pan by running the rolling pin over the top. Or use your fingers to press against the top of the pan to remove the excess pastry dough.

Place the tart pan on a baking sheet and chill in the refrigerator for 15 minutes before baking.

Line the pastry shell with a large piece of aluminum foil that fits well against the bottom and sides. Fill with pie weights or a mixture of rice and beans. Bake for 10 minutes. If the bottom of the pastry shell puffs up, gently pierce it in several places with a fork to release the air. Remove the foil and weights and bake another 10 to 12 minutes, until light golden and set. Remove the pan from the oven and transfer to a rack to cool while preparing the filling.

in the refrigerator, tightly wrapped in a double layer of plastic wrap, up to 4 days. To freeze up to 3 months, wrap the dough snugly in several layers of plastic wrap and place it in a freezer bag. Use a large piece of masking tape and an indelible marker to label and date the contents. If frozen, defrost overnight in the refrigerator before using.

Making a Change
Replace the macadamia nuts with whole blanched almonds or pecans.

VANILLA MACADAMIA NUT FILLING

⅓ cup firmly packed light brown sugar
¼ cup granulated vanilla sugar (see page 552)
¼ cup light corn syrup
¼ cup dark corn syrup
2 extra-large eggs, at room temperature
2 extra-large egg yolks, at room temperature
1 tablespoon pure vanilla extract or vanilla paste

Place the light brown sugar, vanilla sugar, light and dark corn syrups, eggs, egg yolks, and vanilla in a large bowl. Whisk together until thoroughly blended, about 1 minute.

1 tablespoon unsalted butter, softened 2 whole vanilla beans	Place the butter in a small saucepan. Using a sharp knife, split each vanilla bean lengthwise. Scrape out the seeds and add both the seeds and vanilla beans to the butter. Over medium heat, brown the butter until it is just starting to turn amber. This takes about 3 to 4 minutes. Use a fork or tongs to remove the vanilla beans, then add the browned butter to the filling mixture and blend in well.
1²/₃ cups toasted, unsalted, and coarsely chopped macadamia nuts	Add the macadamia nuts to the filling mixture and stir to distribute evenly.
	Transfer the filling to the pastry shell. Smooth and even the top with a rubber spatula. Bake the tart for 30 minutes, until the filling is set and light golden. Remove the tart from the oven and place on a rack to cool completely.

GARNISH

½ cup heavy whipping cream	Place the cream in the chilled bowl of an electric stand mixer or a medium bowl. Use the wire whip attachment or a hand-held mixer to whip the cream until it is frothy.
2 teaspoon granulated vanilla sugar (see page 552) 1 teaspoon pure vanilla extract or vianill paste	Add the vanilla sugar and vanilla and continue to whip until the cream holds soft peaks.
	Remove the sides of the tart pan (see page 42) before serving. Serve each slice of the tart warm with a large dollop of vanilla whipped cream.

Very Vanilla Pound Cake

PURE VANILLA in four forms—sugar, powder, paste, and extract—is used to create the ultimate vanilla taste experience. This is a great cake to serve with tea or coffee in the afternoon. It's excellent served with vanilla ice cream, caramel ice cream, caramel sauce, or raspberry sauce. **Makes one 8¹/₂ × 4¹/₂ × 2¹/₂-inch loaf, 12 servings**

Center a rack in the oven and preheat it to 325°F.

Essential Gear
- 8¹/₂ × 4¹/₂ × 2¹/₂-inch loaf pan
- 1-inch natural-bristle pastry brush or a paper towel
- Electric stand mixer with flat beater attachment and wire whip attachment, or

2 teaspoons unsalted butter, melted and cooled	Use a pastry brush or a paper towel to coat the inside of the loaf pan with the butter.
2 teaspoons all-purpose flour	Sprinkle the inside of the pan with the flour. Shake and tilt the pan to coat it with the flour, then turn it upside down over the sink and shake out the excess.
8 ounces (16 tablespoons, 2 sticks) unsalted butter, softened	Place the butter in the bowl of an electric stand mixer or in a large bowl. Use the flat beater attachment or a hand-held mixer to beat the butter on medium speed until fluffy, about 2 minutes.
1½ cups superfine vanilla sugar (see page 552)	Reduce the mixer speed to low and add the sugar gradually to the butter. Turn the mixer to medium speed and beat the mixture until creamy, about 1 minute. Stop and scrape down the bottom and sides of the bowl with the rubber spatula. This helps the mixture to blend evenly.
4 extra-large eggs, at room temperature	One at a time, add the eggs to the butter mixture, beating well after each addition. Stop frequently and scrape down the bottom and sides of the bowl with the rubber spatula. At first the mixture may look curdled as the eggs are added, but as you scrape down the bowl, the mixture will smooth out.
3 tablespoons milk **2 teaspoons pure vanilla extract** **1 teaspoon pure vanilla paste**	In a liquid measuring cup or small bowl, combine the milk, vanilla extract, and vanilla paste. Stir together to blend, then add to the butter mixture with the mixer on low speed and blend thoroughly.
2 cups cake flour **1 teaspoon baking powder** **1 teaspoon pure vanilla powder** **¼ teaspoon salt**	Over a large piece of waxed or parchment paper or a bowl, sift together the flour and baking powder. Add the vanilla powder and salt and toss to blend together.
	Add the dry ingredients to the butter mixture in 3 stages, beating well after each addition. Stop frequently and scrape down the bottom and sides of the bowl with the rubber spatula.
	Transfer the batter to the prepared pan. Use the rubber spatula to smooth and even the top. Bake the cake for 1 hour and 20 minutes, until a cake tester inserted in the center comes out with no crumbs clinging to it.
	Remove the pan from the oven and cool on a rack for 20 minutes. Invert the pan and turn the cake out. Re-invert the cake, so the top is facing up. Leave the cake to cool completely on the rack. Cut the cake into serving slices and serve at room temperature.

hand-held mixer and large mixing bowl
• Rubber spatula
• Sifter
• Cooling rack

Keeping
Store the cake tightly wrapped in aluminum foil at room temperature up to 4 days. To freeze up to 4 months, wrap the cake tightly in several layers of plastic wrap and aluminum foil. Use a large piece of masking tape and an indelible marker to label and date the contents. If frozen, defrost overnight in the refrigerator, and bring to room temperature before serving.

Making a Change
Add 1½ cups roughly chopped nuts or dried apricots to the batter before turning into the pan to bake.

Adding Style
Serve slices of the cooled cake with Raspberry Sauce (see Meyer Lemon Soufflés, page 143) and mixed berries, Caramel Sauce (see Rum-Raisin Pound Cake, page 614), fudge sauce, vanilla ice cream, or caramel ice cream.

19

HERBS

Herbs are becoming very popular as a main ingredient for baking. I am seeing more herb desserts on restaurant menus and in major food magazines. For me, however, herb desserts go back a long way. I remember using them when I worked in Europe, where some restaurants have their own herb gardens. What I like most about herbs is that they impart a fresh and lively, distinct flavor.

Many people shy away from using herbs. Perhaps it's because they believe that herbs are hard to work with and may not be very exciting. This is just not the case. Herbs are very easy to use and bring flavor complexity that is always satisfying. I encourage you to try all of the recipes in this chapter. You, your family, and your friends won't be disappointed.

I have chosen my favorite herbs for the recipes in this chapter: chocolate mint, cinnamon basil, lavender, lemon verbena, and rosemary. In many of these recipes I give variations using other herbs.

Fresh herbs are usually found in the spring and summer, but often they can also be found throughout the year because they are grown in greenhouses. Fresh herbs are sold in the produce section of supermarkets, natural food stores, and specialty food shops. I'm lucky enough to have my own herb garden right outside my kitchen door. It's surprising how easy it is to grow your own herbs and it's really satisfying when you can snip what you need from your own garden. But if you don't have the space for a garden, herbs grow very easily in pots and will even grow indoors when placed in a sunny window. Start with small plants because they grow quickly and don't require much maintenance.

TIPS AND TECHNIQUES

All of the recipes in this chapter use herbs in their fresh form, with the exception of lavender, which is dried. Selecting herbs from the market should be done with the same care as selecting vegetables and fruits. Make sure they look fresh and vibrant, don't have any imperfections, and are not moldy. Also, smell the herbs to make sure they have their distinct aroma.

If you aren't growing your own, store fresh herbs loosely wrapped in plastic or in their plastic containers in the vegetable bin in the refrigerator for no more than a few days. Use them while they are still fresh-looking. Because herbs impart their flavor and aroma to other foods, try to keep them separate. Dried lavender flowers should be stored in a tightly sealed glass jar in a cool, dry place. I don't recommend freezing fresh herbs because they lose their flavor and color and become limp.

Use whole leaves of chocolate mint and cinnamon basil. Both of these are steeped in either milk or cream, depending on the recipe, and then strained out. Lemon verbena and rosemary leaves are finely chopped before they are added to a dough or batter. Small, dried lavender flowers are simply added to a dough right at the end of mixing.

If you have fresh herbs growing in a pot or in the garden, snip the leaves and wash and dry them right before use. I like to use a salad spinner to dry my herbs after they're washed.

Lemon Verbena and Walnut Tea Cake

LEMON VERBENA has a tangy, lemony flavor and fragrance that comes through very well in this cake. It is especially good with a warm lemon glaze. I like to bake this cake in a grooved tube pan. This is a great cake to serve for afternoon tea. **Makes one 9-inch round tube cake, 12 to 14 servings**

Center a rack in the oven and preheat it to 350°F.

2 teaspoons unsalted butter, melted 2 teaspoons all-purpose flour	Use a pastry brush or a paper towel to butter the inside of the pan, being sure to get into all the grooves. Sprinkle the flour inside the pan and shake and tilt the pan to cover the bottom and sides. Turn the pan upside down over the sink and shake out any excess flour.
8 ounces (16 tablespoons, 2 sticks) unsalted butter, softened	Place the butter in the bowl of an electric stand mixer or in a large bowl. Use the flat beater attachment or hand-held mixer to beat the butter on medium speed until it's fluffy, about 2 minutes.
½ cup firmly packed light brown sugar ¾ cup granulated sugar	Add the brown sugar and granulated sugar to the butter, and cream together well. Stop occasionally and scrape down the sides and bottom of the bowl with a rubber spatula.
3 extra-large eggs, at room temperature	One at a time, add the eggs to the butter mixture, stopping to scrape down the bottom and sides of the bowl after each addition. At first the mixture may look curdled as the eggs are added, but as you scrape down the bowl, the mixture will smooth out.
1 teaspoon pure vanilla extract	Add the vanilla and blend.
2 cups fresh lemon verbena leaves, washed and dried Finely grated zest of 2 lemons	Finely mince the lemon verbena leaves. Add to the butter mixture with the lemon zest and blend thoroughly.
2½ cups all-purpose flour 2 teaspoons baking powder 1 teaspoon baking soda ¼ teaspoon salt	Over a large piece of waxed or parchment paper or a bowl, sift together the flour, baking powder, and baking soda. Add the salt and toss together to blend.
3 tablespoons heavy whipping cream	Add the dry ingredients to the butter mixture alternately with the cream in 3 stages. Stop after each addition and scrape down the sides and bottom of the bowl. Blend the mixture thoroughly.
1½ cups walnuts, roughly chopped	Add the chopped walnuts to the batter and blend thoroughly.

Essential Gear

- 1-inch natural-bristle pastry brush
- 9 × 4-inch tube, kugelhopf, or Bundt pan
- Electric stand mixer with flat beater attachment, or large mixing bowl and hand-held mixer
- Rubber spatula
- Microplane grater or citrus zester
- Sifter
- Cooling rack

Keeping

Store the cake tightly wrapped in plastic up to 4 days at room temperature. To freeze up to 4 months, tightly wrap the cake in several layers of plastic wrap and aluminum foil. Use a large piece of masking tape and an indelible marker to label and date the contents. If frozen, defrost overnight in the refrigerator and bring to room temperature before serving.

Making a Change

Replace the walnuts with pecans or almonds.

Transfer the batter to the prepared pan. Use the rubber spatula to smooth and even the top.

Bake for 50 to 55 minutes, until a cake tester inserted in the center of the cake comes out clean.

Remove the pan from the oven and cool on a rack for 15 minutes. Invert the pan onto the rack and leave it for a few minutes so the cake will drop out of the pan. Remove the pan and let the cake cool completely.

GARNISH

2 tablespoons confectioners' sugar, sifted	Dust the top of the cake with sugar before serving.

WARM LEMON GLAZE

1½ cups confectioners' sugar, sifted **Finely grated zest of 1 large lemon**	Place the sugar and lemon zest in a large bowl.
¼ cup freshly squeezed lemon juice	Warm the lemon juice in a microwave oven on low power for 1 minute. Pour the lemon juice over the sugar and stir together until smooth.

Serve slices of the cake with a spoonful of the warm lemon glaze.

Lemon Verbena Shortbread

L EMON VERBENA adds its tangy, lemony flavor to this classic buttery shortbread. Lemon verbena is an herb that grows easily in a pot on an indoor windowsill, so you can make these even in the winter. **Makes sixty 1 × 2-inch cookies**

Essential Gear
- Electric stand mixer with flat beater attachment or large mixing bowl and hand-held mixer
- Rubber spatula
- 9 × 13-inch baking pan
- Rolling pin
- Ruler
- Two baking sheets
- Two parchment paper sheets or non-stick liners
- Two cooling racks

1 pound (2 cups, 4 sticks) unsalted butter, softened	Place the butter in the bowl of an electric stand mixer or in a large bowl. Using the flat beater attachment or a hand-held mixer, beat the butter on medium speed until light and fluffy, about 2 minutes.
1 cup superfine sugar	Add the sugar and beat together until thoroughly blended, about 2 minutes. Stop occasionally and scrape down the bottom and sides of the bowl with a rubber spatula.

4 cups all-purpose flour **½ teaspoon salt**	In a medium bowl, combine the flour and salt. Toss to blend together. Add to the butter mixture in 4 stages, blending thoroughly after each addition. Stop and scrape down the sides and bottom of the bowl after each addition to ensure even mixing.	

Keeping

Store the shortbread in an airtight plastic container between layers of waxed paper at room temperature up to 1 week. To freeze up to 3 months, wrap the container tightly in several layers of plastic wrap and aluminum foil. Use a large piece of masking tape and an indelible marker to label and date the contents. If frozen, defrost overnight in the refrigerator and bring to room temperature before serving.

Finely grated zest of 1 large lemon
¾ cup loosely packed fresh lemon verbena leaves, washed, dried, and finely chopped

Add the lemon zest and chopped lemon verbena and continue to mix until the dough is smooth and soft.

2 tablespoons all-purpose flour

Sprinkle the inside of the baking pan evenly with the flour, then transfer the shortbread dough to the pan. Use your fingertips and a rolling pin to press and roll the dough evenly into the pan and the corners. Use a ruler and a sharp knife to score the shortbread into 1 × 2-inch rectangles. Use a fork to pierce each shortbread rectangle in 2 places on the diagonal. Cover the baking pan tightly with plastic wrap and chill in the refrigerator for at least 2 hours.

Adjust the oven racks to the upper and lower thirds and preheat the oven to 300°F. Line the baking sheets with parchment paper or nonstick liners.

Use a sharp knife and cut through the scored pieces of shortbread. Transfer the shortbread rectangles to the baking sheets, leaving at least 1 inch of space between them.

Bake the shortbread for 15 minutes, then switch the baking sheets and bake another 15 to 18 minutes, until the shortbread cookies are set and very lightly colored. Remove the baking sheets from the oven and cool the cookies completely on the baking sheets on racks.

Streamlining

The shortbread dough can be made up to 3 days in advance and kept tightly wrapped in a double layer of plastic wrap in the refrigerator. To freeze up to 3 months, wrap the dough snugly in several layers of plastic wrap and place in a freezer bag. Use a large piece of masking tape and an indelible marker to label and date the contents. If frozen, defrost in the refrigerator.

Fresh Rosemary and Lemon Scones with Dried Figs

THESE SCONES have a wonderful balance of flavors. Lemon adds its fresh, tart flavor to the sharp, herbal flavor of the fresh rosemary, and dried figs contribute a touch of sweetness. Serve these with afternoon tea or with lunch or dinner. They are easy to reheat in a 350°F oven for 10 to 15 minutes. **Makes eight 3-inch scones**

Essential Gear
- Baking sheet
- Parchment paper or non-stick liner
- Food processor
- Chef's knife

Center a rack in the oven and preheat it to 400°F. Line a baking sheet with parchment paper or a non-stick liner.

2 cups all-purpose flour **1½ tablespoons finely chopped fresh rosemary** **1 tablespoon granulated sugar** **1 tablespoon baking powder** **¼ teaspoon salt**	In the work bowl of a food processor fitted with the steel blade, combine the flour, rosemary, sugar, baking powder, and salt. Pulse a few times to blend and to chop the rosemary.
3 ounces (6 tablespoons, ¾ stick) unsalted butter, chilled	Cut the butter into small pieces and add to the mixture in the food processor. Pulse until the butter is cut into very tiny pieces, about 30 seconds. The texture should be sandy with very tiny lumps throughout.
⅓ cup heavy whipping cream **1 extra-large egg, at room temperature** **Finely grated zest of 2 large lemons**	Using a fork, lightly beat the cream and egg together in a liquid measuring cup. Add the lemon zest. With the food processor running, pour this mixture through the feed tube and process until the dough forms itself into a ball, about 30 seconds.
¾ cup finely chopped dried figs	Add the figs to the dough and pulse briefly until they are well distributed.

Dust a large piece of waxed or parchment paper with flour and turn the dough out onto it. Knead the dough briefly until it is smooth (see Essential Baking Language, page 45). Dust your hands with flour and shape it into a circle about 6 inches in diameter and 1 inch thick. Using a sharp knife dipped in flour, cut the circle in half and each half into 4 equal triangles.

Transfer the scones to the lined baking sheets, leaving at least 1 inch of space between them so they have room to expand as they bake.

GARNISH

2 teaspoons heavy whipping cream	Using a pastry brush, lightly brush the top of each scone with cream, taking care that it doesn't run down the sides and under the scones.
1 tablespoon granulated sugar	Lightly sprinkle the top of each scone with sugar.

Bake the scones for 18 to 20 minutes, until they are light golden. Remove the baking sheet from the oven and cool briefly. Serve the scones while they are warm. They can be reheated in a 350°F oven on a baking sheet for 10 minutes.

- Microplane grater or citrus zester
- Liquid measuring cup
- 1-inch natural-bristle pastry brush
- Cooling rack

Keeping
Store the scones in an airtight plastic container between layers of waxed paper at room temperature up to 4 days. To freeze up to 4 months, wrap the container tightly in several layers of plastic wrap and aluminum foil. Use a large piece of masking tape and an indelible marker to label and date the contents. If frozen, defrost overnight in the refrigerator and bring to room temperature before serving.

Streamlining
The unbaked scones can be frozen for up to 3 months, wrapped as above. It's not necessary to defrost the scones, but bake them 5 to 6 minutes longer.

Making a Change
Replace the rosemary with fresh thyme, tarragon, or basil.

Replace the figs with dried cranberries, cherries, apricots, or raisins.

Replace the figs with finely chopped walnuts or almonds.

Roasted Peach Tart with Cinnamon Basil Pastry Cream

R OASTED PEACHES sit atop a classic pastry cream filling flavored with cinnamon basil, a type of fresh basil that is easy to grow in a pot or in your herb garden. A delicate cookie crust pastry shell holds the filling. This is a succulent tart with a subtle cinnamon and mint flavor that you will find intriguing. I think this is a perfect tart to serve after a spring or summer meal because it is light and fresh. **Makes one 9½-inch round tart, 12 to 14 servings**

PASTRY DOUGH

1¼ cups all-purpose flour
⅓ cup confectioners' sugar
⅛ teaspoon salt

In the work bowl of a food processor fitted with the steel blade, combine the flour, sugar, and salt. Pulse briefly to blend.

4 ounces (8 tablespoons, 1 stick) unsalted butter, chilled

Cut the butter into small pieces and add to the flour mixture. Pulse until the butter is cut into very tiny pieces, about 30 seconds.

1 extra-large egg yolk, at room temperature
½ teaspoon pure vanilla extract or vanilla paste

In a small bowl, beat the egg yolk with the vanilla. With the food processor running, pour this mixture through the feed tube. Process the dough until the mixture wraps itself around the blade, about 1 minute.

Turn the pastry dough onto a large piece of plastic wrap. Shape into a flat disk and wrap tightly in a double layer of plastic wrap. Chill in the refrigerator until firm before using, at least 2 hours. Chilling the dough relaxes the gluten in the flour so it won't be too elastic and will roll out easily. It also firms up the butter in the dough so it will need less flour when rolled out. If the dough is too firm it will splinter and break when rolled out. Let it stand at room temperature for 10 to 15 minutes before rolling to become more pliable.

Center a rack in the oven and preheat it to 375°F.

On a smooth, flat surface, roll out the pastry dough between sheets of lightly floured waxed or parchment paper to a large circle about 11 inches in diameter. To tell if the dough will fit the tart pan, hold the pan above the dough. If there are about 2 inches of dough that protrude beyond the sides of the pan, it will fit.

Carefully peel the paper off the top of the dough. Brush excess flour off the dough, then loosely roll the pastry dough around the rolling

Essential Gear

- Food processor
- Rolling pin
- Baking sheet
- 9½-inch round, fluted-edge tart pan with removable bottom
- Aluminum foil
- Pie weights
- Cooling rack
- Large mixing bowl
- Large heavy-bottomed saucepan
- Electric stand mixer with wire whip attachment, or large mixing bowl and hand-held mixer
- Rubber spatula
- Ladle
- Whisk, heat-resistant spatula, or wooden spoon
- Small saucepan
- Shallow baking pan
- Parchment paper or non-stick liner

Keeping

Although the tart is best eaten the day it's made, it can last up to 2 days. Store the tart loosely covered with waxed paper, then tightly wrapped with aluminum foil in the refrigerator.

Streamlining

The pastry dough can be made in advance and kept in the refrigerator, tightly wrapped in a double layer of plastic wrap, up to 4 days. To freeze up to 3 months, wrap

pin without the bottom piece of paper. Place the tart pan directly underneath the rolling pin and carefully unroll the pastry dough into the tart pan. Gently lift up the sides and ease the pastry dough into the bottom and sides of the tart pan. Trim off the excess pastry dough at the top of the pan. Transfer the tart pan to a baking sheet and chill for 15 minutes. This helps prevent the dough from shrinking as it bakes.

Line the pastry shell with a large piece of aluminum foil that fits well against the bottom and sides. Fill the pastry shell with pie weights or a mixture of rice and beans. Bake for 10 minutes, then remove the foil and weights. If the bottom of the pastry shell puffs up, gently pierce it in a few places with a fork or the point of a knife to release the air. Bake another 12 to 14 minutes, until light golden and set. Remove the pan from the oven and transfer the tart pan to a rack to cool completely.

CINNAMON BASIL PASTRY CREAM

1 cup milk
⅓ cup fresh cinnamon basil leaves, rinsed and patted dry

Place the milk in the saucepan over medium-high heat. Warm until small bubbles form around the edges. Add the cinnamon basil leaves, cover the pan, and let them infuse for 30 minutes.

3 extra-large egg yolks, at room temperature
⅓ cup granulated sugar

Place the egg yolks in the bowl of an electric stand mixer or a large bowl. Using the wire whip attachment or a hand-held mixer, whip the egg yolks on medium high speed until they are frothy. Add the sugar and whip together until the mixture is very thick and pale colored and holds a slowly dissolving ribbon as the beater is lifted, about 5 minutes.

2 tablespoons cornstarch, sifted

Turn the mixer speed to low and add the cornstarch. Use a rubber spatula to scrape down the bottom and sides of the bowl to encourage even mixing. Return the mixer speed to medium and whip until the cornstarch is thoroughly blended.

Use a slotted spoon, a skimmer, or tongs to remove the cinnamon basil leaves from the milk. Heat the milk on medium-high heat again, until tiny bubbles form around the edges.

Turn the mixer speed to low. Use a ladle to take about ½ cup of the hot milk from the pan and slowly add it to the egg yolk mixture. Whip together to blend. This tempers the egg yolks so they won't curdle when they are added to the milk.

Transfer the egg yolk mixture into the milk in the saucepan. Stir the mixture constantly with a whisk, heat-resistant spatula, or wooden spoon, so it doesn't burn. Cook until the mixture starts to bubble and pop.

the dough snugly in several layers of plastic wrap and place it in a freezer bag. Use a large piece of masking tape and an indelible marker to label and date the contents. If frozen, defrost overnight in the refrigerator before using.

The pastry cream can be made up to 4 days in advance and kept in the refrigerator in a tightly covered bowl or container.

Troubleshooting
Don't roll out the pastry dough before it is chilled. The dough will be too soft and it will require a lot of flour to roll out, which results in a tough dough.

Once the pastry dough is unrolled into the tart pan, don't push it down forcefully. This will stretch the dough, which will shrink as it bakes, making it flat instead of taking the shape of the tart pan.

Making a Change
Replace the peaches with apricots or nectarines.

Remove the saucepan from the heat immediately and transfer the pastry cream to a bowl. Cover the top of the pastry cream with a piece of waxed paper to prevent a skin from forming on top. Cover the bowl with plastic wrap and place the bowl on a cooling rack. Leave the pastry cream to cool to room temperature, then chill it in the refrigerator until cold before using, at least 2 hours.

Stir the pastry cream vigorously before using to remove any lumps.

ROASTED PEACHES

¼ cup granulated sugar
½ cup water

Place the sugar and water together in a small saucepan. Bring to a boil over high heat to dissolve the sugar. Remove from the heat and cool.

1¼ pounds ripe peaches
(5 medium), washed
and dried

Cut the peaches in half along their seams and remove the pits.

Place the peach halves, cut-side down, in a shallow baking pan and pour the sugar syrup over them. Let them soak in the sugar syrup for 15 minutes.

Preheat the oven to 375°F.

Remove the peaches from the sugar syrup and pat dry on paper towels.

Line a baking sheet with parchment paper or a non-stick liner. Place the peach halves on the lined baking sheet, cut sides up. Roast in the oven for 15 to 20 minutes, until soft and the sugar syrup is lightly caramelized on the peaches.

Remove the baking sheet from the oven and cool slightly on a rack.

ASSEMBLY

Use a rubber spatula to evenly spread the pastry cream in the cooled tart shell.

Arrange the roasted peach halves on top of the pastry cream cut sides down, spacing them evenly. Lightly press down on the peach halves and they will spread out slightly.

GARNISH

2 sprigs fresh cinnamon basil,
washed and patted dry

Arrange the sprigs of cinnamon basil between the peaches. Serve the tart at room temperature.

Rolled Chocolate Cake with Minted White Chocolate Ganache

WHITE CHOCOLATE GANACHE, subtly flavored with chocolate mint from the garden, is the filling and icing in this rolled cake. When the cake is cut across the width, you can see the spiral of white rolled up inside the dark chocolate cake. The cake is rolled up while warm, immediately after baking, so it retains the rolled shape when cool. A simple decoration of chocolate mint leaves is all this yummy cake needs. **Makes one 15-inch cake, 12 to 15 servings**

ROLLED CHOCOLATE CAKE

Center a rack in the oven and preheat it to 450°F.

1 tablespoon unsalted butter, melted	Line the jelly-roll pan with a sheet of parchment paper. Use the pastry brush or a paper towel to coat the parchment paper with butter.
2 tablespoons all-purpose flour **¼ cup unsweetened cocoa powder (natural or Dutch-processed)** **⅛ teaspoon salt**	Over a medium piece of waxed or parchment paper or a bowl, sift together the flour and cocoa powder. Add the salt and toss together to blend.
5 extra-large egg whites, at room temperature **¼ teaspoon cream of tartar**	Place the egg whites in the grease-free bowl of an electric stand mixer or in a large grease-free bowl. Using the wire whip attachment or a hand-held mixer, whip the egg whites on medium-high speed until they are frothy. Add the cream of tartar and whip until the egg whites hold soft peaks.
⅓ cup superfine sugar **½ cup firmly packed light brown sugar**	Mix together the superfine sugar and light brown sugar. Sprinkle on 2 tablespoons of this mixture and continue to whip the egg whites on medium-high speed until they hold glossy and firm, but not stiff, peaks.
5 extra-large egg yolks, at room temperature	Place the egg yolks in the clean bowl of an electric stand mixer or in a large bowl. Using the wire whip attachment or a hand-held mixer, whip the egg yolks with the remaining sugar on medium-high speed until they are very thick and pale colored and hold a slowly dissolving ribbon as the beater is lifted, about 5 minutes.
	In 4 stages, alternately fold the whipped egg whites and dry ingredients into the whipped egg yolks, starting with the egg whites.

Essential Gear

- Jelly-roll pan (12 × 17 inches)
- two parchment paper sheets
- 1-inch natural-bristle pastry brush or paper towel
- Electric stand mixer with wire whip attachment and flat beater attachment, or large mixing bowl and hand-held mixer
- Rubber spatula
- Long-blade offset spatula or rubber spatula
- Cocoa dredger or small fine-mesh strainer
- Small sharp knife
- Kitchen towel
- Small saucepan
- Fine-mesh strainer
- Heat-resistant spatula or whisk
- Ruler
- 12- or 14-inch pastry bag and large open star tip
- Serrated knife

Keeping

Store the cake lightly tented with waxed paper and aluminum foil in the refrigerator up to 4 days.

Streamlining

The cake can be baked up to 3 days before filling. When the cake is completely cool wrap it tightly in a double layer of plastic wrap and store in the refrigerator.

Turn the batter out onto the lined jelly-roll pan. Use a long-blade off-set spatula or rubber spatula to spread the mixture smoothly and evenly over the parchment paper and into the corners of the pan.

Bake the cake for 8 to 10 minutes, until the cake looks set and springs back when touched lightly on top.

1 tablespoon unsweetened cocoa powder (natural or Dutch-processed)

Remove the pan from the oven and transfer it to a cooling rack. Lightly dust the top of the cake with cocoa powder in a dredger or fine mesh sifter.

While the cake is still hot, use a small, sharp knife to loosen the edges from the sides of the pan. Place a sheet of parchment paper over the top of the cake and cover with a kitchen towel. Then invert the jelly-roll pan and lift it off the cake. Gently peel the parchment paper off the back of the cake.

Starting at one long end, roll up the cake inside the towel and parchment paper and leave it seam-side down to cool to room temperature.

FILLING

1¼ pounds white chocolate, finely chopped

Place the chopped white chocolate in a large bowl.

¾ cup heavy whipping cream
⅓ cup fresh chocolate mint leaves, washed and dried

Place the cream in a saucepan and bring to a boil over medium heat. Turn off the heat. Add the chocolate mint, cover the pan, and let steep together for 20 minutes.

Remove the cover and bring the cream to a boil again over medium heat. Strain the cream over the white chocolate and let it stand for 1 minute. Stir the mixture together using a heat-resistant spatula, whisk, or immersion blender until very smooth.

Tightly cover the ganache with plastic wrap and chill until thick, but not stiff, about 1 hour.

Take the white chocolate ganache from the refrigerator. If it is very firm, soften it in a microwave oven on low power for 5-second bursts. The consistency should be like thick pudding; that is, you should be able to stick your finger into it easily but it will hold the indentation. Take care not to soften it so much that it becomes liquid.

Place the ganache in the bowl of an electric stand mixer or a large bowl. Use the flat beater attachment or a hand-held mixer to beat the

The ganache for the filling can be made up to 3 weeks in advance and kept in an airtight plastic container away from strong-flavored foods in the refrigerator. Bring it to room temperature before using.

Recovering from a Mishap
If the cake breaks or cracks while it is being rolled, position the cracked part of the cake on the bottom of the roll or patch with whipped cream.

Making a Change
Fold 1 cup toasted and finely ground hazelnuts or pecans into the batter before spreading it on the jelly-roll pan. Sprinkle toasted and finely ground hazelnuts or pecans lightly on top of the cake after decorating with the whipped ganache.

ganache on medium speed until it holds soft peaks, 1 to 2 minutes. Don't beat the ganache too much or it will become grainy.

Unroll the cake and remove the towel. Use the offset spatula or a rubber spatula to evenly spread ⅓ of the filling over the cake, leaving a 1-inch border at the farthest long end of the cake. Use the parchment paper to help roll up the filled cake.

To make a tight cake roll, pull about one-third of the parchment paper over the top of the cake. Then place a ruler flat against the parchment that covers the top of the cake and push it against the roll while pulling the bottom part of the parchment paper toward you. This resistance motion of simultaneously pushing against the cake while pulling the parchment under the cake toward you compresses the roulade.

Using the spatula, transfer the cake to a serving plate or a jelly-roll pan covered with waxed paper. Place the seam side down. Trim off the rough ends of the cake and discard

Fit the pastry bag with the star tip and fill partway with the whipped ganache. Starting at the bottom of the rolled cake and from one end to the other, pipe the ganache in rows on the cake. You will need to turn the plate around to work on the other side.

2 to 3 sprigs of fresh chocolate mint, washed and patted dry

Decorate the top of the cake with a few sprigs of fresh chocolate mint.

2 tablespoons unsweetened cocoa powder (natural or Dutch-processed)

Cut the cake crosswise into 1-inch slices. Place each slice on its side on a plate and dust lightly with cocoa powder. Serve immediately.

VII.

COFFEE, TEA, LIQUEURS, AND SPIRITS

AKING AND EATING what you've made is fun. This couldn't be truer than when using coffee, tea, liqueurs, and spirits. And don't think this is only for adults. The small amount of these ingredients used in baking won't affect children. ✳ Baked desserts made with espresso are a long-time favorite of mine. Tea, not commonly thought of as an ingredient in baked goods, imparts a fantastic flavor, especially green tea. When it comes to using liqueurs and spirits, including whiskey, get ready for the accolades. ✳ There are plenty of great recipes to choose from in this section. What I like to do is serve two or three at a time. This way you're sure to please everyone.

20

COFFEE

STARTING THE DAY with a cup of coffee is something many of us do. I can't exactly remember when I had my first cup of coffee, but I can remember fairly well when I first smelled its wonderful aroma. This was as a young girl, because my parents loved to drink coffee. Using coffee in desserts seems natural because it complements so many other flavors. To get the rich flavor of coffee, I use instant espresso powder mixed with a very small amount of water to create a paste-like consistency. This allows me to achieve deep coffee flavor without having to add much liquid to a recipe. I learned this technique while working in Europe. I also use this method to create the mocha flavor in the recipes in this chapter. This is made by combining either cocoa powder or dark chocolate and espresso. I don't recommend using ground espresso coffee because it doesn't get as finely ground as the instant espresso powder and you can end up with a gritty texture. Also, different espresso beans will produce an inconsistent flavor that may be bitter.

These recipes will delight both coffee lovers and those who may not drink coffee, but enjoy intensely flavored desserts. Instant espresso powder is available year-round. It is found in some supermarkets, specialty food shops, and through many online and catalogue sources.

TIPS AND TECHNIQUES

Instant espresso powder comes in 2-ounce glass jars. When buying espresso powder, make sure that the jar is sealed properly and check the expiration date.

Instant espresso powder should be stored in its original jar, tightly sealed, in a cool, dark, and dry place. Don't use it past its expiration date because it will have lost its full-bodied flavor and will become hard and cakey.

Some recipes call for espresso powder to be used directly from the jar without any further preparation. Others require making a paste-like consistency by mixing the espresso powder with a small amount of water. I do this in a small bowl and stir them together until the mixture is smooth.

Espresso Cheesecake with Chocolate Wafer Cookie Crust

THIS RICH espresso filling nestled in a chocolate wafer cookie crust is the type of cheesecake you dream about. The smooth, creamy filling is the perfect counterpoint to the crunchy chocolate wafer cookie crust. As with all cheesecakes, it's best to make this one at least a day before you plan to serve it so there is plenty of time for it to cool and chill. The cake also freezes very well. **Makes one 9½-inch round cake, 12 to 14 servings**

Center a rack in the oven and preheat it to 300°F.

1 tablespoon unsalted butter, softened

Using a paper towel or your fingertips, generously butter the inside of the springform pan. Use a double layer of heavy-duty aluminum foil to wrap tightly around the bottom of the pan. This prevents any water from seeping into the cake.

COOKIE CRUST

One 9-ounce package chocolate wafers
2 tablespoons granulated sugar

In the work bowl of a food processor fitted with the steel blade, combine the cookies and sugar. Pulse until the cookies are finely ground, about 2 minutes. Or place the cookies in a sturdy plastic bag and seal it. Use a rolling pin to crush the cookies to a very fine crumb consistency. Add the sugar to the cookies, seal the bag, and shake to blend together evenly.

Transfer the cookie crumbs to a medium bowl.

4 ounces (8 tablespoons, 1 stick) unsalted butter, melted and cooled

Add the butter to the cookie crumbs. Use a rubber spatula or a spoon to toss the mixture together to moisten all the cookie crumbs.

Transfer the crust to the prepared springform pan. Using your fingers, press the crumb mixture evenly into the bottom and most of the way up the sides of the pan. Chill the crust while preparing the cheesecake batter.

CHEESECAKE

½ cup heavy whipping cream
2 tablespoons instant espresso powder

Place the cream in a small saucepan and bring to a boil over medium heat. Turn off the heat, add the espresso powder, and whisk until thoroughly blended. Remove from the heat and let cool.

2 pounds cream cheese, softened

Place the cream cheese in the bowl of an electric stand mixer or in a large bowl. Use the flat beater attachment or a hand-held mixer to

Essential Gear

- 9½-inch round spring-form pan
- Heavy-duty aluminum foil
- Food processor or rolling pin
- Small saucepan
- Whisk
- Electric stand mixer with flat beater attachment or large mixing bowl and hand-held mixer
- Rubber spatula
- 12-inch round cake pan or large roasting pan
- Cooling rack

Keeping

Store the cheesecake covered with waxed paper and tightly wrapped in aluminum foil in the refrigerator up to 4 days. To freeze up to 2 months, wrap the cake pan tightly in several layers of plastic wrap and aluminum foil. Use a large piece of masking tape and an indelible marker to label and date the contents. If frozen, defrost overnight in the refrigerator and bring to room temperature at least 30 minutes before serving.

Making a Change

Add 1½ cups finely ground toasted hazelnuts or walnuts to the batter before turning it into the pan.

beat the cream cheese on medium speed until it's fluffy, about 2 minutes.

½ cup firmly packed light brown sugar ⅔ cup granulated sugar	Add the brown sugar and granulated sugar to the cream cheese and beat together until very smooth. Stop occasionally and scrape down the sides and bottom of the bowl with a rubber spatula.
3 extra-large eggs, at room temperature	One at a time, add the eggs to the cream cheese mixture, beating well after each addition. At first the eggs will sit on top of the cream cheese mixture, but stop often to scrape down the sides and bottom of the mixing bowl with a rubber spatula. This will help the mixture to blend. The mixture may also look curdled as the eggs are added, but as you scrape down the bowl, the mixture will smooth out.
2 teaspoons pure vanilla extract or vanilla paste ½ cup sour cream	Add the vanilla and sour cream to the cream cheese mixture and stir together to combine.
	Add the cooled espresso cream to the cream cheese mixture and blend thoroughly.
	Pour the batter into the crust in the springform pan. Use a rubber spatula to smooth and even the top.
1 quart boiling water	Place the springform pan in the larger cake pan or roasting pan and set the pan on the oven rack. Carefully pour the boiling water into the bottom pan until it reaches halfway up the side of the springform pan. Baking the cake in a water bath cushions it from the heat and adds extra moisture to the oven, which keeps the top of the cake from cracking.

Bake the cake for 1 hour and 45 minutes, until the top is set, but jiggles slightly. Remove the pan from the oven and transfer the cheesecake to a rack. Remove the foil from the bottom of the pan and let the cheesecake cool completely.

Cover the top of the cheesecake with waxed paper and wrap the pan tightly in aluminum foil. Refrigerate the cake for at least 6 hours before serving. To unmold the cheesecake, dip a thin-bladed knife in hot water and dry, then run it around the inner edge of the pan; release the clip on the rim of the pan and gently lift it off the cake.

Adding Style

Drizzle the top of the cooled and chilled cheesecake with fine line or designs of dark chocolate (see page 43). Let the chocolate set for 15 minutes in the refrigerator before serving or storing.

Serve each slice of cheesecake with a dollop of lightly sweetened whipped cream and scatter about a teaspoon of shaved dark chocolate over the cream, or place a candy coffee bean on top of the cream.

Espresso Chiffon Cake with Caramel Glaze

THIS CLASSIC AMERICAN cake is flavored with espresso and decorated with a caramel glaze. The flavors of espresso and caramel are natural partners that bring out the best in each other. The cake can be made a couple of days in advance of serving and held at room temperature. Once the glaze is added, the cake should be served within a couple of hours so it doesn't become soggy. **Makes one 10-inch round cake, 12 to 14 servings**

Center a rack in the oven and preheat it to 325°F.

Cut a round of parchment paper to fit the bottom of the pan and cut out a hole in the middle to fit the center tube of the pan. This cake is baked in an ungreased pan because greasing the pan would keep the batter from rising and gripping the sides of the pan as the cake bakes.

2 tablespoons instant espresso powder ²/₃ cup water ¹/₂ cup unflavored vegetable oil (canola or safflower) 2 teaspoons pure vanilla extract or vanilla paste	In a large measuring cup or medium bowl, dissolve the espresso powder in the water. Add the oil and vanilla.
2¹/₄ cups cake flour 1 tablespoon baking powder 1 cup superfine sugar ¹/₄ teaspoon salt	Over a large piece of waxed or parchment paper or a bowl, sift together the flour and baking powder. Add the sugar and salt and stir together.
6 extra-large egg yolks, at room temperature	Make a well in the center of the mixture by pushing the dry ingredients toward the sides of the bowl. Add the espresso mixture and the egg yolks. Using a rubber spatula, stir together until thoroughly combined.
6 extra-large egg whites, at room temperature ¹/₂ teaspoon cream of tartar ¹/₂ cup superfine sugar	Place the egg whites in the grease-free bowl of an electric stand mixer or in a large grease-free bowl. Using the wire whip attachment or a hand-held mixer, whip the egg whites on medium speed until they are frothy. Add the cream of tartar. Slowly sprinkle on the sugar and continue whipping until the egg whites hold glossy and firm, but not stiff, peaks, about 5 minutes.

Fold the egg whites into the cake batter in 3 to 4 stages, blending thoroughly after each addition.

Essential Gear

- 10 × 4-inch tube pan with removable bottom
- Parchment paper
- Scissors
- Sifter
- Electric stand mixer with wire whip attachment, or large mixing bowl and hand-held mixer
- Rubber spatula
- Cooling rack
- Thin-bladed knife
- Medium heavy-bottomed saucepan
- Sugar dredger or fine-mesh sieve

Keeping

Store the unglazed cake tightly wrapped in plastic up to 3 days at room temperature. To freeze up to 4 months, tightly wrap the unglazed cake in several layers of plastic wrap and aluminum foil. Use a large piece of masking tape and an indelible marker to label and date the contents. If frozen, defrost overnight in the refrigerator and bring to room temperature before serving.

Once the cake is glazed, it can be kept, lightly covered with waxed paper and then tightly covered with plastic wrap, at room temperature for 1 day. Place a few toothpicks in the top outer edges of the cake to hold the waxed paper away from it so it won't mar the glaze.

Transfer the batter to the tube pan. Use the rubber spatula to smooth and even the top.

Bake for 1 hour, until a cake tester inserted in the center of the cake comes out clean.

Remove the pan from the oven and invert it over a cooling rack onto its feet or over a funnel or a thin-necked bottle. Let the cake hang to cool completely. Don't set the pan on a cooling rack on its base. This will cause the cake to collapse onto itself.

Don't shake the cake out of the pan before it is cool. Once the cake is cool, use a thin-bladed knife or flexible-blade spatula to run around the outer edge and the inside tube to help release the cake from the pan. Invert the cake onto a rack, then re-invert onto a serving plate.

CARAMEL GLAZE

²/₃ cup firmly packed light brown sugar

2 ounces (4 tablespoons, ¹/₂ stick) unsalted butter, cut into small pieces

3 tablespoons heavy whipping cream

Place the sugar, butter, and cream in the saucepan over medium heat. Stir until the mixture is very smooth. Remove the pan from the heat and cool slightly.

¹/₄ cup confectioners' sugar, sifted

Stir the sugar into the glaze until very smooth.

Place the cake on a rack over a lined baking sheet. Drizzle the glaze over the top of the cake and let it run down the sides. Let the glaze set for 10 minutes, then cut the cake into serving pieces.

Making a Change
Serve the cake in a pool of Caramel Sauce (see Rum-Raisin Pound Cake, page 614) instead of decorating it with the caramel glaze.

Mocha and Hazelnut French-Style Macaroons

THESE ARE FRENCH-STYLE macaroons, with two small round mocha and hazelnut cookies that enclose a smooth mocha-flavored ganache filling. Perfect to serve for afternoon tea or after dinner, these scrumptious cookies are elegant and very satisfying. **Makes about 3 dozen sandwich cookies**

MOCHA HAZELNUT COOKIES

Adjust the oven racks to the upper and lower thirds and preheat the oven to 350°F. Line the jelly-roll pans with aluminum foil with the shiny side up.

Essential Gear
- Two jelly-roll pans
- Aluminum foil
- Electric stand mixer with wire whip attachment and flat beater attachment, or large mixing bowl and hand-held mixer
- Two rubber spatulas

4 extra-large egg whites, at room temperature	Place the egg whites in the grease-free bowl of an electric stand mixer or in a large grease-free bowl. Using the wire whip attachment or a hand-held mixer, beat the egg whites on medium speed until they are frothy. This takes about 1 minute.
¼ teaspoon cream of tartar	Add the cream of tartar to stabilize the egg white foam and continue to whip on medium speed.
1½ cups confectioners' sugar, sifted	Slowly add the sugar and continue to whip the egg whites until they hold firm and glossy, but not stiff, peaks.
¼ cup unsweetened cocoa powder (natural or Dutch-processed), sifted **1⅓ cups toasted and finely ground hazelnuts** **⅛ teaspoon salt**	In a medium bowl, combine the cocoa powder, hazelnuts, and salt. Use a rubber spatula or large spoon and toss to mix together.
	Fold this mixture into the whipped egg whites in 3 stages. Blend thoroughly after each addition. Be sure each batch is mixed in before adding the next or it becomes too difficult to get a smooth mixture.
1 tablespoon instant espresso powder **1 teaspoon warm water** **½ teaspoon pure vanilla extract or vanilla paste**	In a small bowl, combine the espresso powder and water. Stir together until they make a smooth mixture. Add the vanilla and mix together.
	Add this mixture to the batter and blend in thoroughly.
	Fit the pastry bag with a plain round tip. Fill the pastry bag partway with the macaroon mixture. Holding the pastry bag vertically, 1 inch above the jelly-roll pan, pipe out mounds 1 inch in diameter. Leave at least 2 inches space between each mound because they will spread as they bake. As you pipe out the macaroons, concentrate on keeping the size uniform and small. It looks more attractive to have macaroons of the same size when they are assembled.
	Bake the macaroons for 8 minutes. Switch the jelly-roll pans and bake another 7 minutes, until set. Remove the jelly-roll pans from the oven and immediately lift up a corner of the aluminum foil on each pan.
½ cup water	Pour ¼ cup water under the foil on each pan. This creates steam, which makes it easy to remove the macaroons from the foil. Be careful to pour the water under the foil and not on top. Place each pan on a cooling rack and let the macaroons cool completely. Carefully remove the macaroons from the foil.

- Two 12- or 14-inch pastry bags with two ½-inch plain round pastry tips
- Cooling rack
- Small saucepan
- Whisk, heat-resistant spatula, or immersion blender
- Fine-mesh sieve

Keeping

Store the cookies in a single layer, between sheets of waxed paper, tightly covered with plastic wrap in the refrigerator, up to 2 days. The texture will soften slightly, but this doesn't affect their flavor.

Streamlining

The macaroons can be baked up to 2 days in advance. When they're completely cool, store them between layers of waxed paper on a jelly-roll pan or cookie sheet tightly covered with aluminum foil in a cool, dry place.

The ganache filling can be made up to 3 weeks in advance. Store it in an airtight plastic container tightly covered with plastic wrap or a freezer bag in the refrigerator, away from any strong-flavored foods. Bring the ganache to room temperature before using. It should be pliable enough to hold the indentation of your finger, but not so soft that it is liquid.

MOCHA GANACHE FILLING

4 ounces bittersweet chocolate, very finely chopped

Place the finely chopped chocolate in a medium bowl.

½ cup heavy whipping cream

1 tablespoon instant espresso powder

In a small saucepan over medium heat, bring the cream to a boil. Add the espresso powder, cover the pan, turn off the heat, and let the mixture infuse for 10 minutes.

Remove the cover of the pan and again bring the cream to a boil over medium heat.

Immediately strain the hot cream into the chocolate. Let it stand for 1 minute, then blend together with a heat-resistant spatula, whisk, or an immersion blender until very smooth.

Cover the bowl tightly with plastic wrap to prevent a skin from forming on top and let the mixture cool to room temperature. Chill in the refrigerator until thick, but not firm, about 1 hour.

Place the ganache filling in the bowl of an electric stand mixer or in a medium bowl. Use the flat beater attachment or a hand-held mixer and beat the ganache until it holds soft peaks, about 1 minute.

Fit a clean pastry bag with a clean round tip. Fill the pastry bag partway with the whipped ganache. Pipe a small mound of ganache on the flat side of 1 macaroon and top it with the flat side of a similar-sized macaroon. Gently press the cookies together to spread the ganache filling out to the edges.

Serve the cookies immediately or chill in the refrigerator, covered with a sheet of waxed paper, then tightly wrapped with plastic wrap, until 30 minutes before serving.

Making a Change

Fill the macaroons with whipped milk chocolate mocha ganache. To make the ganache, use 5 ounces milk chocolate and ⅓ cup heavy whipping cream. Follow the directions in the recipe for the Mocha Ganache Filling.

Adding Style

Dust the top of the assembled macaroons lightly with a mixture of 2 teaspoons confectioners' sugar and 2 teaspoons unsweetened cocoa powder sifted together.

Mocha Biscotti with Cocoa Nibs

NSTANT ESPRESSO POWDER, coarsely chopped dark chocolate, and cocoa nibs are the ingredients that give these biscotti their rich mocha flavor. They are crisp and crunchy, just right for dipping into a cup of coffee or a glass of milk. **Makes about 3 dozen cookies**

Essential Gear

- Two baking sheets
- Two parchment paper sheets or non-stick liners
- Sifter

Adjust the oven racks to the upper and lower thirds and preheat the oven to 350°F. Line the baking sheets with parchment paper or non-stick liners.

2½ cups all purpose flour
2 teaspoons baking soda
⅛ teaspoon salt

Over a large piece of waxed or parchment paper or a bowl, sift together the flour and baking soda. Add the salt and toss together to blend. Transfer the mixture to the bowl of an electric stand mixer or a large bowl.

½ cup granulated sugar
½ cup firmly packed light brown sugar

Add the granulated sugar and brown sugar to the dry ingredients and use a flat beater attachment or a hand-held mixer to stir together.

1 tablespoon instant espresso powder
1 teaspoon warm water

In a small bowl, combine the instant espresso powder and water. Stir together to thoroughly dissolve the espresso powder and until the mixture becomes a paste.

3 extra-large eggs, at room temperature
1 teaspoon pure vanilla extract or vanilla paste
2 ounces (4 tablespoons, ½ stick) unsalted butter, melted

Using a fork, whisk the eggs with the vanilla in a small bowl. Add the espresso paste and butter. Add this mixture to the dry ingredients. Mix on low speed until thoroughly combined. Stop occasionally and scrape down the sides and bottom of the mixing bowl with a rubber spatula.

2 ounces bittersweet chocolate, coarsely chopped
1 cup cocoa nibs

Add the chopped chocolate and cocoa nibs to the dough and blend thoroughly on low speed. The dough should be smooth and pliable at this point.

Divide the dough into 4 equal pieces. Dust your hands with flour to keep the dough from sticking and shape each piece into a log about 7 inches long, 3 inches wide, and ¾ inch high. Place 2 logs on each baking sheet, leaving at least 2 inches space between them.

Bake for 12 minutes. Switch the baking sheets and bake another 10 to 13 minutes, until set. Remove the baking sheets from the oven and let the dough logs rest on a rack for 10 minutes. Lower the oven temperature to 325°F.

Using a serrated knife, cut the logs on the diagonal into ½-inch-thick slices. Place the slices back on the baking sheet on their sides so the wide part of each slice faces up.

Bake the biscotti again until firm, 12 to 15 minutes, switching the baking sheets halfway through.

Transfer the biscotti to racks to cool.

- Electric stand mixer with flat beater attachment, or large mixing bowl and hand-held mixer
- Rubber spatula
- Two cooling racks
- Serrated knife

Keeping

Store the biscotti in an airtight container between sheets of waxed paper at room temperature up to 2 weeks. A kitchen cupboard or the pantry is the ideal storage place.

To freeze up to 3 months, wrap the container tightly in several layers of plastic wrap and aluminum foil. Use a large piece of masking tape and an indelible marker to label and date the contents. If frozen, defrost overnight in the refrigerator and bring to room temperature before serving.

Making a Change

Replace the cocoa nibs with chopped almonds or walnuts.

Adding Style

Drizzle the biscotti with thin lines of bittersweet, semisweet, milk, or white chocolate after they are completely cool (see page 43). Let the chocolate set for 15 minutes in the refrigerator before serving or storing.

Mocha Bûche de Noël

A CLASSIC FRENCH cake that is served during the Christmas holiday season, this is a mocha rolled cake, filled and decorated with rich mocha buttercream so that it looks like a Yule log. Marzipan holly leaves and berries and a light dusting of confectioners' sugar are the final decorations that add a very festive touch to this cake. There are several steps involved in making this cake and some of them can be done in advance of assembling and decorating it. **Makes one 15-inch cake, 14 to 16 servings**

MOCHA ROLLED CAKE

Center a rack in the oven and preheat it to 375°F.

1 tablespoon unsalted butter, softened	Line the jelly-roll pan with a sheet of parchment paper. Using a paper towel or your fingertips, generously butter the parchment paper or spray it with non-stick baking spray.
4 extra-large eggs, at room temperature ²⁄₃ cup granulated sugar	Place the eggs and sugar in the bowl of an electric stand mixer or in a large bowl. Use the wire whip attachment or a hand-held mixer to whip the eggs and sugar together until they are very thick and pale colored and hold a slowly dissolving ribbon as the beater is lifted, about 5 minutes.
¾ cup all-purpose flour 3 tablespoons cornstarch 2 tablespoons unsweetened Dutch-processed cocoa powder 2 tablespoons instant espresso powder 1 teaspoon baking powder ¼ teaspoon salt	Over a large piece of waxed or parchment paper or a bowl, sift together the flour, cornstarch, cocoa powder, espresso powder, and baking powder. Add the salt and toss to mix. Fold this mixture into the egg mixture in 3 stages, blending well after each addition.
2 tablespoons unsalted butter, melted	Fold the butter into the batter in 2 stages. Pour the cake batter onto the prepared jelly-roll pan. Use the offset spatula to spread the batter out evenly and into the corners of the pan.
	Bake the cake for 18 minutes, until the top springs back when lightly touched.
	Remove the jelly-roll pan from the oven. While the cake is still hot, use a small, sharp knife to loosen the edges from the sides of the pan. Place a sheet of parchment paper over the top of the cake and cover

Essential Gear

- Jelly-roll pan (12 × 17 inches)
- 2 parchment paper sheets
- Rubber spatula
- Electric stand mixer with wire whip attachment, or large mixing bowl and hand-held mixer
- Kitchen towel
- 2-quart heavy-bottomed saucepan
- 1-inch natural-bristle pastry brush
- Sugar or candy thermometer
- Small saucepan
- Offset spatula
- 12- or 14-inch pastry bag and large open star tip
- Holly leaf cookie cutter or stencil

Keeping

Store the cake loosely covered with aluminum foil in the refrigerator for up to 4 days. Place several toothpicks in the cake to hold the foil away from it so it won't damage the buttercream. To freeze for up to 3 months, place the cake on a lined baking sheet in the freezer and let it freeze (about 3 hours). Loosely wrap the cake in layers of plastic wrap and aluminum foil. If frozen, defrost overnight in the refrigerator. Bring the cake to room temperature at least 30 minutes before serving.

with a kitchen towel. Then invert the jelly-roll pan and lift it off the cake. Gently peel the parchment paper off of the back of the cake and discard.

Starting at one long end of the cake, roll it up inside the towel and parchment paper. Leave the cake seam-side down to cool to room temperature.

SUGAR SYRUP

¼ cup granulated sugar
½ cup water
2 tablespoons Grand Marnier or other orange liqueur

Place the sugar and water in a small saucepan and bring to a boil over medium-high heat to dissolve the sugar. Remove the pan from the heat and cool the sugar syrup, then stir in the Grand Marnier.

MOCHA BUTTERCREAM

3 extra-large eggs, at room temperature
3 extra-large egg yolks, at room temperature
¼ cup granulated sugar

Place the eggs, egg yolks, and sugar in the bowl of an electric stand mixer or in a large bowl. Use the wire whip attachment or a hand-held mixer and whip the eggs on medium speed until they are very pale colored and hold a slowly dissolving ribbon as the beater is lifted, about 5 minutes.

1¾ cups granulated sugar
¾ cup water
½ teaspoon cream of tartar

While the eggs are whipping, place the sugar, water, and cream of tartar in the heavy-bottomed saucepan. Bring the mixture to a boil, without stirring. Place a wet pastry brush at the point where the sugar syrup meets the sides of the pan and sweep it around completely. Do this two times. This prevents the sugar from crystallizing by brushing any stray crystals back into the mixture. Cook over high heat until the mixture registers 242°F on a sugar thermometer (soft-ball stage).

Immediately remove the thermometer and place it in a glass of warm water, then remove the pan from the heat so it won't continue to cook.

Adjust the mixer speed to low and pour the sugar syrup into the whipped eggs in a slow, steady stream. Aim the sugar syrup between the beater and the side of the bowl, so it doesn't get caught up in the beater or thrown against the sides of the bowl. Turn the mixer speed up to medium-high and whip until the bowl is cool to the touch, about 8 minutes. Once the cooked sugar syrup is added to the whipped eggs, the mixture must whip until the bowl is completely cool to the touch before the butter is added or the butter will melt. If this happens, the texture and consistency of the buttercream will be too soft and more butter needs to be added to bring it to the right point.

1½ pounds (3 cups, 6 sticks) unsalted butter, softened

Adjust the mixer speed to medium and add the butter, 2 tablespoons at a time. Continue to beat until the buttercream is thoroughly blended and fluffy.

Streamlining

Bake the rolled cake up to 2 days before assembling the cake. After the cake is completely cool, cover it with plastic wrap and hold at room temperature. The cake can be frozen for up to 3 months. To freeze, wrap it snugly in several layers of plastic wrap and place in freezer bags. Use a large piece of masking tape and an indelible marker to label and date the contents. If frozen, defrost the cake overnight in the refrigerator.

The buttercream can be prepared up to 3 days in advance and kept in an airtight plastic container in the refrigerator or for up to 4 months in the freezer. If frozen, defrost overnight in the refrigerator. To reheat the buttercream, break it up into chunks and place in a mixing bowl. Place the bowl in a saucepan of warm water and let the buttercream begin to melt around the bottom. Wipe the bottom of the bowl dry and beat the buttercream with an electric mixer until it is fluffy and smooth.

Recovering from a Mishap

Don't worry if the rolled cake cracks when you unroll it. The cracks will be hidden with the icing. You can always position the cracked part of the cake on the bottom of the roll or patch with icing.

10 ounces bittersweet chocolate, very finely chopped	Place the chocolate in a microwave-proof bowl and melt on low power for 30-second bursts. Stir with a rubber spatula after each burst. When the chocolate is completely melted, stir it to cool for a couple of minutes. Then add it to the buttercream and blend well.
1 tablespoon instant espresso powder **1 teaspoon water**	In a small bowl, dissolve the espresso powder in the water. Add the espresso paste to the buttercream and blend thoroughly.

ASSEMBLY

Unroll the cake and remove the towel. Use a pastry brush to brush the sugar syrup over the inside of the cake.

Use an offset spatula to spread about 1½ cups of the buttercream evenly over the inside of the cake, leaving a 1-inch border at the farthest long end of the cake. Use the parchment paper to help roll up the filled cake.

To make a tight cake roll, pull about one-third of the parchment paper over the top of the cake. Then place a ruler flat against the parchment that covers the top of the cake and push it against the roll while pulling the bottom part of the parchment paper toward you. This resistance motion of simultaneously pushing against the cake while pulling the parchment under the cake toward you compresses the roulade.

Use a serrated knife to trim off the ends and discard. Then cut a diagonal slice about 3 inches thick from each end of the log. Set these aside briefly.

Transfer the rolled cake to a rectangular serving plate with the seam side down.

Fit the pastry bag with the star tip and fill partway with some of the remaining buttercream.

Working from the bottom of one side of the rolled cake and from one end to the other, pipe the buttercream in rows on the log (see page 44). You will need to turn the plate around to work on the other side. Place the diagonal cut ends of the cake on top of the log near each end to look like sawed-off branches. Use the buttercream to build up around these pieces so that they look like they are part of the log.

Confectioners' sugar — Lightly dust the top of the log with sugar so it looks like snow.

3 ounces marzipan

Divide the marzipan into 2 portions, one twice as large as the other.

Green paste food coloring
Red paste food coloring
Confectioners' sugar

Take the larger portion of marzipan and dust a flat work surface with confectioners' sugar. Dip the end of a toothpick into green paste food coloring, then dap it into the marzipan. Knead the marzipan (see Essential Baking Language, page 45) until the color is evenly distributed. Add more confectioners' sugar as needed to keep the marzipan from sticking. Roll out the marzipan to a thickness of about 1/4 inch. Brush off any excess sugar and cut out holly leaf shapes, using a cutter or a cardboard pattern you have made. You will need 6 to 8 holly leaves.

Color the remaining piece of marzipan with red paste food coloring. Pinch off small pieces of red marzipan and roll them into balls to be the holly berries.

Arrange 2 holly leaves together at intervals over the top of the log and place 3 or 4 holly berries where the leaves meet.

Place the cake in the refrigerator to firm up the buttercream, then tent it with foil. Serve slices of the cake at room temperature.

Mocha Cream Puffs

CREAM PUFFS are made from choux pastry (pâte à choux, pronounced "pot ah *shoe*"), also known as cream puff pasty, which is one of the basics of French pastry, and they are traditionally filled with pastry cream. In this recipe, the cream puffs are filled with mocha-flavored pastry cream. The cream puffs can be baked in advance and filled before serving. Once filled, they should be served within a few hours so they don't become soggy. **Makes about 30 cream puffs**

Essential Gear
- Two baking sheets
- Aluminum foil or two non-stick pan liners
- Medium heavy-bottomed saucepan
- Sifter
- Wooden spoon or heat-resistant spatula
- Electric stand mixer with flat beater attachment, or hand-held mixer and large mixing bowl, or food processor
- Rubber spatula

CREAM PUFF PASTRY DOUGH

Adjust the oven racks to the upper and lower thirds and preheat the oven to 425°F. Line the baking sheets with aluminum foil or non-stick pan liners.

²/₃ cup water

4 ounces (8 tablespoons, 1 stick) unsalted butter, cut into small pieces

¹/₃ cup milk

1 tablespoon granulated sugar

¹/₄ teaspoon salt

Place the water, butter, milk, sugar, and salt in the saucepan. Bring to a boil over medium-high heat.

---

1 cup all-purpose flour, sifted

Remove the saucepan from the heat and add the flour all at once. Stir vigorously with a long-handled wooden spoon or heat-resistant spatula until the dough pulls away from the sides of the pan and forms a ball around the spoon. Return the saucepan to medium heat and cook for 3 minutes, stirring continuously, until the dough is smooth. This helps to develop the gluten in the flour, the protein that gives flour its elasticity. The result is that the puffs rise very well as they bake.

Transfer the dough to the bowl of an electric stand mixer or a large bowl. Use the flat beater attachment or a hand-held mixer to beat the dough on medium speed for about 3 minutes to release the heat and steam.

Or transfer the dough to the work bowl of a food processor fitted with the steel blade. Leave the feed tube open to release steam and process the mixture for 30 seconds to 1 minute.

---

4 extra-large eggs, at room temperature

Using a fork, lightly beat each egg in a small bowl, then add to the dough, 1 at a time. Mix completely after each addition, then stop and scrape down the sides and bottom of the bowl with a rubber spatula. Mix or process the dough until it is smooth and glossy, 30 seconds to 1 minute.

Fit the pastry bag with the plain round tip and fill partway with the dough. Holding the pastry bag straight up and down and 1 inch above the baking sheet, pipe out mounds about 2 to 2¹/₄ inches in diameter and ³/₄ inch high, with 2 inches of space between each mound.

Spacing the puffs evenly on each baking sheet helps them bake evenly. If the puffs are crowded on the baking sheet, they may collapse because air won't be able to circulate around them.

Dip a spoon or fork in water and shake off the excess. Lightly smooth the top of each mound with the back of the spoon or fork to even the tops.

- 14-inch pastry bag and ¹/₂-inch plain round pastry tip
- 1-inch natural-bristle pastry brush
- Two cooling racks
- Small sharp knife
- Large heavy-bottomed saucepan
- Ladle
- Serrated knife

Keeping

Store the unfilled cream puffs in a single layer on a cool baking sheet tightly wrapped with aluminum foil at room temperature for 1 day. To freeze up to 2 months, store the puffs in a single layer in freezer bags. Use a large piece of masking tape and an indelible marker to label and date the contents. Place them in a single layer on a baking sheet and warm them in a 300°F oven for 10 minutes before filling.

Streamlining

The puffs can be baked in advance and kept in the freezer up to 2 months before using. They can also be filled and frozen for the same amount of time. If filled and frozen, defrost briefly in the refrigerator before serving so they won't be too firm to eat.

The pastry cream can be made up to 4 days in advance and kept in a bowl tightly covered with plastic wrap or in a tightly covered

EGG WASH

1 extra-large egg
1 teaspoon milk

Using a fork, lightly beat the egg and milk together in a small bowl. Lightly brush the top of each mound with the egg wash. Be careful that the egg wash doesn't run down the sides and get underneath the puffs. If this happens, wipe it up because the puffs will stick to the foil or pan liner.

Bake the puffs for 15 minutes. Reduce the oven temperature to 375°F. Switch the baking sheets and bake another 15 to 20 minutes. The puffs should be deep golden brown. The initial heat of the oven creates steam inside of the puffs, which causes them to rise. If the oven heat is too low, the puffs won't rise properly.

Remove the baking sheets from the oven and put them on racks. Use a small sharp knife to cut a small horizontal slit in the side of each puff, about halfway from the top, to release steam. Return the baking sheets to the oven, turn off the heat, and prop the door open with a wooden spoon. Leave the puffs in the oven for 30 to 45 minutes to dry completely. Test a puff to make sure it is dry inside by slitting it open. If the puffs are not dry, leave them in the oven another 10 to 15 minutes. When the puffs are dry, cool them completely on racks. If the puffs are not properly dried out inside, they will collapse as they cool.

MOCHA PASTRY CREAM FILLING

2 cups milk
½ vanilla bean

Place the milk in the saucepan. Use a small sharp knife to slice the vanilla bean open lengthwise. This exposes the tiny grains inside, which hold the essential vanilla flavor. Add the vanilla bean to the milk and warm over medium heat until tiny bubbles begin to form around the edges of the pan, about 5 minutes.

6 extra-large egg yolks,
** at room temperature**
⅔ cup granulated sugar

Place the egg yolks in the bowl of an electric stand mixer or in a large bowl. Using the wire whip attachment or a hand-held mixer, whip the egg yolks on medium-high speed until they are frothy. Add the sugar and whip together until the mixture is very thick and pale colored and holds a slowly dissolving ribbon as the beater is lifted, about 5 minutes.

¼ cup cornstarch, sifted

Turn the mixer speed to low and add the cornstarch. Use a rubber spatula to scrape down the bottom and sides of the bowl to encourage even mixing. Return the mixer speed to medium and whip until the cornstarch is thoroughly blended in.

Turn the mixer speed to low. Use a ladle to take about ½ cup of the hot milk from the pan and slowly add it to the egg yolk mixture.

plastic container in the refrigerator.

Making a Change
To make chocolate pastry cream, leave out the espresso.

To make espresso pastry cream, leave out the chocolate. Increase the espresso powder to 2 tablespoons and add 2 more teaspoons of water to dissolve it.

Whip together to blend. This tempers the egg yolks so they won't curdle when they are added to the milk.

Transfer the egg yolk mixture into the milk in the saucepan. Stir the mixture constantly with a whisk, heat-resistant rubber spatula, or wooden spoon, so it doesn't burn. Cook until the mixture starts to bubble and pop. Remove the saucepan from the heat immediately and transfer the pastry cream to a bowl.

1 tablespoon instant espresso powder
2 teaspoons water
4 ounces bittersweet chocolate, finely chopped

In a small bowl, combine the espresso powder and water. Stir together until they make a smooth mixture. Stir the finely chopped chocolate and the espresso paste into the pastry cream until thoroughly blended and smooth.

Cover the top of the pastry cream with a piece of waxed paper to prevent a skin from forming on top. Cover the bowl with plastic wrap and place the bowl on a cooling rack. Let the pastry cream cool to room temperature, then chill it in the refrigerator until cold before using.

Stir the pastry cream vigorously before using to remove any lumps, and remove the vanilla bean.

ASSEMBLY

Fit a clean pastry bag with a clean round tip. Fill the pastry bag partway with the mocha pastry cream.

Use a serrated knife to cut each cream puff in half horizontally, leaving the top attached at one side. Pipe a mound of pastry cream into the center of each cream puff, filling it completely.

GARNISH

Confectioners' sugar

Lightly dust the tops of the cream puffs with confectioners' sugar.

Serve the cream puffs immediately, or refrigerate up to 3 hours before serving.

21

TEA

THERE ARE SO MANY wonderful flavors to enjoy from teas. There are all of the green teas, black teas, and specialty teas that offer their distinct and subtle flavors. Usually we experience these flavors by drinking tea, but it's easy enough to carry them over into your baking by steeping tea leaves or bags to make a concentrated flavor. The idea of using teas in baking came to me during my travels in the British Isles. When having tea in the afternoon with cakes, I would take a sip of tea right after a bite and the flavors would mix in my mouth. So I thought to myself, why not put the tea flavor directly into the cakes? In this chapter I have created recipes that use my favorite drinking teas and that impart a delicate yet satisfying flavor. These are black currant tea, green tea, chai tea, Darjeeling, English breakfast, and jasmine tea.

Teas are always available in supermarkets, health or natural food stores, specialty coffee and tea shops, and through many online and catalog sources.

TIPS AND TECHNIQUES

Tea comes in two forms, bags and loose leaves. Bagged teas are sold in boxes or tins. Loose leaf tea is sold in tins or bags and in bulk.

When buying any packaged tea, always check the expiration date and make sure that the container is tightly sealed. When choosing bulk tea, look it over to make sure there is no foreign material mixed with it and that it is consistent. If possible, smell the tea for its distinct aroma.

It's best to store tea bags or loose tea in the original container, tightly sealed, in a cool, dark, dry place. Transfer bulk tea to a tightly sealed container. I like to store my bulk teas in glass jars with latches that seal securely.

To make a concentrate of tea, place the tea bags or loose tea leaves in a 1-quart bowl. Pour boiling water over the tea bags or leaves and leave to steep for 10 minutes. Remove the tea bags, squeezing them to release any liquid, or strain the tea leaves, pushing through as much liquid as possible. Cool the tea to room temperature before adding to the recipe.

Black Currant Tea Pound Cake

T HE NATURALLY SWEET and fruity flavor and aroma of black currant tea stands out in this cake but doesn't overpower it. This cake is larger than a typical pound cake and is baked in a tube pan. I like to use a pan with deep grooves to give the cake a natural design. The cake is served with a glaze or sauce made from black currant tea, and fresh raspberries or strawberries add an extra touch that makes it very special. **Makes one 10-inch round cake, 12 to 14 servings**

POUND CAKE

Center a rack in the oven and preheat it to 350°F.

2 teaspoons unsalted butter, melted 2 teaspoons all-purpose flour	Use a pastry brush or a paper towel to butter the inside of the pan, being sure to get into all the grooves. Sprinkle the flour inside the pan and shake and tilt the pan to cover the bottom and sides. Turn the pan upside down over the sink and shake out any excess flour. Or spray the inside of the pan with non-stick baking spray.
8 black currant tea bags or 8 tablespoons loose black currant tea 1 cup boiling water	Place the tea bags or loose tea leaves in a medium bowl. Pour the boiling water over the tea bags or leaves and leave to steep for 10 minutes. Remove the tea bags, squeezing them to release any liquid, or strain the tea leaves, pushing through as much liquid as possible. Cool the tea in the refrigerator for 30 minutes or in the freezer for 10 minutes. Reserve ⅓ cup of the tea to use for the glaze.
6 ounces (12 tablespoons, 1½ sticks) unsalted butter, softened	Place the butter in the bowl of an electric stand mixer or in a large bowl. Use the flat beater attachment or hand-held mixer to beat the butter on medium speed until it's fluffy, about 2 minutes.
2 cups granulated sugar	Add the sugar to the butter, and cream together thoroughly. Stop occasionally and scrape down the sides and bottom of the bowl with a rubber spatula.
3 extra-large eggs, at room temperature	One at a time, add the eggs to the butter mixture, stopping to scrape down the bottom and sides of the bowl after each addition. At first the mixture may look curdled as the eggs are added, but as you scrape down the bowl, the mixture will smooth out.

Essential Gear

- 10 × 4-inch tube pan or Bundt pan
- Electric stand mixer with flat beater attachment and wire whip attachment, or large mixing bowl and hand-held mixer
- Natural-bristle pastry brush
- Rubber spatula
- Cooling rack
- Sifter
- Thin-bladed knife

Keeping

Store the cake tightly wrapped in plastic up to 4 days at room temperature. To freeze up to 4 months, tightly wrap the cake in several layers of plastic wrap and aluminum foil. Use a large piece of masking tape and an indelible marker to label and date the contents. If frozen, defrost overnight in the refrigerator and bring to room temperature before serving.

Streamlining

The glaze can be made up to 3 days before using. Store it in a tightly sealed container at room temperature.

2 teaspoons pure vanilla extract or vanilla paste	Add the vanilla and blend.
⅓ cup sour cream	Add the sour cream to the butter mixture and blend together thoroughly.
3 cups all-purpose flour **1½ teaspoons baking powder** **¼ teaspoon salt**	Over a large piece of waxed or parchment paper or a bowl, sift together the flour and baking powder. Add the salt and toss to blend.
	Add the dry ingredients to the butter mixture alternately with the tea in 3 stages, starting and ending with the dry ingredients. Stop after each addition and scrape down the sides and bottom of the bowl. Blend the mixture thoroughly. Transfer the mixture to the pan. Use the rubber spatula to smooth and even the top. Bake for 1 hour and 10 minutes, until a cake tester inserted in the center of the cake comes out clean. Remove the pan from the oven and cool on a rack for 15 minutes. Invert the pan onto the rack and leave it for a few minutes so the cake will drop out of the pan. Remove the pan and let the cake cool completely.

GLAZE

1 cup confectioners' sugar, sifted **⅓ cup cooled black currant tea** **½ teaspoon freshly squeezed lemon juice**	Add the sugar and lemon juice to the tea and whisk together until completely smooth.

GARNISH

2 tablespoons confectioners' sugar, sifted	Dust the top of the cake with confectioners' sugar before serving. Serve slices of the cake drizzled with glaze. Scatter a few fresh raspberries or strawberries on the plate.

English Breakfast Tea Angel Food Cake

ENGLISH BREAKFAST TEA is actually a combination of several black teas. It imparts full-bodied flavor to this classic, airy angel food cake that turns light tan from the color of the tea. This cake uses twelve egg whites and is the perfect cake to bake if you have egg whites in your freezer and you're wondering what to do with them. **Makes one 10-inch round cake, 12 to 14 servings**

Center a rack in the oven and preheat it to 325°F.

Cut a round of parchment paper to fit the bottom of the pan and cut out a hole in the middle to fit the center tube of the pan. This cake is baked in an ungreased pan because greasing the pan would keep the batter from rising and gripping the sides of the pan as the cake bakes.

¼ cup loose English breakfast tea leaves
½ cup boiling water

Place the loose tea leaves in a medium bowl. Pour the boiling water over the tea leaves and let them steep for 10 minutes.

Strain the tea leaves, pushing through as much liquid as possible. Cool the tea to room temperature. Cool in the refrigerator for 30 minutes or in the freezer for 10 minutes.

12 extra-large egg whites, at room temperature
1 teaspoon cream of tartar
¾ cup superfine sugar

Place the egg whites in the grease-free bowl of an electric stand mixer or in a large grease-free bowl. Use the wire whip attachment or a hand-held mixer to whip the egg whites on medium speed until frothy. Add the cream of tartar and whip on medium-high speed until the egg whites hold soft peaks. Slowly sprinkle on the sugar and continue to beat the egg whites until they hold glossy and firm, but not stiff, peaks.

Add the cooled tea to the beaten egg whites and blend thoroughly.

1 cup plus 2 tablespoons cake flour
¾ cup superfine sugar
¼ teaspoon salt

Over a large piece of waxed or parchment paper or a bowl, sift together the flour and sugar. Add the salt and toss lightly to blend.

Fold this mixture into the whipped egg white mixture in 3 to 4 stages, blending thoroughly.

Transfer the batter to the tube pan. Use the rubber spatula to smooth and even the top. Gently tap the pan on the countertop a few times to eliminate any air bubbles.

Bake for 50 minutes to 1 hour, until a cake tester inserted in the center of the cake comes out clean.

Essential Gear

- 10 × 4-inch tube pan with removable bottom
- Scissors
- Parchment paper
- Electric stand mixer with wire whip attachment, or large mixing bowl and hand-held mixer
- Sifter
- Rubber spatula
- Thin-bladed knife
- Cooling rack

Keeping

Store the cake tightly wrapped in plastic up to 3 days at room temperature. To freeze up to 4 months, tightly wrap the cake in several layers of plastic wrap and aluminum foil. Use a large piece of masking tape and an indelible marker to label and date the contents. If frozen, defrost overnight in the refrigerator and bring to room temperature before serving.

Making a Change

Replace the English breakfast tea with Irish breakfast or Darjeeling tea.

Remove the pan from the oven and invert it over a cooling rack onto its feet or over a funnel or a thin-necked bottle. Let the cake hang to cool completely. Don't set the pan on a cooling rack on its base. This will cause the cake to collapse onto itself.

Don't shake the cake out of the pan before it is cool. Once it is cool, use a thin-bladed knife or flexible-blade spatula to run around the outer edge and the inside tube to help release the cake from the pan. Invert the cake onto a rack, then re-invert onto a serving plate.

Serve the cake at room temperature.

Chai Tea Spice Cake

CHAI TEA is an Indian black tea perfumed with spices such as cardamom, cinnamon, ginger, and cloves. It lends its intriguing flavor to this quick and easy cake. After the cake is cooled, it's lightly dusted with confectioners' sugar and cut into squares. Chai tea can be found in health food stores and specialty coffee and tea shops. **Makes sixteen 2-inch squares**

CAKE

Center a rack in the oven and preheat it to 350°F.

Non-stick baking spray	Spray the inside of the baking pan with non-stick baking spray.
6 chai tea bags **½ cup boiling water**	Place the tea bags in a medium bowl. Pour the boiling water over the tea bags and leave to steep for 5 minutes. Remove the tea bags, squeezing them to release as much liquid as possible. Cool the tea in the refrigerator for 30 minutes or in the freezer for 10 minutes.
4 ounces (8 tablespoons, 1 stick) unsalted butter, softened	Place the butter in the bowl of an electric stand mixer or a large bowl. Use the flat beater or a hand-held mixer to beat until fluffy, about 2 minutes.
¼ cup granulated sugar **½ cup firmly packed light brown sugar**	Add the granulated sugar and brown sugar to the butter, and cream together well.

Essential Gear
- 8-inch square baking pan
- Electric stand mixer with flat beater attachment and wire whip attachment, or large mixing bowl and hand-held mixer
- Rubber spatula
- Cooling rack
- Sugar dredge or fine-mesh strainer

Keeping

Store the cake in an airtight plastic container between layers of waxed paper at room temperature up 4 days. To freeze up to 3 months, wrap the container tightly in several layers of aluminum foil and plastic wrap. Use a large piece of masking tape and an indelible marker to label and date the contents. If frozen, defrost in the refrigerator.

¼ cup unflavored vegetable oil (canola or safflower)	Add the oil and the cooled tea to the butter mixture and blend thoroughly. Stop occasionally and scrape down the sides and bottom of the bowl with a rubber spatula.
2½ cups all-purpose flour 2 teaspoons ground cinnamon 1 teaspoon baking soda 1 teaspoon ground ginger 1 teaspoon ground cardamom 1 teaspoon ground cloves ½ teaspoon freshly grated nutmeg ¼ teaspoon salt	Over a large piece of waxed or parchment paper or a bowl, sift together the flour, cinnamon, baking soda, ginger, cardamom, and cloves. Add the nutmeg and salt and toss to blend well.
1 cup buttermilk	Alternately add the dry ingredients with the buttermilk to the butter mixture in 4 stages, starting and ending with the dry ingredients. Blend thoroughly after each addition and stop often to scrape down the sides and bottom of the bowl with a rubber spatula.
2 extra-large egg whites, at room temperature ½ teaspoon cream of tartar ¼ cup granulated sugar	Place the egg whites in the grease-free bowl of an electric stand mixer or in a large grease-free bowl. Use the wire whip attachment or a handheld mixer to whip the egg whites on medium speed until frothy. Add the cream of tartar and whip on medium-high speed until the egg whites hold soft peaks. Sprinkle on the sugar and continue to whip the egg whites until they hold glossy and firm, but not stiff, peaks. Gently fold the whipped egg whites into the batter in 3 to 4 stages.
	Transfer the cake batter to the prepared pan. Use a rubber spatula to spread the batter into the corners and even the top. Bake for 40 to 45 minutes, until a cake tester inserted in the center comes out clean. Remove the baking pan from the oven and cool completely on a rack.

GARNISH

Confectioners' sugar	Lightly dust the top of the cake with confectioners' sugar and cut into 2-inch squares.

Darjeeling Chocolate Layer Cake

DARJEELING TEA and cocoa powder blend together very well to give this cake an unexpected, yet delightful, taste. The delicate, tender-textured layers are alternated with a creamy icing. I recommend serving this cake with afternoon tea or after a special meal. **Makes one 9-inch round cake, 12 to 14 servings**

CAKE

Center a rack in the oven and preheat it to 350°F.

1 tablespoon unsalted butter, at room temperature	Using a paper towel or your fingertips, butter the inside of the cake pans.
1 tablespoon all-purpose flour	Dust the inside of each pan with some of the flour, then turn the pans over and shake out the excess over the sink.
	Cut a round of parchment paper to fit the bottom of each pan. Butter each parchment paper round and place it in each pan, butter-side up.
6 tablespoons loose Darjeeling tea leaves **²/₃ cup boiling water**	Place the tea leaves in a medium bowl and pour the boiling water over them. Leave the tea leaves to steep for 10 minutes.
	Strain the tea, using a spoon to push through as much of the liquid as possible.
	Let the tea cool in the refrigerator for 30 minutes or chill in the freezer for 10 minutes.
2 cups cake flour **1 teaspoon baking soda** **¼ teaspoon salt**	Over a large piece of waxed or parchment paper or a bowl, sift together the flour and baking soda. Add the salt and toss to mix.
²/₃ cup unsweetened natural cocoa powder, sifted **²/₃ cup boiling water**	Place the cocoa powder in a medium bowl. Pour the boiling water over the cocoa powder. Use a heatproof spatula or a spoon to blend together until it forms a smooth cocoa paste.
	Chill the cocoa paste in the freezer for 10 minutes.
¼ cup plain non-fat yogurt **2 teaspoons pure vanilla extract or vanilla paste**	Stir the yogurt, vanilla, and cooled tea into the cocoa paste mixture thoroughly.

Essential Gear

- Two 9 × 2-inch round cake pans
- Scissors
- Parchment paper
- Medium fine-mesh strainer
- Sifter or large fine-mesh strainer
- Heat-resistant spatula
- Electric stand mixer with flat beater attachment and wire whip attachment, or hand-held mixer and large mixing bowl
- Two rubber spatulas
- Two cooling racks
- Pie or cake pan
- 8-inch chef's knife
- 10-inch flexible-blade icing spatula

Keeping

Store the cake loosely covered with aluminum foil in the refrigerator up to 4 days. Place several toothpicks in the top outer edges of the cake to hold the foil away from it so it won't mar the icing. To freeze up to 3 months, place the cake in a cake box and wrap the box with several layers of plastic wrap and aluminum foil. Or place the cake on a lined baking sheet on a flat surface in the freezer and let it freeze (about 3 hours). Loosely wrap the cake in layers of plastic wrap and aluminum foil. If frozen, defrost overnight in the refrigerator. Bring the cake

2 ounces (4 tablespoons, ½ stick) unsalted butter, softened	Place the butter in the bowl of an electric stand mixer or in a large bowl. Use the flat beater attachment or a hand-held mixer to beat the butter on medium speed until fluffy, about 2 minutes.
1¼ cups granulated sugar ¾ cup firmly packed light brown sugar	Add the granulated sugar and brown sugar to the butter and beat on medium speed until thoroughly blended. Stop occasionally and scrape down the bottom and sides of the bowl with a rubber spatula.
1 extra-large egg, at room temperature 3 extra-large egg whites, at room temperature	Use a fork to lightly beat together the egg and egg whites in a small bowl. Slowly add the egg mixture to the butter mixture and blend well. Stop occasionally and scrape down the bottom and sides of the bowl with a rubber spatula. At first the mixture may look curdled as the eggs are added, but as you scrape down the bowl, the mixture will smooth out.
	Alternately add the dry ingredients and cocoa/tea mixture to the butter mixture in 3 or 4 stages, blending well after each addition. Stop and scrape down the bottom and sides of the bowl with a rubber spatula frequently.
	Transfer the batter to the cake pans, dividing it evenly between them. Use the rubber spatula to spread the batter evenly in both pans.
	Bake the layers for 30 minutes, until a cake tester inserted in the center comes out clean.
	Remove the pans from the oven and cool on racks for 15 minutes. Invert each pan over a plate and peel the parchment paper from the back. Re-invert the layers onto cooling racks and cool completely.
2 tablespoons sliced almonds	Place the almonds in a pie or cake pan and toast in the oven until light golden, about 5 minutes.
	Remove the pan from the oven and cool on a rack.
	Use a chef's knife to finely chop the almonds.

ICING

5 tablespoons loose Darjeeling tea leaves ½ cup boiling water	Place the tea leaves in a medium bowl and pour the boiling water over them. Leave to steep for 10 minutes.
	Strain the tea, using a spoon to push through as much of the liquid as possible. Cool in the refrigerator for 30 minutes or in the freezer for 10 minutes.

to room temperature at least 30 minutes before serving.

Streamlining
Bake the layers up to 2 days before assembling the cake. After the layers are completely cool, cover them tightly with plastic wrap and hold at room temperature. The layers can be frozen up to 3 months. To freeze, wrap them snugly in several layers of plastic wrap and place them in freezer bags. Use a large piece of masking tape and an indelible marker to label and date the contents. If frozen, defrost the layers overnight in the refrigerator.

Recovering from a Mishap
Don't worry if one of the cake layers breaks during assembly. You can patch it together with some of the icing and no on will know the difference.

Making a Change
Replace the almonds with hazelnuts or walnuts.

2¹/₂ cups confectioners' sugar **¹/₂ cup unsweetened natural** **cocoa powder**	Over a piece of waxed or parchment paper or a bowl, sift together the sugar and cocoa powder.
6 ounces cream cheese, **softened**	Place the cream cheese in the bowl of an electric stand mixer or in a large bowl. Use the flat beater attachment or a hand-held mixer to beat the cream cheese on medium speed until fluffy, about 2 minutes.
	Alternately add the confectioners' sugar mixture and the cooled tea to the cream cheese. Continue to beat the mixture until it is thick enough to spread. If the icing is too thin, chill in the freezer for 5 to 10 minutes. Stir it occasionally to make sure it doesn't become too firm.

ASSEMBLY

Place one cake layer on a serving plate. Place wide strips of waxed paper around the serving plate to protect it while assembling the cake. Use a flexible-blade spatula to evenly spread ¹/₃ of the icing over the cake layer.

Position the second cake layer evenly over the icing. Spread the top of the cake with ¹/₃ of the icing. Then spread the remaining icing over the top and sides of the cake.

Sprinkle the top of the cake with the chopped, toasted almonds.

Let the cake chill for at least 2 hours before serving so it has time to set and will be easier to cut. Serve the cake at room temperature.

Green Tea and Almond Cake
with Green Tea Sorbet

BECAUSE GREEN TEA is more delicate than black tea, use very hot, rather than boiling, water to prepare it. Bring the water to the point where it's just about to boil, then pour it over the tea to steep. Also, don't steep the tea as long as black tea. Green tea and almonds are a superb flavor combination. The green tea sorbet has a delicate flavor and goes very well with the cake. **Makes one 9¹/₂-inch round cake, 12 servings**

Essential Gear
- Medium heavy-bottomed saucepan
- Rubber spatula
- 9¹/₂-inch round spring-form pan
- Scissors
- Parchment paper

GREEN TEA SORBET

6 unflavored green tea bags
or 5 tablespoons
unflavored loose green tea
¾ cup very hot water

Place the green tea bags or loose green tea leaves in a medium bowl. Pour the hot water over the tea bags or leaves and leave to steep for 5 minutes.

Remove the tea bags, squeezing them to release any liquid or strain the tea leaves, pushing through as much liquid as possible. Cool the tea in the refrigerator for 30 minutes or in the freezer for 10 minutes.

1½ cups water
1 cup granulated sugar
1 tablespoon honey

In the saucepan, combine the water, sugar, and honey and bring to a boil over medium heat. Stir briefly and cook until the sugar dissolves.

Remove the pan from the heat and transfer the mixture to a large bowl. Let cool to room temperature.

Combine the tea mixture and the sugar mixture. Cover tightly with plastic wrap and chill in the refrigerator until cold, at least 2 hours.

Pour the mixture into an ice cream freezer and freeze according to the manufacturer's directions. Place the sorbet into a tightly sealed container and freeze until firm, about 3 hours.

GREEN TEA AND ALMOND CAKE

1 tablespoon unsalted butter,
softened

Center a rack in the oven and preheat it to 350°F. Use your fingertips or a paper towel to butter the inside of the springform pan.

1 tablespoon all-purpose
flour

Dust the inside of the pan with the flour. Shake and tilt the pan to evenly distribute the flour, then turn the pan over and shake out the excess over the sink.

Cut a round of parchment paper to fit the bottom of the pan. Butter the parchment paper round and place in the pan, butter-side up.

Or spray the inside of the pan and the parchment paper round with non-stick baking spray.

7 unflavored green tea bags
or 7 tablespoons unflavored
loose green tea leaves
½ cup very hot water

Place the green tea bags or loose green tea leaves in a medium bowl. Pour the hot water over the tea bags or leaves and leave to steep for 5 minutes.

Remove the tea bags, squeezing them to release any liquid, or strain the tea leaves, pushing through as much liquid as possible. Cool in the refrigerator for 30 minutes or in the freezer for 10 minutes.

- Electric stand mixer with flat beater attachment and wire whip attachment, or large mixing bowl and hand-held mixer
- Food processor
- Ice cream machine

Keeping

Store the cake tightly wrapped in aluminum foil at room temperature up to 4 days. To freeze up to 3 months, wrap the cake tightly in several layers of plastic wrap and aluminum foil. Use a large piece of masking tape and an indelible marker to label and date the contents. If frozen, defrost overnight in the refrigerator and bring to room temperature before serving.

Making a Change

Replace the ground almonds with ground macadamia nuts.

1½ **cups whole, blanched almonds**	In the work bowl of a food processor fitted with the steel blade, combine the almonds, sugar, cornstarch, and salt. Pulse until the almonds are very finely ground, about 1 minute.
2 **tablespoons granulated sugar**	
2 **tablespoons cornstarch**	
⅛ **teaspoon salt**	
3 **extra-large egg yolks, at room temperature**	Place the egg yolks and sugar in the bowl of an electric stand mixer or in a large bowl. Use the wire whip attachment or a hand-held mixer to whip together until the mixture is very thick and pale colored and holds a slowly dissolving ribbon as the beater is lifted, about 5 minutes.
1 **cup granulated sugar**	
5 **extra-large egg whites, at room temperature**	Place the egg whites in the grease-free bowl of an electric stand mixer or in a large grease-free bowl. Use the wire whip attachment or a hand-held mixer to whip the egg whites on medium speed until frothy. Add the cream of tartar and whip on medium-high speed until the egg whites hold firm, but not stiff, peaks.
½ **teaspoon cream of tartar**	
	Gently fold the whipped egg whites into the sugar mixture in 4 stages.
	Gently fold the ground almond mixture into the sugar mixture, then fold in the cooled tea.
	Transfer the cake batter to the prepared springform pan. Use a rubber spatula to smooth and even the top.
	Bake the cake for 30 to 35 minutes, until a cake tester inserted into the center comes out clean.
	Remove the pan from the oven and cool completely on a rack. Remove the sides of the springform pan. Use a flexible-blade spatula to loosen the bottom of the cake from the bottom of the pan. Peel the parchment paper off the back of the cake.
	Cut the cake into wedges and serve each with a scoop of green tea sorbet.

Individual Jasmine Tea Cakes

JASMINE TEA has a strong, flowery aroma and flavor that permeates but does not overpower these individual cakes. They are baked in a muffin tin, which makes them very easy to serve. **Makes 12 cakes**

Essential Gear
- 12-cavity 3-inch muffin pan
- 3-inch pleated paper muffin cups
- Food processor

Center a rack in the oven and preheat it to 350°F. Line each cavity of the muffin pan with a paper muffin cup.

¼ cup loose jasmine tea leaves ⅓ cup boiling water	Place the tea leaves in a medium bowl. Pour the boiling water over the leaves and leave to steep for 10 minutes. Strain the tea, pushing through as much of the liquid as possible.
½ cup dried apricots, finely chopped	Soak the apricots in the tea for 10 minutes, then pulse the mixture in the work bowl of a food processor fitted with the steel blade until it forms a thick puree, about 30 seconds.
½ cup buttermilk ¼ cup unflavored vegetable oil (canola or safflower) 3 extra-large egg whites, at room temperature	Place the buttermilk, oil, and egg whites in a medium bowl and whisk together until thoroughly blended. Add the apricot puree and mix thoroughly.
2½ cups all-purpose flour 2 teaspoons baking powder 1 teaspoon baking soda ⅓ cup granulated sugar ¼ cup firmly packed light brown sugar ¼ teaspoon salt	Over a large piece of waxed or parchment paper or a bowl, sift together the flour, baking powder, and baking soda. Add the granulated sugar, brown sugar, and salt and stir to blend thoroughly.
	Stir the egg white mixture into the dry ingredients, blending thoroughly.
½ cup sliced or slivered almonds, finely chopped	Add the almonds to the batter and blend thoroughly.
	Using a spoon or rubber spatula, divide the mixture evenly among the cavities in the muffin pan, filling them almost to the top. Bake for 25 minutes, until a cake tester inserted in the center comes out clean. Remove the baking pan from the oven and cool completely on a rack.

GARNISH

Confectioners' sugar	Lightly dust the top of each tea cake with confectioners' sugar.

- Medium fine-mesh strainer
- Sifter
- Whisk
- Rubber spatula
- Cooling rack

Keeping

Store the tea cakes in an airtight plastic container between layers of waxed paper at room temperature up 4 days. To freeze up to 3 months, wrap the container tightly in several layers of aluminum foil and plastic wrap. Use a large piece of masking tape and an indelible marker to label and date the contents. If frozen, defrost in the refrigerator.

22

LIQUEURS AND

SPIRITS

BAKING WITH liqueurs and spirits is an area where I've had a fair amount of experience. While I was working in hotels and restaurants, especially in Europe, there were always several desserts on the menu that used liqueurs and spirits. I remember at first thinking that these desserts would add even more alcoholic consumption for diners and perhaps not be very palatable. Neither one of these is true, because the amount of liqueurs and spirits used is relatively small. What you get is the great flavor and aroma in a non-drinking form. Although these desserts have a more full-bodied flavor, they are in no way overpowering. And don't think these are just for the colder months. They are great all year round, including for afternoon tea and coffee. I have used a wide variety of liqueurs and spirits, so there is something for everyone in this chapter.

You can always find liqueurs and spirits in supermarkets, liquor stores, special discount warehouse stores, and some gourmet food shops.

TIPS AND TECHNIQUES

Quality is important when selecting liqueurs and spirits for baking. I always buy the best brand possible. Also, if you intend to make only a couple of recipes that are flavored with one liqueur or spirit, you will need to buy only a small amount, such as a pint. However, if you intend to make more than a couple of recipes, it's a better value to buy a larger bottle. What I like to buy are the small bottles, usually 2 ounces, similar to what you are served on an airplane. I like to keep a variety of these on hand. Store liqueurs and spirits in their original bottles, tightly sealed, in a cool, dark place.

Stored properly, they will keep for several months, even years. Of course, smell them and have a little taste before using them to make sure they haven't lost their character.

In most cases, the liqueurs or spirits that you are using in recipes are added directly to a mixture. However, for two of the recipes in this chapter, there is a need to soak dried fruit. To do this, place the dried fruit in a bowl and add the liqueur or spirit. Cover the bowl tightly with plastic wrap and let them steep at least 30 minutes, then strain off any excess liquid.

Amaretto Almond Layer Cake

THE BASE for this layer cake is a classic almond sponge cake. American sponge cake traditionally has no fat and has a light, airy, delicate texture. It is a close relative of the classic French génoise cake, which is made with a small amount of butter. For this cake, the sponge cake layers are brushed with amaretto sugar syrup and amaretto whipped cream is used both as the filling between the layers and as the icing. Toasted sliced almonds finish the sides of the cake and add to the top decoration. The cake is very versatile and can be assembled with fresh fruit, such as strawberries, raspberries, and apricots between the layers. **Makes one 9½-inch round cake, 10 to 12 servings**

ALMOND SPONGE CAKE

Center a rack in the oven and preheat it to 350°F.

1 tablespoon unsalted butter, softened	Using a paper towel or your fingertips, generously butter the inside of the springform pan.
1 tablespoon all-purpose flour	Dust the inside of the pan with the flour. Shake and tilt the pan to evenly distribute the flour, then turn the pan over and shake out the excess over the sink.
	Cut a round of parchment paper to fit the bottom of the pan. Butter the parchment paper round and place in the pan, butter-side up.
1½ cups sliced or slivered almonds **⅓ cup superfine sugar**	In the work bowl of a food processor fitted with the steel blade, combine the almonds and sugar. Pulse until the almonds are very finely ground, about 1 minute.
6 extra-large egg yolks, at room temperature **⅔ cup superfine sugar**	Place the egg yolks and sugar in the bowl of an electric stand mixer or in a large bowl.
	Using the wire whip attachment or a hand-held mixer, whip the eggs and sugar on medium-high speed until they are very thick and pale colored and hold a slowly dissolving ribbon as the beater is lifted, about 5 minutes.
¾ cup sifted cake flour **⅛ teaspoon salt**	Over a large piece of waxed or parchment paper or a bowl, sift the flour and measure out ¾ cup. Transfer this amount to a bowl. Add the salt and the finely ground almonds and stir to blend together.
	Fold this mixture into the beaten eggs and sugar in 3 stages. Fold gently, taking care not to deflate the egg mixture.

Essential Gear

- 9½-inch round spring-form pan
- Scissors
- Parchment paper
- Food processor
- Electric stand mixer with flat beater attachment and wire whip attachment, or large mixing bowl and hand-held mixer
- Sifter
- Two rubber spatulas
- Cooling rack
- 10-inch flexible-blade icing spatula
- Small saucepan
- Serrated knife
- 12- or 14-inch pastry bag and large open star tip

Keeping

Store the cake loosely covered with waxed paper, then wrapped with aluminum foil, in the refrigerator up to 2 days. Place several tooth-picks in the top outer edges of the cake to hold the waxed paper away from it so it won't mar the whipped cream.

Streamlining

Bake the almond sponge cake up to 2 days before assembling and keep it tightly covered with a double layer of plastic wrap at room temperature or in the refrig-erator up to 4 days. To freeze the unassembled cake up to 3 months, wrap it snugly in

6 extra-large egg whites, at room temperature ½ teaspoon cream of tartar	Place the egg whites in the grease-free bowl of an electric stand mixer or a large bowl. Use the wire whip attachment or a hand-held mixer to whip the egg whites on medium speed until frothy. Add the cream of tartar and whip on medium-high speed until the egg whites hold firm, but not stiff, peaks. Fold the whipped egg whites into the yolk mixture in 3 stages. Fold gently, taking care not to deflate the egg whites. The air beaten into the egg whites is what makes this cake rise as it bakes.
2 teaspoons amaretto	Fold the amaretto into the batter and blend thoroughly. Transfer the batter to the springform pan. Smooth the top of the cake with a rubber spatula. Bake the cake for 35 to 40 minutes, until golden and a cake tester inserted into the center comes out clean. Remove the cake pan from the oven and cool completely on a rack. When cool, gently run the flat blade of a flexible-blade spatula between the sides of the cake and the edges of the pan. Release the clip on the springform pan and lift off the sides.

SUGAR SYRUP

¼ cup sugar ½ cup water	Combine the sugar and water in the small saucepan and bring to a boil over medium heat to dissolve the sugar. Remove the saucepan from the heat and let the sugar syrup cool.
2 tablespoons amaretto	Add the amaretto to the cooled sugar syrup.

AMARETTO WHIPPED CREAM

2 cups heavy whipping cream ½ cup confectioners' sugar, sifted	Place the cream in the chilled bowl of an electric stand mixer or a large bowl. Using the wire whip attachment or a hand-held mixer, whip the cream on medium speed until it is frothy. Add the sugar and continue to whip the cream on medium speed until it holds soft peaks.
2 to 3 tablespoons amaretto	Stir 2 tablespoons of amaretto into the whipped cream. Taste the whipped cream to see if another tablespoon of amaretto is needed for flavor. You want flavor to be good, but not overpowering.

ASSEMBLY

With your fingertips, carefully peel the skin off of the top of the cake. Using a serrated knife, cut the cake horizontally into 3 equal layers

several layers of plastic wrap and place in freezer bags. Use a large piece of masking tape and an indelible marker to label and date the contents. If frozen, defrost the cake overnight in the refrigerator.

The sugar syrup can be prepared up to 2 weeks in advance and kept in an airtight plastic container in the refrigerator.

Recovering from a Mishap
If one of the sponge cake layers breaks during assembly, patch it together with some of the whipped cream.

Making a Change
Use 1¾ cups previously ground almonds instead of grinding them when making the cake.

Assemble the cake with thinly sliced strawberries, fresh raspberries, or thinly sliced fresh apricots between the cake layers, pressing the fruit gently into the whipped cream on each layer.

(see page 34). Use a flexible-blade spatula to release the bottom layer of cake from the bottom of the springform pan. Place the bottom layer on a serving plate or cardboard cake circle. Place strips of waxed paper around the bottom edges of the cake to protect the plate while assembling the cake.

½ cup apricot preserves

Brush the layer with the amaretto sugar syrup. Use the flexible-blade spatula to spread the layer evenly with half of the apricot preserves.

Reserve ¼ cup of the whipped cream for the top decoration. With a clean spatula, evenly spread some of the whipped cream over the apricot preserves.

Position the second cake layer evenly over the whipped cream and brush with amaretto sugar syrup. Spread the remaining apricot preserves evenly over the layer. Spread some of the whipped cream over the apricot preserves. Repeat with the top cake layer and spread the remaining whipped cream over the sides and top of the cake.

1¼ cup toasted sliced almonds

Press the toasted almonds into the sides of the cake just up to, but not over, the top edge.

Fit the pastry bag with the star tip and fill partway with the remaining whipped cream. Visually divide the top of the cake into 12 pieces or use a small sharp knife to mark the outer top edge of the cake into serving pieces. Pipe a star or rosette in the center of each marked piece at the outside top edge of the cake and pipe a larger star or rosette in the center (see page 44).

15 sliced almonds, lightly toasted

Place a sliced almond in the center of each star or rosette, pointed end down, and arrange 3 sliced almonds on the center star or rosette.

Serve immediately, cutting the cake into wedges, or refrigerate for up to 4 hours.

Black Forest Cherry Cake

T HIS CLASSIC CAKE takes its name from the *kirschwasser* (cherry brandy) used to make it, which comes from the Black Forest in Germany. Kirsch is readily found in liquor stores or in the liquor section of grocery stores. The base for the cake is a chocolate génoise, which is made with two extra egg yolks that help support the cake's structure, because it becomes heavier

Essential Gear

- 9 × 2-inch round cake pan
- Scissors
- Parchment paper
- Electric stand mixer with flat beater attachment and

than a classic génoise with the addition of cocoa powder. The génoise is cut into three horizontal layers and assembled with kirsch sugar syrup, kirsch whipped cream, and cherries. Use either Morello cherries or canned tart cherries in water, not in sugar syrup. The whole cake is covered in dark chocolate shavings and decorated with whipped cream rosettes. When the cake is cut into serving pieces, the beautiful layers of cake, whipped cream, and cherries are revealed. The chocolate génoise and kirsch sugar syrup can be made a couple of days before assembling the cake. **Makes one 9-inch round cake, 10 to 12 servings**

- wire whip attachment, or large mixing bowl and hand-held mixer
- Large saucepan
- Whisk
- Instant-read thermometer
- Sifter
- Cooling rack
- Small saucepan
- Serrated knife
- 1-inch natural-bristle pastry brush
- Two rubber spatulas
- Fine-mesh strainer
- 10-inch flexible-blade icing spatula
- 12- or 14-inch pastry bag and large open star tip

CHOCOLATE GÉNOISE

Center a rack in the oven and preheat it to 350°F.

1 tablespoon unsalted butter, softened	Using a paper towel or your fingertips, generously butter the inside of the cake pan, coating it thoroughly.
2 teaspoons all-purpose flour	Dust the inside of the pan with the flour. Shake and tilt the pan to evenly distribute the flour, then turn the pan over and shake out the excess over the sink.
	Cut a round of parchment paper to fit the bottom of the pan. Butter the parchment paper round and place in the pan, butter-side up.
6 extra-large eggs, at room temperature **2 extra-large egg yolks, at room temperature** **½ cup granulated sugar**	Place the eggs, egg yolks, and sugar in the bowl of an electric stand mixer or in a large bowl. Place the bowl in a large saucepan of simmering water. Use a whisk to stir together constantly until the mixture registers 110°F on an instant-read thermometer. This process helps the sugar dissolve so it will incorporate thoroughly. Remove the bowl from the water and wipe the bottom dry. Use the wire whip attachment or a hand-held mixer to whip the mixture on medium-high speed until very thick and pale colored and it holds a slowly dissolving ribbon as the beater is lifted, about 5 minutes.
¾ cup cake flour **¼ cup cocoa powder** **⅛ teaspoon salt**	Over a large piece of waxed or parchment paper or a bowl, sift together the flour and cocoa powder. Add the salt and toss to blend. Fold this mixture into the beaten eggs and sugar in 3 stages. Fold gently, taking care not to deflate the egg mixture. The air beaten into the eggs is what makes this cake rise as it bakes.
1 ounce (2 tablespoons, ¼ stick) unsalted butter, melted	Place the butter in a small bowl. Take about 1 cup of the batter and blend it thoroughly with the butter. Then fold this mixture into the cake batter.

Keeping
Store the cake loosely covered with aluminum foil in the refrigerator for up to 2 days. Place several toothpicks in the top outer edge of the cake to hold the foil away from it so it won't mar the whipped cream.

Streamlining
Bake the chocolate génoise up to 2 days before assembling and keep it tightly covered with a double layer of plastic wrap at room temperature or in the refrigerator up to 4 days. To freeze the cake up to 3 months, wrap it snugly in several layers of plastic wrap and place in freezer bags. Use a large piece of masking tape and an indelible marker to label and date the contents. If frozen, defrost the cake overnight in the refrigerator.

½ teaspoon pure vanilla extract or vanilla paste	Fold the vanilla into the batter and blend thoroughly.
	Transfer the cake batter to the prepared cake pan. Smooth the top with a rubber spatula.
	Bake the cake for 30 to 35 minutes, until it springs back when lightly touched on top.
	Remove the cake pan from the oven and cool completely on a rack. Invert the pan to remove the cake, then peel the parchment paper off the back of the layer. Re-invert the cake onto a plate or a cardboard cake circle.

SUGAR SYRUP

¼ cup sugar **½ cup water** **1 tablespoon kirsch**	Combine the sugar and water in the small saucepan and bring to a boil over medium heat to dissolve the sugar. Remove the saucepan from the heat and let the sugar syrup cool, then stir in the kirsch.

KIRSCH WHIPPED CREAM

3 cups heavy whipping cream **½ cup confectioners' sugar, sifted**	Place the cream in the chilled bowl of an electric stand mixer or a large bowl. Using the wire whip attachment or a hand-held mixer, whip the cream on medium speed until it is frothy. Add the sugar and continue to whip the cream on medium speed until it holds soft peaks.
3 to 4 tablespoons kirsch	Add 3 tablespoons of the kirsch and stir in completely. Taste the whipped cream to see if it needs another tablespoon of kirsch. The flavor should be subtle, not powerful, and it is better to have a light hand with the kirsch.

ASSEMBLY

Two 16-ounce cans water-packed Morello or tart cherries	Pour the cherries into a strainer to drain them of their water.
	With your fingertips, carefully peel the skin off of the top of the cake. Using a serrated knife, cut the génoise horizontally into 3 equal layers (see page 34). Place the bottom layer on a serving plate or a cardboard cake circle. Place strips of waxed paper around the bottom edges of the cake to protect the plate while assembling the cake.
	Brush the layer heavily with the kirsch sugar syrup. Use the flexible-blade spatula to spread the layer evenly with about ¼ inch of whipped cream.

The sugar syrup can be prepared up to 2 weeks in advance and kept in an airtight plastic container in the refrigerator.

Recovering from a Mishap
If one of the chocolate génoise layers breaks during assembly, patch it together with some of the whipped cream.

Cover the top of the whipped cream with a layer of cherries and gently press them into the cream. Spread a thin layer of whipped cream over the cherries.

Position the second cake layer evenly over the whipped cream and brush heavily with the kirsch sugar syrup. Spread a thin layer of the whipped cream over the cake layer. Cover the top of the whipped cream with the remaining cherries and gently press them into the cream. Spread a thin layer of whipped cream over the cherries.

Turn the top layer of the cake upside down to create an even surface and press it gently into the whipped cream, lining up the edges so the cake is straight. Brush this layer generously with the remaining kirsch sugar syrup.

Reserve ⅓ cup of the whipped cream for the top decoration and use the remaining cream to cover the top and sides of the cake. Use the flexible-blade spatula to spread the cream evenly and smoothly.

1½ cups shaved dark chocolate

Press the shaved chocolate into the sides of the cake up to, but not over, the top edge and sprinkle the top lightly with shaved chocolate.

Fit the pastry bag with the star tip and fill with the reserved whipped cream. Visually divide the top of the cake into 12 pieces or use a small sharp knife to mark the outer top edge of the cake into serving pieces. Pipe a rosette in the center of each marked piece at the outside top edge of the cake (see page 44).

Lightly sprinkle the top of each rosette with shaved chocolate.

Serve immediately, cutting the cake into wedges, or refrigerate for up to 4 hours.

Chambord Roulade with Fresh Raspberries

THIS CLASSIC SPONGE CAKE is baked in a jelly-roll pan and rolled up tightly while warm. The cake is baked at high heat, which quickly sets its structure, and it has no fat, creating a light, soft texture. When cool, the cake is unrolled and lightly brushed with sugar syrup flavored with Chambord, then spread with a filling of Chambord-flavored whipped cream and fresh raspberries. The cake is rerolled and decorated on the outside with more whipped cream and fresh raspberries. It's a stunning and scrumptious summer dessert. **Makes one 15-inch cake, 12 to 14 servings**

Essential Gear
- Jelly-roll pan (12 × 17 inches)
- Two sheets parchment paper
- Electric stand mixer with wire whip attachment, or a hand-held mixer and a large mixing bowl

ROLLED CAKE

Center a rack in the oven and preheat it to 450°F.

1 tablespoon unsalted butter, softened

Line the jelly-roll pan with a sheet of parchment paper. Use a paper towel or your fingertips to butter the parchment paper. Or spray the parchment paper with non-stick baking spray.

5 extra-large egg yolks, at room temperature
½ cup granulated sugar

Place the egg yolks and sugar in the bowl of an electric stand mixer or a large bowl. Place the bowl in a saucepan of hot water over medium heat and whisk constantly until the mixture registers 110°F on an instant-read thermometer. This process helps the sugar dissolve so it will incorporate thoroughly

Remove the bowl from the water and wipe the bottom and sides dry.

Use the wire whip attachment or a hand-held mixer to whip the mixture on medium-high speed until very thick and pale colored and it holds a slowly dissolving ribbon as the beater is lifted, about 5 minutes.

½ teaspoon pure vanilla extract or vanilla paste
½ teaspoon Chambord

Add the vanilla and Chambord to the egg yolk mixture and blend together thoroughly.

⅔ cup cake flour
⅛ teaspoon salt

Over a large piece of waxed or parchment paper or a bowl, sift the flour. Add the salt and toss to blend. Fold this mixture into the egg mixture in 3 stages, blending well after each addition.

4 extra-large egg whites, at room temperature
½ teaspoon cream of tartar

Place the egg whites in the grease-free bowl of an electric stand mixer or a large grease-free bowl. Use the wire whip attachment or a hand-held mixer to whip the egg whites on medium speed until frothy. Add the cream of tartar and whip on medium-high speed until the egg whites hold firm, but not stiff, peaks.

Fold the whipped egg whites into the yolk mixture in 3 stages, blending thoroughly.

Pour the batter onto the prepared pan and use the rubber spatula or an offset spatula to spread it smoothly and evenly over the parchment and into the corners.

Bake the cake for 7 to 8 minutes, until it is evenly colored and the top springs back when touched lightly.

Confectioners' sugar

Remove the pan from the oven. Dust the top of the cake with the sugar.

- Large saucepan
- Whisk
- Sifter
- Instant-read thermometer
- Rubber spatula
- Offset spatula
- Kitchen towel
- Small sharp knife
- Small saucepan
- 1-inch natural-bristle pastry brush
- 12- or 14-inch pastry bag with large open star tip
- Serrated knife

Keeping

Store the filled and frosted cake tented with waxed paper and topped with aluminum foil in the refrigerator for 1 day. Place several toothpicks in the top of the cake to hold the waxed paper away from it so it won't mar the whipped cream. Store the unfilled and frosted cake tightly wrapped with plastic wrap in the refrigerator up to 4 days before filling. To freeze the cake without the filling and frosting up to 4 months, wrap it tightly in several layers of plastic wrap and aluminum foil. Use a large piece of masking tape and an indelible marker to label and date the contents. If frozen, defrost overnight in the refrigerator and bring to room temperature before serving.

Making a Change

Replace the Chambord with framboise.

While the cake is still hot, use a small, sharp knife to loosen the edges from the sides of the pan. Place a sheet of parchment paper over the top of the cake and cover with a kitchen towel. Then invert the jelly-roll pan and lift it off the cake. Gently peel the parchment paper off of the back of the cake and discard.

Starting at one long end of the cake, immediately roll it up in the towel and parchment paper. Leave the cake seam-side down to cool completely.

CHAMBORD SUGAR SYRUP

2 tablespoons sugar **¼ cup water**	Combine the sugar and water in the small saucepan and bring to a boil over medium heat to dissolve the sugar. Remove the saucepan from the heat and let the sugar syrup cool.
1 tablespoon Chambord	Add the Chambord to the cooled sugar syrup.

WHIPPED CREAM FILLING AND FROSTING

2⅓ cups heavy whipping cream	Place the cream in the chilled bowl of an electric stand mixer or in a large bowl. Use the wire whip attachment or a hand-held mixer to whip the cream on medium speed until frothy.
½ cup confectioners' sugar, sifted	Sprinkle the sugar onto the whipped cream and continue to whip until the cream holds soft peaks.
3 tablespoons Chambord	Add the Chambord and blend together thoroughly
	Unroll the cooled cake and remove the towel. Brush the inside of the cake with the sugar syrup.
½ cup fresh raspberries	Use an offset spatula to spread ¼ of the whipped cream evenly over the inside of the cake, leaving a 1-inch border at the farthest long end of the cake. Sprinkle the raspberries over the top ⅓ of the whipped cream. Roll up the cake, using the parchment paper as a guide.

To make a tight cake roll, pull about one-third of the parchment paper over the top of the cake. Then place a ruler flat against the parchment that covers the top of the cake and push it against the roll while pulling the bottom part of the parchment paper toward you. This resistance motion of simultaneously pushing against the cake while pulling the parchment under the cake toward you compresses the roulade.

Carefully place the roulade on a rectangular serving plate with the seam down and discard the parchment paper. Trim off the rough ends of the cake and discard.

Fit the pastry bag with the star tip and fill partway with some of the remaining whipped cream.

Pipe parallel rows of cream (see page 44) from one end of the roulade to the other, starting from the bottom and moving toward the top of the cake. Turn the plate around and repeat piping the cream on the other side of the roulade.

6 to 8 fresh raspberries

Pipe a row of evenly spaced stars or rosettes across the top of the cake (see page 44). Gently press a fresh raspberry onto the top of each star or rosette.

Use a serrated knife to cut the roulade crosswise for serving pieces. Serve immediately or refrigerate up to 4 hours.

Grand Marnier Soufflé

GRAND MARNIER is the quintessential dessert soufflé. It's very impressive when served because it rises dramatically as it bakes. The soufflé must be served as soon as it comes out of the oven, before it begins to collapse. The soufflé mixture can be partially made several hours in advance and kept in the refrigerator. All you have to do before baking it is to whip the egg whites and fold them in. **Makes one 5-cup soufflé, 6 servings**

1 tablespoon unsalted butter, softened
1 tablespoon granulated sugar

Use a paper towel or your fingertips to butter the inside of the soufflé dish, then sprinkle the inside with sugar. Tilt the dish so the sugar sticks to the butter. Set aside while preparing the soufflé batter.

Adjust an oven rack to the lower third and preheat it to 400°F.

½ cup milk

Place the milk in the saucepan and bring to a boil over medium-high heat.

3 tablespoons all-purpose flour

Add the flour to the milk and whisk or stir together until there are no lumps remaining, about 1 minute.

⅓ cup granulated sugar

Add the sugar and whisk or stir together constantly until the mixture comes to a boil and thickens, about 2 minutes. Remove the pan from the heat.

4 extra-large egg yolks, at room temperature

One at a time, whisk or stir the egg yolks into the milk mixture, blending thoroughly.

Essential Gear
- 5-cup soufflé dish
- 2-quart heavy-bottomed saucepan
- Whisk or heat-resistant spatula
- Microplane grater or citrus zester
- Electric stand mixer with wire whip attachment, or large mixing bowl and hand-held mixer
- Rubber spatula

Streamlining
Prepare the soufflé batter through adding the Grand Marnier and finely grated orange zest. Transfer the batter to a mixing bowl, cover tightly with plastic wrap, and refrigerate up to 8 hours. When ready to bake, whip the egg whites, fold them into the soufflé batter, transfer to the soufflé dish, and bake.

1 tablespoon unsalted butter, softened	Add the butter and stir until it is melted and thoroughly blended into the mixture.
¼ cup Grand Marnier **2 teaspoons finely grated orange zest**	Stir in the Grand Marnier and orange zest.
5 extra-large egg whites, at room temperature **½ teaspoon cream of tartar** **2 tablespoons granulated sugar**	Place the egg whites in the grease-free bowl of an electric stand mixer or in a large grease-free bowl. Using the wire whip attachment or a hand-held mixer, whip the egg whites on medium-high speed until they are frothy. Add the cream of tartar and continue to whip. When soft peaks form, gradually sprinkle on the sugar and continue to whip until the egg whites hold glossy and firm, but not stiff, peaks
	Fold ¼ of the whipped egg whites into the yolk mixture. Gently fold the yolk mixture into the whipped egg whites, blending thoroughly. Be careful not to mix vigorously and deflate the air beaten into the egg whites, which is what makes the soufflé rise as it bakes.
	Transfer the soufflé mixture to the prepared soufflé dish. Use the rubber spatula to sweep around the rim of the dish and slightly mound the soufflé mixture.
	Bake for 30 minutes, until the soufflé is puffed over the top of the dish and looks set, and the center wiggles a little. You can also test for doneness with a cake tester inserted into the center of the soufflé. It should come out moist, but not runny.
1 tablespoon confectioners' sugar	Remove the soufflé dish from the oven, sprinkle the top with sugar, and serve immediately. Use a large spoon to scoop out serving portions so each has both the outer crust and the soft center of the soufflé.

Making a Change

To make raspberry soufflé, replace the Grand Marnier with Chambord or framboise, replace the grated orange zest with grated lemon zest and fold 1½ cups fresh raspberries into the batter before transferring it to the soufflé dish to bake.

Adding Style

Serve the soufflé with a scoop of vanilla or caramel ice cream.

Kahlúa Cupcakes with Kahlúa Ganache Icing

CUPCAKES are great to serve for dessert because they are easy to handle and are just the right portion size. They are very satisfying individual pieces of cake. Kahlúa is a coffee liqueur that flavors both the cake and the dark chocolate ganache icing in these cupcakes. The recipe makes two dozen, so there will be plenty to go around and maybe even enough for a second helping. **Makes 2 dozen cupcakes**

Adjust the oven racks to the upper and lower thirds and preheat the oven to 350°F.

Essential Gear

- Two 12-cavity, 3-inch muffin pans
- 24 pleated paper muffin cups
- Electric stand mixer with wire whip attachment and flat beater attachment, or large mixing bowl and hand-held mixer

Line each cavity of the muffin pans with a paper muffin cup.

CUPCAKES

9 ounces (18 tablespoons, 2¼ sticks) unsalted butter, cut into small pieces	Place the butter in the bowl of an electric stand mixer or in a large bowl. Use the flat beater attachment or a hand-held mixer to beat the butter on medium speed until it's fluffy, about 2 minutes.
1 cup granulated sugar **½ cup firmly packed light brown sugar**	Add the granulated sugar and brown sugar and cream together thoroughly. Stop occasionally and scrape down the sides and bottom of the bowl with a rubber spatula.
6 extra-large eggs, at room temperature	One at a time, add the eggs to the butter mixture, stopping to scrape down the bottom and sides of the bowl after each addition. At first the mixture may look curdled as the eggs are added, but as you scrape down the bowl, the mixture will smooth out.
¼ cup Kahlúa **1 teaspoon pure vanilla extract or vanilla paste**	Add the Kahlúa and the vanilla to the butter mixture and blend thoroughly.
2½ cups all-purpose flour **2 teaspoons baking powder** **½ teaspoon salt**	Over a large piece of waxed or parchment paper or a bowl, sift together the flour and baking powder. Add the salt and toss together to blend.
½ cup milk	In 3 stages, add the flour mixture alternately with the milk to the butter mixture, blending well after each addition. Stop and scrape down the sides and bottom of the bowl with the rubber spatula.
	Pour half of the batter into a 2-cup liquid measuring cup. Divide the batter evenly among the muffin cups, filling them almost to the top. Repeat with the remaining batter and muffin pan.
	Bake the cupcakes for 9 minutes. Switch the pans and bake another 9 to 11 minutes, until a cake tester or toothpick inserted in the center of the cupcakes comes out dry.
	Remove the pans from the oven and cool completely on racks. Lift the cupcakes from the pans.

GANACHE FROSTING

9 ounces bittersweet chocolate, finely chopped	Place the chopped chocolate in a large bowl.
⅔ cup heavy whipping cream	In a small saucepan, bring the cream to a boil over medium heat. Pour the cream over the chopped chocolate. Let it stand for 1 minute,

- Rubber spatula
- Sifter
- 2-cup liquid measuring cup
- Two cooling racks
- Small saucepan

Keeping

Store the unfrosted cupcakes in a single layer in an airtight plastic container at room temperature up to 4 days. To freeze up to 4 months, wrap the container tightly in several layers of plastic wrap and aluminum foil. Use a large piece of masking tape and an indelible marker to label and date the contents. If frozen, defrost overnight in the refrigerator and bring to room temperature before serving.

Store the frosted cupcakes in a single layer on a baking sheet in the refrigerator, loosely covered with waxed paper, then tightly wrapped in aluminum foil. Place a few toothpicks around the top outer edges of the cupcakes to hold the waxed paper away from them so it won't mar the frosting.

then stir together well using a rubber spatula, whisk, or immersion blender until very smooth.

¼ cup Kahlúa

Add the Kahlúa and mix in completely.

Cover the ganache mixture tightly with plastic wrap and cool to room temperature. Chill in the refrigerator until the mixture is firm but pliable, about 1 hour. A good test is to press a finger into the mixture. If it takes the indentation of your finger easily, it's at the right point. If the ganache is too soft, it will feel runny, and if it is too firm, it will be hard to press your finger in it. If the ganache is too firm, let it stand at room temperature until it is ready to use.

3 ounces (6 tablespoons, ¾ stick) unsalted butter, softened

Place the butter in the bowl of an electric stand mixer or in a large bowl. Using the flat beater attachment or a hand-held mixer, beat the butter on medium speed until it is fluffy. Add the ganache in 2 or 3 stages and beat until the mixture holds soft peaks, 1 to 2 minutes. As the ganache beats it becomes lighter in color. Don't beat the ganache too long or it may separate.

Use a small offset spatula, a rubber spatula, or a spoon to spread the top of each cupcake with the ganache frosting.

Serve the cupcakes at room temperature.

Port Chocolate Mousse and Macadamia Nut Tartlets

WHEN MY GOOD FRIEND Nicole Aloni came to town to teach a cooking class that I attended, I was intrigued by the dessert she made using port and dark chocolate. Since I always recommend drinking port with dark chocolate, I thought it was a great idea to combine them, and Nicole's dessert is my inspiration for this recipe. A macadamia nut tartlet shell holds a creamy dark chocolate and port mousse. A sprinkling of toasted and finely chopped macadamia nuts is the only decoration needed. If you really want to dress these up, serve them with a small glass of good-quality port. **Makes six 4½-inch tartlets**

Essential Gear
- Food processor
- Rolling pin
- Six 4½-inch round, fluted-edge tartlet pans with removable bottoms
- Pie weights
- Baking sheet
- Two cooling racks
- Double boiler
- Rubber spatula

PASTRY DOUGH

1½ cups all-purpose flour
¾ cup toasted, unsalted
  macadamia nuts
¼ cup granulated sugar
⅛ teaspoon salt

In the work bowl of a food processor fitted with the steel blade, combine the flour, macadamia nuts, sugar, and salt. Pulse until the macadamia nuts are finely ground, about 2 minutes.

6 ounces (12 tablespoons,
  1½ sticks) unsalted butter,
  chilled

Cut the butter into small pieces and add to the flour mixture. Pulse until the butter is cut into very tiny pieces, about 30 seconds. The texture will be sandy with very tiny lumps throughout.

1 extra-large egg, at room
  temperature
2 teaspoons pure vanilla
  extract

In a small bowl, use a fork to lightly beat the egg with the vanilla. With the food processor running, pour this mixture through the feed tube. Process the dough until the mixture wraps itself around the blade, about 1 minute.

Turn the pastry dough onto a large piece of plastic wrap. Shape into a flat disk and wrap tightly. Chill in the refrigerator until firm before using, at least 2 hours. Chilling the dough relaxes the gluten in the flour so it won't be too elastic and will roll out easily. It also firms up the butter in the dough so it will need less flour when rolled out. If the dough is too firm, it will splinter and break when rolled out. Let it stand at room temperature for 10 to 15 minutes before rolling to become more pliable.

Center a rack in the oven and preheat it to 375°F.

On a smooth, flat surface, roll out the pastry dough between sheets of lightly floured waxed or parchment paper to a large rectangle about 16 × 12 inches. Cut the dough in half horizontally, then into 3 equal sections vertically, making six 6 × 5-inch squares. Carefully peel the squares off the other piece of paper.

Gently place each square in a tart pan. Carefully lift up the sides of the pastry dough and ease the dough into the bottom and sides of each tart pan. Trim off the excess pastry dough at the top of the pan. Transfer the tart pans to a baking sheet and chill for at least 15 minutes to set.

Line each pastry shell with a large piece of aluminum foil that fits well against the bottom and sides. Fill each pastry shell with pie weights or a mixture of rice and beans. Bake for 10 minutes, then remove the foil and weights. If the bottom of the pastry shell puffs up, gently pierce it in a few places with a fork or the point of a knife to release the air. Bake another 12 to 14 minutes, until light golden

• Electric stand mixer with wire whip attachment, or large mixing bowl and hand-held mixer

Keeping

Store the tartlets in a single layer on a baking sheet. Cover the top of the tartlets with a large piece of waxed paper to keep the surface from becoming marred. Tightly wrap the pan with plastic wrap and keep in the refrigerator up to 3 days.

Streamlining

The pastry dough can be made in advance and kept in the refrigerator, tightly wrapped in a double layer of plastic wrap, up to 4 days before using. To freeze up to 4 months, wrap it in a double layer of plastic wrap and place it inside a freezer bag. Use a large piece of masking tape and an indelible marker to label and date the contents. If frozen, defrost in the refrigerator overnight before using. If the dough is too cold to roll out, let it stand at room temperature to become pliable.

The tartlet shells can be baked and held at room temperature up to 2 days before filling. After they are completely cool, place them on a jelly-roll pan between layers of waxed or parchment paper and tightly wrap the pan in aluminum foil.

and set. Remove the pan from the oven and transfer the tartlets to racks to cool completely.

PORT CHOCOLATE MOUSSE

12 ounces bittersweet chocolate

Melt the chocolate in the top of a double boiler over hot water. Stir often with a rubber spatula to help melt evenly. Remove the top pan of the double boiler and wipe the bottom and sides very dry.

Or melt the chocolate in a microwave-safe bowl on low power for 30-second bursts. Stir with a rubber spatula after each burst.

½ cup ruby port

Add the port and stir together until smooth and completely blended.

⅓ cup heavy whipping cream

Place the cream in the chilled bowl of an electric stand mixer or a medium bowl. Using the wire whip attachment or a hand-held mixer, whip the cream on medium speed until it holds soft peaks.

Fold the whipped cream into the chocolate mixture in 3 stages, blending well.

ASSEMBLY

Evenly divide the mousse mixture into the cooled tartlet shells. Gently shake the tartlet shells to spread out the filling evenly.

¼ cup finely chopped, toasted macadamia nuts

Sprinkle the top of each tartlet with the macadamia nuts.

Chill the tartlets for 20 minutes, to set the filling. Let the tartlets stand at room temperature for 20 to 30 minutes before serving.

Rum-Raisin Pound Cake

RUM AND RAISINS are a classic flavor combination that bring out the best in each other and make this pound cake outstanding. Although this cake is yummy on its own, it becomes even better when served with creamy caramel sauce. **Makes one 8½ × 4½ × 2½-inch loaf cake, 12 servings**

Essential Gear
- 8½ × 4½ × 2½-inch loaf pan
- Electric stand mixer with flat beater attachment, or large mixing bowl and hand-held mixer
- Rubber spatula
- Sifter
- Cooling rack

CAKE

⅔ cup raisins
¼ cup dark rum

Place the raisins in a small bowl and pour the rum over them. Cover the bowl tightly with plastic wrap and let the raisins soak for at least 30 minutes.

Drain the raisins, keeping the rum to use in the cake batter.

1 tablespoon unsalted butter, softened	Center a rack in the oven and preheat it to 350°F. Using a paper towel or your fingertips, generously butter the inside of the pan.
2 teaspoons all-purpose flour	Dust the inside of the pan with the flour. Shake and tilt the pan to distribute the flour evenly, then turn the pan over the sink and tap out the excess. Or spray the inside of the pan with non-stick baking spray.
8 ounces (16 tablespoons, 2 sticks) unsalted butter, softened	Place the butter in the bowl of an electric stand mixer or in a large bowl. Use the flat beater attachment or a hand-held mixer to beat the butter on medium speed until it's fluffy, about 2 minutes.
1½ cups superfine sugar	Add the sugar to the butter and cream together thoroughly. Stop occasionally and scrape down the bottom and sides of the bowl with a rubber spatula.
4 extra-large eggs, at room temperature	Add the eggs one at a time to the butter mixture, stopping to scrape down the bottom and sides of the bowl after each addition. At first the mixture may look curdled as the eggs are added, but as you scrape down the bowl, the mixture will smooth out.
	Add the reserved rum to the butter mixture and stir together until completely blended.
2¼ cups cake flour **1 teaspoon baking powder** **¼ teaspoon salt**	Over a large piece of waxed or parchment paper or a bowl, sift together the flour and baking powder. Add the salt and toss to blend. Take 2 tablespoons of this mixture and toss with the rum-soaked raisins. This will prevent the raisins from sinking to the bottom of the batter when they are mixed in. Add the dry ingredients to the butter mixture in 3 stages, blending well after each. Stop after each addition and scrape down the sides and bottom of the bowl to ensure even mixing. Blend in the rum-soaked raisins.
	Transfer the batter to the prepared loaf pan. The batter is very thick, so use a rubber spatula to spread it evenly into the pan.
	Bake for 1 hour and 20 minutes, until the cake is light golden on top and a cake tester inserted into the center comes out with only a few crumbs clinging to it.
	Remove the pan from the oven and cool completely on a rack.
	Invert the pan to remove the cake, then turn the cake top-side up.

- Small saucepan
- 2-quart heavy-bottomed saucepan
- 1-inch natural-bristle pastry brush
- Long-handled spoon or heat-resistant spatula

Keeping

Store the cake tightly wrapped in aluminum foil at room temperature up to 4 days. To freeze up to 3 months, wrap the cake tightly in several layers of plastic wrap and aluminum foil. Use a large piece of masking tape and an indelible marker to label and date the contents. If frozen, defrost overnight in the refrigerator and bring to room temperature before serving.

Store the caramel sauce in a tightly covered plastic container in the refrigerator up to 1 week. Rewarm the sauce in a microwave-safe bowl on low power for 30-second bursts or in the top of a double boiler over hot water, stirring often.

CREAMY CARAMEL SAUCE

¾ cup heavy whipping cream

Place the cream in a small saucepan and heat over medium heat until bubbles form at the edges.

1 cup granulated sugar
¼ cup water
1 tablespoon light corn syrup

While the cream is heating, combine the sugar, water, and corn syrup in the other saucepan. Cook over high heat without stirring until the mixture begins to boil. Place a wet pastry brush at the point where the sugar syrup meets the sides of the pan and sweep it around completely. Do this two times. This prevents the sugar from crystallizing. Cook the mixture without stirring until it turns amber colored, about 10 minutes.

Remove the saucepan from the heat and stir in the hot cream, using a long-handled spoon or heat-resistant spatula. Be very careful because it will bubble and splatter as the cream is added. Return the saucepan to the heat and stir to dissolve any lumps.

2 ounces (4 tablespoons, ½ stick) unsalted butter, softened

Add the butter to the caramel mixture and stir until it is melted.

1½ teaspoons pure vanilla extract

Remove the saucepan from the heat and stir in the vanilla. Stir the sauce to cool slightly.

Slice the cake into serving pieces, about ¾ inch thick. Drizzle the top of each piece with creamy caramel sauce.

Whiskey Bread Pudding with Whiskey Sauce

BREAD PUDDING is a classic comfort food that is a great way to use up leftover bread. But you don't have to wait until you have extra bread on hand to make this delicious dessert. I prefer to use a baguette and dry it in the oven. It is fabulous served warm, but you can also serve it at room temperature. The whiskey sauce adds an extra yummy layer to this dessert. Use good-quality whiskey or bourbon for the best flavor. **Makes 6 to 8 servings**

Essential Gear
- Baking sheet
- 2-quart baking pan
- 3-quart roasting pan or baking dish
- Rubber spatula
- Cooling rack
- Double boiler
- Microplane grater

Keeping
Store the bread pudding tightly covered with plastic

WHISKEY BREAD PUDDING

1 cup dried currants
¼ cup whiskey or bourbon

Place the currants in a bowl and add the whiskey or bourbon. Cover the bowl tightly with plastic wrap and let them soak at least 30 minutes.

Center a rack in the oven and preheat it to 400°F.

**¾ (about 8 ounces) fresh or day-old baguette
or
½ loaf (8 ounces) fresh or day-old good-quality white bread**

Cut the crusts off the bread and cut the bread into 1-inch cubes. If using fresh bread, place the cubes in a shallow layer on a baking sheet and dry in the oven for 15 minutes.

**1 tablespoon unsalted butter, softened
1 tablespoon granulated sugar**

Use a paper towel or your fingertips to butter the inside of the 2-quart baking pan. Sprinkle the inside of the baking pan evenly with the sugar.

Transfer the dry bread cubes to the prepared baking pan

**2 cups milk
1 cup heavy whipping cream
¾ cup granulated sugar
4 extra-large eggs, at room temperature
2 teaspoons pure vanilla extract
¼ teaspoon salt
¼ teaspoon freshly grated nutmeg**

In a large bowl, combine the milk, cream, sugar, eggs, vanilla, salt, and nutmeg. Whisk together to blend thoroughly.

Drain the currants and add the whiskey to the liquid mixture, blending well.

Pour this mixture over the bread in the baking pan. Sprinkle the currants evenly over the top of the bread pudding. Cover the pan tightly with plastic wrap and place in the refrigerator for 30 minutes. This gives the bread time to soak up the liquid.

Adjust the oven heat to 350°F.

1 quart boiling water

Remove the plastic wrap from the baking pan. Place the bread pudding in a roasting pan or larger baking pan. Place the baking pan on the oven rack and pour boiling water halfway up the sides of the pan.

Bake for 35 to 45 minutes, until the pudding is puffed and a cake tester or toothpick inserted in the center comes out clean.

Remove the baking pan from the oven. Remove the bread pudding from the water bath and cool on a rack.

wrap in the refrigerator up to 3 days. Warm it in a 350°F oven for 15 to 20 minutes before serving.

Streamlining
The whiskey sauce can be made up to 1 week in advance and kept in a tightly covered container in the refrigerator. Warm it in the top of a double boiler or in a microwave oven on medium power before serving.

Making a Change
Sprinkle 1 cup finely chopped walnuts or pecans over the top of the bread pudding before baking it in the oven.

1 extra-large egg, at room temperature **¾ cup granulated sugar**	Place the egg and sugar in the top of a double boiler over simmering water and whisk together constantly until the mixture begins to thicken, about 5 minutes.
3 ounces (6 tablespoons, ¾ stick) unsalted butter, melted	Add the butter and continue to stir to blend thoroughly.
¼ cup whiskey or bourbon **¼ teaspoon freshly ground nutmeg**	Remove the top pan of the double boiler and wipe the bottom and sides dry. Add the whiskey and nutmeg to the sauce and stir in thoroughly.

Serve warm scoops of the bread pudding topped with a large spoonful of whiskey sauce, or pass the sauce separately.

Whiskey, Pecan, and Brown Sugar Meringue Cake

I WAS INSPIRED to create this dessert by the classic dacquoise (page 333), a hazelnut meringue cake. The combination of whiskey, pecans, and brown sugar produce a very pleasing flavor experience. Four thin, crisp layers of toasted pecan and brown sugar meringue are filled and decorated with rich whiskey-flavored, French-style buttercream. The top of the cake is decorated with confectioners' sugar and buttercream stars topped with toasted pecan halves, and finely chopped toasted pecans are pressed into the sides. Be sure to use very good-quality Irish or Scotch whiskey for the best flavor. You can also use smooth Kentucky bourbon, which is American whiskey. **Makes one 9-inch round cake, 12 to 14 servings**

Essential Gear

- Jelly-roll pan
- Food processor
- Four baking sheets
- Four aluminum foil sheets
- 9-inch round cardboard cake circle or cake pan
- Electric stand mixer with wire whip attachment, or hand-held mixer and large mixing bowl
- Sifter
- 12- or 14-inch pastry bag with ½-inch plain round pastry tip
- 8- or 10-inch flexible-blade spatula
- 10-inch pastry bag with large open star tip
- 2-quart heavy-bottomed saucepan
- 1-inch natural-bristle pastry brush

PECAN BROWN SUGAR MERINGUE CIRCLES

2⅓ cups raw pecans	Center a rack in the oven and preheat it to 350°F. Place the pecans in a single layer on a jelly-roll pan and toast for 7 to 8 minutes, until the nuts turn golden brown.
	Remove the pan from the oven and transfer to a rack to cool.
	Reduce the oven temperature to 200°F. Adjust the racks to the upper and lower thirds of the oven.

3 tablespoons firmly packed light brown sugar	Place 1⅓ cups of the pecans in the work bowl of a food processor fitted with the steel blade. Add the sugar and pulse until the nuts are very finely ground, about 1 minute.
2 tablespoons cornstarch	Place the finely ground pecans in a small bowl. Add the cornstarch and stir together to blend thoroughly. Finely chop the remaining 1 cup of toasted pecans and reserve for the final decoration.
	Line the baking sheets with aluminum foil. Use the cake circle or cake pan as a guide and trace a 9-inch circle onto the dull side of each piece of foil with a pencil, then turn the foil over onto the baking sheets.
8 extra-large egg whites, at room temperature **1 teaspoon cream of tartar**	Place the egg whites in the grease-free bowl of an electric stand mixer or a large grease-free bowl. Use the wire whip attachment or a hand-held mixer to whip the egg whites on medium speed until frothy. Add the cream of tartar and whip on medium-high speed until the egg whites hold soft peaks.
1 cup firmly packed light brown sugar	Push the sugar through a sifter. Reserve 1 tablespoon of the brown sugar. With the mixer running, gradually sprinkle the remaining sugar on the egg whites and continue to whip until the egg whites hold glossy and firm, but not stiff, peaks. Fold the pecan and cornstarch mixture into the egg whites in 3 stages, blending thoroughly.
	Fit a 12- or 14-inch pastry bag with the plain tip. Fill the pastry bag partway with the pecan meringue mixture. Hold the pastry bag straight and about 1 inch above the center of one of the circles. Pipe out concentric circles of the meringue mixture into the traced circles, filling in each circle completely. Instead of using a pastry bag, you can divide the meringue mixture evenly into four. Place a mound of the meringue in the center of each traced circle. Use an offset spatula to evenly spread the mixture to the edges of each circle, keeping the meringue at least ¼ inch thick. Sprinkle the top of each meringue disk evenly with the reserved tablespoon of brown sugar. On 2 of the baking sheets, place small bowls or cups in each corner and balance a second baking sheet on top of them.

- Sugar or candy thermometer
- Small sharp knife

Keeping

Store the meringue cake tented with aluminum foil in the refrigerator up to 3 days.

Streamlining

The meringue circles can be made up to 2 weeks in advance and stored at room temperature wrapped in aluminum foil. They are subject to humidity and may soften if it is too humid or damp. If this happens, they can be redried. Place them on a baking sheet lined with aluminum foil in the oven at 200°F for 1 hour.

Recovering from a Mishap

If one of the meringue circles cracks or breaks, place it on top of a layer of buttercream and patch it back together with buttercream on top. Use the cracked or broken layer as the center meringue layer of the cake.

Making a Change

Replace the pecans with walnuts.

Place the stacked baking sheets in the oven and dry for 2 hours. Turn off the oven and leave the meringues in the oven with the door closed until it is completely cool.

Very carefully peel the aluminum foil off the back of each meringue circle.

WHISKEY BUTTERCREAM

2 extra-large eggs, at room temperature
2 extra-large egg yolks, at room temperature
¼ cup granulated sugar

Place the eggs, egg yolks, and sugar in the bowl of an electric stand mixer or in a large bowl. Use the wire whip attachment or a handheld mixer and whip the eggs on medium speed until they are very pale colored and hold a slowly dissolving ribbon as the beater is lifted, about 5 minutes.

1¼ cups granulated sugar
½ cup water
¼ teaspoon cream of tartar

While the eggs are whipping, place the sugar, water, and cream of tartar in the saucepan. Bring the mixture to a boil, without stirring. Place a wet pastry brush at the point where the sugar syrup meets the sides of the pan and sweep it around completely. Do this two times. This prevents the sugar from crystallizing by brushing any stray crystals back into the mixture. Cook over high heat until the mixture registers 242°F on a sugar thermometer (soft-ball stage).

Immediately remove the thermometer and place it in a glass of warm water, then remove the pan from the heat so it won't continue to cook.

Adjust the mixer speed to low and pour the sugar syrup into the whipped eggs in a slow, steady stream. Aim the sugar syrup between the beater and the side of the bowl, so it doesn't get caught up in the beater or thrown against the sides of the bowl. Turn the mixer speed up to medium-high and whip until the bowl is cool to the touch, about 8 minutes. Once the cooked sugar syrup is added to the whipped eggs, the mixture must whip until the bowl is completely cool to the touch before the butter is added, or the butter will melt. If this happens, the texture and consistency of the buttercream will be too soft and more butter needs to be added to bring it to the right point.

---

1 pound (2 cups, 4 sticks) unsalted butter, softened

Adjust the mixer speed to medium and add the butter, 2 tablespoons at a time. Continue to beat until the buttercream is thoroughly blended and fluffy.

---

3 to 4 tablespoons whiskey

Add 3 tablespoons of the whiskey and blend thoroughly. Taste the buttercream to see if it needs another tablespoon of whiskey. The flavor should be subtle, not powerful, and it is better to have a light hand with the whiskey. As the cake sits, the flavor of the buttercream develops and deepens.

ASSEMBLY

Place 1 pecan meringue disk on a 9-inch cardboard cake circle or serving plate. Use a small sharp knife to carefully trim the edges to make them even, if necessary. Place strips of waxed paper around the bottom edges of the cake to protect the plate while assembling the cake.

Use a flexible-blade spatula to spread 1/4 of the buttercream evenly over the meringue layer.

Carefully trim the edges of a second meringue layer and position it evenly over the buttercream, lining up the edges with the bottom meringue disk. Spread another 1/4 of the buttercream evenly over the second meringue layer.

Repeat with the third meringue layer.

Carefully trim the edges of the fourth meringue layer and position it over the buttercream with the bottom of the layer facing up. This provides a flat surface for the top of the cake.

Reserve 1/3 cup of the buttercream and use the rest to cover the sides of the cake evenly.

Confectioners' sugar

Heavily dust the top of the cake with sugar. Press the chopped pecans into the sides of the cake just up to, but not over, the top edges. The waxed paper will catch the pecans that don't stick to the sides of the cake.

Fit the 10-inch pastry bag with the star tip. Fill the bag with the reserved buttercream.

Visually divide the top of the cake into 12 pieces or use a small sharp knife to mark the outer top edge of the cake into serving pieces. Pipe a rosette in the center of each marked piece at the outside top edge of the cake (see page 44). Center a pecan half at an angle on each rosette.

12 toasted pecan halves

Let the cake chill for at least 2 hours before serving so it has time to set and will be easier to cut. To cut the cake into serving pieces, dip a knife in hot water and dry after each slice. Serve the cake at room temperature.

Appendices

COMPARATIVE VOLUME OF BAKING PAN SIZES

If there is a recipe you want to bake but don't have the exact size pan called for, check here to see if there is another pan that holds the same volume that you can use.

PAN SIZE	VOLUME
Round Cake Pans	
6 × 2-inch	3¾ cups
7 × 2-inch	5¼ cups
8 × 1½ -inch	4 cups
8 × 2-inch	7 cups
9 × 1½-inch	6 cups
9 × 2-inch	8⅔ cups
10 × 2-inch	10¾ cups
12 × 2-inch	15½ cups
9 × 3-inch Bundt	9 cups
10 × 3⅓-inch Bundt	12 cups
9 × 4-inch kugelhopf/tube	12 cups
9 × 3-inch tube	10 cups
10 × 4-inch tube	16 cups
9 × 2¾-inch springform	10 cups
10 × 2¾-inch springform	12 cups
9 × 3-inch cheesecake with removable bottom	14 cups
3 × 1¼-inch muffin cup	½ cup
Pie Pans	
8 × 1½-inch	3 cups
9 × 1¼-inch	3½ cups
9 × 1½-inch	4 cups
9 × 2-inch	6 cups
9½ × 2-inch	7 cups
Square Pans	
8 × 8 × 1½-inch	6 cups
8 × 8 × 2-inch	8 cups
9 × 9 × 1½-inch	10 cups
9 × 9 × 2-inch	10 cups
10 × 10 × 2-inch	12 cups

Rectangular and Loaf Pans

10½ × 15½ × 1-inch jelly-roll pan	10 cups
12½ × 17½ × 1-inch jelly-roll pan	12 cups
11 × 7 × 2-inch rectangle	8 cups
13 × 9 × 2-inch rectangle	15 cups
8 × 4 × 2½-inch loaf	4 cups
8½ × 4½ × 2½-inch loaf	6 cups
9 × 5 × 3-inch loaf	8 cups

WEIGHT AND MEASUREMENT EQUIVALENTS

U.S. MEASURING SYSTEM	METRIC SYSTEM
Capacity	**Approximate Capacity**
¼ teaspoon	1.25 milliliters
1 teaspoon	5 milliliters
1 tablespoon	15 milliliters
¼ cup	60 milliliters
1 cup (8 fluid ounces)	240 milliliters
2 cups (1 pint; 16 fluid ounces)	470 milliliters
4 cups (1 quart; 32 fluid ounces)	0.95 liter
4 quarts (1 gallon; 64 fluid ounces)	3.8 liters
Weight	**Approximate Weight**
1 dry ounce	15 grams
2 ounces	30 grams
4 ounces (¼ pound)	110 grams
8 ounces (½ pound)	230 grams
16 ounces (1 pound)	454 grams

LIQUID MEASUREMENT

Measurement	Fluid Ounces	Ounces by Weight	Grams
2 tablespoons	1 fluid ounce	½ ounce	14 grams
¼ cup	2 fluid ounces	1¾ ounces	50 grams
⅓ cup	2⅔ fluid ounces	2 ounces	70 grams
½ cup	4 fluid ounces	4 ounces	113 grams
⅔ cup	5⅓ fluid ounces	5 ounces	142 grams
¾ cup	6 fluid ounces	5¼ ounces	177 grams
1 cup	8 fluid ounces	8 ounces	227 grams

Measurement	Equivalent
¼ cup (2 fluid ounces)	5 tablespoons
⅓ cup (2⅔ fluid ounces)	7 tablespoons
½ cup (4 fluid ounces)	11 tablespoons
⅔ cup (5⅓ fluid ounces)	14 tablespoons
¾ cup (6 fluid ounces)	16 tablespoons
1 cup (8 fluid ounces)	20 tablespoons

DRY MEASUREMENT

Measurement	Equivalent
3 teaspoons	1 tablespoon
2 tablespoons	⅛ cup
4 tablespoons	¼ cup
5⅓ tablespoons	⅓ cup
8 tablespoons	½ cup
10⅔ tablespoons	⅔ cup
12 tablespoons	¾ cup
16 tablespoons	1 cup

GRANULATED SUGAR

Measurement	Ounces	Grams
1 teaspoon	⅙ ounce	5 grams
1 tablespoon	½ ounce	15 grams
¼ cup	1¾ ounces	50 grams
⅓ cup	2¼ ounces	65 grams
½ cup	3½ ounces	100 grams
⅔ cup	4½ ounces	130 grams
¾ cup	5 ounces	145 grams
1 cup	7 ounces	200 grams

BROWN SUGAR, PACKED

Measurement	Ounces	Grams
1 tablespoon	¼ ounce	7 grams
¼ cup	1¼ ounces	35 grams
⅓ cup	1¾ ounces	50 grams
½ cup	2¾ ounces	75 grams
⅔ cup	3 ounces	85 grams
¾ cup	3½ ounces	100 grams
1 cup	5 ounces	145 grams

FLOUR (UNSIFTED)

Measurement	Ounces	Grams
1 tablespoon	¼ ounce	7 grams
¼ cup	1¼ ounces	35 grams
⅓ cup	1½ ounces	45 grams
½ cup	2½ ounces	70 grams
⅔ cup	3¼ ounces	90 grams
¾ cup	3½ ounces	100 grams
1 cup	5 ounces	145 grams

NUTS

1 cup, shelled	Ounces	Grams
Almonds, sliced	3½ ounces	100 grams
Almonds, unblanched whole	5¼ ounces	150 grams
Cashews	4½ ounces	130 grams
Hazelnuts	4½ ounces	130 grams
Macadamia nuts	4 ounces	110 grams
Peanuts	4 ounces	110 grams
Pecans	4 ounces	110 grams
Pistachio nuts	5 ounces	145 grams
Walnuts	3½ ounces	100 grams

BUTTER

Measurement	Ounces	Grams
1 tablespoon	½ ounce	15 grams
2 tablespoons	1 ounce	30 grams
4 tablespoons (½ stick, ¼ cup)	2 ounces	60 grams
8 tablespoons (1 stick, ½ cup)	4 ounces (¼ pound)	115 grams
1 cup (2 sticks)	8 ounces (½ pound)	230 grams
2 cups (4 sticks)	1 pound	454 grams

CONVERSIONS TO AND FROM METRIC

WHEN THIS FACTOR IS KNOWN	MULTIPLY BY	TO FIND
Weight		
Ounces	28.35	Grams
Pounds	0.454	Kilograms
Grams	0.035	Ounces
Kilograms	2.2	Pounds
Measurement		
Inches	2.5	Centimeters
Millimeters	0.04	Inches
Centimeters	0.4	Inches
Volume		
Teaspoons	4.93	Milliliters
Tablespoons	14.79	Milliliters
Fluid ounces	29.57	Milliliters
Cups	0.237	Liters
Pints	0.47	Liters
Quarts	0.95	Liters
Gallons	3.785	Liters
Milliliters	0.034	Fluid ounces
Liters	2.1	Pints
Liters	1.06	Quarts
Liters	0.26	Gallons

	DIVIDE BY	
Milliliters	4.93	Teaspoons
Milliliters	14.79	Tablespoons
Milliliters	236.59	Cups
Milliliters	473.18	Pints
Milliliters	946.36	Quarts
Liters	0.236	Cups
Liters	0.473	Pints
Liters	0.946	Quarts
Liters	3.785	Gallons

Sources for Ingredients and Equipment

The following are good places for locating great ingredients and equipment you may not be able to find close to home. Browse their Web sites, catalogs, or shops. Be sure to e-mail or call before ordering to make sure the items you want to order are in stock. Also, watch for specials. Some companies will put you on their e-mail list to receive notification of specials.

A Cook's Wares
211 37th Street
Beaver Falls, PA 15010
Tel: 800-915-9788; 724-846-9490
Fax: 724-846-9490
e-mail: sales@cookswares.com
Web site: www.cookswares.com

This source carries Callebaut chocolate, Bensdrop and Droste cocoa powders, Nielsen-Massey vanilla products; a variety of bakeware, utensils, and equipment, including mixers and food processors, pots and pans, and knives. A catalog is available.

Beryl's Cake Decorating & Pastry Supplies
P.O. Box 1584
North Springfield, VA 22151
Tel: 705-256-6951; 800-488-2749
Fax: 705-750-3779
e-mail: beryl@beryls.com
Web site: www.beryls.com

Beryl's has a very large variety of equipment and utensils including baking pans, thermometers, pastry bags and tips, parchment paper, cookie cutters, scales, graters, and whisks. This source also carries extracts, dried fruit, and chocolate, including Callebaut, Ghirardelli, Lindt, Schokinag, and Valrhona. A catalog is available.

Bridge Kitchenware
711 Third Avenue
New York, NY 10017
Phone: 212-688-4220
Fax: 212-758-5387
e-mail: bridge@ix.netcom.com
Web site: www.bridgekitchenware.com

Bridge carries an extensive selection of equipment and tools, including bowls, cutters, baking pans, knives, measuring cups and spoons, mixers, pastry bags and tips, parchment paper, pastry brushes, pots and pans, rolling pins, spatulas, scales, and thermometers. A catalog is available.

CHEFS Catalog
5070 Centennial Boulevard
Colorado Springs, CO 80919-2402
Tel: 800-884-2433
Fax: 800-967-2433
e-mail: customerservice@ecare.chefscatalog.com
Web site: www.chefscatalog.com

CHEFS catalog carries a large variety of equipment and tools, including baking pans, bowls, measuring cups and spoons, mixers, pots and pans, food processors, rolling pins, non-stick baking mats, sifters, and scales. A catalog is available.

cheftools.com
309 S. Cloverdale Street, C35
Seattle, WA 98108
Phone: 866-716-2433
Fax: 206-716-4414
e-mail: customerservice@ChefTools.com
Web site: www.cheftools.com

Cheftools carries a good selection of bakeware, knives, measuring tools, thermometers, timers, and pots and pans. A catalog is available.

Chocosphere
Chocosphere LLC
P.O. Box 2237
Tualatin, OR 97062
Tel: 877-992-4626; 503-692-3323
Fax: 877-912-4626
e-mail: customer-service@chocosphere.com
Web site: www.chocosphere.com

This supplier carries a large variety of chocolate and cocoa powder from twenty-five companies around the world, including Callebaut, El Rey, Guittard, Scharffen Berger, Schokinag, and Valrhona. They also carry vanilla beans and extract. This is an online source only.

Cooking.com
2850 Ocean Park Blvd., Suite 310
Santa Monica, CA 90405
Tel: (orders) 800-663-8810
Tel: (customer service) 877-999-2433
Tel: (outside of U.S. and Canada) 310-450-3270
e-mail: fill out the form on the Web site
Web site: www.cooking.com

This Web site sells a variety of bakeware, bowls, knives, measuring utensils, scales, thermometers, timers, spatulas, whisks, food processors, mixers, and pots and pans. This is an online source only.

Gourmetsleuth
P.O. Box 508
Los Gatos, CA 95031
Tel: 408-354-8281
Fax: 408-395-8279
e-mail: help_me@gourmetsleuth.com
Web site: www.gourmetsleuth.com

This Web site sells a variety of ingredients, including instant espresso powder and chocolate.

Hayward Enterprises, Inc.
(Perfect Puree of Napa Valley)
2700 Napa Valley Corporate Drive, Suite L
Napa, CA 94558
Tel: 800-556-3707; 707-261-5100
Fax: 707-261-5111

e-mail: info@perfectpuree.com
Web site: www.perfectpuree.com

This source carries a wide variety of fruit concentrates, such as kiwi, guava, passion fruit, pomegranate, peach, and pear.

La Cuisine
323 Cameron Street
Alexandria, VA 22314-3219
Tel: 800-521-1176; 703-836-4435
Fax: 703-836-8925
e-mail: info@lacuisineus.com
Web site: www.lacuisineus.com

La Cuisine carries a variety of chocolate, including Valrhona; Cocoa Barry, and Valrhona cocoa powder; candied and dried fruit; baking pans, including silicone; bowls, cutters, rolling pins, knives, and cookware.

Melissa's/World Variety Produce, Inc.
P.O. Box 21127
Los Angeles, CA 90021
Tel: 800-588-0151
e-mail: hotline@melissas.com
Web site: www.melissas.com

Melissa's carries a huge variety of the freshest fruit and vegetables and is the largest distributor of specialty produce in the U.S. You can buy directly from the company through its Web site or find many of their products in your local supermarket.

New York Cake Supplies
56 West 22nd Street
New York, NY 10010
Tel: 800-942-2539; 212-675-2253
Fax: 212-675-7099
Web site: www.nycake.com

This source has all manner of cake, tart, and muffin pans, madeleine molds, measuring cups and spoons, graters, cooling racks, ramekins, thermometers, whisks, rolling pins, parchment paper, scales, timers, mixing bowls, cake decorating turntables, mixers, spatulas, scoops, pastry brushes, pastry bags and tips, cutters, cake flour, marzipan, extracts, colors, and chocolate, including Valrhona and Callebaut. A catalog is available. Although New York Cake has a Web site, all orders must be placed by phone or fax.

Pastry Chef Central, Inc.
1355 West Palmetto Park Road, Suite 302
Boca Raton, FL 33486-3303
Tel: 888-750-2433; 561-999-9483
Fax: 561-999-1282
e-mail: customer_service@pastrychef.com
Web site: www.pastrychef.com

This online-only source carries a large variety of equipment, including baking pans, scales, copper sugar pans, thermometers, timers, knives, measuring cups and spoons, pastry bags and tips, scoops, rolling pins, whisks, spatulas, graters, cookie cutters, cake decorating turntables, and much more. They also carry a variety of chocolate and cocoa powder, marzipan, coconut, vanilla beans, and vanilla extract.

Penzeys Spices
19300 West Janacek Court
P.O. Box 924
Brookfield, WI 53008-0924
Tel: 800-741-7787; 262-785-7637
Fax: 262-785-7678
Web site: www.penzeys.com

Penzeys is an excellent source for fresh spices, both whole and ground, vanilla beans and extracts, almond, lemon, and orange extracts, and a variety of types of salt. Their cassia cinnamon, very bold in flavor, is my personal favorite. You can order different amounts of spices, ranging from ¼ cup to 1 pound. A catalog is available.

Previn, Inc.
2044 Rittenhouse Square
Philadelphia, PA 19103
Tel: 215-985-1996
Fax: 215-985-0323
e-mail: customerservice@previninc.com
Web site: www.previninc.com

Previn sells a vast variety of professional-quality pots and pans, including copper sugar pots, scales, whisks, spatulas, measuring cups and spoons, mixing bowls, ice cream scoops, zesters and graters, thermometers, knives, ramekins, tart and tartlet pans, cake pans, madeleine plaques, baking sheets, cutters, Silpat pan liners, pastry brushes, pastry bags and tips, pastry crimpers, rolling pins, cake decorating turntables, and more. A catalog is available.

J. B. Prince Company
36 East 31st Street
New York, NY 10016-6821
Tel: 800-473-0577; 212-683-3553
Fax: 212-683-4488
e-mail: Fill out the form on the Web site
Web site: www.jbprince.com

J.B. Prince Company supplies professional-quality equipment and tools, including baking pans, pastry bags and tips, cutters, molds, tart, muffin, and cake pans, cooling racks, rolling pins, thermometers, timers, spatulas, non-stick baking pan liners, pots and pans, scales, mixing bowls, knives, and measuring cups and spoons. A catalog is available.

The King Arthur Flour Baker's Catalog
135 Route 5 South
P.O. Box 1010
Norwich, VT 05055-0876
Tel: 800-827-6836; 802-649-3881
Fax: 800-353-3002
e-mail: bakers@kingarthurflour.com

Web site: www.kingarthurflour.com

This source sells a wide variety of equipment and utensils, including cutters, cake, tart, and muffin pans, baking sheets, cooling racks, silicone baking forms, spatulas, pastry brushes, pastry bags and tips, rolling pins, non-stick baking pan liners, knives, pots and pans, scales, thermometers, measuring cups and spoons, graters, and ingredients, including their own brand of flour, vanilla and other extracts, flower waters, salt, crystallized ginger, candied fruit, and chocolate and cocoa powder.

Scharffen Berger Chocolate Maker
914 Heinz Avenue
Berkeley, CA 94710
Tel: 510-981-4050; 800-930-4528
Fax: 510-981-4051
e-mail: beantobar@scharffenberger.com
Web site: www.scharffenberger.com

Scharffen Berger makes excellent-quality, European-style, dark chocolate in 62 percent, 70 percent, and 82 percent cocoa components, and dark milk chocolate of 41 percent cocoa components. They also make natural cocoa powder and cocoa nibs.

Sur La Table
Corporate Headquarters
Seattle Design Center
5701 Sixth Avenue South, Suite 486
Seattle, WA 98108
Tel: 800-243-0852; 866-328-5412
Fax: 206-682-1026 (orders only)
e-mail: customerservice@surlatable.com
Web site: www.surlatable.com

Sur La Table is an excellent source for all types of baking pans, tart, tartlet, and muffin pans, including silicone, non-stick silicone pan liners, cooling racks, timers, thermometers, food processors, mixers, pastry brushes, pastry bags and tips, pots and pans, serving utensils, scales, spatulas, measuring cups and spoons, graters, knives, cutters, and many other utensils, as well as Nielsen-Massey vanilla extract, Scharffen Berger and E. Guittard chocolate and cocoa powder, marzipan, and food coloring. They have several shops throughout the United States, a catalog, and a Web site.

Surfas
8824 National Boulevard
Culver City, CA 90232
Tel: 310-559-4770; 866-799-4770
e-mail: customerservice@surfasonline.com
Web site: www.surfasonline.com

Surfas, Chef's Paradise, is just that. They sell a vast selection of professional-quality equipment and tools including all manner of baking pans, spatulas, silicone baking items, parchment paper, non-stick pan liners, thermometers, timers, pots and pans, cooling racks, pastry bags and tips, rolling pins, pie weights, knives, scoops, graters, measuring cups and spoons, scales, mixing bowls, whisks, and more. Surfas also stocks vanilla beans, extracts, flavorings, several brands of cocoa powder, a variety of flours, almond paste, and chocolate, including Callebaut, Cocoa Barry, Scharffen Berger, and Valrhona.

Sweet Celebrations
P.O. Box 39426
Edina, MN 55439-0426
Tel: 800-328-6722; 952-943-1508
e-mail: sweetcel@maidofscandinavia.com
Web site: www.maidofscandinavia.com

This source carries a variety of baking pans, rolling pins, pie weights, measuring cups and spoons, molds, scoops, cooling racks, graters, whisks, pastry brushes, spatulas, pastry bags and tips, and a huge variety of cookie cutters. They also carry several ingredients, including Nielsen-Massey vanilla extract, Scharffen Berger, Valrhona, Callebaut, Lindt, Peter's, and Merckens chocolate, almond paste, and crystal sugar.

The Spice House
1512 N. Wells Street
Chicago, IL 60610
Tel: 312-274-0378
Fax: 312-274-0143
e-mail: Fill out the form on the Web site.
Web site: www.thespicehouse.com

This is an excellent source for fresh spices, both whole and ground, and a variety of spice mills and graters. A catalog is available

The Vanilla.COMpany
P.O. Box 3206
Santa Cruz, CA 95063
Tel: 800-757-7511, 831-476-9112
e-mail: info@vanilla.com
Web site: www.vanilla.com

This Web site specializes in all things vanilla. They carry all types of vanilla beans, extract, and powder.

Williams-Sonoma
3250 Van Ness Avenue
San Francisco, CA 94109
Tel: 877-812-6235; 415-421-7900
Tel: 405-717-6131 (outside of the U.S.)
Fax: 702-363-2541
e-mail: Fill out the form on the Web site.
Web site: www.williamssonoma.com

Williams-Sonoma carries a selection of equipment such as blenders, food processors and mixers, baking pans, rolling pins, pots and pans, non-stick baking pan liners, and parchment paper, and a small selection of chocolate, including Scharffen Berger, Valrhona, and Pernigotti cocoa powder. They have a wide variety of utensils and tools, including knives, cookie cutters, timers, thermometers, whisks, measuring cups and spoons, mixing bowls, and scales. Williams-Sonoma has stores throughout the United States, as well as a catalog and Web site.

Wilton Enterprises
2240 W. 75th St.
Woodridge, IL 60517
Phone: 630-963-1818; 800-794-5866
Fax: 630-963-7196; 888-824-9520
e-mail: info@wilton.com
Web site: www.wilton.com

Wilton makes a variety of cake and baking pans, cookie cutters, parchment paper circles and triangles, spatulas, and a large variety of pastry bags and tips. Their products can be found in many stores that carry cake decorating supplies, as well as through their Web site and catalog.

Photography Credits

Food Styling and Prop Styling by Carole Bloom

Prop Styling and Photography by Glenn Cormier

COCONUT MACAROONS
Seafoam green scalloped-edge plate	Sur La Table
White linen cloth w/rust color embroidery trim and flower	Author's collection

COCOA NIB AND WALNUT BISCOTTI
Light tan, round, deep Chinese basket	Author's collection
Orange textured towel	Sur La Table

HAZELNUT SNOWFLAKE COOKIES
Vietri green square plate	Bo Danica
Khaki/tan striped napkin	Sur La Table
Jam jar and knife/spreader	Author's collection

ALMOND BUTTER ROUNDS AND PECAN SHORTBREAD
White long rectangular plate	Author's collection
Bamboo woven place mat	Sur La Table

CHAMPAGNE GRAPE TARTLET
White square plate with curved edges	Author's collection
Yellow/orange striped place mat	Sur La Table

PEANUT BUTTER AND CHOCOLATE TARTLETS
Mustard-colored leaf-shaped plate	Author's collection
Taupe/ivory striped napkin	Sur La Table
Stone base	Author's collection

DRIED CHERRY AND ALMOND SCONES
Light tan rectangular basket with handles	Author's collection
Rust-colored napkin	Sur La Table
Yellow cup and saucer	Author's collection
Small glass bowl	Author's collection

DARK CHOCOLATE MADELEINES
Celadon green rectangular plate	Author's collection
Ivory napkin	Author's collection

PUMPKIN-NUT MUFFINS
White square wavy-edge plate	Author's collection
Ivory-handled Jean Dubost small knife	Sur La Table
Taupe woven place mat	Sur La Table
Rust-colored napkin	Sur La Table

LEMON TEA CAKE WITH PECANS
Glass pedestal cake plate	Author's collection
Ivory textured Ralph Lauren tablecloth	Author's collection

Waterford crystal cake cutter	Author's collection
Yellow placemat	Sur La Table

RED, WHITE, AND BLUE BERRY PIZZA
Small glass bowls	Author's collection
Pale yellow textured towel	Sur La Table

APPLE PIE WITH SOUR CREAM
Soft green, round scalloped-edge plate	Sur La Table
Vietri fork with ivory handle and silver ring	Bo Danica
Glass bowl with apples	Author's collection
Maple wood table	Author's collection

NECTARINE AND ALMOND GALETTE
Square ceramic tile	Author's collection
Square white dessert plates	Author's collection
Dessert forks	Author's collection
Ivory napkin	Author's collection

MOCHA CREAM PUFFS
Revol white rectangular scalloped-edge plate	Sur La Table
Turquoise napkin	Sur La Table

PASSION FRUIT AND MACADAMIA NUT CAKE
Round, pale cream–colored plate	Author's collection
Gold charger	Author's collection
Libbey antique crystal glasses	Author's collection
Fork with yellow handle and silver carved ring	Sur La Table
Ivory and light tan napkins	Author's collection

WHITE CHOCOLATE CUPCAKE WITH WHITE CHOCOLATE FROSTING
Green and white, square Asian-style footed plate	Sur La Table
Light tan woven place mat	Sur La Table

RAISIN AND WALNUT TART
White, square, lace-edged cake stand with curved edges	Author's collection

MILK CHOCOLATE CARAMEL PECAN TART
Clear crystal cake platter with frosted glass leaf handles	Author's collection
Pale yellow and light tan textured towels	Sur La Table
Stainless cake server	Bo Danica

ESPRESSO CHEESECAKE

Small rectangular footed white plate	Sur La Table
Jagged-edge stone piece	Author's collection
Vietri ivory-handled fork with silver band	Bo Danica

DEVILISH CHOCOLATE LAYER CAKE WITH CARAMEL CHOCOLATE BUTTERCREAM

Annieglass clear glass plate with wide band gold-scalloped edge	Bo Danica
Gold charger	Author's collection

ALLSPICE LAYER CAKE

Silver-footed cake stand	Author's collection
Bamboo woven place mat	Sur La Table
Waterford crystal cake server	Author's collection
Ivory textured tablecloth	Author's collection

Index